Morning and Evening

This book is presented to

_____

by

_____

on

_____

"He wakeneth morning by morning. He wakeneth mine ear to hear as the learned."

Isaiah chapter 50 verse 4

". . . my mouth shall praise Thee with joyful lips: when I remember Thee upon my bed, and meditate on Thee in the night watches."

Psalm 63 verses 5, 6

Morning
and
Evening

C. H. Spurgeon

Christian Focus Publications

© 1994 Christian Focus Publications
Reprinted 1996

ISBN 1-85792-104-6 (black)
ISBN 1-85792-125-9 (blue)
ISBN 1-85792-126-7 (burgundy)
ISBN 1-85792-127-5 (green)

Published by
Christian Focus Publications Ltd
Geanies House, Fearn, Ross-shire,
IV20 1TW, Scotland, Great Britain.

Charles Haddon Spurgeon (1834-1892) was born in Essex, England. He became a Christian in 1850 and a year later was the pastor of a small Baptist church. In 1854 he was called to the pastorate of New Park Street Baptist Chapel in Southwark, London. His preaching attracted great crowds, so much so that a new building, the Metropolitan Tabernacle, was erected. During his ministry he built up a congregation which numbered about 6,000. As well as being a popular preacher, Spurgeon was involved in several charitable organisations, including an orphanage at Stockwell. Spurgeon also had an extensive influence through literature, in particular his sermons which appeared in pamphlet form weekly. He also wrote a commentary on the Psalms entitled *Treasury of David* as well as *Morning and Evening*, a compilation of devotional readings.

Morning by Morning

In penning these short reflections upon certain passages of Holy Writ, the author has had in view the assistance of the private meditation of believers. A child may sometimes suggest a consolation which might not otherwise have cheered a desolate heart; and even a flower, smiling upward from the sod, may turn the thoughts heavenward: may we not hope that, by the Holy Spirit's grace, as the reader turns 'morning by morning' to our simple page, he will hear in it 'a still small voice' whose speech shall be the message of God to his soul? The mind wearies of one thing, and we have therefore studied variety, changing our method constantly; sometimes exhorting, then soliloquizing, then conversing; using the first, second, and third persons, and speaking both in the singular and plural, and all with the desire of avoiding sameness and dulness. Our matter also, we venture to hope, is wide in its range, and not altogether without a dash of freshness; readers of our sermons will recognize many thoughts and expressions which they may met with in our discourses; but much is, to the author's view at least, new; and, as far as anything can be which treats of the common salvation, it is original. We have written out of our own heart, and most of the portions are remembrances of words which were refreshing in our own experience; and, therefore, we trust the daily meditations will not be without savour to our brethren; in fact, we know they will not, if the Spirit of God shall rest upon them.

Our ambition has led us to hope that our little volume may also aid the worship of families where God's altar is honoured in the morning. We know that it has been the custom in some households to read Mason, Hawker, Bogatsky, Smith, or Jay; and without wishing to usurp the place of any of these, our *Morning by Morning* aspires to a position among them. Our happiness will overflow should we be made a blessing to Christian households. Family worship is beyond measure important, both for the present and succeeding generations; and to be in part a chaplain in the houses of our friends, we shall esteem to be a very great honour.

Evening by Evening

Having had the seal of our Master's approval set upon our former volume, entitled, *Morning by Morning*, we have felt encouraged to give our best attention to the present series of brief meditations, and we send them forth with importunate prayer for a blessing to rest upon every reader. Already, more than twenty thousand readers are among our morning fellow-worshippers. Oh, that all may receive grace from the Lord by means of the portion read; and when a similar number shall be gathered to read the evening selection, may the Father's smile be their benison!

We have striven to keep out of the common track; and, hence, we have selected unusual texts, and have brought forward neglected subjects. The vice of many religious works is their dulness. From this fault we have striven to be free; our friends must judge how far we have succeeded. If we may lead upward one heart which otherwise would have drooped, or sow in a single mind a holy purpose which else had never been conceived, we shall be grateful. The Lord send us such results in thousands of instances, and His shall be the praise! The longer we live, the more deeply are we conscious that the Holy Spirit alone can make truth profitable to the heart; and, therefore, in earnest prayer, we commit this volume and its companion to His care.

January

*'They did eat of the fruit
of the land of Canaan that year'*
Joshua 5:12

Israel's weary wanderings were all over, and the
promised rest was attained. No more moving tents,
fiery serpents, fierce Amalekites, and howling
wildernesses: they came to the land which flowed with
milk and honey, and they ate the old corn of the land.
Perhaps this year, beloved Christian reader, this may
be thy case or mine. Joyful is the prospect, and if faith
be in active exercise, it will yield unalloyed delight. To
be with Jesus in the rest which remaineth for the people
of God, is a cheering hope indeed, and to expect this
glory so soon is a double bliss. Unbelief shudders at the
Jordan which still rolls between us and the goodly land,
but let us rest assured that we have already experienced
more ills than death at its worst can cause us. Let us
banish every fearful thought, and rejoice with exceeding great joy, in the prospect that this year we shall
begin to be 'for ever with the Lord'.

A part of the host will this year tarry on earth, to
do service for their Lord. If this should fall to our lot,
there is no reason why the New-year's text should not
still be true. 'We who have believed do enter into rest.'
The Holy Spirit is the earnest of our inheritance; He
gives us 'glory begun below'. In heaven they are
secure, and so are we preserved in Christ Jesus; there
they triumph over their enemies, and we have victories
too. Celestial spirits enjoy communion with their
Lord, and this is not denied to us; they rest in His love,
and we have perfect peace in Him: they hymn His
praise, and it is our privilege to bless Him too. We will
this year gather celestial fruits on earthly ground,
where faith and hope have made the desert like the
garden of the Lord. Man did eat angels' food of old, and
why not now? O for grace to feed on Jesus, and so to
eat of the fruit of the land of Canaan this year!

'We will be glad and rejoice in Thee'
Canticles 1:4

We will be glad and rejoice in Thee. We will not open the gates of the year to the dolorous notes of the sackbut, but to the sweet strains of the harp of joy, and the high sounding cymbals of gladness. 'O come, let us sing unto the Lord: let us make a joyful noise unto the rock of our salvation.' WE, the called and faithful and chosen, *we* will drive away our griefs, and set up our banners of confidence in the name of God. Let others lament over their troubles, we who have the sweetening tree to cast into Marah's bitter pool, with joy will magnify the Lord. Eternal Spirit, our effectual Comforter, we who are the temples in which Thou dwellest, will never cease from adoring and blessing the name of Jesus. *We* WILL, we are resolved about it, Jesus must have the crown of our heart's delight; we will not dishonour our Bridegroom by mourning in His presence. We are ordained to be the minstrels of the skies, let us rehearse our everlasting anthem before we sing it in the halls of the New Jerusalem. *We will* BE GLAD AND REJOICE; two words with one sense, double joy, blessedness upon blessedness. Need there be any limit to our rejoicing in the Lord even now? Do not men of grace find their Lord to be camphire and spikenard, calamus and cinnamon even now, and what better fragrance have they in heaven itself? *We will be glad and rejoice* in THEE. That last word is the meat in the dish, the kernel of the nut, the soul of the text. What heavens are laid up in Jesus! What rivers of infinite bliss have their source ay, and every drop of their fulness in Him! Since, O sweet Lord Jesus, Thou art the present portion of Thy people, favour us this year with such a sense of Thy preciousness, that from its first to its last day we may be glad and rejoice in Thee. Let January open with joy in the Lord, and December close with gladness in Jesus!

'Continue in prayer'
Colossians 4:2

It is interesting to remark how large a portion of Sacred Writ is occupied with the subject of prayer, either in furnishing examples, enforcing precepts, or pronouncing promises. We scarcely open the Bible before we read, 'Then began men to call upon the name of the Lord'; and just as we are about to close the volume, the 'Amen' of an earnest supplication meets our ear. Instances are plentiful. Here we find a wrestling Jacob - there a Daniel who prayed three times a day - and a David who with all his heart called upon his God. On the mountain we see Elias; in the dungeon Paul and Silas. We have multitudes of commands, and myriads of promises. What does this teach us, but the sacred importance and necessity of prayer? We may be certain that whatever God has made prominent in His Word, He intended to be conspicuous in our lives. If He has said much about prayer, it is because He knows we have much need of it. So deep are our necessities, that until we are in heaven we must not cease to pray. Dost thou want nothing? Then, I fear thou dost not know thy poverty. Hast thou no mercy to ask of God? Then, may the Lord's mercy show thee thy misery! A prayerless soul is a Christless soul. Prayer is the lisping of the believing infant, the shout of the fighting believer, the requiem of the dying saint falling asleep in Jesus. It is the breath, the watchword, the comfort, the strength, the honour of a Christian. If thou be a child of God, thou wilt seek thy Father's face, and live in thy Father's love. Pray that this year thou mayest be holy, humble, zealous, and patient; have closer communion with Christ, and enter oftener into the banqueting-house of His love. Pray that thou mayest be an example and a blessing unto others, and that thou mayest live more to the glory of thy Master. The motto for this year must be, 'Continue in prayer'.

'Let the people renew their strength'
Isaiah 41:1

All things on earth need to be renewed. No created thing continueth by itself. 'Thou renewest the face of the year', was the Psalmist's utterance. Even the trees, which wear not themselves with care, nor shorten their lives with labour, must drink of the rain of heaven and suck from the hidden treasures of the soil. The cedars of Lebanon, which God has planted, only live because day by day they are full of sap fresh drawn from the earth. Neither can man's life be sustained without renewal from God. As it is necessary to repair the waste of the body by the frequent meal, so we must repair the waste of the soul by feeding upon the Book of God, or by listening to the preached Word, or by the soul-fattening table of the ordinances. How depressed are our graces when means are neglected! What poor starvelings some saints are who live without the diligent use of the Word of God and secret prayer! If our piety can live without God it is not of divine creating; it is but a dream; for if God had begotten it, it would wait upon Him as the flowers wait upon the dew. Without constant restoration we are not ready for the perpetual assaults of hell, or the stern afflictions of heaven, or even for the strifes within. When the whirlwind shall be loosed, woe to the tree that hath not sucked up fresh sap, and grasped the rock with many intertwisted roots. When tempests arise, woe to the mariners that have not strengthened their mast, nor cast their anchor, nor sought the haven. If we suffer the good to grow weaker, the evil will surely gather strength and struggle desperately for the mastery over us; and so, mayhap, a painful desolation, and a lamentable disgrace may follow. Let us draw near to the footstool of divine mercy in humble entreaty, and we shall realise the fulfilment of the promise, 'They that wait on the Lord shall renew their strength'.

'I will give thee for a covenant of the people'
Isaiah 49:8

Jesus Christ is Himself the sum and substance of the covenant, and as one of its gifts He is the property of every believer. Believer, canst thou estimate what thou hast gotten in Christ? 'In Him dwelleth all the fulness of the Godhead bodily.' Consider that word 'God' and its infinity, and then meditate upon 'perfect man' and all his beauty; for all that Christ, as God and man, ever had, or can have, is thine - out of pure free favour, passed over to thee to be thine entailed property for ever. Our blessed Jesus, as God, is omniscient, omnipresent, omnipotent. Will it not console you to know that all these great and glorious attributes are altogether yours? Has he power? That power is yours to support and strengthen you, to overcome your enemies, and to preserve you even to the end. Has He love? Well, there is not a drop of love in His heart which is not yours; you may dive into the immense ocean of His love, and you may say of it all, 'It is mine'. Hath He justice? It may seem a stern attribute, but even that is yours, for He will by His justice see to it that all which is promised to you in the covenant of grace shall be most certainly secured to you. And all that He has as *perfect man* is yours. As a perfect man the Father's delight was upon Him. He stood accepted by the Most High. O believer, God's acceptance of Christ is thine acceptance; for knowest thou not that the love which the Father set on a perfect Christ, He sets on thee *now*? For all that Christ did is thine. That perfect righteousness which Jesus wrought out, when through His stainless life He kept the law and made it honourable, is thine, and is imputed to thee. Christ is in the covenant.

'My God, I am thine - what a comfort divine!
What a blessing to know that the Saviour is mine!
In the heavenly Lamb thrice happy I am,
And my heart it doth dance at the sound of His name.'

*'The voice of one crying in the wilderness, Prepare
ye the way of the Lord, make his paths straight'*
Luke 3:4

The voice crying in the wilderness demanded *a way for
the Lord, a way prepared, and a way prepared in the
wilderness.* I would be attentive to the Master's proclamation, and give Him a road into my heart, cast up by
gracious operations, through the desert of my nature.
The four directions in the text must have my serious
attention.

Every valley must be exalted. Low and grovelling
thoughts of God must be given up; doubting and
despairing must be removed; and self-seeking and
carnal delights must be forsaken. Across these deep
valleys a glorious causeway of grace must be raised.

Every mountain and hill shall be laid low. Proud
creature-sufficiency, and boastful self-righteousness,
must be levelled, to make a highway for the King of
kings. Divine fellowship is never vouchsafed to haughty,
highminded sinners. The Lord hath respect unto the
lowly, and visits the contrite in heart, but the lofty are
an abomination unto Him. My soul, beseech the Holy
Spirit to set thee right in this respect.

The crooked shall be made straight. The wavering
heart must have a straight path of decision for God and
holiness marked out for it. Double-minded men are
strangers to the God of truth. My soul, take heed that
thou be in all things honest and true, as in the sight of
the heart-searching God

The rough places shall be made smooth. Stumbling-blocks of sin must be removed, and thorns and
briars of rebellion must be uprooted. So great a visitor
must not find miry ways and stony places when He
comes to honour His favoured ones with His company.
Oh that this evening the Lord may find in my heart a
highway made ready by His grace, that He may make
a triumphal progress through the utmost bounds of my
soul, from the beginning of this year even to the end of
it.

*'Grow in grace, and in the knowledge of our Lord
and Saviour Jesus Christ'*
2 Peter 3:18

'Grow in grace' - not in one grace only, but in *all* grace.
Grow in that root-grace, *faith*. Believe the promises
more firmly than you have done. Let faith increase in
fulness, constancy, simplicity. Grow also in *love*. Ask
that your love may become extended, more intense,
more practical, influencing every thought, word, and
deed. Grow likewise in *humility*. Seek to lie very low,
and know more of your own nothingness. As you grow
downward in humility, seek also to grow *upward* -
having nearer approaches to God in prayer and more
intimate fellowship with Jesus. May God the Holy
Spirit enable you to '*grow in the knowledge of our Lord
and Saviour*'. He who grows not in the knowledge of
Jesus, refuses to be blessed. To know Him is 'life
eternal', and to advance in the knowledge of Him is to
increase in happiness. He who does not long to know
more of Christ, knows nothing of Him yet. Whoever
hath sipped this wine will thirst for more, for although
Christ doth satisfy, yet it is such a satisfaction, that the
appetite is not cloyed, but whetted. If you know the love
of Jesus - as the hart panteth for the water-brooks, so
will you pant after deeper draughts of His love. If you
do not desire to know Him better, then you love Him
not, for love always cries, 'Nearer, nearer'. Absence
from Christ is hell; but the presence of Jesus is heaven.
Rest not then content without an increasing acquaintance with Jesus. Seek to know more of Him in His
divine nature, in His human relationship, in His finished work, in His death, in His resurrection, in His
present glorious intercession, and in His future royal
advent. Abide hard by the Cross, and search the
mystery of His wounds. An increase of love to Jesus,
and a more perfect apprehension of His love to us, is
one of the best tests of growth in grace.

'*And Joseph knew his brethren,*
but they knew not him'
Genesis 42:8

This morning our desires went forth for growth in our
acquaintance with the Lord Jesus; it may be well
tonight to consider a kindred topic, namely, *our*
heavenly Joseph's knowledge of us. This was most
blessedly perfect long before we had the slightest
knowledge of Him. 'His eyes beheld our substance, yet
being imperfect, and in His book all our members were
written, when as yet there was none of them.' Before
we had a being in the world we had a being in His heart.
When we were enemies to Him, He knew us, our
misery, our madness, and our wickedness. When we
wept bitterly in despairing repentance, and viewed Him
only as a judge and a ruler, He viewed us as His
brethren well beloved, and His bowels yearned towards
us. He never mistook His chosen, but always beheld
them as objects of His infinite affection. 'The Lord
knoweth them that are His', is as true of the prodigals
who are feeding swine as of the children who sit at the
table.

But, alas! *We knew not our royal Brother*, and out
of this ignorance grew a host of sins. We withheld our
hearts from Him, and allowed Him no entrance to our
love. We mistrusted Him, and gave no credit to His
words. We rebelled against Him, and paid Him no
loving homage. The Sun of Righteousness shone forth,
and we could not see Him. Heaven came down to earth,
and earth perceived it not. Let God be praised, those
days are over with us; yet even now it is but little that
we know of Jesus compared with what He knows of us.
We have but begun to study Him, but He knoweth us
altogether. It is a blessed circumstance that the ignorance is not on His side, for then it would be a hopeless
case for us. He will not say to us, 'I never knew you',
but He will confess our names in the day of His
appearing, and meanwhile will manifest Himself to us
as He doth not unto the world.

*'And God saw the light, that it was good:
and God divided the light from the darkness'*
Genesis 1:4

Light might well be good since it sprang from that fiat of goodness, 'Let there be light'. We who enjoy it should be more grateful for it than we are, and see more of God in it and by it. Light *physical* is said by Solomon to be sweet, but *gospel* light is infinitely more precious, for it reveals eternal things, and ministers to our immortal natures. When the Holy Spirit gives us *spiritual* light, and opens our eyes to behold the glory of God in the face of Jesus Christ, we behold sin in its true colours, and ourselves in our real position; we see the Most Holy God as He reveals Himself, the plan of mercy as He propounds it, and the world to come as the Word describes it. Spiritual light has many beams and prismatic colours, but whether they be knowledge, joy, holiness, or life, all are divinely good. If the light received be thus good, what must the *essential* light be, and how glorious must be the place where He reveals Himself! O Lord, since light is so good, give us more of it, and more of Thyself, the true light.

No sooner is there a good thing in the world, than *a division is necessary*. Light and darkness have no communion; God has divided them, let us not confound them. Sons of light must not have fellowship with deeds, doctrines, or deceits of darkness. The children of the day must be sober, honest, and bold in their Lord's work, leaving the works of darkness to those who shall dwell in it for ever. Our Churches should by discipline divide the light from the darkness, and we should by our distinct separation from the world do the same. In judgment, in action, in hearing, in teaching, in association, we must discern between the precious and the vile, and maintain the great distinction which the Lord made upon the world's first day. O Lord Jesus, be Thou our light throughout the whole of this day, for Thy light is the light of men.

'And God saw the light'
Genesis 1:4

This morning we noticed the goodness of the light, and the Lord's dividing it from the darkness, we now note the special eye which the Lord had for the light. 'God saw the light' - He looked at it with complacency, gazed upon it with pleasure, saw that it 'was good'. If the Lord has given you light, dear reader, He looks on that light with peculiar interest; for not only is it dear to Him as His own handiwork, but because it is *like* Himself, for *He is light*. Pleasant it is to the believer to know that God's eye is thus tenderly observant of that work of grace which He has begun. He never loses sight of the treasure which He has placed in our earthen vessels. Sometimes *we* cannot see the light, but *God* always sees the light, and that is much better than our seeing it. Better for the judge to see my innocence than for me to think I see it. It is very comfortable for me to know that I am one of God's people - but whether *I* know it or not, if the Lord knows it, I am still safe. This is the foundation, 'The Lord knoweth them that are His'. You may be sighing and groaning because of inbred sin, and mourning over your darkness, yet the Lord sees 'light' in your heart, for He has put it there, and all the cloudiness and gloom of your soul cannot conceal your light from His gracious eye. You may have sunk low in despondency, and even despair; but if your soul has any longing towards Christ, and if you are seeking to rest in His finished work, God sees the 'light'. He not only *sees* it, but He also *preserves* it in you. 'I, the Lord, do keep it.' This is a precious thought to those who, after anxious watching and guarding of themselves, feel their own powerlessness to do so. The light thus preserved by His grace, He will one day develop into the splendour of noonday, and the fulness of glory. The light within is the dawn of the eternal day.

'Casting all your care upon Him;
for He careth for you'
1 Peter 5:7

It is a happy way of soothing sorrow when we can feel - 'HE careth for *me*'. Christian! do not dishonour your religion by always wearing a brow of care; come, cast your burden upon your Lord. You are staggering beneath a weight which your Father would not feel. What seems to you a crushing burden, would be to Him but as the small dust of the balance. Nothing is so sweet as to

'Lie passive in God's hands,
And know no will but His.'

O child of suffering, be thou patient; God has not passed thee over in His providence. He who is the feeder of sparrows, will also furnish *you* with what you need. Sit not down in despair; hope on, hope ever. Take up the arms of faith against a sea of trouble, and your opposition shall yet end your distresses. *There is* One who careth for you. His eye is fixed on you, His heart beats with pity for your woe, and his hand omnipotent shall yet bring you the needed help. The darkest cloud shall scatter itself in showers of mercy. The blackest gloom shall give place to the morning. He, if thou art one of His family, will bind up thy wounds, and heal thy broken heart. Doubt not His grace because of thy tribulation, but believe that He loveth thee as much in seasons of trouble as in times of happiness. What a serene and quiet life might you lead if you would leave providing to the God of providence! With a little oil in the cruse, and a handful of meal in the barrel, Elijah outlived the famine, and you will do the same. If God cares for you, why need you care too? Can you trust Him for your soul, and not for your body? He has never refused to bear your burdens, He has never fainted under their weight. Come, then, soul! have done with fretful care, and leave all thy concerns in the hand of a gracious God.

> *'Now the hand of the Lord*
> *was upon me in the evening'*
> Ezekiel 33:22

In the way of *judgment* this may be the case, and, if so, be it mine to consider the reason of such a visitation, and hear the rod and Him that hath appointed it. I am not the only one who is chastened in the night season; let me cheerfully submit to the affliction, and carefully endeavour to be profited thereby. But the hand of the Lord may also be felt in another manner, *strengthening* the soul and lifting the spirit upward towards eternal things. O that I may in this sense feel the Lord dealing with me! A sense of the divine presence and indwelling bears the soul towards heaven as upon the wings of eagles. At such times we are full to the brim with spiritual joy, and forget the cares and sorrows of earth; the invisible is near, and the visible loses its power over us; servant-body waits at the foot of the hill, and the master-spirit worships upon the summit in the presence of the Lord. O that a hallowed season of divine communion may be vouchsafed to me this evening! The Lord knows that I need it very greatly. My graces languish, my corruptions rage, my faith is weak, my devotion is cold; all these are reasons why His healing hand should be laid upon me. His hand can cool the heat of my burning brow, and stay the tumult of my palpitating heart. That glorious right hand which moulded the world can new-create my mind; the unwearied hand which bears the earth's huge pillars up can sustain my spirit; the loving hand which incloses all the saints can cherish me; and the mighty hand which breaketh in pieces the enemy can subdue my sins. Why should I not feel that hand touching me this evening? Come, my soul, address thy God with the potent plea, that Jesu's hands were pierced for thy redemption, and thou shalt surely feel that same hand upon thee which once touched Daniel and set him upon his knees that he might see visions of God.

'For me to live is Christ'

Philippians 1:21

The believer did not always live to Christ. He began to do so when God the Holy Spirit convinced him of sin, and when by grace he was brought to see the dying Saviour making a propitiation for his guilt. From the moment of the new and celestial birth the man begins to live to Christ. Jesus is to believers the one pearl of great price, for whom we are willing to part with all that we have. He has so completely won our love, that it beats alone for Him; to His glory we would live, and in defence of His gospel we would die; He is the pattern of our life, and the model after which we would sculpture our character. Paul's words mean more than most men think; they imply that the *aim and end of his life was Christ* - nay, his life itself was Jesus. In the words of an ancient saint, he did eat, and drink, and sleep eternal life. Jesus was his very breath, the soul of his soul, the heart of his heart, the life of his life. Can you say, as a professing Christian, that you live up to this idea? Can you honestly say that for you to live is Christ? Your business - are you doing it *for Christ*? Is it not done for self-aggrandisement and for family advantage? Do you ask, 'Is that a mean reason?' For the *Christian* it is. He professes to live for Christ; how can he live for another object without committing a spiritual adultery? Many there are who carry out this principle in some measure; but who is there that dare say that he hath lived wholly for Christ as the apostle did? Yet, this alone is the true life of a Christian - its source, its sustenance, its fashion, its end, all gathered up in one word - *Christ Jesus*. Lord, accept me; I here present myself, praying to live only in Thee and to Thee. Let me be as the bullock which stands between the plough and the altar, to work or to be sacrificed; and let my motto be, 'Ready for either'.

'My sister, my spouse'
Canticles 4:12

Observe the sweet titles with which the heavenly Solomon with intense affection addresses His bride the church. *'My sister'*, one near to me by ties of nature, partaker of the same sympathies. *My spouse*, nearest and dearest, united to me by the tenderest bands of love; my sweet companion, part of my own self. *My sister*, by my Incarnation, which makes me bone of thy bone and flesh of thy flesh; *my spouse*, by heavenly betrothal, in which I have espoused thee unto myself in righteousness. *My sister*, whom I knew of old, and over whom I watched from her earliest infancy; *my spouse*, taken from among the daughters, embraced by arms of love, and affianced unto me for ever. See how true it is that our royal Kinsman is not ashamed of us, for He dwells with manifest delight upon this two-fold relationship. We have the word 'my' twice in our version; as if Christ dwelt with rapture on His possession of His Church. 'His delights were with the sons of men', because those sons of men were His own chosen ones. He, the Shepherd, sought the sheep, because they were *His* sheep; He has gone about 'to seek and to save that which was lost', because that which was lost was *His* long before it was lost to itself or lost to Him. The church is the exclusive portion of her Lord; none else may claim a partnership, or pretend to share her love. Jesus, thy church delights to have it so! Let every believing soul drink solace out of these wells. Soul! Christ is near to thee in ties of relationship; Christ is dear to thee in bonds of marriage union, and thou art dear to Him; behold He grasps both of thy hands with both His own, saying, *'My sister, my spouse'*. Mark the two sacred holdfasts by which thy Lord gets such a double hold of thee that He neither can nor will ever let thee go. Be not, O beloved, slow to return the hallowed flame of His love.

'*The iniquity of the holy things*'
Exodus 28:38

What a veil is lifted up by these words, and what a disclosure is made! It will be humbling and profitable for us to pause awhile and see this sad sight. The iniquities of our public worship, its hypocrisy, formality, lukewarmness, irreverence, wandering of heart and forgetfulness of God, what a full measure have we there! Our work for the Lord, its emulation, selfishness, carelessness, slackness, unbelief, what a mass of defilement is there! Our private devotions, their laxity, coldness, neglect, sleepiness, and vanity, what a mountain of dead earth is there! If we looked more carefully we should find this iniquity to be far greater than appears at first sight. Dr Payson, writing to his brother, says, 'My parish, as well as my heart, very much resembles the garden of the sluggard; and what is worse, I find that very many of my desires for the melioration of both, proceed either from pride or vanity or indolence. I look at the weeds which overspread my garden, and breathe out an earnest wish that they were eradicated. But why? What prompts the wish? It may be that I may walk out and say to myself, "In that fine order is my garden kept!" This is *pride*. Or, it may be that my neighbours may look over the wall and say, "How finely your garden flourishes!" This is *vanity*. Or I may wish for the destruction of the weeds, because I am weary of pulling them up. This is indolence.' So that even our desires after holiness may be polluted by ill motives. Under the greenest sods worms hide themselves; we need not look long to discover them. How cheering is the thought, that when the High Priest bore the iniquity of the holy things he wore upon his brow the words, 'HOLINESS TO THE LORD': and even so while Jesus bears our sin, He presents before His Father's face not our unholiness, but his own holiness. O for grace to view our great High Priest by the eye of faith!

'Thy love is better than wine'
Canticles 1:2

Nothing gives the believer so much joy as fellowship with Christ. He has enjoyment as others have in the common mercies of life, he can be glad both in God's gifts and God's works; but in all these separately, yea, and in all of them added together, he doth not find such substantial delight as in the matchless person of his Lord Jesus. He has wine which no vineyard on earth ever yielded; he has bread which all the cornfields of Egypt could never bring forth. Where can such sweetness be found as we have tasted in communion with our Beloved? In our esteem, the joys of earth are little better than husks for swine compared with Jesus, the heavenly manna. We would rather have one mouthful of Christ's love, and a sip of his fellowship, than a whole world full of carnal delights. What is the chaff to the wheat? What is the sparkling paste to the true diamond? What is a dream to the glorious reality? What is time's mirth, in its best trim, compared to our Lord Jesus in His most despised estate? If you know anything of the inner life, you will confess that our highest, purest, and most enduring joys must be the fruit of the tree of life which is in the midst of the Paradise of God. No spring yields such sweet water as that well of God which was digged with the soldier's spear. All earthly bliss is of the earth earthy, but the comforts of Christ's presence are like Himself, heavenly. We can review our communion with Jesus, and find no regrets of emptiness therein; there are no dregs in this wine, no dead flies in this ointment. The joy of the Lord is solid and enduring. Vanity hath not looked upon it, but discretion and prudence testify that it abideth the test of years, and is in time and in eternity worthy to be called 'the only true delight'. For nourishment, consolation, exhilaration, and refreshment, no wine can rival the love of Jesus. Let us drink to the full this evening.

'I will be their God'
Jeremiah 31:33

Christian! here is all thou canst require. To make thee happy thou wantest something that shall *satisfy* thee; and is not this enough? If thou canst pour this promise into thy cup, wilt thou not say, with David, 'My cup runneth over; I have more than heart can wish'? When this is fulfilled, '*I am thy God*', art thou not possessor of all things? Desire is insatiable as death, but He who filleth all in all can fill it. The capacity of our wishes who can measure? but the immeasurable wealth of God can more than overflow it. I ask thee if thou art not complete when God is thine? Dost thou want anything but God? Is not His all-sufficiency enough to satisfy thee if all else should fail? But thou wantest more than quiet satisfaction; thou desirest *rapturous delight*. Come, soul, here is music fit for heaven in this thy portion, for God is the Maker of Heaven. Not all the music blown from sweet instruments, or drawn from living strings, can yield such melody as this sweet promise, 'I will be their God'. Here is a deep sea of bliss, a shoreless ocean of delight; come, bathe thy spirit in it; swim an age, and thou shalt find no shore; dive throughout eternity, and thou shalt find no bottom. '*I will be their God.*' If this does not make thine eyes sparkle, and thy heart beat high with bliss, then assuredly thy soul is not in a healthy state. But thou wantest more than present delights - thou cravest something concerning which thou mayest exercise *hope*; and what more canst thou hope for than the fulfilment of this great promise, 'I will be their God'? This is the masterpiece of all the promises; its enjoyment makes a heaven below, and will make a heaven above. Dwell in the light of thy Lord, and let thy soul be always ravished with His love. Get out the marrow and fatness which this portion yields thee. Live up to thy privileges, and rejoice with unspeakable joy.

'Serve the Lord with gladness'
Psalm 100:2

Delight in divine service is a token of acceptance. Those who serve God with a sad countenance, because they do what is unpleasant to them, are not serving Him at all; they bring the form of homage, but the life is absent. Our God requires no slaves to grace His throne; He is the Lord of the empire of love, and would have His servants dressed in the livery of joy. The angels of God serve Him with songs, not with groans; a murmur or a sigh would be a mutiny in their ranks. That obedience which is not voluntary is disobedience, for the Lord looketh at the heart, and if He seeth that we serve Him from force, and not because we love Him, He will reject our offering. Service coupled with cheerfulness is heart-service, and therefore true. Take away joyful willingness from the Christian, and you have removed *the test of his sincerity*. If a man be driven to battle, he is no patriot; but he who marches into the fray with flashing eye and beaming face, singing, 'It is sweet for one's country to die', proves himself to be sincere in his patriotism. Cheerfulness is *the support of our strength*; in the joy of the Lord are we strong. It acts as *the remover of difficulties*. It is to our service what oil is to the wheels of a railway carriage. Without oil the axle soon grows hot, and accidents occur; and if there be not a holy cheerfulness to oil our wheels, our spirits will be clogged with weariness. The man who is cheerful in his service of God, proves that obedience is his element; he can sing,

> 'Make me to walk in Thy commands,
> 'Tis a delightful road.'

Reader, let us put this question - do *you* serve the Lord *with gladness*? Let us show to the people of the world, who think our religion to be slavery, that it is to us a delight and a joy! Let our gladness proclaim that we serve a good Master.

*'There is laid up for me
a crown of righteousness'*
2 Timothy 4:8

Doubting one! thou hast often said, 'I fear I shall never enter heaven'. Fear not! all the people of God shall enter there. I love the quaint saying of a dying man, who exclaimed, 'I have no fear of going home; I have sent all before me; God's finger is on the latch of my door, and I am ready for Him to enter.' 'But,' said one, 'are you not afraid lest you should miss your inheritance?' 'Nay,' said he, 'nay; there is one crown in heaven which the angel Gabriel could not wear; it will fit no head but mine. There is one throne in heaven which Paul the apostle could not fill; it was made for me, and I shall have it.' O Christian, what a joyous thought! thy portion is secure; 'there remaineth a rest'. 'But cannot I forfeit it?' No; it is entailed. If I be a child of God I shall not lose it. It is mine as securely as if I were there. Come with me, believer, and let us sit upon the top of Nebo, and view the goodly land, even Canaan. Seest thou that little river of death glistening in the sunlight, and across it dost thou see the pinnacles of the eternal city? Dost thou mark the pleasant country and all its joyous inhabitants? Know, then, that if thou couldst fly across thou wouldst see written upon one of its many mansions, 'This remaineth for such a one; preserved for him only. He shall be caught up to dwell for ever with God.' Poor doubting one, see the fair inheritance; it is *thine*. If thou believest in the Lord Jesus, if thou hast repented of sin, if thou hast been renewed in heart, thou art one of the Lord's people, and there is a place reserved for thee, a crown laid up for thee, a harp specially provided for thee. No one else shall have thy portion, it is reserved in heaven for thee, and thou shalt have it ere long, for there shall be no vacant thrones in glory when all the chosen are gathered in.

'In my flesh shall I see God'
Job 19:26

Mark the subject of Job's devout anticipation - 'I shall see God'. He does not say, 'I shall see the saints' - though doubtless that will be untold felicity - but, 'I shall see *God*'. It is not - 'I shall see the pearly gates, I shall behold the walls of jasper, I shall gaze upon the crowns of gold', but 'I shall see God'. This is the sum and substance of heaven, this is the joyful hope of all believers. It is their delight to see Him now in the ordinances by faith. They love to behold Him in communion and in prayer; but there in heaven they shall have an open and unclouded vision, and thus seeing, 'Him as He is', shall be made completely like Him. *Likeness to God* - what can we wish for more? And *a sight of God* - what can we desire better? Some read the passage, 'Yet, I shall see God in my flesh', and find here an allusion to Christ, as the 'Word made flesh', and that glorious beholding of Him which shall be the splendour of the latter days. Whether so or not it is certain that Christ shall be the object of our eternal vision; nor shall we ever want any joy beyond that of seeing Him. Think not that this will be a narrow sphere for the mind to dwell in. It is but one source of delight, but that source is infinite. All His attributes shall be subjects for contemplation, and as He is infinite under each aspect, there is no fear of exhaustion. His works, His gifts, His love to us, and His glory in all His purposes, and in all His actions, these shall make a theme which will be ever new. The patriarch looked forward to this sight of God as a *personal* enjoyment. 'Whom mine eye shall behold, and not another.' Take realising views of heaven's bliss; think what it will be *to you*. '*Thine* eyes shall see the King in His beauty.' All earthly brightness fades and darkens as we gaze upon it, but here is a brightness which can never dim, a glory which can never fade - '*I shall see God*'.

'These have no root'
Luke 8:13

My soul, examine thyself this morning by the light of
this text. Thou hast received the word with joy; thy
feelings have been stirred and a lively impression has
been made; but, remember, that to receive the word in
the ear is one thing, and to receive Jesus into thy very
soul is quite another; superficial feeling is often joined
to inward hardness of heart, and a lively impression of
the word is not always a lasting one. In the parable, the
seed in one case fell upon ground having a rocky
bottom, covered over with a thin layer of earth; when
the seed began to take root, its downward growth was
hindered by the hard stone, and therefore it spent its
strength in pushing its green shoot aloft as high as it
could, but having no inward moisture derived from
root nourishment, it withered away. Is this my case?
Have I been making a fair show in the flesh without
having a corresponding inner life? Good growth takes
place upwards and downwards at the same time. Am I
rooted in sincere fidelity and love to Jesus? If my heart
remains unsoftened and unfertilised by grace, the good
seed may germinate for a season, but it must ultimately
wither, for it cannot flourish on a rocky, unbroken,
unsanctified heart. Let me dread a godliness as rapid in
growth and as wanting in endurance as Jonah's gourd;
let me count the cost of being a follower of Jesus, above
all let me feel the energy of His Holy Spirit, and then
I shall possess an abiding and enduring seed in my
soul. If my mind remains as obdurate as it was by
nature, the sun of trial will scorch, and my hard heart
will help to cast the heat the more terribly upon the ill-
covered seed, and my religion will soon die, and my
despair will be terrible; therefore, O heavenly Sower,
plough me first, and then cast the truth into me, and let
me yield Thee a bounteous harvest.

'*I have prayed for thee*'
Luke 22:32

How encouraging is the thought of the Redeemer's never-ceasing intercession for us. When we pray, He pleads for us; and then we are *not* praying, He is advocating our cause, and by His supplications shielding us from unseen dangers. Notice the word of comfort addressed to Peter - 'Simon, Simon, Satan hath desired to have you that he may sift you as wheat; but' - what? 'But go and pray for yourself.' That would be good advice, but it is not so written. Neither does he say, 'But I will keep you watchful, and so you shall be preserved.' That were a great blessing. No, it is, '*But I have prayed for thee*, that thy faith fail not.' We little know what we owe to our Saviour's prayers. When we reach the hilltops of heaven, and look back upon all the way whereby the Lord our God hath led us, how we shall praise Him who, before the eternal throne, undid the mischief which Satan was doing upon earth. How shall we thank Him because He never held His peace, but day and night pointed to the wounds upon His hands, and carried our names upon His breastplate! Even before Satan had begun to tempt, Jesus had forestalled him and entered a plea in heaven. Mercy outruns malice. Mark, He does not say, 'Satan has sifted you, and therefore I will pray', but 'Satan hath *desired* to have you'. He checks Satan even in his very desire, and nips it in the bud. He does not say, 'But I have desired to pray for you.' No, but 'I *have* prayed for you: I have done it already; I have gone to court and entered a counterplea even before an accusation is made.' O Jesus, what a comfort it is that thou hast pleaded our cause against our unseen enemies; countermined their mines, and unmasked their ambushes. Here is a matter for joy, gratitude, hope, and confidence.

'Ye are Christ's'
1 Corinthians 3:23

'Ye are Christ's.' You are His by donation, for the
Father gave you to the Son; His by His bloody purchase, for He counted down the price for your redemption; His by dedication, for you have consecrated
yourself to Him; His by relation, for you are named by
his name, and made one of His brethren and joint-heirs.
Labour practically to show the world that you are the
servant, the friend, the bride of Jesus. When tempted
to sin, reply, 'I cannot do this great wickedness, for I
am Christ's'. Immortal principles forbid the friend of
Christ to sin. When wealth is before you to be won by
sin, say that you are Christ's, and touch it not. Are you
exposed to difficulties and dangers? Stand fast in the
evil day, remembering that you are Christ's. Are you
placed where others are sitting down idly, doing
nothing? Rise to the work with all your powers; and
when the sweat stands upon your brow, and you are
tempted to loiter, cry, 'No, I cannot stop, for I am
Christ's. If I were not purchased by blood, I might be
like Issachar, crouching between two burdens; but I am
Christ's, and cannot loiter.' When the siren song of
pleasure would tempt you from the path of right, reply,
'Thy music cannot charm me; I am Christ's'. When the
cause of God invites thee, give thyself to it; when the
poor require thee, give thy goods and thyself away, for
thou art Christ's. Never belie thy profession. Be thou
ever one of those whose manners are Christian, whose
speech is like the Nazarene, whose conduct and conversation are so redolent of heaven, that all who see you
may know that you are the Saviour's, recognising in
you His features of love and His countenance of
holiness. 'I am a Roman!' was of old a reason for
integrity; far more, then, let it be your argument for
holiness, 'I am Christ's!'

'I have yet to speak on God's behalf'

Job 36:2

We ought not to court publicity for our virtue, or notoriety for our zeal; but, at the same time, it is a sin to be always seeking to hide that which God has bestowed upon us for the good of others. A Christian is not to be a village in a valley, but 'a city set upon a hill'; he is not to be a candle under a bushel, but a candle in a candlestick, giving light to all. Retirement may be lovely in its season, and to hide one's self is doubtless modest, but the hiding of *Christ* in us can never be justified, and the keeping back of truth which is precious to ourselves is a sin against others and an offence against God. If you are of a nervous temperament and of retiring disposition, take care that you do not too much indulge this trembling propensity, lest you should be useless to the church. Seek in the name of Him who was not ashamed of you to do some little violence to your feelings, and tell to others what Christ has told to you. If thou canst not speak with trumpet tongue, use the still small voice. If the pulpit must not be thy tribune, if the press may not carry on its wings thy words, yet say with Peter and John, 'Silver and gold have I none; but such as I have give I thee'. By Sychar's well talk to the Samaritan woman, if thou canst not on the mountain preach a sermon; utter the praises of Jesus in the house, if not in the temple; in the field, if not upon the exchange; in the midst of thine own household, if thou canst not in the midst of the great family of man. From the hidden springs within let sweetly flowing rivulets of testimony flow forth, giving drink to every passer-by. Hide not thy talent; trade with it; and thou shalt bring in good interest to thy Lord and Master. To speak for God will be refreshing to ourselves, cheering to saints, useful to sinners, and honouring to the Saviour. Dumb children are an affliction to their parents. Lord, unloose all Thy children's tongues.

> '*Jehoshaphat made ships of Tharshish to go to
> Ophir for gold: but they went not;
> for the ships were broken at Ezion-geber*'
> 1 Kings 22:48

Solomon's ships had returned in safety, but Jehoshaphat's vessels never reached the land of gold. Providence prospers one, and frustrates the desires of another, in the same business and at the same spot, yet the Great Ruler is as good and wise at one time as another. May we have grace today, in the remembrance of this text, to bless the Lord for ships broken at Ezion-geber, as well as for vessels freighted with temporal blessings; let us not envy the more successful, nor murmur at our losses as though we were singularly and specially tried. Like Jehoshaphat, we may be precious in the Lord's sight, although our schemes end in disappointment.

The secret cause of Jehoshaphat's loss is well worthy of notice, for it is the root of very much of the suffering of the Lord's people; it was his alliance with a sinful family, his fellowship with sinners. In 2 Chronicles 20:37, we are told that the Lord sent a prophet to declare, 'Because thou hast joined thyself with Ahaziah, the Lord hath broken thy works'. This was a fatherly chastisement, which appears to have been blest to him; for in the verse which succeeds our morning's text we find him refusing to allow his servants to sail in the same vessels with those of the wicked king. Would to God that Jehoshaphat's experience might be a warning to the rest of the Lord's people, to avoid being unequally yoked together with unbelievers! A life of misery is usually the lot of those who are united in marriage, or in any other way of their own choosing, with the men of the world. O for such love to Jesus that, like Him, we may be holy, harmless, undefiled, and separate from sinners; for if it be not so with us, we may expect to hear it often said, 'The Lord hath broken thy works.'

'The iron did swim'
2 Kings 6:6

The axe-head seemed hopelessly lost, and as it was borrowed, the honour of the prophetic band was likely to be imperilled, and so the name of their God to be compromised. Contrary to all expectation, the iron was made to mount from the depth of the stream and to swim; for things impossible with man are possible with God. I knew a man in Christ but a few years ago who was called to undertake a work far exceeding his strength. It appeared so difficult as to involve absurdity in the bare idea of attempting it. Yet he was called thereto, and his faith rose with the occasion; God honoured his faith, unlooked-for aid was sent, and the iron did swim. Another of the Lord's family was in grievous financial straits, he was able to meet all claims, and much more if he could have realised a certain portion of his estate, but he was overtaken with a sudden pressure; he sought for friends in vain, but faith led him to the unfailing Helper, and lo, the trouble was averted, his footsteps were enlarged, and the iron did swim. A third had a sorrowful case of depravity to deal with. He had taught, reproved, warned, invited, and interceded, but all in vain. Old Adam was too strong for young Melancthon, the stubborn spirit would not relent. Then came an agony of prayer, and before long a blessed answer was sent from heaven. The hard heart was broken, the iron did swim.

Beloved reader, what is thy desperate case? What heavy matter hast thou in hand this evening? Bring it hither. The God of the prophets lives, and lives to help His saints. He will not suffer thee to lack any good thing. Believe thou in the Lord of hosts! Approach Him pleading the name of Jesus, and the iron shall swim; thou too shalt see the finger of God working marvels for His people. According to thy faith be it unto thee, and yet again the iron shall swim.

'Mighty to save'
Isaiah 63:1

By the words 'to save' we understand the whole of the great work of salvation, from the first holy desire onward to complete sanctification. The words are *multum in parvo*; indeed, here is all mercy in one word. Christ is not only 'mighty to save' those who repent, but He is able to make men repent. He will carry those to heaven who believe; but He is, moreover, mighty to give men new hearts and to work faith in them. He is mighty to make the man who hates holiness love it, and to constrain the despiser of His name to bend the knee before Him. Nay, this is not all the meaning, for the divine power is equally seen in the after-work. The life of a believer is a series of miracles wrought by 'the Mighty God'. The bush burns, but is not consumed. He is mighty to keep His people holy after He has made them so, and to preserve them in his fear and love until he consummates their spiritual existence in heaven. Christ's might doth not lie in making a believer and then leaving him to shift for himself; but He who begins the good work carries it on; He who imparts the first germ of life in the dead soul, prolongs the divine existence, and strengthens it until it bursts asunder every bond of sin, and the soul leaps from earth, perfected in glory. Believer, here is encouragement. Art thou praying for some beloved one? Oh, give not up thy prayers, for Christ is 'mighty to save'. You are powerless to reclaim the rebel, but your Lord is Almighty. Lay hold on that mighty arm and rouse it to put forth its strength. Does your own case trouble you? Fear not, for His strength is sufficient for you. Whether to begin with others, or to carry on the work in you, Jesus is 'mighty to save'; the best proof of which lies in the fact that He has saved *you*. What a thousand mercies that you have not found Him mighty to destroy!

'Beginning to sink, he cried, saying, Lord, save me'
Matthew 14:30

Sinking times are praying times with the Lord's servants. Peter neglected prayer at starting upon his venturous journey, but when he began to sink his danger made him a suppliant, and his cry though late was not too late. In our hours of bodily pain and mental anguish, we find ourselves as naturally driven to prayer as the wreck is driven upon the shore by the waves. The fox hies to its hole for protection; the bird flies to the wood for shelter; and even so the tried believer hastens to the mercy seat for safety. Heaven's great harbour of refuge is All-prayer; thousands of weather-beaten vessels have found a haven there, and the moment a storm comes on, it is wise for us to make for it with all sail.

Short prayers are long enough. There were but three words in the petition which Peter gasped out, but they were sufficient for his purpose. Not length but strength is desirable. A sense of need is a mighty teacher of brevity. If our prayers had less of the tail feathers of pride and more wing they would be all the better. Verbiage is to devotion as chaff to the wheat. Precious things lie in small compass, and all that is real prayer in many a long address might have been uttered in a petition as short as that of Peter.

Our extremities are the Lord's opportunities. Immediately a keen sense of danger forces an anxious cry from us the ear of Jesus hears, and with Him ear and heart go together, and the hand does not long linger. At the last moment we appeal to our Master, but His swift hand makes up for our delays by instant and effectual action. Are we nearly engulfed by the boisterous waters of affliction? Let us then lift up our souls unto our Saviour, and we may rest assured that He will not suffer us to perish. When we can do nothing Jesus can do all things; let us enlist His powerful aid upon our side, and all will be well.

'Do as Thou hast said'
2 Samuel 7:25

God's promises were never meant to be thrown aside
as waste paper; He intended that they should be used.
God's gold is not miser's money, but is minted to be
traded with. Nothing pleases our Lord better than to see
His promises put in circulation; He loves to see His
children bring them up to Him, and say, 'Lord, do as
Thou hast said'. We glorify God when we plead His
promises. Do you think that God will be any the poorer
for giving you the riches He has promised? Do you
dream that He will be any the less holy for giving
holiness to you? Do you imagine He will be any the less
pure for washing you from your sins? He has said,
'Come now, and let us reason together, saith the Lord:
though your sins be as scarlet, they shall be as white as
snow; though they be red like crimson, they shall be as
wool.' Faith lays hold upon the promise of pardon, and
it does not delay, saying, 'This is a precious promise,
I wonder if it be true?' but it goes straight to the throne
with it, and pleads, 'Lord, here is the promise, Do as
Thou hast said'. Our Lord replies, 'Be it unto thee even
as thou wilt.' When a Christian grasps a promise, if he
does not take it to God, he dishonours Him; but when
he hastens to the throne of grace, and cries, 'Lord, I
have nothing to recommend me but this, "Thou hast
said it"'; then his desire shall be granted. Our heavenly
Banker delights to cash His own notes. Never let the
promise rust. Draw the word of promise out of its
scabbard, and use it with holy violence. Think not that
God will be troubled by your importunately reminding
Him of His promises. He loves to hear the loud outcries
of needy souls. It is His delight to bestow favours. He
is more ready to hear than you are to ask. The sun is not
weary of shining, nor the fountain of flowing. It is
God's nature to keep His promises; therefore go at once
to the throne with, 'Do as thou hast said'.

'But I give myself unto prayer'
Psalm 109:4

Flying tongues were busy against the reputation of David, but he did not defend himself; he moved the case into a higher court, and pleaded before the great King Himself. Prayer is the safest method of replying to words of hatred. The Psalmist prayed in no cold-hearted manner, he *gave himself* to the exercise - threw his whole soul and heart into it - straining every sinew and muscle, as Jacob did when wrestling with the angel. Thus, and thus only, shall any of us speed at the throne of grace. As a shadow has no power because there is no substance in it, even so that supplication, in which a man's proper self is not thoroughly present in agonising earnestness and vehement desire, is utterly ineffectual, for it lacks that which would give it force. 'Fervent prayer,' says an old divine, 'like a cannon planted at the gates of heaven, makes them fly open.' The common fault with the most of us is our readiness to yield to distractions. Our thoughts go roving hither and thither, and we make little progress towards our desired end. Like quicksilver our mind will not hold together, but rolls off this way and that. How great an evil this is! It injures us, and what is worse, it insults our God. What would we think of a petitioner, if, while having an audience with a prince, he should be playing with a feather or catching a fly?

Continuance and perseverance are intended in the expression of our text. David did not cry once, and then relapse into silence; his holy clamour was continued till it brought down the blessing. Prayer must not be our chance work, but our daily business, our habit and vocation. As artists give themselves to their models, and poets to their classical pursuits, so must we addict ourselves to prayer. We must be immersed in prayer as in our element, and so pray without ceasing. Lord, teach us so to pray that we may be more and more prevalent in supplication.

'I will help thee, saith the Lord'
Isaiah 41:14

This morning let us hear the Lord Jesus speak to each one of us: 'I will *help* thee'. 'It is but a small thing for Me, thy God, to *help* thee. Consider what I have done already. What! not help thee? Why, I bought thee with My blood. What! not help thee? I have died for thee; and if I have done the greater, will I not do the less? *Help* thee! It is the least thing I will ever do for thee; I *have* done more, and *will* do more. Before the world began I chose thee. I made the covenant for thee. I laid aside My glory and became a man for thee; I gave My life for thee; and if I did all this, I will surely help thee now. In helping thee, I am giving thee what I have bought for thee already. If thou hadst need of a thousand times as much help, I would give it thee; thou requirest little compared with what I am ready to give. 'Tis much for thee to need, but it is nothing for me to bestow. "*Help* thee?" Fear not! If there were an ant at the door of thy granary asking for help, it would not ruin thee to give him a handful of thy wheat; and thou art nothing but a tiny insect at the door of My all sufficiency. "I will help thee".'

O my soul, is not this enough? Dost thou need more strength than the omnipotence of the United Trinity? Dost thou want more wisdom than exists in the Father, more love than displays itself in the Son, or more power than is manifest in the influences of the Spirit? Bring hither thine empty pitcher! Surely this well will fill it. Haste, gather up thy wants, and bring them there - thine emptiness, thy woes, thy needs. Behold, this river of God is full for thy supply; what canst thou desire beside? Go forth, my soul, in this thy might. The Eternal God is thine helper!

'Fear not, I am with thee, oh, be not dismay'd!
I, I am thy God, and will still give thee aid.'

'The Messiah shall be cut off, but not for himself'
Daniel 9:26

Blessed be His name, there was no cause of death in
Him. Neither original nor actual sin had defiled Him,
and therefore death had no claim upon Him. No man
could have taken His life from Him justly, for He had
done no man wrong, and no man could even have slayed
Him by force unless He had been pleased to yield
Himself to die. But lo, one sins and another suffers.
Justice was offended by us, but found its satisfaction
in Him. Rivers of tears, mountains of offerings, seas
of the blood of bullocks, and hills of frankincense,
could not have availed for the removal of sin; but Jesus
was cut off for us, and the cause of wrath was cut off
at once, for sin was put away for ever. Herein is
wisdom, whereby substitution, the sure and speedy
way of atonement, was devised! Herein is condescension, which brought Messiah, the Prince, to wear a
crown of thorns, and die upon the cross! Herein is love,
which led the Redeemer to lay down His life for His
enemies!

It is not enough, however, to admire the spectacle
of the innocent bleeding for the guilty, we must make
sure of our interest therein. The special object of the
Messiah's death was the salvation of His church; have
we a part and a lot among those for whom He gave His
life a ransom? Did the Lord Jesus stand as our
representative? Are we healed by His stripes? It will be
a terrible thing indeed if we should come short of a
portion in His sacrifice; it were better for us that we had
never been born. Solemn as the question is, it is a joyful
circumstance that it is one which may be answered
clearly and without mistake. To all who believe on Him
the Lord Jesus is a present Saviour, and upon them all
the blood of reconciliation has been sprinkled. Let all
who trust in the merit of Messiah's death be joyful at
every remembrance of Him, and let their holy gratitude
lead them to the fullest consecration to His cause.

'And I looked, and lo, a Lamb stood on the mount Sion'
Revelation 14:1

The apostle John was privileged to look within the gates of heaven, and in describing what he saw, he begins by saying, 'I looked, and, lo, a Lamb!' This teaches us that the chief object of contemplation in the heavenly state is 'the Lamb of God, which taketh away the sins of the world'. Nothing else attracted the apostle's attention so much as the person of that Divine Being, who hath redeemed us by his blood. He is the theme of the songs of all glorified spirits and holy angels. Christian, here is joy for thee; thou hast looked, and thou hast seen the Lamb. Through thy tears thine eyes have seen the Lamb of God taking away thy sins. Rejoice, then. In a little while, when thine eyes shall have been wiped from tears, thou wilt see the same Lamb *exalted on His throne*. It is the joy of thy heart to hold daily fellowship with Jesus; thou shalt have the same joy to a higher degree in heaven; thou shalt enjoy the constant vision of His presence; thou shalt dwell with Him for ever. 'I looked, and, lo, a Lamb!' Why, that Lamb is heaven itself; for as good Rutherford says, 'Heaven and Christ are the same thing'; to be with Christ is to be in heaven, and to be in heaven is to be with Christ. That prisoner of the Lord very sweetly writes in one of his glowing letters - 'O my Lord Christ, if I could be in heaven without thee, it would be a hell; and if I could be in hell, and have thee still, it would be a heaven to me, for thou art all the heaven I want.' It is true, is it not, Christian? Does not thy soul say so?

> Not all the harps above
>   Can make a heavenly place,
> If God His residence remove,
>   Or but conceal His face.

All thou needest to make thee blessed, supremely blessed, is 'to be with Christ'.

'And it came to pass in an evening-tide,
that David arose from off his bed,
and walked upon the roof of the king's house'
2 Samuel 11:2

At that hour David saw Bathsheba. We are never out of the reach of temptation. Both at home and abroad we are liable to meet with allurements to evil; the morning opens with peril, and the shades of evening find us still in jeopardy. They are well kept whom God keeps, but woe unto those who go forth into the world, or even dare to walk their own house unarmed. Those who think themselves secure are more exposed to danger than any others. The armour-bearer of Sin is self-confidence.

David should have been engaged in fighting the Lord's battles, instead of which he tarried at Jerusalem, and gave himself up to luxurious repose, for he arose from his bed at eventide. Idleness and luxury are the devil's jackals, and find him abundant prey. In stagnant waters noxious creatures swarm, and neglected soil soon yields a dense tangle of weeds and briars. Oh for the constraining love of Jesus to keep us active and useful! When I see the King of Israel sluggishly leaving his couch at the close of the day, and falling at once into temptation, let me take warning, and set holy watchfulness to guard the door.

Is it possible that the king had mounted his housetop for retirement and devotion? If so, what a caution is given us to count no place, however secret, a sanctuary from sin! While our hearts are so like a tinder-box, and sparks so plentiful, we had need use all diligence in all places to prevent a blaze. Satan can climb housetops, and enter closets, and even if we could shut out that foul fiend, our own corruptions are enough to work our ruin unless grace prevent. Reader, beware of evening temptations. Be not secure. The sun is down but sin is up. We need a watchman for the night as well as a guardian for the day. O blessed Spirit, keep us from all evil this night. Amen.

*'There remaineth therefore
a rest to the people of God'*
Hebrews 4:9

How different will be the state of the believer in heaven from what it is here! Here he is born to toil and suffer weariness, but in the land of the immortal, fatigue is never known. Anxious to serve his Master, he finds his strength unequal to his zeal: his constant cry is, 'Help me to serve Thee, O my God.' If he be thoroughly active, he will have much labour; not too much for his will, but more than enough for his power, so that he will cry out, 'I am not wearied *of* the labour, but I am wearied *in it*'. Ah! Christian, the hot day of weariness lasts not for ever; the sun is nearing the horizon; it shall rise again with a brighter day than thou hast ever seen, upon a land where they serve God day and night, and yet rest from their labours. *Here*, rest is but partial, *there*, it is *perfect*. *Here*, the Christian is always unsettled; he feels that he has not yet attained. *There*, all are at rest; they have attained the summit of the mountain; they have ascended to the bosom of their God. Higher they cannot go. Ah, toil-worn labourer, only think when thou shalt rest for ever! Canst thou conceive it? It is a rest *eternal*; a rest that 'remaineth'. Here, my best joys bear 'mortal' on their brow; my fair flowers fade; my dainty cups are drained to dregs; my sweetest birds fall before Death's arrows; my most pleasant days are shadowed into nights; and the flood-tides of my bliss subside into ebbs of sorrow; but *there*, everything is immortal; the harp abides unrusted, the crown unwithered, the eye undimmed, the voice unfaltering, the heart unwavering, and the immortal being is wholly absorbed in infinite delight. Happy day! happy day! when mortality shall be swallowed up of life, and the Eternal Sabbath shall begin.

'*He expounded unto them in all the Scriptures the
things concerning himself*'
Luke 24:27

The two disciples on the road to Emmaus had a most
profitable journey. Their companion and teacher was
the best of tutors; the interpreter one of a thousand, in
whom are hid all the treasures of wisdom and knowledge. The Lord Jesus condescended to become a
preacher of the gospel, and He was not ashamed to
exercise His calling before an audience of two persons,
neither does He now refuse to become the teacher of
even one. Let us court the company of so excellent an
Instructor, for till He is made unto us wisdom we shall
never be wise unto salvation.

This unrivalled tutor used as His class-book *the
best of books*. Although able to reveal fresh truth, He
preferred to expound the old. He knew by His omniscience what was the most instructive way of teaching,
and by turning at once to Moses and the prophets, He
showed us that the surest road to wisdom is not
speculation, reasoning, or reading human books, but
meditation upon the Word of God. The readiest way to
be spiritually rich in heavenly knowledge is to dig in
this mine of diamonds, to gather pearls from this
heavenly sea. When Jesus Himself sought to enrich
others, He wrought in the quarry of Holy Scripture.

The favoured pair were led to consider *the best of
subjects*, for Jesus spake of Jesus, and expounded the
things concerning Himself. Here the diamond cut the
diamond, and what could be more admirable? The
Master of the House unlocked His own doors, con-
ducted the guests to His table, and placed His own
dainties upon it. He who hid the treasure in the field
Himself guided the searchers to it. Our Lord would
naturally discourse upon the sweetest of topics, and he
could find none sweeter than his own person and work:
with an eye to these we should always search the Word.
O for grace to study the Bible with Jesus as both our
teacher and our lesson!

'I sought him, but I found him not'
Canticles 3:1

Tell me where you lost the company of Christ, and I will tell you the most likely place to find Him. Have you lost Christ in the closet by restraining prayer? Then it is there you must seek and find Him. Did you lose Christ by sin? You will find Christ in no other way but by the giving up of the sin, and seeking by the Holy Spirit to mortify the member in which the lust doth dwell. Did you lose Christ by neglecting the Scriptures? You must find Christ in the Scriptures. It is a true proverb, 'Look for a thing where you dropped it, it is there'. So look for Christ where you lost Him, for He has not gone away. But it is hard work to go back for Christ. Bunyan tells us, the pilgrim found the piece of the road back to the Arbour of Ease, where he lost his roll, the hardest he had ever travelled. Twenty miles onward is easier than to go one mile back for the lost evidence.

Take care, then, when you find your Master, to cling close to Him. But how is it you have lost Him? One would have thought you would never have parted with such a precious friend, whose presence is so sweet, whose words are so comforting, and whose company is so dear to you! How is it that you did not watch him every moment for fear of losing sight of Him? Yet, since you have let Him go, what a mercy that you are seeking Him, even though you mournfully groan, 'O that I knew where I might find Him!' Go on seeking, for it is dangerous to be without thy Lord. Without Christ you are like a sheep without its shepherd; like a tree without water at its roots; like a sere leaf in the tempest - not bound to the tree of life. With thine whole heart seek Him, and He will be found of thee: only give thyself thoroughly up to the search, and verily, thou shalt yet discover Him to thy joy and gladness.

> *'Then opened He their understanding,*
> *that they might understand the Scriptures'*
> Luke 24:45

He whom we viewed last evening as opening Scripture, we here perceive opening the understanding. In the first work He has many fellow-labourers, but in the second He stands alone; many can bring the Scriptures to the mind, but the Lord alone can prepare the mind to receive the Scriptures. Our Lord Jesus differs from all other teachers; they reach the ear, but He instructs the heart; they deal with the outward letter, but He imparts an inward taste for the truth, by which we perceive its savour and spirit. The most unlearned of men become ripe scholars in the school of grace when the Lord Jesus by His Holy Spirit unfolds the mysteries of the kingdom to them, and grants the divine anointing by which they are enabled to behold the invisible. Happy are we if we have had our understandings cleared and strengthened by the Master! How many men of profound learning are ignorant of eternal things! They know the killing letter of revelation, but its living spirit they cannot discern; they have a veil upon their hearts which the eyes of carnal reason cannot penetrate. Such was our case a little time ago; we who now see were once utterly blind; truth was to us as beauty in the dark, a thing unnoticed and neglected. Had it not been for the love of Jesus we should have remained to this moment in utter ignorance, for without His gracious opening of our understanding, we could no more have attained to spiritual knowledge than an infant can climb the Pyramids, or an ostrich fly up to the stars. Jesus' College is the only one in which God's truth can be really learned; other schools may teach us what is to be believed, but Christ's alone can show us how to believe it. Let us sit at the feet of Jesus, and by earnest prayer call in His blessed aid that our dull wits may grow brighter, and our feeble understandings may receive heavenly things.

'Abel was a keeper of sheep'
Genesis 4:2

As a shepherd Abel *sanctified his work to the glory of God, and offered a sacrifice of blood upon his altar, and the Lord had respect unto Abel and his offering.* This early type of our Lord is exceedingly clear and distinct. Like the first streak of light which tinges the east at sunrise, it does not reveal everything, but it clearly manifests the great fact that the sun is coming. As we see Abel, a shepherd and yet a priest, offering a sacrifice of sweet smell unto God, we discern our Lord, who brings before His Father a sacrifice to which Jehovah ever hath respect. Abel was hated by his brother - hated without a cause; and even so was the Saviour: the natural and carnal man hated the accepted man in whom the Spirit of grace was found, and rested not until his blood had been shed. Abel fell, and sprinkled his altar and sacrifice with his own blood, and therein sets forth the Lord Jesus slain by the enmity of man while serving as a priest before the Lord. 'The good Shepherd layeth down His life for the sheep.' Let us weep over Him as we view Him slain by the hatred of mankind, staining the horns of His altar with His own blood. *Abel's blood speaketh.* 'The Lord said unto Cain, The voice of thy brother's blood crieth unto Me from the ground.' The blood of Jesus hath a mighty tongue, and the import of its prevailing cry is not vengeance but mercy. It is precious beyond all preciousness to stand at the altar of our good Shepherd! to see him bleeding there as the slaughtered priest, and then to hear His blood speaking peace to all his flock, peace in our conscience, peace between Jew and Gentile, peace between man and his offended Maker, peace all down the ages of eternity for blood-washed men. Abel is the first shepherd in order of time, but our hearts shall ever place Jesus first in order of excellence. Thou great Keeper of the sheep, we the people of Thy pasture bless Thee with our whole hearts when we see Thee slain for us.

'Turn away mine eyes from beholding vanity; and
quicken Thou me in Thy way'
Psalm 119:37

There are divers kinds of vanity. The cap and bells of
the fool, the mirth of the world, the dance, the lyre, and
the cup of the dissolute, all these men know to be
vanities; they wear upon their forefront their proper
name and title. Far more treacherous are those equally
vain things, the cares of this world and the deceitfulness of riches. A man may follow vanity as truly in the
counting-house as in the theatre. If he be spending his
life in amassing wealth, he passes his days in a vain
show. Unless we follow Christ, and make our God the
great object of life, we only differ in appearance from
the most frivolous. It is clear that there is much need
of the first prayer of our text.

'Quicken Thou me in Thy way.' The Psalmist
confesses that he is dull, heavy, lumpy, all but dead.
Perhaps, dear reader, you feel the same. We are so
sluggish that the best motives cannot quicken us, apart
from the Lord Himself. What! will not hell quicken
me? Shall I think of sinners perishing, and yet not be
awakened? Will not heaven quicken me? Can I think of
the reward that awaiteth the righteous, and yet be cold?
Will not death quicken me? Can I think of dying, and
standing before my God, and yet be slothful in my
Master's service? Will not Christ's love constrain me?
Can I think of His dear wounds, can I sit at the foot of
His cross, and not be stirred with fervency and zeal? It
seems so! No mere consideration can quicken us to
zeal, but God Himself must do it, hence the cry,
'Quicken *Thou* me'. The Psalmist breathes out his
whole soul in vehement pleadings: his body and his
soul unite in prayer. 'Turn away mine eyes,' says the
body: 'Quicken Thou me,' cries the soul. This is a fit
prayer for every day. O Lord, hear it in my case this
night.

'And so all Israel shall be saved'
Romans 11:26

When Moses sang at the Red Sea, it was his joy to know that *all* Israel were safe. Not a drop of spray fell from that solid wall until the last of God's Israel had safely planted his foot on the other side of the flood. That done, immediately, the floods dissolved into their proper place again, but not till then. Part of that song was, 'Thou in thy mercy hast led forth the people which thou hast redeemed'. In the last time, when the elect shall sing the song of Moses, the servant of God, and of the Lamb, it shall be the boast of Jesus, 'Of all whom thou hast given me, I have lost none'. In heaven there shall not be a vacant throne.

'For all the chosen race
Shall meet around the throne,
Shall bless the conduct of His grace,
And make His glories known.'

As many as God hath chosen, as many as Christ hath redeemed, as many as the Spirit hath called, as many as believe in Jesus, shall safely cross the dividing sea. We are not all safely landed yet:

'Part of the host have crossed the flood,
And part are crossing now.'

The vanguard of the army has already reached the shore. We are marching through the depths; we are at this day following hard after our Leader into the heart of the sea. Let us be of good cheer: the rearguard shall soon be where the vanguard already is; the last of the chosen ones shall soon have crossed the sea, and then shall be heard the song of triumph, when all are secure. But oh! if one were absent - oh! if one of his chosen family should be cast away - it would make an everlasting discord in the song of the redeemed, and cut the strings of the harps of paradise, so that music could never be exhorted from them.

'He was sore athirst, and called on the Lord, and said, Thou hast given this great deliverance into the hand of Thy servant, and now shall I die for thirst?'
Judges 15:18

Samson was thirsty and ready to die. The difficulty was totally different from any which the hero had met before. Merely to get thirst assuaged is nothing like so great a matter as to be delivered from a thousand Philistines! but when the thirst was upon him, Samson felt that little present difficulty more weighty than the great past difficulty out of which he had so specially been delivered. It is very usual for God's people, when they have enjoyed a great deliverance, to find a little trouble too much for them. Samson slays a thousand Philistines, and piles them up in heaps, and then faints for a little water! Jacob wrestles with God at Peniel, and overcomes Omnipotence itself, and then goes 'halting on his thigh'! Strange that there *must* be a shrinking of the sinew whenever we win the day. As if the Lord *must* teach us our littleness, our nothingness, in order to keep us within bounds. Samson boasted right loudly when he said, 'I have slain a thousand men'. His boastful throat soon grew hoarse with thirst, and he betook himself to prayer. God has many ways of humbling His people. Dear child of God, if after great mercy you are laid very low, your case is not an unusual one. When David had mounted the throne of Israel, he said, 'I am this day weak, though anointed king'. You must expect to feel weakest when you are enjoying your greatest triumph.

If God has wrought for you great deliverances in the past, your present difficulty is only like Samson's thirst, and the Lord will not let you faint, nor suffer the daughter of the uncircumcised to triumph over you. The road of sorrow is the road to heaven, but there are wells of refreshing water all along the route. So, tried brother, cheer your heart with Samson's words, and rest assured that God will deliver you ere long.

> '*Son of man, What is the vine tree more
> than any tree, or than a branch which is among the
> trees of the forest?*'
> Ezekiel 15:2

These words are for the humbling of God's people;
they are called God's vine, but what are they by nature
more than others? They, by God's goodness, have
become fruitful, having been planted in a good soil; the
Lord hath trained them upon the walls of the sanctuary,
and they bring forth fruit to His glory; but what are they
without their God? What are they without the continual
influence of the Spirit, begetting fruitfulness in them?
O believer, learn to reject pride, seeing that thou hast
no ground for it. Whatever thou art, thou hast nothing
to make thee proud. The more thou hast, the more thou
art in debt to God; and thou shouldst not be proud of
that which renders thee a debtor. Consider thine origin;
look back to what thou wast. Consider what thou
wouldst have been but for divine grace. Look upon
thyself as thou art now. Doth not thy conscience
reproach thee? Do not thy thousand wanderings stand
before thee, and tell thee that thou art unworthy to be
called His son? And if He hath made thee anything, art
thou not taught thereby that it is grace which hath made
thee to differ? Great believer, thou wouldst have been
a great sinner if God had not made thee to differ. O thou
who art valiant for truth, thou wouldst have been as
valiant for error if grace had not laid hold upon thee.
Therefore be not proud, though thou hast a large estate
- a wide domain of grace, thou hadst not once a single
thing to call thine own except thy sin and misery. Oh!
strange infatuation, that thou, who hast borrowed
everything, shouldst think of exalting thyself; a poor
dependent pensioner upon the bounty of thy Saviour,
one who hath a life which dies without fresh streams of
life from Jesus, and yet proud! Fie on thee, O silly
heart!

'Doth Job fear God for nought?'
Job 1:9

This was the wicked question of Satan concerning that upright man of old, but there are many in the present day concerning whom it might be asked with justice, for they love God after a fashion because He prospers them; but if things went ill with them, they would give up all their boasted faith in God. If they can clearly see that since the time of their supposed conversion the world has gone prosperously with them, then they will love God in their poor carnal way; but if they endure adversity, they rebel against the Lord. Their love is the love of the table, not of the host; a love to the cupboard, not to the master of the house. As for the true Christian, he expects to have his reward in the next life, and to endure hardness in this. The promise of the old covenant was prosperity, but the promise of the new covenant is adversity. Remember Christ's words - 'Every branch in Me that beareth not fruit He taketh away, and every branch that beareth fruit' - What? '*He purgeth it, that it may bring forth more fruit.*' If you bring forth fruit, you will have to endure affliction. 'Alas!' you say, 'that is a terrible prospect.' But this affliction works out such precious results, that the Christian who is the subject of it must learn to rejoice in tribulations, because as his tribulations abound, so his consolations abound by Christ Jesus. Rest assured, if you are a child of God, you will be no stranger to the rod. Sooner or later every bar of gold must pass through the fire. Fear not, but rather rejoice that such fruitful times are in store for you, for in them you will be weaned from earth and made meet for heaven; you will be delivered from clinging to the present, and made to long for those eternal things which are so soon to be revealed to you. When you feel that as regards the present you do serve God for nought, you will then rejoice in the infinite reward of the future.

'*I have exalted one chosen out of the people*'
Psalm 89:19

Why was Christ chosen out of the people? Speak, my heart, for heart-thoughts are best. Was it not that He might be able to be *our brother* in the blest tie of kindred blood? Oh, what relationship there is between Christ and the believer! The believer can say, 'I have a Brother in heaven; I may be poor, but I have a Brother who is rich, and is a King, and will He suffer me to want while He is on His throne? Oh, no! He loves me; He is my brother.' Believer wear this blessed thought, like a necklace of diamonds, around the neck of thy memory; put it, as a golden ring, on the finger of recollection, and use it as the King's own seal, stamping the petitions of thy faith with confidence of success. He is a brother born for adversity, treat him as such.

Christ was also chosen out of the people that He might know our wants and sympathise with us. 'He was tempted in all points like as we are, yet without sin.' In all our sorrows we have His sympathy. Temptation, pain, disappointment, weakness, weariness, poverty - He knows them all, for He has felt all. Remember this, Christian, and let it comfort thee. However difficult and painful thy road, it is marked by the footsteps of thy Saviour; and even when thou reachest the dark valley of the shadow of death, and the deep waters of the swelling Jordan, thou wilt find His footprints there. In all places whithersoever we go, He has been our forerunner; each burden we have to carry, has once been laid on the shoulders of Immanuel.

'His way was much rougher and darker than mine;
Did Christ, my Lord, suffer, and shall I repine?'

Take courage! Royal feet have left a blood-red track upon the road, and consecrated the thorny path for ever.

'We will remember Thy love more than wine'
Song of Solomon 1:4

Jesus will not let His people forget His love. If all the love they have enjoyed should be forgotten, He will visit them with fresh love. 'Do you forget My cross?' says He, 'I will cause you to remember it; for at My table I will manifest Myself anew to you. Do you forget what I did for you in the council-chamber of eternity? I will remind you of it, for you shall need a counsellor, and shall find Me ready at your call.' Mothers do not let their children forget them. If the boy has gone to Australia, and does not write home, his mother writes - 'Has John forgotten his mother?' Then there comes back a sweet epistle, which proves that the gentle reminder was not in vain. So is it with Jesus, He says to us, 'Remember Me', and our response is, 'We will remember Thy love'. We *will* remember Thy love and its matchless history. It is ancient as the glory which Thou hadst with the Father before the world was. We remember, O Jesus, Thine eternal love when Thou didst become our Surety, and espouse us as Thy betrothed. We remember the love which suggested the sacrifice of Thyself, the love which, until the fulness of time, mused over that sacrifice, and longed for the hour whereof in the volume of the book it was written of Thee, 'Lo, I come'. We remember Thy love, O Jesus! as it was manifest to us in Thy holy life, from the manger of Bethlehem to the garden of Gethsemane. We track Thee from the cradle to the grave - for every word and deed of Thine was love - and we rejoice in Thy love, which death did not exhaust; Thy love which shone resplendent in Thy resurrection. We remember that burning fire of love which will never let Thee hold Thy peace until Thy chosen ones be all safely housed, until Zion be glorified, and Jerusalem settled on her everlasting foundations of light and love in heaven.

*'Surely he shall deliver thee
from the snare of the fowler'*
Psalm 91:3

God delivers His people from the snare of the fowler
in two senses. *From*, and *out of*. First, He delivers them
from the snare - does not let them enter it; and secondly,
if they should be caught therein, He delivers them *out
of* it. The first promise is the most precious to some;
the second is the best to others.

'He shall deliver thee *from* the snare.' How?
Trouble is often the means whereby God delivers us.
God knows that our backsliding will soon end in our
destruction, and He in mercy sends the rod. We say,
'Lord, why is this?' not knowing that our trouble has
been the means of delivering us from far greater evil.
Many have been thus saved from ruin by their sorrows
and their crosses; these have frightened the birds from
the net. At other times, God keeps His people *from* the
snare of the fowler by giving them great spiritual
strength, so that when they are tempted to do evil they
say, 'How can I do this great wickedness and sin
against God?' But what a blessed thing it is that if the
believer shall, in an evil hour, come into the net, yet
God will bring him *out of* it! O backslider, be cast
down, but do not despair. Wanderer though thou hast
been, hear what thy Redeemer saith - 'Return, O
backsliding children; I will have mercy upon you'. But
you say you cannot return, for you are a captive. Then
listen to the promise - 'Surely He shall deliver thee out
of the snare of the fowler'. Thou shalt yet be brought
out of all evil into which thou hast fallen, and though
thou shalt never cease to repent of thy ways, yet He that
hath loved thee will not cast thee away; He will receive
thee, and give thee joy and gladness, that the bones
which He has broken may rejoice. No bird of paradise
shall die in the fowler's net.

'Martha was cumbered about much serving'
Luke 10:40

Her fault was not that she *served*: the condition of a servant well becomes every Christian. 'I serve', should be the motto of all the princes of the royal family of heaven. Nor was it her fault that she had *'much serving'*. We cannot do too much. Let us do all that we possibly can; let head, and heart, and hands, be engaged in the Master's service. It was no fault of hers that she was busy preparing a feast for the Master. Happy Martha, to have an opportunity of entertaining so blessed a guest; and happy, too, to have the spirit to throw her whole soul so heartily into the engagement. Her fault was that she grew *'cumbered* with much serving', so that she forgot *Him*, and only remembered the service. She allowed service to override communion, and so presented one duty stained with the blood of another. We ought to be Martha and Mary in one: we should do much service, and have much communion at the same time. For this we need great grace. It is easier to serve than to commune. Joshua never grew weary in fighting with the Amalekites; but Moses, on the top of the mountain in prayer, needed two helpers to sustain his hands. The more spiritual the exercise, the sooner we tire in it. The choicest fruits are the hardest to rear: the most heavenly graces are the most difficult to cultivate. Beloved, while we do not neglect external things, which are good enough in themselves, we ought also to see to it that we enjoy living, personal fellowship with Jesus. See to it that sitting at the Saviour's feet is not neglected, even though it be under the specious pretext of doing Him service. The first thing for our soul's health, the first thing for His glory, and the first thing for our own usefulness, is to keep ourselves in perpetual communion with the Lord Jesus, and to see that the vital spirituality of our religion is maintained over and above everything else in the world.

'*I will mention the lovingkindness of the Lord,
and the praises of the Lord, according to all that the
Lord hath bestowed on us*'
Isaiah 63:7

And canst *thou* not do this? Are there no mercies which
thou *hast experienced*? What though thou art gloomy
now, canst thou forget that blessed hour when Jesus
met thee, and said, 'Come unto me'? Canst thou not
remember that rapturous moment when He snapped thy
fetters, dashed thy chains to the earth, and said, 'I came
to break thy bonds and set thee free'? Or if the love of
thine espousals be forgotten, there must surely be some
precious milestone along the road of life not quite
grown over with moss, on which thou canst read a
happy memorial of His mercy towards thee? What,
didst thou never have a sickness like that which thou art
suffering now, and did he not restore thee? Wert thou
never poor before, and did he not supply thy wants?
Wast thou never in straits before, and did He not
deliver thee? Arise, go to the river of thine experience,
and pull up a few bulrushes, and plait them into an ark,
wherein thine infant-faith may float safely on the
stream. Forget not what thy God has done for thee; turn
over the book of thy remembrance, and consider the
days of old. Canst thou not remember the hill Mizar?
Did the Lord never meet with thee at Hermon? Hast
thou never climbed the Delectable Mountains? Hast
thou never been helped in time of need? Nay, I know
thou hast. Go back, then, a little way to the choice
mercies of yesterday, and though all may be dark *now*,
light up the lamps of the past, they shall glitter through
the darkness, and thou shalt trust in the Lord till the day
break and the shadows flee away. 'Remember, O Lord,
thy tender mercies and thy lovingkindnesses, for they
have been ever of old.'

'Do we then make void the law through faith? God
forbid: yea, we establish the law'
Romans 3:31

When the believer is adopted into the Lord's family,
his relationship to old Adam and the law ceases at once;
but then he is under a new rule, and a new covenant.
Believer, you are God's child; it is your first duty to
obey your heavenly Father. A servile spirit you have
nothing to do with: you are not a slave, but a child; and
now, inasmuch as you are a beloved child, you are
bound to obey your Father's faintest wish, the least
intimation of His will. Does He bid you fulfil a sacred
ordinance? It is at your peril that you neglect it, for you
will be disobeying your Father. Does He command you
to seek the image of Jesus? Is it not your joy to do so?
Does Jesus tell you, 'Be ye perfect, even as your Father
which is in heaven is perfect'? Then not because the law
commands, but because your Saviour enjoins, you will
labour to be perfect in holiness. Does He bid his saints
love one another? Do it, not because the law says,
'Love thy neighbour', but because Jesus says, 'If ye
love Me, keep My commandments'; and this is the
commandment that He has given unto you, 'that ye love
one another'. Are you told to distribute to the poor? Do
it, not because charity is a burden which you dare not
shirk, but because Jesus teaches, 'Give to him that
asketh of thee'. Does the Word say, 'Love God with all
your heart'? Look at the commandment and reply, 'Ah!
commandment, Christ hath fulfilled thee already - I
have no need, therefore, to fulfil thee for my salvation,
but I rejoice to yield obedience to thee because God is
my Father now and He has a claim upon me, which I
would not dispute'. May the Holy Ghost make your
heart obedient to the constraining power of Christ's
love, that your prayer may be, 'Make me to go in the
path of Thy commandments; for therein do I delight'.
Grace is the mother and nurse of holiness, and not the
apologist of sin.

'Your heavenly Father'
Matthew 6:26

God's people are doubly His children, they are His offspring by creation, and they are his sons by adoption in Christ. Hence they are privileged to call Him, 'Our Father which art in heaven'. Father! Oh, what a precious word is that, Here is *authority*: 'If I be a Father, where is mine honour?' If ye be sons, where is your obedience? Here is *affection* mingled with authority; an authority which does not provoke rebellion; an obedience demanded which is most cheerfully rendered - which would not be withheld even if it might. The obedience which God's children yield to Him must be *loving* obedience. Do not go about the service of God as slaves to their taskmaster's toil, but run in the way of His commands because it is your *Father*'s way. Yield your bodies as instruments of righteousness, because righteousness is your Father's will, and *His* will should be the will of His child. *Father*! - Here is a kingly attribute so sweetly veiled in love, that the King's crown is forgotten in the King's face, and His sceptre becomes, not a rod of iron, but a silver sceptre of mercy - the sceptre indeed seems to be forgotten in the tender hand of Him who wields it. Father! - Here is honour and love. How great is a Father's love to his children! That which friendship cannot do, and mere benevolence will not attempt, a father's heart and hand must do for his sons. They are his offspring, he must bless them; they are his children, he must show himself strong in their defence. If an earthly father watches over his children with unceasing love and care, how much more does our heavenly Father? Abba, Father! He who can say this, hath uttered better music than cherubim or seraphim can reach. There is heaven in the depth of that word - Father! There is all I can ask; all my necessities can demand; all my wishes can desire. I have all in all to all eternity when I can say, 'Father'.

'All they that heard it wondered at those things'
Luke 2:18

We must not cease to wonder at the great marvels of our
God. It would be very difficult to draw a line between
holy wonder and *real worship*; for when the soul is
overwhelmed with the majesty of God's glory, though
it may not express itself in song, or even utter its voice
with bowed head in humble prayer, yet it silently
adores. Our incarnate God is to be worshipped as 'the
Wonderful'. That God should consider His fallen
creature, man, and instead of sweeping him away with
the besom of destruction, should Himself undertake to
be man's Redeemer, and to pay his ransom price, is,
indeed, marvellous! But to each believer redemption is
most marvellous as he views it in relation to himself.
It is a miracle of grace indeed, that Jesus should forsake
the thrones and royalties above, to suffer ignomini-
ously below *for you*. Let your soul lose itself in
wonder, for wonder is in this way a very practical
emotion. Holy wonder will lead you to *grateful worship* and *heartfelt thanksgiving*. It will cause within
you *godly watchfulness*; you will be afraid to sin
against such a love as this. Feeling the presence of the
mighty God in the gift of His dear Son, you will put off
your shoes from off your feet, because the place
whereon you stand is holy ground. You will be moved
at the same time to *glorious hope*. If Jesus has done
such marvellous things on your behalf, you will feel
that heaven itself is not too great for your expectation.
Who can be astonished at anything, when he has once
been astonished at the manger and the cross? What is
there wonderful left after one has seen the Saviour?
Dear reader, it may be that from the quietness and
solitariness of your life, you are scarcely able to imitate
the shepherds of Bethlehem, who told what they had
seen and heard, but you can, at least, fill up the circle
of the worshippers before the throne, by wondering at
what God has done.

'*And of his fulness have all we received*'
John 1:16

These words tell us that there is a fulness in Christ.
There is a fulness of essential Deity, for 'in Him
dwelleth all the fulness of the Godhead'. There is a
fulness of perfect manhood, for in Him, bodily, that
Godhead was revealed. There is a fulness of atoning
efficacy in His blood, for 'the blood of Jesus Christ,
His Son, cleanseth us from all sin'. There is a fulness
of justifying righteousness in His life, for 'there is
therefore now no condemnation to them that are in
Christ Jesus'. There is a fulness of divine prevalence
in his plea, for 'He is able to save to the uttermost them
that come unto God by Him; seeing He ever liveth to
make intercession for them'. There is a fulness of
victory in His death, for through death He destroyed
him that had the power of death, that is the devil. There
is a fulness of efficacy in His resurrection from the
dead, for by it 'we are begotten again unto a lively
hope'. There is a fulness of triumph in His ascension,
for 'when He ascended up on high, He led captivity
captive, and received gifts for men'. There is a fulness
of blessings of every sort and shape; a fulness of grace
to pardon, of grace to regenerate, of grace to sanctify,
of grace to preserve, and of grace to perfect. There is
a fulness at all times; a fulness of comfort in affliction;
a fulness of guidance in prosperity. A fulness of every
divine attribute, of wisdom, of power, of love; a
fulness which it were impossible to survey, much less
to explore. 'It pleased the Father that in Him should *all*
fulness dwell.' Oh, what a fulness must this be of
which *all* receive! Fulness, indeed, must there be when
the stream is always flowing, and yet the well springs
up as free, as rich, as full as ever. Come, believer, and
get all thy need supplied; ask largely, and thou shalt
receive largely, for this 'fulness' is inexhaustible, and
is treasured up where all the needy may reach it, even
in Jesus, Immanuel - God with us.

> *'But Mary kept all these things,*
> *and pondered them in her heart'*
> Luke 2:19

There was an exercise, on the part of this blessed woman, of three powers of her being: her *memory* - she kept all these things; her *affections* - she kept them in her heart; her *intellect* - she pondered them; so that memory, affection, and understanding, were all exercised about the things which she had heard. Beloved, remember what you have heard of your Lord Jesus, and what He has done for you; make your heart the golden pot of manna to preserve the memorial of the heavenly bread whereon you have fed in days gone by. Let your memory treasure up everything about Christ which you have either felt, or known, or believed, and then let your fond affections hold *Him* fast for evermore. Love the person of your Lord! Bring forth the alabaster box of your heart, even though it be broken, and let all the precious ointment of your affection come streaming on His pierced feet. Let your intellect be exercised concerning the Lord Jesus. Meditate upon what you read: stop not at the surface dive into the depths. Be not as the swallow which toucheth the brook with her wing, but as the fish which penetrates the lowest wave. Abide with your Lord: let Him not be to you as a wayfaring man, that tarrieth for a night, but constrain Him, saying, 'Abide with us, for the day is far spent'. Hold Him, and do not let Him go. The word 'ponder', means to weigh. Make ready the balances of judgment. Oh, but where are the scales that can weigh the Lord Christ? 'He taketh up the isles as a very little thing' - who shall take *Him* up? 'He weigheth the mountains in scales' - in what scales shall we weigh *Him*? Be it so, if your understanding cannot comprehend, let your affections apprehend; and if your spirit cannot compass the Lord Jesus in the grasp of understanding, let it embrace Him in the arms of affection.

'Perfect in Christ Jesus'
Colossians 1:28

Do you not feel in your own soul that perfection is not in you? Does not every day teach you that? Every tear which trickles from your eye, weeps 'imperfection'; every sigh which bursts from your heart, cries 'imperfection'; every harsh word which proceeds from your lip, mutters 'imperfection'. You have too frequently had a view of your own heart to dream for a moment of any perfection *in yourself*. But amidst this sad consciousness of imperfection, here is comfort for you - you are 'perfect *in Christ Jesus*'. In God's sight, you are 'complete in Him'; *even now* you are 'accepted in the beloved'. But there is a second perfection, yet to be realised, which is sure to all the seed. Is it not delightful to look forward to the time when every stain of sin shall be removed from the believer, and he shall be presented faultless before the throne, without spot, or wrinkle, or any such thing? The Church of Christ then will be so pure, that not even the eye of Omniscience will see a spot or blemish in her; so holy and so glorious, that Hart did not go beyond the truth when he said:

'With my Saviour's garments on,
Holy as the Holy One.'

Then shall we know, and taste, and feel the happiness of this vast but short sentence, 'Complete in Christ'. Not till then shall we fully comprehend the heights and depths of the salvation of Jesus. Doth not thy heart leap for joy at the thought of it? Black as thou art, thou shalt be white one day; filthy as thou art, thou shalt be clean. Oh, it is a marvellous salvation this! Christ takes a worm and transforms it into an angel; Christ takes a black and deformed thing and makes it clean and matchless in His glory, peerless in His beauty, and fit to be the companion of seraphs. O my soul, stand and admire this blessed truth of perfection in Christ.

*'And the shepherds returned, glorifying and
praising God for all the things that they had heard
and seen, as it was told unto them'*
Luke 2:20

What was the subject of their praise? They *praised God
for what they had heard* - for the good tidings of great
joy that a Saviour was born unto them. Let us copy
them; let us also raise a song of thanksgiving that we
have heard of Jesus and His salvation. They also
praised God for what they had seen. There is the
sweetest music - what we have experienced, what we
have felt within, what we have made our own - 'the
things which we have made touching the King'. It is not
enough to *hear* about Jesus; mere hearing may tune the
harp, but the fingers of living faith must create the
music. If you have seen Jesus with the God-giving
sight of faith, suffer no cobwebs to linger among the
harpstrings, but loud to the praise of sovereign grace,
awake your psaltery and harp. One point for which they
praised God was *the agreement between what they had
heard and what they had seen*. Observe the last
sentence - 'As it was told unto them'. Have you not
found the gospel to be in yourselves just what the Bible
said it would be? Jesus said he would give you rest -
have you not enjoyed the sweetest peace in Him? He
said you should have joy, and comfort, and life through
believing in Him - have you not received all these? Are
not His ways ways of pleasantness, and His paths paths
of peace? Surely you can say with the queen of Sheba,
'The half has not been told me'. I have found Christ
more sweet than His servants ever said He was. I
looked upon His likeness as they painted it, but it was
a mere daub compared with Himself; for the King in
His beauty outshines all imaginable loveliness. Surely
what we have '*seen*' keeps pace with, nay, far exceeds,
what we have '*heard*'. Let us, then, glorify and praise
God for a Saviour so precious, and so satisfying.

'The things which are not seen'
2 Corinthians 4:18

In our Christian pilgrimage it is well, for the most part, to be looking forward. Forward lies the crown, and onward is the goal. Whether it be for hope, for joy, for consolation, or for the inspiring of our love, the future must, after all, be the grand object of the eye of faith. Looking into the future we see sin cast out, the body of sin and death destroyed, the soul made perfect, and fit to be a partaker of the inheritance of the saints in light. Looking further yet, the believer's enlightened eye can see death's river passed, the gloomy stream forded, and the hills of light attained on which standeth the celestial city; he seeth himself enter within the pearly gates, hailed as more than conqueror, crowned by the hand of Christ, embraced in the arms of Jesus, glorified with Him, and made to sit together with Him on His throne, even as *He* has overcome and has sat down with the Father on His throne. The thought of this future may well relieve the darkness of the past and the gloom of the present. The joys of heaven will surely compensate for the sorrows of earth. Hush, my fears! this world is but a narrow span, and thou shalt soon have passed it. Hush, hush, my doubts! death is but a narrow stream, and thou shalt soon have forded it. Time, how short - eternity, how long! Death, how brief - immortality, how endless! Methinks I even now eat of Eshcol's clusters, and sip of the well which is within the gate. The road is so, so short! I shall soon be there.

'When the world my heart is rending
With its heaviest storm of care,
My glad thoughts to heaven ascending,
Find a refuge from despair.
Faith's bright vision shall sustain me
Till life's pilgrimage is past;
Fears may vex and troubles pain me,
I shall reach my home at last.'

'The dove came in to him in the evening'
Genesis 8:11

Blessed be the Lord for another day of mercy, even though I am now weary with its toils. Unto the preserver of men lift I my song of gratitude. The dove found no rest out of the ark, and therefore returned to it; and my soul has learned yet more fully than ever, this day, that there is no satisfaction to be found in earthly things - God alone can give rest to my spirit. As to my business, my possessions, my family, my attainments, these are all well enough in their way, but they cannot fulfil the desires of my immortal nature. 'Return unto thy rest, O my soul, for the Lord hath dealt bountifully with thee.' It was at the still hour, when the gates of the day were closing, that with weary wing the dove came back to the master. O Lord, enable me this evening thus to return to Jesus. She could not endure to spend a night hovering over the restless waste, nor can I bear to be even for another hour away from Jesus, the rest of my heart, the home of my spirit. She did not merely alight upon the roof of the ark, she 'came in to him'; even so would my longing spirit look into the secret of the Lord, pierce to the interior of truth, enter into that which is within the veil, and reach to my Beloved in very deed. To Jesus must I come: short of the nearest and dearest intercourse with Him my panting spirit cannot stay. Blessed Lord Jesus, be with me, reveal Thyself, and abide with me all night, so that when I awake, I may be still with thee. I note that the dove brought in her mouth an olive branch plucked off, the memorial of the past day, and a prophecy of the future. Have I no pleasing record to bring home? No pledge and earnest of lovingkindness yet to come? Yes, my Lord, I present Thee my grateful acknowledgments for tender mercies which have been new every morning and fresh every evening; and now, I pray Thee, put forth Thy hand and take Thy dove into Thy bosom.

*'When thou hearest the sound of a going in the tops
of the mulberry trees, then thou shalt bestir thyself'*
2 Samuel 5:24

The members of Christ's Church should be very prayerful, always seeking the unction of the Holy One to rest upon their hearts, that the kingdom of Christ may come, and that His 'will be done on earth, even as it is in heaven'; but there are times when God seems especially to favour Zion, such seasons ought to be to them like 'the sound of a going in the tops of the mulberry trees'. We ought then to be doubly prayerful, doubly earnest, wrestling more at the throne than we have been wont to do. Action should then be prompt and vigorous. The tide is flowing - now let us pull manfully for the shore. O for Pentecostal outpourings and Pentecostal labours. Christian, in *yourself* there are times 'when thou hearest the sound of a going in the tops of the mulberry trees'. You have a peculiar power in prayer; the Spirit of God gives you joy and gladness; the Scripture is open to you; the promises are applied; you walk in the light of God's countenance; you have peculiar freedom and liberty in devotion, and more closeness of communion with Christ than was your wont. Now, at such joyous periods when you hear the 'sound of a going in the tops of the mulberry trees', is the time to bestir yourself; now is the time to get rid of any evil habit, while God the Spirit helpeth your infirmities. Spread your sail; but remember what you sometimes sing

'I can only spread the sail;
Thou! Thou! must breathe the auspicious gale.'

Only be sure you have the sail up. Do not miss the gale for want of preparation for it. Seek help of God, that you may be more earnest in duty when made more strong in faith; that you may be more constant in prayer when you have more liberty at the throne; that you may be more holy in your conversation whilst you live more closely with Christ.

'In whom also we have obtained an inheritance'
Ephesians 1:11

When Jesus gave Himself for us, He gave us all the rights and privileges which went with Himself; so that now, although as eternal God, He has essential rights to which no creature may venture to pretend, yet as Jesus, the Mediator, the federal Head of the covenant of grace, He has no heritage apart from us. All the glorious consequences of His obedience unto death are the joint riches of all who are in Him, and on whose behalf He accomplished the divine will. See, He enters into glory, but not for Himself alone, for it is written, 'Whither the Forerunner is *for us* entered' (Hebrews 6:20). Does He stand in the presence of God? - 'He appears in the presence of God *for us*' (Hebrews 9:24). Consider this, believer. You have no right to heaven in yourself: your right lies in Christ. If you are pardoned, it is through *His* blood; if you are justified, it is through *His* righteousness; if you are sanctified, it is because *He* is made of God unto you sanctification; if you shall be kept from falling, it will be because you are preserved in Christ Jesus; and if you are perfected at the last, it will be because you are complete in *Him*. Thus Jesus is magnified - for all is in Him and by Him; thus the inheritance is made certain to us - for it is obtained in Him; thus each blessing is the sweeter, and even heaven itself the brighter, because it is Jesus our Beloved 'in whom' we have obtained all. Where is the man who shall estimate our divine portion? Weigh the riches of Christ in scales, and His treasures in balances, and then think to count the treasures which belong to the saints. Reach the bottom of Christ's sea of joy, and then hope to understand the bliss which God hath prepared for them that love Him. Overleap the boundaries of Christ's possessions, and then dream of a limit to the fair inheritance of the elect. 'All things are yours, for ye are Christ's and Christ is God's.'

'The Lord our Righteousness'
Jeremiah 23:6.

It will always give a Christian the greatest calm, quiet, ease, and peace, to think of the perfect righteousness of Christ. How often are the saints of God downcast and sad! I do not think they ought to be. I do not think they would if they could always see their perfection in Christ. There are some who are always talking about corruption, and the depravity of the heart, and the innate evil of the soul. This is quite true, but why not go a little further, and remember that we are 'perfect in Christ Jesus'. It is no wonder that those who are dwelling upon their own corruption should wear such downcast looks; but surely if we call to mind that 'Christ is made unto us righteousness', we shall be of good cheer. What though distresses afflict me, though Satan assault me, though there may be many things to be experienced before I get to heaven, those are done for me in the covenant of divine grace; there is nothing wanting in my Lord, Christ hath done it all. On the cross He said, 'It is finished!' and if it be finished, then am I complete in him, and can rejoice with joy unspeakable and full of glory, 'Not having mine own righteousness, which is of the law, but that which is through the faith of Christ, the righteousness which is of God by faith'. You will not find on this side of heaven a holier people than those who receive into their hearts the doctrine of Christ's righteousness. When the believer says, 'I live on Christ alone; I rest on him solely for salvation; and I believe that, however unworthy, I am still saved in Jesus'; then there rises up as a motive of gratitude this thought - 'Shall I not live to Christ? Shall I not love Him and serve Him, seeing that I am saved by *His merits*?' 'The love of Christ constraineth us', 'that they which live should not henceforth *live unto* themselves, but unto Him which died for them'. If saved by imputed righteousness, we shall greatly value imparted righteousness.

*'Then Ahimaaz ran by the way of the plain,
and overran Cushi'*
2 Samuel 18:23

Running is not everything, there is much in the way
which we select: a swift foot over hill and down dale
will not keep pace with a slower traveller upon level
ground. How is it with my spiritual journey, am I
labouring up the hill of my own works and down into
the ravines of my own humiliations and resolutions, or
do I run by the plain way of 'Believe and live'? How
blessed is it to wait upon the Lord by faith! The soul
runs without weariness, and walks without fainting, in
the way of believing. Christ Jesus is the way of life, and
He is a plain way, a pleasant way, a way suitable for the
tottering feet and feeble knees of trembling sinners: am
I found in this way, or am I hunting after another track
such as priestcraft or metaphysics may promise me? I
read of the way of holiness, that the wayfaring man,
though a fool, shall not err therein: have I been
delivered from proud reason and been brought as a little
child to rest in Jesus' love and blood? If so, by God's
grace, I shall outrun the strongest runner who chooses
any other path. This truth I may remember to my profit
in my daily cares and needs. It will be my wisest course
to go at once to my God, and not to wander in a
roundabout manner to this friend and that. He knows
my wants and can relieve them, to whom should I repair
but to Himself by the direct appeal of prayer, and the
plain argument of the promise. 'Straightforward makes
the best runner.' I will not parley with the servants, but
hasten to their Master.

In reading this passage, it strikes me that if men vie
with one another in common matters, and one outruns
the other, I ought to be in solemn earnestness so to run
that I may obtain. Lord, help me to gird up the loins of
my mind, and may I press forward towards the mark
for the prize of my high calling of God in Christ Jesus.

February

'They shall sing in the ways of the Lord'
Psalm 138:5

The time when Christians begin to sing in the ways of
the Lord is when they first lose their burden at the foot
of the Cross. Not even the songs of the angels seem so
sweet as the first song of rapture which gushes from the
inmost soul of the forgiven child of God. You know
how John Bunyan describes it. He says, when poor
Pilgrim lost his burden at the Cross, he gave three great
leaps, and went on his way singing:

> 'Blest Cross! blest Sepulchre! blest rather be
> The Man that there was put to shame for me!'

Believer, do you recollect the day when *your* fetters fell
off? Do you remember the place when Jesus met you,
and said, 'I have loved thee with an everlasting love; I
have blotted out as a cloud thy transgressions, and as
a thick cloud thy sins; they shall not be mentioned
against thee any more for ever.' Oh! what a sweet
season is that when Jesus takes away the pain of sin.
When the Lord first pardoned my sin, I was so joyous
that I could scarce refrain from dancing. I thought on
my road home from the house where I had been set at
liberty, that I must tell the stones in the street the story
of my deliverance. So full was my soul of joy, that I
wanted to tell every snowflake that was falling from
heaven of the wondrous love of Jesus, who had blotted
out the sins of one of the chief of rebels. But it is not
only at the commencement of the Christian life that
believers have reason for song; as long as they live they
discover cause to sing in the ways of the Lord, and their
experience of his constant lovingkindness leads them
to say, 'I will bless the Lord at all times: His praise
shall continually be in my mouth'. See to it, brother,
that thou magnifiest the Lord *this day*.

> 'Long as we tread this desert land,
> New mercies shall new songs demand.'

'Thy love to me was wonderful'
2 Samuel 1:26

Come, dear readers, let each one of us speak for himself of the wonderful love, not of Jonathan, but of Jesus. We will not relate what we have been told, but the things which we have tasted and handled - of the love of Christ. Thy love to me, O Jesus, was wonderful when I was a stranger wandering far from Thee, fulfilling the desires of the flesh and of the mind. Thy love restrained me from committing the sin which is unto death, and withheld me from self-destruction. Thy love held back the axe when Justice said, 'Cut it down! why cumbereth it the ground?' Thy love drew me into the wilderness, stripped me there, and made me feel the guilt of my sin and the burden of mine iniquity. Thy love spake thus comfortably to me when I was sore dismayed - 'Come unto Me, and I will give thee rest'. Oh, how matchless Thy love when, in a moment, Thou didst wash my sins away, and make my polluted soul, which was crimson with the blood of my nativity, and black with the grime of my transgressions, to be white as the driven snow, and pure as the finest wool. How Thou didst commend Thy love when Thou didst whisper in my ears, 'I am thine and thou art Mine'. Kind were those accents when Thou saidst, 'The Father Himself loveth you'. And sweet the moments, passing sweet, when Thou declaredst to me 'the love of the Spirit'. Never shall my soul forget those chambers of fellowship where Thou hast unveiled Thyself to me. Had Moses his cleft in the rock, where he saw the train, the back parts of his God? We, too, have had our clefts in the rock, where we have seen the full splendours of the Godhead in the person of Christ. Did David remember the tracks of the wild goat, the land of Jordan and the Hermonites? We, too, can remember spots to memory dear, equal to these in blessedness. Precious Lord Jesus, give us a fresh draught of Thy wondrous love to begin the month with. Amen.

'Without shedding of blood is no remission'
Hebrews 9:22

This is the voice of unalterable truth. In none of the
Jewish ceremonies were sins, even typically, removed
without blood-shedding. In no case, by no means can
sin be pardoned without atonement. It is clear then, that
there is no hope for me out of Christ; for there is no
other blood-shedding which is worth a thought as an
atonement for sin. Am I then believing in Him? Is the
blood of His atonement truly applied to my soul? All
men are on a level as to their need of Him. If we be never
so moral, generous, amiable, or patriotic, the rule will
not be altered to make an exception for us. Sin will yield
to nothing less potent than the blood of Him whom God
hath set forth as a propitiation. What a blessing that
there is the one way of pardon! Why should we seek
another?

Persons of merely formal religion cannot understand how we can rejoice that all our sins are forgiven
us for Christ's sake. Their works, and prayers, and
ceremonies, give them very poor comfort; and well
may they be uneasy, for they are neglecting the one
great salvation, and endeavouring to get remission
without blood. My soul, sit down, and behold the
justice of God as bound to punish sin; see that punishment all executed upon thy Lord Jesus, and fall down
in humble joy, and kiss the dear feet of Him whose
blood has made atonement for thee. It is in vain when
conscience is aroused to fly to feelings and evidences
for comfort: this is a habit which we learned in the
Egypt of our legal bondage. The only restorative for a
guilty conscience is a sight of Jesus suffering on the
cross. 'The blood is the life thereof' says the Levitical
law, and let us rest assured that it is the life of faith and
joy and every other holy grace.

'Oh! how sweet to view the flowing
Of my Saviour's precious blood;
With divine assurance knowing
He has made my peace with God.'

'And these are ancient things'
1 Chronicles 4:22

Yet not so ancient as those precious things which are the delight of our souls. Let us for a moment recount them, telling them over as misers count their gold. *The sovereign choice* of the Father, by which He elected us unto eternal life, or ever the earth was, is a matter of vast antiquity, since no date can be conceived for it by the mind of man. We were chosen from before the foundations of the world. *Everlasting love* went with the choice, for it was not a bare act of divine will by which we were set apart, but the divine affections were concerned. The Father loved us in and from the beginning. Here is a theme for daily contemplation. *The eternal purpose* to redeem us from our foreseen ruin, to cleanse and sanctify us, and at last to glorify us, was of infinite antiquity, and runs side by side with immutable love and absolute sovereignty. *The covenant* is always described as being everlasting, and Jesus, the second party in it, had His goings forth of old; He struck hands in sacred suretyship long ere the first of the stars began to shine, and it was in Him that the elect were ordained unto eternal life. Thus in the divine purpose a most blessed covenant union was established between the Son of God and His elect people, which will remain as the foundation of their safety when time shall be no more. Is it not well to be conversant with these ancient things? Is it not shameful that they should be so much neglected and even rejected by the bulk of professors? If they knew more of their own sin, would they not be more ready to adore distinguishing grace? Let us both admire and adore tonight, as we sing

'A monument of grace,
   A sinner saved by blood;
The streams of love I trace
   Up to the Fountain, God;
And in His sacred bosom see
   Eternal thoughts of love to me.'

'Therefore, brethren, we are debtors'
Romans 8:12

As God's creatures, we are all debtors to Him: to obey Him with all our body, and soul, and strength. Having broken His commandments, as we all have, we are debtors to His justice, and we owe to Him a vast amount which we are not able to pay. But of the *Christian* it can be said that he does not owe God's *justice* anything, for Christ has paid the debt His people owed; for this reason the believer owes the more to *love*. I am a debtor to God's grace and forgiving mercy; but I am no debtor to His justice, for He will never accuse me of a debt already paid. Christ said, 'It is finished!' and by that He meant, that whatever His people owed was wiped away for ever from the book of remembrance. Christ, to the uttermost, has satisfied divine justice; the account is settled; the handwriting is nailed to the cross; the receipt is given, and we are debtors to God's justice no longer. But then, because we are not debtors to our Lord in that sense, we become ten times more debtors to God than we should have been otherwise. Christian, pause and ponder for a moment. What a debtor thou art to divine *sovereignty*! How much thou owest to His disinterested *love*, for He gave His own Son that He might die for thee. Consider how much you owe to His forgiving *grace*, that after ten thousand affronts He loves you as infinitely as ever. Consider what you owe to His *power*; how He has raised you from your death in sin; how He has preserved your spiritual life; how He has kept you from falling; and how, though a thousand enemies have beset your path, you have been able to hold on your way. Consider what you owe to His *immutability*. Though you have changed a thousand times, He has not changed once. Thou art as deep in debt as thou canst be to every attribute of God. To God thou owest thyself, and all thou hast - yield thyself as a living sacrifice, it is but thy reasonable service.

*'Tell me... where Thou feedest, where Thou makest
Thy flock to rest at noon'*
Canticles 1:7

These words express the desire of the believer after Christ, and his longing for *present* communion with Him. Where dost Thou feed Thy flock? In *Thy house*? I will go, if I may find Thee there. In private *prayer*? Then I will pray without ceasing. In the *Word*? Then I will read it diligently. In Thine *ordinances*? Then I will walk in them with all my heart. Tell me where Thou feedest, for wherever Thou standest as the Shepherd, there will I lie down as a sheep; for none but Thyself can supply my need. I cannot be satisfied to be apart from Thee. My soul hungers and thirsts for the refreshment of Thy presence. 'Where dost Thou make Thy flock to rest at noon?' for whether at dawn or noon, my only rest must be where Thou art and Thy beloved flock. My soul's rest must be a grace-given rest, and can only be found in Thee. Where is the shadow of that rock? Why should I not repose beneath it? 'Why should I be as one that turneth aside by the flocks of thy companions?' Thou hast companions - why should I not be one? Satan tells me I am unworthy; but I always was unworthy, and yet Thou hast long loved me; and therefore my unworthiness cannot be a bar to my having fellowship with Thee now. It is true I am weak in faith, and prone to fall, but my very feebleness is the reason why I should always be where Thou feedest Thy flock, that I may be strengthened, and preserved in safety beside the still waters. Why should I turn aside? There is no reason why I should, but there are a thousand reasons why I should not, for Jesus beckons me to come. If He withdraw Himself a little, it is but to make me prize His presence more. Now that I am grieved and distressed at being away from Him, He will lead me yet again to that sheltered nook where the lambs of His fold are sheltered from the burning sun.

'The love of the Lord'
Hosea 3:1

Believer, *look back* through all thine experience, and think of the way whereby the Lord thy God has led thee in the wilderness, and how He hath fed and clothed thee every day - how He hath borne with thine ill manners - how He hath put up with all thy murmurings, and all thy longings after the flesh-pots of Egypt - how He has opened the rock to supply thee, and fed thee with manna that came down from heaven. Think of how His grace has been sufficient for thee in all thy troubles - how His blood has been a pardon to thee in all thy sins - how His rod and His staff have comforted thee. When thou hadst thus looked back upon the love of the Lord, then let faith survey His love *in the future*, for remember that Christ's covenant and blood have something more in them than the *past*. He who has loved thee and pardoned thee, shall never cease to love and pardon. He is Alpha, and He shall be Omega also: He is first, and He shall be *last*. Therefore, bethink thee, when thou shalt pass through the valley of the shadow of death, thou needest fear no evil, for He is with thee. When thou shalt stand in the cold floods of Jordan, thou needest not fear, for death cannot separate thee from His love; and when thou shalt come into the mysteries of eternity thou needest not tremble, 'For I am persuaded, that neither death, nor life, nor angels, nor principalities, nor powers, nor things present, nor things to come, nor height, nor depth, nor any other creature, shall be able to separate us from the love of God, which is in Christ Jesus our Lord'. Now, soul, is not thy love refreshed? Does not this make thee love Jesus? Doth not a flight through illimitable plains of the ether of love inflame thy heart and compel thee to delight thyself in the Lord thy God? Surely as we meditate on 'the love of the Lord', our hearts burn within us, and we long to love Him more.

'Your refuge from the avenger of blood'
Joshua 20:3

It is said that in the land of Canaan, cities of refuge were so arranged, that any man might reach one of them within half a day at the utmost. Even so the word of our salvation is near to us; Jesus is a present Saviour, and the way to him is short; it is but a simple renunciation of our own merit, and a laying hold of Jesus, to be our all in all. With regard to the roads to the city of refuge, we are told that they were strictly preserved, every river was bridged, and every obstruction removed, so that the man who fled might find an easy passage to the city. Once a year the elders went along the roads and saw to their order, so that nothing might impede the flight of any one, and cause him, through delay, to be overtaken and slain. How graciously do the promises of the gospel remove stumbling blocks from the way! Wherever there were by-roads and turnings, there were fixed up hand-posts, with this inscription upon them - 'To the city of refuge!' This is a picture of the road to Christ Jesus. It is no roundabout road of the law; it is no obeying this, that, and the other; it is a straight road: 'Believe, and live'. It is a road so hard, that no self-righteous man can ever tread it, but so easy, that every sinner, who knows himself to be a sinner, may by it find his way to heaven. No sooner did the man-slayer reach the outworks of the city than he was safe; it was not necessary for him to pass far within the walls, but the suburbs themselves were sufficient protection. Learn hence, that if you do but touch the hem of Christ's garment, you shall be made whole; if you do but lay hold upon him with 'faith as a grain of mustard seed', you are safe.

'A little genuine grace ensures
The death of all our sins.'

Only waste no time, loiter not by the way, for the avenger of blood is swift of foot; and it may be he is at your heels at this still hour of eventide.

'The Father sent the Son to be the Saviour of the world'
1 John 4:14

It is a sweet thought that Jesus Christ did not come forth without His Father's permission, authority, consent, and assistance. He was sent of the Father, that He might be the Saviour of men. We are too apt to forget that, while there are distinctions as to the *persons* in the Trinity, there are no distinctions of *honour*. We too frequently ascribe the honour of our salvation, or at least the depths of its benevolence, more to Jesus Christ than we do the Father. This is a very great mistake. What if Jesus came? Did not His Father send Him? If he spake wondrously, did not His Father pour grace into His lips, that He might be an able minister of the new covenant? He who knoweth the Father, and the Son, and the Holy Ghost as he should know them, never setteth one before another in his love; he sees them at Bethlehem, at Gethsemane, and on Calvary, all equally engaged in the work of salvation. O Christian, hast thou put thy confidence in the Man Christ Jesus? Hast thou placed thy reliance solely on Him? And art thou united with Him? Then believe that thou art united unto the God of heaven. Since to the Man Christ Jesus thou art brother, and holdest fellowship, thou art linked thereby with God the Eternal, and 'the Ancient of days' is thy Father and thy friend. Didst thou ever consider the depth of love in the heart of Jehovah, when God the Father equipped His Son for the great enterprise of mercy? If not, be this thy day's meditation. The *Father* sent Him! Contemplate that subject. Think how Jesus works what the *Father* wills. In the wounds of the dying Saviour see the love of the great I AM. Let every thought of Jesus be also connected with the Eternal, ever-blessed God, for 'It pleased the Lord to bruise Him; He hath put Him to grief'.

'At that time Jesus answered'
Matthew 11:25

This is a singular way in which to commence a verse - 'At that time Jesus answered'. If you will look at the context you will not perceive that any person had asked Him a question, or that He was in conversation with any human being. Yet it is written, 'Jesus answered and said, I thank Thee, O Father'. When a man answers, he answers a person who has been speaking to him. Who, then, had spoken to Christ? His Father. Yet there is no record of it; and this should teach us that Jesus had constant fellowship with His Father, and that God spake into His heart so often, so continually, that it was not a circumstance singular enough to be recorded. It was the habit and life of Jesus to talk with God. Even as Jesus was, in this world, so are we; let us therefore learn the lesson which this simple statement concerning Him teaches us. May *we* likewise have silent fellowship with the Father, so that often we may answer Him, and though the world wotteth not to whom we speak, may we be responding to that secret voice unheard of any other ear, which our own ear, opened by the Spirit of God, recognises with joy. God has spoken to us, let us speak to God - either to set to our seal that God is true and faithful to His promise, or to confess the sin of which the Spirit of God has convinced us, or to acknowledge the mercy which God's providence has given, or to express assent to the great truths which God the Holy Ghost has opened to our understanding. What a privilege is intimate communion with the Father of our spirits! It is a secret hidden from the world, a joy with which even the nearest friend intermeddleth not. If we would hear the whispers of God's love, our ear must be purged and fitted to listen to His voice. This very evening may our hearts be in such a state, that when God speaks to us, we, like Jesus, may be prepared at once to *answer* Him.

'Praying always'
Ephesians 6:18

What multitudes of prayers we have put up from the first moment when we learned to pray. Our first prayer was a prayer for ourselves; we asked that God would have mercy upon us, and blot out our sin. He heard us. But when He had blotted out our sins like a cloud, then we had more prayers for ourselves. We have had to pray for sanctifying grace, for constraining and restraining grace; we have been led to crave for a fresh assurance of faith, for the comfortable application of the promise, for deliverance in the hour of temptation, for help in the time of duty, and for succour in the day of trial. We have been compelled to go to God for our souls, as constant beggars asking for everything. Bear witness, children of God, you have never been able to get anything for your souls elsewhere. All the bread your soul has eaten has come down from heaven, and all the water of which it has drunk has flowed from the living rock - Christ Jesus the Lord. Your soul has never grown rich in itself; it has always been a pensioner upon the daily bounty of God; and hence your prayers have ascended to heaven for a range of spiritual mercies all but infinite. Your wants were innumerable, and therefore the supplies have been infinitely great, and your prayers have been as varied as the mercies have been countless. Then have you not cause to say, 'I love the Lord, because He hath heard the voice of my supplication'? For as your prayers have been many, so also have been God's answers to them. He has heard you in the day of trouble, has strengthened you, and helped you, even when you dishonoured Him by trembling and doubting at the mercy-seat. Remember this, and let it fill your heart with gratitude to God, who has thus graciously heard your poor weak prayers. 'Bless the Lord, O my soul, and forget not all His benefits.'

'Pray one for another'
James 5:16

As an encouragement cheerfully to offer intercessory prayer, remember that *such prayer is the sweetest God ever hears*, for the prayer of Christ is of this character. In all the incense which our Great High Priest now puts into the golden censer, there is not a single grain for Himself. His intercession must be the most acceptable of all supplications - and the more like our prayer is to Christ's, the sweeter it will be; thus while petitions for ourselves will be accepted, our pleadings for others, having in them more of the fruits of the Spirit, more love, more faith, more brotherly kindness, will be, through the precious merits of Jesus, the sweetest oblation that we can offer to God, the very fat of our sacrifice. Remember, again, that *intercessory prayer is exceedingly prevalent*. What wonders it has wrought! The Word of God teems with its marvellous deeds. Believer, thou hast a mighty engine in thy hand, use it well, use it constantly, use it with faith, and thou shalt surely be a benefactor to thy brethren. When thou hast the King's ear, speak to Him for the suffering members of His body. When thou art favoured to draw very near to His throne, and the King saith to thee, 'Ask, and I will give thee what thou wilt', let thy petitions be, not for thyself alone, but for the many who need His aid. If thou hast grace at all, and art not an intercessor, that grace must be small as a grain of mustard seed. Thou hast just enough grace to float thy soul clear from the quicksand, but thou hast no deep floods of grace, or else thou wouldst carry in thy joyous bark a weighty cargo of the wants of others, and thou wouldst bring back from thy Lord, for them, rich blessings which but for thee they might not have obtained:

> 'Oh, let my hands forget their skill,
>   My tongue be silent, cold, and still,
> This bounding heart forget to beat,
>   If I forget the mercy-seat!'

'Arise ye, and depart'
Micah 2:10

The hour is approaching when the message will come to us, as it comes to all - 'Arise, and go forth from the home in which thou hast dwelt, from the city in which thou hast done thy business, from thy family, from thy friends. Arise, and take thy last journey.' And what know we of the journey? And what know we of the country to which we are bound? A little we have read thereof, and somewhat has been revealed to us by the Spirit; but how little do we know of the realms of the future! We know that there is a black and stormy river called 'Death'. God bids us cross it, promising to be with us. And, after death, what cometh? What wonder-world will open upon our astonished sight? What scene of glory will be unfolded to our view? No traveller has ever returned to tell. But we know enough of the heavenly land to make us welcome our summons thither with joy and gladness. The journey of death may be dark, but we may go forth on it fearlessly, knowing that God is with us as we walk through the gloomy valley, and therefore we need fear no evil. We shall be departing from all we have known and loved here, but we shall be going to our Father's house - to our Father's home, where Jesus is - to that royal 'city which hath foundations, whose builder and maker is God'. This shall be our *last* removal, to dwell for ever with Him we love, in the midst of His people, in the presence of God. Christian, meditate much on heaven, it will help thee to press on, and to forget the toil of the way. This vale of tears is but the pathway to the better country: this world of woe is but the stepping-stone to a world of bliss.

'Prepare us, Lord, by grace divine,
  For Thy bright courts on high;
Then bid our spirits rise, and join
  The chorus of the sky.'

*'And they heard a great voice from heaven saying
unto them, Come up hither'*
Revelation 11:12

Without considering these words in their prophetical
connection, let us regard them as the invitation of our
great Forerunner to His sanctified people. In due time
there shall be heard 'a great voice from heaven' to every
believer, saying, 'Come up hither'. This should be to
the saints *the subject of joyful anticipation.* Instead of
dreading the time when we shall leave this world to go
unto the Father, we should be panting for the hour of
our emancipation. Our song should be

'My heart is with Him on His throne,
 And ill can brook delay;
Each moment listening for the voice,
 "Rise up, and come away".'

We are not called *down* to the grace, but *up* to the skies.
Our heaven-born spirits should long for their native air. Yet
should the celestial summons be *the object of patient
waiting.* Our God knows best when to bid us 'Come up
hither'. We must not wish to antedate the period of our
departure. I know that strong love will make us cry,

'O Lord of Hosts, the waves divide,
And land us all in heaven;'

but patience must have her perfect work. God ordains
with accurate wisdom the most fitting time for the
redeemed to abide below. Surely, if there could be
regrets in heaven, the saints might mourn that they did not
live longer here to do more good. Oh, for more sheaves for
my Lord's garner! more jewels for His crown! But how,
unless there be more work? True, there is the other side of
it, that, living so briefly, our sins are the fewer; but oh! when
we are fully serving God, and He is giving us to scatter
precious seed, and reap a hundredfold, we would even say
it is well for us to abide where we are. Whether our Master
shall say 'go', or 'stay', let us be equally well pleased
so long as He indulges us with His presence.

'Thou shalt call his name Jesus'
Matthew 1:21

When a person is dear, everything connected with him becomes dear for his sake. Thus, so precious is the person of the Lord Jesus in the estimation of all true believers, that everything about Him they consider to be inestimable beyond all price. 'All Thy garments smell of myrrh, and aloes, and cassia,' said David, as if the very vestments of the Saviour were so sweetened by His person that he could not but love them. Certain it is, that there is not a spot where that hallowed foot hath trodden - there is not a word which those blessed lips have uttered - nor a thought which His loving Word has revealed - which is not to us precious beyond all price. And this is true of the *names* of Christ - they are all sweet in the believer's ear. Whether He be called the Husband of the Church, her Bridegroom, her Friend; whether He be styled the Lamb slain from the foundation of the world - the King, the Prophet, or the Priest - every title of our Master - Shiloh, Emmanuel, Wonderful, the Mighty Counsellor - every name is like the honeycomb dropping with honey, and luscious are the drops that distil from it. But if there be one name sweeter than another in the believer's ear, it is the name of *Jesus*. Jesus! it is the name more charming, more precious than another, it is this name. It is woven into the very warp and woof of our psalmody. Many of our hymns begin with it, and scarcely any, that are good for anything, end without it. It is the sum total of all delights. It is the music with which the bells of heaven ring; a song in a word; an ocean for comprehension, although a drop for brevity: a matchless oratorio in two syllables; a gathering up of the hallelujahs of eternity in five letters.

'Jesus, I love Thy charming name,
'Tis music to mine ear.'

'He shall save His people from their sins'
Matthew 1:21

Many persons, if they are asked what they understand by salvation, will reply, 'Being saved from hell and taken to heaven'. This is one result of salvation, but it is not one tithe of what is contained in that boon. It is true our Lord Jesus Christ does redeem all His people from the wrath to come; He saves them from the fearful condemnation which their sins had brought upon them; but His triumph is far more complete than this. He saves His people 'from their sins'. Oh! sweet deliverance from our worst foes. Where Christ works a saving work, He casts Satan from his throne, and will not let him be master any longer. No man is a true Christian if sin reigns in his mortal body. Sin will be *in* us - it will never be utterly expelled till the spirit enters glory; but it will never have *dominion*. There will be a striving for dominion - a lusting against the new law and the new spirit which God has implanted - but sin will never get the upper hand so as to be absolute monarch of our nature. Christ will be Master of the heart, and sin must be mortified. The Lion of the tribe of Judah shall prevail, and the dragon shall be cast out. Professor! is sin subdued in you? If your *life* is unholy your *heart* is unchanged, and if your heart is unchanged you are an unsaved person. If the Saviour has not sanctified you, renewed you, given you a hatred of sin and a love of holiness, He has done nothing in you of a saving character. The grace which does not make a man better than others is a worthless counterfeit. Christ saves His people, not *in* their sins, but *from* them. 'Without holiness no man shall see the Lord.' 'Let every one that nameth the name of Christ depart from iniquity.' If not saved from sin, how shall we hope to be counted among His people. Lord, save me even now from all evil, and enable me to honour my Saviour.

'And David enquired of the Lord'
2 Samuel 5:23

When David made this enquiry he had just fought the Philistines, and gained a signal victory. The Philistines came up in great hosts, but, by the help of God, David had easily put them to flight. Note, however, that when they came a second time, David did not go up to fight them without enquiring of the Lord. Once he had been victorious, and he might have said, as many have in other cases, 'I shall be victorious again; I may rest quite sure that if I have conquered once I shall triumph yet again. Wherefore should I tarry to seek at the Lord's hands?' Not so, David. He had gained one battle by the strength of the Lord; he would not venture upon another until he had ensured the same. He enquired, 'Shall I go up against them?' He waited until God's sign was given. Learn from David to take no step without God. Christian, if thou wouldst know the path of duty, take God for thy compass; if thou wouldst steer thy ship through the dark billows, put the tiller into the hand of the Almighty. Many a rock might be escaped, if we would let our Father take the helm; many a shoal or quicksand we might well avoid, if we would leave to His sovereign will to choose and to command. The Puritan said, 'As sure as ever a Christian carves for himself, he'll cut his own fingers'; this is a great truth. Said another old divine, 'He that goes before the cloud of God's providence goes on a fool's errand'; and so he does. We must mark God's providence leading us; and if providence tarries, tarry till providence comes. He who goes before providence, will be very glad to run back again. 'I will instruct thee and teach thee in the way which thou shalt go', is God's promise to His people. Let us, then, take all our perplexities to Him, and say, 'Lord, what wilt thou have me to do?' Leave not thy chamber this morning without enquiring of the Lord.

*'Lead us not into temptation; but deliver us from
evil* [or the evil one]*'*
Luke 11:4

What we are taught to seek or shun in prayer, we should
equally pursue or avoid in action. Very earnestly,
therefore, should we avoid temptation, seeking to walk
so guardedly in the path of obedience, that we may
never tempt the devil to tempt us. We are not to enter
the thicket in search of the lion. Dearly might we pay
for such presumption. This lion may cross our path or
leap upon us from the thicket, but we have nothing to
do with hunting him. He that meeteth with him, even
though he winneth the day, will find it a stern struggle.
Let the Christian pray that he may be spared the
encounter. Our Saviour, who had experience of what
temptation meant, thus earnestly admonished His disciples - 'Pray that ye enter not into temptation'.

But let us do as we will, we shall be tempted; hence
the prayer 'deliver us from evil'. God had one Son
without sin; but He has no son without temptation. The
natural man is born to trouble as the sparks fly
upwards, and the Christian man is born to temptation
just as certainly. We must be always on our watch
against Satan, because, like a thief, he gives no intimation of his approach. Believers who have had experience of the ways of Satan, know that there are certain
seasons when he will most probably make an attack,
just as at certain seasons bleak winds may be expected;
thus the Christian is put on a double guard by fear of
danger, and the danger is averted by preparing to meet
it. Prevention is better than cure: it is better to be so well
armed that the devil will not attack you, than to endure
the perils of the fight, even though you come off a
conqueror. Pray this evening first that you may not be
tempted, and next that if temptation be permitted, you
may be delivered from the evil one.

'I know how to abound'
Philippians 4:12

There are many who know 'how to be abased' who have not learned 'how to abound'. When they are set upon the top of a pinnacle their heads grow dizzy, and they are ready to fall. The Christian far oftener disgraces his profession in prosperity than in adversity. It is a dangerous thing to be prosperous. The crucible of adversity is a less severe trial to the Christian than the fining-pot of prosperity. Oh, what leanness of soul and neglect of spiritual things have been brought on through the very mercies and bounties of God! Yet this is not a matter of necessity, for the apostle tells us that he knew how to abound. When he had much he knew how to use it. Abundant grace enabled him to bear abundant prosperity. When he had a full sail he was loaded with much ballast, and so floated safely. It needs more than human skill to carry the brimming cup of mortal joy with a steady hand, yet Paul had learned that skill, for he declares, 'In all things I am instructed both to be full and to be hungry'. It is a divine lesson to know how to be full, for the Israelites were full once, but while the flesh was yet in their mouth, the wrath of God came upon them. Many have asked for mercies that they might satisfy their own hearts' lust. Fulness of bread has often made fulness of blood, and that has brought on wantonness of spirit. When we have much of God's providential mercies, it often happens that we have but little of God's grace, and little gratitude for the bounties we have received. We are full and we forget God: satisfied with earth, we are content to do without heaven. Rest assured it is harder to know how to be full than it is to know how to be hungry - so desperate is the tendency of human nature to pride and forgetfulness of God. Take care that you ask in your prayers that God would teach you 'how to be full'.

'Let not the gifts Thy love bestows
Estrange our hearts from Thee.'

'I have blotted out, as a thick cloud, thy transgressions, and, as a cloud, thy sins: return unto Me; for I have redeemed thee'
Isaiah 44:22

Attentively observe THE INSTRUCTIVE SIMILITUDE: our sins are like a *cloud*. As clouds are of many shapes and shades, so are our transgressions. As clouds obscure the light of the sun, and darken the landscape beneath, so do our sins hide from us the light of Jehovah's face, and cause us to sit in the shadow of death. They are earth-born things, and rise from the miry places of our nature; and when so collected that their measure is full, they threaten us with storm and tempest. Alas! that, unlike clouds, our sins yield us no genial showers, but rather threaten to deluge us with a fiery flood of destruction. O ye black clouds of sin, how can it be fair weather with our souls while ye remain?

Let our joyful eye dwell upon THE NOTABLE ACT of divine mercy - 'blotting out'. God Himself appears upon the scene, and in divine benignity, instead of manifesting His anger, reveals His grace: He at once and for ever effectually removes the mischief, not by blowing away the cloud, but by blotting it out from existence once for all. Against the justified man no sin remains, the great transaction of the cross has eternally removed His transgressions from him. On Calvary's summit the great deed, by which the sin of all the chosen was for ever put away, was completely and effectually performed.

Practically let us obey THE GRACIOUS COMMAND, *'return unto me'*. Why should pardoned sinners live at a distance from their God? If we have been forgiven all our sins, let no legal fear withhold us from the boldest access to our Lord. Let backslidings be bemoaned, but let us not persevere in them. To the greatest possible nearness of communion with the Lord, let us, in the power of the Holy Spirit, strive mightily to return. O Lord, this night restore us!

*'And they took knowledge of them,
that they had been with Jesus'*
Acts 4:13

A Christian should be a striking likeness of Jesus Christ. You have read lives of Christ, beautifully and eloquently written, but the best life of Christ is His living biography, written out in the words and actions of His people. If we were what we profess to be, and what we should be, we should be pictures of Christ; yea, such striking likenesses of Him, that the world would not have to hold us up by the hour together, and say, 'Well, it seems somewhat of a likeness'; but they would, when they once beheld us, exclaim, 'He has been with Jesus; he has been taught of Him; he is like Him; he has caught the very idea of the holy Man of Nazareth, and he works it out in his life and everyday actions'. A Christian should be like Christ in his *boldness*. Never blush to own your religion; your profession will never disgrace you: take care you never disgrace *that*. Be like Jesus, very valiant for your God. Imitate Him in your *loving* spirit; think kindly, speak kindly, and do kindly, that men may say of you, 'He has been with Jesus'. Imitate Jesus in His *holiness*. Was He zealous for His Master? So be you; ever go about doing good. Let not time be wasted: it is too precious. Was He self-denying, never looking to His own interest? Be the same. Was He devout? Be you fervent in your prayers. Had He deference to His Father's will? So submit yourselves to Him. Was He patient? So learn to endure. And best of all, as the highest portraiture of Jesus, try to forgive your enemies, as He did; and let those sublime words of your Master, 'Father, forgive them; for they know not what they do', always ring in your ears. Forgive, as you hope to be forgiven. Heap coals of fire on the head of your foe by your kindness to him. Good for evil, recollect, is godlike. Be godlike, then; and in all ways and by all means, so live that all may say of you, 'He has been with Jesus'.

'Thou hast left thy first love'
Revelation 2:4

Ever to be remembered is that best and brightest of hours, when first we saw the Lord, lost our burden, received the roll of promise, rejoiced in full salvation, and went on our way in peace. It was spring time in the soul; the winter was past; the mutterings of Sinai's thunders were hushed; the flashings of its lightnings were no more perceived; God was beheld as reconciled; the law threatened no vengeance, justice demanded no punishment. Then the flowers appeared in our heart; hope, love, peace, and patience sprung from the sod; the hyacinth of repentance, the snowdrop of pure holiness, the crocus of golden faith, the daffodil of early love, all decked the garden of the soul. The time of the singing of birds was come, and we rejoiced with thanksgiving; we magnified the holy name of our forgiving God, and our resolve was, 'Lord, I am Thine, wholly Thine; all I am, and all I have, I would devote to Thee. Thou hast bought me with Thy blood - let me spend myself and be spent in Thy service. In life and in death let me be consecrated to Thee.' *How have we kept this resolve*? Our espousal love burned with a holy flame of devotedness to Jesus - is it the same *now*? Might not Jesus well say to us, 'I have somewhat against thee, because thou hast left thy first love'? Alas! it is but little we have done for our Master's glory. Our winter has lasted all too long. We are as cold as ice when we should feel a summer's glow and bloom with sacred flowers. We give to God pence when He deserveth pounds, nay, deserveth our heart's blood to be coined in the service of His church and of His truth. But shall we continue thus? O Lord, after Thou hast so richly blessed us, shall we be ungrateful and become indifferent to Thy good cause and work? O quicken us that we may return to our first love, and do our first works! Send us a genial spring, O Sun of Righteousness.

> *'For as the sufferings of Christ abound in us, so
> our consolation also aboundeth by Christ'*
> 2 Corinthians 1:5

Here is a blessed proportion. The Ruler of Providence bears a pair of scales - in this side He puts His people's trials, and in that He puts their consolations. When the scale of trial is nearly empty, you will always find the scale of consolation in nearly the same condition; and when the scale of trials is full, you will find the scale of consolation just as heavy. When the black clouds gather most, the light is the more brightly revealed to us. When the night lowers and the tempest is coming on, the Heavenly Captain is always closest to His crew. It is a blessed thing, that when we are most cast down, then it is that we are most lifted up by the consolations of the Spirit. One reason is, because *trials make more room for consolation.* Great hearts can only be made by great troubles. The spade of trouble digs the reservoir of comfort deeper, and makes more room for consolation. God comes into our heart - He finds it full - He begins to break our comforts and to make it empty; then there is more room for grace. The humbler a man lies, the more comfort he will always have, because he will be more fitted to receive it. Another reason why we are often most happy in our troubles, is this - *then we have the closest dealings with God.* When the barn is full, man can live without God: when the purse is bursting with gold, we try to do without so much prayer. But once take our *gourds* away, and we want our *God*; once cleanse the idols out of the house, then we are compelled to honour Jehovah. 'Out of the depths have I cried unto thee, O Lord.' There is no cry so good as that which comes from the bottom of the mountains; no prayer half so hearty as that which comes up from the depths of the soul, through deep trials and afflictions. Hence they bring us to God, and we are happier; for nearness to God is happiness. Come, troubled believer, fret not over your heavy troubles, for they are the heralds of weighty mercies.

*'He shall give you another Comforter, that He may
abide with you for ever'*
John 14:16

The Great Father revealed Himself to believers of old
before the coming of His Son, and was known to
Abraham, Isaac, and Jacob as the God Almighty. Then
Jesus came, and the ever-blessed Son in His own
proper person, was the delight of His people's eyes. At
the time of the Redeemer's ascension, the Holy Spirit
became the head of the present dispensation, and His
power was gloriously manifested on and after Pentecost. He remains at this hour the present Immanuel -
God with us, dwelling in and with His people, quickening, guiding, and ruling in their midst. Is His
presence recognised as it ought to be? We cannot
control His working; He is most sovereign in all His
operations, but are we sufficiently anxious to obtain
His help, or sufficiently watchful lest we provoke Him
to withdraw His aid? Without Him we can do nothing,
but by His almighty energy the most extraordinary
results can be produced: everything depends upon His
manifesting or concealing His power. Do we always
look up to Him both for our inner life and our outward
service with the respectful dependence which is fitting?
Do we not too often run before His call and act
independently of His aid? Let us humble ourselves this
evening for past neglects, and now entreat the heavenly
dew to rest upon us, the sacred oil to anoint us, the
celestial flame to burn within us. The Holy Ghost is no
temporary gift, He abides with the saints. We have but
to seek Him aright, and He will be found of us. He is
jealous, but He is pitiful; if He leaves in anger, He
returns in mercy. Condescending and tender, He does
not weary of us, but waits to be gracious still.

Sin has been hammering my heart
Unto a hardness, void of love,
Let suppling grace to cross his art
    Drop from above.

*'Behold, what manner of love the Father hath
bestowed upon us, that we should be called the sons
of God: therefore the world knoweth us not,
because it knew Him not.
Beloved, now are we the sons of God'*
1 John 3: 1, 2

'Behold, what manner of love the Father hath bestowed upon *us*.' Consider who we were, and what *we* feel ourselves to be even now when corruption is powerful in us, and you will wonder at our adoption. Yet *we* are called '*the sons of God*'. What a high relationship is that of a son, and what privileges it brings! What care and tenderness the son expects from his father, and what love the father feels towards the son! But all *that*, and more than *that*, we now have through Christ. As for the temporary drawback of suffering with the elder brother, this we accept as an honour: 'Therefore the world knoweth us not, because it knew Him not.' We are content to be unknown with Him in His humiliation, for we are to be exalted with Him. '*Beloved, now are we the sons of God*.' That is easy to read, but it is not so easy to feel. How is it with your heart this morning? Are you in the lowest depths of sorrow? Does corruption rise within your spirit, and grace seem like a poor spark trampled under foot? Does your faith almost fail you? Fear not, it is neither your graces nor feelings on which you are to live: you must live simply by faith on Christ. With all these things against us, *now* - in the very depths of our sorrow, wherever we may be - *now*, as much in the valley as on the mountain, 'Beloved, *now* are we the sons of God'. 'Ah, but,' you say, 'see how I am arrayed! my graces are not bright; my righteousness does not shine with apparent glory.' But read the next: '*It doth not yet appear what we shall be: but we know that, when He shall appear, we shall be like Him*'. The Holy Spirit shall purify our minds, and divine power shall refine our bodies, then shall *we see Him as He is*.

'There is therefore no condemnation'
Romans 8:1

Come, my soul, think thou of this. Believing in Jesus, thou art actually and effectually cleared from guilt; thou art led out of thy prison. Thou art no more in fetters as a bond-slave; thou art delivered *now* from the bondage of the law; thou art freed from sin, and canst walk at large as a freeman, thy Saviour's blood has procured thy full discharge. Thou hast a right now to approach thy Father's throne. No flames of vengeance are there to scare thee now; no fiery sword; justice cannot smite the innocent. Thy disabilities are taken away: thou wast once unable to see thy Father's face: thou canst see it now. Thou couldst not speak with Him; but now thou hast access with boldness. Once there was a fear of hell upon thee; but thou hast no fear of it now, for how can there be punishment for the guiltless? He who believeth is not condemned, and cannot be punished. And more than all, the privileges thou mightst have enjoyed, if thou hadst never sinned, are thine now thou art justified. All the blessings which thou wouldst have had if thou hadst kept the law, and more, are thine, because Christ has kept it for thee. All the love and the acceptance which perfect obedience could have obtained of God, belong to thee, because Christ was perfectly obedient on thy behalf, and hath imputed all His merits to thy account, that thou mightst be exceeding rich through Him, who for thy sake became exceeding poor. Oh! how great the debt of love and gratitude thou owest to thy Saviour!

'A debtor to mercy alone,
  Of covenant mercy I sing;
Nor fear with Thy righteousness on,
  My person and offerings to bring:
The terrors of law and of God,
  With me can have nothing to do;
My Saviour's obedience and blood
  Hide all my transgressions from view.'

'*And his allowance was a continual allowance given
him of the king, a daily rate for every day,
all the days of his life*'
2 Kings 25:30

Jehoiachin was not sent away from the king's palace
with a store to last him for months, but his provision
was given him as a daily pension. Herein he well
pictures the happy position of all the Lord's people. A
daily portion is *all that a man really wants*. We do not
need tomorrow's supplies; that day has not yet dawned,
and its wants are as yet unborn. The thirst which we
may suffer in the month of June does not need to be
quenched in February, for we do not feel it yet; if we
have enough for each day as the days arrive we shall
never know want. Sufficient for the day is *all that we
can enjoy*. We cannot eat or drink or wear more than the
day's supply of food and raiment; the surplus gives us
the care of storing it, and the anxiety of watching
against a thief. One staff aids a traveller, but a bundle
of staves is a heavy burden. Enough is not only as good
as a feast, but is all that the veriest glutton can truly
enjoy. This is *all that we should expect*; a craving for
more than this is ungrateful. When our Father does not
give us more, we should be content with his daily
allowance. Jehoiachin's case is ours, we have a *sure*
portion, a portion *given us of the king*, a *gracious*
portion, and a *perpetual* portion. Here is surely ground
for thankfulness.

Beloved Christian reader, in matters of grace *you
need a daily supply*. You have no store of strength. Day
by day must you seek help from above. It is a very
sweet assurance that *a daily portion is provided for
you*. In the word, through the ministry, by meditation,
in prayer, and waiting upon God you shall receive
renewed strength. In Jesus all needful things are laid up
for you. Then *enjoy your continual allowance*. Never
go hungry while the daily bread of grace is on the table
of mercy.

'She was healed immediately'
Luke 8:47

One of the most touching and teaching of the Saviour's miracles is before us tonight. The woman was very ignorant. She imagined that virtue came out of Christ by a law of necessity, without His knowledge or direct will. Moreover, she was a stranger to the generosity of Jesus' character, or she would not have gone behind to steal the cure which He was so ready to bestow. Misery should always place itself right in the face of mercy. Had she known the love of Jesus' heart, she would have said, 'I have but to put myself where He can see me - His omniscience will teach Him my case, and His love at once will work my cure.' We admire her faith, but we marvel at her ignorance. After she had obtained the cure, she rejoiced with trembling: glad was she that the divine virtue had wrought a marvel in her: but she feared lest Christ should retract the blessing, and put a negative upon the grant of His grace: little did she comprehend the fulness of His love! We have not so clear a view of Him as we could wish; we know not the heights and depths of His love; but we know of a surety that He is too good to withdraw from a trembling soul the gift which it has been able to obtain. But here is the marvel of it: little as was her knowledge, her faith, because it was real faith, saved her, and saved her at once. There was no tedious delay - faith's miracle was instantaneous. If we have faith as a grain of mustard seed, salvation is our present and eternal possession. If in the list of the Lord's children we are written as the feeblest of the family, yet, being heirs through faith, no power, human or devilish, can eject us from salvation. If we cannot clasp the Lord in our hands with Simeon, if we dare not lean our heads upon His bosom with John, yet if we can venture in the press behind Him, and touch the hem of His garment, we are made whole. Courage, timid one! thy faith hath saved thee; go in peace. *'Being* justified by faith, *we have* peace with God.'

> *'To Him be glory both now and for ever'*
> 2 Peter 3:18

Heaven will be full of the ceaseless praises of Jesus. Eternity! thine unnumbered years shall speed their everlasting course, but for ever and for ever, 'to Him be glory'. Is He not a 'Priest for ever after the order of Melchisedek'? 'To Him be glory.' Is He not king for ever? - King of kings and Lord of lords, the everlasting Father? 'To Him be glory *for ever.*' Never shall His praises cease. That which was bought with blood deserves to last while immortality endures. The glory of the cross must never be eclipsed; the lustre of the grave and of the resurrection must never be dimmed. O Jesus! thou shalt be praised for ever. Long as immortal spirits live - long as the Father's throne endures - for ever, for ever, unto Thee shall be glory. Believer, you are anticipating the time when you shall join the saints above in ascribing all glory to Jesus; but are you glorifying Him *now*? The apostle's words are, 'To Him be glory both *now* and for ever'. Will you not this day make it your prayer? 'Lord, help me to glorify Thee; I am poor, help me to glorify Thee by contentment; I am sick, help me to give Thee honour by patience; I have talents, help me to extol Thee by spending them for Thee; I have time, Lord, help me to redeem it, that I may serve thee; I have a heart to feel, Lord, let that heart feel no love but Thine, and glow with no flame but affection for Thee; I have a head to think, Lord, help me to think *of* Thee and *for* Thee; Thou hast put me in this world for something, Lord, show me what that is, and help me to work out my life-purpose: I cannot do much; but as the widow put in her two mites, which were all her living, so, Lord, I cast my time and eternity too into Thy treasury; I am all Thine; take me, and enable me to glorify Thee *now*, in all that I say, in all that I do, and with all that I have.'

'*Whereby they have made Thee glad*'
Psalm 45:8

And who are thus privileged to make the Saviour glad?
His church - His people. But is it possible? He makes
us glad, but how can *we make Him glad*? By *our love*.
Ah! we think it so cold, so faint; and so, indeed, we
must sorrowfully confess it to be, but it is very sweet
to Christ. Hear His own eulogy of that love in the
golden Canticle: 'How fair is thy love, my sister, my
spouse! how much better is thy love than wine!' See,
loving heart, how He delights in you. When you lean
your head on His bosom, you not only receive, but you
give Him joy; when you gaze with love upon His all-
glorious face, you not only obtain comfort, but impart
delight. Our *praise* too, gives Him joy - not the song
of the lips alone, but the melody of the heart's deep
gratitude. Our *gifts*, too, are very pleasant to Him; He
loves to see us lay our time, our talents, our substance
upon His altar, not for the value of what we give, but
for the sake of the motive from which the gift springs.
To Him the lowly offerings of His saints are more
acceptable than thousands of gold and silver. *Holiness*
is like frankincense and myrrh to Him. Forgive your
enemy, and you make Christ glad; distribute of your
substance to the poor, and He rejoices; be the means of
saving souls, and you give Him to see of the travail of
His soul; proclaim His gospel, and you are a sweet
savour unto Him; go among the ignorant and lift up the
cross, and you have given Him honour. It is in your
power even now to break the alabaster box, and pour the
precious oil of joy upon His head, as did the woman of
old, whose memorial is to this day set forth wherever
the gospel is preached. Will you be backward then?
Will you not perfume your beloved Lord with the
myrrh and aloes, and cassia, of your heart's praise?
Yes, ye ivory palaces, ye shall hear the songs of the
saints!

> '*I have learned, in whatsoever state I am,
> therewith to be content*'
> Philippians 4:11.

These words show us that contentment is not a natural propensity of man. 'Ill weeds grow apace.' Covetousness, discontent, and murmuring are as natural to man as thorns are to the soil. We need not sow thistles and brambles; they come up naturally enough, because they are indigenous to earth: and so we need not teach men to complain; they complain fast enough without any education. But the precious things of the earth must be cultivated. If we would have wheat, we must plough and sow; if we want flowers, there must be the garden, and all the gardener's care. Now, contentment is one of the flowers of heaven, and if we would have it, it must be cultivated; it will not grow in us by nature; it is the new nature alone that can produce it, and even then we must be specially careful and watchful that we maintain and cultivate the grace which God has sown in us. Paul says, 'I have *learned*... to be content'; as much as to say, he did not know how at one time. It cost him some pains to attain to the mystery of that great truth. No doubt he sometimes thought he had learned, and then broke down. And when at last he had attained unto it, and could say, 'I have learned in whatsoever state I am, therewith to be content', he was an old, grey-headed man, upon the borders of the grave - a poor prisoner shut up in Nero's dungeon at Rome. We might well be willing to endure Paul's infirmities, and share the cold dungeon with him, if we too might by any means attain unto his good degree. Do not indulge the notion that you can be contented without *learning*, or learn without discipline. It is not a power that may be exercised naturally, but a science to be acquired gradually. We know this from experience. Brother, hush that murmur, natural though it be, and continue a diligent pupil in the College of Content.

'Thy good Spirit'
Nehemiah 9:20

Common, too common is the sin of forgetting the Holy Spirit. This is folly and ingratitude. He deserves well at our hands, for He is good, supremely good. As God, He is *good essentially*. He shares in the threefold ascription of Holy, holy, holy, which ascends to the Triune Jehovah. Unmixed purity, and truth, and grace is He. He is *good benevolently*, tenderly bearing with our waywardness, striving with our rebellious wills; quickening us from our death in sin, and then training us for the skies as a loving nurse fosters her child. How generous, forgiving, and tender is this patient Spirit of God. He is *good operatively*. All His works are good in the most eminent degree: He suggests good thoughts, prompts good actions, reveals good truths, applies good promises, assists in good attainments, and leads to good results. There is no spiritual good in all the world of which He is not the author and sustainer, and heaven itself will owe the perfect character of its redeemed inhabitants to His work. He is *good officially*; whether as Comforter, Instructor, Guide, Sanctifier, Quickener, or Intercessor, he fulfils His office well, and each work is fraught with the highest good to the church of God. They who yield to His influences become good, they who obey His impulses do good, they who live under His power receive good. Let us then act towards so good a person according to the dictates of gratitude. Let us revere His person, and adore Him as God over all, blessed for ever; let us own His power, and our need of Him by waiting upon Him in all our holy enterprises; let us hourly seek His aid, and never grieve Him; and let us speak to His praise whenever occasion occurs. The church will never prosper until more reverently it believes in the Holy Ghost. He is so good and kind, that it is sad indeed that He should be grieved by slights and negligences.

'Isaac dwelt by the well Lahai-roi'
Genesis 25:11

Hagar had once found deliverance there and Ishmael had drunk from the water so graciously revealed by the God who liveth and seeth the sons of men; but this was a merely casual visit, such as worldlings pay to the Lord in times of need, when it serves their turn. They cry to Him in trouble, but forsake Him in prosperity. Isaac *dwelt* there, and made the well of the living and all-seeing God his constant source of supply. The usual tenor of a man's life, the *dwelling* of his soul, is the true test of his state. Perhaps the providential visitation experienced by Hagar struck Isaac's mind, and led him to revere the place; its mystical name endeared it to him; his frequent musings by its brim at eventide made him familiar with the well; his meeting Rebecca there had made his spirit feel at home near the spot; but best of all, the fact that he there enjoyed fellowship with the living God, had made him select that hallowed ground for his dwelling. Let us learn to live in the presence of the living God; let us pray the Holy Spirit that this day, and every other day, we may feel, 'Thou God seest me'. May the Lord Jehovah be as a well to us, delightful, comforting, unfailing, springing up unto eternal life. The bottle of the creature cracks and dries up, but the well of the Creator never fails; happy is he who dwells at the well, and so has abundant and constant supplies near at hand. The Lord has been a sure helper to others: His name is Shaddai, God All-sufficient; our hearts have often had most delightful intercourse with Him; through Him our soul has found her glorious Husband, the Lord Jesus; and in Him this day we live, and move, and have our being; let us, then, dwell in closest fellowship with Him. Glorious Lord, constrain us that we may never leave Thee, but dwell by the well of the living God.

'Whereas the Lord was there'
Ezekiel 35:10

Edom's princes saw the whole country left desolate, and counted upon its easy conquest; but there was one great difficulty in their way - quite unknown to them - *The Lord was there*; and in His presence lay the special security of the chosen land. Whatever may be the machinations and devices of the enemies of God's people, there is still the same effectual barrier to thwart their design. *The saints* are God's heritage, and He is in the midst of them, and will protect His own. What comfort this assurance yields us in our troubles and spiritual conflicts! We are constantly opposed, and yet perpetually preserved! How often Satan shoots his arrows against our *faith*, but our faith defies the power of hell's fiery darts; they are not only turned aside, but they are quenched upon its shield, for 'the Lord is there'. *Our good works* are the subjects of Satan's attacks. A saint never yet had a virtue or a grace which was not the target for hellish bullets: whether it was hope bright and sparkling, or love warm and fervent, or patience all-enduring, or zeal flaming like coals of fire, the old enemy of everything that is good has tried to destroy it. The only reason why anything virtuous or lovely survives in us is this, 'the Lord is there'.

If the Lord be with us through life, we need not fear for our dying confidence; for *when we come to die*, we shall find that 'the Lord is *there*'; where the billows are most tempestuous, and the water is most chill, we shall feel the bottom, and know that it is good: our feet shall stand upon the Rock of Ages when time is passing away. Beloved, from the first of a Christian's life to the last, the only reason why he does not perish is because *the Lord is there*. When the God of everlasting love shall change and leave His elect to perish, then may the Church of God be destroyed; but not till then, because it is written JEHOVAH SHAMMAH, *'the Lord is there'*.

'Shew me wherefore thou contendest with me'
Job 10:2

Perhaps, O tried soul, the Lord is doing this to develop thy graces. There are some of thy graces which would never be *discovered* if it were not for thy trials. Dost thou not know that thy faith never looks so grand in summer weather as it does in winter? Love is too often like a glow-worm, showing but little light except it be in the midst of surrounding darkness. Hope itself is like a star - not to be seen in the sunshine of prosperity, and only to be discovered in the night of adversity. Afflictions are often the black foils in which God doth set the jewels of His children's graces, to make them shine the better. It was but a little while ago that on thy knees thou was saying, 'Lord, I fear I have no faith: let me know that I have faith'. Was not this really, though perhaps unconsciously, praying for trials? - for how canst thou know that thou hast faith until thy faith is exercised? Depend upon it, God often sends us trials that our graces may be discovered, and that we may be certified of their existence. Besides, it is not merely discovery, *real growth* in grace is the result of sanctified trials. God often takes away our comforts and our privileges in order to make us better Christians. He trains His soldiers, not in tents of ease and luxury, but by turning them out and using them to forced marches and hard service. He makes them ford through streams, and swim through rivers, and climb mountains, and walk many a long mile with heavy knapsacks of sorrow on their backs. Well, Christian, may not this account for the troubles through which thou art passing? Is not the Lord bringing out your graces, and making them grow? Is not this the reason why He is contending with you?

'Trials make the promise sweet;
    Trials give new life to prayer;
Trials bring me to His feet,
    Lay me low, and keep me there.'

'Father, I have sinned'
Luke 15:18

It is quite certain that those whom Christ has washed
in His precious blood need not make a confession of
sin, as culprits or criminals, before God the Judge, for
Christ has for ever taken away all their sins in a legal
sense, so that they no longer stand where they can be
condemned, but are once for all accepted in the Beloved; but having become children, and offending as
children, ought they not every day to go before their
heavenly Father and confess their sin, and acknowledge their iniquity in that character? Nature teaches that
it is the duty of erring children to make a confession to
their earthly father, and the grace of God in the heart
teaches us that we, as Christians, owe the same duty to
our heavenly Father. We daily offend, and ought not to
rest without daily pardon. For, supposing that my
trespasses against my Father are not at once taken to
Him to be washed away by the cleansing power of the
Lord Jesus, what will be the consequence? If I have not
sought forgiveness and been washed from these offences against my Father, I shall feel at a distance from
Him; I shall doubt His love to me; I shall tremble at
Him; I shall be afraid to pray to Him: I shall grow like
the prodigal, who, although still a child, was yet far off
from his father. But if, with a child's sorrow at
offending so gracious and loving a Parent, I go to Him
and tell Him all, and rest not till I realise that I am
forgiven, then I shall feel a holy love to my Father, and
shall go through my Christian career, not only as
saved, but as one enjoying present peace in God
through Jesus Christ my Lord. There is a wide distinction between confessing sin *as a culprit*, and confessing sin *as a child*. The Father's bosom is the place for
penitent confessions. We have been cleansed once for
all, but our feet still need to be washed from the
defilement of our daily walk as children of God.

*'Thus saith the Lord God; I will yet for this be
enquired of by the house of Israel, to do it for them'*
Ezekiel 36:37

Prayer is the forerunner of mercy. Turn to sacred
history, and you will find that scarcely ever did a great
mercy come to this world unheralded by supplication.
You have found this true in your own personal experience. God has given you many an unsolicited favour,
but still great prayer has always been the prelude of
great mercy with you. When you first found peace
through the blood of the cross, you had been praying
much, and earnestly interceding with God that He
would remove your doubts, and deliver you from your
distresses. Your assurance was the result of prayer.
When at any time you have had high and rapturous
joys, you have been obliged to look upon them as
answers to your prayers. When you have had great
deliverances out of sore troubles, and mighty helps in
great dangers, you have been able to say, 'I sought the
Lord, and He heard me, and delivered me from all my
fears'. Prayer is always the preface to blessing. It goes
before the blessing *as the blessing's shadow*. When
the sunlight of God's mercies rises upon our necessities, it casts the shadow of prayer far down upon the
plain. Or, to use another illustration, when God piles up
a hill of mercies, He Himself shines behind them, and
He casts on our spirits the shadow of prayer, so that we
may rest certain, if we are much in prayer, our pleadings are the shadows of mercy. Prayer is thus connected with the blessing *to show us the value of it*. If
we had the blessings without asking for them, we
should think them common things; but prayer makes
our mercies more precious than diamonds. The things
we ask for are precious, but we do not realise their
preciousness until we have sought for them earnestly.

'Prayer makes the darken'd cloud withdraw;
   Prayer climbs the ladder Jacob saw;
Gives exercise to faith and love;
   Brings every blessing from above.'

'He first findeth his own brother Simon'
John 1:41

This case is an excellent pattern of all cases where spiritual life is vigorous. *As soon as a man has found Christ, he begins to find others.* I will not believe that thou hast tasted of the honey of the gospel if thou canst eat it all thyself. True grace puts an end to all spiritual monopoly. Andrew *first* found his own brother Simon, and then others. *Relationship has a very strong demand upon our first individual efforts.* Andrew, thou didst well to begin with Simon. I doubt whether there are not some Christians giving away tracts at other people's houses who would do well to give away a tract at their own - whether there are not some engaged in works of usefulness abroad who are neglecting their special sphere of usefulness at home. Thou mayest or thou mayest not be called to evangelise the people in any particular locality, but certainly thou art called to see after thine own servants, thine own kinsfolk and acquaintance. Let thy religion begin at home. Many tradesmen export their best commodities - the Christian should not. He should have all his conversation everywhere of the best savour; but let him have a care to put forth the sweetest fruit of spiritual life and testimony in his own family. When Andrew went to find his brother, he little imagined how eminent Simon would become. *Simon Peter was worth ten Andrews* so far as we can gather from sacred history, and yet Andrew was instrumental in bringing him to Jesus. You may be very deficient in talent yourself, and yet you may be the means of drawing to Christ one who shall become eminent in grace and service. Ah! dear friend, you little know the possibilities which are in you. You may but speak a word to a child, and in that child there may be slumbering a noble heart which shall stir the Christian church in years to come. Andrew has only two talents, but he finds Peter. Go thou and do likewise.

'*God, that comforteth those that are cast down*'
2 Corinthians 7:6

And who comforteth like Him? Go to some poor, melancholy, distressed child of God; tell him sweet promises, and whisper in his ear choice words of comfort; he is like the deaf adder, he listens not to the voice of the charmer, charm he never so wisely. He is drinking gall and wormwood, and comfort him as you may, it will be only a note or two of mournful resignation that you will get from him; you will bring forth no psalms of praise, no hallelujahs, no joyful sonnets. But let *God* come to His child, let Him lift up his countenance, and the mourner's eyes glisten with hope. Do you not hear him sing-

> ''Tis paradise, if thou art here;
> If thou depart, 'tis hell'?

You could not have cheered him: but the Lord has done it; 'He is the God of all comfort'. There is no balm in Gilead, but there is balm in God. There is no physician among the creatures, but the Creator is Jehovah-rophi. It is marvellous how one sweet word of God will make whole songs for Christians. One word of God is like a piece of gold, and the Christian is the goldbeater, and can hammer that promise out for whole weeks. So, then, poor Christian, thou needest not sit down in despair. Go to the Comforter, and ask Him to give thee consolation. Thou art a poor dry well. You have heard it said, that when a pump is dry, go to God, ask Him to shed abroad His joy in thy heart, and then thy joy shall be full. Do not go to earthly acquaintances, for you will find them Job's comforters after all; but go first and foremost to thy 'God, that comforteth those that are cast down', and you will soon say, 'In the multitude of my thoughts within me thy comforts delight my soul'.

*'Then was Jesus led up of the Spirit into the
wilderness to be tempted of the devil'*
Matthew 4:1

A holy character does not avert temptation - Jesus was
tempted. When Satan tempts us, his sparks fall upon
tinder; but in Christ's case, it was like striking sparks
on water; yet the enemy continued his evil work. Now,
if the devil goes on striking when there is no result, how
much more will he do it when he knows what inflam-
mable stuff our hearts are made of! Though you
become greatly sanctified by the Holy Ghost, expect
that the great dog of hell will bark at you still. In the
haunts of men we expect to be tempted, but even
seclusion will not guard us from the same trial. Jesus
Christ was led away from human society into the
wilderness, and was tempted of the devil. Solitude has
its charms and its benefits, and may be useful in
checking the lust of the eye and the pride of life; but the
devil will follow us into the most lovely retreats. Do
not suppose that it is only the worldly-minded who
have dreadful thoughts and blasphemous temptations,
for even spiritual-minded persons endure the same;
and in the holiest position we may suffer the darkest
temptation. The utmost consecration of spirit will not
insure you against Satanic temptation. Christ was
consecrated through and through. It was His meat and
drink to do the will of Him that sent Him: and yet He
was tempted! Your hearts may glow with a seraphic
flame of love to Jesus, and yet the devil will try to bring
you down to Laodicean lukewarmness. If you will tell
me when God permits a Christian to lay aside his
armour, I will tell you when Satan has left off temptation. Like the old knights in war time, we must sleep
with helmet and breastplate buckled on, for the arch-
deceiver will seize our first unguarded hour to make us
his prey. The Lord keep us watchful in all seasons, and
give us a final escape from the jaw of the lion and the
paw of the bear.

'He hath said'
Hebrews 13:5

If we can only grasp these words by faith, we have an all-conquering weapon in our hand. What doubt will not be slain by this two-edged sword? What fear is there which shall not fall smitten with a deadly wound before this arrow from the bow of God's covenant? Will not the distresses of life and the pangs of death; will not the corruptions within, and the snares without; will not the trials from above, and the temptations from beneath, all seem but light afflictions, when we can hide ourselves beneath the bulwark of 'He hath said'? Yes; whether for delight in our quietude, or for strength in our conflict, 'He hath said' must be our daily resort. And this may teach us the extreme value of *searching* the Scriptures. There may be a promise in the Word which would exactly fit your case, but you may not know of it, and therefore you miss its comfort. You are like prisoners in a dungeon, and there may be one key in the bunch which would unlock the door, and you might be free; but if you will not look for it, you may remain a prisoner still, though liberty is so near at hand. There may be a potent medicine in the great pharmaco-poeia of Scripture, and you may yet continue sick unless you will examine and search the Scriptures to discover what 'He hath said'. Should you not, besides reading the Bible, store your memories richly with the promises of God? You can recollect the sayings of great men; you treasure up the verses of renowned poets; ought you not to be profound in your knowledge of the words of God, so that you may be able to quote them readily when you would solve a difficulty, or overthrow a doubt? Since 'He hath said' is the source of all wisdom, and the fountain of all comfort, let it dwell in you richly, as 'A well of water, springing up unto everlasting life'. So shall you grow healthy, strong, and happy in the divine life.

'Understandest thou what thou readest?'
Acts 8:30

We should be abler teachers of others, and less liable to be carried about by every wind of doctrine, if we sought to have a more intelligent understanding of the Word of God. As the Holy Ghost, the Author of the Scriptures, is He who alone can enlighten us rightly to understand them, we should constantly ask His teaching, and His guidance into all truth. When the prophet Daniel would interpret Nebuchadnezzar's dream, what did he do? He set himself to earnest prayer that God would open up the vision. The apostle John, in his vision at Patmos, saw a book sealed with seven seals which none was found worthy to open, or so much as to look upon. The book was afterwards opened by the Lion of the tribe of Judah, who had prevailed to open it; but it is written first - 'I wept much'. The tears of John, which were his liquid prayers, were, so far as he was concerned, the sacred keys by which the folded book was opened. Therefore if, for your own and others' profiting, you desire to be 'filled with the knowledge of God's will in all wisdom and spiritual understanding', remember that prayer is your best means of study: like Daniel, you shall understand the dream, and the interpretation thereof, when you have sought unto God; and like John you shall see the seven seals of precious truth unloosed, after you have wept much. Stones are not broken, except by an earnest use of the hammer; and the stone-breaker must go down on his knees. Use the hammer of diligence, and let the knee of prayer be exercised, and there is not a stony doctrine in revelation which is useful for you to understand, which will not fly into shivers under the exercise of prayer and faith. You may force your way through anything with the leverage of prayer. Thoughts and reasonings are like the steel wedges which give a hold upon truth; but prayer is the lever, the prise which forces open the iron chest of sacred mystery, that we may get the treasure hidden within.

> '*His bow abode in strength,*
> *and the arms of his hands were made strong*
> *by the hands of the mighty God of Jacob*'
> Genesis 49:24.

That strength which God gives to His Josephs is *real* strength; it is not a boasted valour, a fiction, a thing of which men talk, but which ends in smoke; it is true - *divine strength*. Why does Joseph stand against temptation? Because God gives him aid. There is nought that we can do without the power of God. All true strength comes from 'the mighty God of Jacob'. Notice in what a *blessedly familiar way* God gives this strength to Joseph - 'The arms of his hands were made strong by the hands of the mighty God of Jacob'. Thus God is represented as putting His hands on Joseph's hands, placing His arms on Joseph's arms. Like as a father teaches his children, so the Lord teaches them that fear Him. He puts His arms upon them. Marvellous condescension! God Almighty, Eternal, Omnipotent, stoops from His throne and lays His hand upon the child's hand, stretching His arm upon the arm of Joseph, that he may be made strong! This strength was also *covenant strength*, for it is ascribed to 'the mighty *God of Jacob*'. Now, wherever you read of the God of Jacob in the Bible, you should remember the covenant with Jacob. Christians love to think of God's covenant. All the power, all the grace, all the blessings, all the mercies, all the comforts, all the things we have, flow to us from the well-head, through the covenant. If there were no covenant, then we should fail indeed; for all grace proceeds from it, as light and heat from the sun. No angels ascend or descend, save upon that ladder which Jacob saw, at the top of which stood a covenant God. Christian, it may be that the archers have sorely grieved you, and shot at you, and wounded you, but still your bow abides in strength; be sure, then, to ascribe all the glory to Jacob's God.

'The Lord is slow to anger, and great in power'
Nahum 1:3

Jehovah *'is slow to anger'*. When mercy cometh into
the world she driveth winged steeds; the axles of her
chariot wheels are red hot with speed; but when wrath
goeth forth, it toileth on with tardy footsteps, for God
taketh no pleasure in the sinner's death. God's rod of
mercy is ever in His hands outstretched; His sword of
justice is in its scabbard, held down by that pierced
hand of love which bled for the sins of men. 'The Lord
is slow to anger', because He is GREAT IN POWER.
He is truly great in power who hath power over himself.
When God's power doth restrain Himself, then it is
power indeed: the power that binds omnipotence is
omnipotence surpassed. A man who has a strong mind
can bear to be insulted long, and only resents the wrong
when a sense of right demands his action. The weak
mind is irritated at a little: the strong mind bears it like
a rock which moveth not, though a thousand breakers
dash upon it, and cast their pitiful malice in spray upon
its summit. God marketh his enemies, and yet He
bestirs not Himself, but holdeth in His anger. If He
were less divine than He is, He would long ere this have
sent forth the whole of His thunders, and emptied the
magazines of heaven; He would long ere this have
blasted the earth with the wondrous fires of its lower
regions, and man would have been utterly destroyed;
but the greatness of his power brings us mercy. Dear
reader, what is your state this evening? Can you by
humble faith look to Jesus, and say, 'My substitute,
Thou art my rock, my trust'? Then, beloved, be not
afraid of God's power; for now that you are forgiven
and accepted, now that by faith you have fled to Christ
for refuge, the power of God need no more terrify you,
than the shield and sword of the warrior need terrify
those whom he loves. Rather rejoice that He who is
'great in power' is your Father and Friend.

'I will never leave thee'
Hebrews 13:5

No promise is of private interpretation. Whatever God has said to any one saint, He has said to all. When He opens a well for one, it is that all may drink. When He openeth a granary door to give out food, there may be some one starving man who is the occasion of its being opened, but all hungry saints may come and feed too. Whether He gave the word to Abraham or to Moses, matters not, O believer; He has given it to thee as one of the covenanted seed. There is not a high blessing too lofty for thee, nor a wide mercy too extensive for thee. Lift up now thine eyes to the north and to the south, to the east and to the west, for all this is thine. Climb to Pisgah's top, and view the utmost limit of the divine promise, for the land is all thine own. There is not a brook of living water of which thou mayst not drink. If the land floweth with milk and honey, eat the honey and drink the milk, for both are thine. Be thou bold to believe, for He hath said, 'I will never leave *thee*, nor forsake *thee*'. In this promise, God gives to His people everything. '*I* will never leave thee.' Then no attribute of God can cease to be engaged for us. Is He mighty? He will show Himself strong on the behalf of them that trust Him. Is HE love? Then with lovingkindness will He have mercy upon us. Whatever attributes may compose the character of Deity, every one of them to its fullest extent shall be engaged on our side. To put everything in one, there is nothing you can want, there is nothing you can ask for, there is nothing you can need in time or in eternity, there is nothing living, nothing dying, there is nothing in this world, nothing in the next world, there is nothing now, nothing at the resurrection-morning, nothing in heaven which is not contained in this text - 'I will never leave thee, nor forsake thee'.

'Take up the cross, and follow Me'
Mark 10:21

You have not the making of your own cross, although unbelief is a master carpenter at cross-making; neither are you permitted to choose your own cross, although self-will would fain be lord and master; but your cross is prepared and appointed for you by divine love, and you are cheerfully to accept it; you are to *take up* the cross as your chosen badge and burden, and not to stand cavilling at it. This night Jesus bids you submit your shoulder to His easy yoke. Do not kick at it in petulance, or trample on it in vain-glory, or fall under it in despair, or run away from it in fear, but take it up like a true follower of Jesus. Jesus was a cross-bearer; He leads the way in the path of sorrow. Surely you could not desire a better guide! And if He carries a cross, what nobler burden would you desire? The *Via Crucis* is the way of safety; fear not to tread its thorny paths.

Beloved, the cross is not made of feathers, or lined with velvet, it is heavy and galling to disobedient shoulders; but it is not an iron cross, though your fears have painted it with iron colours, it is a wooden cross, and a man can carry it, for the Man of Sorrows tried the load. Take up your cross, and by the power of the Spirit of God, you will soon be so in love with it, that like Moses, you would not exchange the reproach of Christ for all the treasures of Egypt. Remember that Jesus carried it, and it will smell sweetly; remember that it will soon be followed by the crown, and the thought of the coming weight of glory will greatly lighten the present heaviness of trouble. The Lord help you to bow your spirit in submission to the divine will ere you fall asleep this night, that waking with tomorrow's sun, you may go forth to the day's cross with the holy and submissive spirit which becomes a follower of the Crucified.

'*I will cause the shower to come down in his
season; there shall be showers of blessing*'
Ezekiel 34:26

Here is *sovereign mercy* - 'I will give them the shower
in its season'. Is it not sovereign, *divine* mercy? - for
who can say, 'I will give them showers', except God?
There is only one voice which can speak to the clouds,
and bid them beget the rain. Who sendeth down the rain
upon the earth? Who scattereth the showers upon the
green herb? Do not I, the Lord? So grace is the gift of
God, and is not to be created by man. It is also *needed*
grace. What would the ground do without showers?
You may break the clods, you may sow your seeds, but
what can you do without the rain? As absolutely
needful is the divine blessing. In vain you labour, until
God the plenteous shower bestows, and sends salvation down. Then, it is *plenteous grace*. 'I will send
them showers.' It does not say, 'I will send them
drops', but 'showers'. So it is with grace. If God gives
a blessing, He usually gives it in such a measure that
there is not room enough to receive it. Plenteous grace!
Ah! we want plenteous grace to keep us humble, to
make us prayerful, to make us holy; plenteous grace to
make us zealous, to preserve us through this life, and
at last to land us in heaven. We cannot do without
saturating showers of grace. Again, it is *seasonable
grace*. 'I will cause the shower to come down *in his
season*.' What is thy season this morning? Is it the
season of drought? Then that is the season for showers.
Is it a season of great heaviness and black clouds? Then
that is the season for showers. 'As thy days so shall thy
strength be.' And here is a *varied* blessing. 'I will give
thee *showers* of blessing.' The word is in the plural.
All kinds of blessings God will send. All God's
blessings go together, like links in a golden chain. If He
gives converting grace, He will also give comforting
grace. He will send 'showers of blessing'. Look up
today, O parched plant, and open thy leaves and flowers
for a heavenly watering.

*'O Lord of hosts, how long wilt thou not have mercy
upon Jerusalem? ...And the Lord answered the
angel... with good words and comfortable words'*
Zechariah 1:12, 13

What a sweet answer to an anxious enquiry! This night
let us rejoice in it. O Zion, there are good things in store
for thee; thy time of travail shall soon be over; thy
children shall be brought forth; thy captivity shall end.
Bear patiently the rod for a season, and under the
darkness still trust in God, for His love burneth
towards thee. God loves the church with a love too deep
for human imagination: He loves her with all His
infinite heart. Therefore let her sons be of good
courage; she cannot be far from prosperity to whom
God speaketh 'good words and comfortable words'.
What these comfortable words are the prophet goes on
to tell us: 'I am jealous for Jerusalem and for Zion with
a great jealousy'. The Lord loves His church so much
that He cannot bear that she should go astray to others;
and when she has done so, he cannot endure that she
should suffer too much or too heavily. He will not have
his enemies afflict her: He is displeased with them
because they increase her misery. When God seems
most to leave His church, His heart is warm towards
her. History shows us that whenever God uses a rod to
chasten His servants, He always breaks it afterwards,
as if he loathed the rod which gave his children pain. He
feels the smart far more than His people. 'Like as a
father pitieth his children, so the Lord pitieth them that
fear Him.' God hath not forgotten us because He smites
- His blows are no evidences of want of love. If this is
true of His church *collectively*, it is of necessity true
also of *each individual member*. You may fear that the
Lord has passed you by, but it is not so: He who counts
the stars, and calls them by their names, is in no danger
of forgetting His own children. He knows your case as
thoroughly as if you were the only creature He ever
made, or the only saint He ever loved. Approach Him
and be at peace.

'The wrath to come'
Matthew 3:7

It is pleasant to pass over a country after a storm has spent itself; to smell the freshness of the herbs after the rain has passed away, and to note the drops while they glisten like purest diamonds in the sunlight. That is the position of a Christian. He is going through a land where the storm has spent itself upon His Saviour's head, and if there be a few drops of sorrow falling, they distil from clouds of mercy, and Jesus cheers him by the assurance that they are not for his destruction. But how terrible is it to witness the approach of a tempest: to note the forewarnings of the storm; to mark the birds of heaven as they droop their wings; to see the cattle as they lay their heads low in terror; to discern the face of the sky as it groweth black, and look to the sun which shineth not, and the heavens which are angry and frowning! How terrible to await the dread advance of a hurricane - such as occurs, sometimes, in the tropics - to wait in terrible apprehensions till the wind shall rush forth in fury, tearing up trees from their roots, forcing rocks from their pedestals, and hurling down all the dwelling-places of man! And yet, sinner, this is your present position. No hot drops have as yet fallen, but a shower of fire is coming. No terrible winds howl around you, but God's tempest is gathering its dread artillery. As yet the water-floods are dammed up by mercy, but the flood-gates shall soon be opened: the thunderbolts of God are yet in His storehouse, but lo! the tempest hastens, and how awful shall that moment be when God, robed in vengeance, shall march forth in fury! Where, where, where, O sinner, wilt thou hide thy head, or whither wilt thou flee? O that the hand of mercy may now lead you to Christ! He is freely set before you in the gospel: His riven side is the rock of shelter. Thou knowest thy need of Him; believe in Him, cast thyself upon Him, and then the fury shall be overpast for ever.

'*But Jonah rose up to flee unto Tarshish from the
presence of the Lord, and went down to Joppa*'
Jonah 1:3

Instead of going to Nineveh to preach the Word, as God
bade him, Jonah disliked the work, and went down to
Joppa to escape from it. There are occasions when
God's servants shrink from duty. But what is the
consequence? What did Jonah lose by his conduct? *He
lost the presence and comfortable enjoyment of God's
love*. When *we* serve our Lord Jesus as believers
should do, our God is with us; and though we have the
whole world against us, if we have God with us, what
does it matter? But the moment we start back, and seek
our own inventions, we are at sea without a pilot. Then
may we bitterly lament and groan out, 'O my God,
where hast Thou gone? How could I have been so
foolish as to shun Thy service, and in this way to lose
all the bright shinings of Thy face? This is a price too
high. Let me return to my allegiance, that I may rejoice
in Thy presence.' In the next place, Jonah *lost all peace
of mind*. Sin soon destroys a believer's comfort. It is
the poisonous upas tree, from whose leaves distil
deadly drops which destroy the life of joy and peace.
Jonah *lost everything upon which he might have drawn
for comfort in any other case*. He could not plead the
promise of divine protection, for he was not in God's
ways; he could not say, 'Lord, I meet with these
difficulties in the discharge of my duty, therefore help
me through them'. He was reaping his own deeds; he
was filled with his own ways. Christian, do not play the
Jonah, unless you wish to have all the waves and the
billows rolling over your head. You will find in the
long run that it is far harder to shun the work and will
of God than to at once yield yourself to it. *Jonah lost
his time*, for he had to go to Tarshish after all. It is hard
to contend with God; let us yield ourselves at once.

'*Salvation is of the Lord*'
Jonah 2:9

Salvation is the work of God. It is He alone who quickens the soul 'dead in trespasses and sins', and it is He also who maintains the soul in its spiritual life. He is both 'Alpha and Omega'. 'Salvation is of the Lord.' If I am prayerful, God makes me prayerful; if I have graces, they are God's gifts to me; if I hold on in a consistent life, it is because He upholds me with His hand. I do nothing whatever towards my own preservation, except what God himself first does in me. Whatever I have, all my goodness is of the Lord alone. Wherein I sin, that is my own; but wherein I act rightly, that is of God, wholly and completely. If I have repulsed a spiritual enemy, the Lord's strength nerved my arm. Do I live before men a consecrated life? It is not I, but Christ who liveth in me. Am I sanctified? I did not cleanse myself: God's Holy Spirit sanctifies me. Am I weaned from the world? I am weaned by *God*'s chastisements sanctified to my good. Do I grow in knowledge? The great Instructor teaches me. All my jewels were fashioned by heavenly art. I find in God all that I want; but I find in myself nothing but sin and misery. 'He only is my rock and my salvation.' Do I feed on the Word? That Word would be no food for me unless the Lord made it food for my soul, and helped me to feed upon it. Do I live on the manna which comes down from heaven? What is that manna but Jesus Christ himself incarnate, whose body and whose blood I eat and drink? Am I continually receiving fresh increase of strength? Where do I gather my might? My help cometh from heaven's hills: without Jesus I can do nothing. As a branch cannot bring forth fruit except it abide in the vine, no more can I, except I abide in Him. What Jonah learned in the great deep, let me learn this morning in my closet: 'Salvation is of the Lord.'

*'Behold, if the leprosy have covered all his flesh, he
shall pronounce him clean that hath the plague'*
Leviticus 13:13

Strange enough this regulation appears, yet there was
wisdom in it, for the throwing out of the disease proved
that the constitution was sound. This evening it may be
well for us to see the typical teaching of so singular a
rule. We, too, are lepers, and may read the law of the
leper as applicable to ourselves. When a man sees
himself to be altogether lost and ruined, covered all
over with the defilement of sin, and in no part free from
pollution; when he disclaims all righteousness of his
own, and pleads guilty before the Lord, then he is clean
through the blood of Jesus, and the grace of God.
Hidden, unfelt, unconfessed iniquity is the true leprosy; but when sin is seen and felt, it has received its
deathblow, and the Lord looks with eyes of mercy upon
the soul afflicted with it. Nothing is more deadly than
self-righteousness, or more hopeful than contrition.
We must confess that we are 'nothing else but sin', for
no confession short of this will be the whole truth; and
if the Holy Spirit be at work with us, convincing us of
sin, there will be no difficulty about making such an
acknowledgment - it will spring spontaneously from
our lips. What comfort does the text afford to truly
awakened sinners: the very circumstance which so
grievously discouraged them is here turned into a sign
and symptom of a hopeful state! Stripping comes
before clothing; digging out the foundation is the first
thing in building - and a thorough sense of sin is one
of the earliest works of grace in the heart. O thou poor
leprous sinner, utterly destitute of a sound spot, take
heart from the text, and come as thou art to Jesus.

'For let our debts be what they may, however great or small,
As soon as we have nought to pay, our Lord forgives us all.
'Tis perfect poverty alone that sets the soul at large:
While we can call one mite our own, we have no full discharge.'

*'Thou hast made the Lord, which is my refuge, even
the Most High, thy habitation'*
Psalm 91:9

The Israelites in the wilderness *were continually exposed to change.* Whenever the pillar stayed its motion, the tents were pitched; but tomorrow, ere the
morning sun had risen, the trumpet sounded, the ark
was in motion, and the fiery, cloudy pillar was leading
the way through the narrow defiles of the mountain, up
the hillside, or along the arid waste of the wilderness.
They had scarcely time to rest a little before they heard
the sound of 'Away! this is not your rest; you must still
be onward journeying towards Canaan!' They were
never long in one place. Even wells and palm trees
could not detain them. Yet they had an abiding home in
their God, His cloudy pillar was their roof-tree, and its
flame by night their household fire. They must go
onward from place to place, continually changing,
never having time to settle, and to say, 'Now we are
secure; in this place we shall dwell'. 'Yet,' says
Moses, 'though we are always changing, Lord, thou
hast been our dwelling-place throughout all generations.' The Christian knows no change with regard to
God. He may be rich today and poor tomorrow; he may
be sickly today, tomorrow he may be distressed - but
there is no change with regard to his relationship to
God. If He loved me yesterday, He loves me today. My
unmoving mansion of rest is my blessed Lord. Let
prospects be blighted; let hopes be blasted; let joy be
withered; let mildews destroy everything; I have lost
nothing of what I have in God. He is 'my strong
habitation whereunto I can continually resort'. I am a
pilgrim in the world, but at home in my God. In the
earth I wander, but in God I dwell in a quiet habitation.

'Whose goings forth have been from of old,
from everlasting'
Micah 5:2

The Lord Jesus had goings forth for His people *as their representative before the throne, long before they appeared upon the stage of time.* It was 'from everlasting' that He signed the compact with His Father, that He would pay blood for blood, suffering for suffering, agony for agony, and death for death, in the behalf of His people; it was 'from everlasting' that He gave Himself up without a murmuring word, that from the crown of His head to the sole of His foot He might sweat great drops of blood, that He might be spit upon, pierced, mocked, rent asunder, and crushed beneath the pains of death. His goings forth as our Surety were from everlasting. Pause, my soul, and wonder! Thou hadst goings forth in the person of Jesus 'from everlasting'. Not only when thou wast born into the world did Christ love thee, but His delights were with the sons of men before there were any sons of men. Often did He think of them; from everlasting to everlasting He had set His affection upon them. What! my soul, has he been so long about thy salvation, and will not He accomplish it? Has he from everlasting been going forth to save me, and will He lose me now? What! has He carried me in His hand, as His precious jewel, and will He now let me slip from between His fingers? Did He choose me before the mountains were brought forth, or the channels of the deep were digged, and will He reject me now? Impossible! I am sure He would not have loved me so long if He had not been a changeless Lover. If He could grow weary of me, He would have been tired of me long before now. If He had not loved me with a love as deep as hell, and as strong as death, He would have turned from me long ago. Oh, joy above all joys, to know that I am His everlasting and inalienable inheritance, given to Him by His Father or ever the earth was! Everlasting love shall be the pillow for my head this night.

'My expectation is from Him'
Psalm 62:5

It is the believer's privilege to use this language. If he is looking for aught from the world, it is a poor 'expectation' indeed. But if he looks to God for the supply of his wants, whether in temporal or spiritual blessings, his 'expectation' will not be a vain one. Constantly he may draw from the bank of faith, and get his need supplied out of the riches of God's loving-kindness. This I know, I had rather have God for my banker than all the Rothschilds. My Lord never fails to honour his promises; and when we bring them to His throne, He never sends them back unanswered. Therefore I will wait only at His door, for He ever opens it with the hand of munificent grace. At this hour I will try him anew. But we have 'expectations' beyond this life. We shall die soon; and then our 'expectation is from Him'. Do we not expect that when we lie upon the bed of sickness He will send angels to carry us to His bosom? We believe that when the pulse is faint, and the heart heaves heavily, some angelic messenger shall stand and look with loving eyes upon us, and whisper, 'Sister spirit, come away!' As we approach the heavenly gate, we expect to hear the welcome invitation, 'Come, ye blessed of my Father, inherit the kingdom prepared for you from the foundation of the world'. We are expecting harps of gold and crowns of glory; we are hoping soon to be amongst the multitude of shining ones before the throne; we are looking forward and longing for the time when we shall be like our glorious Lord - for 'We shall see Him as He is'. Then if these be thine 'expectations', O my soul, live for God; live with the desire and resolve to glorify Him from whom cometh all thy supplies, and of whose grace in thy election, redemption, and calling, it is that thou hast any 'expectation' of coming glory.

'The barrel of meal wasted not, neither did the cruse of oil fail, according to the word of the Lord, which He spake by Elijah'
1 Kings 17:16

See the faithfulness of divine love. You observe that this woman had *daily necessities*. She had herself and her son to feed in a time of famine; and now, in addition, the prophet Elijah was to be fed too. But though the need was threefold, yet the supply of meal wasted not, for she had *a constant supply*. Each day she made calls upon the barrel, but yet each day it remained the same. You, dear reader, have daily necessities, and because they come so frequently, you are apt to fear that the barrel of meal will one day be empty, and the cruse of oil will fail you. Rest assured that, according to the Word of God, this shall not be the case. Each day, though it bring its trouble, shall bring its help; and though you should live to outnumber the years of Methuselah, and though your needs should be as many as the sands of the seashore, yet shall God's grace and mercy last through all your necessities, and you shall never know a real lack. For three long years, in this widow's days, the heavens never saw a cloud, and the stars never wept a holy tear of dew upon the wicked earth: famine and desolation, and death, made the land a howling wilderness, but this woman never was hungry, but always joyful in abundance. So shall it be with you. You shall see the sinner's hope perish, for he trusts his native strength; you shall see the proud Pharisee's confidence totter, for he builds his hope upon the sand; you shall see even your own schemes blasted and withered, but you yourself shall find that your place of defence shall be the munition of rocks: 'Your bread shall be given you, and your water shall be sure'. Better have God for your guardian, than the Bank of England for your possession. You might spend the wealth of the Indies, but the infinite riches of God you can never exhaust.

'With lovingkindness have I drawn thee'
Jeremiah 31:3

The thunders of the law and the terrors of judgment are all used to bring us to Christ; but the final victory is effected by lovingkindness. The prodigal set out to his father's house from a sense of need; but his father saw him a great way off, and ran to meet him; so that the last steps he took towards his father's house were with the kiss still warm upon his cheek, and the welcome still musical in his ears.

> 'Law and terrors do but harden
> 　All the while they work alone;
> But a sense of blood-bought pardon
> 　Will dissolve a heart of stone.'

The Master came one night to the door, and knocked with the iron hand of the law; the door shook and trembled upon its hinges; but the man piled every piece of furniture which he could find against the door, for he said, 'I will not admit the man'. The Master turned away, but by-and-by He came back, and with His own soft hand, using most that part where the nail had penetrated, he knocked again - oh, so softly and tenderly. This time the door did not shake, but, strange to say, it opened, and there upon his knees the once unwilling host was found rejoicing to receive his guest. 'Come in, come in; thou hast so knocked that my bowels are moved for thee. I could not think of thy pierced hand leaving its blood-mark on my door, and of thy going away houseless, "Thy head filled with dew, and thy locks with the drops of the night". I yield, I yield, Thy love has won my heart.' So in every case: lovingkindness wins the day. What Moses with the tablets of stone could never do, Christ does with His pierced hand. Such is the doctrine of effectual calling. Do I understand it experimentally? Can I say, 'He drew me and I followed on, glad to confess the voice divine'? If so, may He continue to draw me, till at last I shall sit down at the marriage supper of the Lamb.

'Now we have received... the spirit which is of God;
that we might know the things
that are freely given to us of God'
Corinthians 2:12

Dear reader, have you received the spirit which is of God, wrought by the Holy Ghost in your soul? The necessity of the work of the Holy Spirit in the heart may be clearly seen from this fact, that *all which has been done by God the Father, and by God the Son, must be ineffectual to us, unless the Spirit shall reveal these things to our souls.* What effect does the doctrine of election have upon any man until the Spirit of God enters into him? Election is a dead letter in my consciousness until the Spirit of God calls me out of darkness into marvellous light. *Then* through my calling, I see my election, and knowing myself to be called of God, I know myself to have been chosen in the eternal purpose. A covenant was made with the Lord Jesus Christ, by His Father; but what avails that covenant to us until the Holy Spirit brings us its blessings, and opens our hearts to receive them? There hang the blessings on the nail - Christ Jesus; but being short of stature, we cannot reach them; the Spirit of God takes them down and hands them to us, and thus they become actually ours. Covenant blessings in themselves are like the manna in the skies, far out of mortal reach, but the Spirit of God opens the windows of heaven and scatters the living bread around the camp of the spiritual Israel. Christ's finished work is like wine stored in the wine-vat; through unbelief we can neither draw nor drink. The Holy Spirit dips our vessel into this precious wine, and then we drink; but without the Spirit we are as truly dead in sin as though the Father never had elected, and the Son had never bought us with His blood. The Holy Spirit is absolutely necessary to our well-being. Let us walk lovingly towards Him and tremble at the thought of grieving Him.

March

'Awake, O north wind; and come, thou south; blow upon my garden, that the spices thereof may flow out'
Canticles 4:16

Anything is better than the dead calm of indifference. Our souls may wisely desire the north wind of trouble if that alone can be sanctified to the drawing forth of the perfume of our graces. So long as it cannot be said, 'The Lord was not in the wind', we will not shrink from the most wintry blast that ever blew upon plants of grace. Did not the spouse in this verse humbly submit herself to the reproofs of her Beloved; only entreating Him to send forth His grace in some form, and making no stipulation as to the peculiar manner in which it should come? Did she not, like ourselves, become so utterly weary of deadness and unholy calm that she sighed for any visitation which would brace her to action? Yet she desires the warm south wind of comfort too, the smiles of divine love, the joy of the Redeemer's presence; these are often mightily effectual to arouse our sluggish life. She desires either one or the other, or both; so that she may but be able to delight her Beloved with the spices of her garden. She cannot endure to be unprofitable, nor can we. How cheering a thought that Jesus can find comfort in our poor feeble graces. Can it be? It seems far too good to be true. Well may we court trial or even death itself if we shall thereby be aided to make glad Immanuel's heart. O that our heart were crushed to atoms if only by such bruising our sweet Lord Jesus could be glorified. Graces unexercised are as sweet perfumes slumbering in the cups of the flowers; the wisdom of the great Husbandman overrules diverse and opposite causes to produce the one desired result, and makes both affliction and consolation draw forth the grateful odours of faith, love, patience, hope, resignation, joy, and the other fair flowers of the garden. May we know by sweet experience, what this means.

'He is precious'
1 Peter 2:7

As all the rivers run into the sea, so all delights centre in our Beloved. The glances of His eyes outshine the sun: the beauties of His face are fairer than the choicest flowers: no fragrance is like the breath of His mouth. Gems of the mine, and pearls from the sea, are worthless things when measured by His preciousness. Peter tells us that Jesus is precious, but he did not and could not tell us *how* precious, nor could any of us compute the value of God's unspeakable gift. Words cannot set forth the preciousness of the Lord Jesus to His people, nor fully tell how essential He is to their satisfaction and happiness. Believer, have you not found in the midst of plenty a sore famine if your Lord has been absent? The sun was shining, but Christ had hidden Himself, and all the world was black to you; or it was night, and since the bright and morning star was gone, no other star could yield you so much as a ray of light. What a howling wilderness is this world without our Lord! If once He hideth Himself from us, withered are the fruits of our garden; our pleasant fruits decay; the birds suspend their songs, and a tempest overturns our hopes. All earth's candles cannot make daylight if the Sun of Righteousness be eclipsed. He is the soul of our soul, the light of our light, the life of our life. Dear reader, what wouldst thou do in the world without Him, in the midst of its temptations and its cares? What wouldst thou do in the morning without Him, when thou wakest up and lookest forward to the day's battle? What wouldst thou do at night, when thou comest home jaded and weary, if there were no door of fellowship between thee and Christ? Blessed be His name, He will not suffer us to try our lot without Him, for Jesus never forsakes His own. Yet, let the thought of *what life would be without Him* enhance His preciousness.

'But all the Israelites went down to the Philistines,
to sharpen every man his share, and his coulter,
and his axe, and his mattock'
1 Samuel 13:20

We are engaged in a great war with the Philistines of evil. *Every weapon within our reach must be used.* Preaching, teaching, praying, giving, all must be brought into action, and talents which have been thought too mean for service, must now be employed. Coulter, and axe, and mattock, may all be useful in slaying Philistines; rough tools may deal hard blows, and killing need not be elegantly done, so long as it is done effectually. Each moment of time, in season or out of season; each fragment of ability, educated or untutored; each opportunity, favourable or unfavourable, must be used, for our foes are many and our force but slender.
Most of our tools want sharpening; we need quickness of perception, tact, energy, promptness, in a word, complete adaptation for the Lord's work. Practical common sense is a very scarce thing among the conductors of Christian enterprises. We might learn from our enemies if we would, and so *make the Philistines sharpen our weapons*. This morning let us note enough to sharpen our zeal during this day by the aid of the Holy Spirit. See the energy of the Papists, how they compass sea and land to make one proselyte, are they to monopolize all the earnestness? Mark the heathen devotees, what tortures they endure in the service of their idols! are they alone to exhibit patience and self-sacrifice? Observe the prince of darkness, how persevering in his endeavours, how unabashed in his attempts, how daring in his plans, how thoughtful in his plots, how energetic in all! The devils are united as one man in their infamous rebellion, while we believers in Jesus are divided in our service of God, and scarcely ever work with unanimity. O that from Satan's infernal industry we may learn to go about like good Samaritans, seeking whom we may bless!

*'Unto me, who am less than the least of all saints,
is this grace given, that I should preach among the
Gentiles the unsearchable riches of Christ'*
Ephesians 3:8

The apostle Paul felt it a great privilege to be allowed
to preach the gospel. He did not look upon his calling
as a drudgery, but he entered upon it with intense
delight. Yet while Paul was thus thankful for his office,
his success in it greatly humbled him. The fuller a
vessel becomes, the deeper it sinks in the water. Idlers
may indulge a fond conceit of their abilities, because
they are untried; but the earnest worker soon learns his
own weakness. If you seek humility, *try hard work*; if
you would know your nothingness, attempt some great
thing for Jesus. If you would feel how utterly powerless you are apart from the living God, attempt especially the great work of proclaiming the unsearchable
riches of Christ, and you will know, as you never knew
before, what a weak unworthy thing you are. Although
the apostle thus knew and confessed his weakness, he
was never perplexed as to the *subject* of his ministry.
From his first sermon to his last, Paul preached Christ,
and nothing but Christ. He lifted up the cross, and
extolled the Son of God who bled thereon. Follow his
example in all your personal efforts to spread the glad
tidings of salvation, and let 'Christ and Him crucified'
be your ever recurring theme. The Christian should be
like those lovely spring flowers which, when the sun is
shining, open their golden cups, as if saying, 'Fill us
with thy beams!' but when the sun is hidden behind a
cloud, they close their cups and droop their heads. So
should the Christian feel the sweet influence of Jesus;
Jesus must be his sun, and he must be the flower which
yields itself to the Sun of Righteousness. Oh! to speak
of Christ alone, this is the subject which is both 'seed
for the sower, and bread for the eater'. This is the live
coal for the lip of the speaker, and the master-key to the
heart of the hearer.

'*I have chosen thee in the furnace of affliction*'
Isaiah 48:10

Comfort thyself, tried believer, with this thought: God saith, 'I have chosen thee in the furnace of affliction'. Does not the word come like a soft shower, assuaging the fury of the flame? Yea, is it not an asbestos armour, against which the heat hath no power? Let affliction come - God has chosen me. Poverty, thou mayst stride in at my door, but God is in the house already, and He has chosen me. Sickness, thou mayst intrude, but I have a balsam ready - God has chosen me. Whatever befalls me in this vale of tears, I know that He has 'chosen' me. If, believer, thou requirest still greater comfort, remember *that you have the Son of Man with you in the furnace*. In that silent chamber of yours, there sitteth by your side One whom thou hast not seen, but whom thou lovest; and ofttimes when thou knowest it not, He makes all thy bed in thy affliction, and smooths thy pillow for thee. Thou art in poverty; but in that lonely house of thine the Lord of life and glory is a frequent visitor. He loves to come into these desolate places, that He may visit thee. Thy friend sticks closely to thee. Thou canst not see Him, but thou mayst feel the pressure of His hands. Dost thou not hear His voice? Even in the valley of the shadow of death He says, 'Fear not, I am with thee; be not dismayed, for I am thy God.' Remember that noble speech of Caesar: 'Fear not, Christian; Jesus is with thee', is His sure word of promise to His chosen ones in the 'furnace of affliction'. Wilt thou not, then, take fast hold of Christ, and say

'Through floods and flames, if Jesus lead,
I'll follow where he goes.'

'He saw the Spirit of God descending like a dove'
Matthew 3:16

As the Spirit of God descended upon the Lord Jesus, the head, so He also, in measure, descends upon the members of the mystical body. His descent is to us after the same fashion as that in which it fell upon our Lord. There is often a singular *rapidity* about it; or ever we are aware, we are impelled onward and heavenward beyond all expectation. Yet is there none of the hurry of earthly haste, for the wings of the dove are as soft as they are swift. *Quietness* seems essential to many spiritual operations; the Lord is in the still small voice, and like the dew, His grace is distilled in silence. The dove has ever been the chosen type of *purity*, and the Holy Spirit is holiness itself. Where He cometh, everything that is pure and lovely, and of good report, is made to abound, and sin and uncleanness depart. *Peace* reigns also where the Holy Dove comes with power; He bears the olive branch which shows that the waters of divine wrath are assuaged. *Gentleness* is a sure result of the Sacred Dove's transforming power: hearts touched by His benign influence are meek and lowly henceforth and for ever. *Harmlessness* follows, as a matter of course; eagles and ravens may hunt their prey - the turtledove can endure wrong, but cannot inflict it. We must be harmless as doves. The dove is an apt picture of *love*, the voice of the turtle is full of affection; and so, the soul visited by the blessed Spirit, abounds in love to God, in love to the brethren, and in love to sinners; and above all, in love to Jesus. The brooding of the Spirit of God upon the face of the deep, first produced *order and life*, and in our hearts, He causes and fosters new life and light. Blessed Spirit, as Thou didst rest upon our dear Redeemer, even so rest thou upon us from this time forward and for ever.

'My grace is sufficient for thee'
2 Corinthians 12:9

If none of God's saints were poor and tried, we should not know half so well the consolations of divine grace. When we find the wanderer who has not where to lay his head, who yet can say, 'Still will I trust in the Lord'; when we see the pauper starving on bread and water, who still glories in Jesus; when we see the bereaved widow overwhelmed in affliction, and yet having faith in Christ, oh! what honour it reflects on the gospel. God's grace is illustrated and magnified in the poverty and trials of believers. Saints bear up under every discouragement, believing that all things work together for their good, and that out of apparent evils a real blessing shall ultimately spring - that their God will either work a deliverance for them speedily, or most assuredly support them in the trouble, as long as He is pleased to keep them in it. This patience of the saints proves the power of divine grace. There is a lighthouse out at sea: it is a calm night - I cannot tell whether the edifice is firm; the tempest must rage about it, and then I shall know whether it will stand. So with the Spirit's work: if it were not on many occasions surrounded with tempestuous waters, we should not know that it was true and strong; if the winds did not blow upon it, we should not know how firm and secure it was. The master-works of God are those men who stand in the midst of difficulties, steadfast, unmoveable,

'Calm mid the bewildering cry,
Confident of victory.'

He who would glorify his God must set his account upon meeting with many trials. No man can be illustrious before the Lord unless his conflicts be many. If then, yours be a much-tried path, rejoice in it, because you will the better show forth the all-sufficient grace of God. As for His failing you, never dream of it - hate the thought. The God who has been sufficient until now, should be trusted to the end.

> '*They shall be abundantly satisfied
> with the fatness of Thy house*'
> Psalm 36:8

Sheba's queen was amazed at the sumptuousness of
Solomon's table. She lost all heart when she saw the
provision of a single day; and she marvelled equally at
the company of servants who were feasted at the royal
board. But what is this to the hospitalities of the God
of grace? Ten thousand thousand of his people are daily
fed; hungry and thirsty, they bring large appetites with
them to the banquet, but not one of them returns
unsatisfied; there is enough for each, enough for all,
enough for evermore. Though the host that feed at
Jehovah's table is countless as the stars of heaven, yet
each one has his portion of meat. Think how much
grace one saint requires, so much that nothing but the
Infinite could supply him for one day; and yet the Lord
spreads His table, not for one, but many saints, not for
one day, but for many years; not for many years only,
but for generation after generation. Observe the full
feasting spoken of in the text, the guests at mercy's
banquet are satisfied, nay, more 'abundantly satisfied';
and that not with ordinary fare, but with fatness, the
peculiar fatness of God's own house; and such feasting
is guaranteed by a faithful promise to all those children
of men who put their trust under the shadow of
Jehovah's wings. I once thought if I might but get the
broken meat at God's back door of grace I should be
satisfied; like the woman who said, 'The dogs eat of the
crumbs that fall from the master's table'; but no child
of God is ever served with scraps and leavings; like
Mephibosheth, they all eat from the king's own table.
In matters of grace, we all have Benjamin's mess - we
all have ten times more than we could have expected,
and though our necessities are great, yet are we often
amazed at the marvellous plenty of grace which God
gives us experimentally to enjoy.

'Let us not sleep, as do others'
1 Thessalonians 5:6

There are many ways of promoting Christian wakefulness. Among the rest, let me strongly advise Christians to converse together concerning the ways of the Lord. Christian and Hopeful, as they journeyed towards the Celestial City, said to themselves, 'To prevent drowsiness in this place, let us fall into good discourse'. Christian enquired, 'Brother, where shall we begin?' And Hopeful answered, 'Where God began with us.' Then Christian sang this song:

> 'When saints do sleepy grow, let them come hither,
> And hear how these two pilgrims talk together;
> Yea, let them learn of them, in any wise,
> Thus to keep ope their drowsy slumb'ring eyes.
> Saints' fellowship, if it be managed well,
> Keeps them awake, and that in spite of hell.'

Christians who isolate themselves and walk alone, are very liable to grow drowsy. Hold Christian company and you will be kept wakeful by it, and refreshed and encouraged to make quicker progress in the road to heaven. But as you thus take 'sweet counsel' with others in the ways of God, take care that the theme of your converse is the Lord Jesus. Let the eye of faith be constantly looking unto Him; let your heart be full of Him; let your lips speak of His worth. Friend, live near to the cross, and thou wilt not sleep. *Labour to impress thyself with a deep sense of the value of the place to which thou art going.* If thou rememberest that thou art going to heaven, thou wilt not sleep on the road. If thou thinkest that hell is behind thee, and the devil pursuing thee, thou wilt not loiter. Would the manslayer sleep with the avenger of blood behind him, and the city of refuge before him? Christian, wilt thou sleep whilst the pearly gates are open - the songs of angels waiting for thee to join them - a crown of gold ready for thy brow? Ah! no; in holy fellowship continue to watch and pray that ye enter not into temptation.

'Say unto my soul, I am thy salvation'
Psalm 35:3

What does this sweet prayer teach me? It shall be my evening's petition; but first let it yield me an instructive meditation. The text informs me first of all that *David had his doubts*; for why should he pray, 'Say unto my soul, I am thy salvation', if he were not sometimes exercised with doubts and fears? Let me, then, be of good cheer, for I am not the only saint who has to complain of weakness of faith. If David doubted, I need not conclude that *I* am no Christian, because I have doubts. The text reminds me that *David was not content while he had doubts and fears*, but he repaired at once to the mercy-seat to pray for assurance; for he valued it as much fine gold. I too must labour after an abiding sense of my acceptance in the Beloved, and must have no joy when His love is not shed abroad in my soul. When my Bridegroom is gone from me, my soul must and will fast. I learn also that *David knew where to obtain full assurance*. He went to his God in prayer, crying, 'Say unto my soul, I am thy salvation'. I must be much alone with God if I would have a clear sense of Jesus' love. Let my prayers cease, and my eye of faith will grow dim. Much in prayer, much in heaven; slow in prayer, slow in progress. I notice that *David would not be satisfied unless his assurance had a divine source*. '*Say* unto my soul.' Lord, to *Thou* say it! Nothing short of a divine testimony in the soul will ever content the true Christian. Moreover, David could not rest unless his assurance had *a vivid personality* about it. 'Say unto *my* soul, I am *thy* salvation.' Lord, if Thou shouldst say this to all the saints, it were nothing, unless Thou shouldst say it to me. Lord, I have sinned; I deserve not Thy smile; I scarcely dare to ask it; but oh! say to *my* soul, even to *my* soul, 'I am *thy* salvation'. Let me have a present, personal, infallible, indisputable sense that I am Thine, and that Thou art mine.

'Ye must be born again'
John 3:7

Regeneration is a subject which lies at the very basis of salvation, and we should be very diligent to take heed that we really are 'born again', for there are many who fancy they are, who are not. Be assured that the name of a Christian is not the nature of a Christian; and that being born in a Christian land, and being recognised as professing the Christian religion is of no avail whatever, unless there be something more added to it - the being 'born again' by the power of the Holy Spirit. To be 'born again', is a matter so *mysterious*, that human words cannot describe it. 'The wind bloweth where it listeth, and thou hearest the sound thereof, but canst not tell whence it cometh, and whither it goeth: so is every one that is born of the Spirit.' Nevertheless, it is a change which is *known and felt*: known by works of holiness, and felt by a gracious experience. This great work is *supernatural*. It is not an operation which a man performs for himself: a new principle is infused, which works in the heart, renews the soul, and affects the entire man. It is not a change of my name, but a renewal of my nature, so that I am not the man I used to be, but a new man in Christ Jesus. To wash and dress a corpse is a far different thing from making it alive: man can do the one, God alone can do the other. If you have then, been 'born again', your acknowledgement will be, 'O Lord Jesus, the everlasting Father, Thou art my spiritual Parent; unless Thy Spirit had breathed into me the breath of a new, holy, and spiritual life, I had been to this day "dead in trespasses and sins". My heavenly life is wholly derived from Thee, to Thee I ascribe it. "My life is hid with Christ in God." It is no longer I who live, but Christ who liveth in me.' May the Lord enable us to be well assured on this vital point, for to be unregenerate is to be unsaved, unpardoned, without God, and without hope.

'*Before destruction the heart of man is haughty*'
Proverbs 18:12

It is an old and common saying, that 'coming events
cast their shadows before them'; the wise man teaches
us that a haughty heart is the prophetic prelude of evil.
Pride is as safely the sign of destruction as the change
of mercury in the weather-glass is the sign of rain; and
far more infallibly so than that. When men have ridden
the high horse, destruction *has* always overtaken them.
Let David's aching heart show that there is an eclipse
of a man's glory when he doats upon his own greatness.
2 Samuel 24:10. See Nebuchadnezzar, the mighty
builder of Babylon, creeping on the earth, devouring
grass like oxen until his nails had grown like bird's
claws, and his hair like eagle's feathers. Daniel 4:33.
Pride made the boaster a beast, as once before it made
an angel a devil. God hates high looks, and never fails
to bring them down. All the arrows of God are aimed
at proud hearts. O Christian, is thine heart haughty this
evening? For pride can get into the Christian's heart as
well as into the sinner's; it can delude him into
dreaming that he is 'rich and increased in goods, and
hath need of nothing'. Art thou glorying in thy graces
or thy talents? Art thou proud of thyself, that thou hast
had holy frames and sweet experiences? Mark thee,
reader, there is a destruction coming to thee also. Thy
flaunting poppies of self-conceit will be pulled up by
the roots, thy mushroom graces will wither in the
burning heat, and thy self-sufficiency shall become as
straw for the dunghill. If we forget to live at the foot of
the cross in deepest lowliness of spirit, God will not
forget to make us smart under His rod. A destruction
will come to thee, O unduly exalted believer, the
destruction of thy joys and of thy comforts, though
there can be no destruction of thy soul. Wherefore, 'He
that glorieth, let him glory *in the Lord.*'

'Have faith in God'
Mark 11:22

Faith is the foot of the soul by which it can march along the road of the commandments. Love can make the feet move more swiftly; but faith *is* the foot which carries the soul. Faith is the oil enabling the wheels of holy devotion and of earnest piety to move well; and without faith the wheels are taken from the chariot, and we drag heavily. With faith I can do all things; without faith I shall neither have the inclination nor the power to do anything in the service of God. If you would find the men who serve God the best, you must look for the men of the most faith. Little faith will save a man, but little faith cannot do great things for God. Poor Little-faith could not have fought 'Apollyon'; it needed 'Christian' to do that. Poor Little-faith could not have slain 'Giant Despair'; it required 'Great-heart's' arm to knock that monster down. Little-faith will go to heaven most certainly, but it often has to hide itself in a nutshell, and it frequently loses all but its jewels. Little-faith says, 'It is a rough road, beset with sharp thorns, and full of dangers; I am afraid to go'; but Great-faith remembers the promise, 'Thy shoes shall be iron and brass; as thy days, so shall thy strength be': and so she boldly ventures. Little-faith stands desponding, mingling her tears with the flood; but Great-faith sings, 'When thou passest through the waters, I will be with thee; and through the rivers, they shall not overflow thee': and she fords the stream at once. Would you be comfortable and happy? Would you enjoy religion? Would you have the religion of cheerfulness and not that of gloom? Then 'have faith in God'. If you love darkness, and are satisfied to dwell in gloom and misery, then be content with little faith; but if you love the sunshine, and would sing songs of rejoicing, covet earnestly this best gift, 'great faith'.

> '*It is better to trust in the Lord,*
> *than to put confidence in man*'
> Psalm 118:8

Doubtless the reader has been tried with the temptation to rely upon the things which are seen, instead of resting alone upon the invisible God. Christians often look to man for help and counsel, and mar the noble simplicity of their reliance upon their God. Does this evening's portion meet the eye of a child of God anxious about temporals, then would we reason with him awhile. You trust in Jesus, and only in Jesus, for your salvation, then why are you troubled? '*Because of my great care.*' Is it not written, 'Cast thy burden upon the Lord'? 'Be careful for nothing, but in everything by prayer and supplication make known your wants unto God.' Cannot you trust God for temporals? '*Ah! I wish I could.*' If you cannot trust God for temporals, how dare you trust Him for spirituals? Can you trust Him for your soul's redemption, and not rely upon Him for a few lesser mercies? Is not God enough for thy need, or is His all-sufficiency too narrow for thy wants? Dost thou want another eye beside that of Him who sees every secret thing? Is His heart faint? Is His arm weary? If so, seek another God; but if He be infinite, omnipotent, faithful, true, and all-wise, why gaddest thou abroad so much to seek another confidence? Why dost thou rake the earth to find another foundation, when this is strong enough to bear all the weight which thou canst ever build thereon? Christian, mix not thy wine with water, do not alloy thy gold of faith with the dross of human confidence. Wait thou only upon God, and let thine expectation be from Him. Covet not Jonah's gourd, but rest in Jonah's God. Let the sandy foundations of terrestrial trust be the choice of fools, but do thou, like one who foresees the storm, build for thyself an abiding place upon the Rock of Ages.

*'We must through much tribulation
enter into the kingdom of God'*
Acts 14:22

God's people have their trials. It was never designed by God, when He chose His people, that they should be an untried people. They were chosen in the furnace of affliction; they were never chosen to worldly peace and earthly joy. Freedom from sickness and the pains of mortality was never promised them; but when their Lord drew up the charter of privileges, He included chastisements amongst the things to which they should inevitably be heirs. Trials are a part of our lot; they were predestinated for us in God's solemn decrees, and bequeathed us in Christ's last legacy. So surely as the stars are fashioned by his hands, and their orbits fixed by Him, so surely are our trials allotted to us: He has ordained their season and their place, their intensity and the effect they shall have upon us. Good men must never expect to escape troubles; if they do, they will be disappointed, for none of their predecessors have been without them. Mark the patience of Job; remember Abraham, for he had his trials, and by his faith under them, he became the 'Father of the faithful'. Note well the biographies of all the patriarchs, prophets, apostles, and martyrs, and you shall discover none of those whom God made vessels of mercy, who were not made to pass through the fire of affliction. It is ordained of old that the cross of trouble should be engraven on every vessel of mercy, as the royal mark whereby the King's vessels of honour are distinguished. But although tribulation is thus the path of God's children, they have the comfort of knowing that their Master has traversed it before them; they have His presence and sympathy to cheer them, His grace to support them, and His example to teach them how to endure; and when they reach 'the kingdom', it will more than make amends for the 'much tribulation' through which they passed to enter it.

*'She called his name Ben-oni (son of sorrow), but
his father called him Benjamin (son of my right hand)'*
Genesis 35:18

To every matter there is a bright as well as a dark side.
Rachel was overwhelmed with the sorrow of her own
travail and death; Jacob, though weeping the mother's
loss, could see the mercy of the child's birth. It is well
for us if, while the flesh mourns over trials, our faith
triumphs in divine faithfulness. Samson's lion yielded
honey, and so will our adversities, if rightly considered. The stormy sea feeds multitudes with its fishes;
the wild wood blooms with beauteous flowerets; the
stormy wind sweeps away the pestilence, and the biting
frost loosens the soil. Dark clouds distil bright drops,
and black earth grows gay flowers. A vein of good is
to be found in every mine of evil. Sad hearts have
peculiar skill in discovering the most advantageous
point of view from which to gaze upon a trial; if there
were only one slough in the world, they would soon be
up to their necks in it, and if there were only one lion
in the desert they would hear it roar. About us all there
is a tinge of this wretched folly, and we are apt, at times,
like Jacob, to cry, All these things are against me'.
Faith's way of walking is to cast all care upon the Lord,
and then to anticipate good results from the worst
calamities. Like Gideon's men, she does not fret over
the broken pitcher, but rejoices that the lamp blazes
forth the more. Out of the rough oyster-shell of
difficulty she extracts the rare pearl of honour, and
from the deep ocean-caves of distress she uplifts the
priceless coral of experience. When her flood of
prosperity ebbs, she finds treasures hid in the sands;
and when her sun of delight goes down, she turns her
telescope of hope to the starry promises of heaven.
When death itself appears, faith points to the light of
resurrection beyond the grave, thus making our dying
Ben-oni to be our living Benjamin.

'Yea, He is altogether lovely'
Solomon's Song 5:16

The superlative beauty of Jesus is all-attracting; it is not so much to be admired as to be loved. He is more than pleasant and fair, He is LOVELY. Surely the people of God can fully justify the use of this golden word, for He is the object of their warmest love, a love founded on the intrinsic excellence of His person, the complete perfection of His charms. Look, O disciples of Jesus, to your Master's lips and say, 'Are they not most sweet?' Do not His words cause your hearts to burn within you as He talks with you by the way? Ye worshippers of Immanuel, look up to His head of much fine gold, and tell me, are not His thoughts precious unto you? Is not your adoration sweetened with affection as ye humbly bow before that countenance which is as Lebanon, excellent as the cedars? Is there not a charm in His every feature, and is not His whole person fragrant with such a savour of His good ointments, that therefore the virgins love Him? Is there one member of His glorious body which is not attractive? - one portion of His person which is not a fresh loadstone to our souls? - one office which is not as a seal set upon His heart of love alone; it is fastened upon His arm of power also; nor is there a single part of Him upon which it does not fix itself. We anoint His whole person with the sweet spikenard of our fervent love. His whole life we would imitate; His whole character we would transcribe. In all other beings we see some lack, in Him there is all perfection. The best even of His favoured saints have had blots upon their garments and wrinkles upon their brows; he is nothing but loveliness. All earthly suns have their spots: the fair world itself hath its wilderness; we cannot love the whole of the most lovely thing; but Christ Jesus is gold without alloy - light without darkness - glory without cloud - 'Yea, He is *altogether* lovely'.

'Abide in Me'
John 15:4

Communion with Christ is a certain cure for every ill. Whether it be the wormwood of woe, or the cloying surfeit of earthly delight, close fellowship with the Lord Jesus will take bitterness from the one, and satiety from the other. Live near to Jesus, Christian, and it is matter of secondary importance whether thou livest on the mountain of honour or in the valley of humiliation. Living near to Jesus, thou art covered with the wings of God, and underneath thee are the everlasting arms. Let nothing keep thee from that hallowed intercourse, which is the choice privilege of a soul wedded to THE WELL-BELOVED. Be not content with an interview now and then, but seek always to retain His company, for only in His presence hast thou either comfort or safety. Jesus should not be unto us a friend who calls upon us now and then, but one with whom we walk evermore. Thou hast a difficult road before thee: see, O traveller to heaven, that thou go not without thy guide. Thou hast to pass through the fiery furnace, enter it not unless, like Shadrach, Meshach, and Abednego, thou hast the Son of God to be thy companion. Thou hast to storm the Jericho of thine own corruptions: attempt not the warfare until, like Joshua, thou hast seen the Captain of the Lord's host, with His sword drawn in His hand. Thou art to meet the Esau of thy many temptations: meet him not until at Jabbok's brook thou hast laid hold upon the angel, and prevailed. In every case, in every condition, thou wilt need Jesus; but most of all, when the iron gates of death shall open to thee. Keep thou close to thy soul's Husband, lean thy head upon His bosom, ask to be refreshed with the spiced wine of His pomegranate, and thou shalt be found of Him at the last, without spot, or wrinkle, or any such thing. Seeing thou hast lived with Him, and lived in Him here, thou shalt abide with Him for ever.

'In my prosperity I said, I shall never be moved'
Psalm 30:6

'Moab is settled on his lees, he hath not been emptied
from vessel to vessel.' Give a man wealth; let his ships
bring home continually rich freights; let the winds and
waves appear to be his servants to bear his vessels
across the bosom of the mighty deep; let his lands yield
abundantly; let the weather be propitious to his crops;
let uninterrupted success attend him; let him stand
among men as a successful merchant; let him enjoy
continued health; allow him with braced nerve and
brilliant eye to march through the world, and live
happily; give him the buoyant spirit; let him have the
song perpetually on his lips; let his eye be ever
sparkling with joy - and the natural consequence of
such an easy state to any man, let him be the best
Christian who ever breathed, will be *presumption*;
even David said, 'I shall never be moved'; and we are
not better than David, nor half so good. Brother,
beware of the smooth places of the way; if you are
treading them, or if the way be rough, thank God for it.
If God should always rock us in the cradle of prosperity; if we were always dandled on the knees of fortune;
if we had not some stain on the alabaster pillar; if there
were not a few clouds in the sky; if we had not some
bitter drops in the wine of this life, we should become
intoxicated with pleasure, we should dream 'we stand';
and stand we should, but it would be upon a pinnacle;
like the man asleep upon the mast, each moment we
should be in jeopardy.

   We bless God, then, for our afflictions; we thank
Him for our changes; we extol his name for losses of
property; for we feel that had He not chastened us thus,
we might have become too secure. Continued worldly
prosperity is a fiery trial.

'Afflictions, though they seem severe,
   In mercy oft are sent.'

'Man... is of few days, and full of trouble'
Job 14:1

It may be of great service to us, before we fall asleep,
to remember this mournful fact, for it may lead us to
set loose by earthly things. There is nothing very
pleasant in the recollection that we are not above the
shafts of adversity, but it may humble us and prevent
our boasting like the Psalmist in our morning's portion. 'My mountain standeth firm: I shall never be
moved'. It may stay us from taking too deep root in this
soil from which we are so soon to be transplanted into
the heavenly garden. Let us recollect the frail tenure
upon which we hold our *temporal mercies*. If we would
remember that all the trees of earth are marked for the
woodman's axe, we should not be so ready to build our
nests in them. We should love, but we should love with
the love which expects death, and which reckons upon
separations. Our dear relations are but loaned to us, and
the hour when we must return them to the lender's hand
may be even at the door. The like is certainly true of our
worldly goods. Do not riches take to themselves wings
and fly away? Our *health* is equally precarious. Frail
flowers of the field, we must not reckon upon blooming
for ever. There is a time appointed for weakness and
sickness, when we shall have to glorify God by
suffering, and not by earnest activity. There is no
single point in which we can hope to escape from the
sharp arrows of affliction; out of our few days there is
not one secure from sorrow. Man's life is a cask full
of bitter wine; he who looks for joy in it had better seek
for honey in an ocean of brine. Beloved reader, set not
your affections upon things of earth: but seek those
things which are above, for *here* the moth devoureth,
and the thief breaketh through, but *there* all joys are
perpetual and eternal. The path of trouble is the way
home. Lord, make this thought a pillow for many a
weary head!

'Sin... exceedingly sinful'
Romans 7:13

Beware of light thoughts of sin. At the time of conversion, the conscience is so tender, that we are afraid of the slightest sin. Young converts have a holy timidity, a godly fear lest they should offend against God. But alas! very soon the fine bloom upon these first ripe fruits is removed by the rough handling of the surrounding world: the sensitive plant of young piety turns into a willow in after life, too pliant, too easily yielding. It is sadly true, that even a Christian may grow by degrees so callous, that the sin which once startled him does not alarm him in the least. By degrees men get familiar with sin. The ear in which the cannon has been booming will not notice slight sounds. At first a little sin startles us; but soon we say, 'Is it not a little one?' Then there comes another, larger, and then another, until by degrees we begin to regard sin as but a little ill; and then follows an unholy presumption: 'We have not fallen into open sin. True, we tripped a little, but we stood upright in the main. We may have uttered one unholy word, but as for the most of our conversation, it has been consistent'. So we palliate sin; we throw a cloak over it; we call it by dainty names. Christian, beware how thou thinkest lightly of sin. Take heed lest thou fall by little and little. Sin, a *little* thing? Is it not a poison? Who knows its deadliness? Sin, a little thing? Do not the little foxes spoil the grapes? Doth not the tiny coral insect build a rock which wrecks a navy? Do not little strokes fell lofty oaks? Will not continual droppings wear away stones? Sin, a little thing? It girded the Redeemer's head with thorns, and pierced His heart! It made *Him* suffer anguish, bitterness, and woe. Could you weigh the least sin in the scales of eternity, you would fly from it as from a serpent, and abhor *the least appearance of evil*. Look upon all sin as that which crucified the Saviour, and you will see it to be 'exceeding sinful'.

'Thou shalt be called, Sought out'
Isaiah 62:12

The surpassing grace of God is seen very clearly in that we were not only sought, but sought *out*. Men *seek* for a thing which is lost upon the floor of the house, but in such a case there is only seeking, not seeking *out*. The loss is more perplexing and the search more persevering when a thing is sought *out*. We were mingled with the mire: we were as when some precious piece of gold falls into the sewer, and men gather out and carefully inspect a mass of abominable filth, and continue to stir and rake, and search among the heap until the treasure is found. Or, to use another figure, we were lost in a labyrinth; we wandered hither and thither, and when mercy came after us with the gospel, it did not find us at the first coming, it had to search for us and seek us out; for we as lost sheep were so desperately lost, and had wandered into such a strange country, that it did not seem possible that even the Good Shepherd should track our devious roamings. Glory be to unconquerable grace, we were sought *out*! No gloom could hide us, no filthiness could conceal us, we were found and brought home. Glory be to infinite love, God the Holy Spirit restored us!

    The lives of some of God's people, if they could be written would fill us with holy astonishment. Strange and marvellous are the ways which God used in their case to find His own. Blessed be His name, He never relinquishes the search until the chosen are sought out effectually. They are not a people sought today and cast away tomorrow. Almightiness and wisdom combined will make no failures, they shall be called, '*Sought out!*' That *any* should be sought out is matchless grace, but that *we* should be sought out is grace beyond degree! We can find no reason for it but God's own sovereign love, and can only lift up our heart in wonder, and praise the Lord that this night *we* wear the name of '*Sought out*'.

'Thou shalt love thy neighbour'
Matthew 5:43

'Love thy neighbour.' Perhaps he rolls in riches, and thou art poor, and living in thy little cot side-by-side with his lordly mansion; thou seest every day his estates, his fine linen, and his sumptuous banquets; God has given him these gifts, covet not his wealth, and think no hard thoughts concerning him. Be content with thine own lot, if thou canst not better it, but do not look upon thy neighbour, and wish that he were as thyself. Love him, and then thou wilt not envy him.

Mayhap, on the other hand, thou art rich, and near thee reside the poor. Do not scorn to call them neighbours. Own that thou art bound to love them. The world calls them thy inferiors. In what are they inferior? They are far more thine equals than thine inferiors, for 'God hath made of one blood all people that dwell upon the face of the earth'. It is thy coat which is better than theirs, but thou art by no means better than they. They are men, and what art thou more than that? Take heed that thou love thy neighbour even though he be in rags, or sunken in the depths of poverty.

But, perhaps, you say, 'I cannot love my neighbours, because for all I do they return ingratitude and contempt'. So much the more room for the heroism of love. Wouldst thou be a feather-bed warrior, instead of bearing the rough fight of love? He who dares the most, shall win the most; and if rough be thy path of love, tread it boldly, still loving thy neighbours through thick and thin. Heap coals of fire on their heads, and if they be hard to please, seek not to please *them*, but to please *thy Master*; and remember if *they* spurn thy love, thy Master hath not spurned it, and thy deed is as acceptable to Him as if it had been acceptable to them. Love thy neighbour, for in so doing thou art following the footsteps of Christ.

'To whom belongest thou?'
1 Samuel 30:13

No neutralities can exist in religion. We are either ranked under the banner of Prince Immanuel, to serve and fight His battles, or we are vassals of the black prince, Satan. 'To whom belongest thou?' Reader, let me assist you in your response. *Have you been 'born again'*? If you have, you belong to Christ, but without the new birth you cannot be His. *In whom do you trust*? For those who believe in Jesus are the sons of God. *Whose work are you doing*? You are sure to serve your master, for he whom you serve is thereby owned to be your lord. *What company do you keep*? If you belong to Jesus, you will fraternise with those who wear the livery of the cross. 'Birds of a feather flock together.' *What is your conversation*? Is it heavenly or is it earthly? *What have you learned of your Master*? - for servants learn much from their masters to whom they are apprenticed. If you have served your time with Jesus, it will be said of you, as it was of Peter and John, 'They took knowledge of them, that they had been with Jesus'.

We press the question, 'To whom belongest thou?' Answer honestly before you give sleep to your eyes. If you are not Christ's you are in a hard service - *Run away from your cruel master*! Enter into the service of the Lord of Love, and you shall enjoy a life of blessedness. If you *are* Christ's, let me advise you to do four things. You belong to Jesus - *obey Him*; let His word be your law; let His wish be your will. You belong to the Beloved, then *love Him*; let your heart embrace Him; let your whole soul be filled with Him. You belong to the Son of God, then *trust Him*; rest nowhere but on him. You belong to the King of kings, then *be decided for Him*. Thus without your being branded upon the brow, all will know to whom you belong.

'Why sit we here until we die?'
2 Kings 7:3

Dear reader, this little book was mainly intended for the edification of believers, but if you are yet unsaved, our heart yearns over you: and we would fain say a word which may be blessed to you. Open your Bible, and read the story of the lepers, and mark their position, which was much the same as yours. If you remain where you are you must perish; if you go to Jesus you can but die. 'Nothing venture, nothing win', is the old proverb, and in your case the venture is no great one. If you sit still in sullen despair, no one can pity you when your ruin comes; but if you die with mercy sought, if such a thing were possible, you would be the object of universal sympathy. None escape who refuse to look to Jesus; but you know that, at any rate, some are saved who believe in Him, for certain of your own acquaintances have received mercy: then why not you? The Ninevites said, 'Who can tell?' Act upon the same hope, and try the Lord's mercy. To perish is so awful, that if there were but a straw to catch at, the instinct of self-preservation should lead you to stretch out your hand. We have thus been talking to you on your own unbelieving ground, we would now assure you, as from the Lord, that if you seek Him He will be found of you. Jesus casts out none who come unto Him. You shall not perish if you trust Him; on the contrary, you shall find treasure far richer than the poor lepers gathered in Syria's deserted camp. May the Holy Spirit embolden you to go at once, and you shall not believe in vain. When you are saved yourself, publish the good news to others. Hold not your peace; tell the King's house-hold first, and unite with them in fellowship; let the porter of the city, the minister, be informed of your discovery, and then proclaim the good news in every place. The Lord save thee ere the sun goes down this day.

> *'Then he put forth his hand, and took her,*
> *and pulled her in unto him into the ark'*
> Genesis 8:9

Wearied out with her wanderings, the dove returns at length to the ark as her only resting place. How heavily she flies - she will drop - she will never reach the ark! But she struggles on. Noah has been looking out for his dove all day long, and is ready to receive her. She has just strength to reach the edge of the ark, she can hardly alight upon it, and is ready to drop, when Noah puts forth his hand and pulls her in unto him. Mark that: '*pulled her in unto him*'. She did not fly right in herself, but was too fearful, or too weary to do so. She flew as far as she could, and then he put forth his hand and pulled her in unto him. This act of mercy was shown to the wandering dove, and she was not chidden for her wanderings. Just as she was she was pulled into the ark. So you, seeking sinner, with all your sin, will be received. 'Only return' - those are God's two gracious words - 'only return'. What! nothing else? No, 'only return'. She had no olive branch in her mouth this time, nothing at all but just herself and her wanderings; but it is 'only return', and she does return, and Noah pulls her in. Fly, thou wanderer; fly thou fainting one, dove as thou art, though thou thinkest thyself to be black as the raven with the mire of sin, back, back to the Saviour. Every moment thou waitest does but increase thy misery; thine attempts to plume thyself and make thyself fit for Jesus are all vanity. Come thou to Him just as thou art 'Return, thou backsliding Israel'. He does not say, 'Return, thou *repenting* Israel' (there is such an invitation doubtless), but 'thou *backsliding* one', as a backslider with all thy backslidings about thee, Return, return, return! Jesus is waiting for thee! He will stretch forth His hand and 'pull thee in' - in to Himself, thy heart's true home.

> *'Let him that thinketh he standeth*
> *take heed lest he fall'*
> 1 Corinthians 10:12

It is a curious fact, that there is such a thing as being proud of grace. A man says, 'I have great faith, I shall not fall; poor little faith may, but I never shall'. 'I have fervent love,' says another, 'I can stand, there is no danger of my going astray.' He who boasts of grace has little grace to boast of. Some who do this imagine that their graces can keep them, knowing not that the stream must flow constantly from the fountain head, or else the brook will soon be dry. If a continuous stream of oil comes not to the lamp, though it burn brightly today, it will smoke tomorrow, and noxious will be its scent. Take heed that thou gloriest not in thy graces, but let all thy glorying and confidence be in Christ and His strength, for only so canst thou be kept from falling. Be much more in prayer. Spend longer time in holy adoration. Read the Scriptures more earnestly and constantly. Watch your lives more carefully. Live nearer to God. Take the best examples for your pattern. Let your conversation be redolent of heaven. Let your hearts be perfumed with affection for men's souls. So live that men may take knowledge of you that you have been with Jesus, and have learned of Him; and when that happy day shall come, when He whom you love shall say, 'Come up higher', may it be your happiness to hear Him say, 'Thou hast fought a good fight, thou hast finished thy course, and henceforth there is laid up for thee a crown of righteousness which fadeth not away'. On, Christian, with care and caution! On, with holy fear and trembling! On, with faith and confidence in Jesus alone, and let your constant petition be, 'Uphold me according to Thy word'. He is able, and He alone, 'To keep you from falling, and to present you faultless before the presence of His glory with exceeding joy'.

'I will take heed to my ways'
Psalm 39:1

Fellow-pilgrim, say not in your heart, 'I will go hither and thither, and I shall not sin'; for you are never so out of danger of sinning as to boast of security. The road is very miry, it will be hard to pick your path so as not to soil your garments. This is a world of pitch; you will need to watch often, if in handling it you are to keep your hands clean. There is a robber at every turn of the road to rob you of your jewels; there is a temptation in every mercy; there is a snare in every joy; and if you ever reach heaven, it will be a miracle of divine grace to be ascribed entirely to your Father's power. Be on your guard. When a man carries a bomb-shell in his hand, he should mind that he does not go near a candle; and you too must take care that you enter not into temptation. Even your common actions are edged tools; you must mind how you handle them. There is nothing in this world to foster a Christian's piety, but everything to destroy it. How anxious should you be to look up to God, that *He* may keep you! Your prayer should be, 'Hold thou me up, and I shall be safe'. Having prayed, you must also watch; guarding every thought, word, and action, with holy jealousy. Do not expose yourselves unnecessarily; but if called to exposure, if you are bidden to go where the darts are flying, never venture forth without your shield; for if once the devil finds you without your buckler, he will rejoice that his hour of triumph is come, and will soon make you fall down wounded by his arrows. Though slain you cannot be; wounded you may be. 'Be sober; be vigilant, danger may be in an hour when all seemeth securest to thee.' Therefore, take heed to thy ways, and watch unto prayer. No man ever fell into error through being too watchful. May the Holy Spirit guide us in all our ways, so shall they always please the Lord.

'Be strong in the grace that is in Christ Jesus'
2 Timothy 2:1

Christ has grace without measure in Himself, but He hath not retained it for Himself. As the reservoir empties itself into the pipes, so hath Christ emptied out His grace for His people. 'Of His fulness have all we received, and grace for grace.' He seems only to have in order to dispense to us. He stands like the fountain, always flowing, but only running in order to supply the empty pitchers and the thirsty lips which draw nigh unto it. Like a tree, He bears sweet fruit, not to hang on boughs, but to be gathered by those who need. Grace, whether its work be to pardon, to cleanse, to preserve, is ever to be had from Him freely and without price; nor is there one form of the work of grace which He has not bestowed upon His people. As the blood of the body, though flowing from the heart, belongs equally to every member, so the influences of grace are the inheritance of every saint united to the Lamb; and herein there is a sweet communion between Christ and His Church, inasmuch as they both receive the same grace. Christ is the head upon which the oil is first poured; but the same oil runs to the very skirts of the garments, so that the meanest saint has an unction of the same costly moisture as that which fell upon the head. This is true communion when the sap of grace flows from the stem to the branch, and when it is perceived that the stem itself is sustained by the very nourishment which feeds the branch. As we day by day receive grace from Jesus, and more constantly recognise it as coming from Him, we shall behold Him in communion with us, and enjoy the felicity of communion with Him. Let us make daily use of our riches, and ever repair to Him as to our own Lord in covenant, taking from Him the supply of all we need with as much boldness as men take money from their own purse.

'He did it with all his heart and prospered'
2 Chronicles 31:21

This is no unusual occurrence; it is the general rule of
the moral universe that those men prosper who do their
work with all their hearts, while those are almost
certain to fail who go to their labour leaving half their
hearts behind them. God does not give harvests to idle
men except harvests of thistles, nor is He pleased to
send wealth to those who will not dig in the field to find
its hid treasure. It is universally confessed that if a man
would prosper, he must be diligent in business. It is the
same in religion as it is in other things. If you would
prosper in your work for Jesus, let it be *heart* work, and
let it be done with *all* your heart. Put as much force,
energy, heartiness, and earnestness into religion as
ever you do into business, for it deserves far more. The
Holy Spirit helps our infirmities, but He does not
encourage our idleness; He loves active believers. Who
are the most useful men in the Christian church? The
men who do what they undertake for God *with all their
hearts*. Who are the most successful Sabbath-school
teachers? The most talented? No; the most zealous; the
men whose hearts are on fire, those are the men who see
their Lord riding forth prosperously in the majesty of
His salvation. Whole-heartedness shows itself in *perseverance*; there may be failure at first, but the earnest
worker will say, 'It is the Lord's work, and it must be
done; my Lord has bidden me do it, and in His strength
I will accomplish it'. Christian, art thou thus 'with all
thine heart' serving thy Master? Remember the earnestness of Jesus! Think what heart-work was His! He
could say, *'The zeal of Thine house hath eaten Me up'*.
When He sweat great drops of blood, it was no light
burden He had to carry upon those blessed shoulders;
and when He poured out His heart, it was no weak effort
He was making for the salvation of His people. Was
Jesus in earnest, and are we lukewarm?

'I am a stranger with thee'
Psalm 39:12

Yes, O Lord, *with* Thee, but not *to* Thee. All my natural alienation from Thee, Thy grace has effectually removed; and now, in fellowship with Thyself, I walk through this sinful world as a pilgrim in a foreign country. *Thou* art a stranger in Thine own world. Man forgets Thee, dishonours Thee, sets up new laws and alien customs, and knows Thee not. When Thy dear Son came unto His own, His own received Him not. He was in the world, and the world was made by Him, and the world knew Him not. Never was foreigner so speckled a bird among the denizens of any land as Thy beloved Son among His mother's brethren. It is no marvel, then, if I who live the life of Jesus, should be unknown and a stranger here below. Lord, I would not be a citizen where Jesus was an alien. His pierced hand has loosened the cords which once bound my soul to earth, and now I find myself a stranger in the land. My speech seems to these Babylonians among whom I dwell an outlandish tongue, my manners are singular, and my actions are strange. A Tartar would be more at home in Cheapside than I could ever be in the haunts of sinners. But here is the sweetness of my lot: I am a stranger *with Thee*. Thou art my fellow-sufferer, my fellow-pilgrim. Oh, what joy to wander in such blessed society! My heart burns within me by the way when thou dost speak to me, and though I be a sojourner, I am far more blest than those who sit on thrones, and far more at home than those who dwell in their ceiled houses.

> To me remains nor place, nor time:
> My country is in every clime;
> I can be calm and free from care
> On any shore, since God is there.

> While place we seek, or place we shun,
> The soul finds happiness in none;
> But with a God to guide our way,
> 'Tis equal joy to go or stay.

'Keep back Thy servant also from presumptuous sins'
Psalm 19:13.

Such was the *prayer of the 'man after God's own heart'*. Did holy David need to pray thus? How needful, then, must such a prayer be for *us* babes in grace! It is as if he said, 'Keep me back, or I shall rush headlong over the precipice of sin'. Our evil nature, like an ill-tempered horse, is apt to run away. May the grace of God put the bridle upon it, and hold it in, that it rush not into mischief. What might not the best of us do if it were not for the checks which the Lord sets upon us both in providence and in grace! The psalmist's prayer is directed against the worst form of sin - that which is done with deliberation and wilfulness. Even the holiest need to be 'kept back' from the vilest transgressions. It is a solemn thing to find the apostle Paul warning saints against the most loathsome sins. 'Mortify therefore your members which are upon the earth; fornication, uncleanness, inordinate affection, evil concupiscence, and covetousness, which is idolatry.' What! do saints want warning against such sins as these? Yes, they do. The whitest robes, unless their purity be preserved by divine grace, will be defiled by the blackest spots. Experienced Christian, boast not in your experience; you will trip yet if you look away from Him who is able to keep you from falling. Ye whose love is fervent, whose faith is constant, whose hopes are bright, say not, 'We shall never sin', but rather cry, 'Lead us not into temptation'. There is enough tinder in the heart of the best of men to light a fire that shall burn to the lowest hell, unless God shall quench the sparks as they fall. Who would have dreamed that righteous Lot could be found drunken, and committing uncleanness? Hazael said, 'Is Thy servant a dog, that he should do this thing?' and we are very apt to use the same self-righteous question. May infinite wisdom cure us of the madness of self-confidence.

'Remember the poor'
Galatians 2:10

Why does God allow so many of His children to be poor? He could make them all rich if He pleased; He could lay bags of gold at their doors; He could send them a large annual income; or He could scatter round their houses abundance of provisions, as once he made the quails lie in heaps round the camp of Israel, and rained bread out of heaven to feed them. There is no necessity that they should be poor, except that He sees it to be best. 'The cattle upon a thousand hills are His' - He could supply them; He could make the richest, the greatest, and the mightiest bring all their power and riches to the feet of His children, for the hearts of all men are in His control. But He does not choose to do so; He allows them to suffer want, He allows them to pine in penury and obscurity. Why is this? There are many reasons: one is, *to give us, who are favoured with enough, an opportunity of showing our love to Jesus.* We show our love to Christ when we sing of Him and when we pray to Him; but if there were no sons of need in the world we should lose the sweet privilege of evidencing our love, by ministering in almsgiving to His poorer brethren; He has ordained that thus we should prove that our love standeth not in word only, but in deed and in truth. If we truly love Christ, we shall care for those who are loved by Him. Those who are dear to Him will be dear to us. Let us then look upon it not as a duty but as a privilege to relieve the poor of the Lord's flock - remembering the words of the Lord Jesus, 'Inasmuch as ye have done it unto one of the least of these my brethren, ye have done it unto me'. Surely this assurance is sweet enough, and this motive strong enough to lead us to help others with a willing hand and a loving heart - recollecting that all we do for His people is graciously accepted by Christ as done to Himself.

'Blessed are the peacemakers:
for they shall be called the children of God'
Matthew 5:9

This is the seventh of the beatitudes: and seven was the number of perfection among the Hebrews. It may be that the Saviour placed the peacemaker the seventh upon the list because he most nearly approaches the perfect man in Christ Jesus. He who would have perfect blessedness, so far as it can be enjoyed on earth, must attain to this seventh benediction, and become a peacemaker. There is a significance also in the position of the text. The verse which precedes it speaks of the blessedness of 'the pure in heart: for they shall see God'. It is well to understand that we are to be 'first pure, then peaceable'. Our peaceableness is never to be a compact with sin, or toleration of evil. We must set our faces like flints against everything which is contrary to God and His holiness: purity being in our souls a settled matter, we can go on to peaceableness. Not less does the verse that follows seem to have been put there on purpose. However peaceable we may be in this world, yet we shall be misrepresented and misunderstood: and no marvel, for even the Prince of Peace, by His very peacefulness, brought fire upon the earth. He Himself, though He loved mankind, and did no ill, was 'despised and rejected of men, a man of sorrows and acquainted with grief'. Lest, therefore, the peaceable in heart should be surprised when they meet with enemies, it is added in the following verse, 'Blessed are they which are persecuted for righteousness' sake: for theirs is the kingdom of heaven'. Thus the peacemakers are not only pronounced to be blessed, but they are compassed about with blessings. Lord, give us grace to climb to this seventh beatitude! Purify our minds that we may be 'first pure, then peaceable', and fortify our souls, that our peaceableness may not lead us into cowardice and despair, when for Thy sake we are persecuted.

'Ye are all the children of God by faith in Christ Jesus'
Galatians 3:26

The *fatherhood of God is common to all his children.*
Ah! Little-faith, you have often said, 'Oh that I had the
courage of Great-heart, that I could wield his sword and
be as valiant as he! But, alas, I stumble at every straw,
and a shadow makes me afraid.' List thee, Little-faith.
Great-heart is God's child, and you are God's child too;
and Great-heart is not one whit more God's child than
you are. Peter and Paul, the highly-favoured apostles,
were of the family of the Most High; and so are you
also; the weak Christian is as much a child of God as
the strong one.

> 'This cov'nant stands secure,
> Though earth's old pillars bow;
> The strong, the feeble, and the weak,
> Are one in Jesus now.'

All the names are in the same family register. One may
have more grace than another, but God our heavenly
Father has the same tender heart towards all. One may
do more mighty works, and may bring more glory to
his Father, but he whose name is the least in the
kingdom of heaven is as much the child of God as he
who stands among the King's mighty men. Let this
cheer and comfort us, when we draw near to God and
say, 'Our Father'.

Yet, while we are comforted by knowing this, let
us not rest contented with weak faith, but ask, like the
Apostles, to have it increased. However feeble our faith
may be, if it be real faith in Christ, we shall reach
heaven at last, but we shall not honour our Master much
on our pilgrimage, neither shall we abound in joy and
peace. If then you would live to Christ's glory, and be
happy in His service, seek to be filled with the spirit of
adoption more and more completely, till perfect love
shall cast out fear.

'As the Father hath loved Me, so have I loved you'
John 15:9

As the Father loves the Son, in the same manner Jesus loves His people. What is that divine method? He loved Him *without beginning*, and thus Jesus loves His members. '*I have loved thee with an everlasting love.*' You can trace the beginning of human affection; you can easily find the beginning of your love to Christ, but His love to us is a stream whose source is hidden in eternity. God the Father loves Jesus *without any change.* Christian, take this for your comfort, that there is no change in Jesus Christ's love to those who rest in Him. Yesterday you were on Tabor's top, and you said, 'He loves me': today you are in the valley of humiliation, but He loves you still the same. On the hill Mizar, and among the Hermons, you heard His voice, which spake so sweetly with the turtle-notes of love; and now on the sea, or even *in* the sea, when all His waves and billows go over you, His heart is faithful to His ancient choice. The Father loves the Son *without any end*, and thus does the Son love His people. Saint, thou needest not fear the loosing of the silver cord, for His love for thee will never cease. Rest confident that even down to the grave Christ will go with you, and that up again from it He will be your guide to the celestial hills. Moreover, the Father loves the Son *without any measure*, and the same immeasurable love the Son bestows upon His chosen ones. The whole heart of Christ is dedicated to His people. He 'loved us and gave Himself for us'. His is a love which passeth knowledge. Ah! we have indeed an immutable Saviour, a precious Saviour, one who loves without measure, without change, without beginning, and without end, even as the Father loves Him! There is much food here for those who know how to digest it. May the Holy Ghost lead us into its marrow and fatness!

'Strong in faith'
Romans 4:20

Christian, take good care of thy faith; for recollect *faith is the only way whereby thou canst obtain blessings.* If we want blessings from God, nothing can fetch them down but faith. Prayer cannot draw down answers from God's throne except it be the earnest prayer of the man who believes. Faith is the angelic messenger between the soul and the Lord Jesus in glory. Let that angel be withdrawn, we can neither send up prayer, nor receive the answers. Faith is the telegraphic wire which links earth and heaven - on which God's messages of love fly so fast, that before we call He answers, and while we are yet speaking He hears us. But if that telegraphic wire of faith be snapped, how can we receive the promise? Am I in trouble? - I can obtain help for trouble by faith. Am I beaten about by the enemy? - my soul on her dear Refuge leans by faith. But take faith away - in vain I call to God. There is no road betwixt my soul and heaven. In the deepest wintertime faith is a road on which the horses of prayer may travel - ay, and all the better for the biting frost; but blockade the road, and how can we communicate with the Great King? Faith links me with divinity. Faith clothes me with the power of God. Faith engages every attribute of God in my defence. It helps me to defy the hosts of hell. It makes me march triumphant over the necks of my enemies. But without faith how can I receive anything of the Lord? Let not him that wavereth - who is like the wave of the Sea - expect that he will receive anything of God! O, then, Christian, watch well thy faith; for with it thou canst win all things, however poor thou art, but without it thou canst obtain nothing. 'If thou canst believe, all things are possible to him that believeth.'

'And she did eat, and was sufficed, and left'
Ruth 2:14

Whenever we are privileged to eat of the bread which Jesus gives, we are, like Ruth, satisfied with the full and sweet repast. When Jesus is the host no guest goes empty from the table. Our *head* is satisfied with the precious truth which Christ reveals; our *heart* is content with Jesus, as the altogether lovely object of affection; our *hope* is satisfied, for whom have we in heaven but Jesus? and our *desire* is satiated, for what can we wish for more than 'to know Christ and to be found in Him'? Jesus fills our *conscience* till it is at perfect peace; our *judgment* with persuasion of the certainty of His teachings; our *memory* with recollections of what He has done, and our *imagination* with the prospects of what He is yet to do. As Ruth was 'sufficed, *and left*', so is it with us. We have had deep draughts; we have thought that we could take in all of Christ; but when we have done our best we have had to leave a vast remainder. We have sat at the table of the Lord's love, and said, 'Nothing but the infinite can ever satisfy me; I am such a great sinner that I must have infinite merit to wash my sin away'; but we have had our sin removed, and found that there was merit to spare; we have had our hunger relieved at the feast of sacred love, and found that there was a redundance of spiritual meat remaining. There are certain sweet things in the Word of God which we have not enjoyed yet, and which we are obliged to leave for awhile; for we are like the disciples to whom Jesus said, 'I have yet many things to say unto you, but ye cannot bear them now'. Yes, there are graces to which we have not attained; places of fellowship nearer to Christ which we have not reached; and heights of communion which our feet have not climbed. At every banquet of love there are many baskets of fragments left. Let us magnify the liberality of our glorious Boaz.

'My beloved'
Canticles 2:8

This was a golden name which the ancient Church in her most joyous moments was wont to give to the Anointed of the Lord. When the time of the singing of birds was come, and the voice of the turtle was heard in her land, *her* love-note was sweeter than either, as she sung, '*My beloved* is mine and I am His; He feedeth among the lilies'. Ever in her song of songs doth she call Him by that delightful name, 'My beloved!' Even in the long winter, when idolatry had withered the garden of the Lord, her prophets found space to lay aside the burden of the Lord for a little season, and to say, as Esaias did, 'Now will I sing to my well-beloved a song of my beloved touching His vineyard'. Though the saints had never seen His face, though as yet He was not made flesh, nor had dwelt among us, nor had man beheld His glory, yet He was the consolation of Israel, the hope and joy of all the chosen, the 'beloved' of all those who were upright before the Most High. We, in the summer days of the Church, are also wont to speak of Christ as the best beloved of our soul, and to feel that He is very precious, the 'chiefest among ten thousand, and the altogether lovely'. So true is it that the Church loves Jesus, and claims Him as her beloved, that the apostle dares to defy the whole universe to separate her from the love of Christ, and declares that neither persecutions, distress, affliction, peril, or the sword have been able to do it; nay, he joyously boasts, 'In all these things we are more than conquerors through Him that loved us'.

O that we knew more of Thee, Thou ever precious one!

My sole possession is Thy love;
In earth beneath, or heaven above,
I have no other store;
And though with fervent suit I pray,
And importune Thee day by day,
I ask Thee nothing more.

> '*Husbands, love your wives,
> even as Christ also loved the church*'
> Ephesians 5:25

What a golden example Christ gives to His disciples!
Few masters could venture to say, 'If you would
practise my teaching, imitate my life'; but as the life of
Jesus is the exact transcript of perfect virtue, He can
point to Himself as the paragon of holiness, as well as
the teacher of it. The Christian should take nothing
short of Christ for his model. Under no circumstances
ought we to be content unless we reflect the grace which
was in Him. As a husband, the Christian is to look upon
the portrait of Christ Jesus, and he is to paint according
to that copy. The true Christian is to be such a husband
as Christ was to His church. The love of a husband is
special. The Lord Jesus cherishes for the church a
peculiar affection, which is set upon her above the rest
of mankind: 'I pray for them, I pray not for the world'.
The elect church is the favourite of heaven, the treasure
of Christ, the crown of His head, the bracelet of His
arm, the breastplate of His heart, the very centre and
core of His love. A husband should love his wife with
a *constant* love, for thus Jesus loves His church. He
does not vary in His affection. He may change in His
display of affection, but the affection itself is still the
same. A husband should love his wife with an *enduring*
love, for nothing 'shall be able to separate us from the
love of God, which is in Christ Jesus our Lord'. A true
husband loves his wife with a *hearty* love, fervent and
intense. It is not mere lip-service. Ah! beloved, what
more could Christ have done in proof of His love than
He has done? Jesus has a *delighted love* towards His
spouse: He prizes her affection, and delights in her with
sweet complacence. Believer, you wonder at Jesus'
love; you admire it - *are you imitating it*? In your
domestic relationships is the rule and measure of your
love - '*even as Christ loved the church*'?

*'Ye shall be scattered, every man to his own,
and shall leave me alone'*
John 16:32

Few had fellowship with the sorrows of Gethsemane.
The majority of the disciples were not sufficiently
advanced in grace to be admitted to behold the mysteries of 'the agony'. Occupied with the Passover feast at
their own houses, they represent the many who live
upon the letter, but are mere babes as to the spirit of the
gospel. To twelve, nay, to eleven only was the privilege
given to enter Gethsemane and see 'this great sight'.
Out of the eleven, eight were left at a distance; they had
fellowship, but not of that intimate sort to which men
greatly beloved are admitted. Only three highly favoured ones could approach the veil of our Lord's
mysterious sorrow: within that veil even these must not
intrude; a stone's-cast distance must be left between.
He must tread the winepress *alone*, and of the people
there must be none with him. Peter and the two sons of
Zebedee, represent the few eminent, experienced saints,
who may be written down as 'Fathers'; these having
done business on great waters, can in some degree
measure the huge Atlantic waves of their Redeemer's
passion. To some selected spirits it is given, for the
good of others, and to strengthen them for future,
special and tremendous conflict, to enter the inner
circle and hear the pleadings of the suffering High
Priest; they have fellowship with him in his sufferings,
and are made conformable unto his death. Yet even
these cannot penetrate the secret places of the Saviour's
woes. 'Thine unknown sufferings' is the remarkable
expression of the Greek liturgy: there was an inner
chamber in our Master's grief, shut out from human
knowledge and fellowship. There Jesus is '*left alone*'.
Here Jesus was more than ever an 'Unspeakable gift'!
Is not Watts right when he sings:

'And all the unknown joys he gives,
Were bought with agonies unknown'?

'Canst thou bind the sweet influences of Pleiades,
or loose the bands of Orion?'
Job 38:31

If inclined to boast of our abilities, the grandeur of nature may soon show us how puny we are. We cannot move the least of all the twinkling stars, or quench so much as one of the beams of the morning. We speak of power, but the heavens laugh us to scorn. When the Pleiades shine forth in spring with vernal joy we cannot restrain their influences, and when Orion reigns aloft, and the year is bound in winter's fetters, we cannot relax the icy bands. The seasons revolve according to the divine appointment, neither can the whole race of men effect a change therein. Lord, what is man?

In the spiritual, as in the natural world, man's power is limited on all hands. When the Holy Spirit sheds abroad His delights in the soul, none can disturb; all the cunning and malice of men are ineffectual to stay the genial quickening power of the Comforter. When he deigns to visit a church and revive it, the most inveterate enemies cannot resist the good work; they may ridicule it, but they can no more restrain it than they can push back the spring when the Pleiades rule the hour. God wills it, and so it must be. On the other hand, if the Lord in sovereignty, or in justice, bind up a man so that he is in soul bondage, who can give him liberty? He alone can remove the winter of spiritual death from an individual or a people. He looses the bands of Orion, and none but He. What a blessing it is that He can do it. O that He would perform the wonder tonight. Lord, end my winter, and let my spring begin. I cannot with all my longings raise my soul out of her death and dulness, but all things are possible with Thee. I need celestial influences, the clear shinings of Thy love, the beams of Thy grace, the light of Thy countenance, these are the Pleiades to me. I suffer much from sin and temptation, these are my wintry signs, my terrible Orion. Lord, work wonders in me, and for me. Amen.

> *'And He went a little farther,*
> *and fell on His face, and prayed'*
> Matthew 26:39

There are several instructive features in our Saviour's prayer in His hour of trial. It was *lonely prayer*. He withdrew even from His three favoured disciples. Believer, be much in solitary prayer, especially in times of trial. Family prayer, social prayer, prayer in the Church, will not suffice, these are very precious, but the best beaten spice will smoke in your censer in your private devotions, where no ear hears but God's.

It was *humble prayer*. Luke says He knelt, but another evangelist says He 'fell on His face'. Where, then, must be THY place, thou humble servant of the great Master? What dust and ashes should cover *thy* head! Humility gives us good foothold in prayer. There is no hope of prevalence with God unless we abase ourselves that He may exalt us in due time.

It was *filial prayer*. 'Abba, Father.' You will find it a stronghold in the day of trial to plead your adoption. You have no rights as a subject, you have forfeited them by your treason; but nothing can forfeit a child's right to a father's protection. Be not afraid to say, 'My Father, hear my cry'.

Observe that it was *persevering prayer*. He prayed three times. Cease not until you prevail. Be as the importunate widow, whose continual coming earned what her first supplication could not win. Continue in prayer, and watch in the same with thanksgiving.

Lastly, *it was the prayer of resignation*. 'Nevertheless, not as I will, but as thou wilt.' Yield, and God yields. Let it be as God wills, and God will determine for the best. Be thou content to leave thy prayer in his hands, who knows when to give, and how to give, and what to give, and what to withhold. So pleading, earnestly, importunately, yet with humility and resignation, thou shalt surely prevail.

*'Father, I will that they also, whom Thou hast given
Me, be with Me where I am'*
John 17:24

O Death! why dost thou touch the tree beneath whose
spreading branches weariness hath rest? Why dost
thou snatch away the excellent of the earth, in whom is
all our delight? If thou must use thine axe, use it upon
the trees which yield no fruit; thou mightst be thanked
then. But why wilt thou fell the goodly cedars of
Lebanon? O stay thine axe, and spare the righteous. But
no, it must not be; death smites the goodliest of our
friends; the most generous, the most prayerful, the
most holy, the most devoted must die. And why? It is
through Jesus' prevailing prayer - 'Father, I will that
they also, whom Thou hast given Me, be with Me
where I am'. It is *that* which bears them on eagle's
wings to heaven. Every time a believer mounts from
this earth to paradise, it is an answer to Christ's prayer.
A good old divine remarks, 'Many times Jesus and His
people pull against one another in prayer. You bend
your knee in prayer and say, "Father, I will that Thy
saints be with me where *I* am"; Christ says, "Father, I
will that they also, whom Thou hast given Me, be with
Me where *I* am".' Thus the disciple is at cross-
purposes with his Lord. The soul cannot be in both
places: the beloved one cannot be with Christ and with
you too. Now, which pleader shall win the day? If you
had your choice; if the King should step from His
throne, and say, 'Here are two supplicants praying in
opposition to one another, which shall be answered?'
Oh! I am sure, though it were agony, you would start
from your feet, and say, 'Jesus, not my will, but Thine
be done'. You would give up your prayer for your loved
one's life, if you could realise the thought that Christ
is praying in the opposite direction - 'Father, I will that
they also, whom Thou hast given Me, be with Me
where I am'. Lord, Thou shalt have them. By faith we
let them go.

> '*His sweat was as it were great drops of blood*
> *falling down to the ground*'
> Luke 22:44

The mental pressure arising from our Lord's struggle with temptation, so forced his frame to an unnatural excitement, that his pores sent forth great drops of blood which fell down to the ground. This proves *how tremendous must have been the weight of sin* when it was able to crush the Saviour so that he distilled great drops of blood! This demonstrates *the mighty power of his love*. It is a very pretty observation of old Isaac Ambrose that the gum which exudes from the tree without cutting is always the best. This precious camphire tree yielded most sweet spices when it was wounded under the knotty whips, and when it was pierced by the nails on the cross; but see, it giveth forth its best spice when there is no whip, no nail, no wound. This sets forth *the voluntariness of Christ's sufferings*, since without a lance the blood flowed freely. No need to put on the leech, or apply the knife; it flows spontaneously. No need for the rulers to cry, 'Spring up, O well'; of itself it flows in crimson torrents. If men suffer great pain of mind apparently the blood rushes *to* the heart. The cheeks are pale; a fainting fit comes on; the blood has gone inward as if to nourish the inner man while passing through its trial. But see our Saviour in His agony; he is so utterly oblivious of self, that instead of his agony driving his blood to the heart to nourish himself, it drives it outward to bedew the earth. The agony of Christ, inasmuch as it pours him out upon the ground, pictures the fulness of the offering which he made for men.

Do we not perceive how intense must have been the wrestling through which he passed, and will we not hear its voice *to us*? 'Ye have not yet resisted unto blood, striving against sin.' Behold the great Apostle and High Priest of our profession, and sweat even to blood rather than yield to the great tempter of your souls.

*'I tell you that, if these should hold their peace,
the stones would immediately cry out'*
Luke 19:40

But could the stones cry out? Assuredly they could if
He who opens the mouth of the dumb should bid them
lift up their voice. Certainly if they were to speak, they
would have much to testify in praise of Him who
created them by the word of His power; they could extol
the wisdom and power of their *Maker* who called them
into being. Shall not *we* speak well of Him who made
us anew, and out of stones raised up children unto
Abraham? The old rocks could tell of chaos and order,
and the handiwork of God in successive stages of
creation's drama; and cannot *we* talk of God's decrees,
of God's great work in ancient times, in all that He did
for His church in the days of old? If the stones were to
speak, they could tell of their *breaker*, how he took
them from the quarry, and made them fit for the temple,
and cannot we tell of our glorious Breaker, who broke
our hearts with the hammer of His word, that He might
build us into His temple? If the stones should cry out
they would magnify their *builder*, who polished them
and fashioned them after the similitude of a palace; and
shall not we talk of our Architect and Builder, who has
put us in our place in the temple of the living God? If
the stones could cry out, they might have a long, long
story to tell by way of *memorial*, for many a time hath
a great stone been rolled as a memorial before the Lord;
and we too can testify of Ebenezers, stones of help,
pillars of remembrance. The broken stones of the law
cry out against us, but Christ Himself, who has rolled
away the stone from the door of the sepulchre, speaks
for us. Stones might well cry out, but we will not let
them: we will hush their noise with ours; we will break
forth into sacred song, and bless the majesty of the
Most High, all our days glorifying Him who is called
by Jacob the Shepherd and Stone of Israel.

'He was heard in that he feared'
Hebrews 5:7

Did this fear arise from the infernal suggestion *that he was utterly forsaken*? There may be sterner trials than this, but surely it is *one* of the worst to be utterly forsaken? 'See,' said Satan, 'thou hast a friend nowhere! Thy Father hath shut up the bowels of his compassion against thee. Not an angel in His courts will stretch out his hand to help thee. All heaven is alienated from Thee; Thou art left alone. See the companions with whom Thou hast taken sweet counsel, what are they worth? Son of Mary, see there thy brother James, see there Thy loved disciple John, and Thy bold apostle Peter, how the cowards sleep when Thou art in Thy sufferings! Lo! Thou hast no friend left in heaven or earth. All hell is against Thee. I have stirred up mine infernal den. I have sent my missive throughout all regions summoning every prince of darkness to set upon Thee this night, and we will spare no arrows, we will use all our infernal might to overwhelm Thee: and what wilt Thou do, Thou solitary one?' It may be, this was the temptation; we think it was, because the appearance of an angel unto Him strengthening Him removed that fear. He was heard in that He feared; He was no more alone, but heaven was with Him. It may be that this is the reason of His coming three times to His disciples - as Hart puts it:

'Backwards and forwards thrice He ran,
As if He sought some help from man.'

He would see for Himself whether it were really true that all men had forsaken Him; He found them all asleep; but perhaps he gained some faint comfort from the thought that they were sleeping, not from treachery, but from sorrow, the spirit indeed was willing, but the flesh was weak. At any rate He was heard in that he feared. Jesus was heard in His deepest woe; my soul, thou shalt be heard also.

'In that hour Jesus rejoiced in spirit'
Luke 10:21

The Saviour was 'a man of sorrows' but every thoughtful mind has discovered the fact that down deep in His innermost soul He carried an inexhaustible treasury of refined and heavenly joy. Of all the human race, there was never a man who had a deeper, purer, or more abiding peace than our Lord Jesus Christ. 'He was anointed with the oil of gladness above His fellows.' His vast benevolence must, from the very nature of things, have afforded Him the deepest possible delight, for benevolence is joy. There were a few remarkable seasons when this joy manifested itself. 'At that hour Jesus rejoiced in spirit, and said, I thank thee, O Father, Lord of heaven and earth'. Christ had His songs, though it was night with Him; though His face was marred, and His countenance had lost the lustre of earthly happiness, yet sometimes it was lit up with a matchless splendour of unparalleled satisfaction, as He thought upon the recompense of the reward, and in the midst of the congregation sang His praise unto God. In this, the Lord Jesus is a blessed picture of His church on earth. At this hour the church expects to walk in sympathy with her Lord along a thorny road; through much tribulation she is forcing her way to the crown. To bear the cross is her office, and to be scorned and counted an alien by her mother's children is her lot; and yet the church has a deep well of joy, of which none can drink but her own children. There are stores of wine, and oil, and corn, hidden in the midst of our Jerusalem, upon which the saints of God are evermore sustained and nurtured; and sometimes, as in our Saviour's case, we have our seasons of intense delight, for 'There is a river, the streams whereof shall make glad the city of our God'. Exiles though we be, we rejoice in our King; yea, in Him we exceedingly rejoice, while in His name we set up our banners.

'Betrayest thou the Son of Man with a kiss?'
Luke 22:48

'The kisses of an enemy are deceitful.' Let me be on my guard when the world puts on a loving face, for it will, if possible, betray me as it did my Master, with a kiss. Whenever a man is about to stab religion, he usually professes very great reverence for it. Let me beware of the sleek-faced hypocrisy which is armour-bearer to heresy and infidelity. Knowing the deceivableness of unrighteousness, let me be wise as a serpent to detect and avoid the designs of the enemy. The young man, void of understanding, was led astray by the kiss of the strange woman: may my soul be so graciously instructed all this day, that 'the much fair speech' of the world may have no effect upon me. Holy Spirit, let me not, a poor frail son of man, be betrayed with a kiss!

But what if I should be guilty of the same accursed sin as Judas, that son of perdition? I have been baptised into the name of the Lord Jesus; I am a member of His visible Church; I sit at the communion table: all these are so many kisses of my lips. Am I sincere in them? If not, I am a base traitor. Do I live in the world as carelessly as others do, and yet make a profession of being a follower of Jesus? Then I must expose religion to ridicule, and lead men to speak evil of the holy name by which I am called. Surely if I act thus inconsistently I am a Judas, and it were better for me that I had never been born. Dare I hope that I am clear in this matter? Then, O Lord, keep me so. O Lord, make me sincere and true. Preserve me from every false way. Never let me betray my Saviour. I do love Thee, Jesus, and though I often grieve Thee, yet I would desire to abide faithful even unto death. O God, forbid that I should be a high-soaring professor, and then fall at last into the lake of fire, because I betrayed my Master with a kiss.

'The Son of man'
John 3:13

How constantly our Master used the title, the 'Son of man'! If He had chosen, He might always have spoken of Himself as the Son of God, the Everlasting Father, the Wonderful, the Counsellor, the Prince of Peace; but behold the lowliness of Jesus! He prefers to call Himself the Son of man. Let us learn a lesson of humility from our Saviour; let us never court great titles nor proud degrees. There is here, however, a far sweeter thought. Jesus loved manhood so much, that He delighted to honour it; and since it is a high honour, and indeed, the greatest dignity of manhood, that Jesus is the Son of man, He is wont to display this name, that He may as it were hang royal stars upon the breast of manhood, and show forth the love of God to Abraham's seed. *Son of man* - whenever He said that word, He shed a halo round the head of Adam's children. Yet there is perhaps a more precious thought still. Jesus Christ called Himself the Son of man to express His oneness and sympathy with His people. He thus reminds us that He is one whom we may approach without fear. As a man, we may take to Him all our griefs and troubles, for He knows them by experience; in that He Himself hath suffered as the 'Son of man', He is able to succour and comfort us. All hail, Thou blessed Jesus! inasmuch as Thou art evermore using the sweet name which acknowledges that Thou art a brother and a near kinsman, it is to us a dear token of Thy grace, Thy humility, Thy love.

> 'Oh see how Jesus trusts Himself
> Unto our childish love,
> As though by His free ways with us
> Our earnestness to prove!
>
> His sacred name a common word
> On earth He loves to hear;
> There is no majesty in Him
> Which love may not come near.'

'Jesus said unto them, If ye seek Me,
let these go their way'
John 18:8

Mark, my soul, the care which Jesus manifested even
in His hour of trial, towards the sheep of His hand! The
ruling passion is strong in death. He resigns himself to
the enemy, but He interposes a word of power to set His
disciples free. As to himself, like a sheep before her
shearers He is dumb and opened not his mouth, but for
His disciples' sake He speaks with Almighty energy.
Herein is love, constant, self-forgetting, faithful love.
But is there not far more here than is to be found upon
the surface? Have we not the very soul and spirit of the
atonement in these words? The Good Shepherd lays
down His life for the sheep, and pleads that they must
therefore go free. The Surety is bound, and justice
demands that those for whom He stands a substitute
should go their way. In the midst of Egypt's bondage,
that voice rings as a word of power, *'Let these go their
way'*. Out of the slavery of sin and Satan the redeemed
must come. In every cell of the dungeons of Despair,
the sound is echoed, *'Let these go their way'*, and forth
come Despondency and Much-afraid. Satan hears the
well-known voice, and lifts his foot from the neck of
the fallen; and Death hears it, and the grave opens her
gates to let the dead arise. *Their way* is one of progress,
holiness, triumph, glory, and none shall dare to stay
them in it. No lion shall be on their way, neither shall
any ravenous beast go up thereon. 'The hind of the
morning' has drawn the cruel hunters upon himself,
and now the most timid roes and hinds of the field may
graze at perfect peace among the lilies of his loves. The
thundercloud has burst over the Cross of Calvary, and
the pilgrims of Zion shall never be smitten by the bolts
of vengeance. Come, my heart, rejoice in the immunity
which thy Redeemer has secured thee, and bless His
name all the day, and every day.

*'When He cometh in the glory of His Father
with the holy angels'*
Mark 8:38

If we have been partakers with Jesus in His shame, we shall be sharers with Him in the lustre which shall surround Him when He appears again in glory. Art thou, beloved one, with Christ Jesus? Does a vital union knit thee to Him? Then thou art today with Him in His shame; thou hast taken up His cross, and gone with Him without the camp bearing His reproach; thou shalt doubtless be with Him when the cross is exchanged for the crown. But judge thyself this evening; for if thou art not with Him in the regeneration, neither shalt thou be with Him when he shall come in His glory. If thou start back from the black side of communion, thou shalt not understand its bright, its happy period, when the King shall come, and *all His holy angels with Him*. What! are *angels with Him*? And yet He took not up angels - He took up the seed of Abraham. Are the holy angels *with Him*? Come, my soul, if thou art indeed His own beloved, thou canst not be far from Him. If His friends and His neighbours are called together to see His glory, what thinkest thou if thou art married to Him? Shalt thou be distant? Though it be a day of judgment, yet thou canst not be far from that heart which, having admitted angels into intimacy, has admitted thee into union. Has He not said to thee, O my soul, 'I will betroth thee unto Me in righteousness, and in judgment, and in lovingkindness'? Have not His own lips said it, 'I am married unto thee, and My delight is in thee'? If the angels, who are but friends and neighbours, shall be with Him, it is abundantly certain that His own beloved Hephzibah, in whom is all His delight, shall be near to Him, and sit at His right hand. Here is a morning star of hope for thee, of such exceeding brilliance, that it may well light up the darkest and most desolate experience.

'Then all the disciples forsook Him, and fled'
Matthew 26:56

He never deserted them, but they in cowardly fear of their lives, fled from Him in the very beginning of His sufferings. This is but one instructive instance of the frailty of all believers if left to themselves; they are but sheep at the best, and they flee when the wolf cometh. They had all been warned of the danger, and had promised to die rather than leave their Master; and yet they were seized with sudden panic, and took to their heels. It may be, that I, at the opening of this day, have braced up my mind to bear a trial for the Lord's sake, and I imagine myself to be certain to exhibit perfect fidelity; but let me be very jealous of myself, lest having the same evil heart of unbelief, I should depart from my Lord as the apostles did. It is one thing to promise, and quite another to perform. It would have been to their eternal honour to have stood at Jesus' side right manfully; they fled from honour; may I be kept from imitating them! Where else could they have been so safe as near their Master, who could presently call for twelve legions of angels? they fled from their true safety. O God, let me not play the fool also. Divine grace can make the coward brave. The smoking flax can flame forth like fire on the altar when the Lord wills it. These very apostles who were timid as hares, grew to be bold as lions after the Spirit had descended upon them, and even so the Holy Spirit can make my recreant spirit brave to confess my Lord and witness for His truth.

What anguish must have filled the Saviour as He saw His friends so faithless! This was one bitter ingredient in His cup; but that cup is drained dry; let me not put another drop in it. If I forsake my Lord, I shall crucify Him afresh, and put Him to an open shame. Keep me, O blessed Spirit, from an end so shameful.

'And she said. Truth, Lord: yet the dogs eat of the crumbs which fall from their masters' table'
Matthew 15:27

This woman gained comfort in her misery by thinking *great thoughts of Christ*. The Master had talked about the children's bread: 'No,' argued she, 'since Thou art the Master of the table of grace, I know that Thou art a generous housekeeper, and there is sure to be abundance of bread on Thy table; there will be such an abundance for the children that there will be crumbs to throw on the floor for the dogs, and the children will fare none the worse because the dogs are fed.' She thought Him one who kept so good a table that all that she needed would only be a crumb in comparison; yet remember, what she wanted was to have the devil cast out of her daughter. I was a very great thing to her, but she had such a high esteem of Christ, that she said, 'It is nothing to Him, it is but a crumb for Christ to give'. This is the royal road to comfort. Great thoughts of your sin alone will drive you to despair; but great thoughts of Christ will pilot you into the haven of peace. 'My sins are many, but oh! it is nothing to Jesus to take them all away. The weight of my guilt presses me down as a giant's foot would crush a worm, but it is no more than a grain of dust to Him, because He has already borne its curse in His own body on the tree. It will be but a small thing *for Him* to give me full remission, although it will be an infinite blessing *for me* to receive it.' The woman opens her soul's mouth very wide, expecting great things of Jesus and He fills it with His love. Dear reader, do the same. She confessed what Christ laid at her door, but she laid fast hold upon Him, and drew arguments even out of His hard words; she believed great things of Him, and she thus overcame Him. *She won the victory by believing in him.* Her case is an instance of prevailing faith; and if we would conquer like her, we must imitate her tactics.

'The love of Christ which passeth knowledge'
Ephesians 3:19.

The love of Christ in its sweetness, its fulness, its greatness, its faithfulness, passeth all human comprehension. Where shall language be found which shall describe His matchless, His unparalleled love towards the children of men? It is so vast and boundless that, as the swallow but skimmeth the water, and diveth not into its depths, so all descriptive words but touch the surface, while depths immeasurable lie beneath. Well might the poet say, 'O love, thou fathomless abyss!' for this love of Christ is indeed measureless and fathomless; none can attain unto it. Before we can have any right idea of the love of Jesus, we must understand His previous glory in its height of majesty, and His incarnation upon the earth in all its depths of shame. But who can tell us the majesty of Christ? When He was enthroned in the highest heavens He was very God of very God; by Him were the heavens made, and all the hosts thereof. His own almighty arm upheld the spheres; the praises of cherubim and seraphim perpetually surrounded Him; the full chorus of the hallelujahs of the universe unceasingly flowed to the foot of his throne: He reigned supreme above all His creatures, God over all, blessed for ever. Who can tell His height of glory then? And who, on the other hand, can tell how low He descended? To be a man was something, to be a man of sorrows was far more; to bleed, and die, and suffer, these were much for him who was the Son of God; but to suffer such unparalleled agony - to endure a death of shame and desertion by His Father, this is a depth of condescending love which the most inspired mind must utterly fail to fathom. Herein is love! and truly it is love that 'passeth knowledge'. O let this love fill our hearts with adoring gratitude, and lead us to practical manifestations of its power.

'I will accept you with your sweet savour'
Ezekiel 20:41

The merits of our great Redeemer are as sweet savour to the Most High. Whether we speak of the active or passive righteousness of Christ, there is an equal fragrance. There was a sweet savour in His active life by which He honoured the law of God, and made every precept to glitter like a precious jewel in the pure setting of His own person. Such, too, was His passive obedience, when he endured with unmurmuring submission, hunger and thirst, cold and nakedness, and at length sweat great drops of blood in Gethsemane, gave His back to the smiters, and His cheeks to them that plucked out the hair, and was fastened to the cruel wood, that He might suffer the wrath of God in our behalf. These two things are sweet before the Most High; and for the sake of His doing and His dying, His substitutionary sufferings and His vicarious obedience, the Lord our God accepts us. What a preciousness must there be in Him to overcome our want of preciousness! What a sweet savour to put away our ill savour! What a cleansing power in His blood to take away sin such as ours! and what glory in His righteousness to make such unacceptable creatures to be accepted in the Beloved! Mark, believer, how sure and unchanging must be our acceptance, since it is *in Him*! Take care that you never doubt your acceptance in Jesus. You cannot be accepted without Christ; but, when you have received His merit, you cannot be unaccepted. Notwithstanding all your doubts, and fears, and sins, Jehovah's gracious eye never looks upon you in anger; though He sees sin in you, in yourself, yet when He looks at you through Christ, He sees no sin. You are always accepted in Christ, are always blessed and dear to the Father's heart. Therefore lift up a song, and as you see the smoking incense of the merit of the Saviour coming up, this evening, before the sapphire throne, let the incense of your praise go up also.

*'Though He were a Son, yet learned He obedience
by the things which He suffered'*
Hebrews 5:8

We are told that the Captain of our salvation was made perfect through suffering, therefore we who are sinful, and who are far from being perfect, must not wonder if we are called to pass through suffering too. Shall the head be crowned with thorns, and shall the other members of the body be rocked upon the dainty lap of ease? Must Christ pass through seas of His own blood to win the crown, and are we to walk to heaven dryshod in silver slippers? No, our Master's experience teaches us that suffering is necessary, and the true-born child of God must not, would not, escape it if he might. But there is one very comforting thought in the fact of Christ's 'being made perfect through suffering' - it is, that He can have complete sympathy with us. 'He is not an high priest that cannot be touched with the feeling of our infirmities.' In this sympathy of Christ we find a sustaining power. One of the early martyrs said, 'I can bear it all, for Jesus suffered, and He suffers in me now; He sympathizes with me, and this makes me strong'. Believer, lay hold of this thought in all times of agony. Let the thought of Jesus strengthen you as you follow in His steps. Find a sweet support in His sympathy; and remember that, to suffer is an honourable thing - to suffer for Christ is glory. The apostles rejoiced that they were counted worthy to do this. Just so far as the Lord shall give us grace to suffer *for* Christ, to suffer *with* Christ, just so far does he honour us. The jewels of a Christian are his afflictions. The regalia of the kings whom God hath anointed are their troubles, their sorrows, and their griefs. Let us not, therefore, shun being honoured. Let us not turn aside from being exalted. Griefs exalt us, and troubles lift us up. 'If we suffer, we shall also reign with Him.'

'I called Him, but He gave me no answer'
Canticles 5:6

Prayer sometimes tarrieth, like a petitioner at the gate, until the King comes forth to fill her bosom with the blessings which she seeketh. The Lord, when He hath given great faith, has been known to try it by long delayings. He has suffered his servants' voices to echo in their ears as from a brazen sky. They have knocked at the golden gate, but it has remained immovable, as though it were rusted upon its hinges. Like Jeremiah, they have cried, 'Thou hast covered Thyself with a cloud, that our prayer should not pass through'. Thus have true saints continued long in patient waiting without reply, not because their prayers were not vehement, nor because they were unaccepted, but because it so pleased Him who is a Sovereign, and who gives according to His own pleasure. If it pleases Him to bid our patience exercise itself, shall He not do as He wills with His own! Beggars must not be choosers either as to time, place, or form. But we must be careful not to take delays in prayer for denials: God's long-dated bills will be punctually honoured; we must not suffer Satan to shake our confidence in the God of truth by pointing to our unanswered prayers. Unanswered petitions are not unheard. God keeps a file for our prayers - they are not blown away by the wind, they are treasured in the King's archives. There is a registry in the court of heaven wherein every prayer is recorded. Tried believer, thy Lord hath a tear-bottle in which the costly drops of sacred grief are put away, and a book in which thy holy groanings are numbered. By-and-by, thy suit shall prevail. Canst thou not be content to wait a little? Will not thy Lord's time be better than thy time? By-and-by He will comfortably appear, to thy soul's joy, and make thee put away the sackcloth and ashes of long waiting, and put on the scarlet and fine linen of full fruition.

'He was numbered with the transgressors'
Isaiah 53:12

Why did Jesus suffer Himself to be enrolled amongst sinners? This wonderful condescension was justified by many powerful reasons. *In such a character He could the better become their advocate.* In some trials there is an identification of the counsellor with the client, nor can they be looked upon in the eye of the law as apart from one another. Now, when the sinner is brought to the bar, Jesus appears there Himself. *He* stands to answer the accusation. He points to His side, His hands, His feet, and challenges Justice to bring anything against the sinners whom He represents; He pleads his blood, and pleads so triumphantly, being numbered with them and having a part with them, that the Judge proclaims, 'Let them go their way; deliver them from going down into the pit, for He hath found a ransom'. Our Lord Jesus was numbered with the transgressors in order that they might *feel their hearts drawn towards Him.* Who can be afraid of one who is written in the same list with us? Surely we may come boldly to Him, and confess our guilt. He who is numbered with us cannot condemn us. Was he not put down in the transgressor's list *that we might be written in the red roll of the saints*? He was holy, and written among the holy; we were guilty, and numbered among the guilty; He transfers His name from yonder list to this black indictment, and our names are taken from the indictment and written in the roll of acceptance, for there is a complete transfer made between Jesus and His people. All our estate of misery and sin Jesus has taken; and all that Jesus has comes to us. His righteousness, His blood, and everything that He hath He gives us as our dowry. Rejoice, believer, in your union to Him who was numbered among the transgressors; and prove that you are truly saved by being manifestly numbered with those who are new creatures in Him.

'With His stripes we are healed'
Isaiah 53:5

Pilate delivered our Lord to the lictors to be scourged.
The Roman scourge was a most dreadful instrument of
torture. It was made of the sinews of oxen, and sharp
bones were intertwisted every here and there among the
sinews; so that every time the lash came down these
pieces of bone inflicted fearful laceration, and tore off
the flesh from the bone. The Saviour was, no doubt,
bound to the column, and thus beaten. He had been
beaten before; but this of the Roman lictors was
probably the most severe of His flagellations. My soul,
stand here and weep over His poor stricken body.

Believer in Jesus, can you gaze upon Him without
tears, as He stands before you the mirror of agonizing
love? He is at once fair as the lily for innocence, and red
as the rose with the crimson of His own blood. As we
feel the sure and blessed healing which His stripes have
wrought in us, does not our heart melt at once with love
and grief? If ever we have loved our Lord Jesus, surely
we must feel that affection glowing now within our
bosoms.

'See how the patient Jesus stands,
Insulted in His lowest case!
Sinners have bound the Almighty's hands,
And spit in their Creator's face.

With thorns His temples gor'd and gash'd
Send streams of blood from every part;
His back's with knotted scourges lash'd,
But sharper scourges tear His heart.'

We would fain go to our chambers and weep; but since
our business calls us away, we will first pray our
Beloved to print the image of His bleeding self upon the
tablets of our hearts all the day, and at nightfall we will
return to commune with Him, and sorrow that our sin
should have cost Him so dear.

> *'Let us search and try our ways,*
> *and turn again to the Lord'*
> Lamentations 3:40

The spouse who fondly loves her absent husband longs for his return; a long protracted separation from her lord is a semi-death to her spirit: and so with souls who love the Saviour much, they *must* see His face, they cannot bear that He should be away upon the mountains of Bether, and no more hold communion with them. A reproaching glance, an uplifted finger will be grievous to loving children, who fear to offend their tender father, and are only happy in his smile. Beloved, it was so once with you. A text of Scripture, a threatening, a touch of the rod of affliction, and you went to your Father's feet crying, 'Show me wherefore Thou contendest with me?' Is it so now? Are you content to follow Jesus afar off? Can you contemplate suspended communion with Christ without alarm? Can you bear to have your Beloved walking contrary to you, because you walk contrary to Him? Have your sins separated between you and your God, and is your heart at rest? O let me affectionately warn you, for it is a grievous thing when we can live contentedly without the present enjoyment of the Saviour's face. *Let us labour to feel what an evil thing this is* - little love to our own dying Saviour, little joy in our precious Jesus, little fellowship with the Beloved! Hold a true Lent in your souls, while you sorrow over your hardness of heart. Do not stop at sorrow! Remember where you first received salvation. *Go at once to the cross.* There, and there only, can you get your spirit quickened. No matter how hard, how insensible, how dead we may have become, let us go again in all the rags and poverty, and defilement of our natural condition. Let us clasp that cross, let us look into those languid eyes, let us bathe in that fountain filled with blood - this will bring back to us our first love; this will restore the simplicity of our faith, and the tenderness of our heart.

*'And Rizpah the daughter of Aiah took sackcloth, and
spread it for her upon the rock, from the beginning of
harvest until water dropped upon them out of heaven,
and suffered neither the birds of the air to rest on them
by day, nor the beasts of the field by night'*
2 Samuel 21:10

If the love of a woman to her slain sons could make her
prolong her mournful vigil for so long a period, shall
we weary of considering the sufferings of our blessed
Lord? She drove away the birds of prey, and shall not
we chase from our meditations those worldly and
sinful thoughts which defile both our minds and the
sacred themes upon which we are occupied? Away, ye
birds of evil wing! Leave ye the sacrifice alone! She
bore the heats of summer, the night dews and the rains,
unsheltered and alone. Sleep was chased from her
weeping eyes: her heart was too full for slumber.
Behold how she loved her children! Shall Rizpah thus
endure, and shall we start at the first little inconven-
ience or trial? Are we such cowards that we cannot bear
to suffer with our Lord? She chased away even the wild
beasts, with courage unusual in her sex, and will not we
be ready to encounter every foe for Jesus' sake? These
her children were slain by other hands than hers, and
yet she wept and watched; what ought we to do who
have by our sins crucified our Lord? Our obligations
are boundless, our love should be fervent and our
repentance thorough. To watch with Jesus should be
our business, to protect His honour our occupation, to
abide by His cross our solace. Those ghastly corpses
might well have affrighted Rizpah, especially by night,
but in our Lord, at whose cross-foot we are sitting,
there is nothing revolting, but everything attractive.
Never was living beauty so enchanting as a dying
Saviour. Jesus, we will watch with Thee yet awhile,
and do Thou graciously unveil Thyself to us; then shall
we not sit beneath sackcloth, but in a royal pavilion.

April

'*Let Him kiss me with the kisses of His mouth*'
Canticles 1:2

For several days we have been dwelling upon the
Saviour's passion, and for some little time to come we
shall linger there. In beginning a new month, let us seek
the same desires after our Lord as those which glowed
in the heart of the elect spouse. See how she leaps at
once to *Him*; there are no prefatory words; she does not
even mention His name; she is in the heart of her theme
at once, for she speaks of *Him* who was the only Him
in the world to her. How bold is her love! it was much
condescension which permitted the weeping penitent to
anoint His feet with spikenard - it was rich love which
allowed the gentle Mary to sit at His feet and learn of
Him - but here, love, strong, fervent love, aspires to
higher tokens of regard, and closer signs of fellowship.
Esther trembled in the presence of Ahasuerus, but the
spouse in joyful liberty of perfect love knows no fear.
If we have received the same free spirit, we also may
ask the like. By kisses we suppose to be intended those
varied manifestations of affection by which the believer is made to enjoy the love of Jesus. The kiss of
reconciliation we enjoyed at our conversion, and it was
sweet as honey dropping from the comb. The kiss of
acceptance is still warm on our brow, as we know that
He hath accepted our persons and our works through
rich grace. The kiss of daily, present *communion*, is
that which we pant after to be repeated day after day, till
it is changed into the kiss of *reception*, which removes
the soul from earth, and the kiss of *consummation*
which fills it with the joy of heaven. Faith is our walk,
but fellowship sensibly felt is our rest. Faith is the
road, but communion with Jesus is the well from which
the pilgrim drinks. O lover of our souls, be not strange
to us; let the lips of Thy blessing meet the lips of our
asking; let the lips of Thy fulness touch the lips of our
need and straightway the kiss will be effected.

'It is time to seek the Lord'
Hosea 10:12

This month of April is said to derive its name from the Latin verb *aperio*, which signifies *to open*, because all the buds and blossoms are now opening, and we have arrived at the gates of the flowery year. Reader, if you are yet unsaved, may your heart, in accord with the universal awakening of nature, be opened to receive the Lord. Every blossoming flower warns you that *it is time to seek the Lord*; be not out of tune with nature, but let your heart bud and bloom with holy desires. Do not tell me that the warm blood of youth leaps in your veins? Then, I entreat you, give your vigour to the Lord. It was my unspeakable happiness to be called in early youth, and I could fain praise the Lord every day for it. Salvation is priceless, let it come when it may, but oh! an early salvation has a double value in it. Young men and maidens, since you may perish ere you reach your prime, *'It is time to seek the Lord'*. Ye who feel the first signs of decay, quicken your pace: that hollow cough, that hectic flush, are warnings which you must not trifle with; with you *it is indeed time to seek the Lord*. Did I observe a little grey mingled with your once luxurious tresses? Years are stealing on apace, and death is drawing nearer by hasty marches, let each return of spring arouse you to set your house in order. Dear reader, if you are now advanced in life, let me entreat and implore you to delay no longer. There is a day of grace for you now - be thankful for that, but it is a limited season and grows shorter every time that clock ticks. Here in this silent chamber, on this first night of another month, I speak to you as best I can by paper and ink, and from my inmost soul, as God's servant, I lay before you this warning, *'It is time to seek the Lord'*. Slight not that word, it may be your last call from destruction, the final syllable from the lip of grace.

'He answered him to never a word'
Matthew 27:14

He had never been slow of speech when He could bless the sons of men, but He would not say a single word for Himself. 'Never man spake like this Man', and never man was silent like Him. Was this singular silence *the index of His perfect self-sacrifice*? Did it show that He would not utter a word to stay the slaughter of His sacred person, which He had dedicated as an offering for us? Had He so entirely surrendered Himself that He would not interfere in His own behalf, even in the minutest degree, but be bound and slain an unstruggling, uncomplaining victim? Was this silence *a type of the defencelessness of sin*? Nothing can be said in palliation or excuse of human guilt; and, therefore, He who bore its whole weight stood speechless before His judge. Is not patient silence *the best reply to a gainsaying world*? Calm endurance answers some questions infinitely more conclusively than the loftiest eloquence. The best apologists for Christianity in the early days were its martyrs. The anvil breaks a host of hammers by quietly bearing their blows. Did not the silent Lamb of God furnish us with *a grand example of wisdom*? Where every word was occasion for new blasphemy, it was the line of duty to afford no fuel for the flame of sin. The ambiguous and the false, the unworthy and mean, will ere long overthrow and confute themselves, and therefore the true can afford to be quiet, and finds silence to be its wisdom. Evidently our Lord, by His silence, furnished *a remarkable fulfilment of prophecy*. A long defence of Himself would have been contrary to Isaiah's prediction. 'He is led as a lamb to the slaughter, and as sheep before her shearers is dumb, so He openeth not His mouth.' By His quiet He conclusively proved Himself to be the true Lamb of God. As such we salute Him this morning. Be with us, Jesus, and in the silence of our heart, let us hear the voice of Thy love.

*'He shall see His seed; He shall prolong His days, and
the pleasure of the Lord shall prosper in His hand'*
Isaiah 53:10

Plead for the speedy fulfilment of this promise, all ye
who love the Lord. It is easy work to pray when we are
grounded and bottomed, as to our desires, upon God's
own promise. How can He that gave the word refuse to
keep it? Immutable veracity cannot demean itself by a
lie, and eternal faithfulness cannot degrade itself by
neglect. God must bless His Son, His covenant binds
Him to it. That which the Spirit prompts us to ask for
Jesus, is that which God decrees to give Him. Whenever you are praying for the kingdom of Christ, let your
eyes behold the dawning of the blessed day which
draweth near, when the Crucified shall receive His
coronation in the place where men rejected Him.
Courage, you that prayerfully work and toil for Christ
with success of the very smallest kind, it shall not be
so always; better times are before you. Your eyes
cannot see the blissful future: borrow the telescope of
faith; wipe the misty breath of your doubts from the
glass; look through it and behold the coming glory.
Reader, let us ask, *do you* make this your constant
prayer? Remember that the same Christ who tells us to
say, 'Give us this day our daily bread', had first given
us this petition, 'Hallowed be Thy name; Thy kingdom
come; Thy will be done in earth as it is in heaven'. Let
not your prayers be all concerning your own sins, your
own wants, your own imperfections, your own trials,
but let them climb the starry ladder, and get up to Christ
Himself, and then, as you draw nigh to the blood-
besprinkled mercy-seat, offer this prayer continually,
'Lord, extend the kingdom of Thy dear Son'. Such a
petition, fervently presented, will elevate the spirit of
all your devotions. Mind that you prove the sincerity of
your prayer by labouring to promote the Lord's glory.

'They took Jesus, and led Him away'
John 19:16

He had been all night in agony, He had spent the early morning at the hall of Caiaphas, He had been hurried from Caiaphas to Pilate, from Pilate to Herod, and from Herod back again to Pilate; He had, therefore, but little strength left, and yet neither refreshment nor rest were permitted Him. They were eager for His blood, and therefore led Him out to die, loaded with the cross. O dolorous procession! Well may Salem's daughters weep. My soul, do thou weep also.

What learn we here as we see our blessed Lord led forth? Do we not perceive that truth which was set forth in shadow by *the scapegoat*? Did not the high-priest bring the scapegoat, and put both his hands upon its head, confessing the sins of the people, that thus those sins might be laid upon the goat, and cease from the people? Then the goat was led away by a fit man into the wilderness, and it carried away the sins of the people, so that if they were sought for they could not be found. Now we see Jesus brought before the priests and rulers, who pronounce Him guilty; God Himself imputes our sins *to Him*, 'the Lord hath laid on Him the iniquity of us all'; 'He was made sin for us'; and, as the substitute for our guilt, bearing our sin upon His shoulders, represented by the cross; we see the great Scapegoat led away by the appointed officers of justice. Beloved, can you feel assured that He carried *your* sin? As you look at the cross upon His shoulders, does it represent *your* sin? There is one way by which you can tell whether he carried your sin or not. Have you laid your hand upon His head, confessed your sin, and trusted in Him? Then your sin lies not on you; it has all been transferred by blessed imputation to Christ, and He bears it on His shoulder as a load heavier than the cross.

Let not the picture vanish till you have rejoiced in your own deliverance, and adored the loving Redeemer upon whom your iniquities were laid.

*'All we like sheep have gone astray; we have turned
every one to his own way; and the Lord hath laid on
Him the iniquity of us all'*
Isaiah 53:6

Here is a confession of sin *common* to all the elect
people of God. They have all fallen, and therefore, in
common chorus, they all say, from the first who
entered heaven to the last who shall enter there, 'All we
like sheep have gone astray'. The confession, while
thus unanimous, is also *special* and particular: 'We
have turned every one to his own way'. There is a
peculiar sinfulness about every one of the individuals;
all are sinful, but each one with some special aggravation not found in his fellow. It is the mark of genuine
repentance that while it naturally associates itself with
other penitents, it also takes up a position of loneliness.
'We have turned every one to his own way', is a
confession that each man had sinned against light
peculiar to himself, or sinned with an aggravation
which he could not perceive in others. This confession
is *unreserved*; there is not a word to detract from its
force, nor a syllable by way of excuse. The confession
is *a giving up of all pleas of self-righteousness*. It is the
declaration of men who are consciously guilty - guilty
with aggravations, guilty without excuse: they stand
with their weapons of rebellion broken in pieces, and
cry, 'All we like sheep have gone astray; we have
turned every one to his own way'. Yet we hear no
dolorous wailings attending this confession of sin; for
the next sentence makes it almost a song. 'The Lord
hath laid on Him the iniquity of us all.' It is the most
grievous sentence of the three, but it overflows with
comfort. Strange is it that where misery was concentrated mercy reigned; where sorrow reached her climax
weary souls find rest. The Saviour bruised is the
healing of bruised hearts. See how the lowliest penitence gives place to assured confidence through simply
gazing at Christ on the cross!

'*For He hath made Him to be sin for us,
who knew no sin; that we might be made the
righteousness of God in Him*'
2 Corinthians 5:21

Mourning Christian! why weepest thou? Art thou
mourning over thine own corruption? Look to thy
perfect Lord, and remember, thou art complete in Him;
thou art in God's sight as perfect as if thou hadst never
sinned; nay, more than that, the Lord our Righteousness hath put a divine garment upon thee, so that thou
hast more than the righteousness of man - thou hast the
righteousness of God. O thou who art mourning by
reason of inbred sin and depravity, remember, none of
thy sins can condemn thee. Thou hast learned to hate
sin; but thou hast learned also to know that sin is not
thine - it was laid upon Christ's head. Thy standing is
not in thyself - it is in Christ; thine acceptance is not in
thyself, but in thy Lord; thou art as much accepted of
God today, with all thy sinfulness, as thou wilt be when
thou standest before His throne, free from all corruption. O, I beseech thee, lay hold on this precious
thought, *perfection in Christ*! For thou art 'complete in
Him'. With thy Saviour's garment on, thou art holy as
the Holy one, 'Who is he that condemneth? It is Christ
that died, yea rather, that is risen again, who is even at
the right hand of God, who also maketh intercession for
us.' Christian, let thy heart rejoice for thou art 'accepted in the beloved' - what hast thou to fear? Let thy
face ever wear a smile; live near thy Master; live in the
suburbs of the Celestial City; for soon, when thy time
has come, thou shalt rise up where thy Jesus sits, and
reign at His right hand, even as He has overcome and
has sat down at His Father's right hand; and all this
because the divine Lord 'was made to be sin for us, who
knew no sin; that we might be made the righteousness
of God in Him'.

'Come ye, and let us go up to the mountain of the Lord'
Isaiah 2:3

It is exceedingly beneficial to our souls to mount above this present evil world to something nobler and better. The cares of this world and the deceitfulness of riches are apt to choke everything good within us, and we grow fretful, desponding, perhaps proud and carnal. It is well for us to cut down these thorns and briars, for heavenly seed sown among them is not likely to yield a harvest; and where shall we find a better sickle with which to cut them down than communion with God and the things of the kingdom? In the valleys of Switzerland many of the inhabitants are deformed, and all wear a sickly appearance, for the atmosphere is charged with miasma, and is close and stagnant; but up yonder, on the mountain, you find a hardy race, who breathe the clear fresh air as it blows from the virgin snows of the Alpine summits. It would be well if the dwellers in the valley could frequently leave their abodes among the marshes and the fever mists, and inhale the bracing element upon the hills. It is to such an exploit of climbing that I invite you this evening. May the Spirit of God assist us to leave the mists of fear and the fevers of anxiety, and all the ills which gather in this valley of earth, and to ascend the mountains of anticipated joy and blessedness. May God the Holy Spirit cut the cords that keep us here below, and assist us to mount! We sit too often like chained eagles fastened to the rock, only that, unlike the eagle, we begin to love our chain, and would, perhaps, if it came really to the test, be loath to have it snapped. May God now grant us grace, if we cannot escape from the chain as to our flesh, yet to do so as to our spirits; and leaving the body, like a servant, at the foot of the hill, may our soul, like Abraham, attain the top of the mountain, there to indulge in communion with the Most High.

'*On him they laid the cross,
that He might bear it after Jesus*'
Luke 23:26

We see in Simon's carrying the cross a picture of the
work of the Church throughout all generations; she is
the cross-bearer after Jesus. Mark then, Christian,
Jesus does not suffer so as to exclude your suffering.
He bears a cross, not that you may escape it, but that
you may endure it. Christ exempts you from sin, but
not from sorrow. Remember that, and expect to suffer.

But let us comfort ourselves with this thought, that
in our case, as in Simon's, *it is not our cross, but
Christ's cross which we carry*. When you are molested for your piety; when your religion brings the trial
of cruel mockings upon you, then remember it is not
your cross, it is *Christ's* cross; and how delightful is
it to carry the cross of our Lord Jesus!

You carry the cross after Him. You have blessed
company; your path is marked with the footprints of
your Lord. The mark of His blood-red shoulder is upon
that heavy burden. 'Tis *His* cross, and he goes before
you as a shepherd goes before his sheep. Take up your
cross daily, and follow Him.

Do not forget, also, *that you bear this cross in
partnership*. It is the opinion of some that Simon only
carried one end of the cross, and not the whole of it.
That is very possible; Christ may have carried the
heavier part, against the transverse beam, and Simon
may have borne the lighter end. Certainly it is so with
you; you do but carry the light end of the cross, Christ
bore the heavier end.

And remember, *though Simon had to bear the
cross for a very little while, it gave him lasting honour*.
Even so the cross *we* carry is only for a little while at
most, and then we shall receive the crown, the glory.
Surely we should love the cross, and, instead of
shrinking from it, *count it very dear*, when it works out
for us 'a far more exceeding and eternal weight of
glory'.

'Before honour is humility'
Proverbs 15:33

Humiliation of soul always *brings a positive blessing with it*. If we empty our hearts of self God will fill them with His love. He who desires close communion with Christ should remember the word of the Lord, 'To this man will I look, even to him that is poor and of a contrite spirit, and trembleth at My word'. Stoop if you would climb to heaven. Do we not say of Jesus, 'He descended that He might ascend'? So must you. You must grow downwards, that you may grow upwards; for the sweetest fellowship with heaven is to be had by humble souls, and by them alone. God will deny no blessing to a thoroughly humbled spirit. 'Blessed are the poor in spirit: for theirs is the kingdom of heaven', with all its riches and treasures. The whole exchequer of God shall be made over by deed of gift to the soul which is humble enough to be able to receive it without growing proud because of it. God blesses us all up to the full measure and extremity of what it is safe for Him to do. If you do not get a blessing, it is because it is not safe for you to have one. If our heavenly Father were to let your unhumbled spirit win a victory in His holy war, you would pilfer the crown for yourself, and meeting with a fresh enemy you would fall a victim; so that you are kept low for your own safety. When a man is sincerely humble, and never ventures to touch so much as a grain of the praise, there is scarcely any limit to what God will do for him. Humility makes us ready to be blessed by the God of all grace, and fits us to deal efficiently with our fellow men. True humility is a flower which will adorn any garden. This is a sauce with which you may season every dish of life, and you will find an improvement in every case. Whether it be prayer or praise, whether it be work or suffering, the genuine salt of humility cannot be used in excess.

'*Let us go forth therefore unto Him without the camp*'
Hebrews 13:13

Jesus, bearing His cross, went forth to suffer without
the gate. The Christian's reason for leaving the camp
of the world's sin and religion is not because he loves
to be singular, but because *Jesus did so*; and the
disciple must follow his Master. Christ was 'not of the
world': His life and His testimony were a constant
protest against conformity with the world. Never was
such overflowing affection for men as you find in Him;
but still He was separate from sinners. In like manner
Christ's people must 'go forth unto Him'. They must
take their position 'without the camp', as witness-
bearers for the truth. They must be prepared to tread the
straight and narrow path. They must have bold, unflinching, lion-like hearts, loving Christ first, and His
truth next, and Christ and His truth beyond all the
world. Jesus would have His people 'go forth without
the camp' *for their own sanctification.* You cannot
grow in grace to any high degree while you are
conformed to the world. The life of separation may be
a path of sorrow, but it is the highway of safety; and
though the separated life may cost you many pangs, and
make every day a battle, yet it is a happy life after all.
No joy can excel that of the soldier of Christ: Jesus
reveals Himself so graciously, and gives such sweet
refreshment, that the warrior feels more calm and peace
in his daily strife than others in their hours of rest. The
highway of holiness is the highway of communion. It
is thus we shall hope *to win the crown* if we are enabled
by divine grace faithfully to follow Christ 'without the
camp'. The crown of glory will follow the cross of
separation. A moment's shame will be well recom-
pensed by eternal honour; a little while of witness-
bearing will seem nothing when we are 'for ever with
the Lord'.

'In the name of the Lord I will destroy them'
Psalm 118:12

Our Lord Jesus, by His death, did not purchase a right to a *part* of us only, but to the *entire* man. He contemplated in His passion the sanctification of us wholly, spirit, soul, and body; that in this triple kingdom He Himself might reign supreme without a rival. It is the business of the newborn nature which God has given to the regenerate to assert the rights of the Lord Jesus Christ. My soul, so far as thou art a child of God, thou must conquer all the rest of thyself which yet remains unblest; thou must subdue all thy powers and passions to the silver sceptre of Jesus' gracious reign, and thou must never be satisfied till He who is King by purchase becomes also King by gracious coronation, and reigns in thee supreme. Seeing, then, that sin has no right to any part of us, we go about a good and lawful warfare when we seek, in the name of God, to drive it out. O my body, thou art a member of Christ: shall I tolerate thy subjection to the prince of darkness? O my soul, Christ has suffered for thy sins, and redeemed thee with His most precious blood; shall I suffer thy memory to become a storehouse of evil, or thy passions to be firebrands of iniquity? Shall I surrender my judgment to be perverted by error, or my will to be led in fetters of iniquity? No, my soul, thou art Christ's, and sin hath no right to thee.

Be courageous concerning this, O Christian! be not dispirited, as though your spiritual enemies could never be destroyed. You are able to overcome them - not in your own strength - the weakest of them would be too much for you in that; but you can and shall overcome them through the blood of the Lamb. Do not ask, 'How shall I dispossess them, for they are greater and mightier than I?' but go to the strong for strength, wait humbly upon God, and the mighty God of Jacob will surely come to the rescue, and you shall sing of victory through His grace.

*'O ye sons of men,
how long will ye turn my glory into shame?'*
Psalm 4:2

An instructive writer has made a mournful list of the honours which the blinded people of Israel awarded to their long-expected King. (1) They gave Him *a procession of honour*, in which Roman legionaries, Jewish priests, men and women, took a part, He Himself bearing His cross. This is the triumph which the world awards to Him who comes to overthrow man's direst foes. Derisive shouts are His only acclamations, and cruel taunts His only paeans of praise. (2) They presented Him with *the wine of honour*. Instead of a golden cup of generous wine they offered Him the criminal's stupefying death-draught, which He refused because He would preserve an uninjured taste wherewith to taste of death; and afterwards when he cried, 'I thirst', they gave Him vinegar mixed with gall, thrust to His mouth upon a sponge. Oh! wretched detestable inhospitality to the King's Son. (3) He was provided with *a guard of honour*, who showed their esteem of Him by gambling over His garments, which they had seized as their booty. Such was the bodyguard of the adored of heaven; a quaternion of brutal gamblers. (4) *A throne of honour* was found for Him upon the bloody tree; no easier place of rest would rebel men yield to their liege Lord. The cross was, in fact, the full expression of the world's feeling towards Him; 'There,' they seemed to say, 'Thou Son of God, this is the manner in which God Himself should be treated, could we reach Him.' (5) *The title of honour* was nominally 'King of the Jews', but that the blinded nation distinctly repudiated, and really called Him 'King of thieves', by preferring Barabbas, and by placing Jesus in the place of highest shame between two thieves. His glory was thus in all things turned into shame by the sons of men, but it shall yet gladden the eyes of saints and angels, world without end.

> *'Deliver me from bloodguiltiness,*
> *O God, Thou God of my salvation; and*
> *my tongue shall sing aloud of Thy righteousness'*
> Psalm 51:14

In this SOLEMN CONFESSION, it is pleasing to observe that David plainly names his sin. He does not call it manslaughter, nor speak of it as an imprudence by which an unfortunate accident occurred to a worthy man, but he calls it by its true name, bloodguiltiness. He did not actually kill the husband of Bathsheba; but still it was planned in David's heart that Uriah should be slain, and he was before the Lord his murderer. Learn in confession to be honest with God. Do not give fair names to foul sins; call them what you will, they will smell no sweeter. What God sees them to be, that do you labour to feel them to be; and with all openness of heart acknowledge their real character. Observe, that David was evidently oppressed with the heinousness of his sin. It is easy to use words, but it is difficult to feel their meaning. The fifty-first Psalm is the photograph of a contrite spirit. Let us seek after the like brokenness of heart; for however excellent our words may be, if our heart is not conscious of the hell-deservingness of sin, we cannot expect to find forgiveness.

Our text has in it AN EARNEST PRAYER - it is addressed to the God of *salvation*. It is His prerogative to forgive; it is His very name and office to save those who seek His face. Better still, the text calls Him the God of *my* salvation. Yes, blessed be His name, while I am yet going to Him through Jesus' blood, I can rejoice in the God of *my* salvation.

The psalmist ends with A COMMENDABLE VOW; if God will deliver him he will *sing* - nay, more, he will 'sing *aloud*'. Who can sing in any other style of such a mercy as this! But note the subject of the song - 'THY RIGHTEOUSNESS'. We must sing of the finished work of a precious Saviour; and he who knows most of forgiving love will sing the loudest.

'If they do these things in a green tree,
what shall be done in the dry?'
Luke 23:31

Among other interpretations of this suggestive question, the following is full of teaching: 'If I, the innocent substitute for sinners, suffer thus, what will be done when the sinner himself - the dry tree - shall fall into the hands of an angry God?' When God saw Jesus in the sinner's place, He did not spare Him; and when He finds the unregenerate without Christ, He will not spare *them*. O sinner, Jesus was led away by His enemies: so shall you be dragged away by fiends to the place appointed for you. Jesus was deserted of God; and if He, who was only imputedly a sinner, was deserted, how much more shall you be? *'Eloi, Eloi, lama sabachthani?'* what an awful shriek! But what shall be your cry when you shall say, 'O God! O God! why hast Thou forsaken me?' and the answer shall come back, 'Because ye have set at nought all My counsel, and would none of My reproof: I also will laugh at your calamity; I will mock when your fear cometh.' If God spared not His own Son, how much less will He spare you! What whips of burning wire will be yours when conscience shall smite you with all its terrors. Ye richest, ye merriest, ye most self-righteous sinners - who would stand in your place when God shall say, 'Awake, O sword, against the man that rejected Me; smite him, and let him feel the smart for ever'? Jesus was spit upon: sinner, what shame will be yours! We cannot sum up in one word all the mass of sorrows which met upon the head of Jesus who died for us, therefore it is impossible for us to tell you what streams, what oceans of grief must roll over *your* spirit if you die as you now are. You may die so, you may die now. By the agonies of Christ, by His wounds and by His blood, do not bring upon yourselves the wrath to come! Trust in the Son of God, and you shall never die.

'I will fear no evil: for Thou art with me'
Psalm 23:4

Behold how independent of outward circumstances the
Holy Ghost can make the Christian! What a bright light
may shine within us when it is all dark without! How
firm, how happy, how calm, how peaceful we may be,
when the world shakes to and fro, and the pillars of the
earth are removed! Even death itself, with all its
terrible influences, has no power to suspend the music
of a Christian's heart, but rather makes that music
become more sweet, more clear, more heavenly, till the
last kind act which death can do is to let the earthly
strain melt into the heavenly chorus, the temporal joy
into the eternal bliss! Let us have confidence, then, in
the blessed Spirit's power to comfort us. Dear reader,
are you looking forward to poverty? Fear not; the
divine Spirit can give you, in your want, a greater
plenty than the rich have in their abundance. You know
not what joys may be stored up for you in the cottage
around which grace will plant the roses of content. Are
you conscious of a growing failure of your bodily
powers? Do you expect to suffer long nights of languishing and days of pain? O be not sad! That bed may
become a throne to you. You little know how every
pang that shoots through your body may be a refining
fire to consume your dross - a beam of glory to light up
the secret parts of your soul. Are the eyes growing dim?
Jesus will be your light. Do the ears fail you? Jesus'
name will be your soul's best music, and His person
your dear delight. Socrates used to say, 'Philosophers
can be happy without music'; and Christians can be
happier than philosophers when all outward causes of
rejoicing are withdrawn. In Thee, my God, my heart
shall triumph, come what may of ills without! By thy
power, O blessed Spirit, my heart shall be exceedingly
glad, though all things should fail me here below.

'*And there followed Him a great company of people,
and of women, which also bewailed and lamented Him*'
Luke 23:27

Amid the rabble rout which hounded the Redeemer to
His doom, there were some gracious souls whose bitter
anguish sought vent in wailing and lamentations - fit
music to accompany that march of woe. When my soul
can, in imagination, see the Saviour bearing His cross
to Calvary, she joins the godly women and weeps with
them; for, indeed, there is true cause for grief - cause
lying deeper than those mourning women thought.
They bewailed innocence maltreated, goodness persecuted, love bleeding, meekness about to die; but my
heart has a deeper and more bitter cause to mourn. My
sins were the scourges which lacerated those blessed
shoulders, and crowned with thorn those bleeding
brows: my sins cried 'Crucify Him! crucify Him!' and
laid the cross upon His gracious shoulders. His being
led forth to die is sorrow enough for one eternity: but
my having been His murderer, is more, infinitely more,
grief than one poor fountain of tears can express.

Why those women loved and wept it were not hard
to guess: but they could not have had greater reasons
for love and grief than my heart has. Nain's widow saw
her son restored - but I myself have been raised to
newness of life. Peter's wife's mother was cured of the
fever - but I of the greater plague of sin. Out of
Magdalene seven devils were cast - but a whole legion
out of me. Mary and Martha were favoured with visits
- but He dwells with me. His mother bare His body -
but He is formed in me the hope of glory. In nothing
behind the holy women in debt, let me not be behind
them in gratitude or sorrow.

> 'Love and grief my heart dividing,
>   With my tears His feet I'll lave -
> Constant still in heart abiding,
>   Weep for Him who died to save.'

'*Thy gentleness hath made me great*'
Psalm 18:35

The words are capable of being translated, 'Thy *goodness* hath made me great'. David gratefully ascribed all his greatness not to his own goodness, but to the goodness of God. 'Thy *providence*', is another reading; and providence is nothing more than goodness in action. Goodness is the bud of which providence is the flower, or goodness is the seed of which providence is the harvest. Some render it, 'Thy *help*', which is but another word for providence; providence being the firm ally of the saints, aiding them in the service of their Lord. Or again, 'Thy *humility* hath made me great'. 'Thy *condescension*' may, perhaps, serve as a comprehensive reading, combining the ideas mentioned, including that of *humility*. It is God's making Himself little which is the cause of our being made great. We are so little, that if God should manifest His greatness without condescension, we should be trampled under His feet; but God, who must stoop to view the skies, and bow to see what angels do, turns His eye yet lower, and looks to the lowly and contrite, and makes them great. There are yet other readings, as for instance, the Septuagint, which reads, 'Thy discipline' - Thy fatherly correction - 'hath made me great'; while the Chaldee paraphrase reads, 'Thy word hath increased me'. Still the idea is the same. David ascribes all his own greatness to the condescending goodness of his Father in heaven. May this sentiment be echoed in our hearts this evening while we cast our crowns at Jesus' feet, and cry, 'Thy gentleness hath made me great'. How marvellous has been our experience of God's gentleness! How gentle have been His corrections! How gentle His forbearance! How gentle His teachings! How gentle His drawings! Meditate upon this theme, O believer. Let gratitude be awakened; let humility be deepened; let love be quickened ere thou fallest asleep tonight.

'The place which is called Calvary'
Luke 23:33

The hill of comfort is the hill of Calvary; the house of consolation is built with the wood of the cross; the temple of heavenly blessing is founded upon the riven rock - riven by the spear which pierced His side. No scene in sacred history ever gladdens the soul like Calvary's tragedy.

> 'Is it not strange, the darkest hour
> That ever dawned on sinful earth,
> Should touch the heart with softer power,
> For comfort, than an angel's mirth?
> That to the Cross the mourner's eye should turn,
> Sooner than where the stars of Bethlehem burn?'

Light springs from the midday-midnight of Golgotha, and every herb of the field blooms sweetly beneath the shadow of the once accursed tree. In that place of thirst, grace hath dug a fountain which ever gusheth with waters pure as crystal, each drop capable of alleviating the woes of mankind. You who have had your seasons of conflict, will confess that it was not at Olivet that you ever found comfort, not on the hill of Sinai, nor on Tabor; but Gethsemane, Gabbatha, and Golgotha have been a means of comfort to you. The bitter herbs of Gethsemane have often taken away the bitters of your life; the scourge of Gabbatha has often scourged away your cares, and the groans of Calvary have put all other groans to flight. Thus Calvary yields us comfort rare and rich. We never should have known Christ's love in all its heights and depths if He had not died; nor could we guess the Father's deep affection if He had not given His Son to die. The common mercies we enjoy all sing of love, just as the sea-shell, when we put it to our ears, whispers of the deep sea whence it came; but if we desire to hear the ocean itself, we must not look at everyday blessings, but at the transactions of the crucifixion. He who would know love, let him retire to Calvary and see the Man of sorrows die.

'For there stood by me this night the angel of God'
Acts 27:23

Tempest and long darkness, coupled with imminent risk of shipwreck, had brought the crew of the vessel into a sad case; one man alone among them remained perfectly calm, and by his word the rest were reassured. Paul was the only man who had heart enough to say, 'Sirs, be of good cheer'. There were veteran Roman legionaries on board, and brave old mariners, and yet their poor Jewish prisoner had more spirit than they all. He had a secret Friend who kept his courage up. The Lord Jesus despatched a heavenly messenger to whisper words of consolation in the ear of His faithful servant, therefore he wore a shining countenance and spake like a man at ease.

If we fear the Lord, we may look for timely interpositions when our case is at its worst. Angels are not kept from us by storms, or hindered by darkness. Seraphs think it no humiliation to visit the poorest of the heavenly family. If angels' visits are few and far between at ordinary times, they shall be frequent in our nights of tempest and tossing. Friends may drop from us when we are under pressure, but our intercourse with the inhabitants of the angelic world shall be more abundant; and in the strength of love-words, brought to us from the throne by the way of Jacob's ladder, we shall be strong to do exploits. Dear reader, is this an hour of distress with you? Then ask for peculiar help. Jesus is the angel of the covenant, and if His presence be now earnestly sought, it will not be denied. What that presence brings in heart-cheer those remember who, like Paul, have had the angel of God standing by them in a night of storm, when anchors would no longer hold, and rocks were nigh.

'O angel of my God, be near
  Amid the darkness hush my fear:
Loud roars the wild tempestuous sea,
  Thy presence, Lord, shall comfort me.'

'I am poured out like water,
and all my bones are out of joint'
Psalm 22:14

Did earth or heaven ever behold a sadder spectacle of
woe! In soul and body, our Lord felt Himself to be
weak as water poured upon the ground. The placing of
the cross in its socket had shaken Him with great
violence, had strained all the ligaments, pained every
nerve, and more or less dislocated all His bones.
Burdened with His own weight, the august sufferer felt
the strain increasing every moment of those six long
hours. His sense of faintness and general weakness
were overpowering; while to His own consciousness
He became nothing but a mass of misery and swooning
sickness. When Daniel saw the great vision, he thus
describes his sensations, 'There remained no strength
in me, for my vigour was turned into corruption, and
I retained no strength': how much more faint must have
been our greater Prophet when He saw the dread vision
of the wrath of God, and felt it in His own soul! To us,
sensations such as our Lord endured would have been
insupportable, and kind unconsciousness would have
come to our rescue; but in His case, He was wounded,
and *felt* the sword; He drained the cup and *tasted* every
drop.

'O King of Grief! (a title strange, yet true
    To Thee of all kings only due)
O King of Wounds! how shall I grieve for Thee,
    Who in all grief preventest me!'

As we kneel before our now ascended Saviour's
throne, let us remember well the way by which He
prepared it as a throne of grace for us; let us in spirit
drink of His cup, that we may be strengthened for our
hour of heaviness whenever it may come. In His natural
body every member suffered, and so must it be in the
spiritual; but as out of all His griefs and woes His body
came forth uninjured to glory and power, even so shall
His mystical body come through the furnace with not
so much as the smell of fire upon it.

> '*Look upon mine affliction and my pain;*
> *and forgive all my sins*'
> Psalm 25:18

It is well for us when prayers about our sorrows are
linked with pleas concerning our sins - when, being
under God's hand. we are not wholly taken up with our
pain, but remember our offences against God. It is
well, also, to take both sorrow and sin to the same
place. It was to God that David carried his sorrow: it
was to God that David confessed his sin. Observe,
then, *we must take our sorrows to God*. Even your little
sorrows you may roll upon God, for He counteth the
hairs of your head; and your great sorrows you may
commit to Him, for He holdeth the ocean in the hollow
of His hand. Go to Him, whatever your present trouble
may be, and you shall find Him able and willing to
relieve you. *But we must take our sins to God too*. We
must carry them to the cross, that the blood may fall
upon them, to purge away their guilt, and to destroy
their defiling power.

    The special lesson of the text is this: that *we are to
go to the Lord with sorrows and with sins in the right
spirit*. Note that all David asks concerning his sorrow
is, '*Look upon* mine affliction and my pain'; but the
next petition is vastly more express, definite, decided,
plain - '*Forgive* all my sins'. Many sufferers would
have put it, 'Remove my affliction and my pain, and
look at my sins'. But David does not say so; he cries,
'Lord, as for my affliction and my pain, I will not
dictate to Thy wisdom. Lord, look at them, I will leave
them to Thee, I should be glad to have my pain
removed, but do as Thou wilt; but as for my sins, Lord,
I know what I want with them; I must have them
forgiven; I cannot endure to lie under their curse for a
moment.' A Christian counts sorrow lighter in the
scale than sin; he can bear that his troubles should
continue, but he cannot support the burden of his
transgressions.

'My heart is like wax;
it is melted in the midst of my bowels'
Psalm 22:14

Our blessed Lord experienced a terrible sinking and melting of soul. 'The spirit of a man will sustain his infirmity, but a wounded spirt who can bear?' Deep depression of spirit is the most grievous of all trials; all besides is as nothing. Well might the suffering Saviour cry to His God, 'Be not far from me', for above all other seasons a man needs his God when his heart is melted within him because of heaviness. Believer, come near the cross this morning, and humbly adore the King of glory as having once been brought far lower, in mental distress and inward anguish, than any one among us; and mark His fitness to become a faithful High Priest, who can be touched with a feeling of our infirmities. Especially let those of us whose sadness springs directly from the withdrawal of a present sense of our Father's love, enter into near and intimate communion with Jesus. Let us not give way to despair, since through this dark room the Master has passed before us. Our souls may sometimes long and faint, and thirst even to anguish, to behold the light of the Lord's countenance: at such times let us stay ourselves with the sweet fact of the sympathy of our great High Priest. Our drops of sorrow may well be forgotten in the ocean of His griefs; but how high ought our love to rise! Come in, O strong and deep love of Jesus, like the sea at the flood in spring tides, cover all my powers, drown all my sins, wash out all my cares, lift up my earth-bound soul, and float it right up to my Lord's feet, and there let me lie, a poor broken shell, washed up by His love, having no virtue or value; and only venturing to whisper to Him that if He will put His ear to me, He will hear within my heart faint echoes of the vast waves of His own love which have brought me where it is my delight to lie, even at His feet for ever.

'The king's garden'
Nehemiah 3:15

Mention of the king's garden by Nehemiah brings to mind the *paradise* which the King of kings prepared for Adam. Sin has utterly ruined that fair abode of all delights, and driven forth the children of men to till the ground, which yields thorns and briars unto them. My soul, remember the fall, for it was *thy* fall. Weep much because the Lord of love was so shamefully ill-treated by the head of the human race, of which thou art a member, as undeserving as any. Behold how dragons and demons dwell on this fair earth, which once was a garden of delights.

See yonder another King's garden, which the King waters with His bloody sweat - *Gethsemane*, whose bitter herbs are sweeter far to renewed souls than even Eden's luscious fruits. There the mischief of the serpent in the first garden was undone: there the curse was lifted from earth, and borne by the woman's promised seed. My soul, bethink thee much of the agony and the passion; resort to the garden of the olive-press, and view thy great Redeemer rescuing thee from thy lost estate. This is the garden of gardens indeed, wherein the soul may see the guilt of sin and the power of love, two sights which surpass all others.

Is there no other King's garden? Yes, *my heart*, thou art, or shouldst be such. How do the flowers flourish? Do any choice fruits appear? Does the King walk within, and rest in the bowers of my spirit? Let me see that the plants are trimmed and watered, and the mischievous foxes hunted out. Come, Lord, and let the heavenly wind blow at Thy coming, that the spices of Thy garden may flow abroad. Nor must I forget the King's garden of *the church*. O Lord, send prosperity unto it. Rebuild her walls, nourish her plants, ripen her fruits, and from the huge wilderness, reclaim the barren waste, and make thereof 'a King's garden'.

'A bundle of myrrh is my well-beloved unto me'
Canticles 1:13

Myrrh may well be chosen as the type of Jesus on account of its *preciousness*, its *perfume*, its *pleasantness*, its *healing, preserving, disinfecting qualities*, and its *connection with sacrifice*. But why is He compared to 'a *bundle* of myrrh'? First, for *plenty*. He is not a drop of it, He is a casket full. He is not a sprig or flower of it, but a whole bundle. There is enough in Christ for all my necessities; let me not be slow to avail myself of Him. Our well-beloved is compared to a 'bundle' again, for *variety*: for there is in Christ not only the one thing needful, but in 'Him dwelleth all the fulness of the Godhead bodily', everything needful is in Him. Take Jesus in His different characters, and you will see a marvellous variety - Prophet, Priest, King, Husband, Friend, Shepherd. Consider Him in His life, death, resurrection, ascension, second advent; view Him in His virtue, gentleness, courage, self-denial, love, faithfulness, truth, righteousness - everywhere He is a bundle of preciousness. He is a 'bundle of myrrh' for *preservation* - not loose myrrh to be dropped on the floor or trodden on, but myrrh tied up, myrrh to be stored in a casket. We must value Him as our best treasure; we must prize His words and His ordinances; and we must keep our thoughts of Him and knowledge of Him as under lock and key, lest the devil should steal anything from us. Moreover Jesus is a 'bundle of myrrh' *for speciality*. The emblem suggests the idea of distinguishing, discriminating grace. From before the foundation of the world, He was set apart for His people; and He gives forth His perfume only to those who understand how to enter into communion with Him, to have close dealings with Him. Oh! blessed people whom the Lord hath admitted into His secrets, and for whom He sets Himself apart. Oh! choice and happy who are thus made to say, 'A bundle of myrrh is my well-beloved unto me'.

*'And he shall put his hand upon the head of the
burnt-offering; and it shall be accepted for him to
make atonement for him'*
Leviticus 1:4

Our Lord's being made 'sin for us' is set forth here by
the very significant transfer of sin to the bullock, which
was made by the elders of the people. The laying of the
hand was not a mere touch of contact, for in some other
places of Scripture the original word has the meaning
of leaning heavily, as in the expression, 'Thy wrath
lieth hard upon me' (Psalm 88:7). Surely this is the
very essence and nature of faith, which doth not only
bring us into contact with the great Substitute, but
teaches us to lean upon Him with all the burden of our
guilt. Jehovah made to meet upon the head of the
Substitute all the offences of His covenant people, but
each one of the chosen is brought personally to ratify
this solemn covenant act, when by grace he is enabled
by faith to lay his hand upon the head of the 'Lamb slain
from before the foundation of the world'. Believer, do
you remember that rapturous day when you first
realised pardon through Jesus the sin-bearer? Can you
not make glad confession, and join with the writer in
saying, 'My soul recalls her day of deliverance with
delight. Laden with guilt and full of fears, I saw my
Saviour as my Substitute, and I laid my hand upon
Him; oh! how timidly at first, but courage grew and
confidence was confirmed until I leaned my soul
entirely upon Him; and now it is my unceasing joy to
know that my sins are no longer imputed to me, but laid
on Him, and like the debts of the wounded traveller,
Jesus, like the good Samaritan, has said of all my future
sinfulness, "Set that to My account".' Blessed discovery! Eternal solace of a grateful heart!

> My numerous sins transferr'd to Him,
>   Shall never more be found,
> Lost in His blood's atoning stream,
>   Where every crime is drown'd!'

> *'All they that see me laugh me to scorn: they shoot*
> *out the lip, they shake the head'*
> Psalm 22:7

Mockery was a great ingredient in our Lord's woe. Judas mocked Him in the garden; the chief priests and scribes laughed Him to scorn; Herod set Him at nought; the servants and the soldiers jeered at Him, and brutally insulted Him; Pilate and his guards ridiculed His royalty; and on the tree all sorts of horrid jests and hideous taunts were hurled at Him. Ridicule is always hard to bear, but when we are in intense pain it is so heartless, so cruel, that it cuts us to the quick. Imagine the Saviour crucified, racked with anguish far beyond all mortal guess, and then picture that motley multitude, all wagging their heads or thrusting out the lip in bitterest contempt of one poor suffering victim! Surely there must have been something more in the crucified One than they could see, or else such a great and mingled crowd would not unanimously have honoured Him with such contempt. Was it not evil confessing, in the very moment of its greatest apparent triumph, that after all it could do no more than mock at that victorious goodness which was then reigning on the cross? O Jesus, 'despised and rejected of men', how couldst Thou die for men who treated Thee so ill? Herein is love amazing, love divine, yea, love beyond degree. We, too, have despised Thee in the days of our unregeneracy, and even since our new birth we have set the world on high in our hearts, and yet Thou bleedest to heal our wounds, and diest to give us life. O that we could set Thee on a glorious high throne in all men's hearts! We would ring out thy praises over land and sea till men should as universally adore as once they did unanimously reject.

Thy creatures wrong Thee, O Thou sovereign Good!
Thou art not loved, because not understood:
This grieves me most, that vain pursuits beguile
Ungrateful men, regardless of Thy smile.

'Say ye to the righteous, that it shall be well with him'
Isaiah 3:10

It is well with the righteous ALWAYS. If it had said, 'Say ye to the righteous, that it is well with him in his prosperity', we must have been thankful for so great a boon, for prosperity is an hour of peril, and it is a gift from heaven to be secured from its snares: or if it had been written, 'It is well with him when under persecution', we must have been thankful for so sustaining an assurance, for persecution is hard to bear: but when no time is mentioned, all time is included. God's 'shalls' must be understood always in their largest sense. From the beginning of the year to the end of the year, from the first gathering of evening shadows until the day-start shines, in all conditions and under all circumstances, it shall be well with the righteous. It is so well with him that we could not imagine it to be better, for he is *well fed*, he feeds upon the flesh and blood of Jesus; he is *well clothed*, he wears the imputed righteousness of Christ; he is *well housed*, he dwells in God; he is *well married*, his soul is knit in bonds of marriage union to Christ; he is *well provided for*, for the Lord is his Shepherd; he is well endowed, for heaven is his inheritance. It is well with the righteous - *well upon divine authority*; the mouth of God speaks the comforting assurance. O beloved, if God declares that all is well, ten thousand devils may declare it to be ill, but we laugh them all to scorn. Blessed be God for a faith which enables us to believe God when the creatures contradict Him. It is, says the Word, at all times well with thee, thou righteous one; then, beloved, if thou canst not see it, let God's word stand thee in stead of sight; yea, believe it on divine authority more confidently than if thine eyes and thy feelings told it to thee. Whom God blesses is blest indeed, and what His lip declares is truth most sure and steadfast.

> '*My God, my God, why hast Thou forsaken me?*'
> Psalm 22:1

We here behold the Saviour in the depth of His sorrows. No other place so well shows the griefs of Christ as Calvary, and no other moment at Calvary is so full of agony as that in which His cry rends the air - 'My God, my God, why hast thou forsaken me?' At this moment physical weakness was united with acute mental torture from the shame and ignominy through which He had to pass; and to make His grief culminate with emphasis, He suffered spiritual agony surpassing all expression, resulting from the departure of His Father's presence. This was the black midnight of His horror; then it was that He descended the abyss of suffering. No man can enter into the full meaning of these words. Some of us think at times that *we* could cry, 'My God, my God, why hast thou forsaken me?' There are seasons when the brightness of our Father's smile is eclipsed by clouds and darkness; but let us remember that God never does really forsake us. It is only a seeming forsaking with us, but in Christ's case it was a *real* forsaking. We grieve at a little withdrawing of our Father's love; but the real turning away of God's face from His Son, who shall calculate how deep the agony which it caused Him?

In our case, our cry is often dictated by unbelief: in His case, it was the utterance of a dreadful fact, for God had really turned away from Him for a season. O thou poor, distressed soul, who once lived in the sunshine of God's face, but art now in darkness, remember that He has not really forsaken thee. God in the clouds is as much our God as when He shines forth in all the lustre of His grace; but since even the *thought* that He has forsaken us gives us agony, what must the woe of the Saviour have been when He exclaimed, 'My God, my God, why hast thou forsaken me?'

'Lift them up for ever'
Psalm 28:9

God's people need lifting up. They are very heavy by
nature. They have no wings, or, if they have, they are
like the dove of old which lay among the pots; and they
need divine grace to make them mount on wings
covered with silver, and with feathers of yellow gold.
By nature sparks fly upward, but the sinful souls of
men fall downward. O Lord, 'lift them up for ever!'
David himself said, 'Unto Thee, O God, do I lift up my
soul', and he here feels the necessity that other men's
souls should be lifted up as well as his own. When you
ask this blessing for yourself, forget not to seek it for
others also. There are three ways in which God's
people require to be lifted up. *They require to be
elevated in character.* Lift them up, O Lord; do not
suffer Thy people to be like the world's people! The
world lieth in the wicked one; lift them out of it! The
world's people are looking after silver and gold,
seeking their own pleasures, and the gratification of
their lusts; but, Lord, lift Thy people up above all this;
keep them from being 'muck-rakers' as John Bunyan
calls the man who was always scraping after gold! Set
thou their hearts upon their risen Lord and the heavenly
heritage! Moreover, *believers need to be prospered in
conflict.* In the battle, if they seem to fall, O Lord, be
pleased to give them the victory. If the foot of the foe
be upon their necks for a moment, help them to grasp
the sword of the Spirit, and eventually to win the battle.
Lord, lift up Thy children's spirits in the day of
conflict; let them not sit in the dust, mourning for ever.
Suffer not the adversary to vex them sore, and make
them fret; but if they have been, like Hannah, persecuted, let them sing of the mercy of a delivering God.

We may also ask our Lord to *lift them up at the
last!* Lift them up by taking them home; lift their bodies
from the tomb, and raise their souls to Thine eternal
kingdom in glory.

'The precious blood of Christ'
1 Peter 1:19

Standing at the foot of the cross, we see hands, and feet, and side, all distilling crimson streams of precious blood. It is 'precious' because of its *redeeming* and *atoning efficacy*. By it the sins of Christ's people are atoned for; they are redeemed from under the law; they are reconciled to God, made one with Him. Christ's blood is also 'precious' in its *cleansing power*; it 'cleanseth from all sin'. 'Though your sins be as scarlet, they shall be as white as snow.' Through Jesus' blood there is not a spot left upon any believer, no wrinkle nor any such thing remains. O precious blood, which makes us clean, removing the stains of abundant iniquity, and permitting us to stand accepted in the Beloved, notwithstanding the many ways in which we have rebelled against our God. The blood of Christ is likewise 'precious' in its *preserving power*. We are safe from the destroying angel under the sprinkled blood. Remember it is *God's seeing* the blood which is the true reason for our being spared. Here is comfort for us when the eye of faith is dim, for God's eye is still the same. The blood of Christ is 'precious' also in its *sanctifying influence*. The same blood which justifies by taking away sin, does in its afteraction, quicken the new nature and lead it onward to subdue sin and to follow out the commands of God. There is no motive for holiness so great as that which streams from the veins of Jesus. And 'precious', unspeakably precious, is this blood, because it has *an overcoming power*. It is written, 'They overcame through the blood of the Lamb'. How could they do otherwise? The blood of Jesus! Sin dies at its presence, death ceases to be death: heaven's gates are opened. The blood of Jesus! We shall march on, conquering and to conquer, so long as we can trust its power!

*'And his hands were steady until
the going down of the sun'*
Exodus 17:12

So mighty was the prayer of Moses, that all depended
upon it. The petitions of Moses discomfited the enemy
more than the fighting of Joshua. Yet both were
needed. So, in the soul's conflict, force and fervour,
decision and devotion, valour and vehemence, must
join their forces, and all will be well. You must wrestle
with your sin, but the major part of the wrestling must
be done alone in private with God. Prayer, like Moses',
holds up the token of the covenant before the Lord. The
rod was the emblem of God's working with Moses, the
symbol of God's government in Israel. Learn, O
pleading saint, to hold up the promise and the oath of
God before Him. The Lord cannot deny His own
declarations. Hold up the rod of promise, and have
what you will.

Moses grew weary, and then his friends assisted
him. When at any time your prayer flags, let faith
support one hand, and let holy hope uplift the other, and
prayer seating itself upon the stone of Israel, the rock
of our salvation, will persevere and prevail. Beware of
faintness in devotion; if Moses felt it, who can escape?
It is far easier to fight with sin in public, than to pray
against it in private. It is remarked that Joshua never
grew weary in the fighting, but Moses did grow weary
in the praying; the more spiritual the exercise, the more
difficult it is for flesh and blood to maintain it. Let us
cry, then, for special strength, and may the Spirit of
God, who helpeth our infirmities, as He allowed help
to Moses, enable us like him to continue with our hands
steady 'until the going down of the sun'. Intermittent
supplication avails but little, we must wrestle all night,
and hold up our hands, *'until the going down of the
sun'*; till the evening of life is over; till we shall come
to the rising of a better sun in the land where prayer is
swallowed up in praise.

*'We are come to the blood of sprinkling, that
speaketh better things than that of Abel'*
Hebrews 12:24

Reader, have *you* come to the blood of sprinkling? The
question is not whether you have come to a knowledge
of doctrine, or an observance of ceremonies, or to a
certain form of experience, but *have you come to the
blood of Jesus*? The blood of Jesus is the life of all vital
godliness. If you have truly come to Jesus, we know
how you came - the Holy Spirit sweetly brought you
there. You came to the blood of sprinkling with no
merits of your own. Guilty, lost, and helpless, you
came to take that blood, and that blood alone, as your
everlasting hope. You came to the cross of Christ, with
a trembling and an aching heart; and oh! what a
precious sound it was to you to hear the voice of the
blood of Jesus! The dropping of His blood is as the
music of heaven to the penitent sons of earth. We are
full of sin, but the Saviour bids us lift our eyes to Him,
and as we gaze upon His streaming wounds, each drop
of blood, as it falls, cries, 'It is finished; I have made
an end of sin; I have brought in everlasting righteousness'. Oh! sweet language of the precious blood of
Jesus! If you have come to that blood once, you will
come to it constantly. Your life will be 'Looking unto
Jesus'. Your whole conduct will be epitomised in this
- 'To whom coming'. Not to whom I *have* come, but to
whom I am *always coming*. If thou hast ever come to
the blood of sprinkling, thou wilt feel thy need of
coming to it every day. He who does not desire to wash
in that *every day*, has never washed in it at all. The
believer ever feels it to be his joy and privilege that
there is still a fountain opened. Past experiences are
doubtful food for Christians; a present coming to
Christ alone can give us joy and comfort. This morning
let us sprinkle our doorpost fresh with blood, and then
feast upon the Lamb, assured that the destroying angel
must pass us by.

'We would see Jesus'
John 12:21

Evermore the worldling's cry is, 'Who will show us any good?' He seeks satisfaction in earthly comforts, enjoyments and riches. But the quickened sinner knows of only one good. 'O that I knew where I might find HIM'! When he is truly awakened to feel his guilt, if you could pour the gold of India at his feet, he would say, 'Take it away: I want to find HIM'. It is a blessed thing for a man, when he has brought his desires into a focus, so that they all centre in one object. When he has fifty different desires, his heart resembles a mere of stagnant water, spread out into a marsh, breeding miasma and pestilence; but when all his desires are brought into one channel, his heart becomes like a river of pure water, running swiftly to fertilise the fields. Happy is he who hath one desire, if that one desire be set on Christ, though it may not yet have been realised. If Jesus be a soul's desire, it is a blessed sign of divine work within. Such a man will never be content with mere ordinances. He will say, 'I want Christ; I *must* have Him - mere ordinances are of no use to me; I want *Himself*; do not offer me these; you offer me the empty pitcher, while I am dying of thirst; give me water, or I die. Jesus is my soul's desire. I would see Jesus!'

Is this thy condition, my reader, at this moment? Hast thou but one desire, and is that after Christ? Then thou art not far from the kingdom of heaven. Hast thou but one wish in thy heart, and that one wish that thou mayst be washed from all thy sins in Jesus' blood? Canst thou really say, 'I would give all that I have to be a Christian; I would give up everything I have and hope for, if I might but feel that I have an interest in Christ'? Then, despite all thy fears, be of good cheer, the Lord loveth thee, and thou shalt come out into daylight soon, and rejoice in the liberty wherewith Christ makes men free.

'She bound the scarlet line in the window'
Joshua 2:21

Rahab depended for her preservation upon the promise of the spies, whom she looked upon as the representatives of the God of Israel. Her faith was simple and firm, but it was very obedient. To tie the scarlet line in the window was a very trivial act in itself, but she dared not run the risk of omitting it. Come, my soul, is there not here a lesson for thee? Hast thou been attentive to all thy Lord's will, even though some of His commands should seem non-essential? Hast thou observed in his own way the two ordinances of believers' baptism and the Lord's Supper? These neglected, argue much unloving disobedience in thy heart. Be henceforth in all things blameless, even to the tying of a thread, if that be matter of command.

This act of Rahab sets forth a yet more solemn lesson. Have I implicitly trusted in the precious blood of Jesus? Have I tied the scarlet cord, as with a Gordian knot in my window, so that my trust can never be removed? Or can I look out towards the Dead Sea of my sins, or the Jerusalem of my hopes, without seeing the blood, and seeing all things in connection with its blessed power? The passer-by can see a cord of so conspicuous a colour, if it hangs from the window: it will be well for me if my life makes the efficacy of the atonement conspicuous to all onlookers. What is there to be ashamed of? Let me or devils gaze if they will, the blood is my boast and my song. My soul, there is One who will see that scarlet line, even when from weakness of faith thou canst not see it thyself; Jehovah, the Avenger, will see it and pass over thee. Jericho's walls fell flat: Rahab's house was on the wall, and yet it stood unmoved; my nature is built into the wall of humanity, and yet when destruction smites the race, I shall be secure. My soul, tie the scarlet thread in the window afresh, and rest in peace.

'And Thou saidst, I will surely do thee good'
Genesis 32:12

When Jacob was on the other side of the brook Jabbok, and Esau was coming with armed men, he earnestly sought God's protection, and as a master reason he pleaded, 'And Thou saidst, I will surely do thee good'. Oh, the force of that plea! He was holding God to His word - 'Thou saidst'. The attribute of God's faithfulness is a splendid horn of the altar to lay hold upon; but the promise, which has in it the attribute and something more, is a yet mightier holdfast - 'Thou saidst, I will surely do thee good'. And has *He* said, and shall He not do it? 'Let God be true, and every man a liar.' Shall not *He* be true? Shall *He* not keep His word? Shall not every word that cometh out of His lips stand fast and be fulfilled? Solomon, at the opening of the temple, used this same mighty plea. He pleaded with God to remember the word which He had spoken to his father David, and to bless that place. When a man gives a promissory note, his honour is engaged; he signs his hand, and he must discharge it when the due time comes, or else he loses credit. It shall never be said that God dishonours His bills. The credit of the Most High never was impeached, and never shall be. He is punctual to the moment: He never is before His time, but He never is behind it. Search God's word through, and compare it with the experience of God's people, and you shall find the two tally from the first to the last. Many a hoary patriarch has said with Joshua, 'Not one thing hath failed of all the good things which the Lord your God spake concerning you; all are come to pass'. If you have a divine promise, you need not plead it with an 'if', you may urge it with certainty. The Lord meant to fulfil the promise, or He would not have given it. God does not give His words merely to quiet us, and to keep us hopeful for a while with the intention of putting us off at last; but when He speaks, it is because He means to do as He has said.

'Behold, the veil of the temple was rent in twain
from the top to the bottom'
Matthew 27:51

No mean miracle was wrought in the rending of so strong and thick a veil; but it was not intended merely as a display of power - many lessons were herein taught us. *The old law of ordinances was put away*, and like a worn-out vesture, rent and laid aside. When Jesus died, the sacrifices were all finished, because all fulfilled in him, and therefore the place of their presentation was marked with an evident token of decay. That rent also *revealed all the hidden things of the old dispensation*: the mercy-seat could now be seen, and the glory of God gleamed forth above it. By the death of our Lord Jesus we have a clear revelation of God, for He was 'not as Moses, who put a veil over his face'. Life and immortality are now brought to light and things which have been hidden since the foundation of the world are manifest in Him. *The annual ceremony of atonement was thus abolished. The atoning blood* which was once every year sprinkled within the veil, *was now offered once* for all by the great High Priest, and therefore the place of the symbolical rite was broken up. No blood of bullocks or of lambs is needed now, for Jesus has entered within the veil with his own blood. Hence *access to God is now permitted*, and is the privilege of every believer in Christ Jesus. There is no small space laid open through which we may peer at the mercy-seat, but the rent reaches from the top to the bottom. We may come with boldness to the throne of the heavenly grace. Shall we err if we say that the opening of the Holy of Holies in this marvellous manner by our Lord's expiring cry was *the type of the opening of the gates of paradise* to all the saints by virtue of the Passion? Our bleeding Lord hath the key of heaven; He openeth and no man shutteth; let us enter in with him into the heavenly places, and sit with Him there till our common enemies shall be made His footstool.

'*The Amen*'
Revelation 3:14

The word AMEN solemnly confirms that which went before; and Jesus is the great Confirmer; immutable, for ever is 'the Amen' in all *His promises*. *Sinner*, I would comfort thee with this reflection. Jesus Christ said, 'Come unto me all ye that labour and are heavy laden, and I will give you rest.' If you come to Him, He will say, 'Amen' in your soul; His promise shall be true *to you*. He said in the days of His flesh, 'The bruised reed I will not break'. O thou poor, broken, bruised heart, if thou comest to Him, He will say, 'Amen' to thee, and that shall be true in *thy* soul as in hundreds of cases in bygone years. *Christian*, is not this very comforting to thee also, that there is not a word which has gone out of the Saviour's lips which he has ever retracted? The words of Jesus shall stand when heaven and earth shall pass away. If thou gettest a hold of but half a promise, thou shalt find it true. Beware of him who is called 'Clip-promise', who will destroy much of the comfort of God's word.

Jesus is Yea and Amen in all *His offices*. He was a Priest to pardon and cleanse once, He is Amen as Priest still. He was a King to rule and reign for His people, and to defend them with His mighty arm, He is an Amen King, the same still. He was a Prophet of old, to foretell good things to come, His lips are most sweet, and drop with honey still - He is an Amen Prophet. He is Amen as to the merit of His blood; He is Amen as to His righteousness. That sacred robe shall remain most fair and glorious when nature shall decay. He is Amen in every single title which He bears; your Husband, never seeking a divorce; your Friend, sticking closer than a brother; your Shepherd, with you in death's dark vale; your Help and your Deliverer; your Castle and your High Tower; the Horn of your strength, your confidence, your joy, your all in all, and your Yea and Amen in all.

*'That through death He might destroy
him that had the power of death'*
Hebrews 2:14

O child of God, death hath lost its sting, because the
devil's power over it is destroyed. Then cease to fear
dying. Ask grace from God the Holy Ghost, that by an
intimate knowledge and a firm belief of thy Redeemer's death, thou mayst be strengthened for that dread
hour. Living near the cross of Calvary thou mayst think
of death with pleasure, and welcome it when it comes
with intense delight. It is sweet to die in the Lord; it is
a covenant-blessing to sleep in Jesus. Death is no
longer banishment, it is a return from exile, a going
home to the many mansions where the loved ones
already dwell. The distance between glorified spirits in
heaven and militant saints on earth seems great; but it
is not so. We are not far from home - a moment will
bring us there. The sail is spread: the soul is launched
upon the deep. How long will be its voyage? How many
wearying winds must beat upon the sail ere it shall be
reefed in the port of peace? How long shall that soul be
tossed upon the waves before it comes to that sea which
knows no storm? Listen to the answer, 'Absent from
the body, present with the Lord'. Yon ship has just
departed, but it is already at its haven. It did but spread
its sail and it was there. Like that ship of old, upon the
Lake of Galilee, a storm had tossed it, but Jesus said,
'Peace, be still', and *immediately* it came to land. Think
not that a long period intervenes between the instant of
death and the eternity of glory. When the eyes close on
earth they open in heaven. The horses of fire are not an
instant on the road. Then, O child of God, what is there
for thee to fear in death, seeing that through the death
of thy Lord its curse and sting are destroyed? And now
it is but a Jacob's ladder whose foot is in the dark grave,
but its top reaches to glory everlasting.

'Fight the Lord's battles'
1 Samuel 18:17

The sacramental host of God's elect is warring still on earth, Jesus Christ being the Captain of their salvation. He has said, 'Lo! I am with you alway, even unto the end of the world.' Hark to the shouts of war! Now let the people of God stand fast in their ranks, and let no man's heart fail him. It is true that just now in England the battle is turned against us, and unless the Lord Jesus shall lift His sword, we know not what may become of the church of God in this land; but let us be of good courage, and play the man. There never was a day when Protestantism seemed to tremble more in the scales than now that a fierce effort is in the making to restore the Romish antichrist to his ancient seat. We greatly want a bold voice and a strong hand to preach and publish the old gospel for which martyrs bled and confessors died. The Saviour is, by His Spirit, still on earth; let this cheer us. He is ever in the midst of the fight, and therefore the battle is not doubtful. And as the conflict rages, what a sweet satisfaction it is to know that the Lord Jesus, in His office as our great Intercessor, is prevalently pleading for His people! O anxious gazer, look not so much at the battle below, for there thou shalt be enshrouded in smoke, and amazed with garments rolled in blood; but lift thine eyes yonder where the Saviour lives and pleads, for while He intercedes, the cause of God is safe. Let us fight as if it all depended upon us, but let us look up and know that all depends upon Him.

Now, by the lilies of Christian purity, and by the roses of the Saviour's atonement, by the roes and by the hinds of the field, we charge you who are lovers of Jesus, to do valiantly in the Holy War, for truth and righteousness, for the kingdom and crown jewels of your Master. Onward! 'for the battle is not yours but God's'.

'I know that my Redeemer liveth'
Job 19:25

The marrow of Job's comfort lies in that little word 'My' - 'My Redeemer', and in the fact that the Redeemer lives. Oh! to get hold of a living Christ. We must get a property in Him before we can enjoy Him. What is gold in the mine to me? Men are beggars in Peru, and beg their bread in California. It is gold in my purse which will satisfy my necessities, by purchasing the bread I need. So a Redeemer who does not redeem *me*, an avenger who will never stand up for *my* blood, of what avail were such? Rest not content until by faith you can say, 'Yes, I cast myself upon my living Lord; and He is mine'. It may be you hold Him with a feeble hand; you half think it presumption to say, 'He lives as *my* Redeemer'; yet, remember if you have but faith as a grain of mustard seed, that little faith *entitles* you to say it. But there is also another word here, expressive of Job's strong confidence, *'I know'*. To say, 'I hope so, I trust so', is comfortable; and there are thousands in the fold of Jesus who hardly ever get much further. But to reach the essence of consolation you *must* say, 'I know'. Ifs, buts, and perhapses, are sure murderers of peace and comfort. Doubts are dreary things in times of sorrow. Like wasps they sting the soul! If I have any suspicion that Christ is not mine, then there is vinegar mingled with the gall of death; but if I know that Jesus lives for me, then darkness is not dark: even the night is light about me. Surely if Job, in those ages before the coming and advent of Christ, could say, 'I know', *we* should not speak less positively. God forbid that our positiveness should be presumption. Let us see that our evidences are right, lest we build upon an ungrounded hope; and then let us not be satisfied with the mere foundation, for it is from the upper rooms that we get the widest prospect. A living Redeemer, truly mine, is joy unspeakable.

'Who is even at the right hand of God'
Romans 8:34

He who was once despised and rejected of men, now occupies the honourable position of a beloved and honoured Son. The right hand of God is the *place of majesty and favour*. Our Lord Jesus is His people's representative. When He died for them, they had rest; when he rose again for them, they had liberty; when he sat down at His Father's right hand, they had favour, and honour, and dignity. The raising and elevation of Christ is the elevation, the acceptance, the enshrinement, the glorifying of all His people, for He is their head and representative. This sitting at the right hand of God, then, is to be viewed as the acceptance of the person of the Surety, the reception of the Representative, and therefore, the acceptance of *our* souls. O saint, see in this thy sure freedom from condemnation. 'Who is he that condemneth?' Who shall condemn the men who are in Jesus at the right hand of God?

The right hand is *the place of power*. Christ at the right hand of God hath all power in heaven and in earth. Who shall fight against the people who have such power vested in their Captain? O my soul, what can destroy thee if Omnipotence be thy helper? If the aegis of the Almighty cover thee, what sword can smite thee? Rest thou secure. If Jesus is thine all-prevailing King, and hath trodden thine enemies beneath His feet; if sin, death, and hell are all vanquished by Him, and thou art represented in Him, by no possibility canst thou be destroyed.

> Jesu's tremendous name
>   Puts all our foes to flight:
> Jesus, the meek, the angry Lamb,
>   A Lion is in fight.
>
> By all hell's host withstood;
>   We all hell's host o'erthrow;
> And conquering them, through Jesu's blood
>   We still to conquer go.

'Him hath God exalted'
Acts 5:31

Jesus, our Lord, once crucified, dead and buried, now sits upon the throne of glory. The highest place that heaven affords is His by undisputed right. It is sweet to remember that the exaltation of Christ in heaven is a *representative exaltation*. He is exalted at the Father's right hand, and though as Jehovah he has eminent glories, in which finite creatures cannot share, yet as the Mediator, the honours which Jesus wears in heaven are the heritage of all the saints. It is delightful to reflect how close is Christ's union with His people. We are actually one with Him; we are members of His body; and His exaltation is *our* exaltation. He will give us to sit upon His throne, even as He has overcome, and is set down with His Father on His throne; He has a crown, and He gives us crowns too; He has a throne, but He is not content with having a throne to himself, on His right hand there must be His queen, arrayed in 'gold of Ophir'. He cannot be glorified without His bride. Look up, believer, to Jesus now; let the eye of your faith behold Him with many crowns upon His head; and remember that you will one day be like Him, when you shall see Him as He is; you shall not be so great as He is, you shall not be so divine, but still you shall, in a measure, share the same honours, and enjoy the same happiness and the same dignity which He possesses. Be content to live unknown for a little while, and to walk your weary way through the fields of poverty, or up the hills of affliction; for by-and-by you shall reign with Christ, for He has 'made us kings and priests unto God, and we shall reign for ever and ever'. Oh! wonderful thought for the children of God! We have Christ for our glorious representative in heaven's courts *now*, and soon He will come and receive us to Himself, to be with Him there, to behold His glory, and to share His joy.

'Thou shalt not be afraid for the terror by night'
Psalm 91:5

What is this terror? It may be the cry of fire, or the noise of thieves, or fancied appearances, or the shriek of sudden sickness or death. We live in the world of death and sorrow, we may therefore look for ills as well in the night-watches as beneath the glare of the broiling sun. Nor should this alarm us, for be the terror what it may, the promise is that the believer shall not be afraid. Why should he? Let us put it more closely, why should *we*? God our Father is here, and will be here all through the lonely hours; He is an almighty Watcher, a sleepless Guardian, a faithful Friend. Nothing can happen without His direction, for even hell itself is under His control. Darkness is not dark to Him. He has promised to be a wall of fire around His people - and who can break through such a barrier? Worldlings may well be afraid, for they have an angry God above them, a guilty conscience within them, and a yawning hell beneath them; but we who rest in Jesus are saved from all these through rich mercy. If we give way to foolish fear we shall dishonour our profession, and lead others to doubt the reality of godliness. We ought to be afraid of being afraid, lest we should vex the Holy Spirit by foolish distrust. Down, then, ye dismal forebodings and groundless apprehensions, God has not forgotten to be gracious, nor shut up His tender mercies; it may be night in the soul, but there need be no terror, for the God of love changes not. Children of light may walk in darkness, but they are not therefore cast away, nay, they are now enabled to prove their adoption by trusting in their heavenly Father as hypocrites cannot do.

Though the night be dark and dreary,
    Darkness cannot hide from Thee;
Thou art He, who, never weary,
    Watchest where Thy people be.

*'Nay, in all these things we are more than conquer-
ors through Him that loved us'*
Romans 8:37

We go to Christ for forgiveness, and then too often
look to the law for power to fight our sins. Paul thus
rebukes us, 'O foolish Galatians, who hath bewitched
you, that ye should not obey the truth? This only would
I learn of you, Received ye the Spirit by the works of
the law, or by the hearing of faith? are ye so foolish?
having begun in the Spirit, are ye now made perfect by
the flesh?' Take your sins to Christ's cross, for the old
man can only be crucified there: we are crucified *with
Him*. The only weapon to fight sin with is the spear
which pierced the side of Jesus. To give an illustration
- you want to overcome an angry temper, how do you
go to work? It is very possible you have never tried the
right way of going to Jesus with it. How did I get
salvation? I came to Jesus just as I was, and I trusted
Him to save me. I must kill my angry temper in the
same way? It is the only way in which I can ever kill it.
I must go to the cross with it, and say to Jesus, 'Lord,
I trust Thee to deliver me from it'. This is the only way
to give it a death-blow. Are you covetous? Do you feel
the world entangle you? You may struggle against this
evil so long as you please, but if it be your besetting sin,
you will never be delivered from it in any way but by
the blood of Jesus. Take it to Christ. Tell Him, 'Lord,
I have trusted Thee, and Thy name is Jesus, for Thou
dost save Thy people from their sins; Lord, this is one
of my sins, save me from it'! Ordinances are nothing
without Christ as a means of mortification. Your
prayers, and your repentances, and your tears - the
whole of them put together - are worth nothing apart
from Him. 'None but Jesus can do helpless sinners
good'; or helpless saints either. You must be conquerors through Him who hath loved you, if conquerors at
all. Our laurels must grow among His olives in Gethsemane.

> *'Lo, in the midst of the throne...*
> *stood a Lamb as it had been slain'*
> Revelation 5:6

Why should our exalted Lord appear in His wounds in glory? The wounds of Jesus are His glories, His jewels, His sacred ornaments. To the eye of the believer, Jesus is passing fair because He is 'white and ruddy'; white with innocence, and ruddy with his own blood. We see Him as the lily of matchless purity, and as the rose crimsoned with His own gore. Christ is lovely upon Olivet and Tabor, and by the sea, but oh! there never was such a matchless Christ as He that did hang upon the cross. There we behold all His beauties in perfection, all His attributes developed, all His love drawn out, all His character expressed. Beloved, the wounds of Jesus are far more fair in our eyes than all the splendour and pomp of kings. The thorny crown is more than an imperial diadem. It is true that He bears not now the sceptre of reed, but there was a glory in it that never flashed from sceptre of gold. Jesus wears the appearance of a slain Lamb as His court dress in which He wooed our souls, and redeemed them by His complete atonement. Nor are these only the ornaments of Christ: they are the *trophies* of His love and of His victory. He has divided the spoil with the strong. He had redeemed for Himself a great multitude whom no man can number, and these scars are the memorials of the fight. Ah! if *Christ* thus loves to retain the thought of His sufferings for His people, *how precious should his wounds be to us*!

> Behold how every wound of His
> 　A precious balm distils,
> Which heals the scars that sin had made,
> 　And cures all mortal ills.
>
> Those wounds are mouths that preach His grace;
> 　The ensigns of His love;
> The seals of our expected bliss
> 　In paradise above.

'And because of all this we make a sure covenant'
Nehemiah 9:38

There are many occasions in our experience when we
may very rightly, and with benefit, renew our covenant
with God. After *recovery from sickness* when, like
Hezekiah, we have had a new term of years added to
our life, we may fitly do it. After any *deliverance from
trouble*, when our joys bud forth anew, let us again visit
the foot of the cross, and renew our consecration.
Especially, let us do this after any *sin which has
grieved the Holy Spirit*, or brought dishonour upon the
cause of God; let us then look to that blood which can
make us whiter than snow, and again offer ourselves
unto the Lord. We should not only let our troubles
confirm our dedication to God, but *our prosperity*
should do the same. If we ever meet with occasions
which deserve to be called 'crowning mercies', then,
surely, if He hath crowned *us*, we ought also to crown
our God; let us bring forth anew all the jewels of the
divine regalia which have been stored in the jewel-
closet of our heart, and let our God sit upon the throne
of our love, arrayed in royal apparel. If we would learn
to profit by our prosperity, we should not need so much
adversity. If we would gather from a kiss all the good
it might confer upon us, we should not so often smart
under the rod. Have we lately received some blessing
which we little expected? Has the Lord put our feet in
a large room? Can we sing of mercies multiplied? Then
this is the day to put our hand upon the horns of the
altar, and say, 'Bind me here, my God; bind me here
with cords, even for ever'. Inasmuch as we need the
fulfilment of new promises from God, let us offer
renewed prayers that our old vows may not be dishonoured. Let us this morning make with him a sure
covenant, because of the pains of Jesus which for the
last month we have been considering with gratitude.

'The flowers appear on the earth;
the time of the singing of birds is come,
and the voice of the turtle is heard in our land'
Canticles 2:12

Sweet is the season of spring: the long and dreary winter helps us to appreciate its genial warmth, and its promise of summer enhances its present delights. After periods of depression of spirit, it is delightful to behold again the light of the Sun of Righteousness; then our slumbering graces rise from their lethargy, like the crocus and the daffodil from their beds of earth; then is our heart made merry with delicious notes of gratitude, far more melodious than the warbling of birds - and the comforting assurance of peace, infinitely more delightful than the turtle's note, is heard within the soul. Now is the time for the soul to seek communion with her Beloved; now must she rise from her native sordidness, and come away from her old associations. If we do not hoist the sail when the breeze is favourable, we shall be blameworthy: times of refreshing ought not to pass over us unimproved. When Jesus Himself visits us in tenderness, and entreats us to arise, can we be so base as to refuse His request? He has Himself risen that He may draw us after Him: He now by His Holy Spirit has revived us, that we may, in newness of life, ascend into the heavenlies, and hold communion with Himself. Let our wintry state suffice us for coldness and indifference; when the Lord creates a spring within, let our sap flow with vigour, and our branch blossom with high resolve. O Lord, if it be not spring time in my chilly heart, I pray Thee make it so, for I am heartily weary of living at a distance from Thee. Oh! the long and dreary winter, when wilt Thou bring it to an end? Come, Holy Spirit, and renew my soul! Quicken Thou me! Restore me, and have mercy upon me! This very night I would earnestly implore the Lord to take pity upon His servant, and send me a happy revival of spiritual life!

'Rise up, my love, my fair one, and come away'
Canticles 2:10

Lo, I hear the voice of my Beloved! He speaks to *me*! Fair weather is smiling upon the face of the earth, and He would not have me spiritually asleep while nature is all around me awaking from her winter's rest. He bids me, 'Rise up', and well He may, for I have long enough been lying among the pots of worldliness. HE is risen, I am risen in Him, why then should I cleave unto the dust? From lower loves, desires, pursuits, and aspirations, I would rise towards Him. He calls me by the sweet title of 'My love', and counts me fair; this is a good argument for my rising. If He has thus exalted me, and thinks me thus comely, how can I linger in the tents of Kedar and find congenial associates among the sons of men? He bids me, 'Come away'. Further and further from everything selfish, grovelling, worldly, sinful, He calls me; yea, from the outwardly religious world which knows Him not, and has no sympathy with the mystery of the higher life, He calls me. 'Come away' has no harsh sound in it to my ear, for what is there to hold me in this wilderness of vanity and sin? O my Lord, would that I could come away, but I am taken among the thorns, and cannot escape from them as I would. I would, if it were possible, have neither eyes, nor ears, nor heart for sin. Thou callest me to Thyself by saying, 'Come away', and this is a melodious call indeed. To come to Thee is to come home from exile, to come to land out of the raging storm, to come to rest after long labour, to come to the goal of my desires and the summit of my wishes. But Lord, how can a stone rise, how can a lump of clay come away from the horrible pit? O raise me, draw me. Thy grace can do it. Send forth Thy Holy Spirit to kindle sacred flames of love in my heart and I will continue to rise until I leave life and time behind me, and indeed come away.

'If any man hear My voice, and open the door,
I will come in to him'
Revelation 3:20

What is your desire this evening? Is it set upon heavenly things? Do you long to enjoy the high doctrine of eternal love? Do you desire liberty in very close communion with God? Do you aspire to know the heights and depths and lengths, and breadths? Then you must draw near to Jesus; you must get a clear sight of Him in His preciousness and completeness: you must view Him in His work, in His offices, in His person. He who understands Christ, receives an anointing from the Holy One, by which He knows all things. Christ is the great master-key of all the chambers of God: there is no treasure-house of God which will not open and yield up all its wealth to the soul that lives near to Jesus. Are you saying, 'O that He would dwell in my bosom'? 'Would that He would make my heart His dwelling-place for ever'? Open the door, beloved, and He will come into your souls. He has long been knocking, and all with this object, that he may sup with you, and you with Him. *He sups with you* because you find the house or the heart, and *you with Him* because He brings the provision. He could not sup with you if it were not in your heart, you finding the house; nor could you sup with Him, for you have a bare cupboard, if He did not bring the provision with Him. Fling wide, then, the portals of your soul. He will come with that love which you long to feel; He will come with that joy into which you cannot work your poor depressed spirit; He will bring the peace which now you have not; He will come with His flagons of wine and sweet apples of love, and cheer you till you have no other sickness but that of 'love o'erpowering, love divine'. Only open the door to Him, drive out His enemies, give Him the keys of your heart, and He will dwell there for ever. Oh, wondrous love, that brings such a guest to dwell in such a heart!

'This do in remembrance of Me'
1 Corinthians 11:24

It seems then, that Christians may forget Christ! There could be no need for this loving exhortation, if there were not a fearful supposition that our memories might prove treacherous. Nor is this a bare supposition: it is, alas! too well confirmed in our experience, not as a possibility, but as a lamentable fact. It appears almost impossible that those who have been redeemed by the blood of the dying Lamb, and loved with an everlasting love by the eternal Son of God, should forget that gracious Saviour; but, if startling to the ear, it is, alas! too apparent to the eye to allow us to deny the crime. Forget Him who never forgot us! Forget Him who poured His blood forth for our sins! Forget Him who loved us even to the death! Can it be possible? Yes, it is not only possible, but conscience confesses that it is too sadly a fault with all of us, that we suffer Him to be as a wayfaring man tarrying but for a night. He whom we should make the abiding tenant of our memories is but a visitor therein. The cross where one would think that memory would linger, and unmindfulness would be an unknown intruder, is desecrated by the feet of forgetfulness. Does not your conscience say that this is true? Do you not find yourselves forgetful of Jesus? Some creature steals away your heart, and you are unmindful of Him upon whom your affection ought to be set. Some earthly business engrosses your attention when you should fix your eye steadily upon the cross. It is the incessant turmoil of the world, the constant attraction of earthly things which takes away the soul from Christ. While memory too well preserves a poisonous weed, it suffereth the rose of Sharon to wither. Let us charge ourselves to bind a heavenly forget-me-not about our heart for Jesus our Beloved, and, whatever else we let slip, let us hold fast to Him.

'Blessed is he that watcheth'
Revelation 16:15

'We die daily,' said the apostle. This was the life of the early Christians; they went everywhere with their lives in their hands. We are not in this day called to pass through the same fearful persecutions: if we were, the Lord would give us grace to bear the test; but the tests of Christian life, at the present moment, though outwardly not so terrible, are yet more likely to overcome us than even those of the fiery age. We have to bear the sneer of the world - that is little; its blandishments, its soft words, its oily speeches, its fawning, its hypocrisy, are far worse. Our danger is lest we grow rich and become proud, lest we give ourselves up to the fashions of this present evil world, and lose our faith. Or if wealth be not the trial, worldly care is quite as mischievous. If we cannot be torn in pieces by the roaring lion, if we may be hugged to death by the bear, the devil little cares which it is, so long as he destroys our love to Christ, and our confidence in Him. I fear me that the Christian church is far more likely to lose her integrity in these soft and silken days than in those rougher times. We must be awake now, for we traverse the enchanted ground, and are most likely to fall asleep to our own undoing, unless our faith in Jesus be a reality, and our love to Jesus a vehement flame. Many in these days of easy profession are likely to prove tares, and not wheat; hypocrites with fair masks on their faces, but not the true-born children of the living God. Christian, do not think that these are times in which you can dispense with watchfulness or with holy ardour; you need these things more than ever, and may God the eternal Spirit display His omnipotence in you, that you may be able to say, in all these softer things, as well as in the rougher, 'We are more than conquerors through Him that loved us'.

'God, even our own God'
Psalm 67:6

It is strange how little use we make of the spiritual blessings which God gives us, but it is stranger still how little use we make of God Himself. Though He is 'our own God', we apply ourselves but little to Him, and ask but little of Him. How seldom do we ask counsel at the hands of the Lord! How often do we go about our business, without seeking His guidance! In our troubles how constantly do we strive to bear our burdens ourselves, instead of casting them upon the Lord, that He may sustain us! This is not because we may not, for the Lord seems to say, 'I am thine, soul, come and make use of me as thou wilt; thou mayst freely come to my store, and the oftener the more welcome'. It is our own fault if we make not free with the riches of our God. Then, since thou hast such a friend, and He invites thee, draw from Him daily. Never want while thou hast a God to go to; never fear or faint whilst thou hast God to help thee; go to thy treasure and take whatever thou needest - there is all that thou canst want. Learn the divine skill of making God all things to thee. He can supply thee with all, or better still, He can be to thee instead of all. Let me urge thee, then, to make use of thy God. Make use of Him *in prayer*. Go to Him often, because He is *thy* God. O, wilt thou fail to use so great a privilege? Fly to Him, tell Him all thy wants. Use Him constantly *by faith* at all times. If some dark providence has beclouded thee, use thy God as a 'sun'; if some strong enemy has beset thee, find in Jehovah a 'shield', for He is a sun and shield to his people. If thou hast lost thy way in the mazes of life, use Him as a 'guide', for He will direct thee. Whatever thou art, and wherever thou art, remember God is just *what* thou wantest, and just *where* thou wantest, and that He can do *all* thou wantest.

'The Lord is King for ever and ever'
Psalm 10:16

Jesus Christ is no despotic claimant of *divine right*, but He is really and truly the Lord's anointed! 'It hath pleased the Father that in Him should all fulness dwell.' God hath given to Him all power and all authority. As the Son of man, He is now head over all things to His church, and He reigns over heaven, and earth, and hell, with the keys of life and death at His girdle. Certain princes have delighted to call themselves kings by *the popular will*, and certainly our Lord Jesus Christ is such in His church. If it could be put to the vote whether He should be King in the church, every believing heart would crown Him. O that we could crown Him more gloriously than we do! We would count no expense to be wasted that could glorify Christ. Suffering would be pleasure, and loss would be gain, if thereby we could surround His brow with brighter crowns, and make Him more glorious in the eyes of men and angels. Yes, He shall reign. Long live the King! All hail to Thee, King Jesus! Go forth, ye virgin souls who love your Lord, bow at His feet, strew His way with the lilies of your love, and the roses of your gratitude: 'Bring forth the royal diadem, and crown Him Lord of all'. Moreover, our Lord Jesus is King in Zion by *right of conquest*: He has taken and carried by storm the hearts of His people, and has slain their enemies who held them in cruel bondage. In the Red Sea of His own blood, our Redeemer has drowned the Pharaoh of our sins: shall He not be King in Jeshurun? He has delivered us from the iron yoke and heavy curse of the law: shall not the Liberator be crowned? We are His portion, whom He has taken out of the hand of the Amorite with His sword and with His bow: who shall snatch His conquest from His hand? All hail, King Jesus! we gladly own Thy gentle sway! Rule in our hearts for ever, Thou lovely Prince of Peace.

'Remember the word unto Thy servant,
upon which Thou hast caused me to hope'
Psalm 119:49

Whatever your especial need may be, you may readily
find some promise in the Bible suited to it. Are you
faint and feeble because your way is rough and you are
weary? Here is the promise - 'He giveth power to the
faint'. When you read such a promise, take it back to
the great Promiser, and ask Him to fulfil His own word.
Are you seeking after Christ, and thirsting for closer
communion with him? This promise shines like a star
upon you - 'Blessed are they that hunger and thirst after
righteousness, for they shall be filled'. Take that
promise to the throne continually; do not plead anything else, but go to God over and over again with this
- 'Lord, Thou hast said it; do as Thou hast said'. Are
you distressed because of sin, and burdened with the
heavy load of your iniquities? Listen to these words -
'I, even I, am He that blotteth out thy transgressions,
and will no more remember thy sins'. You have no
merit of your own to plead why He should pardon you,
but plead His written engagements and He will perform
them. Are you afraid lest you should not be able to hold
on to the end, lest, after having thought yourself a child
of God, you should prove a castaway? If that is your
state, take this word of grace to the throne and plead it:
'The mountains may depart, and the hills may be
removed, but the covenant of My love shall not depart
from thee'. If you have lost the sweet sense of the
Saviour's presence, and are seeking Him with a sorrowful heart, remember the promises: 'Return unto
Me, and I will return unto you'; 'For a small moment
have I forsaken thee, but with great mercies will I
gather thee.' Banquet your faith upon God's own word,
and whatever your fears or wants, repair to the Bank of
Faith with your Father's note of hand, saying, 'Remember the word unto thy servant, upon which Thou
hast caused me to hope'.

'*All the house of Israel are impudent and hardhearted*'
Ezekiel 3:7

Are there no exceptions? No, not one. Even the favoured race are thus described. Are the best so bad? -
then what must the worst be? Come, my heart, consider
how far thou hast a share in this universal accusation,
and while considering, be ready to take shame unto
thyself wherein thou mayst have been guilty. The first
charge is *impudence*, or hardness of forehead, a want
of holy shame, an unhallowed boldness in evil. Before
my conversion, I could sin and feel no compunction,
hear of my guilt and yet remain unhumbled, and even
confess my iniquity and manifest no inward humiliation on account of it. For a sinner to go to God's house
and pretend to pray to Him and praise Him argues a
brazen-facedness of the worst kind! Alas! since the day
of my new birth I have doubted my Lord to His face,
murmured unblushingly in His presence, worshipped
before Him in a slovenly manner, and sinned without
bewailing myself concerning it. If my forehead were
not as an adamant, harder than flint, I should have far
more holy fear, and a far deeper contrition of spirit.
Woe is me, I am one of the impudent house of Israel.
The second charge is *hardheartedness*, and I must not
venture to plead innocent here. Once I had nothing but
a heart of stone, and although through grace I now have
a new and fleshy heart, much of my former obduracy
remains. I am not affected by the death of Jesus as I
ought to be; neither am I moved by the ruin of my
fellow men, the wickedness of the times, the chastisement of my heavenly Father, and my own failures, as
I should be. Oh that my heart would melt at the recital
of my Saviour's sufferings and death. Would to God
I were rid of this nether millstone within me, this
hateful body of death. Blessed be the name of the Lord,
the disease is not incurable, the Saviour's precious
blood is the universal solvent, and me, even me, it will
effectually soften, till my heart melts as wax before the
fire.

'Thou art my hope in the day of evil'
Jeremiah 17:17

The path of the Christian is not always bright with sunshine; he has his seasons of darkness and of storm. True, it is written in God's Word, 'Her ways are ways of pleasantness, and all her paths are peace'; and it is a great truth, that religion is calculated to give a man happiness below as well as bliss above; but experience tells us that if the course of the just be 'As the shining light that shineth more and more unto the perfect day', yet sometimes *that* light is eclipsed. At certain periods clouds cover the believer's sun, and he walks in darkness and sees no light. There are many who have rejoiced in the presence of God for a season; they have basked in the sunshine in the earlier stages of their Christian career; they have walked along the 'green pastures' by the side of the 'still waters', but suddenly they find the glorious sky is clouded; instead of the Land of Goshen they have to tread the sandy desert; in the place of sweet waters, they find troubled streams, bitter to their taste, and they say, 'Surely, if I were a child of God, this would not happen'. Oh! say not so, thou who art walking in darkness. The best of God's saints must drink the wormwood; the dearest of His children must bear the cross. No Christian has enjoyed perpetual prosperity; no believer can always keep his harp from the willows. Perhaps the Lord allotted you at first a smooth and unclouded path, because you were weak and timid. He tempered the wind to the shorn lamb, but now that you are stronger in the spiritual life, you must enter upon the riper and rougher experience of God's full-grown children. We need winds and tempests to exercise our faith, to tear off the rotten bough of self-dependence, and to root us more firmly in Christ. The day of evil reveals to us the value of our glorious hope.

'The Lord taketh pleasure in His people'
Psalm 149:4

How comprehensive is the love of Jesus! There is no part of His people's interests which He does not consider, and there is nothing which concerns their welfare which is not important to Him. Not merely does He think of you, believer, as an immortal being, but as a mortal being too. Do not deny it or doubt it: 'The very hairs of your head are all numbered'. 'The steps of a good man are ordered by the Lord: and he delighteth in His way.' It were a sad thing for us if this mantle of love did not cover all our concerns, for what mischief might be wrought to us in that part of our business which did not come under our gracious Lord's inspection! Believer, rest assured that the heart of Jesus cares about your meaner affairs. The breadth of His tender love is such that you may resort to Him in all matters; for in all your afflictions He is afflicted, and like as a father pitieth his children, so doth He pity you. The meanest interests of all His saints are all borne upon the broad bosom of the Son of God. Oh, what a heart is His, that doth not merely comprehend the persons of His people, but comprehends also the diverse and innumerable concerns of all those persons! Dost thou think, O Christian, that thou canst measure the love of Christ? Think of what His love has brought thee - justification, adoption, sanctification, eternal life! The riches of His goodness are unsearchable; thou shalt never be able to tell them out or even conceive them. Oh, the breadth of the love of Christ! Shall such a love as this have half our hearts? Shall it have a cold love in return? Shall Jesus' marvellous lovingkindness and tender care meet with but faint response and tardy acknowledgement? O my soul, tune thy harp to a glad song of thanksgiving! Go to thy rest rejoicing, for thou art no desolate wanderer, but a beloved child, watched over, cared for, supplied, and defended by thy Lord.

'And all the children of Israel murmured'
Numbers 14:2

There are murmurers amongst Christians now, as there were in the camp of Israel of old. There are those who, when the rod falls, cry out against the afflictive dispensation. They ask, 'Why am I thus afflicted? What have I done to be chastened in this manner?' A word with thee, O murmurer! Why shouldst thou murmur against the dispensations of thy heavenly Father? Can He treat thee more hardly than thou deservest? Consider what a rebel thou wast once, but he has pardoned thee! Surely, if He in His wisdom sees fit now to chasten thee, thou shouldst not complain. After all, art thou smitten as hardly as thy sins deserve? Consider the corruption which is in thy breast, and then wilt thou wonder that there needs so much of the rod to fetch it out? Weight thyself, and discern how much dross is mingled with thy gold; and dost thou think the fire too hot to purge away so much dross as thou hast? Does not that proud rebellious spirit of thine prove that thy heart is not thoroughly sanctified? Are not those murmuring words contrary to the holy submissive nature of God's children? Is not the correction needed? But if thou *wilt* murmur against the chastening, take heed, for it will go hard with murmurers. God always chastises His children twice, if they do not bear the first stroke patiently. But know one thing - 'He doth not afflict willingly, nor grieve the children of men'. All His corrections are sent in love, to purify thee, and to draw thee nearer to Himself. Surely it must help thee to bear the chastening with resignation if thou art able to recognise thy *Father's* hand. For 'whom the Lord loveth He chasteneth, and scourgeth every son whom He receiveth. If ye endure chastening, God dealeth with you as with sons.' 'Murmur not as some of them also murmured and were destroyed of the destroyer.'

'How precious also are Thy thoughts unto me, O God'
Psalm 139:17

Divine omniscience affords no comfort to the ungodly mind, but to the child of God it overflows with consolation. God is always thinking upon us, never turns aside His mind from us, has us always before His eyes; and this is precisely as we would have it, for it would be dreadful to exist for a moment beyond the observation of our heavenly Father. His thoughts are always tender, loving, wise, prudent, far-reaching, and they bring to us countless benefits: hence it is a choice delight to remember them. The Lord always did think upon His people: hence their election and the covenant of grace by which their salvation is secured; He always will think upon them: hence their final perseverance by which they shall be brought safely to their final rest. In all our wanderings the watchful glance of the Eternal Watcher is evermore fixed upon us - we never roam beyond the Shepherd's eye. In our sorrows He observes us incessantly, and not a pang escapes Him; in our toils He marks all our weariness, and writes in His book all the struggles of His faithful ones. These thoughts of the Lord encompass us in all our paths, and penetrate the innermost region of our being. Not a nerve or tissue, valve or vessel, of our bodily organisation is uncared for, all the littles of our little world are thought upon by the great God.

Dear reader, is this precious to you? Then hold to it. Never be led astray by those philosophic fools who preach up an impersonal God, and talk of self-existent, self-governing matter. The Lord liveth and thinketh upon us, this is a truth far too precious for us to be lightly robbed of it. The notice of a nobleman is valued so highly that he who has it counts his fortune made; but what is it to be thought of by the King of kings! If the Lord thinketh upon us, all is well, and we may rejoice evermore.

May

'His cheeks are as a bed of spices,
as sweet flowers'
Canticles 5:13

Lo, the flowery month is come! March winds and April showers have done their work, and the earth is all bedecked with beauty. Come my soul, put on thine holiday attire and go forth to gather garlands of heavenly thoughts. Thou knowest whither to betake thyself, for to thee 'the beds of spices' are well known, and thou hast so often smelt the perfume of 'the sweet flowers' that thou wilt go at once to thy well-beloved and find all loveliness, all joy in Him. That cheek once so rudely smitten with a rod, oft bedewed with tears of sympathy and then defiled with spittle - that cheek as it smiles with mercy is as fragrant aromatic to my heart. Thou didst not hide thy face from shame and spitting, O Lord Jesus, and therefore I will find my dearest delight in praising thee. Those cheeks were furrowed by the plough of grief, and crimsoned with red lines of blood from thy thorn-crowned temples; such marks of love unbounded cannot but charm my soul far more than 'pillars of perfume'. If I may not see the whole of his face I would behold his cheeks, for the least glimpse of him is exceedingly refreshing to my spiritual sense and yields a variety of delights. In Jesus I find not only fragrance, but a bed of spices; not one flower, but all manner of sweet flowers. He is to me my rose and my lily, my heartsease and my cluster of camphire. When he is with me, it is May all the year round, and my soul goes forth to wash her happy face in the morning-dew of his grace, and to solace herself with the singing of the birds of his promises. Precious Lord Jesus, let me in very deed know the blessedness which dwells in abiding, unbroken fellowship with thee. I am a poor worthless one, whose cheek thou hast deigned to kiss! O let me kiss thee in return with the kisses of my lips.

'*I am the rose of Sharon*'
Solomon's Song 2:1

Whatever there may be of beauty in the material world,
Jesus Christ possesses all that in the spiritual world in
a tenfold degree. Amongst flowers the rose is deemed
the sweetest, but Jesus is infinitely more beautiful in
the garden of the soul than the rose can be in the gardens
of earth. He takes the first place as the fairest among ten
thousand. He is the sun, and all others are the stars: the
heavens and the day are dark in comparison with Him,
for *the King in His beauty transcends all*. 'I am the rose
of Sharon.' This was the best and rarest of roses. Jesus
is not 'the rose' alone, He is 'the rose of Sharon', just
as He calls His righteousness 'gold', and then adds,
'the gold of Ophir' - the best of the best. He is
positively lovely, and superlatively the loveliest. *There
is variety in His charms*. The rose is delightful to the
eye, and its scent is pleasant and refreshing; so each of
the senses of the soul, whether it be the taste or feeling,
the hearing, the sight, or the spiritual smell, finds
appropriate gratification in Jesus. *Even the recollection of His love is sweet*. Take the rose of Sharon and
pull it leaf from leaf, and lay by the leaves in the jar of
memory, and you shall find each leaf fragrant long
afterwards, filling the house with perfume. Christ
satisfies the highest taste of the most educated spirit to
the very full. The greatest amateur in perfumes is quite
satisfied with the rose: and when the soul has arrived
at her highest pitch of true taste, she shall still be
content with Christ, nay, she shall be the better able to
appreciate Him. Heaven itself possesses nothing which
excels the rose of Sharon. What emblem can fully set
forth His beauty? Human speech and earth-born things
fail to tell of Him. Earth's choicest charms commin-
gled, feebly picture His abounding preciousness.
Blessed rose, bloom in my heart for ever!

*'I pray not that Thou shouldest
take them out of the world'*
John 17:15

It is a sweet and blessed event which will occur to all
believers in God's own time - the going home to be with
Jesus. In a few more years the Lord's soldiers, who are
now fighting 'the good fight of faith', will have done
with conflict, and have entered into the joy of their
Lord. But although Christ prays that His people may
eventually be with Him where He is, He does not ask
that they may be taken at once away from this world to
heaven. He wishes them to stay here. Yet how frequently does the wearied pilgrim put up the prayer, 'O
that I had wings like a dove! for then would I fly away
and be at rest'; but Christ does not pray like that, He
leaves us in His Father's hands, until, like shocks of
corn fully ripe, we shall each be gathered into our
Master's garner. Jesus does not plead for our instant
removal by death, for to abide in the flesh is needful for
others if not profitable for ourselves. He asks that we
may be kept from evil, but he never asks for us to be
admitted to the inheritance in glory till we are of full
age. Christians often want to die when they have any
trouble. Ask them why, and they tell you, 'Because we
would be with the Lord'. We fear it is not so much
because they are longing to be with the Lord, as because
they desire to get rid of their troubles; else they would
feel the same wish to die at other times when not under
the pressure of trial. They want to go home, not so
much for the Saviour's company, as to be at rest. Now
it is quite right to desire to depart if we can do it in the
same spirit that Paul did, because to be with Christ is
far better, but the wish to escape from trouble is a
selfish one. Rather let your care and wish be to glorify
God by your life here as long as He pleases, even
though it be in the midst of toil, and conflict, and
suffering, and leave Him to say when 'it is enough'.

'These all died in faith'
Hebrews 11:13

Behold the epitaph of all those blessed saints who fell asleep before the coming of our Lord! It matters nothing how else they died, whether of old age, or by violent means; this one point, in which they all agree, is the most worthy of record, 'they all died in faith'. In faith they lived - it was their comfort, their guide, their motive and their support; and in the same spiritual grace they died, ending their life-song in the sweet strain in which they had so long continued. They did not die resting in the flesh or upon their own attainments; they made no advance from their first way of acceptance with God, but held to the way of faith to the end. Faith is as precious to die by as to live by.

Dying in faith has distinct reference to *the past*. They believed the promises which had gone before, and were assured that their sins were blotted out through the mercy of God. Dying in faith has to do with *the present*. These saints were confident of their acceptance with God, they enjoyed the beams of His love, and rested in His faithfulness. Dying in faith looks into *the future*. They fell asleep, affirming that the Messiah would surely come, and that when He should in the last days appear upon the earth, they would rise from their graves to behold Him. To them the pains of death were but the birth-pangs of a better state. Take courage, my soul, as thou readest this epitaph. Thy course, through grace, is one of faith, and sight seldom cheers thee: this has also been the pathway of the brightest and the best. Faith was the orbit in which these stars of the first magnitude moved all the time of their shining here; and happy art thou that it is thine. Look anew tonight to Jesus, the author and finisher of thy faith, and thank Him for giving thee like precious faith with souls now in glory.

'*In the world ye shall have tribulation*'
John 16:33

Art thou asking the reason of this, believer? Look *upward* to thy heavenly Father, and behold Him pure and holy. Dost thou know that thou art one day to be like Him? Wilt thou easily be conformed to his image? Wilt thou not require much refining in the furnace of affliction to purify thee? Will it be an easy thing to get rid of thy corruptions, and make thee perfect even as thy Father which is in heaven is perfect? Next, Christian, turn thine eye *downward*. Dost thou know what foes thou hast beneath thy feet? Thou wast once a servant of Satan, and no king will willingly lose his subjects. Dost thou think that Satan will let thee alone? No, he will be always at thee, for he 'goeth about like a roaring lion, seeking whom he may devour'. Expect trouble, therefore, Christian, when thou lookest beneath thee. Then look *around thee*. Where art thou? Thou art in an enemy's country, a stranger and a sojourner. The world is not thy friend. If it be, then thou art not God's friend, for he who is the friend of the world is the enemy of God. Be assured that thou shalt find foemen everywhere. When thou sleepest, think that thou art resting on the battlefield; when thou walkest, suspect an ambush in every hedge. As mosquitoes are said to bite strangers more than natives, so will the trials of earth be sharpest to you. Lastly, look *within thee*, into thine own heart and observe what is there. *Sin* and *self* are still within. Ah! if thou hadst no devil to tempt thee, no enemies to fight thee, and no world to ensnare thee, thou wouldst still find in thyself evil enough to be a sore trouble to thee, for 'the heart is deceitful above all things, and desperately wicked'. Expect trouble then, but despond not on account of it, for God is with thee to help and to strengthen thee. He hath said, 'I will be with thee in trouble; I will deliver thee and honour thee'.

'A very present help'
Psalm 46:1

Covenant blessings are not meant to be looked at only, but to be appropriated. Even our Lord Jesus is given to us for our present use. Believer, thou dost not make use of Christ as thou oughtest to do. When thou art in trouble, why dost thou not tell Him all thy grief? Has He not a sympathising heart, and can He not comfort and relieve thee? No, thou art going about to all thy friends, save thy best Friend, and telling thy tale everywhere except into the bosom of thy Lord. Art thou burdened with this day's sins? Here is a fountain filled with blood: use it, saint, use it. Has a sense of guilt returned upon thee? The pardoning grace of Jesus may be proved again and again. Come to Him at once for cleansing. Dost thou deplore thy weakness? He is thy strength: why not lean upon Him? Dost thou feel naked? Come hither, soul; put on the robe of Jesus' righteousness. Stand not looking at it, but wear it. Strip off thine own righteousness, and thine own fears too: put on the fair white linen, for it was meant to *wear*. Dost thou feel thyself sick? Pull the night-bell of prayer, and call up the Beloved Physician! He will give the cordial that will revive thee. Thou art poor, but then thou hast 'a kinsman, a mighty man of wealth'. What! wilt thou not go to Him, and ask Him to give thee of His abundance, when He has given thee this promise, that thou shalt be joint heir with Him, and has made over all that He is and all that He has to be thine? There is nothing Christ dislikes more than for His people to make a show-thing of Him, and not to use Him. He loves to be employed by us. The more burdens we put on His shoulders, the more precious will He be to us.

'Let us be simple with Him, then,
    Not backward, stiff, or cold,
As though our Bethlehem could be
    What Sinai was of old.'

> *'Shall a man make gods unto himself,*
> *and they are no gods?'*
> Jeremiah 16:20

One great besetting sin of ancient Israel was idolatry, and the spiritual Israel are vexed with a tendency to the same folly. Rephan's star shines no longer, and the women weep no more for Tammuz, but Mammon still intrudes his golden calf, and the shrines of pride are not forsaken. Self in various forms struggles to subdue the chosen ones under its dominion, and the flesh sets up its altars wherever it can find space for them. Favourite children are often the cause of much sin in believers; the Lord is grieved when he sees us doting upon them above measure; they will live to be as great a curse to us as Absalom was to David, or they will be taken from us to leave our homes desolate. If Christians desire to grow thorns to stuff their sleepless pillows, let them dote upon their dear ones.

It is truly said that 'they are no gods', for the objects of our foolish love are very doubtful blessings, the solace which they yield us now is dangerous, and the help which they can give us in the hour of trouble is little indeed. Why, then, are we so bewitched with vanities? We pity the poor heathen who adore a god of stone, and yet worship a god of gold. Where is the vast superiority between a god of flesh and one of wood? The principle, the sin, the folly is the same in either case, only that in ours the crime is more aggravated because we have more light, and sin in the face of it. The heathen bows to a false deity, but the true God he has never known; we commit two evils, inasmuch as we forsake the living God and turn unto idols. May the Lord purge us all from this grievous iniquity!

> 'The dearest idol I have known,
>   Whate'er that idol be;
> Help me to tear it from thy throne,
>   And worship only thee.'

'Being born again, not of corruptible seed,
but of incorruptible'
1 Peter 1:23

Peter most earnestly exhorted the scattered saints to love each other 'with a pure heart fervently', and he wisely fetched his argument, not from the law, from nature, or from philosophy, but from that high and divine nature which God hath implanted in His people. Just as some judicious tutor of princes might labour to beget and foster in them a kingly spirit and dignified behaviour, finding arguments in their position and descent, so, looking upon God's people as heirs of glory, princes of the blood royal, descendants of the King of kings, earth's truest and oldest aristocracy, Peter saith to them, 'See that ye love one another, because of your noble birth, being born of incorruptible seed; because of your pedigree, being descended from God, the Creator of all things; and because of your immortal destiny, for you shall never pass away, though the glory of the flesh shall fade, and even its existence shall cease.' It would be well if, in the spirit of humility, we recognised the true dignity of our regenerated nature, and lived up to it. What is a Christian? If you compare him with a king, he adds priestly sanctity to royal dignity. The king's royalty often lieth only in his crown, but with a Christian it is infused into his inmost nature. He is as much above his fellows through his new birth, as a man is above the beast that perisheth. Surely he ought to carry himself, in all his dealings, as one who is not of the multitude, but chosen out of the world, distinguished by sovereign grace, written among 'the peculiar people' and who therefore cannot grovel in the dust as others, nor live after the manner of the world's citizens. Let the dignity of your nature, and the brightness of your prospects, O believers in Christ, constrain you to cleave unto holiness, and to avoid the very appearance of evil.

'*I will be their God, and they shall be my people*'
2 Corinthians 6:16

What a sweet title: 'My people!' What a cheering
revelation: 'Their God!' How much of meaning is
couched in those two words, 'My people!' Here is
speciality. The whole world is God's; the heaven, even
the heaven of heavens is the Lord's, and He reigneth
among the children of men; but of those whom he hath
chosen, whom He hath purchased to himself, He saith
what He saith not of others - 'My people'. In this word
there is the idea of *proprietorship*. In a special manner
the 'Lord's portion is His people; Jacob is the lot of His
inheritance'. All the nations upon earth are His; the
whole world is in His power; yet are His people, His
chosen, more especially His possession; for He has
done more for them than others; He has bought them
with His blood; He has brought them nigh to Himself;
He has set His great heart upon them; He has loved
them with an everlasting love, a love which many
waters cannot quench, and which the revolutions of
time shall never suffice in the least degree to diminish.
Dear friends, can you, by faith, see yourselves in that
number? Can you look up to heaven and say, 'My Lord
and my God: mine by that sweet *relationship* which
entitles me to call Thee Father; mine by that hallowed
fellowship which I delight to hold with Thee when
Thou art pleased to manifest Thyself unto me as Thou
dost not unto the world?' Canst thou read the Book of
Inspiration, and find there the indentures of thy salvation? Canst thou read thy title writ in precious blood?
Canst thou, by humble faith, lay hold of Jesus' garments, and say, 'My Christ'? If thou canst, then God
saith of thee, and of others like thee, 'My people'; for,
if God be your God, and Christ your Christ, the Lord
has a special, peculiar favour to you; you are the object
of His choice, accepted in His beloved Son.

'He that handleth a matter wisely shall find good:
and whoso trusteth in the Lord, happy is he'
Proverbs 16:20

Wisdom is man's true strength; and, under its guidance, he best accomplishes the ends of his being. Wisely handling the matter of life gives to man the richest enjoyment, and presents the noblest occupation for his powers; hence by it he finds good in the fullest sense. Without wisdom, man is as the wild ass's colt, running hither and thither, wasting strength which might be profitably employed. Wisdom is the compass by which man is to steer across the trackless waste of life; without it he is a derelict vessel, the sport of winds and waves. A man must be prudent in such a world as this, or he will find no good, but be betrayed into unnumbered ills. The pilgrim will sorely wound his feet among the briers of the wood of life if he do not pick his steps with the utmost caution. He who is in a wilderness infested with robber bands must handle matters wisely if he would journey safely. If, trained by the Great Teacher, we follow where He leads, we shall find good, even while in this dark abode; there are celestial fruits to be gathered this side of Eden's bowers, and songs of paradise to be sung amid the groves of earth. But where shall this wisdom be found? Many have dreamed of it, but have not possessed it. Where shall we learn it? Let us listen to the voice of the Lord, for He hath declared the secret; He hath revealed to the sons of men wherein true wisdom lieth, and we have it in the text, 'Whoso trusteth in the Lord, happy is he'. *The true way to handle a matter wisely is to trust in the Lord.* This is the sure clue to the most intricate labyrinths of life, follow it and find eternal bliss. He who trusts in the Lord has a diploma for wisdom granted by inspiration: happy is he now, and happier shall he be above. Lord, in this sweet eventide walk with me in the garden, and teach me the wisdom of faith.

'We dwell in Him'
1 John 4:13

Do you want a house for your soul? Do you ask, 'What is the purchase?' It is something less than proud human nature will like to give. It is without money and without price. Ah! you would like to pay a respectable rent! You would love to do something to win Christ? Then you cannot have the house, for it is 'without price'. Will you take my Master's house on a lease for all eternity, with nothing to pay for it, nothing but the ground-rent of loving and serving Him for ever? Will you take Jesus and 'dwell in Him'? See, this house is furnished with all you want; it is filled with riches more than you will spend as long as you live. Here you can have intimate communion with Christ and feast on His love; here are tables well-stored with food for you to live on for ever; in it, when weary, you can find rest with Jesus; and from it you can look out and see heaven itself. Will you have the house? Ah! if you are houseless, you will say, 'I should like to have the house; but may I have it?'. Yes; there is the key - the key is, 'Come to Jesus'. 'But,' you say, 'I am too shabby for such a house.' Never mind; there are garments inside. If you feel guilty and condemned, come; and though the house is too good for you, Christ will make you good enough for the house by-and-by. He will wash you and cleanse you, and you will yet be able to sing, 'We dwell in Him'. Believer: thrice happy art thou to have such a dwelling-place! Greatly privileged thou art, for thou hast a 'strong habitation' in which thou art ever safe. And 'dwelling in Him', thou hast not only a perfect and secure house, but an *everlasting* one. When this world shall have melted like a dream, our house shall live, and stand more imperishable than marble, more solid than granite, self-existent as God, for it is God Himself - 'We dwell in Him'.

'All the days of my appointed time will I wait'
Job 14:14

A little stay on earth will make heaven more heavenly.
Nothing makes rest so sweet as toil; nothing renders
security so pleasant as exposure to alarms. The bitter
quassia cup of earth will give a relish to the new wine
which sparkles in the golden bowls of glory. Our
battered armour and scarred countenance will render
more illustrious our victory above, when we are wel-
comed to the seats of those who have overcome the
world. We should not have full *fellowship with Christ*
if we did not for awhile sojourn below, for He was
baptised with a baptism of suffering among men, and
we must be baptised with the same if we would share
his kingdom. Fellowship with Christ is so honourable
that the sorest sorrow is a light price by which to
procure it. Another reason for our lingering here is *for
the good of others*. We would not wish to enter heaven
till our work is done, and it may be that we are yet
ordained to minister light to souls benighted in the
wilderness of sin. Our prolonged stay here is doubtless
for God's glory. A tried saint, like a well-cut diamond,
glitters much in the King's crown. Nothing reflects so
much honour on a workman as a protracted and severe
trial of his work, and its triumphant endurance of the
ordeal without giving way in any part. We are God's
workmanship, in whom he will be glorified by our
afflictions. It is for the honour of Jesus that we endure
the trial of our faith with sacred joy. Let each man
surrender his own longings to the glory of Jesus, and
feel, 'If my lying in the dust would elevate my Lord by
so much as an inch, let me still lie among the pots of
earth. If to live on earth for ever would make my Lord
more glorious, it should be my heaven to be shut out of
heaven.' Our time is fixed and settled by eternal decree.
Let us not be anxious about it, but wait with patience
till the gates of pearl shall open.

> *'Great multitudes followed Him,
> and He healed them all'*
> Matthew 12:15

What a mass of hideous sickness must have thrust itself under the eye of Jesus! Yet we read not that He was disgusted, but patiently waited on every case. What a singular variety of evils must have met at His feet! What sickening ulcers and putrefying sores! Yet He was ready for every new shape of the monster evil, and was victor over it in every form. Let the arrow fly from what quarter it might, he quenched its fiery power. The heat of fever, or the cold of dropsy; the lethargy of palsy, or the rage of madness; the filth of leprosy, or the darkness of ophthalmia - all knew the power of His word, and fled at His command. In every corner of the field He was triumphant over evil, and received the homage of delivered captives. He came, He saw, He conquered everywhere. It is even so this morning. Whatever my own case may be, the beloved Physician can heal me; and whatever may be the state of others whom I may remember at this moment in prayer, I may have hope in Jesus that He will be able to heal them of their sins. My child, my friend, my dearest one, I can have hope for each, for all, when I remember the healing power of my Lord; and on my own account, however severe my struggle with sins and infirmities, I may yet be of good cheer. He who on earth walked the hospitals, still dispenses his grace, and works wonders among the sons of men: let me go to Him at once in right earnest.

Let me praise Him, this morning, as I remember *how* he wrought His spiritual cures, which bring Him most renown. It was by taking upon Himself our sicknesses. 'By His stripes we are healed.' The Church on earth is full of souls healed by our beloved Physician; and the inhabitants of heaven itself confess that 'He healed them all'. Come, then, my soul, publish abroad the virtue of His grace, and let it be 'to the Lord for a name, for an everlasting sign which shall not be cut off'.

'Jesus saith unto him, Rise,
take up thy bed, and walk'
John 5:8

Like many others, the impotent man had been waiting
for a wonder to be wrought, and a sign to be given.
Wearily did he watch the pool, but no angel came, or
came not for him; yet, thinking it to be his only chance,
he waited still, and knew not that there was One near
him whose word could heal him in a moment. Many are
in the same plight: they are waiting for some singular
emotion, remarkable impression, or celestial vision;
they wait in vain and watch for nought. Even supposing
that, in a few cases, remarkable signs are seen, yet these
are rare, and no man has a right to look for them in his
own case; no man especially who feels his impotency
to avail himself of the moving of the water even if it
came. It is a very sad reflection that tens of thousands
are now waiting in the use of means, and ordinances,
and vows, and resolutions, and have so waited time out
of mind, in vain, utterly in vain. Meanwhile these poor
souls forget the present Saviour, who bids them look
unto Him and be saved. *He* could heal them at once, but
they prefer to wait for an angel and a wonder. To trust
Him is the sure way to every blessing, and He is worthy
of the most implicit confidence; but unbelief makes
them prefer the cold porches of Bethesda to the warm
bosom of His love. O that the Lord may turn His eye
upon the multitudes who are in this case tonight; may
He forgive the slights which they put upon His divine
power, and call them by that sweet constraining voice,
to rise from the bed of despair, and in the energy of faith
take up their bed and walk. O Lord, hear our prayer for
all such at this calm hour of sunset, and ere the day
breaketh may they look and live.

    Courteous reader, is there anything in this portion
for you?

'*He that was healed wist not who it was*'
John 5:13

Years are short to the happy and healthy; but thirty-
eight years of disease must have dragged a very weary
length along the life of the poor impotent man. When
Jesus, therefore, healed him by a word, while he lay at
the pool of Bethesda, he was delightfully *sensible of a
change*. Even so the sinner who has for weeks and
months been paralysed with despair, and has wearily
sighed for salvation, is very conscious of the change
when the Lord Jesus speaks the word of power, and
gives joy and peace in believing. The evil removed is
too great to be removed without our discerning it; the
life imparted is too remarkable to be possessed and
remain inoperative; and the change wrought is too
marvellous not to be perceived. Yet the poor man was
ignorant of the author of his cure; he knew not the
sacredness of His person, the offices which He sustained, or the errand which brought Him among men.
Much ignorance of Jesus may remain in hearts which
yet feel the power of His blood. We must not hastily
condemn men for lack of knowledge; but where we can
see the faith which saves the soul, we must believe that
salvation has been bestowed. The Holy Spirit makes
men penitents long before He makes them divines; and
he who believes what he knows, shall soon know more
clearly what he believes. Ignorance is, however, an
evil; for this poor man was much *tantalised by the
Pharisees*, and was quite unable to cope with them. It
is good to be able to answer gainsayers; but we cannot
do so if we know not the Lord Jesus clearly and with
understanding. The cure of his ignorance, however,
soon followed the cure of his infirmity, for he was
visited by the Lord in the temple; and after that gracious
manifestation, he was *found testifying* that 'it was
Jesus who had made him whole'. Lord, if Thou hast
saved me, show me Thyself, that I may declare Thee to
the sons of men.

'Acquaint now thyself with Him'
Job 22:21

If we would rightly 'acquaint ourselves with God, and be at peace', we must know Him as He has revealed Himself, not only in *the unity of His essence and subsistence*, but also in *the plurality of His persons*. God said, 'Let *us* make man in our *own* image'; let not man be content until he knows something of the 'us' from whom his being was derived. Endeavour to know *the Father*; bury your head in His bosom in deep repentance, and confess that you are not worthy to be called His son; receive the kiss of His love; let the ring which is the token of His eternal faithfulness be on your finger; sit at His table and let your heart make merry in His grace. Then press forward and seek to know much of *the Son* of God who is the brightness of His Father's glory, and yet in unspeakable condescension of grace became man for our sakes; know Him in the singular complexity of His nature: eternal God, and yet suffering, finite man; follow Him as He walks the waters with the tread of deity, and as He sits upon the well in the weariness of humanity. Be not satisfied unless you know much of Jesus Christ as your Friend, your Brother, your Husband, your all. Forget not *the Holy Spirit*; endeavour to obtain a clear view of His nature and character, His attributes, and His works. Behold that Spirit of the Lord, who first of all moved upon chaos, and brought forth order; who now visits the chaos of your soul, and creates the order of holiness. Behold Him as the Lord and giver of spiritual life, the Illuminator, the Instructor, the Comforter, and the Sanctifier. Behold Him as, like holy unction, He descends upon the head of Jesus, and then afterwards rests upon *you* who are as the skirts of His garments. Such an intelligent, scriptural, and experimental belief in the Trinity in Unity is yours if you truly know God; and such knowledge *brings peace indeed*.

'Who hath blessed us with all spiritual blessings'
Ephesians 1:3

All the goodness of the past, the present, and the future, Christ bestows upon His people. In the mysterious ages of the past the Lord Jesus was His Father's first elect, and in His *election* He gave us an interest, for we were chosen in Him from before the foundation of the world. He had from all eternity the prerogatives of *Sonship*, as His Father's only-begotten and well-beloved Son, and He has, in the riches of His grace, by adoption and regeneration, elevated us to sonship also, so that to us He has given 'power to become the sons of God'. The *eternal covenant*, based upon suretyship and confirmed by oath, is ours, for our strong consolation and security. In the *everlasting settlements of predestinating wisdom* and omnipotent decree, the eye of the Lord Jesus was ever fixed on us; and we may rest assured that in the whole roll of destiny there is not a line which militates against the interests of His redeemed. The *great betrothal* of the Prince of Glory is ours, for it is to us that He is affianced, as the sacred nuptials shall ere long declare to an assembled universe. The *marvellous incarnation* of the God of heaven, with all the amazing condescension and humiliation which attended it, is ours. The bloody sweat, the scourge, the cross, are ours for ever. Whatever blissful consequences flow from *perfect obedience, finished atonement, resurrection, ascension, or intercession*, all are ours by His own gift. Upon His breastplate he is now bearing our names; and in His authoritative pleadings at the throne He remembers our persons and pleads our cause. His *dominion* over principalities and powers, and His absolute majesty in heaven, He employs for the benefit of them who trust in Him. His high estate is as much at our service as was His condition of abasement. He who gave Himself for us in the depths of woe and death, doth not withdraw the grant now that He is enthroned in the highest heavens.

'Come, my beloved, let us go forth into the field...
let us see if the vine flourish'
Canticles 7:11, 12

The church was about to engage in earnest labour, and desired her Lord's company in it. She does not say, 'I will go', but 'let us go'. It is blessed working when Jesus is at our side! It is the business of God's people to be trimmers of God's vines. Like our first parents, we are put into the garden of the Lord for usefulness; let us therefore go forth into the field. Observe that the church, when she is in her right mind, in all her many labours desires to enjoy communion with Christ. Some imagine that they cannot serve Christ actively, and yet have fellowship with Him: they are mistaken. Doubtless it is very easy to fritter away our inward life in outward exercises, and come to complain with the spouse, 'They made me keeper of the vineyards; but mine own vineyard have I not kept': but there is no reason why this should be the case except our own folly and neglect. Certain is it that a professor may do nothing, and yet grow quite as lifeless in spiritual things as those who are most busy. Mary was not praised for sitting still; but for her sitting at Jesus' feet. Even so, Christians are not to be praised for neglecting duties under the pretence of having secret fellowship with Jesus: it is not sitting, but *sitting at Jesus' feet* which is commendable. Do not think that activity is in itself an evil: it is a great blessing, and a means of grace to us. Paul called it a grace given to him to be allowed to preach; and every form of Christian service may become a personal blessing to those engaged in it. Those who have most fellowship with Christ are not recluses or hermits, who have much time to spare, but indefatigable labourers who are toiling for Jesus, and who, in their toil, have Him side by side with them, so that they are workers together with God. Let us remember then, in anything we have to do for Jesus, that we can do it, and should do it in close communion with Him.

> '*But now is Christ risen from the dead*'
> 1 Corinthians 15:20

The whole system of Christianity rests upon the fact that 'Christ is risen from the dead'; for, 'If Christ be not risen, then is our preaching vain, and your faith is also vain: ye are yet in your sins'. The *divinity* of Christ finds its surest proof in His resurrection, since He was 'Declared to be the Son of God with power, according to the spirit of holiness, by the resurrection from the dead'. It would not be unreasonable to doubt His Deity if He had not risen. Moreover, Christ's *sovereignty* depends upon His resurrection, 'For to this end Christ both died, and rose, and revived, that He might be Lord both of the dead and living'. Again, our *justification*, that choice blessing of the covenant, is linked with Christ's triumphant victory over death and the grave; for 'He was delivered for our offences, and was raised again for our justification'. Nay, more, our very *regeneration* is connected with His resurrection, for we are 'Begotten again unto a lively hope by the resurrection of Jesus Christ from the dead'. And most certainly our *ultimate resurrection* rests here, for, 'If the Spirit of Him that raised up Jesus from the dead dwell in you, He that raised up Christ from the dead shall also quicken your mortal bodies by His Spirit that dwelleth in you'. If Christ be not risen, then shall we not rise; but if He be risen then they who are asleep in Christ have not perished, but in their flesh shall surely behold their God. Thus, the silver thread of resurrection runs through all the believer's blessings, from his regeneration onwards to his eternal glory, and binds them together. How important then will this glorious fact be in his estimation, and how will he rejoice that beyond a doubt it is established, that 'now is Christ risen from the dead'.

> 'The promise is fulfill'd,
>   Redemption's work is done,
> Justice with mercy's reconciled,
>   For God has raised His Son.'

'*The only begotten of the Father,*
full of grace and truth'
John 1:14

Believer, you can bear your testimony that Christ *is the only begotten of the Father*, as well as the first begotten from the dead. You can say, 'He is divine to me, if He be human to all the world beside. He has done that for me which none but a God could do. He has subdued my stubborn will, melted a heart of adamant, opened gates of brass, and snapped bars of iron. He hath turned for me my mourning into laughter, and my desolation into joy; He hath led my captivity captive, and made my heart rejoice with joy unspeakable and full of glory. Let others think as they will of Him, to me He must be the only begotten of the Father: blessed be His name. And He is *full of grace*. Ah! had He not been I should never have been saved. He drew me when I struggled to escape from His grace; and when at last I came all trembling like a condemned culprit to His mercy-seat He said, "Thy sins which are many are all forgiven thee: be of good cheer." And He is *full of truth*. True have His promises been, not one has failed. I bear witness that never servant had such a master as I have; never brother such a kinsman as He has been to me; never spouse such a husband as Christ has been to my soul; never sinner a better Saviour; never mourner a better comforter than Christ hath been to my spirit. I want none beside Him. In life He is my life, and in death He shall be the death of death; in poverty Christ is my riches; in sickness he makes my bed; in darkness He is my star, and in brightness He is my sun; He is the manna of the camp in the wilderness, and He shall be the new corn of the host when they come to Canaan. Jesus is to me all grace and no wrath, all truth and no falsehood: and of truth and grace He is *full*, infinitely full. My soul, this night, bless with all thy might "the only Begotten".'

'I am with you alway'
Matthew 28:20

It is well there is One who is ever the same, and who is ever with us. It is well there is one stable rock amidst the billows of the sea of life. O my soul, set not thine affections upon rusting, moth-eaten, decaying treasures, but set thine heart upon Him who abides for ever faithful to thee. Build not thine house upon the moving quicksands of a deceitful world, but found thy hopes upon this rock, which, amid descending rain and roaring floods, shall stand immovably secure. My soul, I charge thee, lay up thy treasure in the only secure cabinet; store thy jewels where thou canst never lose them. Put thine all in Christ; set all thine affections on His person, all thy hope in His merit, all thy trust in His efficacious blood, all thy joy in His presence, and so thou mayest laugh at loss, and defy destruction. Remember that all the flowers in the world's garden fade by turns, and the day cometh when nothing will be left but the black, cold earth. Death's black extinguisher must soon put out thy candle. Oh! how sweet to have sunlight when the candle is gone! The dark flood must soon roll between thee and all thou hast; then wed thine heart to Him who will never leave thee; trust thyself with Him who will go with thee through the black and surging current of death's stream, and who will land thee safely on the celestial shore, and make thee sit with Him in heavenly places for ever. Go, sorrowing son of affliction, tell thy secrets to the Friend who sticketh closer than a brother. Trust all thy concerns with Him who never can be taken from thee, who will never leave thee, and who will never let thee leave Him, even 'Jesus Christ, the same yesterday, and today, and for ever'. 'Lo, I am with you alway', is enough for my soul to live upon, let who will forsake me.

'Only be thou strong and very courageous'
Joshua 1:7

Our God's tender love for His servants makes Him
concerned for the state of their inward feelings. He
desires them to be of good courage. Some esteem it a
small thing for a believer to be vexed with doubts and
fears, but God thinks not so. From this text it is plain
that our Master would not have us entangled with fears.
He would have us without carefulness, without doubt,
without cowardice. Our Master does not think so
lightly of our unbelief as we do. When we are desponding we are subject to a grievous malady, not to be trifled
with, but to be carried at once to the beloved Physician.
Our Lord loveth not to see our countenance sad. It was
a law of Ahasuerus that no one should come into the
king's court dressed in mourning: this is not the law of
the King of kings, for we may come mourning as we
are; but still He would have us put off the spirit of
heaviness, and put on the garment of praise, for there
is much reason to rejoice. The Christian man ought to
be of a courageous spirit, in order that he may glorify
the Lord by enduring trials in an heroic manner. If he
be fearful and fainthearted, *it will dishonour his God.*
Besides, *what a bad example it is.* This disease of
doubtfulness and discouragement is an epidemic which
soon spreads amongst the Lord's flock. One downcast
believer makes twenty souls sad. Moreover, unless
your courage is kept up *Satan will be too much for you.*
Let your spirit be joyful in God your Saviour, the joy
of the Lord shall be your strength, and no fiend of hell
shall make headway against you: but cowardice throws
down the banner. Moreover, *labour is light* to a man of
cheerful spirit; and *success waits upon cheerfulness.*
The man who toils, rejoicing in his God, believing with
all his heart, has success guaranteed. He who sows in
hope shall reap in joy; therefore, dear reader, 'be thou
strong, and very courageous'.

'And will manifest myself to him'
John 14:21

The Lord Jesus gives special revelations of Himself to his people. Even if Scripture did not declare this, there are many of the children of God who could testify the truth of it from their own experience. They have had manifestations of their Lord and Saviour Jesus Christ in a peculiar manner, such as no mere reading or hearing could afford. In the biographies of eminent saints, you will find many instances recorded in which Jesus has been pleased, in a very special manner to speak to their souls, and to unfold the wonders of His person; yea, so have their souls been steeped in happiness that they have thought themselves to be in heaven, whereas they were not there, though they were well nigh on the threshold of it - for when Jesus manifests Himself to his people, it is heaven on earth; it is paradise in embryo; it is bliss begun. Especial manifestations of Christ exercise a holy influence on the believer's heart. One effect will be *humility*. If a man says, 'I have had such-and-such spiritual communications, I am a great man', he has never had any communion with Jesus at all; for 'God hath respect unto the lowly: but the proud He knoweth *afar off*'. He does not need to come near them to know them, and will never give them any visits of love. Another effect will be *happiness*; for in God's presence there are pleasures for evermore. *Holiness* will be sure to follow. A man who has no holiness has never had this manifestation. Some men profess a great deal; but we must not believe any one unless we see that his deeds answer to what he says. 'Be not deceived; God is not mocked.' He will not bestow his favours upon the wicked: for while he will not cast away a perfect man, neither will he respect an evil doer. Thus there will be three effects of nearness to Jesus - humility, happiness, and holiness. May God give them to thee, Christian!

> '*Fear not to go down into Egypt;*
> *for I will there make of thee a great nation:*
> *I will go down with thee into Egypt;*
> *and I will also surely bring thee up again*'
> Genesis 46:3, 4

Jacob must have shuddered at the thought of leaving the land of his father's sojourning, and dwelling among heathen strangers. It was *a new scene, and likely to be a trying one*: who shall venture among courtiers of a foreign monarch without anxiety? Yet the way was *evidently appointed* for him, and therefore he resolved to go. This is frequently the position of believers now - they are called to perils and temptations altogether untried; at such seasons *let them imitate Jacob's example* by offering sacrifices of prayer unto God, and seeking His direction; let them not take a step until they have waited upon the Lord for His blessing: then they *will have Jacob's companion* to be their friend and helper. How blessed to feel assured that the Lord is with us in all our ways, and condescends to go down into our humiliations and banishments with us! Even beyond the ocean our Father's love beams like the sun in its strength. We cannot hesitate to go where Jehovah promises His presence; even the valley of deathshade grows bright with the radiance of this assurance. Marching onwards with faith in their God, believers *shall have Jacob's promise*. They shall be brought up again, whether it be from the troubles of life or the chambers of death. Jacob's seed came out of Egypt in due time, and so shall all the faithful pass unscathed through the tribulation of life, and the terror of death. Let us *exercise Jacob's confidence*. '*Fear not*', is the Lord's command and His divine encouragement to those who at His bidding are launching upon new seas; the divine presence and preservation forbid so much as one unbelieving fear. Without our God we should fear to move; but when He bids us go, it would be dangerous to tarry. Reader, go forward, and fear not.

*'Weeping may endure for a night,
but joy cometh in the morning'*
Psalm 30:5

Christian! If thou art in a night of trial, think of the morrow; cheer up thy heart with the thought of the coming of thy Lord. Be patient, for

'Lo! He comes with clouds descending.'

Be patient! The Husbandman waits until he reaps His harvest. Be patient; for you know who has said, 'Behold, I come quickly; and my reward is with me, to give to every man according as his work shall be.' If you are never so wretched now, remember

'A few more rolling suns, at most,
Will land thee on fair Canaan's coast.'

Thy head may be crowned with thorny troubles now, but it shall wear a starry crown ere long; thy hand may be filled with cares - it shall sweep the strings of the harp of heaven soon. Thy garments may be soiled with dust now; they shall be white by-and-by. Wait a little longer. Ah! how despicable our troubles and trials will seem when we look back upon them! Looking at them here in the prospect, they seem immense; but when we get to heaven we shall then

'With transporting joys recount,
The labours of our feet.'

Our trials will then seem light and momentary afflictions. Let us go on boldly; if the night be never so dark, the morning cometh, which is more than they can say who are shut up in the darkness of hell. Do you know what it is thus to live on the future - to live on expectation - to antedate heaven? Happy believer, to have so sure, so comforting a hope. It may be all dark now, but it will soon be light; it may be all trial now, but it will soon be all happiness. What matters it though 'weeping may endure for a night', when 'joy cometh in the morning'?

'Thou art my portion, O Lord'
Psalm 119:57

Look at thy possessions, O believer, and compare thy
portion with the lot of thy fellow-men. Some of them
have their portion in the field; they are rich, and their
harvests yield them a golden increase; but what are
harvests compared with thy God, who is the God of
harvests? What are bursting granaries compared with
Him, who is the Husbandman, and feeds thee with the
bread of heaven? Some have their portion in the city;
their wealth is abundant, and flows to them in constant
streams, until they become a very reservoir of gold; but
what is gold compared with thy God? Thou couldst not
live on it; thy spiritual life could not be sustained by it.
Put it on a troubled conscience, and could it allay its
pangs? Apply it to a desponding heart, and see if it
could stay a solitary groan, or give one grief the less?
But thou hast God, and in Him thou hast more than gold
or riches ever could buy. Some have their portion in
that which most men love - applause and fame; but ask
thyself, is not thy God more to thee than that? What if
a myriad clarions should be loud in thine applause,
would this prepare thee to pass the Jordan, or cheer thee
in prospect of judgment? No, there are griefs in life
which wealth cannot alleviate; and there is the deep
need of a dying hour, for which no riches can provide.
But when thou hast *God* for thy portion, thou hast more
than all else put together. In Him every want is met,
whether in life or in death. With God for thy portion
thou art rich indeed, for He will supply thy need,
comfort thy heart, assuage thy grief, guide thy steps, be
with thee in the dark valley, and then take thee home,
to enjoy Him as thy portion for ever. 'I have enough,'
said Esau; this is the best thing a worldly man can say,
but Jacob replies, 'I have all things', which is a note too
high for carnal minds.

'Joint-heirs with Christ'
Romans 8:17

The boundless realms of His Father's universe are Christ's by prescriptive right. As 'heir of all things', He is the sole proprietor of the vast creation of God, and He has admitted us to claim the whole as ours, by virtue of that deed of joint-heirship which the Lord hath ratified with His chosen people. The golden streets of paradise, the pearly gates, the river of life, the transcendent bliss, and the unutterable glory, are, by our blessed Lord, made over to us for our everlasting possession. All that He has He shares with His people. The crown royal He has placed upon the head of His Church, appointing her a kingdom, and calling her sons a royal priesthood, a generation of priests and kings. He uncrowned Himself that we might have a coronation of glory; He would not sit upon his own throne until he had procured a place upon it for all who overcome by His blood. Crown the head and the whole body shares the honour. Behold here the reward of every Christian conqueror! Christ's throne, crown, sceptre, palace, treasure, robes, heritage, are yours. Far superior to the jealousy, selfishness, and greed, which admit of no participation of their advantages, Christ deems His happiness completed by his people sharing it. 'The glory which thou gavest me have I given them.' 'These things have I spoken unto you, that My joy might remain in you, and that your joy might be full.' The smiles of His Father are all the sweeter to Him, because His people share them. The honours of His kingdom are more pleasing, because His people appear with Him in glory. More valuable to Him are His conquests, since they have taught His people to overcome. He delights in His throne, because on it there is a place for them. He rejoices in His royal robes, since over them His skirts are spread. He delights the more in His joy, because He calls them to enter into it.

> '*He shall gather the lambs with His arm,*
> *and carry them in His bosom*'
> Isaiah 40:11

Who is He of whom such gracious words are spoken?
He is THE GOOD SHEPHERD. *Why* doth He carry the
lambs in His bosom? Because *He hath a tender heart,
and any weakness at once melts His hear*t. The sighs,
the ignorance, the feebleness of the little ones of His
flock draw forth His compassion. *It is His office*, as a
faithful High Priest, to consider the weak. Besides, *He
purchased them with blood, they are His property*: He
must and will care for *that* which cost Him so dear.
Then He is *responsible for each lamb*, bound by
covenant engagements not to lose one. Moreover, *they
are all a part of His glory and reward*.

But how may we understand the expression, 'He
will *carry* them'? Sometimes He carries them by *not
permitting them to endure much trial*. Providence deals
tenderly with them. Often they are 'carried' by being
filled with *an unusual degree of love*, so that they bear
up and stand fast. Though their knowledge may not be
deep, they have great sweetness in what they do know.
Frequently He 'carries' them by giving them *a very
simple faith*, which takes the promise just as it stands,
and believingly runs with every trouble straight to
Jesus. The simplicity of their faith gives them an
unusual degree of confidence, which carries them
above the world.

'He carries the lambs *in His bosom*.' Here is
boundless affection. Would He put them in His bosom
if He did not love them much? Here is *tender nearness*:
so near are they, that they could not possibly be nearer.
Here is *hallowed familiarity*: there are precious love-
passages between Christ and His weak ones. Here is
perfect safety: in His bosom who can hurt them? They
must hurt the Shepherd first. Here is *perfect rest and
sweetest comfort*. Surely we are not sufficiently sensible of the infinite tenderness of Jesus!

'All that believe are justified'
Acts 13:39

The believer in Christ receives a *present* justification.
Faith does not produce this fruit by-and-by, but *now*.
So far as justification is the result of faith, it is given
to the soul in the moment when it closes with Christ,
and accepts Him as its all in all. Are they who stand
before the throne of God justified now? - so are we, as
truly and as clearly justified as they who walk in white
and sing melodious praises to celestial harps. The thief
upon the cross was justified the moment that he turned
the eye of faith to Jesus; and Paul the aged, after years
of service, was not more justified than was the thief
with no service at all. We are *today* accepted in the
Beloved, *today* absolved from sin, *today* acquitted at
the bar of God. Oh! soul-transporting thought! There
are some clusters of Eshcol's vine which we shall not
be able to gather till we enter heaven; but this is a bough
which runneth over the wall. This is not as the corn of
the land, which we can never eat till we cross the
Jordan; but this is part of the manna in the wilderness,
a portion of our daily nutriment with which God
supplies us in our journeying to and fro. We are *now*
- even *now* pardoned; even *now* are our sins put away;
even *now* we stand in the sight of God accepted, as
though we had never been guilty. 'There is therefore
now no condemnation to them which are in Christ
Jesus.' There is not a sin in the Book of God, even *now*,
against one of His people. Who dareth to lay anything
to their charge? There is neither speck, nor spot, nor
wrinkle, nor any such thing remaining upon any one
believer in the matter of justification in the sight of the
Judge of all the earth. Let present privilege awaken us
to present duty, and now, while life lasts, let us spend
and be spent for our sweet Lord Jesus.

'Made perfect'
Hebrews 12:23

Recollect that there are two kinds of perfection which the Christian needs - the perfection of justification in the person of Jesus, and the perfection of sanctification wrought in him by the Holy Spirit. At present, corruption yet remains even in the breasts of the regenerate - experience soon teaches us this. Within us are still lusts and evil imaginations. But I rejoice to know that the day is coming when God shall finish the work which He has begun; and He shall present my soul, not only perfect in Christ, but perfect through the Spirit, without spot or blemish, or any such thing. Can it be true that this poor sinful heart of mine is to become holy even as God is holy? Can it be that this spirit, which often cries, 'O wretched man that I am! who shall deliver me from the body of this sin and death?' shall get rid of sin and death - that I shall have no evil things to vex my ears, and no unholy thoughts to disturb my peace? Oh, happy hour! may it be hastened! When I cross the Jordan, the work of sanctification will be finished; but not till that moment shall I even claim perfection in myself. Then my spirit shall have its last baptism in the Holy Spirit's fire. Methinks I long to die to receive that last and final purification which shall usher me into heaven. Not an angel more pure than I shall be, for I shall be able to say, in a double sense, 'I am clean', through Jesus' blood, and through the Spirit's work. Oh, how should we extol the power of the Holy Ghost in thus making us fit to stand before our father in heaven! Yet let not the hope of perfection hereafter make us content with imperfection now. If it does this, our hope cannot be genuine; for a good hope is a purifying thing, even now. The word of grace must be *abiding in us now* or it cannot be *perfected then*. Let us pray to 'be filled with the Spirit', that we may bring forth *increasingly* the fruits of righteousness.

'Who giveth us richly all things to enjoy'
1 Timothy 6:17

Our Lord Jesus is ever giving, and does not for a
solitary instant withdraw his hand. As long as there is
a vessel of grace not yet full to the brim, the oil shall
not be stayed. He is a sun ever-shining; He is manna
always falling round the camp; He is a rock in the
desert, ever sending out streams of life from his
smitten side; the rain of His grace is always dropping;
the river of His bounty is ever-flowing, and the well-
spring of his love is constantly overflowing. As the
King can never die, so His grace can never fail. Daily
we pluck His fruit, and daily His branches bend down
to our hand with a fresh store of mercy. There are seven
feast-days in His weeks, and as many as are the days,
so many are the banquets in His years. Who has ever
returned from His door unblessed? Who has ever risen
from His table unsatisfied, or from His bosom un-
emparadised? His mercies are new every morning and
fresh every evening. Who can know the number of His
benefits, or recount the list of His bounties? Every sand
which drops from the glass of time is but the tardy
follower of a myriad of mercies. The wings of our
hours are covered with the silver of His kindness, and
with the yellow gold of His affection. The river of time
bears from the mountains of eternity the golden sands
of His favour. The countless stars are but as the
standard bearers of a more innumerable host of blessings. Who can count the dust of the benefits which He
bestows on Jacob, or tell the number of the fourth part
of His mercies towards Israel? How shall my soul extol
Him who daily loadeth us with benefits, and who
crowneth us with loving-kindness? O that my praise
could be as ceaseless as His bounty! O miserable
tongue, how canst thou be silent? Wake up, I pray thee,
lest I call thee no more my glory, but my shame.
'Awake, psaltery and harp: I myself will awake right
early.'

*'And he said, Thus saith the Lord, Make this valley
full of ditches. For thus saith the Lord, Ye shall not
see wind, neither shall ye see rain; yet that valley
shall be filled with water, that ye may drink, both
ye, and your cattle, and your beasts'*
2 Kings 3:16, 17

The armies of the three kings were famishing for want
of water: God was about to send it, and in these words
the prophet announced the coming blessing. Here was
a case of human helplessness: not a drop of water could
all the valiant men procure from the skies or find in the
wells of earth. Thus often the people of the Lord are at
their wits' end; they see the vanity of the creature, and
learn experimentally where their help is to be found.
Still the people were to make *a believing preparation
for the divine blessing*; they were to dig the trenches in
which the precious liquid would be held. The church
must by her varied agencies, efforts, and prayers, make
herself ready to be blessed; she must make the pools,
and the Lord will fill them. This must be done in faith,
in the full assurance that the blessing is about to
descend. By-and-by there was *a singular bestowal of
the needed boon*. Not as in Elijah's case did the shower
pour from the clouds, but in a silent and mysterious
manner the pools were filled. The Lord has His own
sovereign modes of action: He is not tied to manner and
time as we are, but doeth as He pleases among the sons
of men. It is ours thankfully to receive from Him, and
not to dictate to Him. We must also notice *the remarkable abundance of the supply* - there was enough for the
need of all. And so it is in the gospel blessing; all the
wants of the congregation and of the entire church shall
be met by the divine power in answer to prayer; and
above all this, victory shall be speedily given to the
armies of the Lord.

What am I doing for Jesus? What trenches am I
digging? O Lord, make me ready to receive the blessing
which Thou art so willing to bestow.

'So to walk even as He walked'
1 John 2:6

Why should Christians imitate Christ? They should do it for *their own sakes*. If they desire to be in a healthy state of soul - if they would escape the sickness of sin, and enjoy the vigour of growing grace, let Jesus be their model. For their own happiness' sake, if they would drink wine on the lees, well refined; if they would enjoy holy and happy communion with Jesus; if they would be lifted up above the cares and troubles of this world, let them walk even as He walked. There is nothing which can so assist you to walk towards heaven with good speed, as wearing the image of Jesus on your heart to rule all its motions. It is when, by the power of the Holy Spirit, you are enabled to walk with Jesus in His very footsteps, that you are most happy, and most known to be the sons of God. Peter afar off is both unsafe and uneasy. Next, for *religion's sake*, strive to be like Jesus. Ah! poor religion, thou hast been sorely shot at by cruel foes, but thou hast not been wounded one-half so dangerously by thy foes as by thy friends. Who made those wounds in the fair hand of Godliness? The professor who used the dagger of hypocrisy. The man who with pretences, enters the fold, being nought but a wolf in sheep's clothing, worries the flock more than the lion outside. There is no weapon half so deadly as a Judas-kiss. Inconsistent professors injure the gospel more than the sneering critic or the infidel. But, especially for *Christ's own sake*, imitate His example. Christian, lovest thou thy Saviour? Is His name precious to thee? Is His cause dear to thee? Wouldst thou see the kingdoms of the world become His? Is it thy desire that He should be glorified? Art thou longing that souls should be won to Him? If so, *imitate* Jesus; be an 'epistle of Christ, known and read of all men'.

'Thou art My servant; I have chosen thee'
Isaiah 41:9

If we have received the grace of God in our hearts, its
practical effect has been to make us God's *servants*.
We may be unfaithful servants, we certainly are unprofitable ones, but yet, blessed be His name, we *are*
His servants, wearing His livery, feeding at His table,
and obeying His commands. We were once the servants of sin, but He who made us free has now taken us
into His family and taught us obedience to His will. We
do not serve our Master perfectly, but we would if we
could. As we hear God's voice saying unto us, 'Thou
art My servant', we can answer with David, 'I am thy
servant; Thou hast loosed my bonds'. But the Lord
calls us not only His *servants*, but His *chosen* ones - 'I
have chosen thee'. We have not chosen Him first, but
He hath chosen us. If we be God's servants, we were
not always so; to sovereign grace the change must be
ascribed. The eye of sovereignty singled us out, and the
voice of unchanging grace declared, 'I have loved thee
with an everlasting love'. Long ere time began or space
was created God had written upon His heart the names
of His elect people, had predestinated them to be
conformed unto the image of His Son, and ordained
them heirs of all the fulness of His love, His grace, and
His glory. What comfort is here! Has the Lord loved
us so long, and will He yet cast us away? He knew how
stiffnecked we should be; He understood that our
hearts were evil, and yet He made the choice. Ah! our
Saviour is no fickle lover. He doth not feel enchanted
for awhile with some gleams of beauty from His
church's eye, and then afterwards cast her off because
of her unfaithfulness. Nay, He married her in old
eternity; and it is written of Jehovah, 'He hateth putting
away'. The eternal choice is a bond upon *our* gratitude
and upon *His* faithfulness which neither can disown.

*'In Him dwelleth all the fulness of the Godhead
bodily. And ye are complete in Him'*
Colossians 2:9, 10

All the attributes of Christ, as God and man, are at our
disposal. All the fulness of the Godhead, whatever that
marvellous term may comprehend, is ours to make us
complete. He cannot endow us with the attributes of
Deity; but He has done all that can be done, for He has
made even His divine power and Godhead subservient
to our salvation. His omnipotence, omniscience, omni-
presence, immutability and infallibility, are all combined for our defence. Arise, believer, and behold the
Lord Jesus yoking the whole of His divine Godhead to
the chariot of salvation! How vast his grace, how firm
His faithfulness, how unswerving His immutability,
how infinite His power, how limitless His knowledge!
All these are by the Lord Jesus made the pillars of the
temple of salvation; and all, without diminution of their
infinity, are covenanted to us as our perpetual inheritance. The fathomless love of the Saviour's heart is
every drop of it ours; every sinew in the arm of might,
every jewel in the crown of majesty, the immensity of
divine knowledge, and the sternness of divine justice,
all are ours, and shall be employed for us. The whole
of Christ, in His adorable character as the Son of God,
is by Himself made over to us most richly to enjoy. His
wisdom is our direction, His knowledge our instruction, His power our protection, His justice our surety,
His love our comfort, His mercy our solace, and His
immutability our trust. He makes no reserve, but opens
the recesses of the Mount of God and bids us dig in its
mines for the hidden treasures. 'All, all, all are yours,'
saith He, 'be ye satisfied with favour and full of the
goodness of the Lord.' Oh! how sweet thus to behold
Jesus, and to call upon Him with the certain confidence
that in seeking the interposition of His love or power,
we are but asking for that which He has already
faithfully promised.

'*Afterward*'
Hebrews 12:11

How happy are tried Christians, *afterwards*. No calm more deep than that which succeeds a storm. Who has not rejoiced in clear shinings after rain? Victorious banquets are for well-exercised soldiers. After killing the lion, we eat the honey; after climbing the Hill Difficulty, we sit down in the arbour to rest; after traversing the Valley of Humiliation, after fighting with Apollyon, the shining one appears, with the healing branch from the tree of life. Our sorrows, like the passing keels of the vessels upon the sea, leave a silver line of holy light behind them 'afterwards'. It is peace, sweet, deep peace, which follows the horrible turmoil, which once reigned in our tormented, guilty souls. See, then, the happy estate of a Christian! He has his best things last, and he therefore in this world receives his worst things first. But even his worst things are 'afterward' good things, harsh ploughings yielding joyful harvests. Even now he grows rich by his losses, he rises by his falls, he lives by dying, and becomes full by being emptied; if, then, his grievous afflictions yield him so much peaceable fruit in this life, what shall be the full vintage of joy 'afterwards' in heaven? If His dark nights are as bright as the world's days, what shall his days be? If even his starlight is more splendid than the sun, what must his sunlight be? If he can sing in a dungeon, how sweetly will he sing in heaven! If he can praise the Lord in the fires, how will he extol Him before the eternal throne! If evil is good to him *now*, what will the overflowing goodness of God be to him *then*? Oh, blessed 'afterward'! Who would not be a Christian? Who would not bear the present cross for the crown which cometh afterwards? But herein is work for patience, for the rest is not for today, nor the triumph for the present, but 'afterward'. Wait, O soul, and let patience have her perfect work.

*'I have seen servants upon horses,
and princes walking as servants upon the earth'*
Ecclesiastes 10:7

Upstarts frequently usurp the highest places, while the truly great pine in obscurity. This is a riddle in providence whose solution will one day gladden the hearts of the upright; but it is so common a fact, that none of us should murmur if it should fall to our own lot. When our Lord was upon earth, although He is the Prince of the kings of the earth, yet He walked the footpath of weariness and service as the Servant of servants: what wonder is it if His followers, who are princes of the blood, should also be looked down upon as inferior and contemptible persons? The world is upside down, and therefore, the first are last and the last first. See how the servile sons of Satan lord it in the earth! What a high horse they ride! How they lift up their horn on high! Haman is in the court, while Mordecai sits in the gate; David wanders on the mountains, while Saul reigns in state; Elijah is complaining in the cave while Jezebel is boasting in the palace; yet who would wish to take the places of the proud rebels? and who, on the other hand, might not envy the despised saints? When the wheel turns, those who are lowest rise, and the highest sink. Patience, then, believer, eternity will right the wrongs of time.

Let us not fall into the error of letting our passions and carnal appetites ride in triumph, while our nobler powers walk in the dust. Grace must reign as a prince, and make the members of the body instruments of righteousness. The Holy Spirit loves order, and He therefore sets our powers and faculties in due rank and place, giving the highest room to those spiritual faculties which link us with the great King; let us not disturb the divine arrangement, but ask for grace that we may keep under our body and bring it into subjection. We were not new created to allow our passions to rule over us, but that we, as kings, may reign in Christ Jesus over the triple kingdom of our spirit, soul, and body, to the glory of God the Father.

'And he requested for himself that he might die'
1 Kings 19:4

It was a remarkable thing that the man who was never to die, for whom God had ordained an infinitely better lot, the man who should be carried to heaven in a chariot of fire, and be translated, that he should not see death - should thus pray, 'Let me die; I am no better than my fathers'. We have here a memorable proof that God does not always answer prayer in kind, though He always does in effect. He gave Elias something better than that which he asked for, and thus really heard and answered him. Strange was it that the lion-hearted Elijah should be so depressed by Jezebel's threat as to ask to die, and blessedly kind was it on the part of our heavenly Father that he did not take his desponding servant at his word. There is a limit to the doctrine of the prayer of faith. We are not to expect that God will give us everything we choose to ask for. We know that we sometimes ask, and do not receive, because we ask amiss. If we ask for that which is not promised - if we run counter to the spirit which the Lord would have us cultivate - if we ask contrary to His will, or to the decrees of His providence - if we ask merely for the gratification of our own ease, and without an eye to His glory, we must not expect that we shall receive. Yet, when we ask in faith, nothing doubting, if we receive not the precise thing asked for, we shall receive an equivalent, and more than an equivalent, for it. As one remarks, 'If the Lord does not pay in silver, He will in gold; and if He does not pay in gold, He will in diamonds'. If He does not give you precisely what you ask for, He will give you that which is tantamount to it, and that which you will greatly rejoice to receive in lieu thereof. Be then, dear reader, much in prayer, and make this evening a season of earnest intercession, but take heed what you ask.

'Marvellous lovingkindness'
Psalm 17:7

When we give our hearts with our alms, we give well, but we must often plead to a failure in this respect. Not so our Master and our Lord. His favours are always performed with the love of His heart. He does not send to us the cold meat and the broken pieces from the table of His luxury, but He dips our morsel in His own dish, and seasons our provisions with the spices of His fragrant affections. When he puts the golden tokens of His grace into our palms, he accompanies the gift with such a warm pressure of our hand, that the manner of His giving is as precious as the boon itself. He will come into our houses upon His errands of kindness, and He will not act as some austere visitors do in the poor man's cottage, but He sits by our side, not despising our poverty, nor blaming our weakness. Beloved, with what smiles does he speak! What golden sentences drop from His gracious lips! What embraces of affection does He bestow upon us! If He had but given us farthings, the way of His giving would have gilded them; but as it is, the costly alms are set in a golden basket by His pleasant carriage. It is impossible to doubt the sincerity of His charity, for there is a bleeding heart stamped upon the face of all His benefactions. He giveth liberally and upbraideth not. Not one hint that we are burdensome to Him; not one cold look for His poor pensioners; but He rejoices in His mercy, and presses us to His bosom while He is pouring out His life for us. There is a fragrance in His spikenard which nothing but His heart could produce; there is a sweetness in His honeycomb which could not be in it unless the very essence of His soul's affection had been mingled with it. Oh! the rare communion which such singular heartiness effecteth! May we continually taste and know the blessedness of it!

> '*I drew them with cords of a man,*
> *with bands of love*'
> Hosea 11:4

Our heavenly Father often draws us with the cords of love; but ah! how backward we are to run towards Him! How slowly do we respond to His gentle impulses! *He draws us to exercise a more simple faith in Him*; but we have not yet attained to Abraham's confidence; we do not leave our worldly cares with God, but, like Martha, we cumber ourselves with much serving. Our meagre faith brings leanness into our souls; we do not open our mouths wide, though God has promised to fill them. Does He not this evening draw us to trust Him? Can we not hear Him say, 'Come, My child, and trust Me. The veil is rent; enter into My presence, and approach boldly to the throne of My grace. I am worthy of thy fullest confidence, cast thy cares on Me. Shake thyself from the dust of thy cares, and put on thy beautiful garments of joy.' But, alas! though called with tones of love to the blessed exercise of this comforting grace, we will not come. At another time *He draws us to closer communion with Himself.* We have been sitting on the doorstep of God's house, and He bids us advance into the banqueting hall and sup with Him, but we decline the honour. There are secret rooms not yet opened to us; Jesus invites us to enter them, but we hold back. Shame on our cold hearts! We are but poor lovers of our sweet Lord Jesus, not fit to be His servants, much less to be His brides, and yet He hath exalted us to be bone of His bone and flesh of His flesh, married to Him by a glorious marriage-covenant. Herein is love! But it is love which *takes no denial.* If we obey not the gentle drawings of His love, he will send affliction to drive us into closer intimacy with Himself. Have us nearer He will. What foolish children we are to refuse those bands of love, and so bring upon our backs that scourge of small cords, which Jesus knows how to use!

'If so be ye have tasted that the Lord is gracious'
1 Peter 2:3

If - then this is not a matter to be taken for granted concerning every one of the human race. 'If' - then there is a possibility and a probability that some may not have tasted that the Lord is gracious. 'If' - then this is not a general but a special mercy; and it is needful to enquire whether we know the grace of God by inward experience. There is no spiritual favour which may not be a matter for heart-searching.

But while this should be a matter of earnest and prayerful inquiry, no one ought to be content whilst there is any such thing as an 'if' about his having tasted that the Lord is gracious. A jealous and holy distrust of self may give rise to the question even in the believer's heart, but the *continuance* of such a doubt would be an evil indeed. We must not rest without a desperate struggle to clasp the Saviour in the arms of faith, and say, 'I know whom I have believed, and I am persuaded that he is able to keep that which I have committed unto him'. Do not rest, O believer, till thou hast a full assurance of thine interest in Jesus. Let nothing satisfy thee till, by the infallible witness of the Holy Spirit bearing witness with thy spirit, thou art certified that thou art a child of God. Oh, trifle not here; let no 'perhaps' and 'peradventure', and 'if', and 'may be', satisfy thy soul. Build on eternal verities, and verily build upon them. Get the sure mercies of David, and surely get them. Let thine anchor be cast into that which is within the veil, and see to it that thy soul be linked to the anchor by a cable that will not break. Advance beyond these dreary 'ifs'; abide no more in the wilderness of doubts and fears; cross the Jordan of distrust, and enter the Canaan of peace, where the Canaanite still lingers, but where the land ceaseth not to flow with milk and honey.

'There is corn in Egypt'
Genesis 42:2

Famine pinched all the nations, and it seemed inevitable that Jacob and his family should suffer great want; but the God of providence, who never forgets the objects of electing love, had stored a granary for His people by giving the Egyptians warning of the scarcity, and leading them to treasure up the grain of the years of plenty. Little did Jacob expect deliverance from Egypt, but there was the corn in store for him. Believer, though all things are apparently against thee, rest assured that God has made a reservation on thy behalf; in the roll of thy griefs there is a saving clause. Somehow He will deliver thee, and somewhere He will provide for thee. The quarter from which thy rescue shall arise may be a very unexpected one, but help will assuredly come in thine extremity, and thou shalt magnify the name of the Lord. If men do not feed thee, ravens shall; and if earth yield not wheat, heaven shall drop with manna. Therefore be of good courage, and rest quietly in the Lord. God can make the sun rise in the west if He pleases, and make the source of distress the channel of delight. The corn in Egypt was all in the hands of the beloved Joseph; he opened or closed the granaries at will. And so the riches of providence are all in the absolute power of our Lord Jesus, who will dispense them liberally to His people. Joseph was abundantly ready to succour his own family; and Jesus is unceasing in His faithful care for His brethren. Our business is to go after the help which is provided for us: we must not sit still in despondency, but bestir ourselves. Prayer will bear us soon into the presence of our royal Brother: once before His throne we have only to ask and have: His stores are not exhausted, there is corn still: His heart is not hard, He will give the corn to us. Lord, forgive our unbelief, and this evening constrain us to draw largely from Thy fulness and receive grace for grace.

'He led them forth by the right way'
Psalm 107:7

Changeful experience often leads the anxious believer
to enquire 'Why is it thus with me?' I looked for light,
but lo, darkness came; for peace, but behold trouble. I
said in my heart, my mountain standeth firm, I shall
never be moved. Lord, thou dost hide Thy face, and I
am troubled. It was but yesterday that I could read my
title clear; today my evidences are bedimmed, and my
hopes are clouded. Yesterday I could climb to Pisgah's
top, and view the landscape o'er, and rejoice with
confidence in my future inheritance; today, my spirit
has no hopes, but many fears; no joys, but much
distress. Is this part of God's plan with me? Can this
be the way in which God would bring me to heaven?
Yes, it is even so. The eclipse of your faith, the
darkness of your mind, the fainting of your hope, all
these things are but parts of God's method of making
you ripe for the great inheritance upon which you shall
soon enter. These trials are for the testing and strengthening of your faith - they are waves that wash you
further upon the rock - they are winds which waft your
ship the more swiftly towards the desired haven.
According to David's words, so it might be said of you,
'so He bringeth them to their desired haven'. By
honour and dishonour, by evil report and by good
report, by plenty and by poverty, by joy and by distress,
by persecution and by peace, by all these things is the
life of your soul maintained, and by each of these are
you helped on your way. Oh, think not, believer, that
your sorrows are out of God's plan; they are necessary
parts of it. 'We must, through much tribulation, enter
the kingdom.' Learn, then, even to 'count it all joy
when ye fall into divers temptations'.

> 'O let my trembling soul be still,
> And wait Thy wise, Thy holy will!
> I cannot, Lord, Thy purpose see,
> Yet all is well since ruled by Thee.'

'Behold, Thou art fair, my Beloved'
Canticles 1:16

From every point our Well-beloved is most fair. Our various experiences are meant by our heavenly Father to furnish fresh standpoints from which we may view the loveliness of Jesus; how amiable are our trials when they carry us aloft where we may gain clearer views of Jesus than ordinary life could afford us! We have seen Him from the top of Amana, from the top of Shenir and Hermon, and He has shone upon us as the sun in his strength; but we have seen Him also 'from the lions' dens, from the mountains of the leopards', and He has lost none of His loveliness. From the languishing of a sick bed, from the borders of the grave, have we turned our eyes to our soul's spouse, and He has never been otherwise than 'all fair'. Many of His saints have looked upon Him from the gloom of dungeons, and from the red flames of the stake, yet have they never uttered an ill word of Him, but have died extolling His surpassing charms. Oh, noble and pleasant employment to be for ever gazing at our sweet Lord Jesus! Is it not unspeakably delightful to view the Saviour in all His offices, and to perceive Him matchless in each? - to shift the kaleidoscope, as it were, and to find fresh combinations of peerless graces? In the manger and in eternity, on the cross and on His throne, in the garden and in His kingdom, among thieves or in the midst of cherubim, He is everywhere 'altogether lovely'. Examine carefully every little act of His life, and every trait of His character, and He is as lovely in the minute as in the majestic. Judge Him as you will, you cannot censure; weigh Him as you please, and He will not be found wanting. Eternity shall not discover the shadow of a spot in our Beloved, but rather, as ages revolve, His hidden glories shall shine forth with yet more inconceivable splendour, and His unutterable loveliness shall more and more ravish all celestial minds.

'The Lord will perfect that which concerneth me'
Psalm 138:8

Most manifestly the confidence which the Psalmist here expressed was a *divine confidence*. He did not say, *'I* have grace enough to perfect that which concerneth me - my faith is so steady that it will not stagger - my love is so warm that it will never grow cold - my resolution is so firm that nothing can move it;' no, his dependence was on the Lord alone. If we indulge in any confidence which is not grounded on the Rock of ages, our confidence is worse than a dream, it will fall upon us, and cover us with its ruins, to our sorrow and confusion. All that Nature spins time will unravel, to the eternal confusion of all who are clothed therein. The Psalmist was wise, he rested upon nothing short of the *Lord*'s work. It is the Lord who has begun the good work within us; it is He who has carried it on; and if he does not finish it, it never will be complete. If there be one stitch in the celestial garment of our righteousness which we are to insert ourselves, then we are lost; but this is our confidence, the Lord who began will perfect. He *has* done it all, *must* do it all, and *will* do it all. Our confidence must not be in what we have done, nor in what we have resolved to do, but entirely in what *the Lord* will do. Unbelief insinuates - 'You will never be able to stand. Look at the evil of your heart, you can never conquer sin; remember the sinful pleasures and temptations of the world that beset you, you will be certainly allured by them and led astray.' Ah! yes, we should indeed perish if left to our own strength. If we had alone to navigate our frail vessels over so rough a sea, we might well give up the voyage in despair; but, thanks be to God, He will perfect that which concerneth us, and bring us to the desired haven. We can never be too confident when we confide in Him alone, and never too much concerned to *have such* a trust.

'Thou hast bought me no sweet cane with money'
Isaiah 43:24

Worshippers at the temple were wont to bring presents
of sweet perfumes to be burned upon the altar of God:
but Israel, in the time of her backsliding, became
ungenerous, and made but few votive offerings to her
Lord; this was an evidence of coldness of heart towards
God and His house. Reader, does this never occur with
you? Might not the complaint of the text be occasionally, if not frequently, brought against you? Those who
are poor in pocket, if rich in faith, will be accepted none
the less because their gifts are small; but, poor reader,
do you give in fair proportion to the Lord, or is the
widow's mite kept back from the sacred treasury? The
rich believer should be thankful for the talent entrusted
to him, but should not forget his large responsibility,
for where much is given much will be required; but,
rich reader, are you mindful of your obligations, and
rendering to the Lord according to the benefit received?
Jesus gave His blood for us, what shall we give to Him?
We are His, and all that we have, for He has purchased
us unto Himself - can we act as if we were our own? O
for more consecration! and to this end, O for more
love! Blessed Jesus, how good it is of Thee to accept
our sweet cane bought with money! nothing is too
costly as a tribute to Thine unrivalled love, and yet
Thou dost receive with favour the smallest sincere
token of affection! Thou dost receive our poor forget-
me-nots and love-tokens as though they were intrinsi-
cally precious, though indeed they are but as the bunch
of wild flowers which the child brings to its mother.
Never may we grow niggardly towards Thee, and from
this hour never may we hear Thee complain of us again
for withholding the gifts of our love. We will give Thee
the first fruits of our increase, and pay Thee tithes of
all, and then we will confess 'of Thine own have we
given Thee'.

'Blessed be God,
which hath not turned away my prayer'
Psalm 66:20

In looking back upon the character of our prayers, if we do it honestly, we shall be filled with wonder that God has ever answered them. There may be some who think their prayers worthy of acceptance - as the Pharisee did; but the true Christian, in a more enlightened retrospect, weeps over his prayers, and if he could retrace his steps he would desire to pray more earnestly. Remember, Christian, how *cold* thy prayers have been. When in thy closet thou shouldst have wrestled as Jacob did; but instead thereof, thy petitions have been faint and few - far removed from that humble, believing, persevering faith, which cries, 'I will not let Thee go except Thou bless me'. Yet, wonderful to say, God has heard these cold prayers of thine, and not only heard, but answered them. Reflect also, how *unfrequent* have been thy prayers, unless thou hast been in trouble, and *then* thou hast gone often to the mercy-seat: but when deliverance has come, where has been thy constant supplication? Yet, notwithstanding thou hast ceased to pray as once thou didst, God has not ceased to bless. When thou hast neglected the mercy-seat, God has not deserted it, but the bright light of the Shekinah has always been visible between the wings of the cherubim. Oh! it is marvellous that the Lord should regard those intermittent spasms of importunity which come and go with our necessities. What a God is He thus to hear the prayers of those who come to Him when they have pressing wants, but neglect Him when they have received a mercy; who approach Him when they are forced to come, but who almost forget to address Him when mercies are plentiful and sorrows are few. Let His gracious kindness in hearing such prayers touch our hearts, so that we may henceforth be found 'Praying always with all prayer and supplication in the Spirit'.

*'Only let your conversation be as it
becometh the gospel of Christ'*
Philippians 1:27

The word 'conversation' does not merely mean our talk
and converse with one another, but the whole course of
our life and behaviour in the world. The Greek word
signifies the actions and the privileges of citizenship:
and thus we are commanded to let our actions, as
citizens of the New Jerusalem, be such as becometh the
gospel of Christ. What sort of conversation is this? In
the first place, *the gospel is very simple*. So Christians
should be simple and plain in their habits. There should
be about our manner, our speech, our dress, our whole
behaviour, that simplicity which is the very soul of
beauty. The gospel is *pre-eminently true*, it is gold
without dross; and the Christian's life will be lustre-
less and valueless without the jewel of truth. The
gospel is a very *fearless gospel*, it boldly proclaims the
truth, whether men like it or not: we must be equally
faithful and unflinching. But the gospel is also *very
gentle*. Mark this spirit in its Founder: 'a bruised reed
He will not break'. Some professors are sharper than
a thorn-hedge; such men are not like Jesus. Let us seek
to win others by the gentleness of our words and acts.
The gospel is *very loving*. It is the message of the God
of love to a lost and fallen race. Christ's last command
to His disciples was, 'Love one another'. O for more
real, hearty union and love to all the saints; for more
tender compassion towards the souls of the worst and
vilest of men! We must not forget that the gospel of
Christ is *holy*. It never excuses sin: it pardons it, but
only through an atonement. If our life is to resemble the
gospel, we must shun, not merely the grosser vices, but
everything that would hinder our perfect conformity to
Christ. For His sake, for our own sakes, and for the
sake of others, we must strive day by day to let our
conversation be more in accordance with His gospel.

'Forsake me not, O Lord'
Psalm 38:21

Frequently we pray that God would not forsake us in the hour of trial and temptation, but we too much forget that we have need to use this prayer *at all times*. There is no moment of our life, however holy, in which we can do without His constant upholding. Whether in light or in darkness, in communion or in temptation, we alike need the prayer, 'Forsake me not, O Lord'. 'Hold Thou me up, and I shall be safe.' A little child, while learning to walk, always needs the nurse's aid. The ship left by the pilot drifts at once from her course. We cannot do without continued aid from above; let it then be your prayer today, 'Forsake me not. Father, forsake not Thy child, lest he fall by the hand of the enemy. Shepherd, forsake not Thy lamb, lest he wander from the safety of the fold. Great Husbandman, forsake not Thy plant, lest it wither and die. "Forsake me not, O Lord", now; and forsake me not at any moment of my life. Forsake me not in my joys, lest they absorb my heart. Forsake me not in my sorrows, lest I murmur against Thee. Forsake me not in the day of my repentance, lest I lose the hope of pardon, and fall into despair; and forsake me not in the day of my strongest faith, lest faith degenerate into presumption. Forsake me not, for without Thee I am weak, but with Thee I am strong. Forsake me not, for my path is dangerous, and full of snares, and I cannot do without thy guidance. The hen forsakes not her brood, do Thou then evermore cover me with Thy feathers, and permit me under Thy wings to find my refuge. "Be not far from me, O Lord, for trouble is near, for there is none to help." "Leave me not, neither forsake me, O God of my salvation!"'

> 'O ever in our cleansed breast,
> Bid Thine Eternal Spirit rest;
> And make our secret soul to be
> A temple pure and worthy Thee.'

*'And they rose up the same hour, and returned to
Jerusalem... and they told what things were done in
the way, and how He was known of them'*
Luke 24:33, 35

When the two disciples had reached Emmaus, and were
refreshing themselves at the evening meal, the mysterious stranger who had so enchanted them upon the
road, took bread and brake it, made Himself known to
them, and then vanished out of their sight. They had
constrained Him to abide with them, because the day
was far spent; but now, although it was much later,
their love was a lamp to their feet, yea, wings also; they
forgot the darkness, their weariness was all gone, and
forthwith they journeyed back the threescore furlongs
to tell the gladsome news of a risen Lord, who had
appeared to them by the way. They reached the Christians in Jerusalem, and were received by a burst of
joyful news before they could tell their own tale. These
early Christians were all on fire to speak of Christ's
resurrection, and to proclaim what they knew of the
Lord; they made common property of their experiences. This evening let their example impress us
deeply. We too must bear our witness concerning
Jesus. John's account of the sepulchre needed to be
supplemented by Peter; and Mary could speak of
something further still; combined, we have a full
testimony from which nothing can be spared. We have
each of us peculiar gifts and special manifestations; but
the one object God has in view is the perfecting of the
whole body of Christ. We must, therefore, bring our
spiritual possessions and lay them at the apostles' feet,
and make distribution unto all of what God has given
to us. Keep back no part of the precious truth, but speak
what you know, and testify what you have seen. Let not
the toil or darkness, or possible unbelief of your
friends, weigh one moment in the scale. Up, and be
marching to the place of duty, and there tell what great
things God has shown to your soul.

'Cast thy burden upon the Lord,
and He shall sustain thee'
Psalm 55:22

Care, even though exercised upon legitimate objects, if carried to excess, has in it the nature of sin. The precept to avoid anxious care is earnestly inculcated by our Saviour, again and again; it is reiterated by the apostles; and it is one which cannot be neglected without involving transgression: for the very essence of anxious care is the imagining that we are wiser than God, and the thrusting ourselves into His place to do for Him that which He has undertaken to do for us. We attempt to think of that which we fancy He will forget; we labour to take upon ourselves our weary burden, as if He were unable or unwilling to take it for us. Now this disobedience to His plain precept, this unbelief in His Word, this presumption in intruding upon His province, is all sinful. Yet more than this, anxious care often leads to acts of sin. He who cannot calmly leave his affairs in God's hand, but will carry his own burden, is very likely to be tempted to use wrong means to help himself. This sin leads to a forsaking of God as our counsellor, and resorting instead to human wisdom. This is going to the 'broken cistern' instead of to the 'fountain'; a sin which was laid against Israel of old. Anxiety makes us doubt God's lovingkindness, and thus our love to Him grows cold; we feel mistrust, and thus grieve the Spirit of God, so that our prayers become hindered, our consistent example marred, and our life one of self-seeking. Thus want of confidence in God leads us to wander far from Him; but if through simple faith in His promise, we cast each burden as it comes upon Him, and are 'careful for nothing' because He undertakes to care for us, it will keep us close to Him, and strengthen us against much temptation. 'Thou wilt keep him in perfect peace whose mind is stayed on Thee, because he trusteth in Thee.'

'*Continue in the faith*'
Acts 14:22

Perseverance is the badge of true saints. The Christian life is not a *beginning* only in the ways of God, but also a *continuance* in the same as long as life lasts. It is with a Christian as it was with the great Napoleon: he said, 'Conquest has made me what I am, and conquest must maintain me'. So, under God, dear brother in the Lord, conquest has made you what you are, and conquest must sustain you. Your motto must be, 'Excelsior'. He only is a true conqueror, and shall be crowned at the last, who continueth till war's trumpet is blown no more. Perseverance is, therefore, the target of all our spiritual enemies. The *world* does not object to your being a Christian for a time, if she can but tempt you to cease your pilgrimage, and settle down to buy and sell with her in Vanity Fair. The *flesh* will seek to ensnare you, and to prevent your pressing on to glory. 'It is weary work being a pilgrim; come, give it up. Am I always to be mortified? Am I never to be indulged? Give me at least a furlough from this constant warfare.' *Satan* will make many a fierce attack on your perseverance; it will be the mark for all his arrows. He will strive to hinder you *in service*: he will insinuate that you are doing no good; and that you want rest. He will endeavour to make you weary of *suffering*, He will whisper, 'Curse God, and die'. Or he will attack your *steadfastness*; 'What is the good of being so zealous? Be quiet like the rest; sleep as do others, and let your lamp go out as the other virgins do.' Or he will assail your *doctrinal sentiments*: 'Why do you hold to these denominational creeds? Sensible men are getting more liberal; they are removing the old landmarks: fall in with the times.' Wear your shield, Christian, therefore, close upon your armour, and cry mightily unto God, that by His Spirit you may endure to the end.

'*So Mephibosheth dwelt in Jerusalem:
for he did eat continually at the king's table;
and was lame on both his feet*'

2 Samuel 9:13

Mephibosheth was no great ornament to a royal table,
yet he had a continual place at David's board, because
the king could see in his face the features of the beloved
Jonathan. Like Mephibosheth, we may cry unto the
King of Glory, 'What is Thy servant, that Thou
shouldst look upon such a dead dog as I am?', but still
the Lord indulges us with most familiar intercourse
with Himself, because He sees in our countenances the
remembrance of His dearly-beloved Jesus. The Lord's
people are *dear for another's sake.* Such is the love
which the Father bears to His only begotten, that for
His sake He raises His lowly brethren from poverty and
banishment, to courtly companionship, noble rank, and
royal provision. Their *deformity shall not rob them of
their privileges.* Lameness is no bar to sonship; the
cripple is as much the heir as if he could run like
Asahel. Our right does not limp, though our might
may. A king's table is a noble hiding place for lame
legs, and at the gospel feast we learn to glory in
infirmities, because the power of Christ resteth upon
us. Yet grievous *disability may mar the persons of the
best-loved saints.* Here is one feasted by David, and yet
so lame in both his feet that he could not go up with the
king when he fled from the city, and was therefore
maligned and injured by his servant Ziba. Saints whose
faith is weak, and whose knowledge is slender, are
great losers; they are exposed to many enemies, and
cannot follow the king whithersoever he goeth. This
disease frequently arises from falls. Bad nursing in
their spiritual infancy often causes converts to fall into
a despondency from which they never recover, and sin
in other cases brings broken bones. Lord, help the lame
to leap like an hart, and satisfy all Thy people with the
bread of Thy table!

*'What is thy servant, that thou shouldest look upon
such a dead dog as I am?'*
2 Samuel 9:8

If Mephibosheth was thus humbled by David's kindness, what shall we be in the presence of our gracious
Lord? The more grace we have, the less we shall think
of ourselves, for grace, like light, reveals our impurity.
Eminent saints have scarcely known to what to compare themselves, their sense of unworthiness has been
so clear and keen. 'I am,' says holy Rutherford, 'a dry
and withered branch, a piece of dead carcass, dry
bones, and not able to step over a straw.' In another
place he writes, 'Except as to open outbreakings, I want
nothing of what Judas and Cain had'. The meanest
objects in nature appear to the humbled mind to have a
preference above itself, because they have never contracted sin: a dog may be greedy, fierce, or filthy, but
it has no conscience to violate, no Holy Spirit to resist.
A dog may be a worthless animal, and yet by a little
kindness it is soon won to love its master, and is
faithful unto death; but we forget the goodness of the
Lord, and follow not at His call. The term 'dead dog'
is the most expressive of all terms of contempt, but it
is none too strong to express the self-abhorrence of
instructed believers. They do not affect mock modesty,
they mean what they say, they have weighed themselves in the balances of the sanctuary, and found out
the vanity of their nature. At best, we are but clay,
animated dust, mere walking hillocks; but viewed as
sinners, we are monsters indeed. Let it be published in
heaven as a wonder, that the Lord Jesus should set His
heart's love upon such as we are. Dust and ashes
though we be, we must and will 'magnify the exceeding
greatness of his grace'. Could not His heart find rest in
heaven? Must He needs come to these tents of Kedar
for a spouse, and choose a bride upon whom the sun had
looked? O heavens and earth, break forth into a song,
and give all glory to our sweet Lord Jesus.

'Whom He justified, them He also glorified'
Romans 8:30

Here is a precious truth for thee, believer. Thou mayest be poor, or in suffering, or unknown, but for thine encouragement take a review of thy 'calling' and the consequences that flow from it, and especially that blessed result here spoken of. As surely as thou art God's child today, so surely shall all thy trials soon be at an end, and thou shalt be rich to all the intents of bliss. Wait awhile, and that weary head shall wear the crown of glory, and that hand of labour shall grasp the palm branch of victory. Lament not thy troubles, but rather rejoice that ere long thou wilt be where 'there shall be neither sorrow, nor crying, neither shall there be any more pain'. The chariots of fire are at thy door, and a moment will suffice to bear thee to the glorified. The everlasting song is almost on thy lip. The portals of heaven stand open for thee. Think not that thou canst fail of entering into rest. If He hath called thee, nothing can divide thee from His love. Distress cannot sever the bond; the fire of persecution cannot burn the link; the hammer of hell cannot break the chain. Thou art secure; that voice which called thee at first, shall call thee yet again from earth to heaven, from death's dark gloom to immortality's unuttered splendours. Rest assured, the heart of Him who has justified thee beats with infinite love towards thee. Thou shalt soon be with the glorified, where thy portion is; thou art only waiting here to be made meet for the inheritance, and that done, the wings of angels shall waft thee far away, to the mount of peace, and joy, and blessedness, where,

'Far from a world of grief and sin,
  With God eternally shut in',

thou shalt rest for ever and ever.

'This I recall to my mind, therefore have I hope'
Lamentations 3:21

Memory is frequently the bondslave of despondency. Despairing minds call to remembrance every dark foreboding in the past, and dilate upon every gloomy feature in the present; thus memory, clothed in sackcloth, presents to the mind a cup of mingled gall and wormwood. There is, however, no necessity for this. Wisdom can readily transform memory into an angel of comfort. That same recollection which in its left hand brings so many gloomy omens, may be trained to bear in its right a wealth of hopeful signs. She need not wear a crown of iron, she may encircle her brow with a fillet of gold, all spangled with stars. Thus it was in Jeremiah's experience: in the previous verse memory had brought him to deep humiliation of soul: 'My soul hath them still in remembrance, and is humbled in me'; and now this same memory restored him to life and comfort. 'This I recall to my mind, therefore have I hope.' Like a two-edged sword, his memory first killed his pride with one edge, and then slew his despair with the other. As a general principle, if we would exercise our memories more wisely, we might, in our very darkest distress, strike a match which would instantaneously kindle the lamp of comfort. There is no need for God to create a new thing upon the earth in order to restore believers to joy; if they would prayerfully rake the ashes of the past, they would find light for the present; and if they would turn to the book of truth and the throne of grace, their candle would soon shine as aforetime. Be it ours to remember the lovingkindness of the Lord, and to rehearse His deeds of grace. Let us open the volume of recollection which is so richly illuminated with memorials of mercy, and we shall soon be happy. Thus memory may be, as Coleridge calls it, 'the bosom-spring of joy', and when the Divine Comforter bends it to His service, it may be chief among earthly comforters.

'Thou hatest wickedness'
Psalm 45:7

'Be ye angry, and sin not.' There can hardly be
goodness in a man if he be not angry at sin; he who
loves truth must hate every false way. How our Lord
Jesus hated it when the temptation came! Thrice it
assailed Him in different forms, but ever He met it
with, 'Get thee behind me, Satan'. He hated it in others;
none the less fervently because He showed His hate
oftener in tears of pity than in words of rebuke; yet what
language could be more stern, more Elijah-like, than
the words, 'Woe unto you, scribes and Pharisees,
hypocrites! for ye devour widows' houses, and for a
pretence make long prayer'. He hated wickedness so
much that He bled to wound it to the heart; He died that
it might die; He was buried that He might bury it in his
tomb; and He rose that He might for ever trample it
beneath His feet. Christ is in the Gospel, and that
Gospel is opposed to wickedness in every shape.
Wickedness arrays itself in fair garments, and imitates
the language of holiness; but the precepts of Jesus, like
His famous scourge of small cords, chase it out of the
temple, and will not tolerate it in the Church. So, too,
in the heart where Jesus reigns, what war there is
between Christ and Belial! And when our Redeemer
shall come to be our Judge, those thundering words,
'Depart, ye cursed', which are, indeed, but a prolonga-
tion of His life-teaching concerning sin, shall manifest
His abhorrence of iniquity. As warm as is His love to
sinners, so hot is His hatred of sin; as perfect as is His
righteousness, so complete shall be the destruction of
every form of wickedness. O thou glorious champion
of right, and destroyer of wrong, for this cause hath
God, even Thy God, anointed thee with the oil of
gladness above Thy fellows.

> *'Cursed be the man before the Lord,*
> *that riseth up and buildeth this city Jericho'*
> Joshua 6:26.

Since he was cursed who rebuilt Jericho, much more the man who labours to restore Popery among us. In our fathers' days the gigantic walls of Popery fell by the power of their faith, the perseverance of their efforts, and the blast of their gospel trumpets; and now there are some who would rebuild that accursed system upon its old foundations. O Lord, be pleased to thwart their unrighteous endeavours, and pull down every stone which they build. It should be a serious business with us to be thoroughly purged of every error which may have a tendency to foster the spirit of Popery, and when we have made a clean sweep at home we should seek in every way to oppose its all too rapid spread abroad in the church and in the world. This last can be done in secret by fervent prayer, and in public by decided testimony. We must warn with judicious boldness those who are inclined towards the errors of Rome; we must instruct the young in gospel truth, and tell them of the black doings of Popery in the olden times. We must aid in spreading the light more thoroughly through the land, for priests, like owls, hate daylight. Are we doing all we can for Jesus and the gospel? If not, our negligence plays into the hands of priestcraft. What are we doing to spread the Bible, which is the Pope's bane and poison? Are we casting abroad good, sound gospel writings? Luther once said, 'The devil hates goose quills', and, doubtless, he has good reason, for ready writers, by the Holy Spirit's blessing, have done his kingdom much damage. If the thousands who will read this short word this night will do all they can to hinder the rebuilding of this accursed Jericho, the Lord's glory shall speed among the sons of men. Reader, what can you do? What will you do?

*'Take us the foxes,
the little foxes, that spoil the vines'*
Canticles 2:15

A little thorn may cause much suffering. A little cloud may hide the sun. Little foxes spoil the vines; and little sins do mischief to the tender heart. These little sins burrow in the soul, and make it so full of that which is hateful to Christ, that He will hold no comfortable fellowship and communion with us. A great sin cannot destroy a Christian, but a little sin can make him miserable. Jesus will not walk with his people unless they drive out every known sin. He says, 'If ye keep My commandments, ye shall abide in My love, even as I have kept My father's commandments and abide in His love'. Some Christians very seldom enjoy their Saviour's presence. How is this? Surely it must be an affliction for a tender child to be separated from his father. Art thou a child of God, and yet satisfied to go on without seeing thy Father's face? What! thou the spouse of Christ, and yet content without His company! Surely, thou hast fallen into a sad state, for the chaste spouse of Christ mourns like a dove without her mate, when he has left her. Ask, then, the question, what has driven Christ from thee? He hides His face behind the wall of thy sins. That wall may be built up of *little* pebbles, as easily as of great stones. The sea is made of drops; the rocks are made of grains: and the sea which divides thee from Christ may be filled with the drops of thy little sins; and the rock which has well nigh wrecked thy barque, may have been made by the daily working of the coral insects of thy little sins. If thou wouldst live with Christ, and walk with Christ, and see Christ, and have fellowship with Christ, take heed of 'the little foxes that spoil the vines, for our vines have tender grapes'. Jesus invites you to go *with Him* and take them. He will surely, like Samson, take the foxes at once and easily. Go with Him to the hunting.

'That henceforth we should not serve sin'
Romans 6:6

Christian, what hast thou to do with sin? *Hath it not cost thee enough already?* Burnt child, wilt thou play with the fire? What! when thou hast already been between the jaws of the lion, wilt thou step a second time into his den? Hast thou not had enough of the old serpent? Did he not poison all thy veins once, and wilt thou play upon the hole of the asp, and put thy hand upon the cockatrice's den a second time? Oh, be not so mad! so foolish! Did sin ever yield thee real pleasure? Didst thou find solid satisfaction in it? If so, go back to thine old drudgery, and wear the chain again, if it delight thee. But inasmuch as sin did never give thee what it promised to bestow, but deluded thee with lies, be not a second time snared by the old fowler - be free, and let the remembrance of thy ancient bondage forbid thee to enter the net again! *It is contrary to the designs of eternal love,* which all have an eye to thy purity and holiness; therefore run not counter to the purposes of thy Lord. Another thought should restrain thee from sin. *Christians can never sin cheaply*; they pay a heavy price for iniquity. Transgression destroys peace of mind, obscures fellowship with Jesus, hinders prayer, brings darkness over the soul; therefore be not the serf and bondman of sin. There is yet a higher argument: each time you 'serve sin', you have *Crucified the Lord afresh, and put Him to an open shame.* Can you bear *that* thought? Oh! if you have fallen into any special sin during this day, it may be my Master has sent this admonition this evening, to bring you back before you have backslidden very far. Turn thee to Jesus anew; He has not forgotten His love to thee; His grace is still the same. With weeping and repentance, come thou to His footstool, and thou shalt be once more received into His heart; thou shalt be set upon a rock again, and thy goings shall be established.

> *'The king also himself
> passed over the brook Kidron'*
> 2 Samuel 15:23

David passed that gloomy brook when flying with his mourning company from his traitor son. The man after God's own heart was not exempt from trouble, nay, his life was full of it. He was both the Lord's Anointed, and the Lord's Afflicted. Why then should we expect to escape? At sorrow's gates the noblest of our race have waited with ashes on their heads, wherefore then should we complain as though some strange thing had happened unto us?

THE KING of kings himself was not favoured with a more cheerful or royal road. He passed over the filthy ditch of Kidron, through which the filth of Jerusalem flowed. God had one Son without sin, but not a single child without the rod. It is a great joy to believe that Jesus has been tempted in all points like as we are. What is our Kidron this morning? Is it a faithless friend, a sad bereavement, a slanderous reproach, a dark foreboding? The King has passed over all these. Is it bodily pain, poverty, persecution, or contempt? Over each of these Kidrons the King has gone before us. 'In all our afflictions He was afflicted.' The idea of strangeness in our trials must be banished at once and for ever, for He who is the Head of all saints, knows by experience the grief which we think so peculiar. All the citizens of Zion must be free of the Honourable Company of Mourners, of which the Prince Immanuel is Head and Captain.

Notwithstanding the abasement of David, he yet returned in triumph to his city, and David's Lord arose victorious from the grave; let us then be of good courage, for we also shall win the day. We shall yet with joy draw water out of the wells of salvation, though now for a season we have to pass by the noxious streams of sin and sorrow. Courage, soldiers of the Cross, the King himself triumphed after going over Kidron, and so shall you.

'Who healeth all thy diseases'
Psalm 103:3

Humbling as is the statement, yet the fact is certain, that we are all more or less suffering under the disease of sin. What a comfort to know that we have a great Physician who is both able and willing to heal us! Let us think of Him awhile tonight. His cures are very *speedy* - there is life in a look at Him; His cures are *radical* - He strikes at the centre of the disease; and hence, His cures are *sure* and certain. He never fails, and *the disease never returns.* There is no relapse where Christ heals; no fear that His patients should be merely patched up for a season, He makes new men of them: a new heart also does he give them, and a right spirit does He put within them. He is well skilled in *all* diseases. Physicians generally have some *speciality.* Although they may know a little about almost all our pains and ills, there is usually one disease which they have studied above all others; but Jesus Christ is thoroughly acquainted with the whole of human nature. He is as much at home with one sinner as with another, and never yet did He meet with an out-of-the-way case that was difficult to Him. He has had extraordinary complications of strange diseases to deal with, but He has known exactly with one glance of His eye how to treat the patient. He is the only universal doctor; and the medicine He gives is the only true catholicon, healing in every instance. Whatever our spiritual malady may be, we should apply at once to this Divine Physician. There is no brokenness of heart which Jesus cannot bind up. 'His blood cleanseth from all sin.' We have but to think of the myriads who have been delivered from all sorts of diseases through the power and virtue of His touch, and we shall joyfully put ourselves in His hands. We trust Him, and sin dies; we love Him, and grace lives; we wait for Him, and grace is strengthened; we see Him as He is, and grace is perfected for ever.

June

'The evening and the morning were the first day'
Genesis 1:5

Was it so even in the beginning? Did light and darkness divide the realm of time in the first day? Then little wonder is it if I have also changes in my circumstances from the sunshine of prosperity to the midnight of adversity. It will not always be the blaze of noon even in my soul concerns, I must expect at seasons to mourn the absence of my former joys, and seek my Beloved in the night. Nor am I alone in this, for all the Lord's beloved ones have had to sing the mingled song of judgment and of mercy, of trial and deliverance, of mourning and of delight. It is one of the arrangements of Divine providence that day and night shall not cease either in the spiritual or natural creation till we reach the land of which it is written, 'there is no night there'. What our heavenly Father ordains is wise and good. What, then, my soul, is it best for thee to do? Learn first *to be content* with this divine order, and be willing, with Job, to receive evil from the hand of the Lord as well as good. Study next, to *make the outgoings of the morning and the evening to rejoice.* Praise the Lord for the sun of joy when it rises, and for the gloom of evening as it falls. There is beauty both in sunrise and sunset, sing of it, and glorify the Lord. Like the nightingale, pour forth thy notes at all hours. *Believe that the night is as useful as the day.* The dews of grace fall heavily in the night of sorrow. The stars of promise shine forth gloriously amid the darkness of grief. *Continue thy service* under all changes. If in the day thy watchword be *labour,* at night exchange it for *watch.* Every hour has its duty, do thou continue in thy calling as the Lord's servant until He shall suddenly appear in His glory. My soul, thine evening of old age and death is drawing near, dread it not, for it is part of the day; and the Lord has said, 'I will cover him all the day long'.

'He will make her wilderness like Eden'
Isaiah 51:3

Methinks I see in vision a howling wilderness, a great
and terrible desert, like to the Sahara. I perceive
nothing in it to relieve the eye, all around I am wearied
with a vision of hot and arid sand, strewn with ten
thousand bleaching skeletons of wretched men who
have expired in anguish, having lost their way in the
pitiless waste. What an appalling sight! How horrible!
a sea of sand without a bound, and without an oasis, a
cheerless graveyard for a race forlorn! But behold and
wonder! Upon a sudden upspringing from the scorching sand I see a plant of renown; and as it grows it buds,
the bud expands - it is a rose, and at its side a lily bows
its modest head; and, miracle of miracles! as the
fragrance of those flowers is diffused the wilderness is
transformed into a fruitful field, and all around it
blossoms exceedingly, the glory of Lebanon is given
unto it, the excellency of Carmel and Sharon. Call it not
Sahara, call it Paradise. Speak not of it any longer as the
valley of deathshade, for where the skeletons lay
bleaching in the sun, behold a resurrection is proclaimed, and up spring the dead, a mighty army, full of
life immortal. Jesus is that plant of renown, and His
presence makes all things new. Nor is the wonder less
in each individual's salvation. Yonder I behold you,
dear reader, cast out, an infant, unswathed, unwashed,
defiled with your own blood, left to be food for beasts
of prey. But lo, a jewel has been thrown into your
bosom by a divine hand, and for its sake you have been
pitied and tended by divine providence, you are washed
and cleansed from your defilement, you are adopted
into heaven's family, the fair seal of love is upon your
forehead, and the ring of faithfulness is on your hand
- you are now a prince unto God, though once an
orphan, cast away. O prize exceedingly the matchless
power and grace which changes deserts into gardens,
and makes the barren heart to sing for joy.

'*For the flesh lusteth against the Spirit,*
and the Spirit against the flesh'
Galatians 5:17

In every believer's heart there is a constant struggle between the old nature and the new. The old nature is very active, and loses no opportunity of plying all the weapons of its deadly armoury against newborn grace; while on the other hand, the new nature is ever on the watch to resist and destroy its enemy. Grace within us will employ prayer, and faith, and hope, and love, to cast out the evil; it takes unto it the 'whole armour of God', and wrestles earnestly. These two opposing natures will never cease to struggle so long as we are in this world. The battle of 'Christian' with 'Apollyon' lasted three hours, but the battle of Christian with himself lasted all the way from the Wicket Gate to the river Jordan. The enemy is so securely entrenched within us that he can never be driven out while we are in this body: but although we are closely beset, and often in sore conflict, we have an Almighty helper, even Jesus, the Captain of our salvation, who is ever with us, and who assures us that we shall eventually come off more than conquerors through Him. With such assistance the newborn nature is more than a match for its foes. Are you fighting with the adversary today? Are Satan, the world, and the flesh, all against you? Be not discouraged nor dismayed. Fight on! For God Himself is with you; *Jehovah Nissi* is your banner, and *Jehovah Rophi* is the healer of your wounds. Fear not, you shall overcome, for who can defeat Omnipotence? Fight on, 'looking unto Jesus'; and though long and stern be the conflict, sweet will be the victory, and glorious the promised reward.

'From strength to strength go on;
    Wrestle, and fight, and pray,
Tread all the powers of darkness down,
    And win the well-fought day.'

'Good Master'
Matthew 19:16

If the young man in the gospel used this title in speaking to our Lord, how much more fitly may I thus address Him! He is indeed my Master in both senses, a ruling Master and a teaching Master. I delight to run upon His errands, and to sit at His feet. I am both His servant and His disciple, and count it my highest honour to own the double character. If He should ask me why I call Him '*good*', I should have a ready answer. It is true that 'there is none good but one, that is, God', but then He is God, and all the goodness of Deity shines forth in Him. In my experience, I have found Him good, so good, indeed, that all the good I have has come to me through Him. He was good to me when I was dead in sin, for He raised me by His Spirit's power; He has been good to me in all my needs, trials, struggles, and sorrows. Never could there be a better Master, for His service is freedom, His rule is love: I wish I were one thousandth part as good a servant. When He teaches me as my Rabbi, He is unspeakably good, His doctrine is divine, His manner is condescending, His spirit is gentleness itself. No error mingles with His instruction - pure is the golden truth which He brings forth, and all His teachings lead to goodness, sanctifying as well as edifying the disciple. Angels find Him a good Master and delight to pay their homage at His footstool. The ancient saints proved Him to be a good Master, and each of them rejoiced to sing, 'I am Thy servant, O Lord'! My own humble testimony must certainly be to the same effect. I will bear this witness before my friends and neighbours, for possibly they may be led by my testimony to seek my Lord Jesus as their Master. O that they would do so! They would never repent so wise a deed. If they would but take His easy yoke, they would find themselves in so royal a service that they would enlist in it for ever.

*'These were potters,
and those that dwelt among plants and hedges:
there they dwelt with the king for his work'*
1 Chronicles 4:23

Potters were not the very highest grade of workers, but 'the king' needed potters, and therefore they were in *royal service*, although the material upon which they worked was nothing but clay. We, too, may be engaged in the most menial part of the Lord's work, but it is a great privilege to do anything for 'the king'; and therefore we will abide in our calling, hoping that, 'although we have lien among the pots, yet shall we be as the wings of a dove covered with silver, and her feathers with yellow gold'. The text tells us of those who 'dwelt among plants and hedges', having rough, rustic, hedging and ditching work to do. They may have desired to live in the city, amid its life, society, and refinement, but they kept their appointed places, for they also were doing the king's work. The place of our habitation is fixed, and we are not to remove from it out of whim and caprice, but seek to serve the Lord in it, by being a blessing to those among whom we reside. These potters and gardeners had *royal company*, for they dwelt 'with the king', and although among hedges and plants, they dwelt with the king *there*. No lawful place, or gracious occupation, however mean, can debar us from communion with our divine Lord. In visiting hovels, swarming lodging-houses, workhouses, or gaols, we may go *with the king*. In all works of faith we may count upon Jesu's fellowship. It is when we are in His work that we may reckon upon his smile. Ye unknown workers who are occupied for your Lord amid the dirt and wretchedness of the lowest of the low, be of good cheer, for jewels have been found upon dunghills ere now, earthen pots have been filled with heavenly treasure, and ill weeds have been transformed into precious flowers. Dwell ye with the king for his work, and when He writes His chronicles your name shall be recorded.

'He humbled Himself'
Philippians 2:8

Jesus is the great teacher of lowliness of heart. We need daily to learn of Him. See the Master taking a towel and washing His disciples' feet! Follower of Christ, wilt thou not humble thyself? See Him as the Servant of servants, and surely thou canst not be proud! Is not this sentence the compendium of His biography, 'He humbled Himself'? Was He not on earth always stripping off first one robe of honour and then another, till, naked, He was fastened to the cross, and there did He not empty out His inmost self, pouring out His life-blood, giving up for all of us, till they laid Him penniless in a borrowed grave? How low was our dear Redeemer brought! How then can we be proud? Stand at the foot of the cross, and count the purple drops by which you have been cleansed; see the thorn-crown; mark His scourged shoulders, still gushing with encrimsoned rills; see hands and feet given up to the rough iron, and His whole self to mockery and scorn; see the bitterness, and the pangs, and the throes of inward grief, showing themselves in His outward frame; hear the thrilling shriek, 'My God, my God, why hast Thou forsaken Me?'. And if you do not lie prostrate on the ground before that cross, you have never seen it: if you are not humbled in the presence of Jesus, you do not know Him. You were so lost that nothing could save you but the sacrifice of God's only begotten. Think of that, and as Jesus stooped for you, bow yourself in lowliness at His feet. A sense of Christ's amazing love to us has a greater tendency to humble us than even a consciousness of our own guilt. May the Lord bring us in contemplation to Calvary, then our position will no longer be that of the pompous man of pride, but we shall take the humble place of one who loves much because much has been forgiven him. Pride cannot live beneath the cross. Let us sit there and learn our lesson, and then rise and carry it into practice.

'The kindness and love of God our Saviour'
Titus 3:4

How sweet it is to behold the Saviour communing with His own beloved people! There can be nothing more delightful than, by the Divine Spirit, to be led into this fertile field of delight. Let the mind for an instant consider the history of the Redeemer's love, and a thousand enchanting acts of affection will suggest themselves, all of which have had for their design the weaving of the heart into Christ, and the intertwisting of the thoughts and emotions of the renewed soul with the mind of Jesus. When we meditate upon this amazing love, and behold the all-glorious Kinsman of the Church endowing her with all His ancient wealth, our souls may well faint for joy. Who is he that can endure such a weight of love? That partial sense of it which the Holy Spirit is sometimes pleased to afford, is more than the soul can contain; how transporting must be a complete view of it! When the soul shall have understanding to discern all the Saviour's gifts, wisdom wherewith to estimate them, and time in which to meditate upon them, such as the world to come will afford us, we shall then commune with Jesus in a nearer manner than at present. But who can imagine the sweetness of such fellowship? It must be one of the things which have not entered into the heart of man, but which God hath prepared for them that love Him. Oh, to burst open the door of our Joseph's granaries, and see the plenty which he hath stored up for us! This will overwhelm us with love. By faith we see, as in a glass darkly, the reflected image of his unbounded treasures, but when we shall actually see the heavenly things themselves, with our own eyes, how deep will be the stream of fellowship in which our soul shall bathe itself! Till then our loudest sonnets shall be reserved for our loving benefactor, Jesus Christ our Lord, whose love to us is wonderful, passing the love of women.

'Received up into glory'
Timothy 3:16

We have seen our well-beloved Lord in the days of His flesh, humiliated and sore vexed; for He was 'despised and rejected of men, a man of sorrows, and acquainted with grief'. He whose brightness is as the morning, wore the sackcloth of sorrow as His daily dress: shame was His mantle, and reproach was His vesture. Yet now, inasmuch as He has triumphed over all the powers of darkness upon the bloody tree, our faith beholds our King returning with dyed garments from Edom, robed in the splendour of victory. How glorious must He have been in the eyes of seraphs, when a cloud received Him out of mortal sight, and He ascended up to heaven! Now He wears the glory which He had with God or ever the earth was, and yet another glory above all - that which He has well earned in the fight against sin, death, and hell. As victor He wears the illustrious crown. Hark how the song swells high! It is a new and sweeter song: 'Worthy is the Lamb that was slain, for He hath redeemed us unto God by His blood!'. He wears the glory of an Intercessor who can never fail, of a Prince who can never be defeated, of a Conqueror who has vanquished every foe, of a Lord who has the heart's allegiance of every subject. Jesus wears all the glory which the pomp of heaven can bestow upon Him, which ten thousand times ten thousand angels can minister to Him. You cannot with your utmost stretch of imagination conceive His exceeding greatness; yet there will be a further revelation of it when He shall descend from heaven in great power, with all the holy angels - 'Then shall he sit upon the throne of His glory'. Oh, the splendour of that glory! It will ravish His people's hearts. Nor is this the close, for eternity shall sound His praise, 'Thy throne, O God, is for ever and ever'! Reader, if you would joy in Christ's glory hereafter, He must be glorious in your sight now. *Is He so?*

'The Lord shut him in'
Genesis 7:16

Noah was shut in *away from all the world* by the hand of divine love. The door of electing purpose interposes between us and the world which lieth in the wicked ones. We are not of the world even as our Lord Jesus was not of the world. Into the sin, the gaiety, the pursuits of the multitude we cannot enter; we cannot play in the streets of Vanity Fair with the children of darkness, for our heavenly Father has shut us in. Noah was shut in *with his God*. '*Come* thou into the ark,' was the Lord's invitation, by which He clearly showed that He Himself intended to dwell in the ark with His servant and his family. Thus all the chosen dwell in God and God in them. Happy people to be enclosed in the same circle which contains God in the Trinity of His persons, Father, Son, and Spirit. Let us never be inattentive to that gracious call, 'Come, my people, enter thou into thy chambers, and shut thy doors about thee, and hide thyself as it were for a little moment until the indignation be overpast'. Noah was so shut in that *no evil could reach him.* Floods did but lift him heavenward, and winds did but waft him on his way. Outside of the ark all was ruin, but inside all was rest and peace. Without Christ we perish, but in Christ Jesus there is perfect safety. Noah was so shut in that *he could not even desire to come out*, and those who are in Christ Jesus are in Him for ever. They shall go no more out for ever, for eternal faithfulness has shut them in, and infernal malice cannot drag them out. The Prince of the house of David shutteth and no man openeth; and when once in the last days as Master of the house He shall rise up and shut to the door, it will be in vain for mere professors to knock, and cry 'Lord, Lord, open unto us', for that same door which shuts in the wise virgins will shut out the foolish for ever. Lord, shut me in by Thy grace.

'He that loveth not knoweth not God'
1 John 4:8

The distinguishing mark of a Christian is his confidence in the love of Christ, and the yielding of his affections to Christ in return. First, faith sets her seal upon the man by enabling the soul to say with the apostle, 'Christ loved me and gave Himself for me'. Then love gives the countersign, and stamps upon the heart gratitude and love to Jesus in return. 'We love Him because He first loved us.' In those grand old ages, which are the heroic period of the Christian religion, this double mark was clearly to be seen in all believers in Jesus; they were men who knew the love of Christ, and rested upon it as a man leaneth upon a staff whose trustiness he has tried. The love which they felt towards the Lord was not a quiet emotion which they hid within themselves in the secret chamber of their souls, and which they only spake of in their private assemblies when they met on the first day of the week, and sang hymns in honour of Christ Jesus the crucified, but it was a passion with them of such a vehement and all-consuming energy, that it was visible in all their actions, spoke in their common talk, and looked out of their eyes even in their commonest glances. Love to Jesus was a flame which fed upon the core and heart of their being; and, therefore, from its own force burned its way into the outer man, and shone there. Zeal for the glory of King Jesus was the seal and mark of all genuine Christians. Because of their dependence upon Christ's love they *dared* much, and because of their love to Christ they *did* much, and it is the same now. The children of God are ruled in their inmost powers by love - the love of Christ constraineth them; they rejoice that divine love is set upon them, they feel it shed abroad in their hearts by the Holy Ghost, which is given unto them, and then by force of gratitude they love the Saviour with a pure heart, fervently. My reader, do *you* love Him? Ere you sleep give an honest answer to a weighty question!

'Behold, I am Vile'
Job 40:4

One cheering word, poor lost sinner, for thee! You think you must not come to God because you are vile. Now, there is not a saint living on earth but has been made to feel that he is vile. If Job, and Isaiah, and Paul were all obliged to say I am vile, oh, poor sinner, wilt thou be ashamed to join in the same confession? If divine grace does not eradicate all sin from the believer, how dost thou hope to do it thyself? and if God loves His people while they are yet vile, dost thou think thy vileness will prevent His loving thee? Believe on Jesus, thou outcast of the world's society! Jesus calls *thee*, and such as thou art.

> 'Not the righteous, not the righteous;
> Sinners, Jesus came to call.'

Even now say, 'Thou hast died for sinners; I am a sinner, Lord Jesus sprinkle Thy blood on me'; if thou wilt confess thy sin thou shalt find pardon. If, now, with all thy heart, thou wilt say, 'I am vile, wash me', thou shalt be washed *now*. If the Holy Spirit shall enable thee from thy heart to cry

> 'Just as I am, without one plea
> But that Thy blood was shed for me,
> And that Thou bidd'st me come to Thee,
> O Lamb of God, I come!'

thou shalt rise from reading this morning's portion with all thy sins pardoned; and though thou didst wake this morning with every sin that man hath ever committed on thy head, thou shalt rest tonight accepted in the Beloved; though once degraded with the rags of sin, thou shalt be adorned with a robe of righteousness, and appear white as the angels are. For 'now', mark it, '*Now* is the accepted time'. If thou 'believest on Him who justifieth the ungodly thou art saved'. Oh! may the Holy Spirit give thee saving faith in Him who receives the vilest.

'Are they Israelites? so am I'.
2 Corinthians 11:22

We have here A PERSONAL CLAIM, and one that
needs proof. The apostle knew that *His* claim was
indisputable, but there are many persons who have no
right to the title who yet claim to belong to the Israel of
God. If we are with confidence declaring, 'So am I also
an Israelite', let us only say it after having searched our
heart as in the presence of God. But if we can give proof
that we are following Jesus, if we can from the heart
say, 'I trust Him wholly, trust Him only, trust Him
simply, trust Him now, and trust Him ever', then the
position which the saints of God hold belongs to us -
all their enjoyments are our possessions; we may be the
very least in Israel, 'less than the least of all saints', yet
since the mercies of God belong to the saints AS
SAINTS, and not as advanced saints, or well-taught
saints, we may put in our plea, and say, 'Are they
Israelites? so am I; therefore the promises are mine,
grace is mine, glory will be mine'. The claim, right-
fully made, is one which will yield untold comfort.
When God's people are rejoicing that they are His,
what a happiness if they can say, 'SO AM I'! When
they speak of being pardoned, and justified, and accepted in the Beloved, how joyful to respond, *'Through
the grace of God*, SO AM I'. But this claim not only
has its enjoyments and privileges, but also its conditions and duties. We must share with God's people in
cloud as well as in sunshine. When we hear them
spoken of with contempt and ridicule for being Christians, we must come boldly forward and say, 'So am I'.
When we see them working for Christ, giving their
time, their talent, their whole heart to Jesus, we must
be able to say, 'So do I'. O let us prove our gratitude
by our devotion, and live as those who, having claimed
a privilege, are willing to take the responsibility connected with it.

'Ye that love the Lord, hate evil'
Psalm 97:10

Thou hast good reason to 'hate evil', for only consider what harm it has already wrought thee. Oh, what a world of mischief sin has brought into thy heart! Sin blinded thee so that thou couldst not see the beauty of the Saviour; it made thee deaf so that thou couldst not hear the Redeemer's tender invitations. Sin turned thy feet into the way of death, and poured poison into the very fountain of thy being; it tainted thy heart, and made it 'deceitful above all things, and desperately wicked'. Oh, what a creature thou wast when evil had done its utmost with thee, before divine grace interposed! Thou wast an heir of wrath even as others; thou didst 'run with the multitude to do evil'. Such were all of us; but Paul reminds us, 'but ye are washed, but ye are sanctified, but ye are justified in the name of the Lord Jesus, and by the Spirit of our God'. We have good reason, indeed, for hating evil when we look back and trace its deadly workings. Such mischief did evil do us, that our souls would have been lost had not omnipotent love interfered to redeem us. Even now it is an active enemy, ever watching to do us hurt, and to drag us to perdition. Therefore 'hate evil', O Christians, unless you desire trouble. If you would strew your path with thorns, and plant nettles in your death-pillow, then neglect to 'hate evil': but if you would live a happy life, and die a peaceful death, then walk in all the ways of holiness, hating evil, even unto the end. If you truly love your Saviour, and would honour Him, then 'hate evil'. We know of no cure for the love of evil in a Christian like abundant intercourse with the Lord Jesus. Dwell much with Him, and it is impossible for you to be at peace with sin.

'Order my footsteps by Thy Word,
    And make my heart sincere;
Let sin have no dominion, Lord,
    But keep my conscience clear.'

'Be zealous'
Revelation 3:19

If you would see souls converted, if you would hear the cry that 'the kingdoms of this world have become the kingdoms of our Lord'; if you would place crowns upon the head of the Saviour, and see His throne lifted high, then be filled with zeal. For, under God, the way of the world's conversion must be by the zeal of the church. Every grace shall do exploits, but this shall be first; prudence, knowledge, patience, and courage will follow in their places, but zeal must lead the van. It is not the extent of your knowledge, though that is useful; it is not the extent of your talent, though that is not to be despised; it is your zeal that shall do great exploits. This zeal is the fruit of the Holy Spirit: it draws its vital force from *the continued operations of* the Holy Ghost in the soul. If our inner life dwindles, if our heart beats slowly before God, we shall not know zeal; but if all be strong and vigorous within, then we cannot but feel a loving anxiety to see the kingdom of Christ come, and His will done on earth, even as it is in heaven. A deep *sense of gratitude* will nourish Christian zeal. Looking to the hole of the pit whence we were digged, we find abundant reason why we should spend and be spent for God. And zeal is also stimulated by *the thought of the eternal future*. It looks with tearful eyes down to the flames of hell, and it cannot slumber: it looks up with anxious gaze to the glories of heaven, and it cannot but bestir itself. It feels that time is short compared with the work to be done, and therefore it devotes all that it has to the cause of its Lord. And it is ever strengthened by *the remembrance of Christ's example*. He was clothed with zeal as with a cloak. How swift the chariot-wheels of duty went with Him! He knew no loitering by the way. Let us prove that we are His disciples by manifesting the same spirit of zeal.

*'There fell down many slain, because the war was
of God'* 1 Chronicles 5:22

Warrior, fighting under the banner of the Lord Jesus,
observe this verse with holy joy, for as it was in the days
of old so it is now, if the war be of God the victory is
sure. The sons of Reuben, and the Gadites, and the half
tribe of Manasseh could barely muster five and forty
thousand fighting men, and yet in their war with the
Hagarites, they slew 'men, an hundred thousand', 'for
they cried to God in the battle, and He was entreated of
them, because they put their trust in Him'. The Lord
saveth not by many nor by few; it is ours to go forth in
Jehovah's name if we be but a handful of men, for the
Lord of Hosts is with us for our Captain. They did not
neglect buckler, and sword, and bow, neither did they
place their trust in these weapons: we must all use
fitting means, but our confidence must rest in the Lord
alone, for He is the sword and the shield of His people.
The great reason of their extraordinary success lay in
the fact that 'the war was of God'. Beloved, in fighting
with sin without and within, with error doctrinal or
practical, with spiritual wickedness in high places or
low places, with devils and the devil's allies, you are
waging Jehovah's war, and unless He himself can be
worsted, you need not fear defeat. Quail not before superior
numbers, shrink not from difficulties or impossibilities,
flinch not at wounds or death, smite with the two-edged
sword of the Spirit, and the slain shall lie in heaps. The
battle is the Lord's and He will deliver His enemies into
our hands. With steadfast foot, strong hand, dauntless
heart, and flaming zeal, rush to the conflict, and the
hosts of evil shall fly like chaff before the gale.

Stand up! stand up for Jesus!
 The strife will not be long;
This day the noise of battle,
 The next the victor's song:

To him that overcometh,
 A crown of life shall be;
He with the King of glory
 Shall reign eternally.

'Thou shalt see now whether My word
shall come to pass unto thee or not'
Numbers 11:23

God had made a positive promise to Moses that for the
space of a whole month He would feed the vast host in
the wilderness with flesh. Moses, being overtaken by
a fit of unbelief, looks to the outward means, and is at
a loss to know how the promise can be fulfilled. He
looked to the creature instead of the Creator. But doth
the Creator expect the creature to fulfil his promise for
Him? No; He who makes the promise ever fulfils it by
His own unaided omnipotence. If He speaks, it is done
- done by Himself. His promises do not depend for
their fulfilment upon the co-operation of the puny
strength of man. We can at once perceive the mistake
which Moses made. And yet how commonly we do the
same! God has promised to supply our needs, and we
look to the creature to do what God has promised to do;
and then, because we perceive the creature to be weak
and feeble, we indulge in unbelief. Why look we to that
quarter at all? Will you look to the top of the Alps for
summer heat? Will you journey to the north pole to
gather fruits ripened in the sun? Verily, you would act
no more foolishly if ye did this than when you look to
the weak for strength, and to the creature to do the
Creator's work. Let us, then, put the question on the
right footing. The ground of faith is not the sufficiency
of the visible means for the performance of the promise, but the all-sufficiency of the invisible God, who
will most surely do as He hath said. If after clearly
seeing that the onus lies with the Lord and not with the
creature, we dare to indulge in mistrust, the question of
God comes home mightily to us: 'Has the Lord's hand
waxed short?' May it happen, too, in His mercy, that
with the question there may flash upon our souls that
blessed declaration, 'Thou shalt see now whether My
word shall come to pass unto thee or not'.

> '*The Lord hath done great things for us;*
> *whereof we are glad*'
> Psalm 126:3

Some Christians are sadly prone to *look* on the *dark* side of everything, and to dwell more upon what they have gone through than upon what God has done for them. Ask for their impression of the Christian life, and they will describe their continual conflicts, their deep afflictions, their sad adversities, and the sinfulness of their hearts, yet with scarcely any allusion to the mercy and help which God has vouchsafed them. But a Christian whose soul is in a *healthy* state, will come forward joyously, and say, 'I will speak, not about myself, but to the honour of my God. He hath brought me up out of an horrible pit, and out of the miry clay, and set my feet upon a rock, and established my goings: and He hath put a new song in my mouth, even praise unto our God. The Lord hath done great things for me, whereof I am glad.' Such an abstract of experience as this is the very best that any child of God can present. It *is* true that we endure trials, but it is just as true that we are delivered out of them. It *is* true that we have our corruptions, and mournfully do we know this, but it is quite as true that we have an all-sufficient Saviour, who overcomes these corruptions, and delivers us from their dominion. In looking back, it would be wrong to deny that we have been in the Slough of Despond, and have crept along the Valley of Humiliation, but it would be equally wicked to forget that we have been *through* them safely and profitably; we have not remained in them, thanks to our Almighty Helper and Leader, who has brought us 'out into a wealthy place'. The deeper our troubles, the louder our thanks to God, who has led us through all, and preserved us until now. Our griefs cannot mar the melody of our praise, we reckon them to be the bass part of our life's song, 'He hath done great things for us, whereof we are glad'.

'Search the Scriptures'
John 5:39

The Greek word here rendered *search* signifies a strict, close, diligent, curious search, such as men make when they are seeking gold, or hunters when they are in earnest after game. We must not rest content with having given a superficial reading to a chapter or two, but with the candle of the Spirit we must deliberately seek out the hidden meaning of the word. Holy Scripture *requires searching* - much of it can only be learned by careful study. There is milk for babes, but also meat for strong men. The rabbis wisely say that a mountain of matter hangs upon every word, yea, upon every title of Scripture. Tertullian exclaims, 'I adore the fulness of the Scriptures'. No man who merely skims the book of God can profit thereby; we must dig and mine until we obtain the hid treasure. The door of the word only opens to the key of diligence. The Scriptures *claim searching*. They are the writings of God, bearing the divine stamp and imprimatur - who shall dare to treat them with levity? He who despises them despises the God who wrote them. God forbid that any of us should leave our Bibles to become swift witnesses against us in the great day of account. The word of God *will repay searching*. God does not bid us sift a mountain of chaff with here and there a grain of wheat in it, but the Bible is winnowed corn - we have but to open the granary door and find it. Scripture grows upon the student. It is full of surprises. Under the teaching of the Holy Spirit, to the searching eye it glows with splendour of revelation, like a vast temple paved with wrought gold, and roofed with rubies, emeralds, and all manner of gems. No merchandise like the merchandise of Scripture truth. Lastly, *the Scriptures reveal Jesus*: 'They are they which testify of Me'. No more powerful motive can be urged upon Bible readers than this: he who finds Jesus finds life, heaven, all things. Happy he who, searching his Bible, discovers his Saviour.

'We live unto the Lord'
Romans 14:8

If God had willed it, each of us might have entered heaven at the moment of conversion. It was not absolutely necessary for our preparation for immortality that we should tarry here. It is possible for a man to be taken to heaven, and to be found meet to be a partaker of the inheritance of the saints in light, though he has but just believed in Jesus. It is true that our sanctification is a long and continued process, and we shall not be perfected till we lay aside our bodies and enter within the veil; but nevertheless, had the Lord so willed it, He might have changed us from imperfection to perfection, and have taken us to heaven at once. Why then are we here? Would God keep His children out of paradise a single moment longer than was necessary? Why is the army of the living God still on the battle-field when one charge might give them the victory? Why are his children still wandering hither and thither through a maze, when a solitary word from His lips would bring them into the centre of their hopes in heaven? The answer is - they are here that they may *'live unto the Lord'*, and may bring others to know His love. We remain on earth as sowers to scatter good seed; as ploughmen to break up the fallow ground; as heralds publishing salvation. We are here as the 'salt of the earth', to be a blessing to the world. We are here to glorify Christ in our daily life. We are here as workers for Him, and as 'workers together with him'. Let us see that our life answereth its end. Let us live earnest, useful, holy lives, to 'the praise of the glory of His grace'. Meanwhile we long to be with Him, and daily sing

'My heart is with Him on His throne,
    And ill can brook delay;
Each moment listening for the voice,
    "Rise up, and come away".'

'They are they which testify of Me'
John 5:39

Jesus Christ is the Alpha and Omega of the Bible. He is the constant theme of its sacred pages; from first to last they testify of Him. At the creation we at once discern Him as one of the sacred Trinity; we catch a glimpse of Him in the promise of the woman's seed; we see Him typified in the ark of Noah; we walk with Abraham, as He sees Messiah's day; we dwell in the tents of Isaac and Jacob, feeding upon the gracious promise; we hear the venerable Israel talking of Shiloh; and in the numerous types of the law, we find the Redeemer abundantly foreshadowed. Prophets and kings, priests and preachers, all look one way - they all stand as the cherubs did over the ark, desiring to look within, and to read the mystery of God's great propitiation. Still more manifestly in the New Testament we find our Lord the one pervading subject. It is not an ingot here and there, or dust of gold thinly scattered, but here you stand upon a solid floor of gold; for the whole substance of the new Testament is Jesus crucified, and even its closing sentence is bejewelled with the Redeemer's name. We should always read Scripture in this light; we should consider the word to be as a mirror into which Christ looks down from heaven; and then we, looking into it, see His face reflected as in a glass - darkly, it is true, but still in such a way as to be a blessed preparation for seeing Him as we shall see Him face to face. This volume contains Jesus Christ's letters to us, perfumed by his love. These pages are the garments of our King, and they all smell of myrrh, and aloes, and cassia. Scripture is the royal chariot in which Jesus rides, and it is paved with love for the daughters of Jerusalem. The Scriptures are the swaddling bands of the holy child Jesus; unroll them and you find your Saviour. The quintessence of the word of God is Christ.

> *'We love Him, because He first loved us'*
> 1 John 4:19

There is no light in the planet but that which proceedeth from the sun; and there is no true love to Jesus in the heart but that which cometh from the Lord Jesus himself. From this overflowing fountain of the infinite love of God, all our love to God must spring. This must ever be a great and certain truth, that we love Him for no other reason than because He first loved us. Our love to Him is *the fair offspring* of His love to us. Cold admiration, when studying the words of God, anyone may have, but the warmth of love can only be kindled in the heart by God's Spirit. How great the wonder that such as we should ever have been brought to love Jesus at all! How marvellous that when we had rebelled against Him, he should, by a display of such amazing love, seek to draw us back. No! never should we have had a grain of love towards God unless it had been sown in us by the sweet seed of His love to us. Love, then, has for its parent the love of God shed abroad in the heart; but after it is thus divinely born, it must be *divinely nourished*. Love is an exotic; it is not a plant which will flourish naturally in human soil, it must be watered from above. Love to Jesus is a flower of a delicate nature, and if it received no nourishment but that which could be drawn from the rock of our hearts it would soon wither. As love comes from heaven, so it must feed on heavenly bread. It cannot exist in the wilderness unless it be fed by manna from on high. Love must feed on love. The very soul and life of our love to God is His love to us.

> 'I love Thee, Lord, but with no love of mine,
>   For I have none to give;
> I love Thee, Lord; but all the love is Thine,
>   *For by Thy love I live.*
> I am as nothing, and rejoice to be
>   Emptied, and lost, and swallowed up in Thee.'

*'There brake He the arrows of the bow, the shield,
and the sword, and the battle'*
Psalm 76:3

Our Redeemer's glorious cry of 'It is finished', was the death-knell of all the adversaries of His people, the breaking of 'the arrows of the bow, the shield, and the sword, and the battle'. Behold the hero of Golgotha using His cross as an anvil, and His woes as a hammer, dashing to shivers bundle after bundle of our sins, those poisoned 'arrows of the bow'; trampling on every indictment, and destroying every accusation. What glorious blows the mighty Breaker gives with a hammer far more ponderous than the fabled weapon of Thor! How the diabolical darts fly to fragments, and the infernal bucklers are broken like potters' vessels! Behold, he draws from its sheath of hellish workmanship the dread sword of Satanic power! He snaps it across His knee, as a man breaks the dry wood of a faggot, and casts it into the fire. Beloved, no sin of a believer can now be an arrow mortally to wound him, no condemnation can now be a sword to kill him, for the punishment of our sin was borne by Christ, a full atonement was made for all our iniquities by our blessed Substitute and Surety. Who now accuseth? Who now condemneth? Christ hath died, yea rather, hath risen again. Jesus has emptied the quivers of hell, has quenched every fiery dart, and broken off the head of every arrow of wrath; the ground is strewn with the splinters and relics of the weapons of hell's warfare, which are only visible to us to remind us of our former danger, and of our great deliverance. Sin hath no more dominion over us. Jesus has made an end of it, and put it away for ever. O thou enemy, destructions are come to a perpetual end. Talk ye of all the wondrous works of the Lord, ye who make mention of His name, keep not silence, neither by day, nor when the sun goeth to his rest. Bless the Lord, O my soul.

'Thou art weighed in the balances,
and art found wanting'
Daniel 5:27

It is well frequently to weigh ourselves in the scale of God's Word. You will find it a holy exercise to read some psalm of David, and, as you meditate upon each verse, to ask yourself, 'Can I say this? Have I felt as David felt? Has my heart ever been broken on account of sin, as his was when he penned his penitential psalms? Has my soul been full of true confidence in the hour of difficulty as his was when he sang of God's mercies in the cave of Adullam, or in the holds of Engedi? Do I take the cup of salvation and call upon the name of the Lord?' Then turn to the life of Christ, and as you read, ask yourselves how far you are conformed to His likeness. Endeavour to discover whether you have the meekness, the humility, the lovely spirit which He constantly inculcated and displayed. Take, then, the epistles, and see whether you can go with the apostle in what he said of his experience. Have you ever cried out as he did - 'O wretched man that I am! who shall deliver me from the body of this death'? Have you ever felt his self-abasement? Have you seemed to yourself the chief of sinners, and less than the least of all saints? Have you known anything of his devotion? Could you join with him and say, 'For me to live is Christ, and to die is gain'? If we thus read God's Word as a test of our spiritual condition, we shall have good reason to stop many a time and say, 'Lord, I feel I have never yet been here, O bring me here! give me true penitence, such as this I read of. Give me real faith; give me warmer zeal; inflame me with more fervent love; grant me the grace of meekness; make me more like Jesus. Let me no longer be "found wanting", when weighed in the balances of the sanctuary, lest I be found wanting in the scales of judgment.' 'Judge yourselves that ye be not judged.'

> *'Who hath saved us,*
> *and called us with an holy calling'*
> 2 Timothy 1:9

The apostle uses the present tense and says, 'Who *hath* saved us'. Believers in Christ Jesus *are* saved. They are not looked upon as persons who are in a hopeful state, and may ultimately be saved, but they *are* already saved. Salvation is not a blessing to be enjoyed upon the dying bed, and to be sung of in a future state above, but a matter to be obtained, received, promised, and enjoyed now. The Christian is perfectly saved *in God's purpose*; God has ordained him unto salvation, and that purpose is complete. He is saved also as to the *price which has been paid for him*: 'It is finished' was the cry of the Saviour ere He died. The believer is also perfectly saved *in His covenant head*, for as he fell in Adam, so he lives in Christ. This complete salvation is accompanied by a *holy calling*. Those whom the Saviour saved upon the cross are in due time effectually called by the power of God the Holy Spirit unto holiness; they leave their sins; they endeavour to be like Christ; they choose holiness, not out of any compulsion, but from the stress of a new nature, which leads them to rejoice in holiness just as naturally as aforetime they delighted in sin. God neither chose them nor called them because they were holy, but He called them that they might be holy, and holiness is the beauty produced by His workmanship in them. The excellencies which we see in a believer are as much the work of God as the atonement itself. Thus is brought out very sweetly the fulness of the grace of God. Salvation must be of grace, because the Lord is the author of it: and what motive but grace could move Him to save the guilty? Salvation must be of grace, because the Lord works in such a manner that our righteousness is for ever excluded. Such is the believer's privilege - *a present salvation*; such is the evidence that he is called to it - *a holy life*.

*'Whosoever will,
let him take the water of life freely'*
Revelation 22:17

Jesus says, 'take freely'. He wants no payment or preparation. He seeks no recommendation from our virtuous emotions. If you have no good feelings, if you be but willing, you are invited; therefore come! You have no belief and no repentance - come to Him, and He will give them to you. Come just as you are, and take 'Freely', without money and without price. He gives Himself to needy ones. The drinking fountains at the corners of our streets are valuable institutions; and we can hardly imagine any one so foolish as to feel for his purse, when he stands before one of them, and to cry, 'I cannot drink because I have not five pounds in my pocket'. However poor the man is, there is the fountain, and just as he is he may drink of it. Thirsty passengers, as they go by, whether they are dressed in fustian, or in broadcloth, do not look for any warrant for drinking; its being there is their warrant for taking its water freely. The liberality of some good friends has put the refreshing crystal there and we take it, and ask no questions. Perhaps the only persons who need go thirsty through the street where there is a drinking fountain, are the fine ladies and gentlemen who are in their carriages. They are very thirsty, but cannot think of being so vulgar as to get out to drink. It would demean them, they think, to drink at a common drinking fountain: so they ride by with parched lips. Oh, how many there are who are rich in their own good works and cannot therefore come to Christ! 'I will not be saved,' they say, 'in the same way as the harlot or the swearer.' What! go to heaven in the same way as a chimney sweep. Is there no pathway to glory but the path which led the thief there? I will not be saved that way. Such proud boasters must remain without the living water; but, 'WHOSOEVER WILL, LET HIM TAKE THE WATER OF LIFE FREELY'.

'Remove far from me vanity and lies'
Proverbs 30:8
'O my God, be not far from me'
Psalm 38:21

Here we have two great lessons - what to deprecate and what to supplicate. The happiest state of a Christian is the holiest state. As there is the most heat nearest the sun, so there is the most happiness nearest to Christ. No Christian enjoys comfort when his eyes are fixed on vanity - he finds no satisfaction unless his soul is quickened in the ways of God. The world may win happiness elsewhere, but he cannot. I do not blame ungodly men for rushing to their pleasures. Why should I? Let them have their fill. That is all they have to enjoy. A converted wife who despaired of her husband was always very kind to him, for she said, 'I fear that this is the only world in which he will be happy, and therefore I have made up my mind to make him as happy as I can in it.' Christians must seek their delights in a higher sphere than the insipid frivolities or sinful enjoyments of the world. Vain pursuits are dangerous to renewed souls. We have heard of a philosopher who, while he looked *up* to the stars, fell into a pit; but how deeply do they fall who look *down*. Their fall is fatal. No Christian is safe when his soul is slothful, and his God is far from him. Every Christian is always safe as to the great matter of his standing in Christ, but he is not safe as regards his experience in holiness, and communion with Jesus in this life. Satan does not often attack a Christian who is living near to God. It is when the Christian departs from his God, becomes spiritually starved, and endeavours to feed on vanities, that the devil discovers his vantage hour. He may sometimes stand foot to foot with the child of God who is active in his Master's service, but the battle is generally short: he who slips as he goes down into the Valley of Humiliation, every time he takes a false step invites Apollyon to assail him. O for grace to walk humbly with our God!

'Delight thyself also in the Lord'
Psalm 37:4

The teaching of these words must seem very surprising to those who are strangers to vital godliness, but to the sincere believer it is only the inculcation of a recognised truth. The life of the believer is here described as a *delight* in God, and we are thus certified of the great fact that true religion overflows with happiness and joy. Ungodly persons and mere professors never look upon religion as a joyful thing; to them it is service, duty, or necessity, but never pleasure or delight. If they attend to religion at all, it is either that they may gain thereby, or else because they dare not do otherwise. The thought of *delight* in religion is so strange to most men, that no two words in their language stand further apart than 'holiness' and 'delight'. But believers who know Christ, understand that delight and faith are so blessedly united, that the gates of hell cannot prevail to separate them. They who love God with all their hearts, find that his ways are ways of pleasantness, and all His paths are peace. Such joys, such brimful delights, such overflowing blessednesses, do the saints discover in their Lord, that so far from serving Him from custom, they would follow Him though all the world cast out His name as evil. We fear not God because of any compulsion; our faith is no fetter, our profession is no bondage, we are not dragged to holiness, nor driven to duty. No, our piety is our pleasure, our hope is our happiness, our duty is our delight.

Delight and true religion are as allied as root and flower; as indivisible as truth and certainty; they are, in fact, two precious jewels glittering side by side in a setting of gold.

'Tis when we taste Thy love,
  Our joys divinely grow,
Unspeakable like those above,
  And heaven begins below.

*'O Lord, to us belongeth confusion of face...
because we have sinned against Thee'*
Daniel 9:8

A deep sense and clear sight of sin, its heinousness, and
the punishment which it deserves, should make us lie
low before the throne. We have sinned as Christians.
Alas! that it should be so. Favoured as we have been,
we have yet been ungrateful: privileged beyond most,
we have not brought forth fruit in proportion. Who is
there, although he may long have been engaged in the
Christian warfare, that will not blush when he looks
back upon the past? As for our days before we were
regenerate, may they be forgiven and forgotten; but
since then, though we have not sinned as before, yet we
have sinned against light and against love - light which
has really penetrated our minds, and love in which we
have rejoiced. Oh, the atrocity of the sin of a pardoned
soul! An unpardoned sinner sins cheaply compared
with the sin of one of God's own elect ones, who has
had communion with Christ and leaned his head upon
Jesus' bosom. Look at David! Many will talk of his
sin, but I pray you look at his repentance, and hear his
broken bones, as each one of them moans out its
dolorous confession! Mark his tears, as they fall upon
the ground, and the deep sighs with which he accompanies the softened music of his harp! We have erred;
let us, therefore, seek the spirit of penitence. Look,
again, at Peter! We speak much of Peter's denying his
Master. Remember, it is written, 'He wept bitterly'.
Have *we* no denials of our Lord to be lamented with
tears? Alas! these sins of ours before and after conversion, would consign us to the place of inextinguishable
fire if it were not for the sovereign mercy which has
made us to differ, snatching us like brands from the
burning. My soul, bow down under a sense of thy
natural sinfulness, and worship thy God. Admire the
grace which saves thee - the mercy which spares thee
- the love which pardons thee!

*'And Sarah said, God hath made me to laugh, so
that all that hear will laugh with me'*
Genesis 21:6

It was far above the power of nature, and even contrary
to its laws, that the aged Sarah should be honoured with
a son; and even so it is beyond all ordinary rules that
I, a poor, helpless, undone sinner, should find grace to
bear about in my soul the indwelling Spirit of the Lord
Jesus. I, who once despaired, as well I might, for my
nature was as dry, and withered, and barren, and
accursed as a howling wilderness, even I have been
made to bring forth fruit unto holiness. Well may my
mouth be filled with joyous laughter, because of the
singular, surprising grace which I have received of the
Lord, for I have found Jesus, the promised seed, and
He is mine for ever. This day will I lift up psalms of
triumph unto the Lord who has remembered my low
estate, for 'my heart rejoiceth in the Lord; mine horn
is exalted in the Lord; my mouth is enlarged over mine
enemies, because I rejoice in Thy salvation'.

I would have all those that hear of my great
deliverance from hell, and my most blessed visitation
from on high, laugh for joy with me. I would surprise
my family with my abundant peace; I would delight my
friends with my ever-increasing happiness; I would
edify the Church with my grateful confessions; and
even impress the world with the cheerfulness of my
daily conversation. Bunyan tells us that Mercy laughed
in her sleep, and no wonder when she dreamed of Jesus;
my joy shall not stop short of hers while my Beloved
is the theme of my daily thoughts. The Lord Jesus is
a deep sea of joy: my soul shall dive therein, shall be
swallowed up in the delights of His society. Sarah
looked on her Isaac, and laughed with excess of
rapture, and all her friends laughed with her; and thou,
my soul, look on thy Jesus, and bid heaven and earth
unite in thy joy unspeakable.

'He openeth, and no man shutteth'
Revelation 3:7

Jesus is the keeper of the gates of paradise, and before every believing soul He setteth an open door, which no man or devil shall be able to close against it. What joy it will be to find that faith in Him is the golden key to the everlasting doors. My soul, dost thou carry this key in thy bosom, or art thou trusting to some deceitful picklock, which will fail thee at last? Hear this parable of the preacher, and remember it. The great King has made a banquet, and He has proclaimed to all the world that none shall enter but those who bring with them the fairest flower that blooms. The spirits of men advance to the gate by thousands, and they bring each one the flower which he esteems the queen of the garden; but in crowds they are driven from the royal presence, and enter not into the festive halls. Some bear in their hand the deadly nightshade of superstition, or the flaunting poppies of Rome, or the hemlock of self-righteousness, but these are not dear to the King, the bearers are shut out of the pearly gates. My soul, hast thou gathered the rose of Sharon? Dost thou wear the lily of the valley in thy bosom constantly? If so, when thou comest up to the gates of heaven thou wilt know its value, for thou hast only to show this choicest of flowers, and the Porter will open: not for a moment will He deny thee admission, for to that rose the Porter openeth ever. Thou shalt find thy way with the rose of Sharon in thy hand up to the throne of God Himself, for heaven itself possesses nothing that excels its radiant beauty, and of all the flowers that bloom in paradise there is none that can rival the lily of the valleys. My soul, get Calvary's blood-red rose into thy hand by faith, by love wear it, by communion preserve it, by daily watchfulness make it thine all in all, and thou shalt be blessed beyond all bliss, happy beyond a dream. Jesus, be mine for ever, my God, my heaven, my all.

*'And I give unto them eternal life;
and they shall never perish'*
John 10:28

The Christian should never think or speak lightly of unbelief. For a child of God to mistrust His love, His truth, His faithfulness, must be greatly displeasing to Him. How can we ever grieve Him by doubting His upholding grace? Christian! it is contrary to every promise of God's precious Word that thou shouldst ever be forgotten or left to perish. If it could be so, how could He be true who has said, 'Can a woman forget her sucking child, that she should not have compassion on the son of her womb? Yea, they may forget, yet will I never forget thee.' What were the value of that promise - 'The mountains shall depart, and the hills be removed; but My kindness shall not depart from thee, neither shall the covenant of My peace be removed, saith the Lord that hath mercy on thee'? Where were the truth of Christ's words - 'I give unto My sheep eternal life; and they shall never perish, neither shall any man pluck them out of My hand. My Father, which gave them Me, is greater than all; and no man is able to pluck them out of My Father's hand'? Where were the doctrines of grace? They would be all disproved if one child of God should perish. Where were the veracity of God, His honour, His power, His grace, His covenant, His oath, if any of those for whom Christ has died, and who have put their trust in Him, should nevertheless be cast away? Banish those unbelieving fears which so dishonour God. Arise, shake thyself from the dust, and put on thy beautiful garments. Remember it is sinful to doubt His Word wherein He has promised thee that thou shalt never perish. Let the eternal life within thee express itself in confident rejoicing.

'The gospel bears my spirit up:
    A faithful and unchanging God
Lays the foundation for my hope,
    In oaths, and promises, and blood.'

'The Lord is my light and my salvation;
whom shall I fear? the Lord is the strength of my
life; of whom shall I be afraid?'
Psalm 27:1

'*The Lord is my light and my salvation.*' Here is
personal interest, '*my light*', '*my salvation*'; the soul is
assured of it, and therefore declares it boldly. Into the
soul at the new birth divine light is poured as the
precursor of salvation; where there is not enough light
to reveal our own darkness and to make us long for the
Lord Jesus, there is no evidence of salvation. After
conversion our God is our joy, comfort, guide, teacher,
and in every sense our light: He is light within, light
around, light reflected from us, and light to be revealed
to us. Note, it is not said merely that the Lord gives
light, but that He *is* light; nor that He gives salvation,
but that He *is* salvation; he, then, who by faith has laid
hold upon God, has all covenant blessings in his
possession. This being made sure as a fact, the argument drawn from it is put in the form of a question,
'*Whom shall I fear?*' A question which is its own
answer. The powers of darkness are not to be feared,
for the Lord, our light, destroys them; and the damnation of hell is not to be dreaded by us, for the Lord is
our salvation. This is a very different challenge from
that of boastful Goliath, for it rests, not upon the
conceited vigour of an arm of flesh, but upon the real
power of the omnipotent I AM. '*The Lord is the
strength of my life.*' Here is a third glowing epithet, to
show that the writer's hope was fastened with a
threefold cord which could not be broken. We may well
accumulate terms of praise where the Lord lavishes
deeds of grace. Our life derives all its strength from
God; and if He deigns to make us strong, we cannot be
weakened by all the machinations of the adversary. '*Of
whom shall I be afraid?*' The bold question looks into
the future as well as the present. 'If God be for us,' who
can be against us, either now or in time to come?

'Help, Lord'
Psalm 12:1

The prayer itself is remarkable, for it is *short*, but *seasonable*, *sententious*, and *suggestive*. David mourned the fewness of faithful men, and therefore lifted up his heart in supplication; when the creature failed, he flew to the Creator. He evidently felt his own weakness, or he would not have cried for help; but at the same time he intended honestly to exert himself for the cause of truth, for the word 'help' is inapplicable where we ourselves do nothing. There is much of *directness*, *clearness of perception*, and *distinctness of utterance* in this petition of two words; much more, indeed, than in the long rambling outpourings of certain professors. The Psalmist runs straightforward to his God, with a well-considered prayer; he knows what he is seeking, and where to seek it. Lord, teach us to pray in the same blessed manner.

The occasions for the use of this prayer are frequent. In *providential afflictions* how suitable it is for tried believers who find all helpers failing them. Students, in *doctrinal difficulties*, may often obtain aid by lifting up this cry of 'Help, Lord', to the Holy Spirit, the great Teacher. Spiritual warriors in *inward conflicts* may send to the throne for reinforcements, and this will be a model for their request. Workers in *heavenly labour* may thus obtain grace in time of need. Seeking sinners, in *doubts and alarms*, may offer up the same weighty supplication; in fact, in all cases, times, and places, this will serve the turn of needy souls. 'Help, Lord', will suit us living and dying, suffering or labouring, rejoicing or sorrowing. In Him our help is found, let us not be slack to cry to Him.

The answer to the prayer is certain, if it be sincerely offered through Jesus. The Lord's character assures us that He will not leave His people; His relationship as Father and Husband guarantee us His aid; His gift of Jesus is a pledge of every good thing; and His sure promise stands, 'Fear not, I WILL HELP THEE'.

'Then Israel sang this song, Spring up, O well;
sing ye unto it'
Numbers 21:17

Famous was the well of Beer in the wilderness, because
it was *the subject of a promise*: 'That is the well
whereof the Lord spake unto Moses, Gather the people
together, and I will give them water'. The people
needed water, and it was promised by their gracious
God. We need fresh supplies of heavenly grace, and in
the covenant the Lord has pledged Himself to give all
we require. The well next became *the cause of a song*.
Before the water gushed forth, cheerful faith prompted
the people to sing; and as they saw the crystal fount
bubbling up, the music grew yet more joyous. In like
manner, we who believe the promise of God should
rejoice in the prospect of divine revivals in our souls,
and as we experience them our holy joy should overflow. Are we thirsting? Let us not murmur, but sing.
Spiritual thirst is bitter to bear, but we need not bear it
- the promise indicates a well; let us be of good heart,
and look for it. Moreover, the well was *the centre of
prayer*. 'Spring up, O well.' What God has engaged to
give, we must enquire after, or we manifest that we
have neither desire nor faith. This evening let us ask
that the Scripture we have read, and our devotional
exercises, may not be an empty formality, but a channel
of grace to our souls. O that God the Holy Spirit would
work in us with all His mighty power, filling us with
all the fulness of God. Lastly, the well was *the object
of effort*. 'The nobles of the people digged it with their
staves.' The Lord would have us active in obtaining
grace. Our staves are ill adapted for digging in the sand,
but we must use them to the utmost of our ability.
Prayer must not be neglected; the assembling of ourselves together must not be forsaken: ordinances must
not be slighted. The Lord will give us His grace most
plenteously, but not in a way of idleness. Let us, then,
bestir ourselves to seek Him in whom are all our fresh
springs.

'*Thy Redeemer*'
Isaiah 54:5

Jesus, the Redeemer, is altogether ours and ours for ever. All the *offices* of Christ are held on our behalf. He is king for us, priest for us, and prophet for us. Whenever we read a new title of the Redeemer, let us appropriate Him as ours under that name as much as under any other. The shepherd's staff, the father's rod, the captain's sword, the priest's mitre, the prince's sceptre, the prophet's mantle, all are ours. Jesus hath no dignity which he will not employ for our exaltation, and no prerogative which he will not exercise for our defence. His fulness of *Godhead* is our unfailing, inexhaustible treasure-house.

His *manhood* also, which he took upon him for us, is ours in all its perfection. To us our gracious Lord communicates the spotless virtue of a stainless character; to us he gives the meritorious efficacy of a devoted life; on us he bestows the reward procured by obedient submission and incessant service. He makes the unsullied garment of his life our covering beauty; the glittering virtues of his character our ornaments and jewels; and the superhuman meekness of his death our boast and glory. He bequeaths us his manger, from which to learn how God came down to man; and his Cross to teach us how man may go up to God. All his thoughts, emotions, actions, utterances, miracles, and intercessions, were for us. He trod the road of sorrow on our behalf, and hath made over to us as his heavenly legacy the full results of all the labours of his life. He is now as much ours as heretofore; and he blushes not to acknowledge himself '*our* Lord Jesus Christ', though he is the blessed and only Potentate, the King of kings, and Lord of lords. Christ everywhere and every way is our Christ, for ever and ever most richly to enjoy. O my soul, by the power of the Holy Spirit! call him this morning, 'thy Redeemer'.

'I am come into my garden, my sister, my spouse'
Canticles 5:1

The heart of the believer is Christ's garden. He bought it with His precious blood, and He enters it and claims it as His own. A garden *implies separation*. It is not the open common; it is not a wilderness; it is walled around, or hedged in. Would that we could see the wall of separation between the church and the world made broader and stronger. It makes one sad to hear Christians saying, 'Well, there is no harm in this; there is no harm in that', thus getting as near to the world as possible. Grace is at a low ebb in that soul which can even raise the question of how far it may go in worldly conformity. A garden is *a place of beauty*, it far surpasses the wild uncultivated lands. The genuine Christian must seek to be more excellent in his life than the best moralist, because Christ's garden ought to produce the best flowers in all the world. Even the best is poor compared with Christ's deservings: let us not put Him off with withering and dwarf plants. The rarest, richest, choicest lilies and roses ought to bloom in the place which Jesus calls His own. The garden is *a place of growth*. The saints are not to remain undeveloped, always mere buds and blossoms. We should grow in grace, and in the knowledge of our Lord and Saviour Jesus Christ. Growth should be rapid where Jesus is the Husbandman, and the Holy Spirit the dew from above. A garden is *a place of retirement*. So the Lord Jesus Christ would have us reserve our souls as a place in which He can manifest Himself, as He doth not unto the world. O that Christians were more retired, that they kept their hearts more closely shut up for Christ! We often worry and trouble ourselves, like Martha, with much serving, so that we have not the room for Christ that Mary had, and do not sit at His feet as we should. The Lord grant the sweet showers of His grace to water His garden this day.

'And they were all filled with the Holy Ghost'
Acts 2:4

Rich were the blessings of this day if all of us were filled with the Holy Ghost. The consequences of this sacred filling of the soul it would be impossible to overestimate. Life, comfort, light, purity, power, peace; and many other precious blessings are inseparable from the Spirit's benign presence. As sacred *oil*, he anoints the head of the believer, sets him apart to the priesthood of saints, and gives him grace to execute his office aright. As the only truly purifying *water* He cleanses us from the power of sin and sanctifies us unto holiness, working in us to will and to do of the Lord's good pleasure. As the *light*, he manifested to us at first our lost estate, and now He reveals the Lord Jesus to us and in us, and guides us in the way of righteousness. Enlightened by his pure celestial ray, we are no more darkness but light in the Lord. *As fire*, he both purges us from dross, and sets our consecrated nature on a blaze. He is the sacrificial flame by which we are enabled to offer our whole souls as a living sacrifice unto God. As heavenly *dew*, He removes our barrenness and fertilises our lives. O that He would drop from above upon us at this early hour! Such morning dew would be a sweet commencement for the day. As the *dove*, with wings of peaceful love He broods over His Church and over the souls of believers, and as a Comforter He dispels the cares and doubts which mar the peace of His beloved. He descends upon the chosen as upon the Lord in Jordan, and bears witness to their sonship by working in them a filial spirit by which they cry Abba, Father. As the *wind*, he brings the breath of life to men; blowing where He listeth He performs the quickening operations by which the spiritual creation is animated and sustained. Would to God, that we might feel His presence this day and every day.

> '*My Beloved is mine, and I am His: He feedeth*
> *among the lilies. Until the day break, and the*
> *shadows flee away, turn, my Beloved,*
> *and be Thou like a roe or a young hart*
> *upon the mountains of Bether*'
> Solomon's Song 2:16, 17

Surely if there be a happy verse in the Bible it is this
- 'My Beloved is mine, and I am His'. So peaceful, so
full of assurance, so overrunning with happiness and
contentment is it, that it might well have been written
by the same hand which penned the twenty-third
Psalm. Yet though the prospect is exceeding fair and
lovely - earth cannot show its superior - it is not entirely
a sunlit landscape. There is a cloud in the sky which
casts a shadow over the scene. Listen, 'Until the day
break, and the shadows flee away'.

There is a word, too, about the 'mountains of
Bether', or, 'the mountains of division', and to our
love, anything like division is bitterness. Beloved, this
may be your present state of mind; you do not doubt
your salvation; you know that Christ is yours, but you
are not feasting with Him. You understand your vital
interest in Him, so that you have no shadow of a doubt
of your being His, and of His being yours, but still his
left hand is not under your head, nor doth His right hand
embrace you. A shade of sadness is cast over your
heart, perhaps by affliction, certainly by the temporary
absence of your Lord, so even while exclaiming, 'I am
His', you are forced to take to your knees and to pray,
'Until the day break, and the shadows flee away, turn,
my Beloved'.

'Where is He?' asks the soul. And the answer
comes, 'He feedeth among the lilies.' If we would find
Christ, we must get into communion with His people,
we must come to the ordinances with His saints. Oh,
for an evening glimpse of Him! Oh, to sup with him
tonight!

*'For, lo, I will command, and I will sift the house of
Israel among all nations, like as corn is sifted in a
sieve, yet shall not the least grain fall upon the earth'*
Amos 9:9

Every sifting comes by *divine command and permission*. Satan must ask leave before he can lay a finger
upon Job. Nay, more, in some sense our siftings are
directly the work of heaven, for the text says, 'I will sift
the house of Israel'. Satan, like a drudge, may hold the
sieve, hoping to destroy the corn; but the overruling
hand of the Master is accomplishing the purity of the
grain by the very process which the enemy intended to
be destructive. Precious, but much sifted corn of the
Lord's floor, be comforted by the blessed fact that the
Lord directeth both flail and sieve to His own glory,
and to thine eternal profit.

The Lord Jesus will surely use the fan which is in
His hand, and will *divide the precious from the vile*. All
are not Israel that are of Israel; the heap on the barn
floor is not clean provender, and hence the winnowing
process must be performed. In the sieve true weight
alone has power. Husks and chaff being devoid of
substance must fly before the wind, and only solid corn
will remain.

Observe the *complete safety of the Lord's wheat*;
even the least grain has a promise of preservation. God
Himself sifts, and therefore it is stern and terrible
work; He sifts them in all places, 'among all nations';
He sifts them in the most effectual manner, 'like as
corn is sifted in a sieve'; and yet for all this, not the
smallest, lightest, or most shrivelled grain, is permitted to fall to the ground. Every individual believer is
precious in the sight of the Lord; a shepherd would not
lose one sheep, nor a jeweller one diamond, nor a
mother one child, nor a man one limb of his body, nor
will the Lord lose one of his redeemed people. However little we may be, if we are the Lord's we may
rejoice that we are preserved in Christ Jesus.

'Straightway they forsook their nets,
and followed Him'
Mark 1:18

When they heard the call of Jesus, Simon and Andrew obeyed at once without demur. If we would always, punctually and with resolute zeal, put in practice what we hear upon the spot, or at the first fit occasion, our attendance at the means of grace, and our reading of good books, could not fail to enrich us spiritually. He will not lose his loaf who has taken care at once to eat it, neither can he be deprived of the benefit of the doctrine who has already acted upon it. Most readers and hearers become moved so far as to purpose to amend; but, alas! the proposal is a blossom which has not been knit, and therefore no fruit comes of it; they wait, they waver, and then they forget, till, like the ponds in nights of frost, when the sun shines by day, they are only thawed in time to be frozen again. That fatal *tomorrow* is blood-red with the murder of fair resolutions; it is the slaughter-house of the innocents. We are very concerned that our little book of 'Evening Readings' should not be fruitless, and therefore we pray that readers may not be readers only, but doers, of the word. *The practice of truth is the most profitable reading of it.* Should the reader be impressed with any duty while perusing these pages, let him hasten to fulfil it before the holy glow has departed from his soul, and let him leave his nets, and all that he has, sooner than be found rebellious to the Master's call. Do not give place to the devil by delay! Haste while opportunity and quickening are in happy conjunction. Do not be caught in your own nets, but break the meshes of worldliness, and away where glory calls you. Happy is the writer who shall meet with readers resolved to carry out his teachings: his harvest shall be a hundredfold, and his Master shall have great honour. Would to God that such might be our reward upon these brief meditations and hurried hints. Grant it, O Lord, unto thy servant!

'Thou art fairer than the children of men'
Psalm 45:2

The entire person of Jesus is but as one gem, and His life is all along but one impression of the seal. He is altogether complete; not only in His several parts, but as a gracious all-glorious whole. His character is not a mass of fair colours mixed confusedly, nor a heap of precious stones laid carelessly one upon another; He is a picture of beauty and a breastplate of glory. In Him, all the 'things of good repute' are in their proper places, and assist in adorning each other. Not one feature in His glorious person attracts attention at the expense of others; but he is perfectly and altogether lovely.

Oh, Jesus! Thy power, Thy grace, Thy justice, Thy tenderness, Thy truth, Thy majesty, and Thine immutability make up such a man, or rather such a God-man, as neither heaven nor earth hath seen elsewhere. Thy infancy, Thy eternity, Thy sufferings, Thy triumphs, Thy death, and Thine immortality, are all woven in one gorgeous tapestry, without seam or rent. Thou art music without discord; Thou art many, and yet not divided; Thou art all things, and yet not diverse. As all the colours blend into one resplendent rainbow, so all the glories of heaven and earth meet in Thee, and unite so wondrously, that there is none like Thee in all things; nay, if all the virtues of the most excellent were bound in one bundle, they could not rival Thee, Thou mirror of all perfection. Thou hast been anointed with the holy oil of myrrh and cassia, which Thy God hath reserved for Thee alone; and as for Thy fragrance, it is as the holy perfume, the like of which none other can ever mingle, even with the art of the apothecary; each spice is fragrant, but the compound is divine.

'Oh, sacred symmetry! oh, rare connection
Of many perfects, to make one perfection!
Oh, heavenly music, where all parts do meet
In one sweet strain, to make one perfect sweet!'

'The foundation of God standeth sure'
2 Timothy 2:19

The foundation upon which our faith rests is this, that 'God was in Christ reconciling the world unto himself, not imputing their trespasses unto them'. The great fact on which genuine faith relies is, that 'the Word was made flesh and dwelt among us', and that 'Christ also hath suffered for sin, the just for the unjust, that He might bring us to God'; 'Who Himself bare our sins in His own body on the tree'; 'For the chastisement of our peace was upon Him and by His stripes we are healed'. In one word, the great pillar of the Christian's hope is *substitution*. The vicarious sacrifice of Christ for the guilty, Christ being made sin for us that we might be made the righteousness of God in Him, Christ offering up a true and proper expiatory and substitutionary sacrifice in the room, place, and stead of as many as the Father gave Him, who are known to God by name, and are recognised in their own hearts by their trusting in Jesus - this is the cardinal fact of the gospel. If this foundation were removed, what could we do? But it standeth firm as the throne of God. We know it; we rest on it; we rejoice in it; and our delight is to hold it, to meditate upon it, and to proclaim it, while we desire to be actuated and moved by gratitude for it in every part of our life and conversation. In these days a direct attack is made upon the doctrine of the atonement. Men cannot bear substitution. They gnash their teeth at the thought of the Lamb of God bearing the sin of man. But we, who know by experience the preciousness of this truth, will proclaim it in defiance of them confidently and unceasingly. We will neither dilute it nor change it, nor fritter it away in any shape or fashion. It shall still be Christ, a *positive substitute*, bearing human guilt and suffering in the stead of men. We cannot, dare not, give it up, for it is our life, and despite every controversy we feel that 'Nevertheless the foundation of God standeth sure'.

'He shall build the temple of the Lord;
and He shall bear the glory'
Zechariah 6:13

Christ Himself is the builder of His spiritual temple,
and He has built it on the mountains of His unchangeable affection, His omnipotent grace, and His infallible
truthfulness. But as it was in Solomon's temple, so in
this; the materials need making ready. There are the
'Cedars of Lebanon', but they are not framed for the
building; they are not cut down, and shaped, and made
into those planks of cedar, whose odiferous beauty
shall make glad the courts of the Lord's house in
Paradise. There are also the rough stones still in the
quarry, they must be hewn thence, and squared. All this
is Christ's own work. Each individual believer is being
prepared, and polished, and made ready for his place in
the temple; but Christ's own hand performs the prepa-
ration-work. Afflictions cannot sanctify, excepting as
they are used by Him to this end. Our prayers and
efforts cannot make us ready for heaven, apart from the
hand of Jesus, who fashioneth our hearts aright.

As in the building of Solomon's temple, 'there was
neither hammer, nor axe, nor any tool of iron, heard in
the house', because all was brought perfectly ready for
the exact spot it was to occupy - so is it with the temple
which Jesus builds; the making ready is all done on
earth. When we reach heaven, there will be no sanctifying us there, no squaring us with affliction, no
planing us with suffering. No, we must be made meet
here - all *that* Christ will do beforehand; and when He
has done it, we shall be ferried by a loving hand across
the stream of death, and brought to the heavenly
Jerusalem, to abide as eternal pillars in the temple of
our Lord.

> Beneath His eye and care,
>   The edifice shall rise,
> Majestic, strong, and fair,
>   And shine above the skies.

'That those things which cannot be shaken may remain'
Hebrews 12:27

We have many things in our possession at the present
moment which *can* be shaken, and it ill becomes a
Christian man to set much store by them, for there is
nothing stable beneath these rolling skies; change is
written upon all things. Yet, we have certain 'things
which *cannot* be shaken', and I invite you this evening
to think of them, that if the things which can be shaken
should all be taken away, you may derive real comfort
from the things that cannot be shaken, which will
remain. Whatever your losses have been, or may be,
you enjoy *present salvation*. You are standing at the
foot of His cross, trusting alone in the merit of Jesus'
precious blood, and no rise or fall of the markets can
interfere with your salvation in Him; no breaking of
banks, no failures and bankruptcies can touch that.
Then you are *a child of God* this evening. God is your
Father. No change of circumstances can ever rob you
of *that*. Although by losses brought to poverty, and
stripped bare, you can say, 'He is my Father still. In my
Father's house are many mansions; therefore will I not
be troubled'. You have another permanent blessing,
namely, *the love of Jesus Christ*. He who is God and
Man loves you with all the strength of His affectionate
nature - nothing can affect *that*. The fig tree may not
blossom, and the flocks may cease from the field, it
matters not to the man who can sing, 'My Beloved is
mine, and I am His'. Our best portion and richest
heritage we cannot lose. Whatever troubles come, let
us play the man; let us show that we are not such little
children as to be cast down by what may happen in this
poor fleeting state of time. Our country is Immanuel's
land, our hope is above the sky, and, therefore, calm as
the summer's ocean; we will see the wreck of everything earthborn, and yet rejoice in the God of our
salvation.

'Ephraim is a cake not turned'
Hosea 7:8

A cake not turned is *uncooked on one side*; and so Ephraim was, in many respects, untouched by divine grace: though there was some partial obedience, there was very much rebellion left. My soul, I charge thee, see whether this be thy case. Art thou thorough in the things of God? Has grace gone through the very centre of thy being so as to be felt in its divine operations in all thy powers, thy actions, thy words, and thy thoughts? To be sanctified, spirit, soul, and body, should be thine aim and prayer; and although sanctification may not be perfect in thee anywhere in degree, yet it must be universal in its action; there must not be the appearance of holiness in one place and reigning sin in another, else thou, too, wilt be a cake not turned.

A cake not turned *is soon burnt on the side nearest the fire*, and although no man can have too much religion, there are some who seem burnt black with bigoted zeal for that part of truth which they have received, or are charred to a cinder with a vainglorious Pharisaic ostentation of those religious performances which suit their humour. The assumed appearance of superior sanctity frequently accompanies a total absence of all vital godliness. The saint in public is a devil in private. He deals in flour by day and in soot by night. The cake which is burned on one side, is dough on the other.

If it be so with me, O Lord, turn me! Turn my unsanctified nature to the fire of Thy love and let it feel the sacred glow, and let my burnt side cool a little while I learn my own weakness and want of heat when I am removed from thy heavenly flame. Let me not be found a double-minded man, but one entirely under the powerful influence of reigning grace; for well I know if I am left like a cake unturned, and am not on both sides the subject of Thy grace, I must be consumed for ever amid everlasting burnings.

'Waiting for the adoption'
Romans 8:23

Even in this world saints are God's children, but men cannot discover them to be so, except by certain moral characteristics. The adoption is not manifested, the children are not yet openly declared. Among the Romans a man might adopt a child, and keep it private for a long time: but there was a second adoption in public; when the child was brought before the constituted authorities its former garments were taken off, and the father who took it to be his child gave it raiment suitable to its new condition of life. 'Beloved, now are we the sons of God, and it doth not yet appear what we shall be.' We are not yet arrayed in the apparel which befits the royal family of heaven; we are wearing in this flesh and blood just what we wore as the sons of Adam; but we know that 'when He shall appear' who is the 'first-born among many brethren', we shall be like Him, we shall see Him as He is. Cannot you imagine that a child taken from the lowest ranks of society, and adopted by a Roman senator, would say to himself, 'I long for the day when I shall be publicly adopted. Then I shall leave off these plebeian garments, and be robed as becomes my senatorial rank'? Happy in what he has received, for that very reason he groans to get the fulness of what is promised him. So it is with us today. We are waiting till we shall put on our proper garments, and shall be manifested as the children of God. We are young nobles, and have not yet worn our coronets. We are young brides, and the marriage day is not yet come, and by the love our Spouse bears us, we are led to long and sigh for the bridal morning. Our very happiness makes us groan after more; our joy, like a swollen spring, longs to well up like an Iceland geyser, leaping to the skies, and it heaves and groans within our spirit for want of space and room by which to manifest itself to men.

'A certain woman of the company lifted up her
voice, and said unto Him, Blessed is the womb that
bare Thee, and the paps which thou hast sucked.
But He said, Yea, rather, blessed are they that hear
the word of God, and keep it'
Luke 11:27, 28

It is fondly imagined by some that it must have
involved very special privileges to have been the
mother of our Lord, because they supposed that she had
the benefit of looking into His very heart in a way in
which we cannot hope to do. There may be an appearance of plausibility in the supposition, but not much.
We do not know that Mary knew more than others;
what she did know she did well to lay up in her heart;
but she does not appear from anything we read in the
Evangelists to have been a better-instructed believer
than any other of Christ's disciples. All that she knew
we also may discover. Do you wonder that we should
say so? Here is a text to prove it: 'The secret of the Lord
is with them that fear Him, and he will show them His
covenant'. Remember the Master's words - 'Henceforth I call you not servants; for the servant knoweth
not what his Lord doeth: but I have called you friends:
for all things that I have heard of my Father I have made
known unto you'. So blessedly does this Divine Re-
vealer of secrets tell us His heart, that He keepeth back
nothing which is profitable to us; His own assurance is,
'If it were not so, I would have told you'. Doth He not
this day manifest Himself unto us as He doth not unto
the world? It is even so; and therefore we will not
ignorantly cry out, 'Blessed is the womb that bare
thee', but we will intelligently bless God that, having
heard the Word and kept it, we have first of all as true
a communion with the Saviour as the Virgin had, and
in the second place as true an acquaintance with the
secrets of His heart as she can be supposed to have
obtained. Happy soul to be thus privileged!

*'Shadrach, Meshach, and Abed-nego, answered and
said... Be it known unto thee, O king,
that we will not serve thy gods'*
Daniel 3:16, 18

The narrative of the manly courage and marvellous
deliverance of the three holy children, or rather cham-
pions, is well calculated to excite in the minds of
believers firmness and steadfastness in upholding the
truth in the teeth of tyranny and in the very jaws of
death. Let young Christians especially learn from their
example, both in matters of faith in religion, and
matters of uprightness in business, never to sacrifice
their consciences. Lose all rather than lose your integrity, and when all else is gone, still hold fast a clear
conscience as the rarest jewel which can adorn the
bosom of a mortal. Be not guided by the will-o'-the-
wisp of policy, but by the pole-star of divine authority.
Follow the right at all hazards. When you see no
present advantage, walk by faith and not by sight. Do
God the honour to trust Him when it comes to matters
of loss for the sake of principle. See whether He will
be your debtor! See if He doth not even in this life prove
His word that 'Godliness, with contentment, is great
gain', and that they who 'seek first the kingdom of God
and His righteousness, shall have all these things added
unto them'. Should it happen that, in the providence of
God, you are a loser by conscience, you shall find that
if the Lord pays you not back in the silver of earthly
prosperity, He will discharge His promise in the gold
of spiritual joy. Remember that a man's life consisteth
not in the abundance of that which he possesseth. To
wear a guileless spirit, to have a heart void of offence,
to have the favour and smile of God, is greater riches
than the mines of Ophir could yield, or the traffic of
Tyre could win. 'Better is a dinner of herbs where love
is, than a stalled ox and inward contention therewith.'
An ounce of heart's-ease is worth a ton of gold.

'Get thee up into the high mountain'
Isaiah 40:9

Our knowledge of Christ is somewhat like climbing
one of our Welsh mountains. When you are at the base
you see but little: the mountain itself appears to be but
one-half as high as it really is. Confined in a little
valley, you discover scarcely anything but the rippling
brooks as they descend into the stream at the foot of the
mountain. Climb the first rising knoll, and the valley
lengthens and widens beneath your feet. Go higher, and
you see the country for four or five miles round, and
you are delighted with the widening prospect. Mount
still, and the scene enlarges; till at last, when you are
on the summit, and look east, west, north and south,
you see almost all England lying before you. Yonder is
a forest in some distant county, perhaps two hundred
miles away, and here the sea, and there a shining river
and the smoking chimneys of a manufacturing town, or
the masts of the ships in a busy port. All these things
please and delight you, and you say, 'I could not have
imagined that so much could be seen at this elevation'.
Now, the Christian life is of the same order. When we
first believe in Christ we see but little of Him. The
higher we climb the more we discover of His beauties.
But who has ever gained the summit? Who has known
all the heights and depths of the love of Christ which
passes knowledge? Paul, when grown old, sitting grey-
haired, shivering in a dungeon in Rome, could say with
greater emphasis than we can, 'I know whom I have
believed', for each experience had been like the climbing of a hill, each trial had been like ascending another
summit, and his death seemed like gaining the top of
the mountain, from which he could see the whole of the
faithfulness and the love of Him to whom he had
committed his soul. Get thee up, dear friend, into the
high mountain.

'The dove found no rest for the sole of her foot'
Genesis 8:9

Reader, can you find rest apart from the ark, Christ
Jesus? Then be assured that your religion is vain. Are
you satisfied with anything short of a conscious knowledge of your union and interest in Christ? Then woe
unto you. If you profess to be a Christian, yet find full
satisfaction in worldly pleasures and pursuits, your
profession is false. If your soul can stretch herself at
rest, and find the bed long enough, and the coverlet
broad enough to cover her in the chambers of sin, then
you are a hypocrite, and far enough from any right
thoughts of Christ or perception of His preciousness.
But if, on the other hand, you feel that if you could
indulge in sin without punishment, yet it would be a
punishment of itself, and that if you could have the
whole world, and abide in it for ever, it would be quite
enough misery not to be parted from it; for your God
- your God - is what your soul craves after; then be of
good courage, thou art a child of God. With all thy sins
and imperfections, take this to thy comfort: if thy soul
has no rest in sin, thou art not as the sinner is! If thou
art still crying after and craving after something better,
Christ has not forgotten thee, for thou hast not quite
forgotten Him. The believer cannot do without his
Lord; words are inadequate to express his thoughts of
Him. We cannot live on the sands of the wilderness, we
want the manna which drops from on high; our skin
bottles of creature confidence cannot yield us a drop of
moisture, but we drink of the rock which follows us,
and that rock is Christ. When you feed on Him your
souls can sing, 'He hath satisfied my mouth with good
things, so that my youth is renewed like the eagle's',
but if you have Him not, your bursting wine vat and
well-filled barn can give you no sort of satisfaction:
rather lament over them in the words of wisdom,
'Vanity of vanities, all is vanity!'.

'Art thou become like unto us?'
Isaiah 14:10

What must be the apostate professor's doom when his naked soul appears before God? How will he bear that voice, 'Depart, ye cursed; thou hast rejected me, and I reject thee; thou hast played the harlot, and departed from Me: I also have banished thee for ever from my presence, and will not have mercy upon thee'. What will be this wretch's shame at the last great day when, before assembled multitudes, the apostate shall be unmasked? See the profane, and sinners who never professed religion, lifting themselves up from their beds of fire to point at him. 'There he is,' says one, 'will he preach the gospel in hell?' 'There he is,' says another, 'he rebuked me for cursing, and was a hypocrite himself!' 'Aha!' says another, 'here comes a psalm-singing Methodist - one who was always at his meeting; he is the man who boasted of his being sure of everlasting life; and here he is!' No greater eagerness will ever be seen among Satanic tormentors, than in that day when devils drag the hypocrite's soul down to perdition. Bunyan pictures this with massive but awful grandeur of poetry when he speaks of the backway to hell. Seven devils bound the wretch with nine cords, and dragged him from the road to heaven, in which he had professed to walk, and thrust him through the back door into hell. Mind that backway to hell, professors! 'Examine yourselves, whether ye be in the faith.' Look well to your state; see whether you be in Christ or not. It is the easiest thing in the world to give a lenient verdict when oneself is to be tried; but O, be just and true here. Be just to all, but be rigorous to yourself. Remember if it be not a rock on which you build, when the house shall fall, great will be the fall of it. O may the Lord give you sincerity, constancy, and firmness; and in no day, however evil, may you be led to turn aside.

'*Having escaped the corruption
that is in the world through lust*'
2 Peter 1:4

Banish for ever all thought of indulging the flesh if you would live in the power of your risen Lord. It were ill that a man who is alive in Christ should dwell in the corruption of sin. 'Why seek ye the living among the dead?' said the angel to Magdalene. Should the living dwell in the sepulchre? Should divine life be immured in the charnel-house of fleshly lust? How can we partake of the cup of the Lord and yet drink the cup of Belial? Surely, believer, from open lusts and sins you are delivered: have you also escaped from the more secret and delusive lime-twigs of the Satanic fowler? Have you come forth from the lust of pride? Have you escaped from slothfulness? Are you seeking day by day to live above worldliness, the pride of life, and the ensnaring vice of avarice? Remember, it is for this that you have been enriched with the treasures of God. If you be indeed the chosen of God, and beloved by Him, do not suffer all the lavish treasures of grace to be wasted upon you. Follow after holiness; it is the Christian's crown and glory. An unholy church! it is useless to the world, and of no esteem among men. It is an abomination, hell's laughter, heaven's abhorrence. The worst evils which have ever come upon the world have been brought upon her by an unholy church. O Christian, the vows of God are upon you. You are God's priest: act as such. You are God's king: reign over your lusts. You are God's chosen: do not associate with Belial. Heaven is your portion: live like a heavenly spirit, so shall you prove that you have true faith in Jesus, for there cannot be faith in the heart unless there be holiness in the life.

> Lord, I desire to live as one
>   Who bears a blood-bought name,
> As one who fears but grieving Thee,
>   And knows no other shame.

'Only ye shall not go very far away'
Exodus 8:28

This is a crafty word from the lip of the arch-tyrant
Pharaoh. If the poor bondaged Israelites must needs go
out of Egypt, then he bargains with them that it shall not
be very far away; not too far for them to escape the
terror of his arms, and the observation of his spies.
After the same fashion, the world loves not the nonconformity of nonconformity, or the dissidence of dissent,
it would have us be more charitable and not carry
matters with too severe a hand. Death to the world, and
burial with Christ, are experiences which carnal minds
treat with ridicule, and hence the ordinance which sets
them forth is almost universally neglected, and even
contemned. Worldly wisdom recommends the path of
compromise, and talks of 'moderation'. According to
this carnal policy, purity is admitted to be very desirable, but we are warned against being too precise; truth
is of course to be followed, but error is not to be
severely denounced. 'Yes,' says the world, 'be spiritually minded by all means, but do not deny yourself a
little gay society, an occasional ball, and a Christmas
visit to a theatre. What's the good of crying down a
thing when it is so fashionable, and everybody does it?'
Multitudes of professors yield to this cunning advice,
to their own eternal ruin. If we would follow the Lord
wholly, we must go right away into the wilderness of
separation, and leave the Egypt of the carnal world
behind us. We must leave its maxims, its pleasures,
and its religion too, and go far away to the place where
the Lord calls His sanctified ones. When the town is on
fire, our house cannot be too far from the flames. When
the plague is abroad, a man cannot be too far from its
haunts. The further from a viper the better, and the
further from worldly conformity the better. To all true
believers let the trumpet-call be sounded, 'Come ye out
from among them, be ye separate'.

> '*Let every man abide in the same calling
> wherein he was called*'
> 1 Corinthians 7:20

Some persons have the foolish notion that the only way
in which they can live for God is by becoming ministers, missionaries, or Bible women. Alas! how many
would be shut out from any opportunity of magnifying
the Most High if this were the case. Beloved, it is not
office, it is earnestness; it is not position, it is grace
which will enable us to glorify God. God is most surely
glorified in that cobbler's stall, where the godly worker,
as he plies the awl, sings of the Saviour's love, ay,
glorified far more than in many a prebendal stall where
official *religiousness* performs its scanty duties. The
name of Jesus is glorified by the poor unlearned carter
as he drives his horse, and blesses his God, or speaks
to his fellow labourer by the roadside, as much as by
the popular divine who, throughout the country, like
Boanerges, is thundering out the gospel. God is glorified by our serving Him in our proper vocations. Take
care, dear reader, that you do not forsake the path of
duty by leaving your occupation, and take care you do
not dishonour your profession while in it. Think little
of yourselves, but do not think too little of your
callings. Every lawful trade may be sanctified by the
gospel to noblest ends. Turn to the Bible, and you will
find the most menial forms of labour connected either
with most daring deeds of faith, or with persons whose
lives have been illustrious for holiness. Therefore be
not discontented with your calling. Whatever God has
made your position, or your work, abide in that, unless
you are *quite sure* that he calls you to something else.
Let your first care be to glorify God to the utmost of
your power where you are. Fill your present sphere to
His praise, and if He needs you in another He will show
it you. This evening lay aside vexatious ambition, and
embrace peaceful content.

'*Looking unto Jesus*'
Hebrews 12:2

It is ever the Holy Spirit's work to turn our eyes away
from self to Jesus; but Satan's work is just the opposite
of this, for he is constantly trying to make us regard
ourselves instead of Christ. He insinuates, 'Your sins
are too great for pardon; you have no faith; you do not
repent enough; you will never be able to continue to the
end; you have not the joy of His children; you have such
a wavering hold of Jesus.' All these are thoughts about
self, and we shall never find comfort or assurance by
looking within. But the Holy Spirit turns our eyes
entirely away from self: He tells us that we are nothing,
but that 'Christ is all in all'. Remember, therefore, it
is not *thy hold* of Christ that saves thee - it is Christ;
it is not *thy joy* in Christ that saves thee - it is Christ;
it is not even faith in Christ, though that be the
instrument - it is Christ's blood and merits; therefore,
look not so much to thy hand with which thou art
grasping Christ, as to Christ; look not to thy hope, but
to Jesus, the author and finisher of thy faith. We shall
never find happiness by looking at our prayers, our
doings, or our feelings; it is what *Jesus* is, not what *we*
are, that gives rest to the soul. If we would at once
overcome Satan and have peace with God, it must be by
'looking unto Jesus'. Keep thine eye simply on Him;
let His death, His sufferings, His merits, His glories,
His intercession, be fresh upon thy mind; when thou
wakest in the morning look to Him; when thou liest
down at night look to Him. Oh! let not thy hopes or
fears come between thee and Jesus; follow hard after
Him, and He will never fail thee.

'My hope is built on nothing less
        Than Jesu's blood and righteousness:
I dare not trust the sweetest frame,
        But wholly lean on Jesu's name.'

'But Aaron's rod swallowed up their rods'
Exodus 7:12

This incident is an instructive emblem of the sure victory of the divine handiwork over all opposition. Whenever a divine principle is cast into the heart, though the devil may fashion a counterfeit, and produce swarms of opponents, as sure as ever God is in the work, it will swallow up all its foes. If God's grace takes possession of a man, the world's magicians may throw down all their rods; and every rod may be as cunning and poisonous as a serpent, but Aaron's rod will swallow up their rods. The sweet attractions of the cross will woo and win the man's heart, and he who lived only for this deceitful earth will now have an eye for the upper spheres, and a wing to mount into celestial heights. When grace has won the day the worldling seeks the world to come. The same fact is to be observed in the life of the believer. What multitudes of foes has our faith had to meet! Our old sins - the devil threw them down before us, and they turned to serpents. What hosts of them! Ah, but the cross of Jesus destroys them all. Faith in Christ makes short work of all our sins. Then the devil has launched forth another host of serpents in the form of worldly trials, temptations, unbelief; but faith in Jesus is more than a match for them, and overcomes them all. The same absorbing principle shines in the faithful service of God! with an enthusiastic love for Jesus difficulties are surmounted, sacrifices become pleasures, sufferings are honours. But, if religion is thus a consuming passion in the heart, then it follows that there are many persons who profess religion but have it not; for what they have will not bear this test. Examine yourself, my reader, on this point. Aaron's rod *proved* its heaven-given power. Is your religion doing so? If Christ be anything He must be everything. O rest not till love and faith in Jesus be the master passions of your soul!

'*Them also which sleep in Jesus
will God bring with Him*'
1 Thessalonians 4:14

Let us not imagine that *the soul* sleeps in insensibility.
'Today shalt thou be with me in paradise,' is the
whisper of Christ to every dying saint. They 'sleep in
Jesus', but their souls are before the throne of God,
praising Him day and night in His temple, singing
hallelujahs to Him who washed them from their sins in
His blood. The body sleeps in its lonely bed of earth,
beneath the coverlet of grass. But what is this sleep?
The idea connected with sleep is '*rest*', and that is the
thought which the Spirit of God would convey to us.
Sleep makes each night a Sabbath for the day. Sleep
shuts fast the door of the soul, and bids all intruders
tarry for a while, that the life within may enter its
summer garden of ease. The toilworn believer quietly
sleeps, as does the weary child when it slumbers on its
mother's breast. Oh! happy they who die in the Lord;
they rest from their labours, and their works do follow
them. Their quiet repose shall never be broken until
God shall rouse them to give them their full reward.
Guarded by angel watchers, curtained by eternal mysteries, they sleep on, the heritors of glory, till the
fulness of time shall bring the fulness of redemption.
What an awaking shall be theirs! They were laid in their
last resting place, weary and worn, but such they shall
not rise. They went to their rest with the furrowed
brow, and the wasted features, but they wake up in
beauty and glory. The shrivelled seed, so destitute of
form and comeliness, rises from the dust a beauteous
flower. The winter of the grave gives way to the spring
of redemption and the summer of glory. Blessed is
death, since it, through the divine power, disrobes us
of this work-day garment, to clothe us with the wedding garment of incorruption. Blessed are those who
'sleep in Jesus'.

'Howbeit, in the business of the ambassadors of
the princes of Babylon, who sent unto him to
enquire of the wonder that was done in the land,
God left him, to try him,
that He might know all that was in his heart'
2 Chronicles 32:31

Hezekiah was growing so inwardly great, and priding himself so much upon the favour of God, that self-righteousness crept in, and through his carnal security, the grace of God was for a time, in its more active operations, withdrawn. Here is quite enough to account for his folly with the Babylonians; for if the grace of God should leave the best Christian, there is enough of sin in his heart to make him the worst of transgressors. If left to yourselves, you who are warmest for Christ would cool down like Laodicea into sickening lukewarmness: you who are sound in the faith would be white with the leprosy of false doctrine; you who now walk before the Lord in excellency and integrity would reel to and fro, and stagger with a drunkenness of evil passion. Like the moon, we borrow our light; bright as we are when grace shines on us, we are darkness itself when the Sun of Righteousness withdraws Himself. *Therefore let us cry to God never to leave us.* 'Lord, take not thy Holy Spirit from us! withdraw not from us Thine indwelling grace! Hast Thou not said, I the Lord do keep it; I will water it every moment: lest any hurt it, I will keep it night and day? Lord, keep us everywhere. Keep us when in the valley, that we murmur not against Thy humbling hand; keep us when on the mountain, that we wax not giddy through being lifted up; keep us in youth, when our passions are strong; keep us in old age, when becoming conceited of our wisdom, we may therefore prove greater fools than the young and giddy; keep us when we come to die, lest, at the very last, we should deny Thee! Keep us living, keep us dying, keep us labouring, keep us suffering, keep us fighting, keep us resting, keep us everywhere, for everywhere we need Thee, O our God!'

> *'And the glory which Thou*
> *gavest me I have given them'*
> John 17:22

Behold the superlative liberality of the Lord Jesus, for He hath given us His all. Although a tithe of His possessions would have made a universe of angels rich beyond all thought, yet was He not content until He had given us all that He had. It would have been surprising grace if He had allowed us to eat the crumbs of His bounty beneath the table of His mercy; but He will do nothing by halves, He makes us sit with Him and share the feast. Had He given us some small pension from His royal coffers, we should have had cause to love Him eternally; but no, He will have His bride as rich as Himself, and He will not have a glory or a grace in which she shall not share. He has not been content with less than making us joint-heirs with Himself, so that we might have equal possessions. He has emptied all His estate into the coffers of the Church, and hath all things common with His redeemed. There is not one room in His house the key of which He will withhold from His people. He gives them full liberty to take all that He hath to be their own; He loves them to make free with His treasure, and appropriate as much as they can possibly carry. The boundless fulness of His all-sufficiency is as free to the believer as the air he breathes. Christ hath put the flagon of His love and grace to the believer's lip, and bidden him drink on for ever; for could he drain it, he is welcome to do so, and as he cannot exhaust it, he is bidden to drink abundantly, for it is all his own. What truer proof of fellowship can heaven or earth afford?

> 'When I stand before the throne
>   Dressed in beauty not my own;
> When I see Thee as Thou art,
>   Love Thee with unsinning heart;
> Then, Lord, shall I fully know -
>   Not till then - how much I owe.'

'Ah, Lord God, behold, Thou hast made the heaven
and the earth by thy great power and stretched out
arm, and there is nothing too hard for Thee'
Jeremiah 32:17

At the very time when the Chaldeans surrounded
Jerusalem, and when the sword, famine and pestilence
had desolated the land, Jeremiah was commanded by
God to purchase a field, and have the deed of transfer
legally sealed and witnessed. This was a strange
purchase for a rational man to make. Prudence could
not justify it, for it was buying with scarcely a probability that the person purchasing could ever enjoy the
possession. But it was enough for Jeremiah that his
God had bidden him, for well he knew that God will be
justified of all His children. He reasoned thus: 'Ah,
Lord God! Thou canst make this plot of ground of use
to me; Thou canst rid this land of these oppressors;
Thou canst make me yet sit under my vine and my fig-
tree in the heritage which I have bought; for Thou didst
make the heavens and the earth, and there is nothing too
hard for Thee.' This gave a majesty to the early saints,
that they dared to do at God's command things which
carnal reason would condemn. Whether it be a Noah
who is to build a ship on dry land, an Abraham who is
to offer up his only son, or a Moses who is to despise
the treasures of Egypt, or a Joshua who is to besiege
Jericho seven days, using no weapons but the blasts of
rams' horns, they all act upon God's command, contrary to the dictates of carnal reason; and the Lord gives
them a rich reward as the result of their obedient faith.
Would to God we had in the religion of these modern
times a more potent infusion of this heroic faith in God.
If we would venture more upon the naked promise of
God, we should enter a world of wonders to which as
yet we are strangers. Let Jeremiah's place of confidence be ours - nothing is too hard for the God that
created the heavens and the earth.

July

'In summer and in winter shall it be'
Zechariah 14:8

The streams of living water which flow from Jerusalem are not dried up by the parching heats of sultry midsummer any more than they were frozen by the cold winds of blustering winter. Rejoice, O my soul, that thou art spared to testify of the faithfulness of the Lord. The seasons change and thou changest, but thy Lord abides evermore the same, and the streams of His love are as deep, as broad and as full as ever. The heats of business cares and scorching trials make me need the cooling influences of the river of His grace; I may go at once and drink to the full from the inexhaustible fountain, for in summer and in winter it pours forth its flood. The upper springs are never scanty, and blessed be the name of the Lord, the nether springs cannot fail either. Elijah found Cherith dry up, but Jehovah was still the same God of providence. Job said his brethren were like deceitful brooks, but he found his God an overflowing river of consolation. The Nile is the great confidence of Egypt, but its floods are variable; our Lord is evermore the same. By turning the course of the Euphrates, Cyrus took the city of Babylon, but no power, human or infernal, can divert the current of divine grace. The tracks of ancient rivers have been found all dry and desolate, but the streams which take their rise on the mountains of divine sovereignty and infinite love shall ever be full to the brim. Generations melt away, but the course of grace is unaltered. The river of God may sing with greater truth than the brook in the poem:

'Men may come, and men may go,
But I go on for ever.'

How happy art thou, my soul, to be led beside such still waters! Never wander to other streams, lest thou hear the Lord's rebuke, 'What hast thou to do in the way of Egypt to drink of the muddy river?'

'The voice of the Lord God walking
in the garden in the cool of the day'
Genesis 3:8

My soul, now that the cool of the day has come, retire awhile and hearken to the voice of thy God. He is always ready to speak with thee when thou art prepared to hear. If there be any slowness to commune it is not on His part, but altogether on thine own, for He stands at the door and knocks, and if His people will but open He rejoices to enter. But in what state is my heart, which is my Lord's garden? May I venture to hope that it is well trimmed and watered, and is bringing forth fruit fit for Him? If not, He will have much to reprove, but still I pray Him to come unto me, for nothing can so certainly bring my heart into a right condition as the presence of the Sun of Righteousness, who brings healing in His wings. Come, therefore, O Lord, my God, my soul invites Thee earnestly, and waits for thee eagerly. Come to me, O Jesus, my well-beloved, and plant fresh flowers in my garden, such as I see blooming in such perfection in Thy matchless character! Come, O my Father, who art the Husbandman, and deal with me in Thy tenderness and prudence! Come, O Holy Spirit, and bedew my whole nature, as the herbs are now moistened with the evening dews. O that God would speak to me. Speak, Lord, for Thy servant heareth! O that He would walk with me; I am ready to give up my whole heart and mind to Him, and every other thought is hushed. I am only asking what He delights to give. I am sure that He will condescend to have fellowship with me, for He has given me His Holy Spirit to abide with me for ever. Sweet is the cool twilight, when every star seems like the eye of heaven, and the cool wind is as the breath of celestial love. My Father, my elder Brother, my sweet Comforter, speak now in loving-kindness, for Thou hast opened mine ear and I am not rebellious.

'Our heart shall rejoice in Him'
Psalm 33:21

Blessed is the fact that Christians can rejoice even in
the deepest distress; although trouble may surround
them, they still sing; and, like many birds, they sing
best in their cages. The waves may roll over them, but
their souls soon rise to the surface and see the light of
God's countenance; they have a buoyancy about them
which keeps their head always above the water, and
helps them to sing amid the tempest, 'God is with me
still'. To whom shall the glory be given? Oh! to *Jesus*
- it is all by Jesus. Trouble does not necessarily bring
consolation with it to the believer, but the presence of
the Son of God in the fiery furnace with him fills his
heart with joy. He is sick and suffering, but Jesus visits
him and makes his bed for him. He is dying, and the
cold chilly waters of Jordan are gathering about him up
to the neck, but Jesus puts His arms around him, and
cries, 'Fear not, beloved; to die is to be blessed; the
waters of death have their fountain-head in heaven;
they are not bitter, they are sweet as nectar, for they
flow from the throne of God.' As the departing saint
wades through the stream, and the billows gather
around him, and heart and flesh fail him, the same voice
sounds in his ears, 'Fear not; I am with thee; be not
dismayed; I am thy God'. As he nears the borders of the
infinite unknown, and is almost afrighted to enter the
realm of shades, Jesus says, 'Fear not, it is your
Father's good pleasure to give you the kingdom.' Thus
strengthened and consoled, the believer is not afraid to
die; nay, he is even willing to depart, for since he has
seen Jesus as the morning star, he longs to gaze upon
Him as the sun in his strength. Truly, the presence of
Jesus is all the heaven we desire. He is at once

'The glory of our brightest days;
The comfort of our nights.'

'Unto Thee will I cry, O Lord my rock;
be not silent to me: lest, if Thou be silent to me,
I become like them that go down into the pit'
Psalm 28:1

A cry is the natural expression of sorrow, and a suitable utterance when all other modes of appeal fail us; but the cry must be alone directed to the Lord, for to cry to man is to waste our entreaties upon the air. When we consider the readiness of the Lord to hear, and His ability to aid, we shall see good reason for directing all our appeals at once to the God of our salvation. It will be in vain to call to the rocks in the day of judgment, but our Rock attends to our cries.

'*Be not silent to me.*' Mere formalists may be content without answers to their prayers, but genuine suppliants cannot; they are not satisfied with the results of prayer itself in calming the mind and subduing the will - they must go further, and obtain actual replies from heaven, or they cannot rest; and those replies they long to receive at once, they dread even a little of God's silence. God's voice is often so terrible that it shakes the wilderness; but His silence is equally full of awe to an eager suppliant. When God seems to close His ear, we must not therefore close our mouths, but rather cry with more earnestness; for when our note grows shrill with eagerness and grief, He will not long deny us a hearing. What a dreadful case should we be in if the Lord should become for ever silent to our prayers? '*Lest, if Thou be silent to me, I become like them that go down into the pit.*' Deprived of the God who answers prayer, we should be in a more pitiable plight than the dead in the grave, and should soon sink to the same level as the lost in hell. We *must* have answers to prayer: ours is an urgent case of dire necessity; surely the Lord will speak peace to our agitated minds, for He never can find it in His heart to permit His own elect to perish.

*'The ill-favoured and leanfleshed kine did eat up the
seven well-favoured and fat kine'*
Genesis 41:4

Pharaoh's dream has too often been my waking experience. My days of sloth have ruinously destroyed all that I had achieved in times of zealous industry; my seasons of coldness have frozen all the genial glow of my periods of fervency and enthusiasm; and my fits of worldliness have thrown me back from my advances in the divine life. I had need to beware of lean prayers, lean praises, lean duties, and lean experiences, for these will eat up the fat of my comfort and peace. If I neglect prayer for never so short a time, I lose all the spirituality to which I had attained; if I draw no fresh supplies from heaven, the old corn in my granary is soon consumed by the famine which rages in my soul. When the caterpillars of indifference, the cankerworms of worldliness, and the palmerworms of self-indulgence, lay my heart completely desolate, and make my soul to languish, all my former fruitfulness and growth in grace avails me nothing whatever. How anxious should I be to have no lean-fleshed days, no ill-favoured hours! If every day I journeyed towards the goal of my desires I should soon reach it, but backsliding leaves me still far off from the prize of my high calling, and robs me of the advances which I had so laboriously made. The only way in which all my days can be as the 'fat kine', is to feed them in the right meadow, to spend them with the Lord, in His service, in His company, in His fear, and in His way. Why should not every year be richer than the past, in love, and usefulness, and joy? - I am nearer the celestial hills, I have had more experience of my Lord, and should be more like Him. O Lord, keep far from me the curse of leanness of soul; let me not have to cry, 'My leanness, my leanness, woe unto me!' but may I be well-fed and nourished in Thy house, that I may praise Thy name.

'If we suffer, we shall also reign with Him'
2 Timothy 2:12

We must not imagine that we are suffering for Christ, and with Christ, if we are not in Christ. Beloved friend, are you trusting to Jesus only? If not, whatever you may have to mourn over on earth, you are not 'suffering with Christ', and have no hope of reigning with Him in heaven. Neither are we to conclude that all a Christian's sufferings are sufferings with Christ, for *it is essential that he be called by God to suffer.* If we are rash and imprudent, and run into positions for which neither providence nor grace has fitted us, we ought to question whether we are not rather sinning than communing with Jesus. If we let passion take the place of judgment, and self-will reign instead of Scriptural authority, we shall fight the Lord's battles with the devil's weapons, and if we cut our own fingers we must not be surprised. Again, *in troubles which come upon us as the result of sin, we must not dream that we are suffering with Christ.* When Miriam spoke evil of Moses, and the leprosy polluted her, she was not suffering for God. Moreover, suffering which God accepts *must have God's glory as its end.* If I suffer that I may earn a name, or win applause, I shall get no other reward than that of the Pharisee. It is requisite also *that love to Jesus, and love to his elect, be ever the mainspring of all our patience. We must manifest the Spirit of Christ* in meekness, gentleness, and forgiveness. Let us search and see if we truly *suffer with Jesus.* And if we do thus suffer, what is our 'light affliction' compared with *reigning with Him*? Oh it is so blessed to be in the furnace with Christ, and such an honour to stand in the pillory with Him, that if there were no future reward, we might count ourselves happy in present honour; but when the recompense is so eternal, so infinitely more than we had any right to expect, shall we not take up the cross with alacrity, and go on our way rejoicing?

'Sanctify them through Thy truth'
John 17:17

Sanctification begins in regeneration. The Spirit of God infuses into man that new living principle by which he becomes 'a new creature' in Christ Jesus. This work, which begins in the new birth, is carried on in two ways - mortification, whereby the lusts of the flesh are subdued and kept under; and vivification, by which the life which God has put within us is made to be a well of water springing up unto everlasting life. This is carried on every day in what is called 'perseverance', by which the Christian is preserved and continued in a gracious state, and is made to abound in good works unto the praise and glory of God; and it culminates or comes to perfection, in 'glory', when the soul, being thoroughly purged, is caught up to dwell with holy beings at the right hand of the Majesty on high. But while the Spirit of God is thus the author of sanctification, yet there is a visible agency employed which must not be forgotten. 'Sanctify them,' said Jesus, 'through thy *truth*: thy word is truth.' The passages of Scripture which prove that the instrument of our sanctification is the Word of God are very many. The Spirit of God brings to our mind the precepts and doctrines of truth, and applies them with power. These are heard in the ear, and being received in the heart, they work in us to will and to do of God's good pleasure. The truth is the sanctifier, and if we do not hear or read the truth, we shall not grow in sanctification. We only progress in sound living as we progress in sound understanding. 'Thy word is a lamp unto my feet and a light unto my path.' Do not say of any error, 'It is a mere matter of opinion'. No man indulges an error of judgment, without sooner or later tolerating an error in practice. Hold fast the truth, for by so holding the truth shall you be sanctified by the Spirit of God.

> *'He that hath clean hands, and a pure heart;*
> *who hath not lifted up his soul unto vanity,*
> *nor sworn deceitfully'*
> Psalm 24:4

Outward practical holiness is a very precious mark of grace. It is to be feared that many professors have perverted the doctrine of justification by faith in such a way as to treat good works with contempt; if so, they will receive everlasting contempt at the last great day. If our hands are not clean, let us wash them in Jesus' precious blood, and so let us lift up pure hands unto God. But *'clean hands'* will not suffice, unless they are connected with *'a pure heart'*. True religion is heart-work. We may wash the outside of the cup and the platter as long as we please, but if the inward parts be filthy, we are filthy altogether in the sight of God, for our hearts are more truly ourselves than our hands are; the very life of our being lies in the inner nature, and hence the imperative need of purity within. The pure in heart shall see God, all others are but blind bats.

The man who is born for heaven *'hath not lifted up his soul unto vanity'*. All men have their joys, by which their souls are lifted up; the worldling lifts up his soul in carnal delights, which are mere empty vanities; but the saint loves more substantial things; like Jehoshaphat, he is lifted up in the ways of the Lord. He who is content with husks, will be reckoned with the swine. Does the world satisfy thee? Then thou hast thy reward and portion in this life; make much of it, for thou shalt know no other joy.

'Nor sworn deceitfully.' The saints are men of honour still. The Christian man's word is his only oath; but that is as good as twenty oaths of other men. False speaking will shut any man out of heaven, for a liar shall not enter into God's house, whatever may be his professions or doings. Reader, does the text before us condemn thee, or dost thou hope to ascend into the hill of the Lord?

'Called to be saints'
Romans 1:7

We are very apt to regard the apostolic saints as if they were 'saints' in a more especial manner than the other children of God. All are 'saints' whom God has called by His grace, and sanctified by His Spirit; but we are apt to look upon the *apostles* as extraordinary beings, scarcely subject to the same weaknesses and temptations as ourselves. Yet in so doing we are forgetful of this truth, that the nearer a man lives to God the more intensely has he to mourn over his own evil heart; and the more his Master honours him in His service, the more also doth the evil of the flesh vex and tease him day by day. The fact is, if we had seen the apostle Paul, we should have thought him remarkably like the rest of the chosen family: and if we had talked with him, we should have said, 'We find that his experience and ours are much the same. He is more faithful, more holy, and more deeply taught than we are, but he has the selfsame trials to endure. Nay, in some respects he is more sorely tried than ourselves.' Do not, then, look upon the ancient saints as being exempt either from infirmities or sins; and do not regard them with that mystic reverence which will almost make us idolaters. Their holiness is attainable even by us. We are 'called to be saints' by that same voice which constrained them to their high vocation. It is a Christian's duty to force his way into the inner circle of saintship; and if these saints were superior to us in their attainments, as they certainly were, let us follow them; let us emulate their ardour and holiness. We have the same light that they had, the same grace is accessible to us, and why should we rest satisfied until we have equalled them in heavenly character? They lived *with* Jesus, they lived *for* Jesus, therefore they grew *like* Jesus. Let us live by the same Spirit as they did, 'looking unto Jesus', and our saintship will soon be apparent.

'*Trust ye in the Lord for ever:*
for in the Lord Jehovah is everlasting strength'
Isaiah 26:4

Seeing that we have such a God to trust to, let us rest
upon him with all our weight; let us resolutely drive out
all unbelief, and endeavour to get rid of doubts and
fears, which so much mar our comfort; since there is
no excuse for fear where God is the foundation of our
trust. A loving parent would be sorely grieved if his
child could not trust him; and how ungenerous, how
unkind is our conduct when we put so little confidence
in our heavenly Father who has never failed us, and
who never will. It were well if doubting were banished
from the household of God; but it is to be feared that
old Unbelief is as nimble nowadays as when the
psalmist asked, 'Is His mercy clean gone for ever? Will
He be favourable no more?' David had not made any
very lengthy trial of the mighty sword of the giant
Goliath, and yet he said, 'There is none like it'. He had
tried it once in the hour of his youthful victory, and it
had proved itself to be of the right metal, and therefore
he praised it ever afterwards; even so should we speak
well of our God, there is none like unto Him in the
heaven above or the earth beneath; 'To whom then will
ye liken Me, or shall I be equal? saith the Holy One'.
There is no rock like unto the rock of Jacob, our
enemies themselves being judges. So far from suffering doubts to live in our hearts, we will take the whole
detestable crew, as Elijah did the prophets of Baal, and
slay them over the brook; and for a stream to kill them
at, we will select the sacred torrent which wells forth
from our Saviour's wounded side. We have been in
many trials, but we have never yet been cast where we
could not find in our God all that we needed. Let us then
be encouraged to trust in the Lord for ever, assured that
His everlasting strength will be, as it has been, our
succour and stay.

> '*Whoso hearkeneth unto me shall dwell safely, and*
> *shall be quiet from fear of evil*'
> Proverbs 1:33

Divine love is rendered conspicuous when it shines in
the midst of judgments. Fair is that lone star which
smiles through the rifts of the thunder clouds; bright is
the oasis which blooms in the wilderness of sand; so
fair and so bright is love in the midst of wrath. When
the Israelites provoked the Most High by their continued idolatry, He punished them by withholding both
dew and rain, so that their land was visited by a sore
famine; but while He did this, he took care that His own
chosen ones should be secure. If all other brooks are
dry, yet shall there be one reserved for Elijah; and when
that fails, God shall still preserve for him a place of
sustenance; nay, not only so, the Lord had not simply
one 'Elijah', but He had a remnant according to the
election of grace, who were hidden by fifties in a cave,
and though the whole land was subject to famine, yet
these fifties in the cave were fed, and fed from Ahab's
table too by His faithful, God-fearing steward, Obadiah. Let us from this draw the inference, that come
what may, God's people are safe. Let convulsions
shake the solid earth, let the skies themselves be rent
in twain, yet amid the wreck of worlds the believer shall
be as secure as in the calmest hour of rest. If God cannot
save His people *under* heaven, He will save them *in*
heaven. If the world becomes too hot to hold them, then
heaven shall be the place of their reception and their
safety. Be ye then confident, when ye hear of wars, and
rumours of wars. Let no agitation distress you, but be
quiet from fear of evil. Whatsoever cometh upon the
earth, you, beneath the broad wings of Jehovah, shall
be secure. Stay yourself upon His promise; rest in His
faithfulness, and bid defiance to the blackest future, for
there is nothing in it direful for you. Your sole concern
should be to show forth to the world the blessedness of
hearkening to the voice of wisdom.

'How many are mine iniquities and sins?'
Job 13:23

Have you ever really weighed and considered how great
the sin of God's people is? Think how heinous is your
own transgression, and you will find that not only does
a sin here and there tower up like an alp, but that your
iniquities are heaped upon each other, as in the old fable
of the giants who piled Pelian upon Ossa, mountain
upon mountain. What an aggregate of sin there is in the
life of one of the most sanctified of God's children!
Attempt to multiply this, the sin of one only, by the
multitude of the redeemed, 'a number which no man
can number', and you will have some conception of the
great mass of the guilt of the people for whom Jesus
shed His blood. But we arrive at a more adequate idea
of the magnitude of sin by the greatness of the remedy
provided. It is the blood of Jesus Christ, God's only
and well-beloved Son. God's Son! Angels cast their
crowns before Him! All the choral symphonies of
heaven surround His glorious throne. 'God over all,
blessed for ever. Amen.' And yet He takes upon
Himself the form of a servant, and is scourged and
pierced, bruised and torn, and at last slain; since
nothing but the blood of the incarnate Son of God could
make atonement for our offences. No human mind can
adequately estimate the infinite value of the divine
sacrifice, for great as is the sin of God's people, the
atonement which takes it away is immeasurably greater.
Therefore, the believer, even when sin rolls like a black
flood, and the remembrance of the past is bitter, can yet
stand before the blazing throne of the great and holy
God, and cry, 'Who is he that condemneth? It is Christ
that died, yea rather, that hath risen again.' While the
recollection of his sin fills him with shame and sorrow,
he at the same time makes it a foil to show the
brightness of mercy - guilt is the dark night in which
the fair star of divine love shines with serene splendour.

'Brethren, pray for us'
1 Thessalonians 5:25

This one morning in the year we reserved to refresh the reader's memory upon the subject of prayer for ministers, and we do most earnestly implore every Christian household to grant the fervent request of the text first uttered by an apostle and now repeated by us. Brethren, our work is solemnly momentous, involving weal or woe to thousands; we treat with souls for God on eternal business, and our word is either a savour of life unto life, or of death unto death. A very heavy responsibility rests upon us, and it will be no small mercy if at the last we be found clear of the blood of all men. As officers in Christ's army, we are the especial mark of the enmity of men and devils; they watch for our halting, and labour to take us by the heels. Our sacred calling involves us in temptations from which you are exempt, above all it too often draws us away from our personal enjoyment of truth into a ministerial and official consideration of it. We meet with many knotty cases, and our wits are at a non plus; we observe very sad backslidings, and our hearts are wounded; we see millions perishing, and our spirits sink. We wish to profit you by our preaching; we desire to be blest to your children; we long to be useful both to saints and sinners; therefore, dear friends, intercede for us with our God. Miserable men are we if we miss the aid of your prayers, but happy are we if we live in your supplications. You do not look to us but to our Master for spiritual blessings, and yet how many times has He given those blessings through His ministers; ask then, again and again, that we may be the earthen vessels into which the Lord may put the treasure of the gospel. We, the whole company of missionaries, ministers, city missionaries, and students, do in the name of Jesus beseech you

'BRETHREN, PRAY FOR US.'

'When I passed by thee, I said unto thee, Live'
Ezekiel 16:6

Saved one, consider gratefully this mandate of mercy. Note that this fiat of God is *majestic*. In our text, we perceive a sinner with nothing in him but sin, expecting nothing but wrath; but the eternal Lord passes by in His glory; He looks, He pauses, and He pronounces the solitary but royal word, 'Live'. There speaks a God. Who but He could venture thus to deal with life and dispense it with a single syllable? Again, this fiat is *manifold*. When He saith 'Live', it includes many things. Here is judicial life. The sinner is ready to be condemned, but the mighty One saith, 'Live', and he rises pardoned and absolved. It is spiritual life. We knew not Jesus - our eyes could not see Christ, our ears could not hear His voice - Jehovah said, 'Live', and we were quickened who were dead in trespasses and sins. Moreover, it includes glory-life, which is the perfection of spiritual life. 'I said unto thee, Live': and that word rolls on through all the years of time till death comes, and in the midst of the shadows of death, the Lord's voice is still heard, 'Live'! In the morning of the resurrection it is that self-same voice which is echoed by the archangel, 'Live', and as holy spirits rise to heaven to be blest for ever in the glory of their God, it is in the power of this same word, 'Live'. Note again, that it is an *irresistible* mandate. Saul of Tarsus is on the road to Damascus to arrest the saints of the living God. A voice is heard from heaven and a light is seen above the brightness of the sun, and Saul is crying out, 'Lord, what wilt Thou have me to do?' This mandate is a mandate of *free grace*. When sinners are saved, it is only and solely because God *will* do it to magnify His free, unpurchased, unsought grace. Christians, see your position, debtors to grace; show your gratitude by earnest, Christlike lives, and as God has bidden you live, see to it that you live in earnest.

*'Tell me, I pray thee,
wherein thy great strength lieth'*
Judges 16:6

Where lies the secret strength of faith? It lies in the
food it feeds on; for faith studies *what the promise is*
- an emanation of divine grace, an overflowing of the
great heart of God; and faith says, 'My God could not
have given this promise, except from love and grace;
therefore it is quite certain His Word will be fulfilled'.
Then faith thinketh, *'Who gave* this promise?' It
considereth not so much its greatness, as, 'Who is the
author of it?' She remembers that it is God who cannot
lie - God omnipotent, God immutable; and therefore
concludeth that the promise must be fulfilled; and
forward she advances in this firm conviction. She
remembereth *why the promise was given* - namely, for
God's glory, and she feels perfectly sure that God's
glory is safe, that He will never stain His own escutch-
eon, nor mar the lustre of His own crown; and therefore
the promise must and will stand. Then faith also
considereth the amazing *work of Christ* as being a clear
proof of the Father's intention to fulfil His word. 'He
that spared not His own Son, but freely delivered Him
up for us all, how shall He not with Him also freely give
us all things?' Moreover faith looks back upon *the
past*, for her battles have strengthened her, and her
victories have given her courage. She remembers that
God never has failed her; nay, that He never did once
fail any of His children. She recollecteth times of great
peril, when deliverance came; hours of awful need,
when as her day her strength was found, and she cries,
'No, I never will be led to think that He can change and
leave His servant now. Hitherto the Lord hath helped
me, and He will help me still.' Thus faith views each
promise in its connection with the promise-giver, and,
because she does so, can with assurance say, 'Surely
goodness and mercy shall follow me all the days of my
life!'

'Lead me in Thy truth, and teach me:
for Thou art the God of my salvation;
on Thee do I wait all the day'
Psalm 25:5

When the believer has begun with trembling feet to walk in the way of the Lord, he asks to be still led onward like a little child upheld by its parent's helping hand, and he craves to be further instructed in the alphabet of truth. Experimental teaching is the burden of this prayer. David knew much, but he felt his ignorance, and desired to be still in the Lord's school: four times over in two verses he applies for a scholarship in the college of grace. It were well for many professors if instead of following their own devices, and cutting out new paths of thought for themselves, they would enquire for the good old ways of God's own truth, and beseech the Holy Ghost to give them sanctified understandings and teachable spirits. '*For thou art the God of my salvation.*' The Three-One Jehovah is the Author and Perfecter of salvation to His people. Reader, is He the God of *your* salvation? Do you find in the Father's election, in the Son's atonement, and in the Spirit's quickening, all the grounds of your eternal hopes? If so, you may use this as an argument for obtaining further blessings; if the Lord has ordained to save you, surely He will not refuse to instruct you in His ways. It is a happy thing when we can address the Lord with the confidence which David here manifests, it gives us great power in prayer, and comfort in trial. '*On Thee do I wait all the day.*' Patience is the fair handmaid and daughter of faith; we cheerfully wait when we are certain that we shall not wait in vain. It is our duty and our privilege to wait upon the Lord in service, in worship, in expectancy, in trust all the days of our life. Our faith will be tried faith, and if it be of the true kind, it will bear continued trial without yielding. We shall not grow weary of waiting upon God if we remember how long and how graciously He once waited for us.

'Forget not all His benefits'
Psalm 103:2

It is a delightful and profitable occupation to mark the hand of God in the lives of ancient saints, and to observe His goodness in delivering them, His mercy in pardoning them, and His faithfulness in keeping His covenant with them. But would it not be even more interesting and profitable for us to remark the hand of God in our own lives? Ought we not to look upon our own history as being at least as full of God, as full of His goodness and of His truth, as much a proof of His faithfulness and veracity, as the lives of any of the saints who have gone before? We do our Lord an injustice when we suppose that He wrought all His mighty acts, and showed Himself strong for those in the early time, but doth not perform wonders or lay bare his arm for the saints who are now upon the earth. Let us review our own lives. Surely in these we may discover some happy incidents, refreshing to ourselves and glorifying to our God. Have you had no *deliverances*? Have you passed through no rivers, supported by the divine presence? Have you walked through no fires unharmed? Have you had no *manifestations*? Have you had no *choice favours*? The God who gave Solomon the desire of his heart, hath He never listened to you and answered your requests? That God of lavish bounty of whom David sang, 'Who satisfieth thy mouth with good things', hath He never satiated *you* with fatness? Have you never been made to lie down in green pastures? Have you never been led by the still waters? Surely the goodness of God has been the same to us as to the saints of old. Let us then weave His mercies into a song. Let us take the pure gold of thankfulness, and the jewels of praise and make them into another crown for the head of Jesus. Let our souls give forth music as sweet and as exhilarating as came from David's harp, while we praise the Lord whose mercy endureth for ever.

'And God divided the light from the darkness'
Genesis 1:4

A believer has two principles at work within him. In his
natural estate he was subject to one principle only,
which was darkness; now light has entered, and the two
principles disagree. Mark the apostle Paul's words in
the seventh chapter of Romans: 'I find then a law, that,
when I would do good, evil is present with me. For I
delight in the law of God after the inward man: but I see
another law in my members, warring against the law of
my mind, and bringing me into captivity to the law of
sin, which is in my members.' How is this state of
things occasioned? 'The Lord divided the light from
the darkness.' Darkness, by itself, is quiet and undisturbed, but when the Lord sends in light, there is a
conflict, for the one is in opposition to the other: a
conflict which will never cease till the believer is
altogether light in the Lord. If there be a division *within*
the individual Christian, there is certain to be *a division
without.* So soon as the Lord gives to any man light, he
proceeds to separate himself from the darkness around;
he secedes from a merely worldly religion of outward
ceremonial, for nothing short of the gospel of Christ
will now satisfy him, and he withdraws himself from
worldly society and frivolous amusements, and seeks
the company of the saints, for 'We know we have
passed from death unto life, because we love the
brethren'. The light gathers to itself, and the darkness
to itself. What God has divided, let us never try to
unite, but as Christ went without the camp, bearing His
reproach, so let us come out from the ungodly, and be
a peculiar people. He was holy, harmless, undefiled,
separate from sinners; and, as He was, so we are to be
nonconformists to the world, dissenting from all sin,
and distinguished from the rest of mankind by our
likeness to our Master.

'Fellow citizens with the saints'
Ephesians 2:19

What is meant by our being citizens in heaven? It means that *we are under heaven's government*. Christ the king of heaven reigns in our hearts; our daily prayer is, 'Thy will be done on earth as it is in heaven'. The proclamations issued from the throne of glory are freely received by us: the decrees of the Great King we cheerfully obey. Then as citizens of the New Jerusalem, *we share heaven's honours*. The glory which belongs to beatified saints belongs to us, for we are already sons of God, already princes of the blood imperial; already we wear the spotless robe of Jesu's righteousness; already we have angels for our servitors, saints for our companions, Christ for our Brother, God for our Father, and a crown of immortality for our reward. We share the honours of citizenship, for we have come to the general assembly and Church of the first-born whose names are written in heaven. As citizens, we have *common rights to all the property of heaven*. Ours are its gates of pearl and walls of chrysolite; ours the azure light of the city that needs no candle nor light of the sun; ours the river of the water of life, and the twelve manner of fruits which grow on the trees planted on the banks thereof; there is nought in heaven that belongeth not to us. 'Things present, or things to come', all are ours. Also as citizens of heaven we *enjoy its delights*. Do they there rejoice over sinners that repent - prodigals that have returned? So do we. Do they chant the glories of triumphant grace? We do the same. Do they cast their crowns at Jesu's feet? Such honours as we have we cast there too. Are they charmed with His smile? It is not less sweet to us who dwell below. Do they look forward, waiting for His second advent? We also look and long for His appearing. If, then, we are thus *citizens of heaven*, let our walk and actions be consistent with our high dignity.

'And the evening and the morning were the first day'
Genesis 1:5

The evening was 'darkness' and the morning was 'light', and yet *the two together are called by the name that is given to the light alone!* This is somewhat remarkable, but it has an exact analogy in spiritual experience. In every believer, there is darkness and light, and yet he is not to be named a sinner because there is sin in him, but he is to be named a saint because he possesses some degree of holiness. This will be a most comforting thought to those who are mourning their infirmities, and who ask, 'Can I be a child of God while there is so much darkness in me?' Yes; for you, like the day, take not your name from the evening, but from the morning; and you are spoken of in the word of God as if you were even now perfectly holy as you will be soon. You are called the child of light, though there is darkness in you still. You are named after what is the predominating quality in the sight of God, which will one day be the only principle remaining. Observe that *the evening comes first*. Naturally we are darkness first in order of time, and the gloom is often first in our mournful apprehension, driving us to cry out in deep humiliation, 'God be merciful to me, a sinner'. The place of the morning is second, it dawns when grace overcomes nature. It is a blessed aphorism of John Bunyan, 'That which is last, lasts for ever'. That which is first, yields in due season to the last; but nothing comes after the last. So that though you are naturally darkness, when once you become light in the Lord, there is no evening to follow; 'thy sun shall no more go down'. The first day in this life is an evening and a morning; but the second day, when we shall be with God for ever, shall be a day with no evening, but one, sacred, high, eternal noon.

> '*After that ye have suffered awhile, make you*
> *perfect, stablish, strengthen, settle you*'
> 1 Peter 5:10

You have seen the arch of heaven as it spans the plain: glorious are its colours, and rare its hues. It is beautiful, but, alas, it passes away, and lo, it is not. The fair colours give way to the fleecy clouds, and the sky is no longer brilliant with the tints of heaven. It is not *established*. How can it be? A glorious show made up of transitory sunbeams and passing raindrops, how can it abide? The graces of the Christian character must not resemble the rainbow in its transitory beauty, but, on the contrary, must be stablished, settled, abiding. Seek, O believer, that every good thing you have may be an abiding thing. May your character not be a writing upon the sand, but an inscription upon the rock! May your faith be no 'baseless fabric of a vision', but may it be builded of material able to endure that awful fire which shall consume the wood, hay, and stubble of the hypocrite. May you be rooted and grounded in love. May your convictions be deep, your love real, your desires earnest. May your whole life be so settled and established, that all the blasts of hell, and all the storms of earth shall never be able to remove you. But notice how this blessing of being 'stablished in the faith' is gained. The apostle's words point us to *suffering* as the means employed - '*After that ye have suffered awhile.*' It is of no use to hope that we shall be well rooted if no rough winds pass over us. Those old gnarlings on the root of the oak tree, and those strange twistings of the branches, all tell of the many storms that have swept over it, and they are also indicators of the depth into which the roots have forced their way. So the Christian is made strong, and firmly rooted by all the trials and storms of life. Shrink not then from the tempestuous winds of trial, but take comfort, believing that by their rough discipline God is fulfilling this benediction to you.

'Tell ye your children of it, and let your children tell their children, and their children another generation'
Joel 1:3

In this simple way, by God's grace, a living testimony for truth is always to be kept alive in the land - the beloved of the Lord are to hand down their witness for the gospel, and the covenant to their heirs, and these again to their next descendants. This is our *first* duty, we are to begin at the family hearth: he is a bad preacher who does not commence his ministry at home. The heathen are to be sought by all means, and the highways and hedges are to be searched, but home has a prior claim, and woe unto those who reverse the order of the Lord's arrangements. To teach our children is a *personal* duty; we cannot delegate it to Sunday School teachers, or other friendly aids, these can assist us, but cannot deliver us from the sacred obligation; proxies and sponsors are wicked devices in this case; mothers and fathers must, like Abraham, command their households in the fear of God, and talk with their offspring concerning the wondrous works of the Most High. Parental teaching is a *natural* duty - who so fit to look to the child's wellbeing as those who are the authors of his actual being? To neglect the instruction of our offspring is worse than brutish. Family religion is *necessary* for the nation, for the family itself, and for the church of God. By a thousand plots Popery is covertly advancing in our land, and one of the most effectual means for resisting its inroads is left almost neglected, namely, the instruction of children in the faith. Would that parents would awaken to a sense of the importance of this matter. It is a *pleasant* duty to talk of Jesus to our sons and daughters, and the more so because it has so often proved to be an *accepted* work, for God has saved the children through the parents' prayers and admonitions. May every house into which this volume shall come honour the Lord and receive His smile.

'Sanctified by God the Father' Jude 1
'Sanctified in Christ Jesus' 1 Corinthians 1:2
'Through sanctification of the Spirit' 1 Peter 1:2

Mark the union of the Three Divine Persons in all their gracious acts. How unwisely do those believers talk who make preferences in the Persons of the Trinity; who think of Jesus as if He were the embodiment of everything lovely and gracious, while the Father they regard as severely just, but destitute of kindness. Equally wrong are those who magnify the decree of the Father, and the atonement of the Son, so as to depreciate the work of the Spirit. In deeds of grace none of the Persons of the Trinity act apart from the rest. They are as united in their deeds as in their essence. In their love towards the chosen they are one, and in the actions which flow from that great central source they are still undivided. Specially notice this in the matter of sanctification. While we may without mistake speak of sanctification as the work of the Spirit, yet we must take heed that we do not view it as if the Father and the Son had no part therein. It is correct to speak of sanctification as the work of the Father, of the Son, and of the Spirit. Still doth Jehovah say, 'Let *us* make man in our own image after our likeness', and thus we are '*his*' workmanship, created in Christ Jesus unto good works, which God hath before ordained that we should walk in them'. See the value which God sets upon real holiness since the Three Persons in the Trinity are represented as co-working to produce a Church without 'spot, or wrinkle, or any such thing'. And you, believer, as the follower of Christ, must also set a high value on holiness - upon purity of life and godliness of conversation. Value the blood of Christ as the foundation of your hope, but never speak disparagingly of the work of the Spirit which is your meetness for the inheritance of the saints in light. This day let us so live as to manifest the work of the Triune God in us.

'His heavenly kingdom'
2 Timothy 4:18

Yonder city of the great King is a place of *active service*. Ransomed spirits serve Him day and night in His temple. They never cease to fulfil the good pleasure of their King. They always 'rest', so far as ease and freedom from care is concerned; and never 'rest', in the sense of indolence or inactivity. Jerusalem the golden is the place of *communion* with all the people of God. We shall sit with Abraham, Isaac, and Jacob, in eternal fellowship. We shall hold high converse with the noble host of the elect, all reigning with Him who by His love and His potent arm has brought them safely home. We shall not sing solos, but in chorus shall we praise our King. Heaven is a place of *victory realised*. Whenever, Christian, thou hast achieved a victory over thy lusts - whenever after hard struggling, thou hast laid a temptation dead at thy feet - thou hast in that hour a foretaste of the joy that awaits thee when the Lord shall shortly tread Satan under thy feet, and thou shalt find thyself more than conqueror through Him who hath loved thee. Paradise is a place of *security*. When you enjoy the full assurance of faith, you have the pledge of that glorious security which shall be yours when you are a perfect citizen of the heavenly Jerusalem. O my sweet home, Jerusalem, thou happy harbour of my soul! Thanks, even now, to Him whose love hath taught me to long for Thee; but louder thanks in eternity, when I shall possess thee.

'My soul has tasted of the grapes,
   And now it longs to go
Where my dear Lord His vineyard keeps
   And all the clusters grow.

'Upon the true and living vine
   My famish'd soul would feast,
And banquet on the fruit divine,
   An everlasting guest.'

'*God said to Jonah, Doest thou well to be angry?*'
Jonah 4:9

Anger is not always or necessarily sinful, but it has such a tendency to run wild that whenever it displays itself, we should be quick to question its character, with this enquiry, 'Doest thou well to be angry?' It may be that we can answer, 'YES'. Very frequently anger is the madman's firebrand, but sometimes it is Elijah's fire from heaven. We do well when we are angry with sin, because of the wrong which it commits against our good and gracious God; or with ourselves because we remain so foolish after so much divine instruction; or with others when the sole cause of anger is the evil which they do. He who is not angry at transgression becomes a partaker in it. Sin is a loathsome and hateful thing, and no renewed heart can patiently endure it. God himself is angry with the wicked every day, and it is written in His Word, 'Ye that love the Lord, hate evil'.

Far more frequently it is to be feared that our anger is not commendable or even justifiable, and then we must answer, 'NO'. Why should we be fretful with children, passionate with servants, and wrathful with companions? Is such anger honourable to our Christian profession, or glorifying to God? Is it not the old evil heart seeking to gain dominion, and should we not resist it with all the might of our newborn nature? Many professors give way to temper as though it were useless to attempt resistance; but let the believer remember that he must be a conqueror in every point, or else he cannot be crowned. If we cannot control our tempers, what has grace done for us? Someone told Mr Jay that grace was often grafted on a crab-stump. 'Yes,' said he, 'but the fruit will not be crabs.' We must not make natural infirmity an excuse for sin, but we must fly to the cross and pray the Lord to crucify our tempers, and renew us in gentleness and meekness after his own image.

*'When I cry unto Thee, then shall mine enemies turn
back: this I know; for God is for me'*
Psalm 56:9

It is impossible for any human speech to express the
full meaning of this delightful phrase, *'God is for me'*.
He was 'for us' before the worlds were made; He was
'for us', or He would not have given His well-beloved
Son; He was 'for us' when he smote the Only-begotten,
and laid the full weight of His wrath upon Him - He was
'for *us*', though He was against *Him*; He was 'for us',
when we were ruined in the fall - He loved us notwithstanding all; He was 'for us', when we were rebels
against Him, and with a high hand were bidding Him
defiance; He was 'for us', or He would not have
brought us humbly to seek His face. He has been 'for
us' in many struggles; we have been summoned to
encounter hosts of dangers; we have been assailed by
temptations from without and within - how could we
have remained unharmed to this hour if He had not been
'for us'? He is 'for us', with all the infinity of His
being; with all the omnipotence of His love; with all the
infallibility of His wisdom; arrayed in all His divine
attributes; He is 'for us', - eternally and immutably 'for
us'; 'for us' when yon blue skies shall be rolled up like
a worn out vesture; 'for us' throughout eternity. And
because He is 'for us', the voice of prayer will always
ensure His help. *'When I cry unto Thee, then shall mine
enemies be turned back.'* This is no uncertain hope, but
a well grounded assurance - *'this I know'*. I will direct
my prayer unto Thee, and will look up for the answer,
assured that it will come, and that mine enemies shall
be defeated, 'for God is for me'. O believer, how happy
art thou with the King of kings on thy side! How safe
with such a Protector! How sure thy cause pleaded by
such an Advocate! If God be for thee, who can be
against thee?

'If thou lift up thy tool upon it, thou hast polluted it'
Exodus 20:25

God's altar was to be built of unhewn stones, that no trace of human skill or labour might be seen upon it. Human wisdom delights to trim and arrange the doctrines of the cross into a system more artificial and more congenial with the depraved tastes of fallen nature; instead, however, of improving the gospel carnal wisdom pollutes it, until it becomes another gospel, and not the truth of God at all. All alterations and amendments of the Lord's own Word are defilements and pollutions. The proud heart of man is very anxious to have a hand in the justification of the soul before God; preparations for Christ are dreamed of, humblings and repentings are trusted in, good works are cried up, natural ability is much vaunted, and by all means the attempt is made to lift up human tools upon the divine altar. It were well if sinners would remember that so far from perfecting the Saviour's work, their carnal confidences only pollute and dishonour it. The Lord alone must be exalted in the work of atonement, and not a single mark of man's chisel or hammer will be endured. There is an inherent blasphemy in seeking to add to what Christ Jesus in His dying moments declared to be finished, or to improve that in which the Lord Jehovah finds perfect satisfaction. Trembling sinner, away with thy tools, and fall upon thy knees in humble supplication; and accept the Lord Jesus to be the altar of thine atonement and rest in Him alone.

Many professors may take warning from this morning's text as to the doctrines which they believe. There is among Christians far too much inclination to square and reconcile the truths of revelation; this is a form of irreverence and unbelief, let us strive against it, and receive truth as we find it; rejoicing that the doctrines of the Word are unhewn stones, and so are all the more fit to build an altar for the Lord.

*'As it began to dawn, came Mary Magdalene,
to see the sepulchre'*
Matthew 28:1

Let us learn from Mary Magdalene how to obtain
fellowship with the Lord Jesus. Notice how she sought.
She sought the Saviour *very early* in the morning. If
thou canst wait for Christ, and be patient in the hope of
having fellowship with Him at some distant season,
thou wilt never have fellowship at all; for the heart that
is fitted for communion is a hungering and a thirsting
heart. She sought Him also with *very great boldness*.
Other disciples fled from the sepulchre, for they
trembled and were amazed; but Mary, it is said, 'stood'
at the sepulchre. If you would have Christ with you,
seek Him boldly. Let nothing hold you back. Defy the
world. Press on where others flee. She sought Christ
faithfully - she stood *at the sepulchre*. Some find it hard
to stand by a living Saviour, but she stood by a dead
one. Let us seek Christ after this mode, cleaving to the
very least thing that has to do with Him, remaining
faithful though all others should forsake Him. Note
further, she sought Jesus *earnestly* - she stood '*weeping*'. Those tear-droppings were as spells that led the
Saviour captive, and made Him come forth and show
Himself to her. If you desire Jesus' presence, weep
after it! If you cannot be happy unless He come and say
to you, 'Thou art My beloved', you will soon hear His
voice. Lastly, she sought the Saviour *only*. What cared
she for angels, she turned herself back from them; her
search was only for her Lord. If Christ be your one and
only love, if your heart has cast out all rivals, you will
not long lack the comfort of His presence. Mary
Magdalene sought thus *because she loved much*. Let us
arouse ourselves to the same intensity of affection; let
our heart, like Mary's, be full of Christ, and our love,
like hers, will be satisfied with nothing short of
Himself. O Lord, reveal Thyself to us this evening!

> *'The fire shall ever be burning upon the altar;*
> *it shall never go out'*
> Leviticus 6:13

Keep the altar of *private prayer* burning. This is the very life of all piety. The sanctuary and family altars borrow their fires here, therefore let this burn well. Secret devotion is the very essence, evidence, and barometer, of vital and experimental religion.

Burn here the fat of your sacrifices. Let your closet seasons be, if possible, regular, frequent, and undisturbed. Effectual prayer availeth much. Have you nothing to pray for? Let us suggest the Church, the ministry, your own soul, your children, your relations, your neighbours, your country, and the cause of God and truth throughout the world. Let us examine ourselves on this important matter. Do we engage with lukewarmness in private devotion? Is the fire of devotion burning dimly in our hearts? Do the chariot wheels drag heavily? If so, let us be alarmed at this sign of decay. Let us go with weeping, and ask for the Spirit of grace and of supplications. Let us set apart special seasons for extraordinary prayer. For if this fire should be smothered beneath the ashes of a worldly conformity, it will dim the fire on the family altar, and lessen our influence both in the Church and in the world.

The text will also apply to *the altar of the heart*. This is a golden altar indeed. God loves to see the hearts of His people glowing towards Himself. Let us give to God our hearts, all blazing with love, and seek his grace, that the fire may never be quenched; for it will not burn if the Lord does not keep it burning. Many foes will attempt to extinguish it; but if the unseen hand behind the wall pour thereon the sacred oil, it will blaze higher and higher. Let us use texts of Scripture as fuel for our heart's fire, they are live coals; let us attend sermons, but above all, let us be much alone with Jesus.

'He appeared first to Mary Magdalene'
Mark 16:9

Jesus 'appeared first to Mary Magdalene', probably not only on account of her great love and persevering seeking, but because, as the context intimates, *she had been a special trophy of Christ's delivering power*. Learn from this, that the greatness of our sin before conversion should not make us imagine that we may not be specially favoured with the very highest grade of fellowship. She was one who had left all to become *a constant attendant on the Saviour*. He was her first, her chief object. Many who were on Christ's side did not take up Christ's cross; *she* did. *She spent her substance in relieving His wants*. If we would see much of Christ, let us *serve* Him. Tell me who they are that sit oftenest under the banner of His love, and drink deepest draughts from the cup of communion, and I am sure they will be those who give most, who serve best, and who abide closest to the bleeding heart of their dear Lord. But notice how Christ revealed Himself to this sorrowing one - by *a word*, 'Mary'. It needed but one word *in His voice*, and at once she knew Him, and *her heart owned allegiance by another word*, her heart was too full to say more. That one word would naturally be the most fitting for the occasion. It implies obedience. She said, *'Master'*. There is no state of mind in which this confession of allegiance will be too cold. No, when your spirit glows most with the heavenly fire, then you will say, 'I am Thy servant, Thou hast loosed my bonds'. If you can say, 'Master', if you feel that His will is your will, then you stand in a happy, holy place. He must have said, 'Mary', or else you could not have said, 'Rabboni'. See, then, from all this, how Christ honours those who honour Him, how love draws our Beloved, how it needs out one word of His to turn our weeping to rejoicing, how His presence makes the heart's sunshine.

'They gathered manna every morning'
Exodus 16:21

Labour to maintain a sense of thine entire dependence upon the Lord's good will and pleasure for the continuance of thy richest enjoyments. Never try to live on the old manna, nor seek to find help in Egypt. All must come from Jesus, or thou art undone for ever. Old anointings will not suffice to impart unction to thy spirit; thine head must have fresh oil poured upon it from the golden horn of the sanctuary, or it will cease from its glory. Today thou mayest be upon the summit of the mount of God, but he who has put thee there must keep thee there, or thou wilt sink far more speedily than thou dreamest. Thy mountain only stands firm when He settles it in its place; if He hide His face, thou wilt soon be troubled. If the Saviour should see fit, there is not a window through which thou seest the light of heaven which He could not darken in an instant. Joshua bade the sun stand still, but Jesus can shroud it in total darkness. He can withdraw the joy of thine heart, the light of thine eyes, and the strength of thy life; in His hand thy comforts lie, and at His will they can depart from thee. This hourly dependence our Lord is determined that we shall feel and recognise, for He only permits us to pray for 'daily bread', and only promises that 'as our days our strength shall be'. Is it not best for us that it should be so, that we may often repair to His throne, and constantly be reminded of His love? Oh! how rich the grace which supplies us so continually, and doth not refrain itself because of our ingratitude! The golden shower never ceases, the cloud of blessing tarries evermore above our habitation. O Lord Jesus, we would bow at Thy feet, conscious of our utter inability to do anything without Thee, and in every favour which we are privileged to receive, we would adore Thy blessed name and acknowledge Thine unexhausted love.

'Thou shalt arise, and have mercy upon Zion:
for the time to favour her, yea, the set time, is come.
For Thy servants take pleasure in her stones,
and favour the dust thereof'
Psalm 102:13, 14

A selfish man in trouble is exceedingly hard to comfort, because the springs of his comfort lie entirely within himself, and when he is sad all his springs are dry. But a large-hearted man full of Christian philanthropy, has other springs from which to supply himself with comfort beside those which lie within. He can go to his God first of all, and there find abundant help; and he can discover arguments for consolation in things relating to the world at large, to his country, and, above all, to the church. David in this Psalm was exceedingly sorrowful; he wrote, 'I am like an owl of the desert. I watch and am as a sparrow alone upon the house top'. The only way in which he could comfort himself, was in the reflection that God would arise, and have mercy upon Zion: though *he* was sad, yet Zion should prosper; however low his own estate, yet Zion should arise. Christian man! learn to comfort thyself in God's gracious dealing towards the church. That which is so dear to thy Master, should it not be dear above all else to thee? What though thy way be dark, canst thou not gladden thine heart with the triumphs of His cross and the spread of His truth? Our own personal troubles are forgotten while we look, not only upon what God *has* done, and *is* doing for Zion, but on the glorious things He *will yet do* for His church. Try this receipt, O believer, whenever thou art sad of heart and in heaviness of spirit: forget thyself and thy little concerns, and seek the welfare and prosperity of Zion. When thou bendest thy knee in prayer to God, limit not thy petition to the narrow circle of thine own life, tried though it be, but send out thy longing prayers for the church's prosperity, 'Pray for the peace of Jerusalem', and thine own soul shall be refreshed.

'Knowing, brethren beloved, your election of God'
1 Thessalonians 1:4

Many persons want to know their election before they look to Christ, but they cannot learn it thus, it is only to be discovered by 'looking unto Jesus'. If you desire to ascertain your own election; after the following manner, shall you assure your heart before God. Do you feel yourself to be a lost, guilty sinner? go straightway to the cross of Christ, and tell Jesus so, and tell Him that you have read in the Bible, 'Him that cometh unto me, I will in no wise cast out'. Tell Him that He has said, 'This is a faithful saying, and worthy of all acceptation, that Christ Jesus came into the world to save sinners'. Look to Jesus and believe on Him, and you shall make proof of your election directly, for so surely as thou believest, thou art elect. If you will give yourself wholly up to Christ and trust Him, then you are one of God's chosen ones; but if you stop and say, 'I want to know first whether I am elect', you ask you know not what. Go to Jesus, be you never so guilty, just as you are. Leave all curious inquiry about election alone. Go straight to Christ and hide in His wounds, and you shall know your election. The assurance of the Holy Spirit shall be given to you, so that you shall be able to say, 'I know whom I have believed, and I am persuaded that he is able to keep that which I have committed to Him'. Christ was at the everlasting council: He can tell you whether you were chosen or not; but you cannot find it out in any other way. Go and put your trust in Him, and His answer will be - 'I have loved thee with an everlasting love, therefore with loving-kindness have I drawn thee'. There will be no doubt about His having chosen *you*, when you have chosen *Him.*

'Sons we are through God's election,
　Who in Jesus Christ believe.'

'Let not one of them escape'
1 Kings 18:40

When the prophet Elijah had received the answer to his prayer, and the fire from heaven had consumed the sacrifice in the presence of all the people, he called upon the assembled Israelites to take the priests of Baal, and sternly cried, 'Let not one of them escape'. He took them all down to the brook Kishon, and slew them there. So must it be with our sins - they are all doomed, not one must be preserved. Our darling sin must die. Spare it not for its much crying. Strike, though it be as dear as an Isaac. Strike, for God struck at sin when it was laid upon His own Son. With stern unflinching purpose must you condemn to death that sin which was once the idol of your heart. Do you ask how you are to accomplish this? Jesus will be your power. You have grace to overcome sin given you in the covenant of grace; you have strength to win the victory in the crusade against inward lusts, because Christ Jesus has promised to be with you even unto the end. If you would triumph over darkness, set yourself in the presence of the Sun of Righteousness. There is no place so well adapted for the discovery of sin, and recovery from its power and guilt, as the immediate presence of God. Job never knew how to get rid of sin half so well as he did when his eye of faith rested upon God, and then he abhorred himself, and repented in dust and ashes. The fine gold of the Christian is oft becoming dim. We need the sacred fire to consume the dross. Let us fly to our God, He is a consuming fire; He will not consume our spirit, but our sins. Let the goodness of God excite us to a sacred jealousy, and to a holy revenge against those iniquities which are hateful in His sight. Go forth to battle with Amalek in His strength, and utterly destroy the accursed crew: let not one of them escape.

'They shall go hindmost with their standards'
Numbers 2:31

The camp of Dan brought up the rear when the armies of Israel were on the march. The Danites occupied *the hindmost place*, but what mattered the position, since they were as truly part of the host as were the foremost tribes; they followed the same fiery cloudy pillar, they ate of the same manna, drank of the same spiritual rock, and journeyed to the same inheritance. Come, my heart, cheer up, though last and least; it is thy privilege to be in the army, and to fare as they fare who lead the van. Someone must be hindmost in honour and esteem, someone must do menial work for Jesus, and why should not I? In a poor village, among an ignorant peasantry; or in a back street, among degraded sinners, I will work on, and 'go hindmost with my standard'.

The Danites occupied *a very useful place*. Stragglers have to be picked up upon the march, and lost property has to be gathered from the field. Fiery spirits may dash forward over untrodden paths to learn fresh truth, and win more souls to Jesus; but some of a more conservative spirit may be well engaged in reminding the Church of her ancient faith, and restoring her fainting sons. Every position has its duties, and the slowly moving children of God will find their peculiar state one in which they may be eminently a blessing to the whole host.

The rear guard is a *place of honour*. There are foes behind us as well as before us. Attacks may come from any quarter. We read that Amalek fell upon Israel, and slew some of the hindmost of them. The experienced Christian will find much work for his weapons in aiding those poor doubting, desponding, wavering, souls, who are hindmost in faith, knowledge, and joy. These must not be left unaided, and therefore be it the business of well-taught saints to bear their standards among the hindmost. My soul, do thou tenderly watch to help the hindmost this day.

> *'Neither shall one thrust another;*
> *they shall walk every one in his path'*
> Joel 2:8

Locusts legion, they do not crowd upon each other, so as to throw their columns into confusion. This remarkable fact in natural history shows how thoroughly the Lord has infused the spirit of order into His universe, since the smallest animate creatures are as much controlled by it as are the rolling spheres or the seraphic messengers. It would be wise for believers to be ruled by the same influence in all their spiritual life. *In their Christian graces* no one virtue should usurp the sphere of another, or eat out the vitals of the rest for its own support. Affection must not smother honesty, courage must not elbow weakness out of the field, modesty must not jostle energy, and patience must not slaughter resolution. So also with *our duties*, one must not interfere with another; public usefulness must not injure private piety; church work must not push family worship into a corner. It is ill to offer God one duty stained with the blood of another. Each thing is beautiful in its season, but not otherwise. It was to the Pharisee that Jesus said, 'This ought ye to have done, and not to have left the other undone'. The same rule applies to *our personal position*, we must take care to know our place, take it, and keep to it. We must minister as the Spirit has given us ability, and not intrude upon our fellow servant's domain. Our Lord Jesus taught us not to covet the high places, but to be willing to be the least among the brethren. Far from us be an envious, ambitious spirit, let us feel the force of the Master's command, and do as He bids us, keeping rank with the rest of the host. Tonight let us see whether we are keeping the unity of the Spirit in the bonds of peace, and let our prayer be that, in all the churches of the Lord Jesus, peace and order may prevail.

'The Lord our God hath shewed us His glory'
Deuteronomy 5:24

God's great design in all His works is the manifestation
of His own glory. Any aim less than this were unworthy of Himself. But how shall the glory of God be
manifested to such fallen creatures as we are? Man's
eye is not single, he has ever a side glance towards his
own honour, has too high an estimate of his own
powers, and so is not qualified to behold the glory of
the Lord. It is clear, then, that self must stand out of the
way, that there may be room for God to be exalted; and
this is the reason why He bringeth His people ofttimes
into straits and difficulties, that, being made conscious
of their own folly and weakness, they may be fitted to
behold the majesty of God when he comes forth to work
their deliverance. He whose life is one even and smooth
path, will see but little of the glory of the Lord, for he
has few occasions of self-emptying, and hence, but
little fitness for being filled with the revelation of God.
They who navigate little streams and shallow creeks,
know but little of the God of tempests; but they who 'do
business in great waters', these see His 'wonders in the
deep'. Among the huge Atlantic-waves of bereavement, poverty, temptation, and reproach, we learn the
power of Jehovah, because we feel the littleness of
man. Thank God, then, if you have been led by a rough
road: it is this which has given you your experience of
God's greatness and loving-kindness. Your troubles
have enriched you with a wealth of knowledge to be
gained by no other means: your trials have been the
cleft of the rock in which Jehovah has set you, as He did
His servant Moses, that you might behold His glory as
it passed by. Praise God that you have not been left to
the darkness and ignorance which continued prosperity
might have involved, but that in the great fight of
affliction, you have been capacitated for the outshinings
of His glory in His wonderful dealings with you.

'*A bruised reed shall He not break, and smoking
flax shall He not quench*'
Matthew 12:20

What is weaker than the bruised reed or the smoking
flax? A *reed* that groweth in the fen or marsh, let but
the wild duck light upon it, and it snaps; let but the foot
of man brush against it, and it is bruised and broken;
every wind that flits across the river moves it to and fro.
You can conceive of nothing more frail or brittle, or
whose existence is more in jeopardy, than a bruised
reed. Then look at the smoking flax - what is it? It has
a spark within it, it is true, but it is almost smothered;
an infant's breath might blow it out; nothing has a more
precarious existence than its flame. *Weak things* are
here described, yet Jesus says of them, 'The smoking
flax I will not quench; the bruised reed I will not break'.
Some of God's children are made strong to do mighty
works for Him; God has His Samsons here and there
who can pull up Gaza's gates, and carry them to the top
of the hill; He has a few mighties who are lion-like men,
but the majority of His people are a timid, trembling
race. They are like starlings, frightened at every passer-
by; a little fearful flock. If temptation comes, they are
taken like birds in a snare; if trial threatens, they are
ready to faint; their frail skiff is tossed up and down by
every wave, they are drifted along like a sea bird on the
crest of the billows - weak things, without strength,
without wisdom, without foresight. Yet, weak as they
are, and *because* they are so weak, they have this
promise made specially to them. Herein is grace and
graciousness! Herein is love and loving-kindness!
How it opens to us the compassion of Jesus - so gentle,
tender, considerate! We need never shrink back from
His touch. We need never fear a harsh word from *Him*;
though He might well chide us for our weakness, He
rebuketh not. Bruised reeds shall have no blows from
Him, and the smoking flax no damping frowns.

'The earnest of our inheritance'
Ephesians 1:14

Oh! what enlightenment, what joys, what consolation, what delight of heart is experienced by that man who has learned to feed on Jesus, and on Jesus alone. Yet the realisation which we have of Christ's preciousness is, in this life, imperfect at the best. As an old writer says, ''Tis but a taste!'. We have tasted 'that the Lord is gracious', but we do not yet know *how* good and gracious He is, although what we know of His sweetness makes us long for more. We have enjoyed the firstfruits of the Spirit, and they have set us hungering and thirsting for the fulness of the heavenly vintage. We groan within ourselves, waiting for the adoption. *Here* we are like Israel in the wilderness, who had but one cluster from Eshcol, *there* we shall be in the vineyard. Here we see the manna falling small, like coriander seed, but there shall we eat the bread of heaven and the old corn of the kingdom. We are but beginners now in spiritual education; for although we have learned the first letters of the alphabet, we cannot read words yet, much less can we put sentences together; but as one says, 'He that has been in heaven but five minutes, knows more than the general assembly of divines on earth'. We have many ungratified desires at present, but soon every wish shall be satisfied; and all our powers shall find the sweetest employment in that eternal world of joy. O Christian, antedate heaven for a few years. Within a very little time thou shalt be rid of all thy trials and thy troubles. Thine eyes now suffused with tears shall weep no longer. Thou shalt gaze in ineffable rapture upon the splendour of Him who sits upon the throne. Nay, more, upon His throne shalt thou sit. The triumph of His glory shall be shared by thee; His crown, His joy, His paradise, these shall be thine, and thou shalt be co-heir with Him who is the heir of all things.

'And now what hast thou to do in the way of Egypt,
to drink the waters of Sihor?'
Jeremiah 2:18

By sundry miracles, by divers mercies, by strange
deliverances Jehovah had proved Himself to be worthy
of Israel's trust. Yet they broke down the hedges with
which God had enclosed them as a sacred garden; they
forsook their own true and living God, and followed
after false gods. Constantly did the Lord reprove them
for this infatuation, and our text contains one instance
of God's expostulating with them, 'What hast thou to
do in the way of Egypt, to drink the waters of the muddy
river?' - for so it may be translated. 'Why dost thou
wander afar and leave thine own cool stream from
Lebanon? Why dost thou forsake Jerusalem to turn
aside to Noph and to Tahapanes? Why art thou so
strangely set on mischief, that thou canst not be content
with the good and healthful, but woudst follow after
that which is evil and deceitful?' Is there not here a
word of expostulation and warning to the Christian? O
true believer, called by grace and washed in the precious blood of Jesus, thou hast tasted of better drink
than the muddy river of this world's pleasure can give
thee; thou hast had fellowship with Christ; thou hast
obtained the joy of seeing Jesus, and leaning thine head
upon His bosom. Do the trifles, the songs, the honours,
the merriment of this earth content thee after that? Hast
thou eaten the bread of angels, and canst thou live on
husks? Good Rutherford once said, 'I have tasted of
Christ's own manna, and it hath put my mouth out of
taste for the brown bread of this world's joys'. Methinks
it should be so with thee. If thou art wandering after the
waters of Egypt, O return quickly to the one living
fountain: the waters of Sihor may be sweet to the
Egyptians, but they will prove only bitterness to thee.
What hast *thou* to do with them? *Jesus asks thee this*
question this evening - what wilt thou answer Him?

> '*The daughter of Jerusalem*
> *hath shaken her head at thee*'
> Isaiah 37:22

Reassured by the Word of the Lord, the poor trembling citizens of Zion grew bold, and shook their heads at Sennacherib's boastful threats. Strong faith enables the servants of God to look with calm contempt upon their most haughty foes. *We know that our enemies are attempting impossibilities*. They seek to destroy the eternal life, which cannot die while Jesus lives; to overthrow the citadel, against which the gates of hell shall not prevail. They kick against the pricks to their own wounding, and rush upon the bosses of Jehovah's buckler to their own hurt.

We know their weakness. What are they but men? And what is man but a worm? They roar and swell like waves of the sea, foaming out their own shame. When the Lord ariseth, they shall fly as chaff before the wind, and be consumed as crackling thorns. Their utter powerlessness to do damage to the cause of God and His truth, may make the weakest soldiers in Zion's ranks laugh them to scorn.

Above all, *we know that the Most High is with us*, and when He dresses Himself in arms, where are His enemies? If He cometh forth from His place, the potsherds of the earth will not long contend with their Maker. His rod of iron shall dash them in pieces like a potter's vessel, and their very remembrance shall perish from the earth. Away, then, all fears, the kingdom is safe in the King's hands. Let us shout for joy, for the Lord reigneth, and His foes shall be as straw for the dunghill.

> 'As true as God's own word is true;
>> Nor earth, nor hell, with all their crew,
> Against us shall prevail.
>> A jest, and by-word, are they grown;
> God *is* with us, we *are* his own,
>> Our victory cannot fail.'

'Why go I mourning?'
Psalm 42:9

Canst thou answer this, believer? Canst thou find any reason why thou art so often mourning instead of rejoicing? Why yield to gloomy anticipations? Who told thee that the night would never end in day? Who told thee that the sea of circumstances would ebb out till there should be nothing left, but long leagues of the mud of horrible poverty? Who told thee that the winter of thy discontent would proceed from frost to frost, from snow, and ice, and hail, to deeper snow, and yet more heavy tempest of despair? Knowest thou not that day follows night, that flood comes after ebb, that spring and summer succeed to winter? Hope thou then! Hope thou ever! for God fails thee not. Dost thou not know that thy God loves thee in the midst of all this? Mountains, when in darkness hidden, are as real as in day, and God's love is as true to thee now as it was in thy brightest moments. No father chastens always: thy Lord hates the rod as much as thou dost; He only cares to use it for that reason which should make thee willing to receive it, namely, that it works thy lasting good. Thou shalt yet climb Jacob's ladder with the angels, and behold Him who sits at the top of it - thy covenant God. Thou shalt yet, amidst the splendours of eternity, forget the trials of time or only remember them to bless the God who led thee through them, and wrought thy lasting good by them. Come, sing in the midst of tribulation. Rejoice even while passing through the furnace. Make the wilderness to blossom like the rose! Cause the desert to ring with thine exulting joys, for these light afflictions will soon be over, and then 'for ever with the Lord', thy bliss shall never wane.

'Faint not nor fear, His arms are near,
　　He changeth not, and thou art dear;
Only believe and thou shalt see,
　　That Christ is all in all to thee.'

'I am married unto you'
Jeremiah 3:14

Christ Jesus is joined unto His people in marriage
union. In love He espoused His Church as a chaste
virgin, long before she fell under the yoke of bondage.
Full of burning affection He toiled, like Jacob for
Rachel, until the whole of her purchase-money had
been paid, and now, having sought her by His Spirit,
and brought her to know and love Him, He awaits the
glorious hour when their mutual bliss shall be con-
summated at the marriage-supper of the Lamb. Not yet
hath the glorious Bridegroom presented His betrothed,
perfected and complete, before the Majesty of heaven;
not yet hath she actually entered upon the enjoyment of
her dignities as His wife and queen: she is as yet a
wanderer in a world of woe, a dweller in the tents of
Kedar; but she is even now the bride, the spouse of
Jesus, dear to His heart, precious in His sight, written
on His hands, and united with His person. On earth he
exercises towards her all the affectionate offices of
Husband. He makes rich provision for her wants, pays
all her debts, allows her to assume His name, and to
share in all His wealth. Nor will He ever act otherwise
to her. The word divorce He will never mention, for
'He hateth putting away'. Death must sever the conju-
gal tie between the most loving mortals, but it cannot
divide the links of this immortal marriage. In heaven
they marry not, but are as the angels of God; yet there
is this one marvellous exception to the rule, for in
Heaven Christ and His Church shall celebrate their
joyous nuptials. This affinity as it is more lasting, so
is it more near than earthly wedlock. Let the love of
husband be never so pure and fervent, it is but a faint
picture of the flame which burns in the heart of Jesus.
Passing all human union is that mystical cleaving unto
the Church, for which Christ left His Father, and
became one flesh with her.

'Behold the Man!'
John 19:5

If there be one place where our Lord Jesus most fully becomes the joy and comfort of His people, it is where he plunged deepest into the depths of woe. Come hither, gracious souls, and behold the Man in the garden of Gethsemane; behold His heart so brimming with love that He cannot hold it in - so full of sorrow that it must find a vent. Behold the bloody sweat as it distils from every pore of His body, and falls upon the ground. Behold the Man as they drive the nails into His hands and feet. Look up, repenting sinners, and see the sorrowful image of your suffering Lord. Mark Him, as the ruby drops stand on the thorn-crown, and adorn with priceless gems the diadem of the King of Misery. Behold the Man when all His bones are out of joint, and He is poured out like water and brought into the dust of death; God hath forsaken Him, and hell compasseth Him about. Behold and see, was there ever sorrow like unto His sorrow that is done unto Him? All ye that pass by draw near and look upon this spectacle of grief, unique, unparalleled, a wonder to men and angels, a prodigy unmatched. Behold the Emperor of Woe who had no equal or rival in His agonies! Gaze upon Him, ye mourners, for if there be not consolation in a crucified Christ there is no joy in earth or heaven. If in the ransom price of His blood there be not hope, ye harps of heaven, there is no joy in you, and the right hand of God shall know no pleasures for evermore. We have only to sit more continually at the cross foot to be less troubled with our doubts and woes. We have but to see *His* sorrows, and *our* sorrows we shall be ashamed to mention; we have but to gaze into His wounds and heal our own. If we would live aright it must be by the contemplation of His death; if we would rise to dignity it must be by considering His humiliation and His sorrow.

'Even thou wast as one of them'
Obadiah 1:11

Brotherly kindness was due from Edom to Israel in the time of need, but instead thereof, the men of Esau made common cause with Israel's foes. Special stress in the sentence before us is laid upon the word *thou*; as when Caesar cried to Brutus, 'and *thou* Brutus'; a bad action may be all the worse, because of the person who has committed it. When *we* sin, who are the chosen favourites of heaven, we sin with an emphasis; ours is a crying offence, because we are so peculiarly indulged. If an angel should lay his hand upon us when we are doing evil, he need not use any other rebuke than the question, 'What *thou*? What dost *thou* here?' Much forgiven, much delivered, much instructed, much enriched, much blessed, shall we dare to put forth our hand unto evil? God forbid!

A few minutes of confession may be beneficial to thee, gentle reader, this morning. Hast thou never been as the wicked? At an evening party certain men laughed at uncleanness, and the joke was not altogether offensive to thine ear, *even thou wast as one of them*. When hard things were spoken concerning the ways of God, thou wast bashfully silent; and so, to onlookers, *thou wast as one of them*. When worldlings were bartering in the market, and driving hard bargains, wast thou not as one of them? When they were pursuing vanity with a hunter's foot, wert thou not as greedy for gain as they were? Could any difference be discerned between thee and them? *Is there any difference?* Here we come to close quarters. Be honest with thine own soul, and make sure that thou art a new creature in Christ Jesus; but when this is sure, walk jealously, lest any should again be able to say, 'Even thou wast as one of them'. Thou wouldst not desire to share their eternal doom, why then be like them here? Come not thou into their secret, lest thou come into their ruin. Side with the afflicted people of God, and not with the world.

> *'The blood of Jesus Christ His Son*
> *cleanseth us from all sin'*
> 1 John 1:7

'Cleanseth,' says the text - not *'shall* cleanse'. There are multitudes who think that as a dying hope they may look forward to pardon. Oh! how infinitely better to have cleansing now than to depend on the bare possibility of forgiveness when I come to die. Some imagine that a sense of pardon is an attainment only obtainable after many years of Christian experience. But forgiveness of sin is a *present* thing - a privilege for this day, a joy for this very hour. The moment a sinner trusts Jesus he is fully forgiven. The text, being written in the present tense, also indicates *continuance*; it was 'cleanseth' yesterday, it is 'cleanseth' today, it will be 'cleanseth' tomorrow: it will be always so with you, Christian, until you cross the river; every hour you may come to this fountain, for it cleanseth still. Notice, likewise, *the completeness* of the cleansing, 'The blood of Jesus Christ His Son cleanseth us from *all sin'* - not only from sin, but 'from *all* sin'. Reader, I cannot tell you the exceeding sweetness of this word, but I pray God the Holy Ghost to give you a taste of it. Manifold are our sins against God. Whether the bill be little or great, the same receipt can discharge one as the other. The blood of Jesus Christ is as blessed and divine a payment for the transgressions of blaspheming Peter as for the shortcomings of loving John; our iniquity is gone, all gone at once, and all gone for ever. Blessed completeness! What a sweet theme to dwell upon as one gives himself to sleep

> 'Sins against a holy God;
>   Sins against His righteous laws;
> Sins against His love, His blood;
>   Sins against His name and cause;
> Sins immense as is the sea -
>   From them all He cleanseth me.'

'Stand still, and see the salvation of the Lord'
Exodus 14:13

These words contain God's command to the believer when he is reduced to great straits and brought into extraordinary difficulties. He cannot retreat; he cannot go forward; he is shut up on the right hand and on the left; what is he now to do? The Master's word to him is, 'Stand still'. It will be well for him if at such times he listens only to his Master's word, for other and evil advisers come with their suggestions. *Despair* whispers, 'Lie down and die; give it all up'. But God would have us put on a cheerful courage, and even in our worst times, rejoice in His love and faithfulness. *Cowardice* says, 'Retreat; go back to the worldling's way of action; you cannot play the Christian's part, it is too difficult. Relinquish your principles'. But, however much Satan may urge this course upon you, you cannot follow it if you are a child of God. His divine fiat has bid thee go from strength to strength, and so thou shalt, and neither death nor hell shall turn thee from thy course. What, if for a while thou art called to stand still, yet this is but to renew thy strength for some greater advance in due time. *Precipitancy* cries, 'Do something. Stir yourself; to stand still and wait is sheer idleness'. We *must* be doing something at once - *we* must do it so we think - instead of looking to the Lord, who will not only do something but will do everything. *Presumption* boasts, 'If the sea be before you, march into it and expect a miracle'. But Faith listens neither to Presumption, nor to Despair, nor to Cowardice, nor to Precipitancy, but it hears God say, 'Stand still', and immoveable as a rock it stands. '*Stand* still'; keep the posture of an upright man, ready for action, expecting further orders, cheerfully and patiently awaiting the directing voice; and it will not be long ere God shall say to you, as distinctly as Moses said it to the people of Israel, 'Go forward'.

'His camp is very great'

Joel 2:11

Consider, my soul, the mightiness of the Lord who is thy glory and defence. He is a man of war, Jehovah is His name. All *the forces of heaven* are at His beck, legions wait at his door, cherubim and seraphim, watchers and holy ones, principalities and powers, are all attentive to His will. If our eyes were not blinded by the ophthalmia of the flesh, we should see horses of fire and chariots of fire round about the Lord's beloved. *The powers of nature* are all subject to the absolute control of the Creator: stormy wind and tempest, lightning and rain, and snow and hail, and the soft dews and cheering sunshine, come and go at His decree. The bands of Orion He looseth, and bindeth the sweet influences of the Pleiades. Earth, sea, and air, and the places under the earth, are the barracks for Jehovah's great armies; space is His camping ground, light is His banner, and flame is His sword. When He goeth forth to war, famine ravages the land, pestilence smites the nations, hurricane sweeps the sea, tornado shakes the mountains, and earthquake makes the solid world to tremble. As for *animate creatures*, they all own His dominion, and from the great fish which swallowed the prophet, down to 'all manner of flies' which plagued the field of Zoan, all are His servants, and like the palmer-worm, the caterpillar, and the cankerworm, are squadrons of His great army, for His camp is very great. My soul, see to it that thou be at peace with this mighty King, yea, more, be sure to enlist under His banner, for to war against Him is madness, and to serve Him is glory. Jesus, Immanuel, God with us, is ready to receive recruits for the army of the Lord: if I am not already enlisted let me go to Him ere I sleep, and beg to be accepted through His merits; and if I be already, as I hope I am, a soldier of the cross, let me be of good courage; for the enemy is powerless compared with my Lord, whose camp is very great.

> *'He left his garment in her hand,*
> *and fled, and got him out'*
> Genesis 39:12

In contending with certain sins there remains no mode
of victory but by flight. The ancient naturalists wrote
much of basilisks, whose eyes fascinated their victims
and rendered them easy victims; so the mere gaze of
wickedness puts us in solemn danger. He who would
be safe from acts of evil must haste away from
occasions of it. A covenant must be made with our eyes
not even to look upon the cause of temptation, for such
sins only need a spark to begin with and a blaze follows
in an instant. Who would wantonly enter the leper's
prison and sleep amid its horrible corruption? He only
who desires to be leprous himself would thus court
contagion. If the mariner knew how to avoid a storm,
he would do anything rather than run the risk of
weathering it. Cautious pilots have no desire to try how
near the quicksand they can sail, or how often they may
touch a rock without springing a leak; their aim is to
keep as nearly as possible in the midst of a safe channel.

This day I may be exposed to great peril, let me
have the serpent's wisdom to keep out of it and avoid
it. The wings of a dove may be of more use to me today
than the jaws of a lion. It is true I may be an apparent
loser by declining evil company, but I had better leave
my cloak than lose my character; it is not needful that
I should be rich, but it is imperative upon me to be pure.
No ties of friendship, no chains of beauty, no flashings
of talent, no shafts of ridicule must turn me from the
wise resolve to flee from sin. The devil I am to resist
and he will flee from me, but the lusts of the flesh, *I*
must flee, or they will surely overcome me. O God of
holiness preserve thy Josephs, that Madam Bubble
bewitch them not with her vile suggestions. May the
horrible trinity of the world, the flesh and the devil,
never overcome us!

'In their affliction they will seek Me early'
Hosea 5:15

Losses and adversities are frequently the means which the great Shepherd uses to fetch home His wandering sheep; like fierce dogs they worry the wanderers back to the fold. There is no making lions tame if they are too well fed; they must be brought down from their great strength, and their stomachs must be lowered, and then they will submit to the tamer's hand; and often have we seen the Christian rendered obedient to the Lord's will by straitness of bread and hard labour. When rich and increased in goods many professors carry their heads much too loftily, and speak exceeding boastfully. Like David, they flatter themselves, 'My mountain standeth fast; I shall never be moved.' When the Christian groweth wealthy, is in good repute, hath good health, and a happy family, he too often admits Mr Carnal Security to feast at his table, and then if he be a true child of God there is a rod preparing for him. Wait awhile, and it may be you will see his substance melt away as a dream. There goes a portion of his estate - how soon the acres change hands. That debt, that dishonoured bill - how fast his losses roll in, where will they end? It is a blessed sign of divine life if when these embarrassments occur one after another he begins to be distressed about his backslidings, and betakes himself to his God. Blessed are the waves that wash the mariner upon the rock of salvation! Losses in business are often sanctified to our soul's enriching. If the chosen soul will not come to the Lord full-handed, it shall come empty. If God, in His grace, findeth no other means of making us honour Him among men, He will cast us into the deep; if we fail to honour Him on the pinnacle of riches, he will bring us into the valley of poverty. Yet faint not, heir of sorrow, when thou art thus rebuked, rather recognise the loving hand which chastens, and say, 'I will arise, and go unto my Father'.

> '*Giving all diligence, add to your faith virtue;*
> *and to virtue knowledge, etc*'
> 2 Peter 1:5, 6

If thou wouldest enjoy the eminent grace of the full assurance of faith, under the blessed Spirit's influence, and assistance, do what the Scripture tells thee, '*Give diligence*'. Take care that thy *faith* is of the right kind - that it is not a mere belief of doctrine, but a simple faith, depending on Christ, and on Christ alone. Give diligent heed to thy *courage*. Plead with God that He would give thee the face of a lion, that thou mayest, with a consciousness of right, go on boldly. Study well the Scriptures, and get *knowledge*; for a knowledge of doctrine will tend very much to confirm faith. Try to understand God's Word; let it dwell in thy heart richly.

When thou hast done this, 'Add to thy knowledge *temperance*'. Take heed to thy body: be temperate without. Take heed to thy soul: be temperate within. Get temperance of lip, life, heart, and thought. Add to this, by God's Holy Spirit, *patience*; ask Him to give thee that patience which endureth affliction, which, when it is tried, shall come forth as gold. Array yourself with patience, that you may not murmur nor be depressed in your afflictions. When that grace is won look to *godliness*. Godliness is something more than religion. Make God's glory your object in life; live in His sight; dwell close to Him; seek for fellowship with Him; and thou hast 'godliness'; and to that add *brotherly love*. Have a love to all the saints: and add to that a *charity*, which openeth its arms to all men, and loves their souls. When you are adorned with these jewels, and just in proportion as you practise these heavenly virtues, will you come to know by clearest evidence 'your calling and election'. 'Give diligence' if you would get assurance, for lukewarmness and doubting very naturally go hand in hand.

'That He may set him with princes'
Psalm 113:8

Our spiritual privileges are of the highest order. 'Among princes' *is the place of select society.* 'Truly our fellowship is with the Father, and with His Son Jesus Christ.' Speak of select society, there is none like this! 'We are a chosen generation, a peculiar people, a royal priesthood.' 'We are come unto the general assembly and church of the first-born, whose names are written in heaven.' The saints *have courtly audience*: princes have admittance to royalty when common people must stand afar off. The child of God has free access to the inner courts of heaven. 'For through Him we both have access by one Spirit unto the Father.' 'Let us come boldly,' says the apostle, '*to the throne* of the heavenly grace.' Among princes there is *abundant wealth*, but what is the abundance of princes compared with the riches of believers? for 'all things are yours, and ye are Christ's, and Christ is God's'. 'He that spared not his own Son, but delivered Him up for us all, how shall He not with Him also freely give us all things?' Princes have *peculiar power*. A prince of heaven's empire has great influence: he wields a sceptre in his own domain; he sits upon Jesus' throne, for 'He hath made us kings and priests unto God, and we shall reign for ever and ever'. We reign over the united kingdom of time and eternity. Princes, again, have *special honour*. We may look down upon all earth-born dignity from the eminence upon which grace has placed us. For what is human grandeur to this, 'He hath raised us up together, and made us sit together in heavenly places in Christ Jesus'? We share the honour of Christ, and compared with this, earthly splendours are not worth a thought. Communion with Jesus is a richer gem than ever glittered in imperial diadem. Union with the Lord is a coronet of beauty outshining all the blaze of imperial pomp.

'Exceeding great and precious promises'
2 Peter 1:4

If you would know experimentally the preciousness of the promises, and enjoy them in your own heart, *meditate much upon them.* There are promises which are like grapes in the wine-press; if you will tread them the juice will flow. Thinking over the hallowed words will often be the prelude to their fulfilment. While you are musing upon them, the boon which you are seeking will insensibly come to you. Many a Christian who has thirsted for the promise has found the favour which it ensured gently distilling into his soul even while he has been considering the divine record; and he has rejoiced that ever he was led to lay the promise near his heart.

But besides *meditating* upon the promises, *seek in thy soul to receive them as being the very words of God.* Speak to thy soul thus, 'If I were dealing with a man's promise, I should carefully consider the ability and the character of the man who had covenanted with me. So with the promise of God; my eye must not be so much fixed upon the greatness of the mercy - that may stagger me; as upon the greatness of the Promiser - that will cheer me. My soul, it is God, even thy God, God that cannot lie, who speaks to thee. This word of His which thou art now considering is as true as His own existence. He is a God unchangeable. He has not altered the thing which has gone out of His mouth, nor called back one single consolatory sentence. Nor doth he lack any power; it is the God that made the heavens and the earth who has spoken thus. Nor can he fail in wisdom as to the time when he will bestow the favours, for He knoweth when it is best to give and when better to withhold. Therefore, seeing that it is the word of a God so true, so immutable, so powerful, so wise, I will and must believe the promise'. If we thus meditate upon the promises, and consider the Promiser, we shall experience their sweetness, and obtain their fulfilment.

'Who shall lay anything to the charge of God's elect?'
Romans 8:33

Most blessed challenge! How unanswerable it is! Every sin of the elect was laid upon the great Champion of our salvation, and by the atonement carried away. There is no sin in God's book against His people: He seeth no sin in Jacob, neither iniquity in Israel; they are justified in Christ for ever. When the guilt of sin was taken away, the punishment of sin was removed. For the Christian there is no stroke from God's angry hand - nay, not so much as a single frown of punitive justice. The believer may be chastised by his Father, but God the Judge has nothing to say to the Christian, except 'I have absolved thee: thou art acquitted'. For the Christian there is no penal death in this world, much less any second death. He is completely freed from all the punishment as well as the guilt of sin, and the power of sin is removed too. It may stand in our way, and agitate us with perpetual warfare; but sin is a conquered foe to every soul in union with Jesus. There is no sin which a Christian cannot overcome if he will only rely upon his God to do it. They who wear the white robe in heaven overcame through the blood of the Lamb, and we may do the same. No lust is too mighty, no besetting sin too strongly entrenched; we can overcome through the power of Christ. Do believe it, Christian, that thy sin is a condemned thing. It may kick and struggle, but it is doomed to die. God has written condemnation across its brow. Christ has crucified it, 'nailing it to His cross'. Go now and mortify it, and the Lord help you to live to His praise, for sin with all its guilt, shame, and fear, is gone.

> 'Here's pardon for transgressions past,
>   It matters not how black their cast;
> And, O my soul, with wonder view,
>   For sins to come here's pardon too.'

> *'So foolish was I, and ignorant;*
> *I was as a beast before Thee'*
> Psalm 73:22

Remember this is the confession of the man after God's own heart; and in telling us his inner life, he writes, 'So foolish was I, and ignorant'. The word *'foolish'*, here, means more than it signifies in ordinary language. David, in a former verse of the Psalm, writes, 'I was envious at *the foolish* when I saw the prosperity of the wicked', which shows that the folly he intended had *sin* in it. He puts himself down as being thus 'foolish', and adds a word which is to give intensity to it; 'so foolish was I'. *How foolish* he could not tell. It was a sinful folly, a folly which was not to be excused by frailty, but to be condemned because of its perverseness and wilful ignorance, for he had been envious of the present prosperity of the ungodly, forgetful of the dreadful end awaiting all such. And are we better than David that *we* should call ourselves wise! Do we profess that we have attained perfection, or to have been so chastened that the rod has taken all our wilfulness out of us? Ah, this were pride indeed! If *David* was foolish, how foolish should *we* be in our own esteem if we could but see ourselves! Look back, believer: think of your doubting God when he has been so faithful to you - think of your foolish outcry of 'Not so, my Father', when he crossed his hands in affliction to give you the larger blessing; think of the many times when you have read His providences in the dark, misinterpreted His dispensations, and groaned out, 'All these things are against me', when they are all working together for your good! Think how often you have chosen sin because of its pleasure, when indeed, that pleasure was a root of bitterness to you! Surely if we know our own heart we must plead guilty to the indictment of a sinful folly; and conscious of this 'foolishness', we must make David's consequent resolve our own - *'Thou shalt guide me with Thy counsel'*.

'Who went about doing good'
Acts 10:38

Few words, but yet an exquisite miniature of the Lord
Jesus Christ. There are not many touches, but they are
the strokes of a master's pencil. Of the Saviour and
only of the Saviour is it true in the fullest, broadest, and
most unqualified sense. 'He went about doing good.'
From this description it is evident that He did good
personally. The evangelists constantly tell us that He
touched the leper with His own finger, that He anointed
the eyes of the blind, and that in cases where He was
asked to speak the word only at a distance, he did not
usually comply, but went Himself to the sick bed, and
there personally wrought the cure. A lesson to us, if we
would do good, to do it ourselves. Give alms with your
own hand; a kind look or word, will enhance the value
of the gift. Speak to a friend about his soul; your loving
appeal will have more influence than a whole library of
tracts. Our Lord's mode of doing good sets forth His
incessant activity! He did not only the good which came
close to hand, but He 'went about' on his errands of
mercy. Throughout the whole land of Judaea there was
scarcely a village or a hamlet which was not gladdened
by the sight of Him. How this reproves the creeping,
loitering manner, in which many professors serve the
Lord. Let us gird up the loins of our mind, and be not
weary in well doing. Does not the text imply that Jesus
Christ *went out of His way to do good*? 'He went *about*
doing good.' He was never deterred by danger or
difficulty. He sought out the objects of His gracious
intentions. So must we. If old plans will not answer, we
must try new ones, for fresh experiments sometimes
achieve more than regular methods. Christ's *perseverance* and the *unity* of His purpose, are also hinted at,
and the practical application of the subject may be
summed up in the words, 'He hath left us an example
that we should follow in His steps'.

'Nevertheless I am continually with Thee'
Psalm 73:23

Nevertheless - as if, notwithstanding all the foolishness and ignorance which David had just been confessing to God, not one atom the less was it true and certain
that David was saved and accepted, and that the
blessing of being constantly in God's presence was
undoubtedly his. Fully conscious of his own lost
estate, and of the deceitfulness and vileness of his
nature, yet, by a glorious outburst of faith, he sings
'nevertheless I am continually with thee'. Believer,
you are forced to enter into Asaph's confession and
acknowledgment, endeavour in like spirit to say 'nevertheless, since I belong to Christ I am continually with
God'! By this is meant continually upon His *mind*, He
is always thinking of me for my good. Continually
before His *eye* - the eye of the Lord never sleepeth, but
is perpetually watching over my welfare. Continually
in His *hand*, so that none shall be able to pluck me
thence. Continually on His *heart*, worn there as a
memorial, even as the high priest bore the names of the
twelve tribes upon his heart for ever. Thou always
thinkest of me, O God. The bowels of Thy love
continually yearn towards me. Thou art always making
providence work for my good. Thou hast set me as a
signet upon thine arm; thy love is strong as death, many
waters cannot quench it; neither can the floods drown
it. Surprising grace! Thou seest me in Christ, and
though in myself abhorred, Thou beholdest me as
wearing Christ's garments, and washed in His blood,
and thus I stand accepted in Thy presence. I am thus
continually in Thy favour - 'continually with Thee'.
Here is comfort for the tried and afflicted soul; vexed
with the tempest within - look at the calm without.
Nevertheless - O say it in thy heart, and take the peace
it gives. 'Nevertheless I am continually with thee.'

'All that the Father giveth Me shall come to Me'
John 6:37

This declaration involves *the doctrine of election*: there are some whom the Father gave to Christ. It involves *the doctrine of effectual calling*: these who are given to Christ are not saved except they come to Jesus. Even *they* must come, for there is no other way to heaven but by the door, Christ Jesus. All that the Father gives to our Redeemer *must come to Him*, therefore none can come to heaven except they come to Christ.

Oh! the power and majesty which rest in the words *'shall come'*. He does not say they have power to come, nor they may come if they will, but they *'shall come'*. The Lord Jesus doth by his messengers, His word, and His Spirit, sweetly and graciously compel men to come that they may eat of His marriage supper; and this He does, not by any violation of the free agency of man, but by the power of His grace. I may exercise power over another man's will, and yet that other man's will may be perfectly free, because the constraint is exercised in a manner accordant with the laws of the human mind. Jehovah Jesus knows how, by irresistible arguments addressed to the understanding, by mighty reasons appealing to the affections, and by the mysterious influence of His Holy Spirit operating upon all the powers and passions of the soul, so to subdue the whole man, that whereas he was once rebellious, he yields cheerfully to His government, subdued by sovereign love. But how shall those be known whom God hath chosen? By this result: that they do willingly and joyfully accept Christ, and come to Him with simple and unfeigned faith, resting upon Him as all their salvation and all their desire. Reader, have you thus come to Jesus?

'And when he thought thereon, he wept'
Mark 14:72

It has been thought by some that as long as Peter lived, the fountain of his tears began to flow whenever he remembered his denying his Lord. It is not unlikely that it was so, for his sin was very great and grace in him had afterwards a perfect work. This same experience is common to all the redeemed family according to the degree in which the Spirit of God has removed the natural heart of stone. We, like Peter, remember *our boastful promise*: 'Though all men shall forsake Thee, yet will not I'. We eat our own words with the bitter herbs of repentance. When we think of what we vowed we would be, and of what we have been, we may weep whole showers of grief. He thought on *his denying his Lord*. The place in which he did it, the little cause which led him into such heinous sin, the oaths and blasphemies with which he sought to confirm his falsehood, and the dreadful hardness of heart which drove him to do so again and yet again. Can we, when we are reminded of our sins, and their exceeding sinfulness, remain stolid and stubborn? Will we not make our house a Bochim, and cry unto the Lord for renewed assurances of pardoning love? May we never take a dry-eyed look at sin, lest ere long we have a tongue parched in the flames of hell. Peter also thought upon *his Master's look of love*. The Lord followed up the cock's warning voice with an admonitory look of sorrow, pity, and love. That glance was never out of Peter's mind so long as he lived. It was far more effectual than ten thousand sermons would have been without the Spirit. The penitent apostle would be sure to weep when he recollected the *Saviour's full forgiveness*, which restored him to his former place. To think that we have offended so kind and good a Lord is more than sufficient reason for being constant weepers. Lord, smite our rocky hearts, and make the waters flow.

'Him that cometh to Me I will in no wise cast out'
John 6:37

No limit is set to *the duration* of this promise. It does not merely say, 'I will not cast out a sinner at his first coming', but, 'I will in no wise cast out'. The original reads, 'I will *not, not* cast out', or 'I will never, never cast out'. The text means, that Christ will not *at first* reject a believer; and that as he will not do it at first, so He will not *to the last*.

But suppose the believer sins after coming? 'If any man sin we have an advocate with the Father, Jesus Christ the righteous'. But suppose that believers backslide? 'I will heal their backsliding, I will love them freely: for Mine anger is turned away from him.' But believers may fall under temptation! 'God is faithful, who will not suffer you to be tempted above that ye are able; but will with the temptation also make a way to escape, that ye may be able to bear it.' But the believer may fall into sin as David did! Yes, but He will 'Purge them with hyssop, and they shall be clean; He will wash them and they shall be whiter than snow'; 'From all their iniquities will I cleanse them.'

'Once in Christ, in Christ for ever,
Nothing from His love can sever.'

'I give unto My sheep,' saith He, 'eternal life; and they shall never perish, neither shall any man pluck them out of My hand.' What sayest thou to this, O trembling feeble mind? Is not this a precious mercy, that coming to Christ, thou dost not come to one who will treat thee well for a little while, and then send thee about thy business, but He will receive thee and make thee His bride, and thou shalt be His for ever? Receive no longer the spirit of bondage again to fear, but the spirit of adoption whereby thou shalt cry, Abba, Father! Oh! the grace of these words: 'I will in no wise cast out'.

'I in them'
John 17:23

If such be the union which subsists between our souls and the person of our Lord, how deep and broad is the channel of our communion! This is no narrow pipe through which a thread-like stream may wind its way, it is a channel of amazing depth and breadth, along whose glorious length a ponderous volume of living water may roll its floods. Behold he hath set before us an open door, let us not be slow to enter. This city of communion hath many pearly gates, every several gate is of one pearl, and each gate is thrown open to the uttermost that we may enter, assured of welcome. If there were but one small loophole through which to talk with Jesus, it would be a high privilege to thrust a word of fellowship through the narrow door; how much we are blessed in having so large an entrance! Had the Lord Jesus been far away from us, with many a stormy sea between, we should have longed to send a messenger to Him to carry Him our loves, and bring us tidings from his Father's house; but see His kindness, He has built His house next door to ours, nay, more, He takes lodging with us, and tabernacles in poor humble hearts, that so He may have perpetual intercourse with us. O how foolish must we be, if we do not live in habitual communion with Him. When the road is long, and dangerous, and difficult, we need not wonder that friends seldom meet each other, but when they live together, shall Jonathan forget his David? A wife may when her husband is upon a journey, abide many days without holding converse with him, but she could never endure to be separated from him if she knew him to be in one of the chambers of her own house. Why, believer, dost not thou sit at His banquet of wine? Seek thy Lord, for He is near; embrace Him, for He is thy Brother. Hold Him fast, for He is thine Husband; and press Him to thine heart, for He is of thine own flesh.

'And these are the singers... they were employed in that work day and night'
1 Chronicles 9:33

Well was it so ordered in the temple that the sacred chant never ceased: for evermore did the singers praise the Lord, whose mercy endureth for ever. As mercy did not cease to rule either by day or by night, so neither did music hush its holy ministry. My heart, there is a lesson sweetly taught to thee in the ceaseless song of Zion's temple, thou too art a constant debtor, and see thou to it that thy gratitude, like charity, never faileth. God's praise is constant in heaven, which is to be thy final dwelling-place, learn thou to practise the eternal hallelujah. Around the earth as the sun scatters his light, his beams awaken grateful believers to tune their morning hymn, so that by the priesthood of the saints perpetual praise is kept up at all hours, they swathe our globe in a mantle of thanksgiving, and girdle it with a golden belt of song.

The Lord always deserves to be praised for what He is in Himself, for His works of creation and providence, for His goodness towards His creatures, and especially for the transcendent act of redemption, and all the marvellous blessing flowing therefrom. It is always beneficial to praise the Lord; it cheers the day and brightens the night; it lightens toil and softens sorrow; and over earthly gladness it sheds a sanctifying radiance which makes it less liable to blind us with its glare. Have we not something to sing about at this moment? Can we not weave a song out of our present joys, or our past deliverances, or our future hopes? Earth yields her summer fruits: the hay is housed, the golden grain invites the sickle, and the sun tarrying long to shine upon a fruitful earth, shortens the interval of shade that we may lengthen the hours of devout worship. By the love of Jesus, let us be stirred up to close the day with a psalm of sanctified gladness.

August

'Let me now go to the field, and glean ears of corn'
Ruth 2:2

Downcast and troubled Christian, come and glean
today in the broad field of promise. Here are abundance
of precious promises, which exactly meet thy wants.
Take this one: 'He will not break the bruised reed, nor
quench the smoking flax'. Doth not that suit thy case?
A reed, helpless, insignificant, and weak; a bruised
reed, out of which no music can come; weaker than
weakness itself; a reed, and that reed bruised, yet, He
will not break thee; but on the contrary, will restore and
strengthen thee. Thou art like the smoking flax: no
light, no warmth, can come from thee; but he will not
quench thee; He will blow with His sweet breath of
mercy till He fans thee to a flame. Wouldst thou glean
another ear? 'Come unto Me all ye that labour and are
heavy laden, and I will give you rest'. What soft words!
Thy heart is tender, and the Master knows it, and
therefore He speaketh so gently to thee. Wilt thou not
obey Him, and come to Him even now? Take another
ear of corn: 'Fear not, thou worm Jacob, I will help
thee, saith the Lord and thy Redeemer, the Holy One of
Israel'. How canst thou fear with such a wonderful
assurance as this? Thou mayest gather ten thousand
such golden ears as these! 'I have blotted out thy sins
like a cloud, and like a thick cloud thy transgressions.'
Or this, 'Though your sins be as scarlet, they shall be
as white as snow; though they be red like crimson, they
shall be as wool'. Or this, 'The Spirit and the Bride say,
Come, and let him that is athirst come, and whosoever
will let him take the water of life freely'. Our Master's
field is very rich; behold the handfuls. See, there they
lie before thee, poor timid believer! Gather them up,
make them thine own, for Jesus bids thee take them. Be
not afraid, only believe! Grasp these sweet promises,
thresh them out by meditation and feed on them with
joy.

'*Thou crownest the year with Thy goodness*'
Psalm 65:11

All the year round, every hour of every day, God is richly blessing us; both when we sleep and when we wake His mercy waits upon us. The sun may leave us a legacy of darkness, but our God never ceases to shine upon His children with beams of love. Like a river, His loving-kindness is always flowing, with a fulness inexhaustible as His own nature. Like the atmosphere which constantly surrounds the earth, and is always ready to support the life of man, the benevolence of God surrounds all His creatures; in it, as in their element, they live, and move, and have their being. Yet as the sun on summer days gladdens us with beams more warm and bright than at other times, and as rivers are at certain seasons swollen by the rain, and as the atmosphere itself is sometimes fraught with more fresh, more bracing, or more balmy influences than heretofore, so is it with the mercy of God; it hath its golden hours; its days of overflow, when the Lord magnifieth His grace before the sons of men. Amongst the blessings of the nether springs, *the joyous days of harvest* are a special season of excessive favour. It is the glory of autumn that the ripe gifts of providence are then abundantly bestowed; it is the mellow season of realisation, whereas all before was but hope and expectation. Great is the joy of harvest. Happy are the reapers who fill their arms with the liberality of heaven. The Psalmist tells us that the harvest is the crowning of the year. Surely these crowning mercies call for crowning thanksgiving! Let us render it by the *inward emotions of gratitude*. Let our hearts be warmed; let our spirits remember, meditate, and think upon this goodness of the Lord. Then let us *praise him with our lips*, and laud and magnify His name from whose bounty all this goodness flows. Let us glorify God by yielding *our gifts* to His cause. A practical proof of our gratitude is a special thank-offering to the Lord of the harvest.

'*Who worketh all things*
after the counsel of His own will'
Ephesians 1:11

Our belief in God's wisdom supposes and necessitates
that He has a settled purpose and plan in the work of
salvation. What would *creation* have been without His
design? Is there a fish in the sea, or a fowl in the air,
which was left to chance for its formation? Nay, in
every bone, joint, and muscle, sinew, gland, and blood-
vessel, you mark the presence of a God working
everything according to the design of infinite wisdom.
And shall God be present in creation, ruling over all,
and not in *grace*? Shall the new creation have the fickle
genius of free will to preside over it when divine
counsel rules the old creation? Look at *Providence*!
Who knoweth not that not a sparrow falleth to the
ground without your Father? Even the hairs of your
head are all numbered. God weighs the mountains of
our grief in scales, and the hills of our tribulation in
balances. And shall there be a God in providence and
not in grace? Shall the shell be ordained by wisdom and
the kernel be left to blind chance? No; he knows the end
from the beginning. He sees in its appointed place, not
merely the cornerstone which He has laid in fair
colours, in the blood of His dear Son, but He beholds
in their ordained position each of the chosen stones
taken out of the quarry of nature, and polished by His
grace; He sees the whole from corner to cornice, from
base to roof, from foundation to pinnacle. He hath in
His mind a clear knowledge of every stone which shall
be laid in its prepared space, and how vast the edifice
shall be, and when the top-stone shall be brought forth
with shoutings of 'Grace! Grace! unto it'. At the last it
shall be clearly seen that in every chosen vessel of
mercy, Jehovah did as He willed with His own; and that
in every part of the work of grace He accomplished His
purpose, and glorified His own name.

'So she gleaned in the field until even'
Ruth 2:17

Let me learn from Ruth, the gleaner. As she went out
to gather the ears of corn, so must I go forth into the
fields of prayer, meditation, the ordinances, and hearing the word to gather spiritual food. *The gleaner
gathers her portion ear by ear*; her gains are little by
little: so must I be content to search for single truths,
if there be no greater plenty of them. Every ear helps
to make a bundle, and every gospel lesson assists in
making us wise unto salvation. *The gleaner keeps her
eyes open*: if she stumbled among the stubble in a
dream, she would have no load to carry home rejoicingly at eventide. I must be watchful in religious
exercises lest they become unprofitable to me; I fear I
have lost much already - O that I may rightly estimate
my opportunities, and glean with greater diligence. *The
gleaner stoops for all she finds*, and so must I. High
spirits criticise and object, but lowly minds glean and
receive benefit. A humble heart is a great help towards
profitably hearing the gospel. The engrafted soul-
saving word is not received except with meekness. A
stiff back makes a bad gleaner; down, master pride,
thou art a vile robber, not to be endured for a moment.
What the gleaner gathers she holds: if she dropped one
ear to find another, the result of her day's work would
be but scant; she is as careful to retain as to obtain, and
so at last her gains are great. How often do I forget all
that I hear; the second truth pushes the first out of my
head, and so my reading and hearing end in much ado
about nothing! Do I feel duly the importance of storing
up the truth? A hungry belly makes the gleaner wise; if
there be no corn in her hand, there will be no bread on
her table; she labours under the sense of necessity, and
hence her tread is nimble and her grasp is firm; I have
even a greater necessity, Lord, help me to feel it, that
it may urge me onward to glean in fields which yield so
plenteous a reward to diligence.

'The Lamb is the light thereof'
Revelation 21:23

Quietly contemplate the Lamb as the light of heaven. Light in Scripture is the emblem of *joy*. The joy of the saints in heaven is comprised in this: *Jesus* chose us, loved us, bought us, cleansed us, robed us, kept us, glorified us: we are here entirely through the Lord Jesus. Each one of these thoughts shall be to them like a cluster of the grapes of Eshcol. Light is also the cause of *beauty*. Nought of beauty is left when light is gone. Without light no radiance flashes from the sapphire, no peaceful ray proceedeth from the pearl; and thus all the beauty of the saints above comes from Jesus. As planets, they reflect the light of the Sun of Righteousness; they live as beams proceeding from the central orb. If He withdrew, they must die; if His glory were veiled, their glory must expire. Light is also the emblem of *knowledge*. In heaven our knowledge will be perfect, but the Lord Jesus Himself will be the fountain of it. Dark providences, never understood before, will then be clearly seen, and all that puzzles us now will become plain to us in the light of the Lamb. Oh! what unfoldings there will be and what glorifying of the God of love! Light also means *manifestation*. Light manifests. In this world it doth not yet appear what we shall be. God's people are a hidden people, but when Christ receives his people into heaven, he will touch them with the wand of his own love, and change them into the image of his manifested glory. They were poor and wretched, but what a transformation! They were stained with sin, but one touch of his finger, and they are bright as the sun, and clear as crystal. Oh! what a manifestation! All this proceeds from the exalted Lamb. Whatever there may be of effulgent splendour, Jesus shall be the centre and soul of it all. Oh! to be present and to see him in his own light, the King of kings, and Lord of lords!

'*But as He went*'
Luke 8:42

Jesus is passing through the throng to the house of
Jairus, to raise the ruler's dead daughter; but He is so
profuse in goodness that he works another miracle
while upon the road. While yet this rod of Aaron bears
the blossom of an unaccomplished wonder, it yields the
ripe almonds of a perfect work of mercy. It is enough
for us, if we have some one purpose, straightway to go
and accomplish it; it were imprudent to expend our
energies by the way. Hastening to the rescue of a
drowning friend, we cannot afford to exhaust our
strength upon another in like danger. It is enough for
a tree to yield one sort of fruit, and for a man to fulfil
his own peculiar calling. But our Master knows no
limit of power or boundary of mission. He is so prolific
of grace, that like the sun which shines as it rolls
onward in its orbit, His path is radiant with loving-
kindness. He is a swift arrow of love, which not only
reaches its ordained target, but perfumes the air through
which it flies. Virtue is evermore going out of Jesus,
as sweet odours exhale from flowers; and it always will
be emanating from him, as water from a sparkling
fountain. What delightful encouragement this truth
affords us! If our Lord is so ready to heal the sick and
bless the needy, then, my soul, be not thou slow to put
thyself in His way, that He may smile on thee. Be not
slack in asking, if he be so abundant in bestowing. Give
earnest heed to His word now, and at all times, that
Jesus may speak through it to thy heart. Where He is
to be found there make thy resort, that thou mayest
obtain His blessing. When He is present to heal, may
He not heal Thee? But surely He is present even now,
for He always comes to hearts which need Him. And
dost not thou need Him? Ah, *He* knows how much!
Thou Son of David, turn Thine eye and look upon the
distress which is now before Thee, and make Thy
suppliant whole.

'The people that do know their God shall be strong'
Daniel 11:32

Every believer understands that to know God is the
highest and best form of knowledge; and this spiritual
knowledge is a source of strength to the Christian. It
strengthens his *faith*. Believers are constantly spoken
of in the Scriptures as being persons who are enlightened and taught of the Lord; they are said to 'have an
unction from the Holy One', and it is the Spirit's
peculiar office to lead them into all truth, and all this for
the increase and the fostering of their faith. Knowledge
strengthens *love*, as well as faith. Knowledge opens the
door, and then through that door we see our Saviour.
Or, to use another similitude, knowledge paints the
portrait of Jesus, and when we see that portrait then we
love Him, we cannot love a Christ whom we do not
know, at least, in some degree. If we know but little of
the excellences of Jesus, what He has done for us, and
what He is doing now, we cannot love Him much; but
the more we know Him, the more we shall love Him.
Knowledge also strengthens *hope*. How can we hope
for a thing if we do not know of its existence? Hope may
be the telescope, but till we receive instruction, our
ignorance stands in the front of the glass, and we can
see nothing whatever; knowledge removes the inter-
posing object, and when we look through the bright
optic glass we discern the glory to be revealed, and
anticipate it with joyous confidence. Knowledge supplies us reasons for *patience*. How shall we have
patience unless we know something of the sympathy of
Christ, and understand the good which is to come out
of the correction which our heavenly Father sends us?
Nor is there one single grace of the Christian which,
under God, will not be fostered and brought to perfection by holy knowledge. How important, then, is it that
we should grow not only in grace, but in the 'knowledge' of our Lord and Saviour Jesus Christ.

*'I smote you with blasting and with mildew and
with hail in all the labours of your hands'*
Haggai 2:17

How destructive is the hail to the standing crops,
beating out the precious grain upon the ground! How
grateful ought we to be when the corn is spared so
terrible a ruin! Let us offer unto the Lord thanksgiving.
Even more to be dreaded are those mysterious destroy-
ers - smut, bunt, rust, and mildew. These turn the ear
into a mass of soot, or render it putrid, or dry up the
grain, and all in a manner so beyond all human control
that the farmer is compelled to cry, 'This is the finger
of God'. Innumerable minute fungi cause the mischief,
and were it not for the goodness of God, the rider on the
black horse would soon scatter famine over the land.
Infinite mercy spares the food of men, but in view of
the active agents which are ready to destroy the harvest,
right wisely are we taught to pray, 'Give us this day our
daily bread'. The curse is abroad; we have constant
need of the blessing. When blight and mildew come
they are chastisements from heaven, and men must
learn to hear the rod, and Him that hath appointed it.

Spiritually, mildew is no uncommon evil. When
our work is most promising this blight appears. We
hoped for many conversions, and lo! a general apathy,
an abounding worldliness, or a cruel hardness of heart!
There may be no open sin in those for whom we are
labouring, but there is a deficiency of sincerity and
decision sadly disappointing our desires. We learn
from this our dependence upon the Lord, and the need
of prayer that no blight may fall upon our work.
Spiritual pride or sloth will soon bring upon us the
dreadful evil, and only the Lord of the harvest can
remove it. Mildew may even attack our own hearts, and
shrivel our prayers and religious exercises. May it
please the great Husbandman to avert so serious a
calamity. Shine, blessed Sun of Righteousness, and
drive the blights away.

> '*We know that all things work together*
> *for good to them that love God*'
> Romans 8:28

Upon some points a believer is absolutely sure. He knows, for instance, that God sits in the stern-sheets of the vessel when it rocks most. He believes that an invisible hand is always on the world's tiller, and that wherever providence may drift, Jehovah steers it. That reassuring knowledge prepares him for everything. He looks over the raging waters and sees the spirit of Jesus treading the billows, and he hears a voice saying, 'It is I, be not afraid'. He knows too that God is always wise, and, knowing this, he is confident that there can be no accidents, no mistakes; that nothing can occur which ought not to arise. He can say, 'If I should lose all I have, it is better that I should lose than have, if God so wills: the worst calamity is the wisest and the kindest thing that could befall to me if God ordains it.' 'We know that all things work together for good to them that love God.' The Christian does not merely hold this as a theory, but *he knows it* as a matter of fact. Everything *has* worked for good as yet; the poisonous drugs mixed in fit proportions have worked the cure; the sharp cuts of the lancet have cleansed out the proud flesh and facilitated the healing. Every event as yet has worked out the most divinely blessed results; and so, believing that God rules all, that He governs wisely, that He brings good out of evil, the believer's heart is assured, and he is enabled calmly to meet each trial as it comes. The believer can in the spirit of true resignation pray, 'Send me what thou wilt, my God, so long as it comes from Thee; never came there an ill portion from Thy table to any of Thy children'.

'Say not my soul, "From whence can God relieve my care?"
  Remember that Omnipotence has servants everywhere.
His method is sublime, His heart profoundly kind,
  God never is before His time, and never is behind.'

*'Shall your brethren go to war,
and shall ye sit here?'*
Numbers 32:6

Kindred has its obligations. The Reubenites and Gadites
would have been most unbrotherly if they had claimed
the land which had been conquered, and had left the rest
of the people to fight for their portions alone. We have
received much by means of the efforts and sufferings
of the saints in years gone by, and if we do not make
some return to the church of Christ by giving her our
best energies, we are unworthy to be enrolled in her
ranks. Others are combating the errors of the age
manfully, or excavating perishing ones from amid the
ruins of the fall, and if we fold our hands in idleness we
had need be warned, lest the curse of Meroz fall upon
us. The Master of the vineyard saith, 'Why stand ye
here all the day idle?' What is the idler's excuse?
Personal service of Jesus becomes all the more the duty
of all because it is cheerfully and abundantly rendered
by some. The toils of devoted missionaries and fervent
ministers shame us if we sit still in indolence. Shrinking from trial is the temptation of those who are at ease
in Zion: they would fain escape the cross and yet wear
the crown; to them the question for this evening's
meditation is very applicable. If the most precious are
tried in the fire, are we to escape the crucible? If the
diamond must be vexed upon the wheel, are we to be
made perfect without suffering? Who hath commanded
the wind to cease from blowing because our bark is on
the deep? Why and wherefore should we be treated
better than our Lord? The firstborn felt the rod, and
why not the younger brethren? It is a cowardly pride
which would choose a downy pillow and a silken couch
for a soldier of the cross. Wiser far is he who, being
first resigned to the divine will, groweth by the energy
of grace to be pleased with it, and so learns to gather
lilies at the cross foot, and, like Samson, to find honey
in the lion.

'Watchman, what of the night?'
Isaiah 21:11

What enemies are abroad? Errors are a numerous horde, and new ones appear every hour; against what heresy am I to be on my guard? Sins creep from their lurking places when the darkness reigns; I must myself mount the watch-tower, and watch unto prayer. Our heavenly Protector foresees all the attacks which are about to be made upon us, and when as yet the evil designed us is but in the desire of Satan, He prays for us that our faith fail not, when we are sifted as wheat. Continue O gracious Watchman, to forewarn us of our foes, and for Zion's sake hold not Thy peace.

'Watchman, what of the night?' *What weather is coming* for the Church? Are the clouds lowering, or is it all clear and fair overhead? We must care for the Church of God with anxious love; and now that Popery and infidelity are both threatening, let us observe the signs of the times and prepare for conflict.

'Watchman, what of the night?' *What stars are visible*? What precious promises suit our present case? You sound the alarm, give us the consolation also. Christ, the pole-star, is ever fixed in His place, and all the stars are secure in the right hand of their Lord.

But, watchman, *when comes the morning*? The Bridegroom tarries. Are there no signs of His coming forth as the Sun of Righteousness? Has not the morning star arisen as the pledge of day? When will the day dawn, and the shadows flee away? O Jesus, if Thou come not in person to thy waiting Church this day, yet come in Spirit to my sighing heart, and make it sing for joy.

'Now all the earth is bright and glad
    With the fresh morn;
      But all my heart is cold, and dark and sad:
Sun of the soul, let me behold Thy dawn!
Come, Jesus, Lord,
    O quickly come, according to Thy word.'

*'Let the whole earth be filled with His glory;
Amen, and Amen'*
Psalm 72:19

This is a large petition. To intercede for a whole city
needs a stretch of faith, and there are times when a
prayer for one man is enough to stagger us. But how
far-reaching was the psalmist's dying intercession!
How comprehensive How sublime! 'Let the whole
earth be filled with His glory.' It doth not exempt a
single country however crushed by the foot of superstition; it doth not exclude a single nation however
barbarous. For the cannibal as well as for the civilised,
for all climes and races this prayer is uttered: the whole
circle of the earth it encompasses, and omits no son of
Adam. We must be up and doing for our Master, or we
cannot honestly offer such a prayer. The petition is not
asked with a sincere heart unless we endeavour, as God
shall help us, to extend the kingdom of our Master. Are
there not some, who *neglect* both to plead and to
labour? Reader, is it *your* prayer? Turn your eyes to
Calvary. Behold the Lord of Life nailed to a cross, with
the thorn-crown about His brow, with bleeding head,
and hands, and feet. What! can you look upon this
miracle of miracles, the death of the Son of God,
without feeling within your bosom a marvellous adoration that language never can express? And when you
feel the blood applied to your conscience, and know
that He has blotted out your sins, *you are not a man*
unless you start from your knees and cry, 'Let the
whole earth be filled with His glory; Amen, and
Amen'. Can you bow before the Crucified in loving
homage, and not wish to see your Monarch master of
the world? Out on you if you can pretend to love your
Prince, and desire not to see him the universal ruler.
Your piety is worthless unless it leads you to wish that
the same mercy which has been extended to you may
bless the whole world. Lord, it is harvest-time, put in
Thy sickle and reap.

'The upright love Thee'
Canticles 1:4

Believers love Jesus with a deeper affection than they dare to give to any other being. They would sooner lose father and mother than part with Christ. They hold all earthly comforts with a loose hand, but they carry him fast locked in their bosoms. They voluntarily deny themselves for His sake, but they are not to be driven to deny *Him*. It is scant love which the fire of persecution can dry up; the true believer's love is a deeper stream than this. Men have laboured to divide the faithful from their Master, but their attempts have been fruitless in every age. Neither crowns of honour, nor frowns of anger, have untied this more than Gordian knot. This is no everyday attachment which the world's power may at length dissolve. Neither man nor devil have found a key which opens this lock. Never has the craft of Satan been more at fault than when he has exercised it in seeking to rend in sunder this union of two divinely welded hearts. It is written, and nothing can blot out the sentence, *'The upright love Thee'*. The intensity of the love of the upright, however, is not so much to be judged by what it appears as by what the upright long for. It is our daily lament that we cannot love enough. Would that our hearts were capable of holding more, and reaching further. Like Samuel Rutherford, we sigh and cry, 'Oh, for as much love as would go round about the earth, and over heaven- yea, the heaven of heavens, and ten thousand worlds - that I might let all out upon fair, fair, only fair Christ'. Alas! our longest reach is but a span of love, and our affection is but as a drop of a bucket compared with His deserts. Measure our love by our intentions, and it is high indeed; 'tis thus, we trust, our Lord doth judge of it. Oh, that we could give all the love in all hearts in one great mass, a gathering together of all loves to Him who is altogether lovely!

'Satan hindered us'
1 Thessalonians 2:18

Since the first hour in which goodness came into conflict with evil, it has never ceased to be true in spiritual experience, that Satan hinders us. From all points of the compass, all along the line of battle, in the vanguard and in the rear, at the dawn of day and in the midnight hour, Satan hinders us. If we toil in the field, he seeks to break the ploughshare; if we build the wall, he labours to cast down the stones; if we would serve God in suffering or in conflict - everywhere Satan hinders us. He hinders us when we are first coming to Jesus Christ. Fierce conflicts we had with Satan when we first looked to the cross and lived. Now that we are saved, he endeavours to hinder the completeness of our personal character. You may be congratulating yourself, 'I have hitherto walked consistently; no man can challenge my integrity'. Beware of boasting, for your virtue will yet be tried; Satan will direct his engines against that very virtue for which you are the most famous. If you have been hitherto a firm believer, your faith will ere long be attacked; if you have been meek as Moses, expect to be tempted to speak unadvisedly with your lips. The birds will peck at your ripest fruit, and the wild boar will dash his tusks at your choicest vines. Satan is sure to hinder us when we are earnest in prayer. He checks our importunity, and weakens our faith in order that, if possible, we may miss the blessing. Nor is Satan less vigilant in obstructing Christian effort. There was never a revival of religion without a revival of his opposition. As soon as Ezra and Nehemiah begin to labour, Sanballat and Tobiah are stirred up to hinder them. What then? We are not alarmed because Satan hindereth us, for it is a proof that we are on the Lord's side, and are doing the Lord's work, and in His strength we shall win the victory, and triumph over our adversary.

'They weave the spider's web'
Isaiah 59:5

See the spider's web, and behold in it a most suggestive picture of the hypocrite's religion. *It is meant to catch his prey*: the spider fattens himself on flies, and the Pharisee has his reward. Foolish persons are easily entrapped by the loud professions of pretenders, and even the more judicious cannot always escape. Philip baptised Simon Magus, whose guileful declaration of faith was so soon exploded by the stern rebuke of Peter. Custom, reputation, praise, advancement, and other flies, are the small game which hypocrites take in their nets. A spider's web is *a marvel of skill*: look at it and admire the cunning hunter's wiles. Is not a deceiver's religion equally wonderful? How does he make so barefaced a lie appear to be a truth? How can he make his tinsel answer so well the purpose of gold? A spider's web *comes all from the creature's own bowels*. The bee gathers her wax from flowers, the spider sucks no flowers, and yet she spins out her material to any length. Even so hypocrites find their trust and hope within themselves; their anchor was forged on their own anvil, and their cable twisted by their own hands. They lay their own foundation, and hew out the pillars of their own house, disdaining to be debtors to the sovereign grace of God. But a spider's web is *very frail*. It is curiously wrought, but not enduringly manufactured. It is no match for the servant's broom, or the traveller's staff. The hypocrite needs no battery of Armstrongs to blow his hope to pieces, a mere puff of wind will do it. Hypocritical cobwebs will soon come down when the besom of destruction begins its purifying work. Which reminds us of one more thought, viz, that such cobwebs *are not to be endured in the Lord's house*: He will see to it that they and those who spin them shall be destroyed for ever. O my soul, be thou resting on something better than a spider's web. Be the Lord Jesus thine eternal hiding-place.

'All things are possible to him that believeth'
Mark 9:23

Many professed Christians are always doubting and fearing, and they forlornly think that this is the necessary state of believers. This is a mistake, for 'all things are possible to him that believeth'; and it is possible for us to mount into a state in which a doubt or a fear shall be but as a bird of passage flitting across the soul, but never lingering there. When you read of the high and sweet communions enjoyed by favoured saints, you sigh and murmur in the chamber of your heart, 'Alas! these are not for me'. O climber, if thou hast but faith, thou shalt yet stand upon the sunny pinnacle of the temple, for 'all things are possible to him that believeth'. You hear of exploits which holy men have done for Jesus; what they have enjoyed of Him; how much they have been like Him; how they have been able to endure great persecutions for His sake; and you say, 'Ah! as for me, I am but a worm; I can never attain to this'. But there is nothing which one saint was, that you may not be. There is no elevation of grace, no attainment of spirituality, no clearness of assurance, no post of duty, which is not open to you if you have but the power to believe. Lay aside your sackcloth and ashes, and rise to the dignity of your true position; you are little in Israel because you will be so, not because there is any necessity for it. It is not meet that thou shouldst grovel in the dust, O child of a King. Ascend! The golden throne of assurance is waiting for you! The crown of communion with Jesus is ready to bedeck your brow. Wrap yourself in scarlet and fine linen, and fare sumptuously every day for if thou believest, thou mayest eat the fat of kidneys of wheat; thy land shall flow with milk and honey, and thy soul shall be satisfied as with marrow and fatness. Gather golden sheaves of grace, for they await thee in the fields of faith. 'All things are possible to him that believeth.'

*'The city had no need of the sun,
neither of the moon, to shine in it'*
Revelation 21:23

Yonder in the better world, the inhabitants are independent of all creature comforts. They have no need of raiment; their white robes never wear out, neither shall they ever be defiled. They need no medicine to heal diseases, 'for the inhabitant shall not say, I am sick'. They need no sleep to recruit their frames - they rest not day nor night, but unweariedly praise Him in His temple. They need no social relationship to minister comfort, and whatever happiness they may derive from association with their fellows is not essential to their bliss, for their Lord's society is enough for their largest desires. They need no teachers there; they doubtless commune with one another concerning the things of God, but they do not require this by way of instruction; they shall all be taught of the Lord. Ours are the alms at the king's gate, but they feast at the table itself. Here we lean upon the friendly arm, but there they lean upon their Beloved and upon Him alone. Here we must have the help of our companions, but there they find all they want in Christ Jesus. Here we look to the meat which perisheth, and to the raiment which decays before the moth, but there they find everything in God. We use the bucket to fetch us water from the well, but there they drink from the fountain head, and put their lips down to the living water. Here the angels bring us blessings, but we shall want no messengers from heaven then. They shall need no Gabriels there to bring their love-notes from God, for there they shall see *Him* face to face. Oh! what a blessed time shall that be when we shall have mounted above every second cause and shall rest upon the bare arm of God! What a glorious hour when God, and not His creatures; the Lord, and not His works, shall be our daily joy! Our souls shall then have attained the perfection of bliss.

*'He appeared first to Mary Magdalene,
out of whom He had cast seven devils'*
Mark 16:9

Mary of Magdala was *the victim of a fearful evil*. She was possessed by not one devil only, but seven. These dreadful inmates caused much pain and pollution to the poor frame in which they had found a lodging. Hers was a hopeless, horrible case. She could not help herself, neither could any human succour avail. But Jesus passed that way, and unsought, and probably even resisted by the poor demoniac, He uttered the word of power, and Mary of Magdala became *a trophy of the healing power of Jesus*. All the seven demons left her, left her never to return, forcibly ejected by the Lord of all. What a blessed deliverance! What a happy change! From delirium to delight, from despair to peace, from hell to heaven! Straightway she became *a constant follower of Jesus*, catching His every word, following His devious steps, sharing His toilsome life; and withal she became *His generous helper*, first among that band of healed and grateful women who ministered unto Him of their substance. When Jesus was lifted up in crucifixion, Mary remained *the sharer of His shame*: we find her first beholding from afar, and then drawing near to the foot of the cross. She could not die on the cross with Jesus, but she stood as near it as she could, and when His blessed body was taken down, she watched to see how and where it was laid. She was *the faithful and watchful believer*, last at the sepulchre where Jesus slept, first at the grave whence He arose. Her holy fidelity made her *a favoured beholder of her beloved Rabboni*, who deigned to call her by her name, and to make her *His messenger of good news* to the trembling disciples and Peter. Thus grace found her a maniac and made her a minister, cast out devils and gave her to behold angels, delivered from Satan, and united her for ever to the Lord Jesus. May I also be such a miracle of grace!

'Christ, who is our life'
Colossians 3:4

Paul's marvellously rich expression indicates, that Christ is the *source* of our life. 'You hath He quickened who were dead in trespasses and sins'. That same voice which brought Lazarus out of the tomb raised us to newness of life. He is now the *substance* of our spiritual life. It is by His life that we live; He is in us, the hope of glory, the spring of our actions, the central thought which moves every other thought. *Christ is the sustenance of our life.* What can the Christian feed upon but Jesus' flesh and blood? 'This is the bread which cometh down from heaven, that a man may eat thereof, and not die.' O wayworn pilgrims in this wilderness of sin, you never get a morsel to satisfy the hunger of your spirits, except ye find it in Him! *Christ is the solace of our life.* All our true joys come from Him; and in times of trouble, His presence is our consolation. There is nothing worth living for but Him; and His loving-kindness is better than life! *Christ is the object of our life.* As speeds the ship towards the port, so hastes the believer towards the haven of his Saviour's bosom. As flies the arrow to its goal, so flies the Christian towards the perfecting of his fellowship with Christ Jesus. As the soldier fights for his captain, and is crowned in his captain's victory, so the believer contends for Christ, and gets his triumph out of the triumphs of his Master. 'For him to live is Christ.' *Christ is the exemplar of our life.* Where there is the same life within, there will, there must be, to a great extent, the same developments without; and if we live in near fellowship with the Lord Jesus we shall grow like Him. We shall set Him before us as our Divine copy, and we shall seek to tread in His footsteps, until He shall become *the crown of our life* in glory. Oh! how safe, how honoured, how happy is the Christian, since Christ is our life!

'The Son of Man hath power on earth to forgive sins'
Matthew 9:6

Behold one of the great Physician's mightiest arts: He has power to forgive sin! While here He lived below, before the ransom had been paid, before the blood had been literally sprinkled on the mercy-seat, He had power to forgive sin. Hath He not power to do it now that He hath died? What power must dwell in Him who to the utmost farthing has faithfully discharged the debts of His people! He has boundless power now that He has finished transgression and made an end of sin. If ye doubt it, see Him rising from the dead! Behold Him in ascending splendour raised to the right hand of God! Hear Him pleading before the eternal Father, pointing to His wounds, urging the merit of His sacred passion! What power to forgive is here! 'He hath ascended on high, and received gifts for men.' 'He is exalted on high to give repentance and remission of sins.' The most crimson sins are removed by the crimson of His blood. At this moment, dear reader, whatever thy sinfulness, Christ has power to pardon, power to pardon *thee*, and millions such as thou art. A word will speak it. He has nothing more to do to win thy pardon; all the atoning work is done. He can, in answer to thy tears, forgive thy sins today, and make thee know it. He can breathe into thy soul at this very moment a peace with God which passeth all understanding, which shall spring from perfect remission of thy manifold iniquities. Dost thou believe that? I trust thou believest it. Mayest thou experience now the power of Jesus to forgive sin! Waste no time in applying to the Physician of souls, but hasten to Him with words like these:

'Jesus! Master! hear my cry;
    Save me, heal me with a word;
Fainting at Thy feet I lie,
    Thou my whisper'd plaint hast heard.'

'Oh that I were as in months past'
Job 29:2

Numbers of Christians can view the past with pleasure, but regard the present with dissatisfaction; they look back upon the days which they have passed in communing with the Lord as being the sweetest and the best they have ever known, but as to the present, it is clad in a sable garb of gloom and dreariness. Once they lived near to Jesus, but now they feel that they have wandered from him, and they say, 'O that I were as in months past!'. They complain that they have lost their evidences, or that they have not present peace of mind, or that they have no enjoyment in the means of grace, or that conscience is not so tender, or that they have not so much zeal for God's glory. The causes of this mournful state of things are manifold. It may arise through a comparative *neglect of prayer*, for a neglected closet is the beginning of all spiritual decline. Or it may be the result of *idolatry*. The heart has been occupied with something else, more than with God; the affections have been set on the things of earth, instead of the things of heaven. A jealous God will not be content with a divided heart; He must be loved first and best. He will withdraw the sunshine of his presence from a cold, wandering heart. Or the cause may be found in *self-confidence* and *self-righteousness*. Pride is busy in the heart, and self is exalted instead of lying low at the foot of the cross. Christian, if you are not now as you 'were in months past', do not rest satisfied with *wishing* for a return of former happiness, but go at once to seek your Master, and tell Him your sad state. Ask His grace and strength to help you to walk more closely with Him; humble yourself before Him, and He will lift you up, and give you yet again to enjoy the light of His countenance. Do not sit down to sigh and lament; while the beloved Physician lives there is hope, nay there is a certainty of recovery for the worst cases.

'Everlasting consolation'
2 Thessalonians 2:16

'Consolation.' There is music in the word: like David's harp, it charms away the evil spirit of melancholy. It was a distinguished honour to Barnabas to be called 'the son of consolation'; nay, it is one of the illustrious names of a greater than Barnabas, for the Lord Jesus is 'the consolation of Israel'. *'Everlasting* consolation' - here is the cream of all, for the eternity of comfort is the crown and glory of it. What is this 'everlasting consolation'? It includes a sense of pardoned sin. A Christian man has received in his heart the witness of the Spirit that his iniquities are put away like a cloud, and his transgressions like a thick cloud. If sin be pardoned, is not that an everlasting consolation? Next, the Lord gives His people an abiding sense of acceptance in Christ. The Christian knows that God looks upon him as standing in union with Jesus. Union to the risen Lord is a consolation of the most abiding order; it is, in fact, everlasting. Let sickness prostrate us, have we not seen hundreds of believers as happy in the weakness of disease as they would have been in the strength of hale and blooming health? Let death's arrows pierce us to the heart, our comfort dies not, for have not our ears full often heard the songs of saints as they have rejoiced because the living love of God was shed abroad in their hearts in dying moments? Yes, a sense of acceptance in the Beloved is an everlasting consolation. Moreover, the Christian has a conviction of his security. God has promised to save those who trust in Christ: the Christian does trust in Christ, and he believes that God will be as good as His word, and will save him. He feels that he is safe by virtue of his being bound up with the person and work of Jesus.

'The Lord reigneth, let the earth rejoice'
Psalm 97:1

Causes for disquietude there are none so long as this blessed sentence is true. *On earth* the Lord's power as readily controls the rage of the wicked as the rage of the sea; His love as easily refreshes the poor with mercy as the earth with showers. Majesty gleams in flashes of fire amid the tempest's horrors, and the glory of the Lord is seen in its grandeur in the fall of empires, and the crash of thrones. In all our conflicts and tribulations, we may behold the hand of the divine King.

'God is God; He sees and hears
All our troubles, all our tears.
Soul, forget not, 'mid thy pains,
God o'er all for ever reigns.'

In hell, evil spirits own, with misery, His undoubted supremacy. When permitted to roam abroad, it is with a chain at their heel; the bit is in the mouth of behemoth, and the hook in the jaws of leviathan. Death's darts are under the Lord's lock, and the grave's prisons have divine power as their warder. The terrible vengeance of the Judge of all the earth makes fiends cower down and tremble, even as dogs in the kennel fear the hunter's whip.

'Fear not death, nor Satan's thrusts,
God defends who in Him trusts;
Soul, remember, in thy pains,
God o'er all for ever reigns.'

In heaven none doubt the sovereignty of the King Eternal, but all fall on their faces to do Him homage. Angels are His courtiers, the redeemed His favourites, and all delight to serve Him day and night. May we soon reach the city of the great King!

'For this life's long night of sadness
He will give us peace and gladness.
Soul, remember, in thy pains,
God o'er all for ever reigns.'

'The bow shall be seen in the cloud'
Genesis 9:14

The rainbow, the symbol of the covenant with Noah, is typical of our Lord Jesus, who is the Lord's witness to the people. When may we *expect to see the token of the covenant*? The rainbow is only to be seen painted upon a *cloud*. When the sinner's conscience is dark with clouds, when he remembers his past sin, and mourneth and lamenteth before God, Jesus Christ is revealed to him as the covenant Rainbow, displaying all the glorious hues of the divine character and betokening peace. To the believer, when his trials and temptations surround him, it is sweet to behold the person of our Lord Jesus Christ - to see Him bleeding, living, rising, and pleading for us. God's rainbow is hung over the cloud of our sins, our sorrows, and our woes, to prophesy deliverance. Nor does a *cloud* alone give a rainbow, there must be the *crystal drops* to reflect the light of the sun. So, our sorrows must not only threaten, but they must really fall upon us. There had been no Christ for us if the vengeance of God had been merely a threatening cloud: punishment must fall in terrible drops upon the Surety. Until there is a *real* anguish in the sinner's conscience, there is no Christ for him; until the chastisement which he feels becomes grievous, he cannot see Jesus. But there must also be *a sun*; for clouds and drops of rain make not rainbows unless the sun shineth. Beloved, our God, who is as the sun to us, always shines, but we do not always see Him - clouds hide His face; but no matter what drops may be falling, or what clouds may be threatening, if *He* does but shine there will be a rainbow at once. It is said that when we see the rainbow the shower is over. Certain it is, that when Christ comes, our troubles remove; when we behold Jesus, our sins vanish, and our doubts and fears subside. When Jesus walks the waters of the sea, how profound the calm!

'The cedars of Lebanon which He hath planted'
Psalm 104:16

Lebanon's cedars are emblematic of the Christian, in that *they owe their planting entirely to the Lord*. This is quite true of every child of God. He is not man-planted, nor self-planted, but God-planted. The mysterious hand of the divine Spirit dropped the living seed into a heart which He had Himself prepared for its reception. Every true heir of heaven owns the great Husbandman as his planter. Moreover, the cedars of Lebanon *are not dependent upon man for their watering*; they stand on the lofty rock, unmoistened by human irrigation; and yet our heavenly Father supplieth them. Thus it is with the Christian who has learned to live by faith. He is independent of man, even in temporal things; for his continued maintenance he looks to the Lord his God, and to Him alone. The dew of heaven is his portion, and the God of heaven is his fountain. Again, the cedars of Lebanon are *not protected by any mortal power*. They owe nothing to man for their preservation from stormy wind and tempest. They are God's trees, kept and preserved by Him, and by Him alone. It is precisely the same with the Christian. He is not a hot-house plant, sheltered from temptation; he stands in the most exposed position; he has no shelter, no protection, except this, that the broad wings of the eternal God always cover the cedars which He Himself has planted. Like cedars, believers *are full of sap*, having vitality enough to be ever green, even amid winter's snows. Lastly, the flourishing and majestic condition of the cedar is *to the praise of God only*. The Lord, even the Lord alone hath been everything unto the cedars, and, therefore David very sweetly puts it in one of the psalms, 'Praise ye the Lord, fruitful trees and all cedars'. In the believer there is nothing that can magnify man; he is planted, nourished, and protected by the Lord's own hand, and to Him let all the glory be ascribed.

'And I will remember My covenant'
Genesis 9:15

Mark the form of the promise. God does not say, 'And when *ye* shall look upon the bow, and *ye* shall remember My covenant, *then* I will not destroy the earth', but it is gloriously put, not upon *our* memory, which is fickle and frail, but upon *God's* memory, which is infinite and immutable. 'The bow shall be in the cloud; and *I* will look upon it, that *I* may remember the everlasting covenant'. Oh! it is not *my* remembering God, it is God's remembering *me* which is the ground of my safety; it is not *my* laying hold of His covenant, but His covenant's laying hold on me. Glory be to God! The whole of the bulwarks of salvation are secured by divine power, and even the minor towers, which we may imagine might have been left to man, are guarded by almighty strength. Even the *remembrance* of the covenant is not left to our memories, for *we* might forget, but our Lord cannot forget the saints whom He has graven on the palms of His hands. It is with us as with Israel in Egypt; the blood was upon the lintel and the two side-posts, but the Lord did not say, 'When *you* see the blood I will pass over you', but 'When *I* see the blood I will pass over you'. My looking to Jesus brings me joy and peace, but it is God's looking to Jesus which secures my salvation and that of all His elect, since it is impossible for our God to look at Christ, our bleeding Surety, and then to be angry with us for sins already punished in Him. No, it is not left with *us* even to be saved by remembering the covenant. There is no linsey-wolsey here - not a single thread of the creature mars the fabric. It is not *of* man, neither *by* man, but of the Lord alone. We *should* remember the covenant, and we *shall* do it, through divine grace; but the hinge of our safety does not hang there - it is God's remembering *us*, not our remembering *him*; and hence the covenant is *an everlasting covenant*.

'Thou, Lord, hast made me glad through Thy work'
Psalm 92:4

Do you believe that your sins are forgiven, and that
Christ has made a full atonement for them? Then what
a joyful Christian *you ought to be*! How you should live
above the common trials and troubles of the world!
Since sin is forgiven, can it matter what happens to you
now? Luther said, 'Smite, Lord, smite, for my sin is
forgiven; if Thou hast but forgiven me, smite as hard
as Thou wilt'; and in a similar spirit you may say,
'Send sickness, poverty, losses, crosses, persecution,
what Thou wilt, *Thou hast forgiven me*, and my soul is
glad'. Christian, if thou art thus saved, whilst thou art
glad, *be grateful and loving*. Cling to that cross which
took thy sin away; serve thou Him who served thee. 'I
beseech you therefore, by the mercies of God, that ye
present your bodies a living sacrifice, holy, acceptable
unto God, which is your reasonable service.' Let not
your zeal evaporate in some little ebullition of song.
Show your love in expressive tokens. Love the brethren of Him who loved you. If there be a Mephibosheth
anywhere who is lame or halt, help him for Jonathan's
sake. If there be a poor tried believer, weep with him,
and bear his cross for the sake of Him who wept for thee
and carried thy sins. Since thou art thus forgiven freely
for Christ's sake, go and tell to others the joyful news
of pardoning mercy. Be not contented with this unspeakable blessing for thyself alone, but publish abroad
the story of the cross. Holy gladness and holy boldness
will make you a good preacher, and all the world will
be a pulpit for you to preach in. Cheerful holiness is the
most forcible of sermons, but the Lord must give it to
you. Seek it this morning before you go into the world.
When it is the Lord's work in which we rejoice, we
need not be afraid of being too glad.

'*I know their sorrows*'
Exodus 3:7

The child is cheered as he sings, 'This my father knows'; and shall not we be comforted as we discern that our dear Friend and tender soul-husband knows all about us?

1. *He is the Physician*, and if He knows all, there is no need that the patient should know. Hush, thou silly, fluttering heart, prying, peeping, and suspecting! What thou knowest not now, thou shalt know hereafter, and meanwhile Jesus, the beloved Physician, knows thy soul in adversities. Why need the patient analyse all the medicine, or estimate all the symptoms? This is the Physician's work, not mine; it is my business to trust, and his to prescribe. If He shall write His prescription in uncouth characters which I cannot read, I will not be uneasy on that account, but rely upon His unfailing skill to make all plain in the result, however mysterious in the working.

2. *He is the Master*, and His knowledge is to serve us instead of our own; we are to obey, not to judge: 'The servant knoweth not what his lord doeth'. Shall the architect explain his plans to every hodman on the works? If he knows his own intent, is it not enough? The vessel on the wheel cannot guess to what pattern it shall be conformed, but if the potter understands his art, what matters the ignorance of the clay? My Lord must not be cross-questioned any more by one so ignorant as I am.

3. *He is the Head*. All understanding centres there. What judgment has the arm? What comprehension has the foot? All the power to know lies in the head. Why should the member have a brain of its own when the head fulfils for it every intellectual office? Here, then, must the believer rest his comfort in sickness, not that he himself can see the end, but that Jesus knows all. Sweet Lord, be thou for ever eye, and soul, and head for us, and let us be content to know only what Thou choosest to reveal.

*'Isaac went out to meditate
in the field at the eventide'*
Genesis 24:63

Very admirable was his occupation. If those who spend so many hours in idle company, light reading, and useless pastimes, could learn wisdom, they would find more profitable society and more interesting engagements in meditation than in the vanities which now have such charms for them. We should all know more, live nearer to God, and grow in grace, if we were more alone. Meditation chews the cud and extracts the real nutriment from the mental food gathered elsewhere. When Jesus is the theme, meditation is sweet indeed. Isaac found Rebecca while engaged in private musings; many others have found their best beloved there.

Very admirable was the choice of place. In the field we have a study hung round with texts for thought. From the cedar to the hyssop, from the soaring eagle down to the chirping grasshopper, from the blue expanse of heaven to a drop of dew, all things are full of teaching, and when the eye is divinely opened, that teaching flashes upon the mind far more vividly than from written books. Our little rooms are neither so healthy, so suggestive, so agreeable, or so inspiring as the fields. Let us count nothing common or unclean, but feel that all created things point to their Maker, and the field will at once be hallowed.

Very admirable was the season. The season of sunset as it draws a veil over the day, befits that repose of the soul when earthborn cares yield to the joys of heavenly communion. The glory of the setting sun excites our wonder, and the solemnity of approaching night awakens our awe. If the business of this day will permit it, it will be well, dear reader, if you can spare an hour to walk in the field at eventide, but if not, the Lord is in the town too, and will meet with thee in thy chamber or in the crowded street. Let thy heart go forth to meet Him.

'*And I will give you an heart of flesh*'
Ezekiel 36:26

A heart of flesh is known by its *tenderness concerning sin*. To have indulged a foul imagination, or to have allowed a wild desire to tarry even for a moment, is quite enough to make a heart of flesh grieve before the Lord. The heart of stone calls a great iniquity nothing, but not so the heart of flesh.

> If to the right or left I stray,
> That moment, Lord, reprove;
> And let me weep my life away,
> For having grieved thy love.

The heart of flesh is *tender of God's will*. My Lord Will-be-will is a great blusterer, and it is hard to subject him to God's will; but when the heart of flesh is given, the will quivers like an aspen leaf in every breath of heaven, and bows like an osier in every breeze of God's Spirit. The natural will is cold, hard iron, which is not to be hammered into form, but the renewed will, like molten metal, is soon moulded by the hand of grace. In the fleshy heart there is a *tenderness of the affections*. The hard heart does not love the Redeemer, but the renewed heart burns with affection towards Him. The hard heart is selfish and coldly demands, 'Why should I weep for sin? Why should I love the Lord?' But the heart of flesh says, 'Lord, Thou knowest that I love Thee; help me to love Thee more'! Many are the privileges of this renewed heart; ''Tis here the Spirit dwells, 'tis here that Jesus rests'. It is fitted to receive every spiritual blessing, and every blessing comes to it. It is prepared to yield every heavenly fruit to the honour and praise of God, and therefore the Lord delights in it. A tender heart is the best defence against sin, and the best preparation for heaven. A renewed heart stands on its watchtower looking for the coming of the Lord Jesus. Have you this heart of flesh?

'Give unto the Lord the glory due unto His name'
Psalm 29:2

God's glory is the result of His nature and acts. He is glorious in His character, for there is such a store of everything that is holy, and good, and lovely in God, that He must be glorious. The actions which flow from His character are also glorious; but while He intends that they should manifest to His creatures His goodness, and mercy, and justice, He is equally concerned that the glory associated with them should be given only to Himself. Nor is there aught in ourselves in which we may glory; for who maketh us to differ from another? And what have we that we did not receive from the God of all grace? Then how careful ought we to be *to walk humbly before the Lord*! The moment we glorify ourselves, since there is room for one glory only in the universe, we set ourselves up as rivals to the Most High. Shall the insect of an hour glorify itself against the sun which warmed it into life? Shall the potsherd exalt itself above the man who fashioned it upon the wheel? Shall the dust of the desert strive with the whirlwind? Or the drops of the ocean struggle with the tempest? Give unto the Lord, all ye righteous, give unto the Lord glory and strength; give unto Him the honour that is due unto His name. Yet it is, perhaps, one of the hardest struggles of the Christian life to learn this sentence - 'Not unto us, not unto us, but unto Thy name be glory'. It is a lesson which God is ever teaching us, and teaching us sometimes by most painful discipline. Let a Christian begin to boast, 'I can do all things', without adding 'through Christ which strengtheneth me', and before long he will have to groan, 'I can do nothing', and bemoan himself in the dust. When we do anything for the Lord, and He is pleased to accept of our doings, let us lay our crown at His feet, and exclaim, 'Not I, but the grace of God which was with me!'.

'Ourselves also,
which have the firstfruits of the Spirit'
Romans 8:23

Present possession is declared. At this present moment we have the firstfruits of the Spirit. We have repentance, that gem of the first water; faith, that priceless pearl; hope, the heavenly emerald; and love, the glorious ruby. We are already made 'new creatures in Christ Jesus', by the effectual working of God the Holy Ghost. This is called the firstfruit because *it comes first*. As the wave-sheaf was the first of the harvest, so the spiritual life, and all the graces which adorn that life, are the first operations of the Spirit of God in our souls. *The firstfruits were the pledge of the harvest.* As soon as the Israelite had plucked the first handful of ripe ears, he looked forward with glad anticipation to the time when the wain should creak beneath the sheaves. So, brethren, when God gives us things which are pure, lovely, and of good report, as the work of the Holy Spirit, these are to us the prognostics of the coming glory. *The firstfruits were always holy to the Lord*, and our new nature, with all its powers, is a consecrated thing. The new life is not ours that we should ascribe its excellence to our own merit: it is Christ's image and creation, and is ordained for His glory. But *the firstfruits were not the harvest*, and the works of the Spirit in us at this moment are not the consummation - the perfection is yet to come. We must not boast that we have attained, and so reckon the wave-sheaf to be all the produce of the year: we must hunger and thirst after righteousness, and pant for the day of full redemption. Dear reader, this evening open your mouth wide, and God will fill it. Let the boon in present possession excite in you a sacred avarice for more grace. Groan within yourself for higher degrees of consecration, and your Lord will grant them to you, for He is able to do exceeding abundantly above what we ask or even think.

'The mercy of God'
Psalm 52:8

Meditate a little on this mercy of the Lord. It is *tender mercy*. With gentle, loving touch, He healeth the broken in heart, and bindeth up their wounds. He is as gracious in the manner of His mercy as in the matter of it. It *is great mercy*. There is nothing little in God; His mercy is like Himself - it is infinite. You cannot measure it. His mercy is so great that it forgives great sins to great sinners, after great lengths of time, and then gives great favours and great privileges, and raises us up to great enjoyments in the great heaven of the great God. It is *undeserved* mercy, as indeed all true mercy must be, for deserved mercy is only a misnomer for justice. There was no right on the sinner's part to the kind consideration of the Most High; had the rebel been doomed at once to eternal fire he would have richly merited the doom, and if delivered from wrath, sovereign love alone has found a cause, for there was none in the sinner himself. It *is rich mercy*. Some things are great, but have little efficacy in them, but this mercy is a cordial to your drooping spirits; a golden ointment to your bleeding wounds; a heavenly bandage to your broken bones; a royal chariot for your weary feet; a bosom of love for your trembling heart. It *is manifold mercy*. As Bunyan says, 'All the flowers in God's garden are double'. There is no single mercy. You may think you have but one mercy, but you shall find it to be a whole cluster of mercies. It *is abounding mercy*. Millions have received it, yet far from its being exhausted, it is as fresh, as full, and as free as ever. It *is unfailing mercy*. It will never leave thee. If mercy be thy friend, mercy will be with thee in temptation to keep thee from yielding; with thee in trouble to prevent thee from sinking; with thee living to be the light and life of thy countenance; and with thee dying to be the joy of thy soul when earthly comfort is ebbing fast.

'This sickness is not unto death'
John 11:4

From our Lord's words we learn that there is a limit to
sickness. Here is an 'unto' within which its ultimate
end is restrained, and beyond which it cannot go.
Lazarus might pass through death, but death was not to
be the ultimatum of his sickness. In all sickness, the
Lord saith to the waves of pain, 'Hitherto shall ye go,
but no further'. His fixed purpose is not the destruction, but the instruction of His people. Wisdom hangs
up the thermometer at the furnace mouth, and regulates
the heat.

1. *The limit is encouragingly comprehensive.* The
God of providence has limited the time, manner,
intensity, repetition, and effects of all our sicknesses;
each throb is decreed, each sleepless hour predestinated, each relapse ordained, each depression of spirit
foreknown, and each sanctifying result eternally pur-
posed. Nothing great or small escapes the ordaining
hand of Him who numbers the hairs of our head.

2. *This limit is wisely adjusted* to our strength, to
the end designed, and to the grace apportioned. Affliction comes not at haphazard - the weight of every stroke
of the rod is accurately measured. He who made no
mistakes in balancing the clouds and meting out the
heavens, commits no errors in measuring out the
ingredients which compose the medicine of souls. We
cannot suffer too much nor be relieved too late.

3. *The limit is tenderly appointed.* The knife of the
heavenly Surgeon never cuts deeper than is absolutely
necessary. 'He doth not afflict willingly, nor grieve the
children of men.' A mother's heart cries, 'Spare my
child'; but no mother is more compassionate than our
gracious God. When we consider how hard-mouthed
we are, it is a wonder that we are not driven with a
sharper bit. The thought is full of consolation, that He
who has fixed the bounds of our habitation, has also
fixed the bounds of our tribulation.

> *'Strangers are come into the*
> *sanctuaries of the Lord's house'*
> Jeremiah 51:51

On this account the faces of the Lord's people were covered with shame, for it was a terrible thing that men should intrude into the Holy Place reserved for the priests alone. Everywhere about us we see like cause for sorrow. How many ungodly men are now educating with the view of entering into the ministry! What a crying sin is that solemn lie by which our whole population is nominally comprehended in a National Church! How fearful it is that ordinances should be pressed upon the unconverted, and that among the more enlightened churches of our land there should be such laxity of discipline. If the thousands who will read this portion shall all take this matter before the Lord Jesus this day, He will interfere and avert the evil which else will come upon His Church. To adulterate the Church is to pollute a well, to pour water upon fire, to sow a fertile field with stones. May we all have grace to maintain in our own proper way the purity of the Church, as being an assembly of believers, and not a nation, an unsaved community of unconverted men.

Our zeal must, however, begin at home. Let us examine *ourselves* as to our right to eat at the Lord's table. Let us see to it that we have on our wedding garment, lest we ourselves be intruders in the Lord's sanctuaries. Many are called, but few are chosen; the way is narrow, and the gate is strait. O for grace to come to Jesus aright, with the faith of God's elect. He who smote Uzzah for touching the ark is very jealous of his two ordinances; as a true believer I may approach them freely, as an alien I must not touch them lest I die. Heart-searching is the duty of all who are baptised or come to the Lord's table. 'Search me, O God, and know my way, try me and know my heart.'

*'And they gave Him to drink wine mingled with
myrrh: but He received it not'*
Mark 15:23

A golden truth is couched in the fact that the Saviour put
the myrrhed wine-cup from His lips. On the heights of
heaven the Son of God stood of old, and as He looked
down upon our globe He measured the long descent to
the utmost depths of human misery; He cast up the sum
total of all the agonies which expiation would require,
and abated not a jot. He solemnly determined that to
offer a sufficient atoning sacrifice He must go the
whole way, from the highest to the lowest, from the
throne of highest glory to the cross of deepest woe.
This myrrhed cup, with its soporific influence, would
have stayed Him within a little of the utmost limit of
misery, therefore He refused it. He would not stop
short of all he had undertaken to suffer for His people.
Ah, how many of us have pined after reliefs to our grief
which would have been injurious to us! Reader, did you
never pray for a discharge from hard service or suffering with a petulant and wilful eagerness? Providence
has taken from you the desire of your eyes with a
stroke. Say, Christian, if it had been said, 'If you so
desire it, that loved one of yours shall live, but God will
be dishonoured', could you have put away the temptation, and said, 'Thy will be done'? Oh, it is sweet to be
able to say, 'My Lord, if for other reasons I need not
suffer, yet if I can honour Thee more by suffering, and
if the loss of my earthly all will bring Thee glory, then
so let it be. I refuse the comfort, if it comes in the way
of Thine honour'. O that we thus walked more in the
footsteps of our Lord, cheerfully enduring trial for His
sake, promptly and willingly putting away the thought
of self and comfort when it would interfere with our
finishing the work which He has given us to do. Great
grace is needed, but great grace is provided.

'He shall stand and feed in the strength of the Lord'
Micah 5:4

Christ's reign in His Church is that of a *shepherd-king*. He has supremacy, but it is the superiority of a wise and tender shepherd over his needy and loving flock; He commands and receives obedience, but it is the willing obedience of the well-cared-for sheep, rendered joyfully to their beloved Shepherd, whose voice they know so well. He rules by the force of love and the energy of goodness.

His reign is *practical in its character*. It is said, 'He shall stand *and feed*.' The great Head of the Church is actively engaged in providing for His people. He does not sit down upon the throne in empty state, or hold a sceptre without wielding it in government. No, He stands and feeds. The expression 'feed', in the original, is like an analogous one in the Greek, which means to shepherdize, to do everything expected of a shepherd: to guide, to watch, to preserve, to restore, to tend, as well as to feed.

His reign is *continual in its duration*. It is said, '*He shall stand* and feed'; not 'He shall feed now and then, and leave His position'; not, 'He shall one day grant a revival, and then next day leave His Church to barrenness'. His eyes never slumber, and His hands never rest; His heart never ceases to beat with love, and His shoulders are never weary of carrying His people's burdens.

His reign is *effectually powerful in its action*; 'He shall feed in the strength of Jehovah'. Wherever Christ is, there is God; and whatever Christ does is the act of the Most High. Oh! it is a joyful truth to consider that He who stands today representing the interests of His people is very God of very God, to whom every knee shall bow. Happy are we who belong to such a shepherd, whose humanity communes with us, and whose divinity protects us. Let us worship and bow down before Him as the people of His pasture.

*'Pull me out of the net that they have laid privily for
me: for Thou art my strength'*
Psalm 31:4

Our spiritual foes are of the serpent's brood, and seek
to ensnare us by subtlety. The prayer before us supposes the possibility of the believer being caught like
a bird. So deftly does the fowler do his work, that
simple ones are soon surrounded by the net. The text
asks that even out of Satan's meshes the captive one
may be delivered; this is a proper petition, and one
which can be granted: from between the jaws of the
lion, and out of the belly of hell, can eternal love rescue
the saint. It may need a sharp *pull* to save a soul from
the net of temptation, and a mighty pull to extricate a
man from the snares of malicious cunning, but the Lord
is equal to every emergency, and the most skilfully
placed nets of the hunter shall never be able to hold His
chosen ones. Woe unto those who are so clever at net
laying; they who tempt others shall be destroyed
themselves.

'*For Thou art my strength.*' What an inexpressible
sweetness is to be found in these few words! How
joyfully may we encounter toils, and how cheerfully
may we endure sufferings, when we can lay hold upon
celestial strength. Divine power will rend asunder all
the toils of our enemies, confound their politics, and
frustrate their knavish tricks; he is a happy man who
has such matchless might engaged upon his side. Our
own strength would be of little service when embar-
rassed in the nets of base cunning, but the Lord's
strength is ever available; we have but to invoke it, and
we shall find it near at hand. If by faith we are
depending alone upon the strength of the mighty God
of Israel, we may use our holy reliance as a plea in
supplication.

'Lord, evermore Thy face we seek:
    Tempted we are, and poor, and weak;
Keep us with lowly hearts, and meek.
    Let us not fall. Let us not fall.'

'The sweet psalmist of Israel'
2 Samuel 23:1

Among all the saints whose lives are recorded in Holy Writ, David possesses an experience of the most striking, varied, and instructive character. In his history we meet with trials and temptations not to be discovered, as a whole, in other saints of ancient times, and hence he is all the more suggestive a type of our Lord. David knew the trials of all ranks and conditions of men. Kings have their troubles, and David wore a crown: the peasant has his cares, and David handled a shepherd's crook: the wanderer has many hardships, and David abode in the caves of Engedi: the captain has his difficulties, and David found the sons of Zeruiah too hard for him. The psalmist was also tried in his friends, his counsellor Ahithophel forsook him, 'He that eateth bread with me, hath lifted up his heel against me'. His worst foes were they of his own household: his children were his greatest affliction. The temptations of poverty and wealth, of honour and reproach, of health and weakness, all tried their power upon him. He had temptations from without to disturb his peace, and from within to mar his joy. David no sooner escaped from one trial than he fell into another; no sooner emerged from one season of despondency and alarm, than he was again brought into the lowest depths, and all God's waves and billows rolled over him. It is probably from this cause that David's psalms are so universally the delight of experienced Christians. Whatever our frame of mind, whether ecstasy or depression, David has exactly described our emotions. He was an able master of the human heart, because he had been tutored in the best of all schools - the school of heart-felt, personal experience. As we are instructed in the same school, as we grow matured in grace and in years, we increasingly appreciate David's psalms, and find them to be 'green pastures'. My soul, let David's experience cheer and counsel thee this day.

'And they fortified Jerusalem unto the broad wall'
Nehemiah 3:8

Cities well fortified have broad walls, and so had Jerusalem in her glory. The New Jerusalem must, in like manner, be surrounded and preserved by a broad wall of nonconformity to the world, and *separation* from its customs and spirit. The tendency of these days is to break down the holy barrier, and make the distinction between the church and the world merely nominal. Professors are no longer strict and Puritanical, questionable literature is read on all hands, frivolous pastimes are currently indulged, and a general laxity threatens to deprive the Lord's peculiar people of those sacred singularities which separate them from sinners. It will be an ill day for the church and the world when the proposed amalgamation shall be complete, and the sons of God and the daughters of men shall be as one: then shall another deluge of wrath be ushered in. Beloved reader, be it your aim in heart, in word, in dress, in action to maintain the broad wall, remembering that the friendship of this world is enmity against God.

The broad wall afforded a pleasant place of *resort* for the inhabitants of Jerusalem, from which they could command prospects of the surrounding country. This reminds us of the Lord's exceeding broad commandments, in which we walk at liberty in communion with Jesus, overlooking the scenes of earth, and looking out towards the glories of heaven. Separated from the world, and denying ourselves all ungodliness and fleshly lusts, we are nevertheless not in prison, nor restricted within narrow bounds; nay, we walk at liberty, because we keep His precepts. Come, reader, this evening walk with God in His statutes. As friend met friend upon the city wall, so meet thou thy God in the way of holy prayer and meditation. The bulwarks of salvation thou hast a right to traverse, for thou art a freeman of the royal burgh, a citizen of the metropolis of the universe.

'He that watereth shall be watered also himself'
Proverbs 11:25

We are here taught the great lesson, that to get, we must give; that to accumulate, we must scatter; that to make ourselves happy, we must make others happy; and that in order to become spiritually vigorous, we must seek the spiritual good of others. In watering others, we are ourselves watered. How? Our efforts to be useful, *bring out our powers for usefulness.* We have latent talents and dormant faculties, which are brought to light by exercise. Our strength for labour is hidden even from ourselves, until we venture forth to fight the Lord's battles, or to climb the mountains of difficulty. We do not know what tender sympathies we possess until we try to dry the widow's tears, and soothe the orphan's grief.

We often find in attempting to teach others, that we *gain instruction for ourselves.* Oh, what gracious lessons some of us have learned at sick beds! We went to teach the Scriptures, we came away blushing that we knew so little of them. In our converse with poor saints, we are taught the way of God more perfectly for ourselves and get a deeper insight into divine truth. So that watering others *makes us humble.* We discover how much grace there is where we had not looked for it; and how much the poor saint may outstrip us in knowledge. Our own *comfort is also increased* by our working for others. We endeavour to cheer them, and the consolation gladdens our own heart. Like the two men in the snow; one chafed the other's limbs to keep him from dying, and in so doing kept his own blood in circulation, and saved his own life. The poor widow of Sarepta gave from her scanty store a supply for the prophet's wants, and from that day she never again knew what want was. Give then, and it shall be given unto you, good measure, pressed down, and running over.

*'I said not unto the seed of Jacob,
Seek ye Me in vain'*
Isaiah 45:19

We may gain much solace by considering what God has
not said. What He *has* said is inexpressibly full of
comfort and delight; what He has *not* said is scarcely
less rich in consolation. It was one of these *'said nots'*
which preserved the kingdom of Israel in the days of
Jeroboam the son of Joash, for 'the Lord said not that
He would blot out the name of Israel from under
heaven' (2 Kings 14:27). In our text we have an
assurance that God *will* answer prayer, because He hath
'not said unto the seed of Israel, Seek ye Me in vain'.
You who write bitter things against yourselves should
remember that, let your doubts and fears say what they
will, if *God* has not cut you off from mercy, there is no
room for despair: even the voice of conscience is of
little weight if it be not seconded by the voice of God.
What God *has* said, tremble at! But suffer not your
vain imaginings to overwhelm you with despondency
and sinful despair. Many timid persons have been
vexed by the suspicion that there may be something in
God's decree which shuts *them* out from hope, but here
is a complete refutation to that troublesome fear, for no
true seeker can be decreed to wrath. 'I have not spoken
in secret, in a dark place of the earth; I have not said',
even in the secret of my unsearchable decree, 'Seek ye
Me in vain'. God has clearly revealed that He *will* hear
the prayer of those who call upon Him, and that
declaration cannot be contravened. He has so firmly, so
truthfully, so righteously spoken, that there can be no
room for doubt. He does not reveal His mind in
unintelligible words, but He speaks plainly and positively, 'Ask, and ye shall receive'. Believe, O trembler,
this sure truth - that prayer must and shall be heard, and
that never, even in the secrets of eternity, has the Lord
said unto any living soul, 'Seek ye Me in vain'.

'I charge you, O daughters of Jerusalem, if ye find my beloved, that ye tell him, that I am sick of love'
Solomon's Song 5:8

Such is the language of the believer panting after present fellowship with Jesus, *he is sick for his Lord.* Gracious souls are never perfectly at ease except they are in a state of nearness to Christ; for when they are away from him they lose their peace. The nearer to Him, the nearer to the perfect calm of heaven; the nearer to Him, the fuller the heart is, not only of peace, but of life, and vigour, and joy, for these all depend on constant intercourse with Jesus. What the sun is to the day, what the moon is to the night, what the dew is to the flower, such is Jesus Christ to us. What bread is to the hungry, clothing to the naked, the shadow of a great rock to the traveller in a weary land, such is Jesus Christ to us; and, therefore, if we are not consciously one with Him, little marvel if our spirit cries in the words of the Song, 'I charge you, O ye daughters of Jerusalem, if ye find my beloved, tell Him that I am sick of love'. *This earnest longing after Jesus has a blessing attending it*: 'Blessed are they that do hunger and thirst after righteousness'; and therefore, supremely blessed are they who thirst after the Righteous One. Blessed is that hunger, since it comes from God: if I may not have the full-blown blessedness of being filled, I would seek the same blessedness in its sweet bud-pining in emptiness and eagerness till I am filled with Christ. If I may not feed on Jesus, it shall be next door to heaven to hunger and thirst after Him. There is a hallowedness about that hunger, since it sparkles among the beatitudes of our Lord. But the blessing *involves a promise.* Such hungry ones *'shall be filled'* with what they are desiring. If Christ thus causes us to long after Himself, He will certainly satisfy those longings; and when he does come to us, as come He will, *oh, how sweet it will be!*

'The unsearchable riches of Christ'
Ephesians 3:8

My Master has riches beyond the count of arithmetic, the measurement of reason, the dream of imagination, or the eloquence of words. They are *unsearchable!* You may look, and study, and weigh, but Jesus is a greater Saviour than you think Him to be when your thoughts are at the greatest. My Lord is more ready to pardon than you to sin, more able to forgive than you to transgress. My Master is more willing to supply your wants than you are to confess them. Never tolerate low thoughts of my Lord Jesus. When you put the crown on His head, you will only crown Him with silver when He deserves gold. *My Master has riches of happiness to bestow upon you now.* He can make you to lie down in green pastures, and lead you beside still waters. There is no music like the music of His pipe, when He is the Shepherd and you are the sheep, and you lie down at His feet. There is no love like His, neither earth nor heaven can match it. To know Christ and to be found in Him - oh! this is life, this is joy, this is marrow and fatness, wine on the lees well refined. My Master does not treat His servants churlishly; He gives to them as a king giveth to a king; He gives them two heavens - a heaven below in serving Him here, and a heaven above in delighting in Him for ever. *His unsearchable riches will be best known in eternity.* He will give you on the way to heaven all you need; your place of defence shall be the munitions of rocks, your bread shall be given you, and your waters shall be sure; but it is there, THERE, where you shall hear the song of them that triumph, the shout of them that feast, and shall have a face-to-face view of the glorious and beloved One. The unsearchable riches of Christ! This is the tune for the minstrels of earth, and the song for the harpers of heaven. Lord, teach us more and more of Jesus, and we will tell out the good news to others.

'The voice of weeping shall be no more heard'
Isaiah 65:19

The glorified weep no more, for *all outward causes of grief are gone*. There are no broken friendships, nor blighted prospects in heaven. Poverty, famine, peril, persecution, and slander, are unknown there. No pain distresses, no thought of death or bereavement saddens. They weep no more, for *they are perfectly sanctified*. No 'evil heart of unbelief' prompts them to depart from the living God; they are without fault before His throne, and are fully conformed to His image. Well may they cease to mourn who have ceased to sin. They weep no more, because *all fear of change is past*. They know that they are eternally secure. Sin is shut out, and they are shut in. They dwell within a city which shall never be stormed; they bask in a sun which shall never set; they drink of a river which shall never dry; they pluck fruit from a tree which shall never wither. Countless cycles may revolve, but eternity shall not be exhausted, and while eternity endures, their immortality and blessedness shall coexist with it. They are for ever with the Lord. They weep no more, because *every desire is fulfilled*. They cannot wish for anything which they have not in possession. Eye and ear, heart and hand, judgment, imagination, hope, desire, will, all the faculties, are completely satisfied; and imperfect as our present ideas are of the things which God hath prepared for them that love him, yet we know enough, by the revelation of the Spirit, that the saints above are supremely blessed. The joy of Christ, which is an infinite fulness of delight, is in them. They bathe themselves in the bottomless, shoreless sea of infinite beatitude. That same joyful rest remains for us. It may not be far distant. Ere long the weeping willow shall be exchanged for the palm-branch of victory, and sorrow's dewdrops will be transformed into the pearls of everlasting bliss. 'Wherefore comfort one another with these words.'

'That Christ may dwell in your hearts by faith'
Ephesians 3:17

Beyond measure it is desirable that we, as believers, should have the person of Jesus constantly before us, to inflame our love towards Him, and to increase our knowledge of Him. I would to God that my readers were all entered as diligent scholars in Jesus' college, students of Corpus Christi, or the body of Christ, resolved to attain unto a good degree in learning of the cross. But to have Jesus ever near, the heart must be full of Him, welling up with His love, even to overrunning; hence the apostle prays 'that Christ may *dwell in your hearts*'. See how near he would have Jesus to be! You cannot get a subject closer to you than to have it in the heart itself. *'That He may dwell'*; not that He may call upon you sometimes, as a casual visitor enters into a house and tarries for a night, but that He may *dwell*; that Jesus may become the Lord and Tenant of your inmost being, never more to go out.

Observe the words - that He may dwell *in your heart*, that best room of the house of manhood; not in your thoughts alone, but in your affections; not merely in the mind's meditations, but in the heart's emotions. We should pant after love to Christ of a most abiding character, not a love that flames up and then dies out into the darkness of a few embers, but a constant flame, fed by sacred fuel, like the fire upon the altar which never went out. This cannot be accomplished except by faith. Faith must be strong, or love will not be fervent; the root of the flower must be healthy, or we cannot expect the bloom to be sweet. Faith is the lily's root, and love is the lily's bloom. Now, reader, Jesus cannot be in your heart's love except you have a firm hold of Him by your heart's faith; and, therefore, pray that you may always trust Christ in order that you may always love Him. If love be cold, be sure that faith is drooping.

'*The breaker is come up before them*'
Micah 2:13

Inasmuch as Jesus has gone before us, things remain not as they would have been had he never passed that way. He has *conquered every foe* that obstructed the way. Cheer up now thou faint-hearted warrior. Not only has Christ travelled the road, but He has slain thine enemies. Dost thou dread sin? He has nailed it to his cross. Dost thou fear death? He has been the death of Death. Art thou afraid of hell? He has barred it against the advent of any of His children; they shall never see the gulf of perdition. Whatever foes may be before the Christian, they are all overcome. There are lions, but their teeth are broken; there are serpents, but their fangs are extracted; there are rivers, but they are bridged or fordable; there are flames, but we wear that matchless garment which renders us invulnerable to fire. The sword that has been forged against us is already blunted; the instruments of war which the enemy is preparing have already lost their point. God has taken away in the person of Christ all the power that anything can have to hurt us. Well then, the army may safely march on, and you may go joyously along your journey, for all your enemies are conquered beforehand. What shall you do but march on to take the prey? They are beaten, they are vanquished; all you have to do is to divide the spoil. You shall, it is true, often engage in combat; but your fight shall be with a vanquished foe. His head is broken; he may attempt to injure you, but his strength shall not be sufficient for his malicious design. Your victory shall be easy, and your treasure shall be beyond all count.

'Proclaim aloud the Saviour's fame,
    Who bears *the Breaker's* wond'rous name;
  Sweet name; and it becomes him well,
    Who breaks down earth, sin, death, and hell.'

'If fire break out, and catch in thorns, so that the
stacks of corn, or the standing corn, or the field,
be consumed therewith; he that kindled the fire
shall surely make restitution'
Exodus 22:6

But what restitution can he make who casts abroad the
firebrands of error, or the coals of lasciviousness, and
sets men's souls on a blaze with the fire of hell? The
guilt is beyond estimate, and the result is irretrievable.
If such an offender be forgiven, what grief it will cause
him in the retrospect, since he cannot undo the mischief
which he has done! An ill example may kindle a flame
which years of amended character cannot quench. To
burn the food of man is bad enough, but how much
worse to destroy the soul! It may be useful to us to
reflect how far we may have been guilty in the past, and
to enquire whether, even in the present, there may not
be evil in us which has a tendency to bring damage to
the souls of our relatives, friends, or neighbours.

The fire of strife is a terrible evil when it breaks out
in a Christian church. Where converts were multiplied,
and God was glorified, jealousy and envy do the devil's
work most effectually. Where the golden grain was
being housed, to reward the toil of the great Boaz, the
fire of enmity comes in and leaves little else but smoke
and a heap of blackness. Woe unto those by whom
offences come. May they never come through us, for
although we cannot make restitution, we shall certainly
be the chief sufferers if we are the chief offenders.
Those who feed the fire deserve just censure, but he
who first kindles it is most to blame. Discord usually
takes first hold upon the thorns; it is nurtured among
the hypocrites and base professors in the church, and
away it goes among the righteous, blown by the winds
of hell, and no one knows where it may end. O Thou
Lord and giver of peace, make us peacemakers, and
never let us aid and abet the men of strife, or even
unintentionally cause the least division among Thy
people.

'His fruit was sweet to my taste'
Canticles 2:3

Faith, in the Scripture, is spoken of under the emblem of all the senses. It is *sight*: 'Look unto me and be ye saved'. It is *hearing*: 'Hear, and your soul shall live'. Faith is *smelling*: 'All thy garments smell of myrrh, and aloes, and cassia'; 'thy name is as ointment poured forth'. Faith is spiritual *touch*. By this faith the woman came behind and touched the hem of Christ's garment, and by this we handle the things of the good word of life. Faith is equally the spirit's *taste*. 'How sweet are Thy words to my taste! yea, sweeter than honey to my lips.' 'Except a man eat my flesh,' saith Christ, 'and drink my blood, there is no life in him.'

This *'taste'* is faith *in one of its highest operations*. One of the first performances of faith is *hearing*. We hear the voice of God, not with the outward ear alone, but with the inward ear; we hear it as God's Word, and we believe it to be so; that is the 'hearing' of faith. Then our mind *looketh* upon the truth as it was presented to us; that is to say, we understand it, we perceive its meaning; that is the 'seeing' of faith. Next we discover its preciousness; we begin to admire it, and find how fragrant it is; that is faith in its *'smell'*. Then we appropriate the mercies which are prepared for us in Christ; that is faith in its *'touch'*. Hence follow the enjoyments, peace, delight, communion; which are faith in its 'taste'. Any one of these acts of faith is saving. To hear Christ's voice as the sure voice of God in the soul will save us; but that which gives true enjoyment is the aspect of faith wherein Christ, by holy taste, is received into us, and made, by inward and spiritual apprehension of His sweetness and preciousness, to be the food of our souls. It is then we sit 'under His shadow with great delight', and find His fruit sweet to our taste.

'If thou believest with all thine heart, thou mayest'
Acts 8:37

These words may answer your scruples, devout reader, concerning *the ordinances*. Perhaps you say, 'I should be afraid to be baptised; it is such a solemn thing to avow myself to be dead with Christ, and buried with Him. I should not feel at liberty to come to the Master's table; I should be afraid of eating and drinking damnation unto myself, not discerning the Lord's body'. Ah! poor trembler, Jesus has given you liberty, be not afraid. If a stranger came to your house, he would stand at the door, or wait in the hall; he would not dream of intruding unbidden into your parlour - he is not at home: but your child makes himself very free about the house; and so is it with the child of God. A stranger may not intrude where a child may venture. When the Holy Ghost has given you to feel the spirit of adoption, you may come to Christian ordinances without fear. The same rule holds good of the *Christian's inward privileges*. You think, poor seeker, that you are not allowed to rejoice with joy unspeakable and full of glory; if you are permitted to get inside Christ's door, or sit at the bottom of His table, you will be well content. Ah! but you shall not have less privileges than the very greatest. God makes no difference in His love to His children. A child is a child to Him; He will not make him a hired servant; but he shall feast upon the fatted calf, and shall have the music and the dancing as much as if he had never gone astray. When Jesus comes into the heart, he issues a general licence to be glad in the Lord. No chains are worn in the court of King Jesus. Our admission into full privileges may be gradual, but it is sure. Perhaps our reader is saying, 'I wish I could enjoy the promises, and walk at liberty in my Lord's commands'. 'If thou believest with all thine heart, thou mayest.' Loose the chains of thy neck, O captive daughter, for Jesus makes thee free.

'He hath commanded His covenant for ever'
Psalm 111:9

The Lord's people delight in the covenant itself. It is
an unfailing source of consolation to them so often as
the Holy Spirit leads them into its banqueting house
and waves its banner of love. They delight to contemplate *the antiquity* of that covenant, remembering that
before the daystar knew its place, or planets ran their
round, the interests of the saints were made secure in
Christ Jesus. It is peculiarly pleasing to them to
remember *the sureness* of the covenant, while meditating upon 'the sure mercies of David'. They delight to
celebrate it as 'signed, and sealed, and ratified, in all
things ordered well'. It often makes their hearts dilate
with joy to think of its *immutability*, as a covenant
which neither time nor eternity, life nor death, shall
ever be able to violate - a covenant as old as eternity and
as everlasting as the Rock of ages. They rejoice also to
feast upon *the fulness* of this covenant, for they see in
it all things provided for them. God is their portion,
Christ their companion, the Spirit their Comforter,
earth their lodge, and heaven their home. They see in
it an inheritance reserved and entailed to every soul
possessing an interest in its ancient and eternal deed of
gift. Their eyes sparkled when they saw it as a treasure-
trove in the Bible; but oh! how their souls were
gladdened when they saw in the last will and testament
of their divine kinsman, that it was bequeathed to them!
More especially it is the pleasure of God's people to
contemplate *the graciousness* of this covenant. They
see that the law was made void because it was a
covenant of works and depended upon merit, but this
they perceive to be enduring because grace is the basis,
grace the condition, grace the strain, grace the bulwark,
grace the foundation, grace the topstone. The covenant
is a treasury of wealth, a granary of food, a fountain of
life, a storehouse of salvation, a charter of peace, and
a haven of joy.

'The people, when they beheld Him, were greatly
amazed, and running to Him saluted Him'
Mark 9:15

How great the difference between Moses and Jesus!
When the prophet of Horeb had been forty days upon
the mountain, he underwent a kind of transfiguration,
so that his countenance shone with exceeding brightness, and he put a veil over his face, for the people could
not endure to look upon his glory. Not so our Saviour.
He had been transfigured with a greater glory than that
of Moses, and yet, it is not written that the people were
blinded by the blaze of His countenance, but rather they
were amazed, and running to Him they saluted Him.
The glory of the law repels, but the greater glory of
Jesus attracts. Though Jesus is holy and just, yet
blended with His purity there is so much of truth and
grace, that sinners run to Him amazed at His goodness,
fascinated by His love; they salute Him, become His
disciples, and take Him to be their Lord and Master.
Reader, it may be that just now you are blinded by the
dazzling brightness of the law of God. You feel its
claims on your conscience, but you cannot keep it in
your life. Not that you find fault with the law, on the
contrary, it commands your profoundest esteem, still
you are in nowise drawn by it to God; you are rather
hardened in heart, and are verging towards desperation.
Ah, poor heart! turn thine eye from Moses, with all his
repelling splendour, and look to Jesus, resplendent
with milder glories. Behold His flowing wounds and
thorn-crowned head! He is the Son of God, and therein
He is greater than Moses, but He is the Lord of love,
and therein more tender than the lawgiver. He bore the
wrath of God, and in His death revealed more of God's
justice than Sinai on a blaze, but that justice is now
vindicated, and henceforth it is the guardian of believers in Jesus. Look, sinner, to the bleeding Saviour, and
as thou feelest the attraction of His love, fly to His
arms, and thou shalt be saved.

'*How long will it be ere they believe me?*'
Numbers 14:11

*Strive with all diligence to keep out that monster
unbelief.* It so dishonours Christ, that he will withdraw
his visible presence if we insult him by indulging it. It
is true it is a weed, the seeds of which we can never
entirely extract from the soil, but we must aim at its
root with zeal and perseverance. Among hateful things
it is the most to be abhorred. Its injurious nature is so
venomous that he that exerciseth it and he upon whom
it is exercised are both hurt thereby. In thy case, O
believer! it is most wicked, for the mercies of thy Lord
in the past, increase thy guilt in doubting Him now.
When thou dost distrust the Lord Jesus, He may well
cry out, 'Behold I am pressed under you, as a cart is
pressed that is full of sheaves.' This is crowning his
head with thorns of the sharpest kind. It is very cruel
for a well-beloved wife to mistrust a kind and faithful
husband. The sin is needless, foolish, and unwar-
ranted. Jesus has never given the slightest ground for
suspicion, and it is hard to be doubted by those to whom
our conduct is uniformly affectionate and true. Jesus is
the Son of the Highest, and has unbounded wealth; it is
shameful to doubt Omnipotence and distrust all-sufficiency. The cattle on a thousand hills will suffice for
our most hungry feeding, and the granaries of heaven
are not likely to be emptied by our eating. If Christ were
only a cistern, we might soon exhaust His fulness, but
who can drain a fountain? Myriads of spirits have
drawn their supplies from Him, and not one of them has
murmured at the scantiness of his resources. Away,
then, with this lying traitor unbelief, for his only errand
is to cut the bonds of communion and make us mourn
an absent Saviour. Bunyan tells us that unbelief has 'as
many lives as a cat': if so, let us kill one life now, and
continue the work till the whole nine are gone. Down
with thee, thou traitor, my heart abhors thee.

'Into Thine hand I commit my spirit:
Thou hast redeemed me, O Lord God of truth'
Psalm 31:5

These words have been frequently used by holy men in
their hour of departure. We may profitably consider
them this evening. The object of the faithful man's
solicitude in life and death is not his body or his estate,
but his spirit; this is his choice treasure - if this be safe,
all is well. What is this mortal state compared with the
soul? The believer commits his soul to the hand of his
God; it came from him, it is his own, he has aforetime
sustained it, he is able to keep it, and it is most fit that
he should receive it. All things are safe in Jehovah's
hands; what we entrust to the Lord will be secure, both
now and in that day of days towards which we are
hastening. It is peaceful living, and glorious dying, to
repose in the care of heaven. At all times we should
commit our all to Jesus' faithful hand; then, though life
may hang on a thread, and adversities may multiply as
the sands of the sea, our soul shall dwell at ease, and
delight itself in quiet resting places.

'Thou hast redeemed me, O Lord God of truth.'
Redemption is a solid basis for confidence. David had
not known Calvary as we have done, but temporal
redemption cheered him; and shall not eternal redemption yet more sweetly console us? Past deliverances are
strong pleas for present assistance. What the Lord has
done He will do again, for He changes not. He is
faithful to His promises, and gracious to His saints; He
will not turn away from His people.

'Though Thou slay me I will trust,
  Praise Thee even from the dust,
Prove, and tell it as I prove,
  Thine unutterable love.

Thou mayst chasten and correct,
  But Thou never canst neglect;
Since the ransom price is paid,
  On Thy love my hope is stay'd.'

'Oil for the light'
Exodus 25:6

My soul, how much thou needest this, for thy lamp will not long continue to burn without it. Thy snuff will smoke and become an offence if light be gone, and gone it will be if oil be absent. Thou hast no oil well springing up in thy human nature, and therefore thou must go to them that sell and buy for thyself, or like the foolish virgins, thou wilt have to cry, 'My lamp is gone out'. Even the consecrated lamps could not give light without oil; though they shone in the tabernacle they needed to be fed, though no rough winds blew upon them they required to be trimmed, and thy need is equally as great. Under the most happy circumstances thou canst not give light for another hour unless fresh oil of grace be given thee.

It was not every oil that might be used in the Lord's service; neither the petroleum which exudes so plentifully from the earth, nor the produce of fishes, nor that extracted from nuts would be accepted; one oil only was selected, and that the best olive oil. Pretended grace from natural goodness, fancied grace from priestly hands, or imaginary grace from outward ceremonies will never serve the true saint of God; he knows that the Lord would not be pleased with rivers of such oil. He goes to the olive-press of Gethsemane, and draws his supplies from Him who was crushed therein. The oil of gospel grace is pure and free from lees and dregs, and hence the light which is fed thereon is clear and bright. Our churches are the Saviour's golden candelabra, and if they are to be lights in this dark world, they must have much holy oil. Let us pray for ourselves, our ministers, and our churches, that they may never lack oil for the light. Truth, holiness, joy, knowledge, love, these are all beams of the sacred light, but we cannot give them forth unless in private we receive oil from God the Holy Ghost.

'*Sing, O barren*'
Isaiah 54:1

Though we have brought forth some fruit unto Christ, and have a joyful hope that we are 'plants of His own right hand planting', yet there are times when we feel very barren. Prayer is lifeless, love is cold, faith is weak, each grace in the garden of our heart languishes and droops. We are like flowers in the hot sun, requiring the refreshing shower. In such a condition what are we to do? The text is addressed to us in just such a state. '*Sing, O barren, break forth and cry aloud.*' But what can I sing about? I cannot talk about the present, and even the past looks full of barrenness. Ah! I *can* sing of *Jesus Christ*. I can talk of visits which the Redeemer has aforetimes paid to me; or if not of these, I can magnify the great love wherewith He loved His people when He came from the heights of heaven for their redemption. I will go to the cross again. Come, my soul, heavy laden thou wast once, and thou didst lose thy burden there. Go to Calvary again. Perhaps that very cross which gave thee life may give thee fruitfulness. What is my barrenness? It is the platform for His fruit-creating power. What is my desolation? It is the black setting for the sapphire of His everlasting love. I will go in poverty, I will go in helplessness, I will go in all my shame and backsliding, I will tell Him that I am still His child, and in confidence in His faithful heart, even I, the barren one, will sing and cry aloud.

Sing, believer, for it will cheer thine own heart, and the hearts of other desolate ones. Sing on, for now that thou art really ashamed of being barren, thou wilt be fruitful soon; now that God makes thee *loath* to be without fruit He will soon cover thee with clusters. The experience of our barrenness is painful, but the Lord's visitations are delightful. A sense of our own poverty drives us to Christ, and that is where we need to be, for in Him is our fruit found.

'Have mercy upon me, O God'
Psalm 51:1

When Dr Carey was suffering from a dangerous illness, the enquiry was made, 'If this sickness should prove fatal, what passage would you select as the text for your funeral sermon?' He replied, 'Oh, I feel that such a poor sinful creature is unworthy to have anything said about him; but if a funeral sermon must be preached, let it be from the words, "Have mercy upon me, O God, according to Thy loving-kindness; according unto the multitude of Thy tender mercies blot out my transgressions".' In the same spirit of humility he directed in his will that the following inscription and nothing more should be cut on his gravestone:

WILLIAM CAREY, BORN AUGUST 17th, 1761: DIED -
'A wretched, poor, and helpless worm
On Thy kind arms I fall.'

Only on the footing of free grace can the most experienced and most honoured of the saints approach their God. The best of men are conscious above all others that they are men at the best. Empty boats float high, but heavily laden vessels are low in the water; mere professors can boast, but true children of God cry for mercy upon their unprofitableness. We have need that the Lord should have mercy upon our good works, our prayers, our preachings, our almsgivings, and our holiest things. The blood was not only sprinkled upon the doorposts of Israel's dwelling houses, but upon the sanctuary, the mercy-seat, and the altar, because as sin intrudes into our holiest things, the blood of Jesus is needed to purify them from defilement. If mercy be needed to be exercised towards our duties, what shall be said of our sins? How sweet the remembrance that inexhaustible mercy is waiting to be gracious to us, to restore our backslidings, and make our broken bones rejoice!

*'All the days of his separation shall he eat nothing
that is made of the vine tree,
from the kernels even to the husk'*
Numbers 6:4

Nazarites had taken, among other vows, one which
debarred them from the use of wine. In order that they
might not violate the obligation, they were forbidden to
drink the vinegar of wine or strong liquors, and to make
the rule still more clear, they were not to touch the
unfermented juice of grapes, nor even to eat the fruit
either fresh or dried. In order, altogether, to secure the
integrity of the vow, they were not even allowed
anything that had to do with the vine; they were, in fact,
to avoid the appearance of evil. Surely this is a lesson
to the Lord's separated ones, teaching them to come
away from sin in every form, to avoid not merely its
grosser shapes, but even its spirit and similitude. Strict
walking is much despised in these days, but rest
assured, dear reader, it is both the safest and the
happiest. He who yields a point or two to the world is
in fearful peril; he who eats the grapes of Sodom will
soon drink the wine of Gomorrah. A little crevice in the
sea-bank in Holland lets in the sea, and the gap speedily
swells till a province is drowned. Worldly conformity,
in any degree, is a snare to the soul, and makes it more
and more liable to presumptuous sins. Moreover, as
the Nazarite who drank grape juice could not be quite
sure whether it might not have endured a degree of
fermentation, and consequently could not be clear in
heart that his vow was intact, so the yielding, tempo-
rising Christian cannot wear a conscience void of
offence, but must feel that the inward monitor is in
doubt of him. Things doubtful we need not doubt
about; they are wrong to us. Things tempting we must
not dally with, but flee from them with speed. Better be
sneered at as a Puritan than be despised as a hypocrite.
Careful walking may involve much self-denial, but it
has pleasures of its own which are more than a
sufficient recompense.

'Wait on the Lord'
Psalm 27:14

It may seem an easy thing to *wait*, but it is one of the postures which a Christian soldier learns not without years of teaching. Marching and quick-marching are much easier to God's warriors than standing still. There are hours of perplexity when the most willing spirit, anxiously desirous to serve the Lord, knows not what part to take. Then what shall it do? Vex itself by despair? Fly back in cowardice, turn to the right hand in fear, or rush forward in presumption? No, but simply wait. *Wait in prayer*, however. Call upon God, and spread the case before Him; tell Him your difficulty, and plead His promise of aid. In dilemmas between one duty and another, it is sweet to be humble as a child, and *wait with simplicity of soul* upon the Lord. It is sure to be well with us when we feel and know our own folly, and are heartily willing to be guided by the will of God. But *wait in faith*. Express your unstaggering confidence in Him; for unfaithful, untrusting waiting, is but an insult to the Lord. Believe that if He keep you tarrying even till midnight, yet He will come at the right time; the vision shall come and shall not tarry. *Wait in quiet patience*, not rebelling because you are under the affliction, but blessing your God for it. Never murmur against the second cause, as the children of Israel did against Moses; never wish you could go back to the world again, but accept the case as it is, and put it as it stands, simply and with your whole heart, without any self-will, into the hand of your covenant God, saying, 'Now, Lord, not my will, but Thine be done. I know not what to do; I am brought to extremities, but I will wait until Thou shalt cleave the floods, or drive back my foes. I will wait, if Thou keep me many a day, for my heart is fixed upon thee alone, O God, and my spirit waiteth for thee in the full conviction that Thou wilt yet be my joy and my salvation, my refuge and my strong tower.'

> '*Heal me, O Lord, and I shall be healed*'
> Jeremiah 17:14
> '*I have seen His ways, and will heal him*'
> Isaiah 57:18

It is the sole prerogative of God to remove spiritual disease. Natural disease may be instrumentally healed by men, but even then the honour is to be given to God who giveth virtue unto medicine, and bestoweth power unto the human frame to cast off disease. As for spiritual sicknesses, these remain with the great Physician alone; He claims it as His prerogative, 'I kill and I make alive, I wound and I heal'; and one of the Lord's choice titles is Jehovah-Rophi, the Lord that healeth thee. 'I will heal thee of thy wounds', is a promise which could not come from the lip of man, but only from the mouth of the eternal God. On this account the psalmist cried unto the Lord, 'O Lord, heal me, for my bones are sore vexed', and again, 'Heal my soul, for I have sinned against thee'. For this, also, the godly praise the name of the Lord, saying, 'He healeth all our diseases'. He who made man can restore man; He who was at first the creator of our nature can new create it. What a transcendent comfort it is that in the person of Jesus 'dwelleth all the fulness of the Godhead bodily'! My soul, whatever thy disease may be, this great Physician can heal thee. If He be God, there can be no limit to His power. Come then with the blind eye of darkened understanding, come with the limping foot of wasted energy, come with the maimed hand of weak faith, the fever of an angry temper, or the ague of shivering despondency, come just as thou art, for He who is God can certainly restore thee of thy plague. None shall restrain the healing virtue which proceeds from Jesus our Lord. Legions of devils have been made to own the power of the beloved Physician, and never once has He been baffled. All His patients have been cured in the past and shall be in the future, and thou shalt be one among them, my friend, if thou wilt but rest thyself in Him this night.

'On mine arm shall they trust'
Isaiah 51:5

In seasons of severe trial, the Christian has nothing on earth that he can trust to, and is therefore compelled to cast himself on his God alone. When his vessel is on its beam-ends, and no human deliverance can avail, he must simply and entirely entrust himself to the providence and care of God. Happy storm that wrecks a man on such a rock as this! O blessed hurricane that drives the soul to God and God alone! There is no getting at our God sometimes because of the multitude of our friends; but when a man is so poor, so friendless, so helpless that he has nowhere else to turn, he flies into his Father's arms, and is blessedly clasped therein! When he is burdened with troubles so pressing and so peculiar, that he cannot tell them to any but his God, he may be thankful for them; for he will learn more of his Lord then than at any time. Oh, tempest-tossed believer, it is a happy trouble that drives thee to thy Father! Now that thou hast only thy God to trust to, see that thou puttest thy full confidence in Him. Dishonour not thy Lord and Master by unworthy doubts and fears; but be strong in faith, giving glory to God. Show the world that thy God is worth ten thousand worlds to thee. Show rich men how rich thou art in thy poverty when the Lord God is thy helper. Show the strong man how strong thou art in thy weakness when underneath thee are the everlasting arms. Now is the time for feats of faith and valiant exploits. Be strong and very courageous, and the Lord thy God shall certainly, as surely as He built the heavens and the earth, glorify Himself in thy weakness, and magnify his might in the midst of thy distress. The grandeur of the arch of heaven would be spoiled if the sky were supported by a single visible column, and your faith would lose its glory if it rested on anything discernible by the carnal eye. May the Holy Spirit give you to rest in Jesus this closing day of the month.

'If we walk in the light, as He is in the light'
1 John 1:7

As He is in the light! Can we ever attain to this? Shall we ever be able to walk as clearly in the light as He is whom we call 'Our Father', of whom it is written, 'God is light, and in Him is no darkness at all'? Certainly, this is the model which is set before us, for the Saviour Himself said, 'Be ye perfect, even as your Father who is in heaven is perfect', and although we may feel that we can never rival the perfection of God, yet we are to seek after it, and never to be satisfied until we attain to it. The youthful artist, as he grasps his early pencil, can hardly hope to equal Raphael or Michael Angelo, but still, if he did not have a noble *beau ideal* before his mind, he would only attain to something very mean and ordinary. But what is meant by the expression that the Christian is to walk in light as God is in the light? We conceive it to import *likeness*, but not *degree*. We are as truly in the light, we are as heartily in the light, we are as sincerely in the light, as honestly in the light, though we cannot be there in the same measure. I cannot dwell in the sun, it is too bright a place for my residence, but I can *walk* in the light of the sun; and so, though I cannot attain to that perfection of purity and truth which belongs to the Lord of hosts by nature as the infinitely good, yet I can set the Lord always before me, and strive, by the help of the indwelling Spirit, after conformity to his image. That famous old commentator, John Trapp, says, 'We may be in the light as God is in the light for *quality*, but not for *equality*'. We are to have the same light, and are as truly to have it and walk in it as God does, though, as for equality with God in his holiness and purity, that must be left until we cross the Jordan and enter into the perfection of the Most High. Mark that the blessings of sacred fellowship and perfect cleansing are bound up with walking in the light.

September

*'Thou shalt guide me with Thy counsel,
and afterward receive me to glory'*
Psalm 73:24

The Psalmist felt his need of divine guidance. He had just been discovering the foolishness of his own heart, and lest he should be constantly led astray by it, he resolved that God's counsel should henceforth guide him. A sense of our own folly is a great step towards being wise, when it leads us to rely on the wisdom of the Lord. The blind man leans on his friend's arm and reaches home in safety, and so would we give ourselves up implicitly to divine guidance, nothing doubting; assured that though we cannot see, it is always safe to trust the All-seeing God. *'Thou shalt'*, is a blessed expression of confidence. He was sure that the Lord would not decline the condescending task. There is a word for thee, O believer; rest thou in it. Be assured that thy God will be thy counsellor and friend; He shall guide thee; He will direct all thy ways. In His written Word thou hast this assurance in part fulfilled, for holy Scripture is His counsel to thee. Happy are we to have God's Word always to guide us! What were the mariner without his compass? And what were the Christian without the Bible? This is the unerring chart, the map in which every shoal is described, and all the channels from the quicksands of destruction to the haven of salvation mapped and marked by one who knows the way. Blessed be Thou, O God, that we may trust Thee to guide us now, and guide us even to the end! After this guidance through life, the Psalmist anticipates a divine reception at last - *'and afterward receive me to glory'*. What a thought for thee, believer! *God* Himself will receive *thee* to glory - *thee*! Wandering, erring, straying, yet He will bring thee safe at last *to glory*! This is thy portion; live on it this day, and if perplexities should surround thee, go in the strength of this text straight to the throne.

'Trust in Him at all times'
Psalm 62:8

Faith is as much the rule of temporal as of spiritual life; we ought to have faith in God for our earthly affairs as well as for our heavenly business. It is only as we learn to trust in God for the supply of all our daily need that we shall live above the world. We are not to be idle, *that* would show we did *not* trust in God, who worketh hitherto, but in the devil, who is the father of idleness. We are not to be imprudent or rash; that were to trust chance, and not the living God, who is a God of economy and order. Acting in all prudence and uprightness, we are to rely simply and entirely upon the Lord at all times.

Let me commend to you a life of trust in God in temporal things. Trusting in God, you will not be compelled to mourn because you have used sinful means to grow rich. Serve God with integrity, and if you achieve no success, at least no sin will lie upon your conscience. Trusting God, you will not be guilty of self-contradiction. He who trusts in craft, sails this way today, and that way the next, like a vessel tossed about by the fickle wind; but he that trusteth in the Lord is like a vessel propelled by steam, she cuts through the waves, defies the wind, and makes one bright silvery straightforward track to her destined haven. Be you a man with living principles within; never bow to the varying customs of worldly wisdom. Walk in your path of integrity with steadfast steps, and show that you are invincibly strong in the strength which confidence in God alone can confer. Thus you will be delivered from carking care, you will not be troubled with evil tidings, your heart will be fixed, trusting in the Lord. How pleasant to float along the stream of providence! There is no more blessed way of living than a life of dependence upon a covenant-keeping God. We have no care, for He careth for us; we have no troubles, because we cast our burdens upon the Lord.

*'But Simon's wife's mother lay sick of a fever,
and anon they tell Him of her'*
Mark 1:30

Very interesting is this little peep into the house of the
Apostolic Fisherman. We see at once that household
joys and cares are no hindrance to the full exercise of
ministry, nay, that since they furnish an opportunity
for personally witnessing the Lord's gracious work
upon one's own flesh and blood, they may even instruct
the teacher better than any other earthly discipline.
Papists and other sectaries may decry marriage, but
true Christianity and household life agree well together. Peter's house was probably a poor fisherman's
hut, but the Lord of Glory, entered it, lodged in it, and
wrought a miracle in it. Should our little book be read
this morning in some very humble cottage, let this fact
encourage the inmates to seek the company of King
Jesus. God is oftener in little huts than in rich palaces.
Jesus is looking round your room now, and is waiting
to be gracious to you. Into Simon's house sickness had
entered, fever in a deadly form had prostrated his
mother-in-law, and as soon as Jesus came they told
Him of the sad affliction, and He hastened to the
patient's bed. Have you any sickness in the house this
morning? You will find Jesus by far the best physician,
go to Him at once and tell Him all about the matter.
Immediately lay the case before Him. It concerns one
of His people, and therefore will not be trivial to Him.
Observe, that *at once* the Saviour restored the sick
woman; none can heal as He does. We may not make
sure that the Lord will at once remove all disease from
those we love, but we may know that believing prayer
for the sick is far more likely to be followed by
restoration than anything else in the world; and where
this avails not, we must meekly bow to His will by
whom life and death are determined. The tender heart
of Jesus waits to hear our griefs, let us pour them into
His patient ear.

> *'Except ye see signs and wonders,*
> *ye will not believe'*
> John 4:48

A craving after marvels was a symptom of the sickly state of men's minds in our Lord's day; they refused solid nourishment, and pined after mere wonder. The gospel which they so greatly needed they would not have; the miracles which Jesus did not always choose to give they eagerly demanded. Many nowadays must see signs and wonders, or they will not believe. Some have said in their heart, 'I must feel deep horror of soul, or I never will believe in Jesus'. But what if you never should feel it, as probably you never may? Will you go to hell out of spite against God, because He will not treat you like another? One has said to himself, 'If I had a dream, or if I could feel a sudden shock of I know not what, then I would believe'. Thus you undeserving mortals dream that my Lord is to be dictated to by you! You are beggars at His gate, asking for mercy, and you must needs draw up rules and regulations as to how He shall give that mercy. Think you that he will submit to this? My Master is of a generous spirit, but He has a right royal heart, he spurns all dictation, and maintains his sovereignty of action. Why, dear reader, if such be your case, do you crave for signs and wonders? Is not the gospel its own sign and wonder? Is not this a miracle of miracles, that 'God so loved the world that he gave His only begotten Son, that whosoever believeth in him might not perish'? Surely that precious word, 'Whosoever will, let him come and take the water of life freely' and that solemn promise, 'Him that cometh unto Me, I will in no wise cast out', are better than signs and wonders! A truthful Saviour ought to be believed. He is truth itself. Why will you ask proof of the veracity of one who cannot lie? The devils themselves declared Him to be the Son of God; will you mistrust Him?

'Thou whom my soul loveth'
Canticles 1:7

It is well to be able, without any 'if' or 'but', to say of the Lord Jesus - *'Thou whom my soul loveth'*. Many can only say of Jesus that they *hope* they love Him; they *trust* they love Him; but only a poor and shallow experience will be content to stay here. No one ought to give any rest to his spirit till he feels quite sure about a matter of such vital importance. We ought not to be satisfied with a superficial *hope* that Jesus loves us, and with a bare trust that we love Him. The old saints did not generally speak with 'buts', and 'ifs', and 'hopes', and 'trusts', but they spoke positively and plainly. 'I know whom I have believed,' saith Paul. 'I know that my Redeemer liveth,' saith Job. Get positive knowledge of your love of Jesus, and be not satisfied till you can speak of your interest in Him as a reality, which you have made sure by having received the witness of the Holy Spirit, and His seal upon your soul by faith.

True love to Christ is in every case the Holy Spirit's work, and must be wrought in the heart by Him. He is the *efficient cause* of it; but the logical reason why we love Jesus lies in *Himself. Why* do we love Jesus? *Because He first loved us. Why* do we love Jesus? Because He *gave Himself for us*. We have life through His death; we have peace through His blood. Though He was rich, yet *for our sakes* he became poor. *Why* do we love Jesus? Because of the *excellency of His person*. We are filled with a sense of His beauty! an admiration of his charms! a consciousness of His infinite perfection! His greatness, goodness, and love-liness, in one resplendent ray, combine to enchant the soul till it is so ravished that it exclaims, 'Yea, He is altogether lovely'. Blessed love this - a love which binds the heart with chains more soft than silk, and yet more firm than adamant!

'The Lord trieth the righteous'
Psalm 11:5

All events are under the control of Providence; consequently all the trials of our outward life are traceable at once to the great First Cause. Out of the golden gate of God's ordinance the armies of trial march forth in array, clad in their iron armour, and armed with weapons of war. All providences are doors to trial. Even our mercies, like roses, have their thorns. Men may be drowned in seas of prosperity as well as in rivers of affliction. Our mountains are not too high, and our valleys are not too low for temptations: trials lurk on all roads. Everywhere, above and beneath, we are beset and surrounded with dangers. Yet no shower falls unpermitted from the threatening cloud; every drop has its order ere it hastens to the earth. The trials which come from God are sent to prove and strengthen our graces, and so at once to illustrate the power of divine grace, to test the genuineness of our virtues, and to add to their energy. Our Lord in His infinite wisdom and superabundant love, sets so high a value upon His people's faith that He will not screen them from those trials by which faith is strengthened. You would never have possessed the precious faith which now supports you if the trial of your faith had not been like unto fire. You are a tree that never would have rooted so well if the wind had not rocked you to and fro, and made you take firm hold upon the precious truths of the covenant of grace. Worldly ease is a great foe to faith; it loosens the joints of holy valour, and snaps the sinews of sacred courage. The balloon never rises until the cords are cut; affliction doth this sharp service for believing souls. While the wheat sleeps comfortably in the husk it is useless to man, it must be threshed out of its resting place before its value can be known. Thus it is well that Jehovah trieth the righteous, for it causeth them to grow rich towards God.

'I will; be thou clean'
Mark 1:41

Primeval darkness heard the Almighty fiat, 'light be', and straightway light was, and the word of the Lord Jesus is equal in majesty to that ancient word of power. Redemption like Creation has its word of might. Jesus speaks and it is done. Leprosy yielded to no human remedies, but it fled at once at the Lord's 'I will'. The disease exhibited no hopeful signs or tokens of recovery, nature contributed nothing to its own healing, but the unaided word effected the entire work on the spot and for ever. The sinner is in a plight more miserable than the leper; let him imitate his example and go to Jesus, 'beseeching Him and kneeling down to Him'. Let him exercise what little faith he has, even though it should go no further than 'Lord, if thou wilt, thou canst make me clean'; and there need be no doubt as to the result of the application. Jesus heals all who come, and casts out none. In reading the narrative in which our morning's text occurs, it is worthy of devout notice that Jesus touched the leper. This unclean person had broken through the regulations of the ceremonial law and pressed into the house, but Jesus so far from chiding him broke through the law himself in order to meet him. He made an interchange with the leper, for while he cleansed him, he contracted by that touch a Levitical defilement. Even so Jesus Christ was made sin for us, although in Himself He knew no sin, that we might be made the righteousness of God in Him. O that poor sinners would go to Jesus, believing in the power of His blessed substitutionary work, and they would soon learn the power of his gracious touch. That hand which multiplied the loaves, which saved sinking Peter, which upholds afflicted saints, which crowns believers, that same hand will touch every seeking sinner, and in a moment make him clean. The love of Jesus is the source of salvation. He loves, He looks, He touches us, WE LIVE.

> *'Just balances, just weights, a just ephah,*
> *and a just hin, shall ye have'*
> Leviticus 19:36

Weights, and scales, and measures were to be all according to the standard of justice. Surely no Christian man will need to be reminded of this in his business, for if righteousness were banished from all the world beside, it should find a shelter in believing hearts. There are, however, other balances which weigh moral and spiritual things, and these often need examining. We will call in the officer tonight.

The balances in which we weigh our own and other men's characters, are they quite accurate? Do we not turn our own ounces of goodness into pounds, and other persons' bushels of excellence into pecks? See to weights and measures here, Christian. The scales in which we measure our trials and troubles, are they according to standard? Paul, who had more to suffer than we have, called his afflictions light, and yet we often consider ours to be heavy - surely something must be amiss with the weights! We must see to this matter, lest we get reported to the court above for unjust dealing. Those weights with which we measure our doctrinal belief, are they quite fair? The doctrines of grace should have the same weight with us as the precepts of the word, no more and no less; but it is to be feared that with many one scale or the other is unfairly weighted. It is a grand matter to give just measure in truth. Christian, be careful here. Those measures in which we estimate our obligations and responsibilities look rather small. When a rich man gives no more to the cause of God than the poor contribute, is that a just ephah and a just hin? When ministers are half starved, is that honest dealing? When the poor are despised, while ungodly rich men are held in admiration, is that a just balance? Reader, we might lengthen the list, but we prefer to leave it as your evening's work to find out and destroy all unrighteous balances, weights and measures.

'Woe is me, that I sojourn in Mesech,
that I dwell in the tents of Kedar!'
Psalm 120:5

As a Christian you have to live in the midst of an ungodly world, and it is of little use for you to cry, 'Woe is me'. Jesus did not pray that you should be taken out of the world, and what He did not pray for, you need not desire. Better far in the Lord's strength to meet the difficulty, and glorify Him in it. The enemy is ever on the watch to detect inconsistency in your conduct; be therefore very *holy*. Remember that the eyes of all are upon you, and that more is expected from you than from other men. Strive to give no occasion for blame. Let your goodness be the only fault they can discover in you. Like Daniel, compel them to say of you, 'We shall not find any occasion against this Daniel, except we find it against him concerning the law of his God'. Seek to be *useful* as well as consistent. Perhaps you think, 'If I were in a more favourable position I might serve the Lord's cause, but I cannot do any good where I am': but the worse the people are among whom you live, the more need have they of your exertions; if they be crooked, the more necessity that you should set them straight; and if they be perverse, the more need have you to turn their proud hearts to the truth. Where should the physician be but where there are many sick? Where is honour to be won by the soldier but in the hottest fire of the battle? And when weary of the strife and sin that meets you on every hand, consider that all the saints have endured the same trial. They were not carried on beds of down to heaven, and you must not expect to travel more easily than they. They had to hazard their lives unto the death in the high places of the field, and you will not be crowned till you also have endured hardness as a good soldier of Jesus Christ. Therefore, 'stand fast in the faith, quit you like men, be strong'.

'Hast thou entered into the springs of the sea?'
Job 38:16

Some things in nature must remain a mystery to the most intelligent and enterprising investigators. Human knowledge has bounds beyond which it cannot pass. Universal knowledge is for God alone. If this be so in the things which are seen and temporal, I may rest assured that it is even more so in matters spiritual and eternal. Why, then, have I been torturing my brain with speculations as to destiny and will, fixed fate, and human responsibility? These deep and dark truths I am no more able to comprehend than to find out the depth which coucheth beneath, from which old ocean draws her watery stores. Why am I so curious to know the reason of my Lord's providences, the motive of His actions, the design of His visitations? Shall I ever be able to clasp the sun in my fist, and hold the universe in my palm? Yet these are as a drop of a bucket compared with the Lord my God. Let me not strive to understand the infinite, but spend my strength in love. What I cannot gain by intellect I can possess by affection, and let that suffice me. I cannot penetrate the heart of the sea, but I can enjoy the healthful breezes which sweep over its bosom, and I can sail over its blue waves with propitious winds. If I could enter the springs of the sea, the feat would serve no useful purpose either to myself or others, it would not save the sinking bark, or give back the drowned mariner to his weeping wife and children; neither would my solving deep mysteries avail me a single whit, for the least love to God, and the simplest act of obedience to Him, are better than the profoundest knowledge. My Lord, I leave the infinite to Thee, and pray Thee to put far from me such love for the tree of knowledge as might keep me from the tree of life.

*'In the midst of a crooked and perverse nation,
among whom ye shine as lights in the world'*
Philippians 2:15

We use lights to *make manifest*. A Christian man should so shine in his life, that a person could not live with him a week without knowing the gospel. His conversation should be such that all who are about him should clearly perceive whose he is, and whom he serves; and should see the image of Jesus reflected in his daily actions. Lights are intended for *guidance*. We are to help those around us who are in the dark. We are to hold forth to them the Word of life. We are to point sinners to the Saviour, and the weary to a divine resting-place. Men sometimes read their Bibles, and fail to understand them; we should be ready, like Philip, to instruct the inquirer in the meaning of God's Word, the way of salvation, and the life of godliness. Lights are also used for *warning*. On our rocks and shoals a lighthouse is sure to be erected. Christian men should know that there are many false lights shown everywhere in the world, and therefore the right light is needed. The wreckers of Satan are always abroad, tempting the ungodly to sin under the name of pleasure; they hoist the wrong light, be it ours to put up the true light upon every dangerous rock, to point out every sin, and tell what it leads to, that so we may be clear of the blood of all men, shining as lights in the world. Lights also have a very *cheering* influence, and so have Christians. A Christian ought to be a comforter, with kind words on his lips, and sympathy in his heart; he should carry sunshine wherever he goes, and diffuse happiness around him.

Gracious Spirit dwell with me;
I myself would gracious be,
And with words that help and heal
Would thy life in mine reveal,
And with actions bold and meek
Would for Christ my Saviour speak.

'*If ye be led of the Spirit, ye are not under the law*'
Galatians 5:18

He who looks at his own character and position from
a legal point of view, will not only despair when he
comes to the *end* of his reckoning, but if he be a wise
man he will despair at the *beginning*; for if we are to be
judged on the footing of the law, there shall no flesh
living be justified. How blessed to know that we dwell
in the domains of grace and not of law! When thinking
of my state before God the question is not, 'Am I
perfect in myself before the law?' but, 'Am I perfect in
Christ Jesus?' That is a very different matter. We need
not enquire, 'Am I without sin naturally?' but, 'Have
I been washed in the fountain opened for sin and for
uncleanness?' It is not 'Am I in myself well pleasing
to God?' but it is 'Am I accepted in the Beloved?' The
Christian views his evidences from the top of Sinai,
and grows alarmed concerning his salvation; it were
better far if he read his title by the light of Calvary.
'Why,' saith he, 'my faith has unbelief in it, it is not
able to save me.' Suppose he had considered *the object*
of his faith instead of his faith, then he would have said,
'There is no failure in *Him*, and therefore I am safe.'
He sighs over his hope: 'Ah! my hope is marred and
dimmed by an anxious carefulness about present things;
how can I be accepted?' Had he regarded *the ground* of
his hope, he would have seen that the promise of God
standeth sure, and that whatever our doubts may be, the
oath and promise never fail. Ah! believer, it is safer
always for you to be led of the Spirit into gospel liberty
than to wear legal fetters. Judge yourself at what *Christ*
is rather than at what *you* are. Satan will try to mar your
peace by reminding you of your sinfulness and imperfections: you can only meet his accusations by faithfully adhering to the gospel and refusing to wear the
yoke of bondage.

*'And when they could not come nigh unto Him for
the press, they uncovered the roof where he was:
and when they had broken it up, they let down the
bed wherein the sick of the palsy lay'*
Mark 2:4

Faith is full of inventions. The house was full, a crowd
blocked up the door, but faith found a way of getting at
the Lord and placing the palsied man before Him. If we
cannot get sinners where Jesus is by ordinary methods
we must use extraordinary ones. It seems, according to
Luke 5:19, that a tiling had to be removed, which would
make dust and cause a measure of danger to those
below, but where the case is very urgent we must not
mind running some risks and shocking some proprie-
ties. Jesus was there to heal, and therefore fall what
might, faith ventured all so that her poor paralysed
charge might have his sins forgiven. O that we had
more daring faith among us! Cannot we, dear reader,
seek it this morning for ourselves and for our fellow-
workers, and will we not try today to perform some
gallant act for the love of souls and the glory of the
Lord?

The world is constantly inventing; genius serves
all the purposes of human desire: cannot faith invent
too, and reach by some new means the outcasts who lie
perishing around us? It was the presence of Jesus
which excited victorious courage in the four bearers of
the palsied man: is not the Lord among us now? Have
we seen His face for ourselves this morning? Have we
felt His healing power in our own souls? If so, then
through door, through window, or through roof, let us,
breaking through all impediments, labour to bring poor
souls to Jesus. All means are good and decorous when
faith and love are truly set on winning souls. If hunger
for bread can break through stone walls, surely hunger
for souls is not to be hindered in its efforts. O Lord,
make us quick to suggest methods of reaching thy poor
sin-sick ones, and bold to carry them out at all hazards.

'There is sorrow on the sea; it cannot be quiet'
Jeremiah 49:23

Little know we what sorrow may be upon the sea at this moment. We are safe in our quiet chamber, but far away on the salt sea the hurricane may be cruelly seeking for the lives of men. Hear how the death fiends howl among the cordage; how every timber starts as the waves beat like battering rams upon the vessel! God help you, poor drenched and wearied ones! My prayer goes up to the great Lord of sea and land, that he will make the storm a calm, and bring you to your desired haven! Nor ought I to offer prayer alone, I should try to benefit those hardy men who risk their lives so constantly. Have I ever done anything for them? What can I do? How often does the boisterous sea swallow up the mariner! Thousands of corpses lie where pearls lie deep. There is death-sorrow on the sea, which is echoed in the long wail of widows and orphans. The salt of the sea is in many eyes of mothers and wives. Remorseless billows, ye have devoured the love of women, and the stay of households. What a resurrection shall there be from the caverns of the deep when the sea gives up her dead! Till then there will be sorrow on the sea. As if in sympathy with the woes of earth, the sea is for ever fretting along a thousand shores, wailing with a sorrowful cry like her own birds, booming with a hollow crash of unrest, raving with uproarious discontent, chafing with hoarse wrath, or jangling with the voices of ten thousand murmuring pebbles. The roar of the sea may be joyous to a rejoicing spirit, but to the son of sorrow the wide, wide ocean is even more forlorn than the wide, wide world. This is not our rest, and the restless billows tell us so. There is a land where there is no more sea - our faces are steadfastly set towards it; we are going to the place of which the Lord hath spoken. Till then, we cast our sorrows on the Lord who trod the sea of old, and who maketh a way for His people through the depths thereof.

'From Me is thy fruit found'
Hosea 14:8

Our fruit is found from our God as to *union*. The fruit
of the branch is directly traceable to the root. Sever the
connection, the branch dies, and no fruit is produced.
By virtue of our union with Christ we bring forth fruit.
Every bunch of grapes has been first in the root, it has
passed through the stem, and flowed through the sap
vessels, and fashioned itself externally into fruit, but it
was first in the stem; so also every good work was first
in Christ, and then is brought forth in us. O Christian,
prize this precious union to Christ; for it must be the
source of all the fruitfulness which thou canst hope to
know. If thou wert not joined to Jesus Christ, thou
wouldst be a barren bough indeed.

Our fruit comes from God as to *spiritual providence*. When the dew-drops fall from heaven, when the
cloud looks down from on high, and is about to distil
its liquid treasure, when the bright sun swells the
berries of the cluster, each heavenly boon may whisper
to the tree and say, 'From me is thy fruit found'. The
fruit owes much to the root - that is essential to
fruitfulness - but it owes very much also to external
influences. How much we owe to God's grace-provi-
dence! In which He provides us constantly with quickening, teaching, consolation, strength, or whatever else
we want. To this we owe our all of usefulness or virtue.

Our fruit comes from God as to *wise husbandry*.
The gardener's sharp-edged knife promotes the fruitfulness of the tree, by thinning the clusters, and by
cutting off superfluous shoots. So is it, Christian, with
that pruning which the Lord gives to thee. 'My Father
is the husbandman. Every branch in Me that beareth not
fruit He taketh away; and every branch that beareth fruit
He purgeth it, that it may bring forth more fruit.' Since
our God is the author of our spiritual graces, let us give
to Him all the glory of our salvation.

*'The exceeding greatness of His power to us-ward
who believe according to the working of His mighty
power, which He wrought in Christ, when He
raised Him from the dead'*
Ephesians 1:19, 20

In the resurrection of Christ, as in our salvation, there
was put forth nothing short of a *divine power*. What
shall we say of those who think that conversion is
wrought by the free will of man, and is due to his own
betterness of disposition? When we shall see the dead
rise from the grave by their own power, then may we
expect to see ungodly sinners of their own free will
turning to Christ. It is not the word preached, nor the
word read in itself; all quickening power proceeds from
the Holy Ghost. This power was *irresistible*. All the
soldiers and the high priests could not keep the body of
Christ in the tomb. Death himself could not hold Jesus
in his bonds: even thus irresistible is the power put
forth in the believer when he is raised to newness of
life. No sin, no corruption, no devils in hell nor sinners
upon earth, can stay the hand of God's grace when it
intends to convert a man. If God omnipotently says,
'Thou shalt', man shall not say, 'I will not'. Observe
that the power which raised Christ from the dead was
glorious. It reflected honour upon God and wrought
dismay in the hosts of evil. So there is great glory to
God in the conversion of every sinner. It was *everlasting power*. 'Christ being raised from the dead dieth no
more; death hath no more dominion over Him.' So we,
being raised from the dead, go not back to our dead
works nor to our old corruptions, but we live unto God.
'Because He lives we live also.' 'For we are dead, and
our life is hid with Christ in God.' 'Like as Christ was
raised up from the dead by the glory of the Father, even
so we also should walk in newness of life.' Lastly, in
the text mark the *union of the new life to Jesus*. The
same power which raised the Head works life in the
members. What a blessing to be quickened together
with Christ!

*'I will answer thee, and shew thee great and mighty
things which thou knowest not'*
Jeremiah 33:3

There are different translations of these words. One
version renders it, 'I will shew thee great and fortified
things'. Another, 'Great and reserved things'. Now,
there are reserved and special things in Christian
experience: all the developments of spiritual life are not
alike easy of attainment. There are the common frames
and feelings of repentance, and faith, and joy, and hope,
which are enjoyed by the entire family; but there is an
upper realm of rapture, of communion, and conscious
union with Christ, which is far from being the common
dwelling-place of believers. We have not all the high
privilege of John, to lean upon Jesus' bosom; nor of
Paul, to be caught up into the third heaven. There are
heights in experimental knowledge of the things of God
which the eagle's eye of acumen and philosophic
thought hath never seen: God alone can bear us there;
but the chariot in which He takes us up, and the fiery
steeds with which that chariot is dragged, are prevailing prayers. Prevailing prayer is victorious over the
God of mercy, 'By his strength he had power with God:
yea, he had power over the angel, and prevailed: he
wept, and made supplication unto Him: he found Him
in Beth-el, and there He spake with us'. Prevailing to
cover heaven with clouds of blessing, and earth with
floods of mercy. Prevailing prayer bears the Christian
aloft to Pisgah, and shows him the inheritance reserved; it elevates us to Tabor and transfigures us, till
in the likeness of his Lord, as he is, so are we also in
this world. If you would reach to something higher than
ordinary grovelling experience, look to the Rock that is
higher than you, and gaze with the eye of faith through
the window of importunate prayer. When you open the
window on your side, it will not be bolted on the other.

*'And round about the throne were four and twenty
seats: and upon the seats I saw four and twenty
elders sitting, clothed in white raiment'*
Revelation 4:4

These representatives of the saints in heaven are said
to be *around the throne*. In the passage in Canticles,
where Solomon sings of the King sitting at his table,
some render it 'a round table'. From this, some
expositors, I think, without straining the text, have
said, 'There is an equality among the saints'. That idea
is conveyed by the equal nearness of the four and
twenty elders. The condition of glorified spirits in
heaven is that of nearness to Christ, clear vision of His
glory, constant access to His court, and familiar fellowship with His person: nor is there any difference in
this respect between one saint and another, but all the
people of God, apostles, martyrs, ministers, or private
and obscure Christians, shall all be seated *near the
throne*, where they shall for ever gaze upon their
exalted Lord, and be satisfied with His love. They shall
all be near to Christ, all ravished with His love, all
eating and drinking at the same table with Him, all
equally beloved as His favourites and friends even if
not all equally rewarded as servants.

Let believers on earth imitate the saints in heaven
in their nearness to Christ. Let us on earth be as the
elders are in heaven, sitting around the throne. May
Christ be the object of our thoughts, the centre of our
lives. How can we endure to live at such a distance from
our Beloved? Lord Jesus, draw us nearer to Thyself!
Say unto us, 'Abide in Me, and I in you'; and permit
us to sing, 'His left hand is under my head, and His
right hand doth embrace me'.

O lift me higher, nearer Thee,
　　And as I rise more pure and meet,
O let my soul's humility
　　Make me lie lower at Thy feet;
Less trusting self, the more I prove
　　The blessed comfort of Thy love.

'And he goeth up into a mountain, and calleth unto him whom he would: and they came unto him'
Mark 3:13

Here was sovereignty. Impatient spirits may fret and fume, because they are not called to the highest places in the ministry; but reader be it thine to rejoice that Jesus calleth whom He wills. If He shall leave me to be a doorkeeper in His house, I will cheerfully bless Him for His grace in permitting me to do anything in His service. The call of Christ's servants comes from above. Jesus stands on the mountain, evermore above the world in holiness, earnestness, love and power. Those whom He calls must go up the mountain to Him, they must seek to rise to His level by living in constant communion with Him. They may not be able to mount to classic honours, or attain scholastic eminence, but they must like Moses go up into the mount of God and have familiar intercourse with the unseen God, or they will never be fitted to proclaim the gospel of peace. Jesus went apart to hold high fellowship with the Father, and we must enter into the same divine companionship if we would bless our fellow-men. No wonder that the apostles were clothed with power when they came down fresh from the mountain where Jesus was. This morning we must endeavour to ascend the mount of communion, that there we may be ordained to the life-work for which we are set apart. Let us not see the face of man today till we have seen Jesus. Time spent with Him is laid out at blessed interest. We too shall cast out devils and work wonders if we go down into the world girded with that divine energy which Christ alone can give. It is of no use going to the Lord's battle till we are armed with heavenly weapons. We *must* see Jesus, this is essential. At the mercy-seat we will linger till He shall manifest himself unto us as He doth not unto the world, and until we can truthfully say, 'We were with Him in the Holy Mount'.

'Evening wolves'
Habakkuk 1:8

While preparing the present volume, this particular expression recurred to me so frequently, that in order to be rid of its constant importunity I determined to give a page to it. The evening wolf, infuriated by a day of hunger, was fiercer and more ravenous than he would have been in the morning. May not the furious creature represent our doubts and fears after a day of distraction of mind, losses in business, and perhaps ungenerous tauntings from our fellow men? How our thoughts howl in our ears, 'Where is now thy God?' How voracious and greedy they are, swallowing up all suggestions of comfort, and remaining as hungry as before. Great Shepherd, slay these evening wolves, and bid Thy sheep lie down in green pastures, undisturbed by insatiable unbelief How like are the fiends of hell to evening wolves, for when the flock of Christ are in a cloudy and dark day, and their sun seems going down, they hasten to tear and to devour. They will scarcely attack the Christian in the daylight of faith, but in the gloom of soul conflict they fall upon him. O Thou who hast laid down Thy life for the sheep, preserve them from the fangs of the wolf.

False teachers who craftily and industriously hunt for the precious life, devouring men by their falsehoods, are as dangerous and detestable as evening wolves. Darkness is their element, deceit is their character, destruction is their end. We are most in danger from them when they wear the sheep's skin. Blessed is he who is kept from them, for thousands are made the prey of grievous wolves that enter within the fold of the church.

What a wonder of grace it is when fierce persecutors are converted, for then the wolf dwells with the lamb, and men of cruel ungovernable dispositions become gentle and teachable. O Lord, convert many such: for such we will pray tonight.

'Be ye separate' - 2 Corinthians 6:17

The Christian, while in the world, is not to be of the world. He should be distinguished from it in *the great object of his life*. To him, 'to live', should be 'Christ'. Whether he eats, or drinks, or whatever he does, he should do all to God's glory. You may lay up treasure; but lay it up in heaven, where neither moth nor rust doth corrupt, where thieves break not through nor steal. You may strive to be rich; but be it your ambition to be 'rich in faith', and good works. You may have pleasure; but when you are merry, sing psalms and make melody in your hearts to the Lord. In your *spirit*, as well as in your aim, you should differ from the world. Waiting humbly before God, always conscious of His presence, delighting in communion with Him, and seeking to know His will, you will prove that you are of heavenly race. And you should be separate from the world in your *actions*. If a thing be right, though you lose by it, it must be done; if it be wrong, though you would gain by it, you must scorn the sin for your Master's sake. You must have no fellowship with the unfruitful works of darkness, but rather reprove them. Walk worthy of your high calling and dignity. Remember, O Christian, that thou art a son of the King of kings. Therefore, keep thyself unspotted from the world. Soil not the fingers which are soon to sweep celestial strings; let not these eyes become the windows of lust which are soon to see the King in His beauty - let not those feet be defiled in miry places, which are soon to walk the golden streets - let not those hearts be filled with pride and bitterness which are ere long to be filled with heaven, and to overflow with ecstatic joy.

> Then rise my soul! and soar away,
>   Above the thoughtless crowd;
> Above the pleasures of the gay,
>   And splendours of the proud;
> Up where eternal beauties bloom,
>   And pleasures all divine;
> Where wealth, that never can consume,
>   And endless glories shine.

*'Lead me, O Lord, in Thy righteousness
because of mine enemies'*
Psalm 5:8

Very bitter is the enmity of the world against the people of Christ. Men will forgive a thousand faults in others, but they will magnify the most trivial offence in the followers of Jesus. Instead of vainly regretting this, let us turn it to account, and since so many are watching for our halting, let this be a special motive for walking very carefully before God. If we live carelessly, the lynx-eyed world will soon see it, and with its hundred tongues, it will spread the story, exaggerated and emblazoned by the zeal of slander. They will shout triumphantly. 'Aha! So would we have it! See how these Christians act! They are hypocrites to a man.' Thus will much damage be done to the cause of Christ, and much insult offered to His name. The cross of Christ is in itself an offence to the world; let us take heed that we add no offence of our own. It is 'to the Jews a stumblingblock': let us mind that we put no stumblingblocks where there are enough already. 'To the Greeks it is foolishness': let us not add our folly to give point to the scorn with which the world-wise deride the gospel. How jealous should we be of ourselves! How rigid with our consciences! In the presence of adversaries who will misrepresent our best deeds, and impugn our motives where they cannot censure our actions, how circumspect should we be! Pilgrims travel as suspected persons through Vanity Fair. Not only are we under surveillance, but there are more spies than we reck of. The espionage is every-where, at home and abroad. If we fall into the enemies' hands we may sooner expect generosity from a wolf, or mercy from a fiend, than anything like patience with our infirmities from men who spice their infidelity towards God with scandals against His people. O Lord, lead us ever, lest our enemies trip us up!

'God is jealous'
Nahum 1:2

Your Lord is very jealous of your love, O believer. Did He choose you? He cannot bear that you should choose another. Did He buy you with His own blood? He cannot endure that you should think that you are your own, or that you belong to this world. He loved you with such a love that He would not stop in heaven without you; He would sooner die than you should perish, and He cannot endure that anything should stand between your heart's love and Himself. *He is very jealous of your trust.* He will not permit you to trust in an arm of flesh. He cannot bear that you should hew out broken cisterns, when the overflowing fountain is always free to you. When we lean upon Him, He is glad, but when we transfer our dependence to another, when we rely upon our own wisdom, or the wisdom of a friend - worst of all, when we trust in any works of our own, He is displeased, and will chasten us that He may bring us to Himself. *He is also very jealous of our company.* There should be no one with whom we converse so much as with Jesus. To abide in Him only, this is true love; but to commune with the world, to find sufficient solace in our carnal comforts, to prefer even the society of our fellow Christians to secret intercourse with Him, this is grievous to our jealous Lord. He would fain have us abide in Him, and enjoy constant fellowship with Himself; and many of the trials which He sends us are for the purpose of weaning our hearts from the creature, and fixing them more closely upon Himself. Let this jealousy which should keep us near to Christ *be also a comfort* to us, for if He loves us so much as to care thus about *our* love we may be sure that He will suffer nothing to harm us, and will protect us from all our enemies. Oh that we may have grace this day to keep our hearts in sacred chastity for our Beloved alone, with sacred jealousy shutting our eyes to all the fascinations of the world!

> *'I will sing of mercy and judgment'*
> Psalm 101:1

Faith triumphs in trial. When reason is thrust into the inner prison, with her feet made fast in the stocks, faith makes the dungeon walls ring with her merry notes as she cries, 'I will sing of mercy and of judgment. Unto thee, O Lord, will I sing'. Faith pulls the black mask from the face of trouble, and discovers the angel beneath. Faith looks up at the cloud, and sees that

> "'Tis big with mercy and shall break
>   In blessings on her head.'

There is a subject for song even in the judgments of God towards us. For, first, the trial is *not so heavy as it might have been*; next, the trouble is *not so severe as we deserved to have borne*; and our affliction is *not so crushing as the burden which others have to carry*. Faith sees that in her worst sorrow there is nothing penal; there is not a drop of God's wrath in it; it is all sent in love. Faith discerns love gleaming like a jewel on the breast of an angry God. Faith says of her grief, 'This is a badge of honour, for the child must feel the rod'; and then she sings of the sweet result of her sorrows, because they work her spiritual good. Nay, more, says Faith, 'These light afflictions, which are but for a moment, work out for me a far more exceeding and eternal weight of glory'. So Faith rides forth on the black horse, conquering and to conquer, trampling down carnal reason and fleshly sense, and chanting notes of victory amid the thickest of the fray.

> 'All I meet I find assists me
>   In my path to heavenly joy:
> Where, though trials now attend me,
>   Trials never more annoy.

> 'Blest there with a weight of glory,
>   Still the path I'll ne'er forget,
> But, exulting, cry, it led me
>   To my blessed Saviour's seat.'

*'Who passing through the valley of Baca make it a
well; the rain also filleth the pools'*
Psalm 84:6

This teaches us that the *comfort* obtained by one may
often prove serviceable to another; just as wells would
be used by the company who came after. We read some
book full of consolation, which is like Jonathan's rod,
dropping with honey. Ah! we think our brother has
been here before us, and digged this well for us as well
as for himself. Many a 'Night of Weeping', 'Midnight
Harmonies', an 'Eternal Day', 'A Crook in the Lot', a
'Comfort for Mourners', has been a well digged by a
pilgrim for himself, but has proved quite as useful to
others. Specially we notice this in the Psalms, such as
that beginning, 'Why art thou cast down, O my soul?'
Travellers have been delighted to see the footprint of
man on a barren shore, and we love to see the waymarks
of pilgrims while passing through the vale of tears.

The pilgrims dig the well, but, strange enough, it
fills from the top instead of the bottom. We use the
means, but the blessing does not spring from the
means. We dig a well, but heaven fills it with rain. The
horse is prepared against the day of battle, but safety is
of the Lord. The means are connected with the end, but
they do not of themselves produce it. See here the rain
fills the pools, so that the wells become useful as
reservoirs for the water; labour is not lost, but yet it
does not supersede divine help.

Grace may well be compared to rain for its purity,
for its refreshing and vivifying influence, for its
coming alone from above, and for the sovereignty with
which it is given or withheld. May our readers have
showers of blessing, and may the wells they have
digged be filled with water! Oh, what are means and
ordinances without the smile of heaven! They are
clouds without rain, and pools without water. O God of
love, open the windows of heaven and pour us out a
blessing!

'This man receiveth sinners'
Luke 15:2

Observe *the condescension* of this fact. This Man, who towers above all other men, holy, harmless, undefiled, and separate from sinners - *this* Man receiveth sinners. This man, who is no other than the eternal God, before whom angels veil their faces - *this* Man receiveth sinners. It needs an angel's tongue to describe such a mighty stoop of love. That any of *us* should be willing to seek after the lost is nothing wonderful - they are of our own race; but that He, the offended God, against whom the transgression has been committed, should take upon Himself the form of a servant, and bear the sin of many, and should then be willing to receive the vilest of the vile, this is marvellous.

'This Man receiveth sinners'; not, however, that they may remain sinners, but He receives them that He may pardon their sins, justify their persons, cleanse their hearts by His purifying word, preserve their souls by the indwelling of the Holy Ghost, and enable them to serve him, to show forth His praise, and to have communion with Him. Into His heart's love He receives sinners, takes them from the dunghill, and wears them as jewels in His crown; plucks them as brands from the burning, and preserves them as costly monuments of His mercy. None are so precious in Jesus' sight as the sinners for whom He died. When Jesus receives sinners, He has not some out-of-doors reception place, no casual ward where He charitably entertains them as men do passing beggars, but He opens the golden gates of His royal heart, and receives the sinner right into Himself - yea, He admits the humble penitent into personal union and makes Him a member of His body, of His flesh, and of His bones. There was never such a reception as this! This fact is still most sure this evening, He is still receiving sinners: would to God sinners would receive Him.

'There were also with Him other little ships'
Mark 4:36

Jesus was the Lord High Admiral of the sea that night, and His presence preserved the whole convoy. It is well to sail with Jesus, even though it be in a little ship. When we sail in Christ's company, we may not make sure of fair weather, for great storms may toss the vessel which carries the Lord Himself, and we must not expect to find the sea less boisterous around our little boat. If we go with Jesus we must be content to fare as He fares; and when the waves are rough to Him, they will be rough to us. It is by tempest and tossing that we shall come to land, as He did before us.

When the storm swept over Galilee's dark lake all faces gathered blackness, and all hearts dreaded shipwreck. When all creature help was useless, the slumbering Saviour arose, and with a word, transformed the riot of the tempest into the deep quiet of a calm; then were the little vessels at rest as well as that which carried the Lord. Jesus is the star of the sea; and though there be sorrow upon the sea, when Jesus is on it there is joy too. May our hearts make Jesus their anchor, their rudder, their lighthouse, their lifeboat, and their harbour. His Church is the Admiral's flagship, let us attend her movements, and cheer her officers with our presence. He Himself is the great attraction; let us follow ever in His wake, mark His signals, steer by His chart, and never fear while He is within hail. Not one ship in the convoy shall suffer wreck; the great Commodore will steer every barque in safety to the desired haven. By faith we will slip our cable for another day's cruise, and sail forth with Jesus into a sea of tribulation. Winds and waves will not spare us, but they all obey Him; and, therefore, whatever squalls may occur without, faith shall feel a blessed calm within. He is ever in the centre of the weather-beaten company: let us rejoice in Him. His vessel has reached the haven, and so shall ours.

'I acknowledged my sin unto Thee,
and mine iniquity have I not hid. I said,
I will confess my transgressions unto the Lord;
and Thou forgavest the iniquity of my sin'
Psalm 32:5

David's grief for sin was bitter. Its effects were visible upon his outward frame: 'his bones waxed old'; 'his moisture was turned into the drought of summer'. No remedy could he find, until he made a full confession before the throne of the heavenly grace. He tells us that for a time he kept silence, and his heart became more and more filled with grief: like a mountain tarn whose outlet is blocked up, his soul was swollen with torrents of sorrow. He fashioned excuses; he endeavoured to divert his thoughts, but it was all to no purpose; like a festering sore his anguish gathered, and as he would not use the lancet of confession, his spirit was full of torment, and knew no rest. At last it came to this, that he must return unto his God in humble penitence, or die outright; so he hastened to the mercy-seat, and there unrolled the volume of his iniquities before the all-seeing One, acknowledging all the evil of his ways in language such as you read in the fifty-first and other penitential Psalms. Having done this, a work so simple and yet so difficult to pride, he received at once the token of divine forgiveness; the bones which had been broken were made to rejoice, and he came forth from his closet to sing the blessedness of the man whose transgression is forgiven. See the value of a grace-wrought confession of sin! It is to be prized above all price, for in every case where there is a genuine, gracious confession, mercy is freely given, not because the repentance and confession *deserve* mercy, but for *Christ's sake*. Blessed be God, there is always healing for the broken heart; the fountain is ever flowing to cleanse us from our sins. Truly, O Lord, Thou art a God 'ready to pardon'! Therefore will we acknowledge our iniquities.

'He shall not be afraid of evil tidings'
Psalm 112:7

Christian, you ought not to dread the arrival of evil tidings; because if you are distressed by them, *what do you more than other men*? Other men have not your God to fly to; they have never proved His faithfulness as you have done, and it is no wonder if they are bowed down with alarm and cowed with fear: but you profess to be of another spirit; you have been begotten again unto a lively hope, and your heart lives in heaven and not on earthly things; now, if you are seen to be distracted as other men, what is the value of that grace which you profess to have received? Where is the dignity of that new nature which you claim to possess?

Again, if you should be filled with alarm, as others are, *you would, doubtless, be led into the sins so common to others under trying circumstances*. The ungodly, when they are overtaken by evil tidings, rebel against God; they murmur, and think that God deals hardly with them. Will you fall into that same sin? Will you provoke the Lord as they do?

Moreover, unconverted men often run to wrong means in order to escape from difficulties, and you will be sure to do the same if your mind yields to the present pressure. Trust in the Lord, and wait patiently for Him. Your wisest course is to do as Moses did at the Red Sea, 'Stand still and see the salvation of God'. For if you give way to fear when you hear of evil tidings, you will be unable to meet the trouble with that calm composure which nerves for duty, and sustains under adversity. How can you glorify God if you play the coward? Saints have often sung God's high praises in the fires, but will your doubting and desponding, as if you had none to help you, magnify the Most High? Then take courage, and relying in sure confidence upon the faithfulness of your covenant God, 'let not your heart be troubled, neither let it be afraid'.

'A people near unto him'
Psalm 148:14

The dispensation of the old covenant was that of distance. When God appeared even to His servant Moses, He said, 'Draw not nigh hither: put off thy shoes from off thy feet'; and when He manifested Himself upon Mount Sinai, to His own chosen and separated people, one of the first commands was, 'Thou shalt set bounds about the mount'. Both in the sacred worship of the tabernacle and the temple, the thought of distance was always prominent. The mass of the people did not even enter the outer court. Into the inner court none but the priests might dare to intrude; while into the innermost place, or the holy of holies, the high priest entered but once in the year. It was as if the Lord in those early ages would teach man that sin was so utterly loathsome to Him, that He must treat men as lepers put without the camp; and when He came nearest to them, He yet made them feel the width of the separation between a holy God and an impure sinner. When the gospel came, we were placed on quite another footing. The word 'Go' was exchanged for 'Come'; distance was made to give place to nearness, and we who aforetime were afar off, were made nigh by the blood of Jesus Christ. Incarnate Deity has no wall of fire about it. 'Come unto me, all ye that labour and are heavy laden, and I will give you rest', is the joyful proclamation of God as He appears in human flesh. Not now does He teach the leper his leprosy by setting him at a distance, but by Himself suffering the penalty of His defilement. What a state of safety and privilege is this nearness to God through Jesus! Do you know it by experience? If you know it, are you living in the power of it? Marvellous is this nearness, yet it is to be followed by a dispensation of greater nearness still, when it shall be said, 'The tabernacle of God is with men, and He doth dwell among them'. Hasten it, O Lord.

'Partakers of the divine nature'
2 Peter 1:4

To be a partaker of the divine nature is not, of course, to become God. That cannot be. The essence of Deity is not to be participated in by the creature. Between the creature and the Creator there must ever be a gulf fixed in respect of essence; but as the first man Adam was made in the image of God, so we, by the renewal of the Holy Spirit, are in a yet diviner sense made in the image of the Most High, and are partakers of the divine nature. We are, by grace, made like God. 'God is love'; we become love - 'He that loveth is born of God'. God is truth; we become true, and we love that which is true: God is good, and He makes us good by His grace, so that we become the pure in heart who shall see God. Moreover, we become partakers of the divine nature in even a higher sense than this - in fact, in as lofty a sense as can be conceived, short of our being absolutely divine. Do we not become members of the body of the divine person of Christ? Yes, the same blood which flows in the head flows in the hand: and the same life which quickens Christ quickens His people, for 'Ye are dead, and your life is hid with Christ in God'. Nay, as if this were not enough, we are married unto Christ. He hath betrothed us unto Himself in righteousness and in faithfulness, and he who is joined unto the Lord is one spirit. Oh! marvellous mystery! we look into it, but who shall understand it? One with Jesus - so one with Him that the branch is not more one with the vine than we are a part of the Lord, our Saviour, and our Redeemer! While we rejoice in this, let us remember that those who are made partakers of the divine nature will manifest their high and holy relationship in their intercourse with others, and make it evident by their daily walk and conversation that they have escaped the corruption that is in the world through lust. O for more divine holiness of life!

'Am I a sea, or a whale,
that Thou settest a watch over me?'
Job 7:12

This was a strange question for Job to ask of the Lord. He felt himself to be too insignificant to be so strictly watched and chastened, and he hoped that he was not so unruly as to need to be so restrained. The enquiry was natural from one surrounded with such insupportable miseries, but after all, it is capable of a very humbling answer. It is true man is not the sea, but he is even more troublesome and unruly. The sea obediently respects its boundary, and though it be but a belt of sand, it does not overleap the limit. Mighty as it is, it hears the divine *hitherto*, and when most raging with tempest it respects the word; but self-willed man defies heaven and oppresses earth, neither is there any end to his rebellious rage. The sea, obedient to the moon, ebbs and flows with ceaseless regularity, and thus renders an active as well as a passive obedience; but man, restless beyond his sphere, sleeps within the lines of duty, indolent where he should be active. He will neither come nor go at the divine command, but sullenly prefers to do what he should not, and to leave undone that which is required of him. Every drop in the ocean, every beaded bubble, and every yeasty foam-flake, every shell and pebble, feel the power of law and yield or move at once. O that our nature were but one thousandth part as much conformed to the will of God! We call the sea fickle and false, but how constant it is! Since our fathers' days, and the old time before them, the sea is where it was, beating on the same cliffs to the same tune; we *know* where to find it, it forsakes not its bed, and changes not in its ceaseless boom; but where is man - vain, fickle man? Can the wise man guess by what folly he will next be seduced from his obedience? We need more watching than the billowy sea, and are far more rebellious. Lord, rule us for Thine own glory. Amen.

'Bring him unto me'
Mark 9:19

Despairingly the poor disappointed father turned away from the disciples to their Master. His son was in the worst possible condition, and all means had failed, but the miserable child was soon delivered from the evil one when the parent in faith obeyed the Lord Jesus' word, 'Bring him unto me'. Children are a precious gift from God, but much anxiety comes with them. They may be a great joy or a great bitterness to their parents; they may be filled with the Spirit of God, or possessed with the spirit of evil. In all cases, the Word of God gives us one receipt for the curing of all their ills, 'Bring him unto me'. O for more agonising prayer on their behalf while they are yet babes! Sin is there, let our prayers begin to attack it. Our cries for our offspring should precede those cries which betoken their actual advent into a world of sin. In the days of their youth we shall see sad tokens of that dumb and deaf spirit which will neither pray aright, nor hear the voice of God in the soul, but Jesus still commands, 'Bring them unto me'. When they are grown up they may wallow in sin and foam with enmity against God; then when our hearts are breaking we should remember the great Physician's words, 'Bring them unto me'. Never must we cease to pray until they cease to breathe. No case is hopeless while Jesus lives.

The Lord sometimes suffers his people to be driven into a corner that they may experimentally know how necessary He is to them. Ungodly children, when they show us our own powerlessness against the depravity of their hearts, drive us to flee to the strong for strength, and this is a great blessing to us. Whatever our morning's need may be, let it like a strong current bear us to the ocean of divine love. Jesus can soon remove our sorrow, he delights to comfort us. Let us hasten to Him while He waits to meet us.

'Encourage him'
Deuteronomy 1:38

God employs His people to encourage one another. He did not say to an angel, 'Gabriel, my servant Joshua is about to lead my people into Canaan - go, encourage him'. God never works needless miracles; if his purposes can be accomplished by ordinary means, He will not use miraculous agency. Gabriel would not have been half so well fitted for the work as Moses. A brother's sympathy is more precious than an angel's embassy. The angel, swift of wing, had better known the Master's bidding than the people's temper. An angel had never experienced the hardness of the road, nor seen the fiery serpents, nor had he led the stiff-necked multitude in the wilderness as Moses had done. We should be glad that God usually works for man by man. It forms a bond of brotherhood, and being mutually dependent on one another, we are fused more completely into one family. Brethren, take the text as God's message to you. Labour to help others, and especially strive to *encourage* them. Talk cheerily to the young and anxious enquirer, lovingly try to remove stumbling-blocks out of his way. When you find a spark of grace in the heart, kneel down and blow it into a flame. Leave the young believer to discover the roughness of the road by degrees, but tell him of the strength which dwells in God, of the sureness of the promise, and of the charms of communion with Christ. Aim to comfort the sorrowful, and to animate the desponding. Speak a word in season to him that is weary, and encourage those who are fearful to go on their way with gladness. God encourages you by His promises; Christ encourages *you* as He points to the heaven He has won for you, and the Spirit encourages *you* as He works in you to will and to do of His own will and pleasure. Imitate divine wisdom, and encourage others, according to the word of this evening.

> '*If we live in the Spirit,*
> *let us also walk in the Spirit*'
> Galatians 5:25

The two most important things in our holy religion are the *life of faith* and the *walk of faith*. He who shall rightly understand these is not far from being a master in experimental theology, for they are vital points to a Christian. You will never find true faith unattended by true godliness; on the other hand, you will never discover a truly holy life which has not for its root a living faith upon the righteousness of Christ. Woe unto those who seek after the one without the other! There are some who cultivate faith and forget holiness; these may be very high in orthodoxy, but they shall be in very deep in condemnation, for they hold the truth in unrighteousness: and there are others who have strained after holiness of life, but have denied the faith, like the Pharisees of old, of whom the Master said, they were 'whitewashed sepulchres'. We must have faith, for this is the foundation; we must have holiness of life, for this is the superstructure. Of what service is the mere foundation of a building to a man in the day of tempest? Can he hide himself therein? He wants a house to cover him, as well as a foundation for that house. Even so we need the superstructure of spiritual life if we would have comfort in the day of doubt. But seek not a holy life without faith, for that would be to erect a house which can afford no permanent shelter, because it has no foundation on a rock. Let faith and life be put together, and, like the two abutments of an arch, they will make our piety enduring. Like light and heat streaming from the same sun, they are like full of blessing. Like the two pillars of the temple, they are for glory and for beauty. They are two streams from the fountain of grace; two lamps lit with holy fire; two olive trees watered by heavenly care. O Lord, give us this day life within, and it will reveal itself without to thy glory.

'And they follow me'
John 10:27

We should follow our Lord as unhesitatingly as sheep follow their shepherd, for *He has a right to lead us wherever He pleases.* We are not our own, we are bought with a price - let us recognise the rights of the redeeming blood. The soldier follows his captain, the servant obeys his master, much more must we follow our Redeemer, to whom we are a purchased possession. We are not true to our profession of being Christians, if we question the bidding of our Leader and Commander. Submission is our duty, cavilling is our folly. Often might our Lord say to us as to Peter, 'What is that to thee? follow thou Me'. Wherever Jesus may lead us, *He goes before us.* If we know not where we go, we know *with whom* we go. With such a companion, who will dread the perils of the road? The journey may be long, but His everlasting arms will carry us to the end. The presence of Jesus is the assurance of eternal salvation, because He lives, we shall live also. We should follow Christ in simplicity and faith, because *the paths in which He leads us all end in glory and immortality.* It is true they may not be *smooth* paths - they may be covered with sharp flinty trials, but they lead to the 'city which hath foundations, whose builder and maker is God'. 'All the paths of the Lord are mercy and truth unto such as keep His covenant.' Let us put full trust in our Leader, since we know that, come prosperity or adversity, sickness or health, popularity or contempt, his purpose shall be worked out, and that purpose shall be pure, unmingled good to every heir of mercy. We shall find it sweet to go up the bleak side of the hill with Christ; and when rain and snow blow into our faces, His dear love will make us far more blest than those who sit at home and warm their hands at the world's fire. To the top of Amana, to the dens of lions, or to the hills of leopards, we will follow our Beloved Precious Jesus, draw us, and we will run after Thee.

'The liberty wherewith Christ hath made us free'
Galatians 5:1

This 'liberty' makes us *free to* heaven's charter - *the Bible*. Here is a choice passage, believer, 'When thou passest through the rivers I will be with thee'. You are free to that. Here is another: 'The mountains shall depart, and the hills be removed, but my kindness shall not depart from thee'; you are free to that. You are a welcome guest at the table of the promises. Scripture is a never-failing treasury filled with boundless stores of grace. It is the bank of heaven; you may draw from it as much as you please, without let or hindrance. Come in faith and you are welcome to all *covenant blessings*. There is not a promise in the Word which shall be withheld. In the depths of tribulations let this freedom comfort you; amidst waves of distress let it cheer you; when sorrows surround thee let it be thy solace. This is thy Father's love-token; thou art free to it at all times. Thou art also *free to the throne of grace*. It is the believer's privilege to have access at all times to His heavenly Father. Whatever our desires, our difficulties, our wants, we are at liberty to spread all before Him. It matters not how much we may have sinned, we may ask and expect pardon. It signifies nothing how poor we are, we may plead His promise that He will provide all things needful. We have permission to approach His throne at all times - in midnight's darkest hour, or in noontide's most burning heat. Exercise thy right, O believer, and live up to thy privilege. Thou art free to all that is treasured up *in Christ* - wisdom, righteousness, sanctification, and redemption. It matters not what thy need is, for there is fulness of supply in Christ, and it is there *for thee*. O what a 'freedom' is thine! Freedom from condemnation, freedom to the promises, freedom to the throne of grace, and at last freedom to enter heaven!

'For this child I prayed'
1 Samuel 1:27

Devout souls delight to look upon those mercies which
they have obtained in answer to supplication, for they
can see God's especial love in them. When we can
name our blessings, Samuel, that is, 'asked of God',
they will be as dear to us as her child was to Hannah.
Peninnah had many children, but they came as common
blessings unsought in prayer: Hannah's one heaven-
given child was dearer far, because he was the fruit of
earnest pleadings. How sweet was that water to Samson which he found at 'the well of him that prayed'!
Quassia cups turn all waters bitter, but the cup of prayer
puts a sweetness into the draughts it brings. Did we
pray for the conversion of our children? How doubly
sweet, when they are saved, to see in them our own
petitions fulfilled! Better to rejoice over them as the
fruit of our pleadings than as the fruit of our bodies.
Have we sought of the Lord some choice spiritual gift?
When it comes to us it will be wrapped up in the gold
cloth of God's faithfulness and truth, and so be doubly
precious. Have we petitioned for success in the Lord's
work? How joyful is the prosperity which comes flying
upon the wings of prayer! It is always best to get
blessings into our house in the legitimate way, by the
door of prayer; then they are blessings indeed, and not
temptations. Even when prayer speeds not, the blessings grow all the richer for the delay; the child Jesus
was all the more lovely in the eyes of Mary when she
found Him after having sought Him sorrowing. That
which we win by prayer we should dedicate to God, as
Hannah dedicated Samuel. The gift came from heaven,
let it go to heaven. Prayer brought it, gratitude sung
over it, let devotion consecrate it. Here will be a special
occasion for saying, 'Of Thine own have I given unto
Thee'. Reader, is prayer your element or your weariness? Which?

'The sword of the Lord, and of Gideon'
Judges 7:20

Gideon ordered his men to do two things: covering up a torch in an earthen pitcher, he bade them, at an appointed signal, break the pitcher and let the light shine, and then sound with the trumpet, crying, 'The sword of the Lord, and of Gideon! the sword of the Lord, and of Gideon!' This is precisely what all Christians must do. First, *you must shine*; break the pitcher which conceals your light; throw aside the bushel which has been hiding your candle, and shine. Let your light shine before men; let your good works be such, that when men look upon you, they shall know that you have been with Jesus. Then *there must be the sound*, the blowing of the trumpet. There must be active exertions for the ingathering of sinners by proclaiming Christ crucified. Take the gospel to them; carry it to their door; put it in their way; do not suffer them to escape it; blow the trumpet right against their ears. Remember that the true war-cry of the Church is Gideon's watchword, *'The sword of the Lord*, and of Gideon!'. God must do it, it is His own work. But we are not to be idle; instrumentality is to be used - 'The sword of the Lord, *and of Gideon*!'. If we only cry, 'The sword of the Lord!' we shall be guilty of an idle presumption; and if we shout, 'The sword of Gideon!' alone, we shall manifest idolatrous reliance on an arm of flesh: we must blend the two in practical harmony, 'The sword of the Lord, and of Gideon!'. We can do nothing of ourselves, but we can do everything by the help of our God; let us, therefore, in His name determine to go out personally and serve with our flaming torch of holy example, and with our trumpet tones of earnest declaration and testimony, and God shall be with us, and Midian shall be put to confusion, and the Lord of hosts shall reign for ever and ever.

'In the evening withhold not thy hand'
Ecclesiastes 11:6

In *the evening of the day* opportunities are plentiful: men return from their labour, and the zealous soul-winner finds time to tell abroad the love of Jesus. Have I no evening work for Jesus? If I have not, let me no longer withhold my hand from a service which requires abundant labour. Sinners are perishing for lack of knowledge; he who loiters may find his skirts crimson with the blood of souls. Jesus gave both his hands to the nails, how can I keep back one of mine from His blessed work? Night and day he toiled and prayed for me, how can I give a single hour to the pampering of my flesh with luxurious ease? Up, idle heart; stretch out thy hand to work, or uplift it to pray; heaven and hell are in earnest, let me be so, and this evening sow good seed for the Lord my God.

The evening of life has also its calls. Life is so short that a morning of manhood's vigour, and an evening of decay, make the whole of it. To some it seems long, but a fourpence is a great sum of money to a poor man. Life is so brief that no man can afford to lose a day. It has been well said that if a great king should bring us a great heap of gold, and bid us take as much as we could count in a day, we should make a long day of it; we should begin early in the morning, and in the evening we should not withhold our hand; but to win souls is far nobler work, how is it that we so soon withdraw from it? Some are spared to a long evening of green old age; if such be my case, let me use such talents as I still retain, and to the last hour serve my blessed and faithful Lord. By His grace I will die in harness, and lay down my charge only when I lay down my body. Age may instruct the young, cheer the faint, and encourage the desponding; if eventide has less of vigorous heat, it should have more of calm wisdom, therefore in the evening I will not withhold my hand.

'I will rejoice over them to do them good'
Jeremiah 32:41

How heart-cheering to the believer is the delight which God has in His saints! We cannot see any reason in ourselves why the Lord should take pleasure in us; we cannot take delight in ourselves, for we often have to groan, being burdened; conscious of our sinfulness, and deploring our unfaithfulness; and we fear that God's people cannot take much delight in us, for they must perceive so much of our imperfections and our follies, that they may rather lament our infirmities than admire our graces. But we love to dwell upon this transcendent truth, this glorious mystery: that as the bridegroom rejoiceth over the bride, so does the Lord rejoice over us. We do not read anywhere that God delighteth in the cloud-capped mountains, or the sparkling stars, but we do read that He delighteth in the habitable parts of the earth, and that His delights are with the sons of men. We do not find it written that even angels give His soul delight; nor doth He say, concerning cherubim and seraphim, 'Thou shalt be called Hephzibah, for the Lord delighteth in thee'; but He does say all that to poor fallen creatures like ourselves, debased and depraved by sin, but saved, exalted, and glorified by His grace. In what strong language He expresses His delight in his people! Who could have conceived of the eternal One as bursting forth into a song? Yet it is written, 'He will rejoice over thee with joy, He will rest in His love, He will joy over thee with singing'. As He looked upon the world He had made, He said, 'It is very good'; but when He beheld those who are the purchase of Jesus' blood, His own chosen ones, it seemed as if the great heart of the Infinite could restrain itself no longer, but overflowed in divine exclamations of joy. Should not we utter our grateful response to such a marvellous declaration of His love, and sing, 'I will rejoice in the Lord, I will joy in the God of my salvation'?

'Gather not my soul with sinners'
Psalm 26:9

Fear made David pray thus, for something whispered, 'Perhaps after all, thou mayest be gathered with the wicked'. That fear, although marred by unbelief, springs, in the main, from holy anxiety, arising from the recollection of past sin. Even the pardoned man will enquire, 'What if at the end my sins should be remembered, and I should be left out of the catalogue of the saved?' He recollects his present unfruitfulness - so little grace, so little love, so little holiness, and looking forward to the future, he considers his weakness and the many temptations which beset him, and he fears that he may fall, and become a prey to the enemy. A sense of sin and present evil, and his prevailing corruptions, compel him to pray, in fear and trembling, 'Gather not my soul with sinners'. Reader, if you have prayed this prayer, and if your character be rightly described in the Psalm from which it is taken, you need not be afraid that you shall be gathered with sinners. Have you the two virtues which David had - the outward walking in integrity, and the inward trusting in the Lord? Are you resting upon Christ's sacrifice, and can you compass the altar of God with humble hope. If so, rest assured, with the wicked you never shall be gathered, for that calamity is impossible. The gathering at the judgment is like to like. 'Gather ye together first the tares, and bind them in bundles to burn them: but gather the wheat into my barn.' If, then, thou art *like* God's people, thou shalt be *with* God's people. You cannot be gathered with the wicked, for you are too dearly bought. Redeemed by the blood of Christ, you are His for ever, and where He is, there must His people be. You are loved too much to be cast away with reprobates. Shall one dear to Christ perish? Impossible! Hell cannot hold thee! Heaven claims thee! Trust in thy Surety and fear not!

'Let Israel rejoice in him'
Psalm 149:2

Be glad of heart, O believer, but take care that thy gladness has its spring *in the Lord*. Thou hast much cause for gladness in thy God, for thou canst sing with David, 'God, my exceeding joy'. Be glad that the Lord reigneth, that Jehovah is King! Rejoice that He sits upon the throne, and ruleth all things! Every attribute of God should become a fresh ray in the sunlight of our gladness. That He is *wise* should make us glad, knowing as we do our own foolishness. That He is *mighty*, should cause us to rejoice who tremble at our weakness. That He is *everlasting*, should always be a theme of joy when we know that *we* wither as the grass. That He is *unchanging*, should perpetually yield us a song, since *we* change every hour. That He is full of grace, that He is overflowing with it, and that this grace in covenant He has given to us; that it is ours to cleanse us, ours to keep us, ours to sanctify us, ours to perfect us, ours to bring us to glory - all this should tend to make us glad in Him. This gladness in God is as a deep river; we have only as yet touched its brink, we know a little of its clear sweet, heavenly streams, but onward the depth is greater, and the current more impetuous in its joy. The Christian feels that he may delight himself not only in what God *is*, but also in all that God *has done* in the past. The Psalms show us that God's people in olden times were wont to think much of God's actions, and to have a song concerning each of them. So let God's people now rehearse the deeds of the Lord! Let them tell of His mighty acts, and 'sing unto the Lord, for He hath triumphed gloriously'. Nor let them ever cease to sing, for as new mercies flow to them day by day, so should their gladness in the Lord's loving acts in providence and in grace show itself in continued thanksgiving. Be glad ye children of Zion and rejoice in the Lord your God.

'When my heart is overwhelmed:
lead me to the Rock that is higher than I'
Psalm 61:2

Most of us know what it is to be overwhelmed in heart;
emptied as when a man wipeth a dish and turneth it
upside down; submerged and thrown on our beam ends
like a vessel mastered by the storm. Discoveries of
inward corruption will do this, if the Lord permits the
great deep of our depravity to become troubled and cast
up mire and dirt. Disappointments and heartbreaks will
do this when billow after billow rolls over us, and we
are like a broken shell hurled to and fro by the surf.
Blessed be God, at such seasons we are not without an
all-sufficient solace, our God is the harbour of weather-
beaten sails, the hospice of forlorn pilgrims. Higher
than we are is He, His mercy higher than our sins, His
love higher than our thoughts. It is pitiful to see men
putting their trust in something lower than themselves;
but our confidence is fixed upon an exceeding high and
glorious Lord. A Rock He is since He changes not, and
a high Rock, because the tempests which overwhelm us
roll far beneath at His feet; He is not disturbed by them,
but rules them at His will. If we get under the shelter
of this lofty Rock we may defy the hurricane; all is calm
under the lee of that towering cliff. Alas! such is the
confusion in which the troubled mind is often cast, that
we need piloting to this divine shelter. Hence the prayer
of the text. O Lord, our God, by Thy Holy Spirit, teach
us the way of faith, lead us into Thy rest. The wind
blows us out to sea, the helm answers not to our puny
hand; Thou, Thou alone canst steer us over the bar
between yon sunken rocks, safe into the fair haven.
How dependent we are upon Thee - we need Thee to
bring us to Thee. To be wisely directed and steered into
safety and peace is Thy gift, and Thine alone. This
night be pleased to deal well with Thy servants.

'Accepted in the beloved'
Ephesians 1:6

What a state of privilege! It includes our *justification* before God, but the term 'acceptance' in the Greek means more than that. It signifies that we are the objects of *divine complacency*, nay, even of *divine delight*. How marvellous that we, worms, mortals, sinners, should be the objects of divine love! But it is only '*in the beloved*'. Some Christians seem to be accepted in their own experience, at least, that is their apprehension. When their spirit is lively, and their hopes bright, they think God accepts them, for they feel so high, so heavenly-minded, so drawn above the earth! But when their souls cleave to the dust, they are the victims of the fear that they are no longer accepted. If they could but see that all their high joys do not exalt them, and all their low despondencies do not really depress them in their Father's sight, but that they stand accepted in one who never alters, in one who is always the beloved of God, always perfect, always without spot or wrinkle, or any such thing, how much happier they would be, and how much more they would honour the Saviour! Rejoice then, believer, in this: thou art accepted 'in the beloved'. Thou lookest within, and thou sayest, 'There is nothing acceptable *here*!' But look at Christ, and see if there is not everything acceptable *there*. Thy sins trouble thee; but God has cast thy sins behind His back, and thou art accepted in the Righteous One. Thou hast to fight with corruption, and to wrestle with temptation, but thou art already accepted in Him who has overcome the powers of evil. The devil tempts thee; be of good cheer, he cannot destroy thee, for thou art accepted in Him who has broken Satan's head. Know by full assurance thy glorious standing. Even glorified souls are not more accepted than thou art. They are only accepted in heaven 'in the beloved', and thou art even now accepted in Christ after the same manner.

'Jesus said unto him, If thou canst believe'
Mark 9:23

A certain man had a demoniac son, who was afflicted with a dumb spirit. The father, having seen the futility of the endeavours of the disciples to heal his child, had little or no faith in Christ, and therefore, when he was bidden to bring his son to Him, he said to Jesus, 'If Thou canst do anything, have compassion on us, and help us'. Now there was an 'if' in the question, but the poor trembling father had put the 'if' in the wrong place: Jesus Christ, therefore, without commanding him to retract the 'if', kindly puts it in its legitimate position. 'Nay, verily,' He seemed to say, 'there should be no "if" about My power, nor concerning My willingness, the "if" lies somewhere else.' *'If thou canst believe,* all things are possible to him that believeth.' The man's trust was strengthened, he offered a humble prayer for an increase of faith, and instantly Jesus spoke the word, and the devil was cast out, with an injunction never to return. There is a lesson here which we need to learn. We, like this man, often see that there is an 'if' somewhere, but we are perpetually blundering by putting it in the wrong place. *If* Jesus can help me - *if* He can give me grace to overcome temptation - *if* He can give me pardon - *if* He can make me successful? Nay, *if* you can believe, He both can and will. You have misplaced your 'if'. If you can confidently trust, even as all things are possible to Christ, so shall all things be possible to you. Faith standeth in God's power, and is robed in God's majesty; it weareth the royal apparel, and rideth on the King's horse, for it is the grace which the King delighteth to honour. Girding itself with the glorious might of the all-working Spirit, it becomes, in the omnipotence of God, mighty to do, to dare, and to suffer. All things, without limit, are possible to him that believeth. My soul, canst thou believe thy Lord tonight?

'*For I was ashamed to require of the king a band of soldiers and horsemen to help us against the enemy in the way: because we had spoken unto the king, saying, The hand of our God is upon all them for good that seek Him; but His power and his wrath is against all them that forsake Him*'

Ezra 8:22

A convoy on many accounts would have been desirable for the pilgrim band, but a holy shamefacedness would not allow Ezra to seek one. He feared lest the heathen king should think his professions of faith in God to be mere hypocrisy, or imagine that the God of Israel was not able to preserve His own worshippers. He could not bring his mind to lean on an arm of flesh in a matter so evidently of the Lord, and therefore the caravan set out with no visible protection, guarded by Him who is the sword and shield of His people. It is to be feared that few believers feel this holy jealousy for God; even those who in a measure walk by faith, occasionally mar the lustre of their life by craving aid from man. It is a most blessed thing to have no props and no buttresses, but to stand upright on the Rock of Ages, upheld by the Lord alone. Would any believers seek state endowments for their Church, if they remembered that the Lord is dishonoured by their asking Caesar's aid? As if the Lord could not supply the needs of His own cause! Should we run so hastily to friends and relations for assistance, if we remembered that the Lord is magnified by our implicit reliance upon His solitary arm? My soul, wait thou only upon God. 'But,' says one, 'are not means to be used?' Assuredly they are; but our fault seldom lies in their neglect: far more frequently it springs out of foolishly believing in them instead of believing in God. Few run too far in neglecting the creature's arm; but very many sin greatly in making too much of it. Learn, dear reader, to glorify the Lord by leaving means untried, if by using them thou wouldst dishonour the name of the Lord.

'I sleep, but my heart waketh'
Solomon's Song 5:2

Paradoxes abound in Christian experience, and here is one - the spouse was asleep, and yet she was awake. He only can read the believer's riddle who has ploughed with the heifer of his experience. The two points in this evening's text are - a mournful sleepiness and a hopeful wakefulness. *I sleep.* Through sin that dwelleth in us we may become lax in holy duties, slothful in religious exercises, dull in spiritual joys, and altogether supine and careless. This is a shameful state for one in whom the quickening Spirit dwells; and it is dangerous to the highest degree. Even wise virgins sometimes slumber, but it is high time for all to shake off the bands of sloth. It is to be feared that many believers lose their strength as Samson lost his locks, while sleeping on the lap of carnal security. With a perishing world around us, to sleep is cruel; with eternity so near at hand, it is madness. Yet we are none of us so much awake as we should be; a few thunder-claps would do us all good, and it may be, unless we soon bestir ourselves, we shall have them in the form of war, or pestilence, or personal bereavements and losses. O that we may leave for ever the couch of fleshly ease, and go forth with flaming torches to meet the coming Bridegroom! *My heart waketh.* This is a happy sign. Life is not extinct, though sadly smothered. When our renewed heart struggles against our natural heaviness, we should be grateful to sovereign grace for keeping a little vitality within the body of this death. Jesus will hear our hearts, will help our hearts, will visit our hearts; for the voice of the wakeful heart is really the voice of our Beloved, saying, 'Open to me'. Holy zeal will surely unbar the door.

> Oh lovely attitude! He stands
> With melting heart and laden hands;
> My soul forsakes her every sin,
> And lets the heavenly stranger in.

'*Just, and the justifier of him which believeth*'
Romans 3:26

Being justified by faith, we have peace with God. Conscience accuses no longer. Judgment now decides for the sinner instead of against him. Memory looks back upon past sins, with deep sorrow for the sin, but yet with no dread of any penalty to come; for Christ has paid the debt of his people to the last jot and tittle, and received the divine receipt; and unless God can be so unjust as to demand double payment for one debt, no soul for whom Jesus died as a substitute can ever be cast into hell. It seems to be one of the very principles of our enlightened nature to believe that God is just; we feel that it must be so, and this gives us our terror at first; but is it not marvellous that this very same belief that God is just, becomes afterwards the pillar of our confidence and peace! If God be just, I, a sinner, alone and without a substitute, must be punished; but Jesus stands in my stead, and is punished for me; and now, if God be just, I, a sinner, standing in Christ, can never be punished. God must change His nature before one soul, for whom Jesus was a substitute, can ever by any possibility suffer the lash of the law. Therefore, Jesus having taken the place of the believer - having rendered a full equivalent to divine wrath for all that His people ought to have suffered as the result of sin, the believer can shout with glorious triumph, 'Who shall lay anything to the charge of God's elect?' Not God, for He hath justified; not Christ, for He hath died, 'yea, rather hath risen again'. My hope lives not because I am not a sinner, but because I am a sinner for whom Christ died; my trust is not that I am holy, but that being unholy, *He* is my righteousness. My faith rests not upon what I am, or shall be, or feel, or know, but in what Christ is, in what He has done, and in what He is now doing for me. On the lion of justice the fair maid of hope rides like a queen.

'Who of God is made unto us wisdom'
1 Corinthians 1:30

Man's intellect seeks after rest, and by nature seeks it apart from the Lord Jesus Christ. Men of education are apt, even when converted, to look upon the simplicities of the cross of Christ with an eye too little reverent and loving. They are snared in the old net in which the Grecians were taken, and have a hankering to mix philosophy with revelation. The temptation with a man of refined thought and high education is to depart from the simple truth of Christ crucified, and to invent, as the term is, a more *intellectual* doctrine. This led the early Christian churches into Gnosticism, and bewitched them with all sorts of heresies. This is the root of Neology, and the other fine things which in days gone by were so fashionable in Germany, and are now so ensnaring to certain classes of divines. Whoever you are, good reader, and whatever your education may be, if you be the Lord's, be assured you will find no rest in philosophising divinity. You may receive this dogma of one great thinker, or that dream of another profound reasoner, but what the chaff is to the wheat, that will these be to the pure word of God. All that reason, when best guided, can find out is but the ABC of truth, and even that lacks certainty, while in Christ Jesus there is treasured up all the fulness of wisdom and knowledge. All attempts on the part of Christians to be content with systems such as Unitarian and Broad-church thinkers would approve of, must fail; true heirs of heaven must come back to the grandly simple reality which makes the ploughboy's eye flash with joy, and glads the pious pauper's heart - 'Jesus Christ came into the world to save sinners'. Jesus satisfies the most elevated intellect when he is believingly received, but apart from Him the mind of the regenerate discovers no rest. 'The fear of the Lord is the beginning of knowledge.' 'A good understanding have all they that do His commandments.'

'The myrtle trees that were in the bottom'
Zechariah 1:8

The vision in this chapter describes the condition of Israel in Zechariah's day; but being interpreted in its aspect towards *us*, it describes the Church of God as we find it now in the world. The Church is compared to a myrtle grove flourishing in a valley. It is *hidden*, unobserved, secreted; courting no honour and attracting no observation from the careless gazer. The Church, like her head, has a glory, but it is concealed from carnal eyes, for the time of her breaking forth in all her splendour is not yet come. The idea of *tranquil security* is also suggested to us: for the myrtle grove in the valley is still and calm, while the storm sweeps over the mountain summits. Tempests spend their force upon the craggy peaks of the Alps, but down yonder where flows the stream which maketh glad the city of our God, the myrtles flourish by the still waters, all unshaken by the impetuous wind. How great is the inward tranquillity of God's Church! Even when opposed and persecuted, she has a peace which the world gives not, and which, therefore, it cannot take away: the peace of God which passeth all understanding keeps the hearts and minds of God's people. Does not the metaphor forcibly picture the peaceful, *perpetual growth* of the saints? The myrtle sheds not her leaves, she is always green; and the Church in her worst time still hath a blessed verdure of grace about her; nay, she has sometimes exhibited *most* verdure when her winter has been sharpest. She has prospered most when her adversities have been most severe. Hence the text *hints at victory*. The myrtle is the emblem of peace, and a significant token of *triumph*. The brows of conquerors were bound with myrtle and with laurel; and is not the Church ever victorious? Is not every Christian more than a conqueror through Him that loved him? Living in peace, do not the saints fall asleep in the arms of victory?

'Howl, fir tree; for the cedar is fallen'
Zechariah 11:2

When in the forest there is heard the crash of a falling oak, it is a sign that the woodman is abroad, and every tree in the whole company may tremble lest tomorrow the sharp edge of the axe should find it out. We are all like trees marked for the axe, and the fall of one should remind us that for every one, whether great as the cedar, or humble as the fir, the appointed hour is stealing on apace. I trust we do not, by often hearing of death, become callous to it. May we never be like the birds in the steeple, which build their nests when the bells are tolling, and sleep quietly when the solemn funeral peals are startling the air. May we regard death as the most weighty of all events, and be sobered by its approach. It ill behoves us to sport while our eternal destiny hangs on a thread. The sword is out of its scabbard - let us not trifle; it is furbished, and the edge is sharp - let us not play with it. He who does not prepare for death is more than an ordinary fool, he is a madman. When the voice of God is heard among the trees of the garden, let fig tree and sycamore, and elm and cedar, alike hear the sound thereof.

Be ready, servant of Christ, for thy Master comes on a sudden, when an ungodly world least expects Him. See to it that thou be faithful in His work, for the grave shall soon be digged for thee. Be ready, parents, see that your children are brought up in the fear of God, for they must soon be orphans; be ready, men of business, take care that your affairs are correct, and that you serve God with all your hearts, for the days of your terrestrial service will soon be ended, and you will be called to give account for the deeds done in the body, whether they be good or whether they be evil. May we all prepare for the tribunal of the great King with a care which shall be rewarded with the gracious commendation, 'Well done, good and faithful servant'.

'Happy art thou, O Israel; who is like unto thee,
O people saved by the Lord?'
Deuteronomy 33:29

He who affirms that Christianity makes men miserable, is himself an utter stranger to it. It were strange indeed, if it made us wretched, for see *to what a position it exalts us*! It makes us sons of God. Suppose you that God will give all the happiness to His enemies, and reserve all the mourning for His own family? Shall His foes have mirth and joy, and shall His home-born children inherit sorrow and wretchedness? Shall the sinner, who has no part in Christ, call himself rich in happiness, and shall we go mourning as if we were penniless beggars? No, we will rejoice in the Lord always, and glory in our inheritance, for we 'have not received the spirit of bondage again to fear; but we have received the spirit of adoption, whereby we cry, Abba, Father'. The rod of chastisement must rest upon us in our measure, but it worketh for us the comfortable fruits of righteousness; and therefore by the aid of the divine Comforter, we, the 'people saved of the Lord', will joy in the God of our salvation. We are married unto Christ; and shall our great Bridegroom permit His spouse to linger in constant grief? Our hearts are knit unto Him: we are His members, and though for awhile we may suffer as our Head once suffered, yet we are even now blessed with heavenly blessings in Him. We have the earnest of our inheritance in the comforts of the Spirit, which are neither few nor small. Heritors of joy for ever, we have foretastes of our portion. There are streaks of the light of joy to herald our eternal sun rising. Our riches are beyond the sea; our city with firm foundations lies on the other side the river; gleams of glory from the spirit-world cheer our hearts, and urge us onward. Truly is it said of us, 'Happy art thou, O Israel; who is like unto thee, O people saved by the Lord?'.

*'My Beloved put in His hand by the hole of the door,
and my bowels were moved for Him'*
Solomon's Song 5:4

Knocking was not enough, for my heart was too full of
sleep, too cold and ungrateful to arise and open the
door, but the touch of His effectual grace has made my
soul bestir itself. Oh, the longsuffering of my Beloved,
to tarry when He found Himself shut out, and me asleep
upon the bed of sloth! Oh, the greatness of His
patience, to knock and knock again, and to add His
voice to His knockings, beseeching me to open to Him!
How could I have refused Him! Base heart, blush and
be confounded! But what greatest kindness of all is
this, that He becomes His own porter and unbars the
door Himself! Thrice blessed is the hand which condescends to lift the latch and turn the key. Now I see that
nothing but my Lord's own power can save such a
naughty mass of wickedness as I am; ordinances fail,
even the gospel has no effect upon me, till His hand is
stretched out. Now, also, I perceive that His hand is
good where all else is unsuccessful, He can open when
nothing else will. Blessed be His name, I feel His
gracious presence even now. Well may my bowels
move for Him, when I think of all that He has suffered
for me, and of my ungenerous return. I have allowed
my affections to wander. I have set up rivals. I have
grieved Him. Sweetest and dearest of all beloveds, I
have treated Thee as an unfaithful wife treats her
husband. Oh, my cruel sins, my cruel self! What can
I do? Tears are a poor show of my repentance, my
whole heart boils with indignation at myself. Wretch
that I am, to treat my Lord, my All in All, my exceeding
great joy, as though He were a stranger. Jesus, thou
forgivest freely, but this is not enough, prevent my
unfaithfulness in the future. Kiss away these tears, and
then purge my heart and bind it with sevenfold cords to
Thyself, never to wander more.

'The Lord looketh from heaven;
He beholdeth all the sons of men'
Psalm 33:13

Perhaps no figure of speech represents God in a more gracious light than when He is spoken of as stooping from His throne, and coming down from heaven to attend to the wants and to behold the woes of mankind. We love Him, who, when Sodom and Gomorrah were full of iniquity, would not destroy those cities until he had made a personal visitation of them. We cannot help pouring out our heart in affection for our Lord who inclines his ear from the highest glory, and puts it to the lip of the dying sinner, whose failing heart longs after reconciliation. How can we but love Him when we know that he numbers the very hairs of our heads, marks our path, and orders our ways? Specially is this great truth brought near to our heart, when we recollect how attentive He is, not merely to the temporal interests of His creatures, but to their spiritual concerns. Though leagues of distance lie between the finite creature and the infinite Creator, yet there are links uniting both. When a tear is wept by thee, think not that God doth not behold; for, 'Like as a father pitieth his children, so the Lord pitieth them that fear Him'. Thy sigh is able to move the heart of Jehovah; thy whisper can incline His ear unto thee; thy prayer can stay His hand; thy faith can move His arm. Think not that God sits on high taking no account of thee. Remember that however poor and needy thou art, yet the Lord thinketh upon thee. For the eyes of the Lord run to and fro throughout the whole earth, to show himself strong in the behalf of them whose heart is perfect towards Him.

Oh! then repeat the truth that never tires;
No God is like the God my soul desires;
He at whose voice heaven trembles, even He,
Great as He is, knows how to stoop to me.

'Once again seven times'
Kings 18:43

Success is certain when the Lord has promised it.
Although you may have pleaded month after month
without evidence of answer, it is not possible that the
Lord should be deaf when His people are earnest in a
matter which concerns His glory. The prophet on the
top of Carmel continued to wrestle with God, and never
for a moment gave way to a fear that he should be non-
suited in Jehovah's courts. Six times the servant
returned, but on each occasion no word was spoken but
'Go again'. We must not dream of unbelief, but hold
to our faith even to seventy times seven. Faith sends
expectant hope to look from Carmel's brow, and if
nothing is beheld, she sends again and again. So far
from being crushed by repeated disappointment, faith
is animated to plead more fervently with her God. She
is humbled but not abashed: her groans are deeper, and
her sighings more vehement, but she never relaxes her
hold or stays her hand. It would be more agreeable to
flesh and blood to have a speedy answer, but believing
souls have learned to be submissive, and to find it good
to wait for as well as upon the Lord. Delayed answers
often set the heart searching itself, and so lead to
contrition and spiritual reformation: deadly blows are
thus struck at our corruption, and the chambers of
imagery are cleansed. The great danger is lest men
should faint, and miss the blessing. Reader, do not fall
into that sin, but continue in prayer and watching. At
last the little cloud was seen, the sure forerunner of
torrents of rain, and even so with you, the token for
good shall surely be given, and you shall rise as a
prevailing prince to enjoy the mercy you have sought.
Elijah was a man of like passions with us: his power
with God did not lie in his own merits. If his believing
prayer availed so much, why not yours? Plead the
precious blood with unceasing importunity, and it shall
be with you according to your desire.

*'Behold, if the leprosy have co red all his flesh, he
shall pronounce him clean th   hath the plague'*
Leviticus 13   3

Strange enough this regulation   pears, yet there was
wisdom in it, for the throwing ou f the disease proved
that the constitution was sound This morning it may
be well for us to see the typical t ching of so singular
a rule. We, too, are lepers, and m   read the law of leper
as applicable to ourselves. Whe   man sees himself to
be altogether lost and ruined, co red all over with the
defilement of sin, and no part fre rom pollution; when
he disclaims all righteousness   his own, and pleads
guilty before the Lord, then is   e clean through the
blood of Jesus, and the grace o od. Hidden, unfelt,
unconfessed iniquity is the true prosy, but when sin
is seen and felt it has received i   death blow, and the
Lord looks with eyes of mercy   on the soul afflicted
with it. Nothing is more deadl   han self-righteousness, or more hopeful than con ition. We must confess that we are 'nothing else b   sin', for no confession short of this will be the who truth, and if the Holy
Spirit be at work with us, conv cing us of sin, there
will be no difficulty about makin such an acknowledgment - it will spring spontaneou   from our lips. What
comfort does the text afford to th e under a deep sense
of sin! Sin mourned and confess d, however black and
foul, shall never shut a man ou rom the Lord Jesus.
Whosoever cometh unto Him,   e will in no wise cast
out. Though dishonest as the thi , though unchaste as
the woman who was a sinner, th ugh fierce as Saul of
Tarsus, though cruel as Manas h, though rebellious
as the prodigal, the great heart   love will look upon
the man who feels himself to hav no soundness in him,
and will pronounce him clean,   en he trusts in Jesus
crucified. Come to Him, then,   or heavy-laden sinner,

Come needy, come guilty, co loathsome and bare;
You can't come too filthy - co e just as you are.

'I found Him whom my soul loveth:
I held Him, and would not let Him go'
Canticles 3:4

Does Christ receive us when we come to Him, notwith-standing all our past sinfulness? Does He never chide us for having tried all other refuges first? And is there none on earth like Him? Is He the best of all the good, the fairest of all the fair? Oh, then let us praise him! Daughters of Jerusalem, extol Him with timbrel and harp! Down with your idols, up with the Lord Jesus. Now let the standards of pomp and pride be trampled under foot, but let the cross of Jesus, which the world frowns and scoffs at, be lifted on high. O for a throne of ivory for our King Solomon! let Him be set on high for ever, and let my soul sit at His footstool, and kiss His feet, and wash them with my tears. Oh, how precious is Christ! How can it be that I have thought so little of Him? How is it I can go abroad for joy or comfort when He is so full, so rich, so satisfying. Fellow believer, make a covenant with thine heart that thou wilt never depart from Him, and ask thy Lord to ratify it. Bid Him set thee as a signet upon His finger, and as a bracelet upon His arm. Ask Him to bind thee about Him, as the bride decketh herself with orna-ments, and as the bridegroom putteth on his jewels. I would live in Christ's heart; in the clefts of that rock my soul would eternally abide. The sparrow hath made a house, and the swallow a nest for herself where she may lay her young, even thine altars, O Lord of hosts, my King and my God; and so too would I make my nest, my home, in Thee, and never from Thee may the soul of Thy turtle dove go forth again, but may I nestle close to Thee, O Jesus, my true and only rest.

When my precious Lord I find,
All my ardent passions glow;
Him with cords of love I bind,
Hold and will not let Him go.

*'Sing forth the honour of His name:
make His praise glorious'*
Psalm 66:2

It is not left to our own option whether we shall praise God or not. Praise is God's most righteous due, and every Christian, as the recipient of His grace, is bound to praise God from day to day. It is true we have no authoritative rubric for daily praise; we have no commandment prescribing certain hours of song and thanksgiving: but the law written upon the heart teaches us that it is right to praise God; and the unwritten mandate comes to us with as much force as if it had been recorded on the tables of stone, or handed to us from the top of thundering Sinai. Yes, it is the Christian's *duty* to praise God. It is not only a pleasurable exercise, but it is the absolute obligation of his life. Think not ye who are always mourning, that ye are guiltless in this respect, or imagine that ye can discharge your duty to your God without songs of praise. You are bound by the bonds of his love to bless His name so long as you live, and His praise should continually be in your mouth, for you are blessed, in order that you may bless Him; 'this people have I formed for myself, they shall show forth my praise'; and if you do not praise God, you are not bringing forth the fruit which He, as the Divine Husbandman, has a right to expect at your hands. Let not your harp then hang upon the willows, but take it down, and strive, with a grateful heart, to bring forth its loudest music. Arise and chant His praise. With every morning's dawn, lift up your notes of thanksgiving, and let every setting sun be followed with your song. Girdle the earth with your praises; surround it with an atmosphere of melody, and God Himself will hearken from heaven and accept your music.

E'en so I love Thee, and will love,
   And in Thy praise will sing,
Because Thou art my loving God,
   And my redeeming King.

'*A living dog is better than a dead lion*'
Ecclesiastes 9:4

Life is a precious thing, and in its humblest form it is superior to death. This truth is eminently certain in spiritual things. It is better to be the least in the kingdom of heaven than the greatest out of it. The lowest degree of grace is superior to the noblest development of unregenerate nature. Where the Holy Ghost implants divine life in the soul, there is a precious deposit which none of the refinements of education can equal. The thief on the cross excels Caesar on his throne; Lazarus among the dogs is better than Cicero among the senators; and the most unlettered Christian is in the sight of God superior to Plato. Life is the badge of nobility in the realm of spiritual things, and men without it are only coarser or finer specimens of the same lifeless material, needing to be quickened, for they are dead in trespasses and sins.

A living, loving, gospel sermon, however unlearned in matter and uncouth in style, is better than the finest discourse devoid of unction and power. A living dog keeps better watch than a dead lion, and is of more service to his master; and so the poorest spiritual preacher is infinitely to be preferred to the exquisite orator who has no wisdom but that of words, no energy but that of sound. The like holds good of our prayers and other religious exercises; if we are quickened in them by the Holy Spirit, they are acceptable to God through Jesus Christ, though we may think them to be worthless things; while our grand performances in which our hearts were absent, like dead lions, are mere carrion in the sight of the living God. O for living groans, living sighs, living despondencies, rather than lifeless songs and dead calms. Better anything than death. The snarlings of the dog of hell will at least keep us awake, but dead faith and dead profession, what greater curses can a man have? Quicken us, quicken us, O Lord!

October

'Pleasant fruits, new and old,
which I have laid up for thee, O my beloved'
Canticles 7:13

The spouse desires to give to Jesus all that she produces. Our heart has 'all manner of pleasant fruits', both 'new and old', and they are laid up for our Beloved. At this rich autumnal season of fruit, let us survey our stores. We have *new* fruits. We desire to feel new life, new joy, new gratitude; we wish to make new resolves and carry them out by new labours; our heart blossoms with new prayers, and our soul is pledging herself to new efforts. But we have some *old* fruits too. There is our first love: a choice fruit that! and Jesus delights in it. There is our first faith: that simple faith by which, having nothing, we became possessors of all things. There is our joy when first we knew the Lord: let us revive it. We have our old remembrances of the promises. How faithful has God been! In sickness, how softly did He make our bed! In deep waters, how placidly did He buoy us up! In the flaming furnace, how graciously did He deliver us. Old fruits, indeed! we have many of them, for His mercies have been more than the hairs of our head. Old sins we must regret, but then we have had repentances which He has given us, by which we have wept our way to the cross, and learned the merit of His blood. We have fruits, this morning both new and old; but here is the point - *they are all laid up for Jesus*. Truly, those are the best and most acceptable services in which Jesus is the solitary aim of the soul, and His glory, without any admixture whatever, the end of all our efforts. Let our many fruits be laid up only for our Beloved; let us display them when He is with us, and not hold them up before the gaze of men. Jesus, we will turn the key in our garden door, and none shall enter to rob Thee of one good fruit from the soil which Thou hast watered with Thy bloody sweat. Our all shall be Thine, Thine only, O Jesus, our Beloved!

'He will give grace and glory'
Psalm 84:11

Bounteous is Jehovah in His nature; to give is His delight. His gifts are beyond measure precious, and are as freely given as the light of the sun. He gives grace to His elect because He wills it, to His redeemed because of His covenant, to the called because of His promise, to believers because they seek it, to sinners because they need it. He gives grace abundantly, seasonably, constantly, readily, sovereignly; doubly enhancing the value of the boon by the manner of its bestowal. Grace in all its forms He freely renders to His people: comforting, preserving, sanctifying, directing, instructing, assisting grace, He generously pours into their souls without ceasing, and He always will do so, whatever may occur. Sickness may befall, but the Lord will give grace; poverty may happen to us, but grace will surely be afforded; death must come, but grace will light a candle at the darkest hour. Reader, how blessed it is as years roll round, and the leaves begin again to fall, to enjoy such an unfading promise as this, 'The Lord will give grace'.

The little conjunction *and* in this verse is a diamond rivet binding the present with the future: grace and glory always go together. God has married them, and none can divorce them. The Lord will never deny a soul glory to whom He has freely given to live upon His grace; indeed, glory is nothing more than grace in its Sabbath dress, grace in full bloom, grace like autumn fruit, mellow and perfected. How soon we may have glory none can tell! It may be before this month of October has run out we shall see the Holy City; but be the interval longer or shorter, we shall be glorified ere long. Glory, the glory of heaven, the glory of eternity, the glory of Jesus, the glory of the Father, the Lord will surely give to His chosen. Oh, rare promise of a faithful God!

Two golden links of one celestial chain:
Who owneth grace shall surely glory gain.

'The hope which is laid up for you in heaven'
Colossians 1:5

Our hope in Christ for the future is the mainspring and the mainstay of our joy here. It will animate our hearts to think often of heaven, for all that we can desire is promised there. Here we are weary and toilworn, but yonder is the land of *rest* where the sweat of labour shall no more bedew the worker's brow, and fatigue shall be for ever banished. To those who are weary and spent, the word 'rest' is full of heaven. We are always in the field of battle; we are so tempted within, and so molested by foes without, that we have little or no peace; but in heaven we shall enjoy the *victory*, when the banner shall be waved aloft in triumph, and the sword shall be sheathed, and we shall hear our Captain say, 'Well done, good and faithful servant'. We have suffered bereavement after bereavement, but we are going to the land of the *immortal* where graves are unknown things. Here sin is a constant grief to us, but there we shall be perfectly *holy*, for there shall by no means enter into that kingdom anything which defileth. Hemlock springs not up in the furrows of celestial fields. Oh! is it not joy, that you are not to be in banishment for ever, that you are not to dwell eternally in this wilderness, but shall soon inherit Canaan? Nevertheless let it never be said of us, that we are dreaming about the *future* and forgetting the *present*, let the future sanctify the present to highest uses. Through the Spirit of God the hope of heaven is the most potent force for the product of virtue; it is a fountain of joyous effort, it is the cornerstone of cheerful holiness. The man who has this hope in him goes about his work with vigour, for the joy of the Lord is his strength. He fights against temptation with ardour, for the hope of the next world repels the fiery darts of the adversary. He can labour without present reward, for he looks for a reward in the world to come.

'A man greatly beloved'
Daniel 10:11

Child of God, do you hesitate to appropriate this title? Ah! has your unbelief made you forget that *you* are greatly beloved too? Must you not have been greatly beloved, to have been bought with the precious blood of Christ, as of a lamb without blemish and without spot? When God smote His only begotten Son for you, what was this but being greatly beloved? You lived in sin, and rioted in it, must you not have been greatly beloved for God to have borne so patiently with you? You were called by grace and led to a Saviour, and made a child of God and an heir of heaven. All this proves, does it not, a very great and superabounding love? Since that time, whether your path has been rough with troubles, or smooth with mercies, it has been full of proofs that you are a man greatly beloved. If the Lord has chastened you, yet not in anger; if He has made you poor, yet in grace you have been rich. The more unworthy you feel yourself to be, the more evidence have you that nothing but unspeakable love could have led the Lord Jesus to save such a soul as yours. The more demerit you feel, the clearer is the display of the abounding love of God in having chosen you, and called you, and made you an heir of bliss. Now, if there be such love between God and us let us live in the influence and sweetness of it, and use the privilege of our position. Do not let us approach our Lord as though we were strangers, or as though He were unwilling to hear us - for we are greatly beloved by our loving Father. 'He that spared not His own Son, but delivered Him up for us all, how shall He not with Him also freely give us all things?' Come boldly, O believer, for despite the whisperings of Satan and the doubtings of thine own heart, thou art greatly beloved. Meditate on the exceeding greatness and faithfulness of divine love this evening, and so go to thy bed in peace.

> *'Are they not all ministering spirits, sent forth to minister for them who shall be heirs of salvation?'*
> Hebrews 1:14

Angels are the unseen attendants of the saints of God; they bear us up in their hands, lest we dash our foot against a stone. Loyalty to their Lord leads them to take a deep interest in the children of His love; they rejoice over the return of the prodigal to his father's house below, and they welcome the advent of the believer to the King's palace above. In olden times the sons of God were favoured with their visible appearance, and at this day, although unseen by us, heaven is still opened, and the angels of God ascend and descend upon the Son of man, that they may visit the heirs of salvation. Seraphim still fly with live coals from off the altar to touch the lips of men greatly beloved. If our eyes could be opened, we should see horses of fire and chariots of fire about the servants of the Lord; for we have come to an innumerable company of angels, who are all watchers and protectors of the seed-royal. Spenser's line is no poetic fiction, where he sings:

> How oft do they with golden pinions cleave
> The flitting skies, like flying pursuivant
> Against foul fiends to aid us militant!

To what dignity are the chosen elevated when the brilliant courtiers of heaven become their willing servitors! Into what communion are we raised since we have intercourse with spotless celestials! How well are we defended since all the twenty thousand chariots of God are armed for our deliverance! To whom do we owe all this? Let the Lord Jesus Christ be for ever endeared to us, for through Him we are made to sit in heavenly places far above principalities and powers. He it is whose camp is round about them that fear Him; He is the true Michael whose foot is upon the dragon. All hail, Jesus! thou Angel of Jehovah's presence, to Thee this family offers its morning vows.

'He Himself hath suffered being tempted'
Hebrews 2:18

It is a commonplace thought, and yet it tastes like nectar to the weary heart - Jesus was tempted as I am. You have heard that truth many times: have you grasped it? He was tempted to the very same sins into which we fall. Do not dissociate Jesus from our common manhood. It is a dark room which you are going through, but Jesus went through it before. It is a sharp fight which you are waging, but Jesus has stood foot to foot with the same enemy. Let us be of good cheer, Christ has borne the load before us, and the bloodstained footsteps of the King of glory may be seen along the road which we traverse at this hour. There is something sweeter yet - Jesus was tempted, but Jesus never sinned. Then, my soul, it is not needful for thee to sin, for Jesus was a man, and if one man endured these temptations and sinned not, then in His power His members may also cease from sin. Some beginners in the divine life think that they cannot be tempted without sinning, but they mistake; there is no sin in *being tempted*, but there *is* sin in *yielding to temptation*. Herein is comfort for the sorely tempted ones. There is still more to encourage them if they reflect that the Lord Jesus, though tempted, gloriously triumphed, and as He overcame, so surely shall His followers also, for Jesus is the representative man for His people; the Head has triumphed, and the members share in the victory. Fears are needless, for Christ is with us, armed for our defence. Our place of safety is the bosom of the Saviour. Perhaps we are tempted just now, in order to drive us nearer to Him. Blessed be any wind that blows us into the port of our Saviour's love! Happy wounds, which make us seek the beloved Physician. Ye tempted ones, come to your tempted Saviour, for He can be touched with a feeling of your infirmities, and will succour every tried and tempted one.

'At evening time it shall be light'
Zechariah 14:7

Oftentimes we look forward with forebodings to *the time of old age*, forgetful that at eventide it shall be light. To many saints, old age is the choicest season in their lives. A balmier air fans the mariner's cheek as he nears the shore of immortality, fewer waves ruffle his sea, quiet reigns, deep, still and solemn. From the altar of age the flashes of the fire of youth are gone, but the more real flame of earnest feeling remains. The pilgrims have reached the land Beulah, that happy country, whose days are as the days of heaven upon earth. Angels visit it, celestial gales blow over it, flowers of paradise grow in it, and the air is filled with seraphic music. Some dwell here for years, and others come to it but a few hours before their departure, but it is an Eden on earth. We may well long for the time when we shall recline in its shady groves and be satisfied with hope until the time of fruition comes. The setting sun seems larger than when aloft in the sky, and a splendour of glory tinges all the clouds which surround his going down. Pain breaks not the calm of the sweet twilight of age, for strength made perfect in weakness bears up with patience under it all. Ripe fruits of choice experience are gathered as the rare repast of life's evening, and the soul prepares itself for rest.

The Lord's people shall also enjoy light in *the hour of death*. Unbelief laments; the shadows fall, the night is coming, existence is ending. Ah no, crieth faith, the night is far spent, the true day is at hand. Light is come, the light of immortality, the light of a Father's countenance. Gather up thy feet in the bed, see the waiting band of spirits! Angels waft thee away. Farewell, beloved one, thou art gone, thou wavest thine hand. Ah, now it is light. The pearly gates are open, the golden streets shine in the jasper light. We cover our eyes but thou beholdest the unseen; adieu, brother, thou hast light at eventide, such as we have not yet.

*'If any man sin, we have an advocate with the
Father, Jesus Christ the righteous'*
1 John 2:1

'If any man sin, we *have* an advocate.' Yes, though we sin; we have Him still. John does not say, 'If any man sin he has forfeited his advocate', but 'we *have* an advocate', sinners though we be. All the sin that a believer ever did, or can be allowed to commit, cannot destroy his interest in the Lord Jesus Christ as his advocate. The name here given to our Lord is suggestive. '*Jesus.*' Ah! then He is an advocate such as we need, for Jesus is the name of one whose business and delight it is to save. 'They shall call His name Jesus, for *He shall save* His people from their sins.' His sweetest name implies His success. Next, it is 'Jesus *Christ*' - Christos, the anointed. This shows *His authority* to plead. The Christ has a right to plead, for He is the Father's own appointed advocate and elected priest. If He were of our choosing He might fail, but if God hath laid help upon one that is mighty, we may safely lay our trouble where God has laid his help. He is Christ, and therefore authorised; He is Christ, and therefore *qualified*, for the anointing has fully fitted Him for His work. He can plead so as to move the heart of God and prevail. What words of tenderness, what sentences of persuasion will the anointed use when He stands up to plead for me! One more letter of His name remains, 'Jesus Christ *the righteous*'. This is not only His character, BUT His plea. It is His character, and if the Righteous One be my advocate, then my cause is good, or He would not have espoused it. It is His plea, for He meets the charge of unrighteousness against me by the plea that *He* is righteous. He declares Himself my substitute and puts His obedience to my account. My soul, thou hast a friend well fitted to be thine advocate, He cannot but succeed; leave thyself entirely in His hands.

*'He arose, and did eat and drink, and went in the
strength of that meat forty days and forty nights'*
1 Kings 19:8

All the strength supplied to us by our gracious God is
meant for service, not for wantonness or boasting.
When the prophet Elijah found the cake baked on the
coals, and the cruse of water placed at his head, as he
lay under the juniper tree, he was no gentleman to be
gratified with dainty fare that he might stretch himself
at his ease; far otherwise, he was commissioned to go
forty days and forty nights in the strength of it,
journeying towards Horeb, the mount of God. When
the Master invited the disciples to 'Come and dine'
with Him, after the feast was concluded He said to
Peter, 'Feed my sheep'; further adding, 'Follow me'.
Even thus it is with us; we eat the bread of heaven, that
we may expend our strength in the Master's service.
We come to the Passover, and eat of the paschal lamb
with loins girt and staff in hand, so as to start off at once
when we have satisfied our hunger. Some Christians
are for living *on* Christ, but are not so anxious to live
for Christ. Earth should be a preparation for heaven;
and heaven is the place where saints feast most and
work most. They sit down at the table of our Lord, and
they serve Him day and night in His temple. They eat
of heavenly food and render perfect service. Believer,
in the strength you daily gain from Christ labour for
Him. Some of us have yet to learn much concerning the
design of our Lord in giving us His grace. We are not
to retain the precious grains of truth as the Egyptian
mummy held the wheat for ages, without giving it an
opportunity to grow: we must sow it and water it. Why
does the Lord send down the rain upon the thirsty earth,
and give the genial sunshine? Is it not that these may all
help the fruits of the earth to yield food for man? Even
so the Lord feeds and refreshes our souls that we may
afterwards use our renewed strength in the promotion
of His glory.

'He that believeth and is baptised shall be saved'
Mark 16:16

Mr Macdonald asked the inhabitants of the island of St Kilda how a man must be saved. An old man replied, 'We shall be saved if we repent, and forsake our sins, and turn to God.' 'Yes,' said a middle-aged female, 'and with a true heart too.' 'Ay,' replied a third, 'and with prayer.' And, added a fourth, 'It must be the prayer of the heart.' 'And we must be diligent too,' said a fifth, 'in keeping the commandments.' Thus, each having contributed his mite, feeling that a very decent creed had been made up, they all looked and listened for the preacher's approbation, but they had aroused his deepest pity. The carnal mind always maps out for itself a way in which self can work and become great, but the Lord's way is quite the reverse. Believing and being baptised are no matters of merit to be gloried in - they are so simple that boasting is excluded, and free grace bears the palm. It may be that the reader is unsaved - what is the reason? Do you think the way of salvation as laid down in the text to be dubious? How can that be when God has pledged His own word for its certainty? Do you think it too easy? Why, then, do you not attend to it? Its ease leaves those without excuse who neglect it. To believe is simply to trust, to depend, to rely upon Christ Jesus. To be baptised is to submit to the ordinance which our Lord fulfilled at Jordan, to which the converted ones submitted at Pentecost, to which the jailer yielded obedience the very night of his conversion. The outward sign saves not, but it sets forth to us our death, burial, and resurrection with Jesus, and, like the Lord's Supper, is not to be neglected. Reader, do you believe in Jesus? Then, dear friend, dismiss your fears, you shall be saved. Are you still an unbeliever, then remember there is but one door, and if you will not enter by it you will perish in your sins.

*'Whosoever drinketh of the water that I
shall give him shall never thirst'*
John 4:14

He who is a believer in Jesus finds enough in his Lord
to satisfy him now, and to content him for evermore.
The believer is not the man whose days are weary for
want of comfort, and whose nights are long from
absence of heart-cheering thought, for he finds in
religion such a spring of joy, such a fountain of
consolation, that he is content and happy. Put him in a
dungeon and he will find good company; place him in
a barren wilderness, he will eat the bread of heaven;
drive him away from friendship, he will meet the
'friend that sticketh closer than a brother'. Blast all his
gourds, and he will find shadow beneath the Rock of
Ages; sap the foundation of his earthly hopes, but his
heart will still be fixed, trusting in the Lord. The heart
is as insatiable as the grave till Jesus enters it, and then
it is a cup full to overflowing. There is such a fulness
in Christ that he alone is the believer's all. The true
saint is so completely satisfied with the all-sufficiency
of Jesus that he thirsts no more - except it be for deeper
draughts of the living fountain. In that sweet manner,
believer, shalt thou thirst; it shall not be a thirst of pain,
but of loving desire; thou wilt find it a sweet thing to
be panting after a fuller enjoyment of Jesus' love. One
in days of yore said, 'I have been sinking my bucket
down into the well full often, but now my thirst after
Jesus has become so insatiable, that I long to put the
well itself to my lips, and drink right on'. Is this the
feeling of thine heart now, believer? Dost thou feel that
all thy desires are satisfied in Jesus, and that thou hast
no want now, but to know more of Him, and to have
closer fellowship with Him? Then come continually to
the fountain, and take of the water of life freely. Jesus
will never think you take too much, but will ever
welcome you, saying, 'Drink, yea, drink abundantly, O
beloved'.

'He had married an Ethiopian woman'
Numbers 12:1

Strange choice of Moses, but how much more strange
the choice of Him who is a prophet like unto Moses,
and greater than he! Our Lord, who is fair as the lily,
has entered into marriage union with one who confesses herself to be black, because the sun has looked
upon her. It is the wonder of angels that the love of
Jesus should be set upon poor, lost, guilty men. Each
believer must, when filled with a sense of Jesus' love,
be also overwhelmed with astonishment that such love
should be lavished on an object so utterly unworthy of
it. Knowing as we do our secret guiltiness, unfaithfulness, and black-heartedness, we are dissolved in grateful admiration of the matchless freeness and sovereignty of grace. Jesus must have found the cause of His
love in His own heart, He could not have found it in us,
for it is not there. Even since our conversion we have
been black, though grace has made us comely. Holy
Rutherford said of himself what we must each sub-
scribe to - 'His relation to me is that I am sick, and He
is the Physician of whom I stand in need. Alas! how
often I play fast and loose with Christ! He bindeth, I
loose; He buildeth, I cast down; I quarrel with Christ,
and He agreeth with me twenty times a day!' Most
tender and faithful Husband of our souls, pursue Thy
gracious work of conforming us to Thine image, till
Thou shalt present even us poor Ethiops unto Thyself,
without spot, or wrinkle, or any such thing. Moses met
with opposition because of his marriage, and both
himself and his spouse were the subjects of an evil eye.
Can we wonder if this vain world opposes Jesus and
His spouse, and especially when great sinners are
converted? For this is ever the Pharisee's ground of
object, 'This man receiveth sinners'. Still is the old
cause of quarrel revived, 'Because he had married an
Ethiopian woman'.

'Wherefore hast Thou afflicted Thy servant?'
Numbers 11:11

Our heavenly Father sends us frequent troubles *to try our faith*. If our faith be worth anything, it will stand the test. Gilt is afraid of fire, but gold is not: the *paste* gem dreads to be touched by the diamond, but the true jewel fears no test. It is a poor faith which can only trust God when friends are true, the body full of health, and the business profitable; but that is true faith which holds by the Lord's faithfulness when friends are gone, when the body is sick, when spirits are depressed, and the light of our Father's countenance is hidden. A faith which can say, in the direst trouble, 'Though he slay me, yet will I trust in Him', is heaven-born faith. The Lord afflicts His servants *to glorify Himself*, for He is greatly glorified in the graces of His people, which are His own handiwork. When 'tribulation worketh patience; and patience, experience; and experience, hope', the Lord is honoured by these growing virtues. We should never know the music of the harp if the strings were left untouched; nor enjoy the juice of the grape if it were not trodden in the winepress; nor discover the sweet perfume of cinnamon if it were not pressed and beaten; nor feel the warmth of fire if the coals were not utterly consumed. The wisdom and power of the great Workman are discovered by the trials through which His vessels of mercy are permitted to pass. Present afflictions *tend also to heighten future joy*. There must be shades in the picture to bring out the beauty of the lights. Could we be so supremely blessed in heaven, if we had not known the curse of sin and the sorrow of earth? Will not peace be sweeter after conflict, and rest more welcome after toil? Will not the recollection of past sufferings enhance the bliss of the glorified? There are many other comfortable answers to the question with which we opened our brief meditation, let us muse upon it all day long.

'Now on whom dost thou trust?'
Isaiah 36:5

Reader, this is an important question. Listen to the Christian's answer, and see if it is yours. 'On whom dost thou trust?' 'I trust,' says the Christian, 'in a triune God. I trust *the Father*, believing that He has chosen me from before the foundations of the world; I trust Him to provide for me in providence, to teach me, to guide me, to correct me if need be, and to bring me home to His own house where the many mansions are. I trust *the Son*. Very God of very God is He - the man Christ Jesus. I trust in Him to take away all my sins by His own sacrifice, and to adorn me with His perfect righteousness. I trust Him to be my Intercessor, to present my prayers and desires before His Father's throne, and I trust Him to be my Advocate at the last great day, to plead my cause, and to justify me. I trust Him for what He is, for what He has done, and for what He has promised yet to do. And I trust *the Holy Spirit* - He has begun to save me from my inbred sins; I trust Him to drive them all out; I trust Him to curb my temper, to subdue my will, to enlighten my understanding, to check my passions, to comfort my despondency, to help my weakness, to illuminate my darkness; I trust Him to dwell in me as my life, to reign in me as my King, to sanctify me wholly, spirit, soul, and body, and then to take me up to dwell with the saints in light for ever.'

Oh, blessed trust! To trust Him whose power will never be exhausted, whose love will never wane, whose kindness will never change, whose faithfulness will never fail, whose wisdom will never be nonplussed, and whose perfect goodness can never know a diminution! Happy art thou, reader, if this trust is thine! So trusting, thou shalt enjoy sweet peace now, and glory hereafter, and the foundation of thy trust shall never be removed.

> *'Launch out into the deep,*
> *and let down your nets for a draught'*
> Luke 5:4

We learn from this narrative, the *necessity of human agency*. The draught of fishes was miraculous, yet neither the fisherman nor his boat, nor his fishing tackle were ignored; but all were used to take the fishes. So in the saving of souls, God worketh by means; and while the present economy of grace shall stand, God will be pleased by the foolishness of preaching to save them that believe. When God worketh without instruments, doubtless He is glorified; but He hath Himself selected the plan of instrumentality as being that by which He is most magnified in the earth. *Means of themselves are utterly unavailing.* 'Master, we have toiled all the night and have taken nothing.' What was the reason of this? Were they not fishermen plying their special calling? Verily, they were no raw hands; they understood the work. Had they gone about the toil unskilfully? No. Had they lacked industry? No, they had *toiled.* Had they lacked perseverance? No, they had toiled *all the night.* Was there a deficiency of fish in the sea? Certainly not, for as soon as the Master came, they swam to the net in shoals. What then, is the reason? Is it because there is no power in the means of themselves apart from the presence of Jesus? 'Without Him we can do nothing.' But with Christ we can do all things. *Christ's presence confers success.* Jesus sat in Peter's boat, and His will, by a mysterious influence, drew the fish to the net. When Jesus is lifted up in His Church, His presence is the Church's power - the shout of a king is in the midst of her. 'I, if I be lifted up, will draw all men unto me.' Let us go out this morning on our work of soul fishing, looking up in faith, and around us in solemn anxiety. Let us toil till night comes, and we shall not labour in vain, for He who bids us let down the net, will fill it with fishes.

'*Praying in the Holy Ghost*'
Jude 20

Mark the grand characteristic of true prayer - '*In the Holy Ghost*'. The seed of acceptable devotion must come from heaven's storehouse. Only the prayer which comes from God can go to God. We must shoot the Lord's arrows back to Him. That desire which He writes upon our heart will move His heart and bring down a blessing, but the desires of the flesh have no power with Him.

Praying in the Holy Ghost is praying in *fervency*. Cold prayers ask the Lord not to hear them. Those who do not plead with fervency, plead not at all. As well speak of lukewarm fire as of lukewarm prayer - it is essential that it be red hot. It is praying *perseveringly*. The true suppliant gathers force as he proceeds, and grows more fervent when God delays to answer. The longer the gate is closed, the more vehemently does he use the knocker, and the longer the angel lingers the more resolved is he that he will never let him go without the blessing. Beautiful in God's sight is tearful, agonising, unconquerable importunity. It means praying *humbly*, for the Holy Spirit never puffs us up with pride. It is His office to convince of sin, and so to bow us down in contrition and brokenness of spirit. We shall never sing *Gloria in excelsis* except we pray to God *De profundis*: out of the depths must we cry, or we shall never behold glory in the highest. It is *loving* prayer. Prayer should be perfumed with love, saturated with love - love to our fellow saints, and love to Christ. Moreover, it must be a prayer full of *faith*. A man prevails only as he believes. The Holy Spirit is the author of faith, and strengthens it, so that we pray believing God's promise. O that this blessed combination of excellent graces, priceless and sweet as the spices of the merchant, might be fragrant within us because the Holy Ghost is in our hearts! Most blessed Comforter, exert Thy mighty power within us, helping our infirmities in prayer.

'Able to keep you from falling'
Jude 24

In some sense the path to heaven is very safe, but in other respects there is *no road so dangerous*. It is beset with difficulties. One false step (and how easy it is to take that if grace be absent), and down we go. What a slippery path is that which some of us have to tread! How many times have we to exclaim with the Psalmist, 'My feet were almost gone; my steps had well nigh slipped'. If we were strong, sure-footed mountaineers, this would not matter so much; but in ourselves, *how weak we are*! In the best roads *we soon falter*, in the smoothest paths we quickly stumble. These feeble knees of ours can scarcely support our tottering weight. A straw may throw us, and a pebble can wound us; we are mere children tremblingly taking our first steps in the walk of faith, our heavenly Father holds us by the arms or we should soon be down. Oh, if we are kept from falling, how must we bless the patient power which watches over us day by day! Think, how prone we are to sin, how apt to choose danger, how strong our tendency to cast ourselves down, and these reflections will make us sing more sweetly than we have ever done, 'Glory be to Him, who is able to keep us from falling'. *We have many foes* who try to push us down. The road is rough and we are weak, but in addition to this, enemies lurk in ambush, who rush out when we least expect them, and labour to trip us up, or hurl us down the nearest precipice. Only an Almighty arm can preserve us from these unseen foes who are seeking to destroy us. Such an arm is engaged for our defence. He is faithful that hath promised, and He is able to keep us from falling, so that with a deep sense of our utter weakness, we may cherish a firm belief in our perfect safety, and say, with joyful confidence,

Against me earth and hell combine,
But on my side is power divine;
Jesus is all, and He is mine!

'But He answered her not a word'
Matthew 15:23

Genuine seekers who as yet have not obtained the blessing, may take comfort from the story before us. The Saviour did not at once bestow the blessing, even though the woman had great faith in Him. He intended to give it, but He waited awhile. 'He answered her not a word.' Were not her prayers good? Never better in the world. Was not her case needy? Sorrowfully needy. Did she not *feel* her need sufficiently? She felt it overwhelmingly. Was she not earnest enough? She was intensely so. Had she no faith? She had such a high degree of it that even Jesus wondered, and said, 'O woman, great is thy faith'. See then, although it is true that faith brings peace, yet it does not always bring it instantaneously. There may be certain reasons calling for the trial of faith, rather than the reward of faith. Genuine faith may be in the soul like a hidden seed, but as yet it may not have budded and blossomed into joy and peace. A painful silence from the Saviour is the grievous trial of many a seeking soul, but heavier still is the affliction of a harsh cutting reply such as this, 'It is not meet to take the children's bread, and to cast it to dogs'. Many in waiting upon the Lord find immediate delight, but this is not the case with all. Some, like the jailer, are in a moment turned from darkness to light, but others are plants of slower growth. A deeper sense of sin may be given to you instead of a sense of pardon, and in such a case you will have need of patience to bear the heavy blow. Ah! poor heart, though Christ beat and bruise thee, or even slay thee, trust Him; though he should give thee an angry word, believe in the love of His heart. Do not, I beseech thee, give up seeking or trusting my Master, because thou hast not yet obtained the conscious joy which thou longest for. Cast thyself on Him, and perseveringly depend even where thou canst not rejoicingly hope.

'Faultless before the presence of His glory'
Jude 24

Revolve in your mind that wondrous word, *'fault-less!'*. We are far off from it now; but as our Lord never stops short of perfection in His work of love, we shall reach it one day. The Saviour who will keep His people to the end, will also present them at last to Himself, as 'a glorious church, not having spot, or wrinkle, or any such thing, but holy and without blemish'. All the jewels in the Saviour's crown are of the first water and without a single flaw. All the maids of honour who attend the Lamb's wife are pure virgins without spot or stain. But how will Jesus make us faultless? He will wash us from our sins in His own blood until we are white and fair as God's purest angel; and we shall be clothed in His righteousness, that righteousness which makes the saint who wears it positively faultless; yea, perfect in the sight of God. We shall be unblameable and unreprovable even in His eyes. His law will not only have no charge against us, but it will be magnified in us. Moreover, the work of the Holy Spirit within us will be altogether complete. He will make us so perfectly holy, that we shall have no lingering tendency to sin. Judgment, memory, will - every power and passion shall be emancipated from the thraldom of evil. We shall be holy even as God is holy, and in His presence we shall dwell for ever. Saints will not be out of place in heaven, their beauty will be as great as that of the place prepared for them. Oh the rapture of that hour when the everlasting doors shall be lifted up, and we, being made meet for the inheritance, shall dwell with the saints in light. Sin gone, Satan shut out, temptation past for ever, and ourselves 'faultless' before God, this will be heaven indeed! Let us be joyful now as we rehearse the song of eternal praise so soon to roll forth in full chorus from all the bloodwashed host; let us copy David's exultings before the ark as a prelude to our ecstasies before the throne.

'And I will deliver thee out of the hand of the wicked,
and I will redeem thee out of the hand of the terrible'
Jeremiah 15:21

Note the glorious personality of the promise, *I* will, *I* will. The Lord Jehovah Himself interposes to deliver and redeem His people. He pledges Himself personally to rescue them. His own arm shall do it, that He may have the glory. Here is not a word said of any effort of our own which may be needed to assist the Lord. Neither our strength nor our weakness is taken into the account, but the lone *I*, like the sun in the heavens, shines out resplendent in all-sufficiency. Why then do we calculate our forces, and consult with flesh and blood to our grievous wounding? Jehovah has power enough without borrowing from our puny arm. Peace, ye unbelieving thoughts, be still, and know that the Lord reigneth. Nor is there a hint concerning secondary means and causes. The Lord says nothing of friends and helpers: He undertakes the work alone, and feels no need of human arms to aid Him. Vain are all our lookings around to companions and relatives; they are broken reeds if we lean upon them - often unwilling when able, and unable when they are willing. Since the promise comes alone from God, it would be well to wait only upon Him; and when we do so, our expectation never fails us. Who are the wicked that we should fear them? The Lord will utterly consume them; they are to be pitied rather than feared. As for terrible ones, they are only terrors to those who have no God to fly to, for when the Lord is on our side, whom shall we fear? If we run into sin to please the wicked, we have cause to be alarmed, but if we hold fast our integrity, the rage of tyrants shall be overruled for our good. When the fish swallowed Jonah, he found him a morsel which he could not digest; and when the world devours the church, it is glad to be rid of it again. In all times of fiery trial, in patience let us possess our souls.

> *'Let us lift up our heart with*
> *our hands unto God in the heavens'*
> Lamentations 3:41

The act of prayer *teaches us our unworthiness*, which is a very salutary lesson for such proud beings as we are. If God gave us favours without constraining us to pray for them we should never know how poor we are, but a true prayer is an inventory of wants, a catalogue of necessities, a revelation of hidden poverty. While it is an application to divine wealth, it is a confession of human emptiness. The most healthy state of a Christian is to be always empty in self and constantly depending upon the Lord for supplies; to be always poor in self and rich in Jesus; weak as water personally, but mighty through God to do great exploits; and hence the use of prayer, because, while it adores God, it lays the creature where it should be, in the very dust. Prayer is in itself, apart from the answer which it brings, a great benefit to the Christian. As the runner gains strength for the race by daily exercise, so for the great race of life we acquire energy by the hallowed labour of prayer. Prayer plumes the wings of God's young eaglets, that they may learn to mount above the clouds. Prayer girds the loins of God's warriors, and sends them forth to combat with their sinews braced and their muscles firm. An earnest pleader cometh out of his closet, even as the sun ariseth from the chambers of the east, rejoicing like a strong man to run his race. Prayer is that uplifted hand of Moses which routs the Amalekites more than the sword of Joshua; it is the arrow shot from the chamber of the prophet foreboding defeat to the Syrians. Prayer girds human weakness with divine strength, turns human folly into heavenly wisdom, and gives to troubled mortals the peace of God. We know not what prayer cannot do! We thank thee, great God, for the mercy-seat, a choice proof of thy marvellous lovingkindness. Help us to use it aright throughout this day!

'Whom He did predestinate, them He also called'
Romans 8:30

In the second epistle to Timothy, first chapter and ninth verse, are these words - 'Who hath saved us, and called us with an *holy* calling'. Now, here is a touchstone by which we may try our calling. It is 'an holy calling, not according to our works, but according to his own purpose and grace'. This calling forbids all trust in our own doings, and conducts us to Christ alone for salvation, but it afterwards purges us from dead works to serve the living and true God. As he that hath called you is holy, so must you be holy. If you are living in sin, you are not called, but if you are truly Christ's, you can say, 'Nothing pains me so much as sin; I desire to be rid of it; Lord, help me to be holy'. Is this the panting of thy heart? Is this the tenor of thy life towards God, and His divine will? Again, in Philippians 3:13, 14, we are told of 'The *high* calling of God in Christ Jesus'. Is then your calling a high calling? Has it ennobled your heart, and set it upon heavenly things? Has it elevated your hopes, your tastes, your desires? Has it upraised the constant tenor of your life, so that you spend it with God and for God? Another test we find in Hebrews 3:1 - 'Partakers of the *heavenly* calling'. Heavenly calling means a call *from* heaven. If man alone call thee, thou art uncalled. Is thy calling of God? Is it a call *to* heaven as well as from heaven? Unless thou art a stranger here, and heaven thy home, thou hast not been called with a heavenly calling; for those who have been so called, declare that they look for a city which hath foundations, whose builder and maker is God, and they themselves are strangers and pilgrims upon the earth. Is thy calling thus holy, high, heavenly? Then, beloved, thou hast been called of God, for such is the calling wherewith God doth call His people.

'I will meditate in Thy precepts'
Psalm 119:15

There are times when solitude is better than society, and silence is wiser than speech. We should be better Christians if we were more alone, waiting upon God, and gathering through meditation on His Word spiritual strength for labour in His service. We ought to muse *upon the things of God, because we thus get the real nutriment out of them.* Truth is something like the cluster of the vine: if we would have wine from it, we must bruise it; we must press and squeeze it many times. The bruisers' feet must come down joyfully upon the bunches, or else the juice will not flow; and they must well tread the grapes, or else much of the precious liquid will be wasted. So we must, by meditation, tread the clusters of truth, if we would get the wine of consolation therefrom. Our bodies are not supported by merely taking food into the mouth, but the process which really supplies the muscle, and the nerve, and the sinew, and the bone, is the process of digestion. It is by digestion that the outward food becomes assimilated with the inner life. Our souls are not nourished merely by listening awhile to this, and then to that, and then to the other part of divine truth. Hearing, reading, marking, and learning, all require inward digesting to complete their usefulness, and the inward digesting of the truth lies for the most part in meditating upon it. Why is it that some Christians, although they hear many sermons, make but slow advances in the divine life? Because they neglect their closets, and do not thoughtfully meditate on God's Word. They love the wheat, but they do not grind it; they would have the corn, but they will not go forth into the fields to gather it; the fruit hangs upon the tree, but they will not pluck it; the water flows at their feet, but they will not stoop to drink it. From such folly deliver us, O Lord, and be this our resolve this morning, 'I will meditate in Thy precepts'.

'The Comforter, which is the Holy Ghost'
John 14:26

This age is peculiarly the dispensation of the Holy Spirit, in which Jesus cheers us, not by His personal presence, as He shall do by-and-by, but by the indwelling and constant abiding of the Holy Ghost, who is evermore the Comforter of the church. It is His office to console the hearts of God's people. He convinces of sin; He illuminates and instructs; but still the main part of His work lies in making glad the hearts of the renewed, in confirming the weak, and lifting up all those that be bowed down. He does this by revealing Jesus to them. The Holy Spirit consoles, but Christ *is the consolation.* If we may use the figure, the Holy Spirit is the Physician, but Jesus is the medicine. *He* heals the wound, but it is by applying the holy ointment of Christ's name and grace. He takes not of His own things, but of the things of Christ. So if we give to the Holy Spirit the Greek name of *Paraclete,* as we sometimes do, then our heart confers on our blessed Lord Jesus the title of the *Paraclesis.* If the one be the Comforter, the other is the Comfort. Now, with such rich provision for his need, why should the Christian be sad and desponding? The Holy Spirit has graciously engaged to be thy Comforter: dost thou imagine, O thou weak and trembling believer, that he will be negligent of His sacred trust? Canst thou suppose that He has undertaken what he cannot or will not perform? If it be His especial work to strengthen thee, and to comfort thee, dost thou suppose He has forgotten His business, or that He will fail in the loving office which he sustains towards thee? Nay, think not so hardly of the tender and blessed Spirit whose name is 'the Comforter'. He delights to give the oil of joy for mourning, and the garment of praise for the spirit of heaviness. Trust thou in Him, and He will surely comfort thee till the house of mourning is closed for ever, and the marriage feast has begun.

'Godly sorrow worketh repentance'
2 Corinthians 7:10

Genuine, spiritual mourning for sin is *the work of the Spirit of God*. Repentance is too choice a flower to grow in nature's garden. Pearls grow naturally in oysters, but penitence never shows itself in sinners except divine grace works it in them. If thou hast one particle of real hatred for sin, God must have given it thee, for human nature's thorns never produced a single fig. 'That which is born of the flesh is flesh.'

True repentance *has a distinct reference to the Saviour*. When we repent of sin, we must have one eye upon sin and another upon the cross, or it will be better still if we fix both our eyes upon Christ and see our transgressions only, in the light of His love.

True sorrow for sin is *eminently practical*. No man may say he hates sin, if he lives in it. Repentance makes us see the evil of sin, not merely as a theory, but experimentally - as a burnt child dreads fire. We shall be as much afraid of it, as a man who has lately been stopped and robbed is afraid of the thief upon the highway; and we shall shun it - shun it in everything - not in great things only, but in little things, as men shun little vipers as well as great snakes. True mourning for sin will make us very jealous over our tongue, lest it should say a wrong word; we shall be very watchful over our daily actions, lest in anything we offend, and each night we shall close the day with painful confessions of shortcoming, and each morning awaken with anxious prayers, that this day God would hold us up that we may not sin against Him.

Sincere repentance is *continual*. Believers repent until their dying day. This dropping well is not intermittent. Every other sorrow yields to time, but this dear sorrow grows with our growth, and it is so sweet a bitter, that we thank God we are permitted to enjoy and to suffer it until we enter our eternal rest.

'Love is strong as death'
Solomon's Song 8:6

Whose love can this be which is as mighty as the conqueror of monarchs, the destroyer of the human race? Would it not sound like satire if it were applied to my poor, weak, and scarcely living love to Jesus my Lord? I do love Him, and perhaps by His grace, I could even die for Him, but as for my love in itself, it can scarcely endure a scoffing jest, much less a cruel death. Surely it is my Beloved's love which is here spoken of - the love of Jesus, the matchless lover of souls. His love was indeed stronger than the most terrible death, for it endured the trial of the cross triumphantly. It was a lingering death, but love survived the torment; a shameful death, but love despised the shame; a penal death, but love bore our iniquities; a forsaken, lonely death, from which the eternal Father hid His face, but love endured the curse, and gloried over all. Never such love, never such death. It was a desperate duel, but love bore the palm. What then, my heart? Hast thou no emotions excited within thee at the contemplation of such heavenly affection? Yes, my Lord, I long, I pant to feel Thy love flaming like a furnace within me. Come Thou Thyself and excite the ardour of my spirit,

> For every drop of crimson blood
> Thus shed to make me live,
> O wherefore, wherefore have not I
> A thousand lives to give?

Why should I despair of loving Jesus with a love as strong as death? He deserves it: I desire it. The martyrs felt such love, and they were but flesh and blood, then why not I? They mourned their weakness, and yet out of weakness were made strong. Grace gave them all their unflinching constancy - there is the same grace for me. Jesus, lover of my soul, shed abroad such love, even Thy love in my heart, this evening.

*'I count all things but loss for the excellency of the
knowledge of Christ Jesus my Lord'*
Philippians 3:8

Spiritual knowledge of Christ will be a *personal*
knowledge. I cannot know Jesus through another
person's acquaintance with Him. No, *I* must know Him
myself; I must know Him on my own account. It will
be an *intelligent* knowledge - I must know *Him*, not as
the visionary dreams of Him, but as the Word reveals
Him. I must know His natures, divine and human. I
must know His offices - His attributes - His works -
His shame - His glory. I must meditate upon Him until
I 'comprehend with all saints what is the breadth, and
length, and depth, and height; and know the love of
Christ, which passeth knowledge'. It will be an *affectionate* knowledge of Him; indeed, if I know Him at all,
I must love Him. An ounce of heart knowledge is worth
a ton of head learning. Our knowledge of Him will be
a *satisfying* knowledge. When I know my Saviour, my
mind will be full to the brim - I shall feel that I have that
which my spirit panted after. 'This is that bread
whereof if a man eat he shall never hunger.' At the same
time it will be an *exciting* knowledge; the more I know
of my Beloved, the more I shall want to know. The
higher I climb the loftier will be the summits which
invite my eager footsteps. I shall want the more as I get
the more. Like the miser's treasure, my gold will make
me covet more. To conclude; this knowledge of Christ
Jesus will be a most *happy* one; in fact, so elevating,
that sometimes it will completely bear me up above all
trials, and doubts, and sorrows; and it will, while I
enjoy it, make me something more than 'Man that is
born of woman, who is of few days, and full of
trouble'; for it will fling about me the immortality of
the everliving Saviour, and gird me with the golden
girdle of His eternal joy. Come, my soul, sit at Jesus'
feet and learn of Him all this day.

'And be not conformed to this world'
Romans 12:2

If a Christian can by possibility be saved while he conforms to this world, at any rate it must be so as by fire. Such a bare salvation is almost as much to be dreaded as desired. Reader, would you wish to leave this world in the darkness of a desponding death bed, and enter heaven as a shipwrecked mariner climbs the rocks of his native country? then be worldly; be mixed up with Mammonites, and refuse to go without the camp bearing Christ's reproach. But would you have a heaven below as well as a heaven above? Would you comprehend with all saints what are the heights and depths, and know the love of Christ which passeth knowledge? Would you receive an abundant entrance into the joy of your Lord? Then come ye out from among them, and be ye separate, and touch not the unclean thing. Would you attain the full assurance of faith? You cannot gain it while you commune with sinners. Would you flame with vehement love? Your love will be damped by the drenchings of godless society. You cannot become a great Christian - you may be a babe in grace, but you never can be a perfect man in Christ Jesus while you yield yourself to the worldly maxims and modes of business of men of the world. It is ill for an heir of heaven to be a great friend with the heirs of hell. It has a bad look when a courtier is too intimate with his king's enemies. Even small inconsistencies are dangerous. Little thorns make great blisters, little moths destroy fine garments, and little frivolities and little rogueries will rob religion of a thousand joys. O professor, too little separated from sinners, you know not what you lose by your conformity to the world. It cuts the tendons of your strength, and makes you creep where you ought to run. Then, for your own comfort's sake, and for the sake of your growth in grace, if you be a Christian, be a Christian, and be a marked and distinct one.

'But who may abide the day of his coming?'
Malachi 3:2

His first coming was without external pomp or show of power, and yet in truth there were few who could abide its testing might. Herod and all Jerusalem with him were stirred at the news of the wondrous birth. Those who supposed themselves to be waiting for him, showed the fallacy of their professions by rejecting him when he came. His life on earth was a winnowing fan, which tried the great heap of religious profession, and few enough could abide the process. But what will his second advent be? What sinner can endure to think of it? 'He shall smite the earth with the rod of His mouth, and with the breath of His lips shall He slay the wicked.' When in His humiliation he did but say to the soldiers, 'I am He', they fell backward; what will be the terror of His enemies when He shall more fully reveal Himself as the '*I am*'? His death shook earth and darkened heaven, what shall be the dreadful splendour of that day in which as the living Saviour, He shall summon the quick and the dead before Him? O that the terrors of the Lord would persuade men to forsake their sins and kiss the Son lest He be angry! Though a lamb, He is yet the lion of the tribe of Judah, rending the prey in pieces; and though He breaks not the bruised reed, yet will He break His enemies with a rod of iron, and dash them in pieces like a potter's vessel. None of His foes shall bear up before the tempest of His wrath, or hide themselves from the sweeping hail of His indignation; but His beloved bloodwashed people look for His appearing with joy, and hope to abide it without fear: to them He sits as a refiner even now, and when He has tried them they shall come forth as gold. Let us search ourselves this morning and make our calling and election sure, so that the coming of the Lord may cause no dark forebodings in our mind. O for grace to cast away all hypocrisy, and to be found of Him sincere and without rebuke in the day of His appearing.

*'But the firstling of an ass thou shalt redeem with a
lamb: and if thou redeem him not,
then shalt thou break his neck'*
Exodus 34:20

Every firstborn creature must be the Lord's, but since
the ass was unclean, it could not be presented in
sacrifice. What then? Should it be allowed to go free
from the universal law? By no means. God admits of
no exceptions. The ass is His due, but He will not
accept it; He will not abate the claim, but yet He cannot
be pleased with the victim. No way of escape remained
but redemption - the creature must be saved by the
substitution of a lamb in its place; or if not redeemed,
it must die. My soul, here is a lesson for thee. That
unclean animal is thyself; thou art justly the property
of the Lord who made thee and preserves thee, but thou
art so sinful that God will not, cannot, accept thee; and
it has come to this, the Lamb of God must stand in thy
stead, or thou must die eternally. Let all the world know
of thy gratitude to that spotless Lamb who has already
bled for thee, and so redeemed thee from the fatal curse
of the law. Must it not sometimes have been a question
with the Israelite which should die, the ass or the lamb?
Would not the good man pause to estimate and compare? Assuredly there was no comparison between the
value of the soul of man and the life of the Lord Jesus,
and yet the Lamb dies, and man the ass is spared. My
soul, admire the boundless love of God to thee and
others of the human race. Worms are bought with the
blood of the Son of the Highest! Dust and ashes
redeemed with a price far above silver and gold! What
a doom had been mine had not plenteous redemption
been found! The breaking of the neck of the ass was but
a momentary penalty, but who shall measure the wrath
to come to which no limit can be imagined? Inestimably
dear is the glorious Lamb who has redeemed us from
such a doom.

'Jesus saith unto them, Come and dine'
John 21:12

In these words the believer is invited to a holy *nearness to Jesus*. 'Come and dine', implies the same table, the same meat; ay, and sometimes it means to sit side by side, and lean our head upon the Saviour's bosom. It is being brought into the banqueting-house, where waves the banner of redeeming love. 'Come and dine', gives us a vision of *union with Jesus*, because the only food that we can feast upon when we dine with Jesus is *Himself*. Oh, what union is this! It is a depth which reason cannot fathom, that we thus feed upon Jesus. 'He that eateth My flesh, and drinketh My blood, dwelleth in Me, and I in him.' It is also an invitation to enjoy *fellowship with the saints*. Christians may differ on a variety of points, but they have all one spiritual appetite; and if we cannot all *feel* alike, we can all *feed* alike on the bread of life sent down from heaven. At the table of fellowship with Jesus we are one bread and one cup. As the loving cup goes round we pledge one another heartily therein. Get nearer to Jesus, and you will find yourself linked more and more in spirit to all who are like yourself, supported by the same heavenly manna. If we were more near to Jesus we should be more near to one another. We likewise see in these words the *source of strength* for every Christian. To look at Christ is to live, but for strength to serve Him you must 'come and dine'. We labour under much unnecessary weakness on account of neglecting this precept of the Master. We none of us need to put ourselves on low diet; on the contrary, we should fatten on the marrow and fatness of the gospel that we may accumulate strength therein, and urge every power to its full tension in the Master's service. Thus, then, if you would realise *nearness* to Jesus, *union* with Jesus, *love* to His people and *strength* from Jesus, 'come and dine' with Him by faith.

'With Thee is the fountain of life'
Psalm 36:9

There are times in our spiritual experience when human counsel or sympathy, or religious ordinances, fail to comfort or help us. Why does our gracious God permit this? Perhaps it is because we have been living too much without Him, and He therefore takes away everything upon which we have been in the habit of depending, that He may drive us to Himself. It is a blessed thing to live at the fountain head. While our skin-bottles are full, we are content, like Hagar and Ishmael, to go into the wilderness; but when those are dry, nothing will serve us but 'Thou God seest me'. We are like the prodigal, we love the swine-troughs and forget our Father's house. Remember, we can make swine-troughs and husks even out of the forms of religion; they are blessed things, but we may put them in God's place, and then they are of no value. Anything becomes an idol when it keeps us away from God: even the brazen serpent is to be despised at 'Nehushtan', if we worship it instead of God. The prodigal was never safer than when he was driven to his father's bosom, because he could find sustenance nowhere else. Our Lord favours us with a famine in the land that it may make us seek after Himself the more. The best position for a Christian is living wholly and directly on God's grace - still abiding where he stood at first - 'Having nothing, and yet possessing all things'. Let us never for a moment think that our standing is in our sanctification, our mortification, our graces, or our feelings, but know that because Christ offered a full atonement, therefore we are saved; for we are complete in Him. Having nothing of our own to trust to, but resting upon the merits of Jesus - His passion and holy life furnish us with the only sure ground of confidence. Beloved, when we are brought to a thirsting condition, we are sure to turn to the fountain of life with eagerness.

*'And David said in his heart,
I shall now perish one day by the hand of Saul'*
1 Samuel 27:1

The thought of David's heart at this time was a *false* thought, because he certainly had no ground for thinking that God's anointing him by Samuel was intended to be left as an empty unmeaning act. On no one occasion had the Lord deserted His servant; he had been placed in perilous positions very often, but not one instance had occurred in which divine interposition had not delivered him. The trials to which he had been exposed had been varied; they had not assumed one form only, but many - yet in every case He who sent the trial had also graciously ordained a way of escape. David could not put his finger upon any entry in his diary, and say of it, 'Here is evidence that the Lord will forsake me', for the entire tenor of his past life proved the very reverse. He should have argued from what God *had* done for him, that God would be his defender still. But is it not just in the same way that *we* doubt God's help? Is it not *mistrust without a cause*? Have we ever had the shadow of a reason to doubt our Father's goodness? Have not His lovingkindnesses been marvellous? Has He *once* failed to justify our trust? Ah, no! our God has not left us at any time. We have had dark nights, but the star of love has shone forth amid the blackness; we have been in stern conflicts, but over our head He has held aloft the shield of our defence. We have gone through many trials, but never to our detriment, always to our advantage; and the conclusion from our past experience is, that He who has been with us in six troubles, will not forsake us in the seventh. What we have known of our faithful God, proves that he will keep us to the end. Let us not, then, reason contrary to evidence. How can we ever be so ungenerous as to *doubt* our God? Lord, throw down the Jezebel of our unbelief, and let the dogs devour it.

'He shall gather the lambs with His arm'
Isaiah 40:11

Our good Shepherd has in His flock a variety of experiences, some are strong in the Lord, and others are weak in faith, but He is impartial in His care for all His sheep, and the weakest lamb is as dear to Him as the most advanced of the flock. Lambs are wont to lag behind, prone to wander, and apt to grow weary, but from all the danger of these infirmities the Shepherd protects them with His arm of power. He finds newborn souls, like young lambs, ready to perish - He nourishes them till life becomes vigorous; He finds weak minds ready to faint and die - He consoles them and renews their strength. All the little ones He gathers, for it is not the will of our heavenly Father that one of them should perish. What a quick eye He must have to see them all! What a tender heart to care for them all! What a far-reaching and potent arm, to gather them all! In His lifetime on earth He was a great gatherer of the weaker sort, and now that He dwells in heaven, His loving heart yearns towards the meek and contrite, the timid and feeble, the fearful and fainting here below. How gently did He gather me to Himself, to His truth, to His blood, to His love, to His church! With what effectual grace did He compel me to come to Himself! Since my first conversion, how frequently has He restored me from my wanderings, and once again folded me within the circle of His everlasting arm! The best of all is, that He does it all Himself personally, not delegating the task of love, but condescending Himself to rescue and preserve His most unworthy servant. How shall I love Him enough or serve Him worthily? I would fain make His name great unto the ends of the earth, but what can my feebleness do for Him? Great Shepherd, add to Thy mercies this one other, a heart to love Thee more truly as I ought.

'Thy paths drop fatness'
Psalm 65:11

Many are 'the paths of the Lord' which 'drop fatness', but an especial one is the *path of prayer*. No believer, who is much in the closet, will have need to cry, 'My leanness, my leanness; woe unto me'. Starving souls live at a distance from the mercy-seat, and become like the parched fields in times of drought. Prevalence with God in wrestling prayer is sure to make the believer strong - if not happy. The nearest place to the gate of heaven is the throne of the heavenly grace. Much alone, and you will have much assurance; little alone with Jesus, your religion will be shallow, polluted with many doubts and fears, and not sparkling with the joy of the Lord. Since the soul-enriching path of prayer is open to the very weakest saint; since no high attainments are required; since you are not bidden to come because you are an advanced saint, but freely invited if you be a saint at all; see to it, dear reader, that you are often in the way of private devotion. Be much on your knees, for so Elijah drew the rain upon famished Israel's fields.

There is another especial path dropping with fatness to those who walk therein, it is the secret walk of *communion*. Oh! the delights of fellowship with Jesus! Earth hath no words which can set forth the holy calm of a soul leaning on Jesus' bosom. Few Christians understand it, they live in the lowlands and seldom climb to the top of Nebo: they live in the outer court, they enter not the holy place, they take not up the privilege of priesthood. At a distance they see the sacrifice, but they sit not down with the priest to eat thereof, and to enjoy the fat of the burnt offering. But, reader, sit thou ever under the shadow of Jesus; come up to that palm tree, and take hold of the branches thereof; let thy beloved be unto thee as the apple tree among the trees of the wood, and thou shalt be satisfied as with marrow and fatness. O Jesus, visit us with Thy salvation!

'Behold, to obey is better than sacrifice'
1 Samuel 15:22

Saul has been commanded to slay utterly all the
Amalekites and their cattle. Instead of doing so, he
preserved the king, and suffered his people to take the
best of the oxen and of the sheep. When called to
account for this, he declared that he did it with a view
of offering sacrifice to God; but Samuel met him at
once with the assurance that sacrifices were no excuse
for an act of direct rebellion. The sentence before us is
worthy to be printed in letters of gold, and to be hung
up before the eyes of the present idolatrous generation,
who are very fond of the fineries of will-worship, but
utterly neglect the laws of God. Be it ever in your
remembrance, that to keep strictly in the path of your
Saviour's command is better than any outward form of
religion; and to hearken to His precept with an attentive
ear is better than to bring the fat of rams, or any other
precious thing to lay upon His altar. If you are failing
to keep the least of Christ's commands to His disciples, I pray you be disobedient no longer. All the
pretensions you make of attachment to your Master,
and all the devout actions which you may perform, are
no recompense for disobedience. 'To obey', even in the
slightest and smallest thing, 'is better than sacrifice',
however pompous. Talk not of Gregorian chants,
sumptuous robes, incense, and banners; the first thing
which God requires of His child is obedience; and
though you should give your body to be burned, and all
your goods to feed the poor, yet if you do not hearken
to the Lord's precepts all your formalities shall profit
you nothing. It is a blessed thing to be teachable as a
little child, but it is a much more blessed thing when
one has been taught the lesson, to carry it out to the
letter. How many adorn their temples and decorate their
priests, but refuse to obey the word of the Lord! My
soul, come not thou into their secret.

'Babes in Christ'
1 Corinthians 3:1

Are you mourning, believer, because you are so weak
in the divine life: because your faith is so little, your
love so feeble? Cheer up, for you have cause for
gratitude. Remember *that in some things you are equal
to the greatest and most full-grown Christian.* You are
as much bought with blood as he is. You are as much
an adopted child of God as any other believer. An infant
is as truly a child of its parents as is the full-grown man.
You are as completely justified, for your justification
is not a thing of degrees: your little faith has made you
clean every whit. You have as much right to the
precious things of the covenant as the most advanced
believers, for your right to covenant mercies lies not in
your growth, but in the covenant itself; and your faith
in Jesus is not the measure, but the token of your
inheritance in Him. You are as rich as the richest, if not
in enjoyment, yet in real possession. The smallest star
that gleams is set in heaven; the faintest ray of light has
affinity with the great orb of day. In the family register
of glory the small and the great are written with the
same pen. You are as dear to your Father's heart as the
greatest in the family. Jesus is very tender over you.
You are like the smoking flax; a rougher spirit would
say, 'put out that smoking flax, it fills the room with
an offensive odour' but the smoking flax *He* will not
quench. You are like a bruised reed; and any less tender
hand than that of the Chief Musician would tread upon
you or throw you away, but He will never break the
bruised reed. Instead of being downcast by reason of
what you are, you should triumph in Christ. Am I but
little in Israel? Yet in Christ I am made to sit in
heavenly places. Am I poor in faith? Still in Jesus I am
heir of all things. Though 'less than nothing I can
boast, and vanity confess', yet, if the root of the matter
be in me I will rejoice in the Lord, and glory in the God
of my salvation.

'God, my Maker, who giveth songs in the night'
Job 35:10

Any man can sing in the day. When the cup is full, man draws inspiration from it. When wealth rolls in abundance around him, any man can praise the God who gives a plenteous harvest or sends home a loaded argosy. It is easy enough for an Aeolian harp to whisper music when the winds blow - the difficulty is for music to swell forth when no wind is stirring. It is easy to sing when we can read the notes by daylight; but he is skilful who sings when there is not a ray of light to read by - who sings from his heart. No man can make a song in the night of himself; he may attempt it, but he will find that a song in the night must be divinely inspired. Let all things go well, I can weave songs, fashioning them wherever I go out of the flowers that grow upon my path; but put me in a desert, where no green thing grows, and wherewith shall I frame a hymn of praise to God? How shall a mortal man make a crown for the Lord where no jewels are? Let but this voice be clear, and this body full of health, and I can sing God's praise: silence my tongue, lay me upon the bed of languishing, and how shall I then chant God's high praises, unless He Himself give me the song? No, it is not in man's power to sing when all is adverse, unless an altar-coal shall touch his lip. It was a divine song, which Habakkuk sang, when in the night he said, 'Although the fig-tree shall not blossom, neither shall fruit be in the vines; the labour of the olive shall fail, and the fields shall yield no meat; the flock shall be cut off from the fold, and there shall be no herd in the stalls: yet I will rejoice in the Lord, I will joy in the God of my salvation'. Then, since our Maker gives *songs in the night*, let us wait upon Him for the music. O Thou chief musician, let us not remain songless because affliction is upon us, but tune Thou our lips to the melody of thanksgiving.

'Grow up into Him in all things'
Ephesians 4:15

Many Christians remain stunted and dwarfed in spiritual things, so as to present the same appearance year after year. No up-springing of advanced and refined feeling is manifested in them. They *exist* but do not *'grow up into Him in all things'*. But should we rest content with being in the 'green blade', when we might advance to 'the ear', and eventually ripen into the 'full corn in the ear'? Should we be satisfied to believe in Christ, and to say, 'I am safe', without wishing to know in our own experience more of the fulness which is to be found in Him? It should not be so; we should, as good traders in heaven's market, covet to be enriched in the knowledge of Jesus. It is all very well to keep other men's vineyards, but we must not neglect our own spiritual growth and ripening. Why should it always be winter time in our hearts? We must have our seed time, it is true, but O for a spring time - yea, a summer season, which shall give promise of an early harvest. If we would ripen in grace, we must live near to Jesus - in His presence - ripened by the sunshine of His smiles. We must hold sweet communion with Him. We must leave the distant view of His face and come near, as John did, and pillow our head on His breast; then shall we find ourselves advancing in holiness, in love, in faith, in hope - yea, in every precious gift. As the sun rises first on mountain-tops and gilds them with his light, and presents one of the most charming sights to the eye of the traveller; so is it one of the most delightful contemplations in the world to mark the glow of the Spirit's light on the head of some saint, who has risen up in spiritual stature, like Saul, above his fellows, till, like a mighty Alp, snow-capped, he reflects first among the chosen, the beams of the Sun of Righteousness, and bears the sheen of His effulgence high aloft for all to see, and seeing it, to glorify His Father which is in heaven.

'*Keep not back*'
Isaiah 43:6

Although this message was sent to the south, and
referred to the seed of Israel, it may profitably be a
summons to ourselves. Backward we are naturally to
all good things, and it is a lesson of grace to learn to go
forward in the ways of God. Reader, are you unconverted, but do you desire to trust in the Lord Jesus?
Then *keep not back*. Love invites you, the promises
secure you success, the precious blood prepares the
way. Let not sins or fears hinder you, but come to Jesus
just as you are. Do you long to pray? Would you pour
out your heart before the Lord? *Keep not back*. The
mercy-seat is prepared for such as need mercy; a
sinner's cries will prevail with God. You are invited,
nay, you are commanded to pray, come therefore with
boldness to the throne of grace.

Dear friend, are you already saved? Then *keep not
back* from union with the Lord's people. Neglect not
the ordinances of baptism and the Lord's Supper. You
may be of a timid disposition, but you must strive
against it, lest it lead you into disobedience. There is a
sweet promise made to those who confess Christ - by
no means miss it, lest you come under the condemnation of those who deny Him. If you have talents *keep
not back* from using them. Hoard not your wealth,
waste not your time; let not your abilities rust or your
influence be unused. Jesus kept not back, imitate Him
by being foremost in self-denials and self-sacrifices.
Keep not back from close communion with God, from
boldly appropriating covenant blessings, from advancing in the divine life, from prying into the precious
mysteries of the love of Christ. Neither, beloved
friend, be guilty of keeping others back by your
coldness, harshness, or suspicions. For Jesus' sake go
forward yourself, and encourage others to do the like.
Hell and the leaguered bands of superstition and
infidelity are forward to the fight. O soldiers of the
cross, keep not back.

'The love of Christ constraineth us'
2 Corinthians 5:14

How much owest thou unto my Lord? Has He ever done anything for thee? Has He forgiven thy sins? Has He covered thee with a robe of righteousness? Has He set thy feet upon a rock? Has He established thy goings? Has He prepared heaven for thee? Has He prepared thee for heaven? Has He written thy name in His book of life? Has He given thee countless blessings? Has He laid up for thee a store of mercies, which eye hath not seen nor ear heard? Then do something for Jesus worthy of His love. Give not a mere wordy offering to a dying Redeemer. How will you feel when your Master comes, if you have to confess that you *did* nothing for Him, but kept your love shut up, like a stagnant pool, neither flowing forth to His poor or to His work? Out on such love as that! What do men think of a love which never shows itself in action? Why, they say, 'Open rebuke is better than secret love'. Who will accept a love so weak that it does not actuate you to a single deed of self-denial, of generosity, of heroism, or zeal! Think how *He* has loved you, and given Himself for you! Do you know the power of that love? Then let it be like a rushing mighty wind to your soul to sweep out the clouds of your worldliness, and clear away the mists of sin. 'For Christ's sake' be this the tongue of fire that shall sit upon you: 'for Christ's sake' be this the divine rapture, the heavenly afflatus to bear you aloft from earth, the divine spirit that shall make you bold as lions and swift as eagles in your Lord's service. Love should give wings to the feet of service, and strength to the arms of labour. Fixed on God with a constancy that is not to be shaken, resolute to honour Him with a determination that is not to be turned aside, and pressing on with an ardour never to be wearied, let us manifest the constraints of love to Jesus. May the divine loadstone draw us heavenward towards itself!

*'Why are ye troubled?
and why do thoughts arise in your hearts?'*
Luke 24:38

'Why sayest thou, O Jacob, and speakest O Israel, My way is hid from the Lord, and my judgment is passed over from my God?' The Lord cares for all things, and the meanest creatures share in His universal providence, but His particular providence is over His saints. 'The angel of the Lord encampeth round about them that fear Him.' 'Precious shall their blood be in His sight.' 'Precious in the sight of the Lord is the death of His saints.' 'We know that all things work together for good to them that love God, to them that are the called according to His purpose.' Let the fact that, while He is the Saviour of all men, He is specially the Saviour of them that believe, cheer and comfort you. You are His peculiar care; His regal treasure which He guards as the apple of His eye; His vineyard over which He watches day and night. 'The very hairs of your head are all numbered.' Let the thought of His special love *to you* be a spiritual painkiller, a dear quietus to your woe: 'I will never leave *thee*, nor forsake *thee*'. God says that as much to you as to any saint of old. 'Fear not, I am thy shield, and thy exceeding great reward.' We lose much consolation by the habit of reading His promises for the whole church, instead of taking them directly home to ourselves. Believer, grasp the divine word with a personal, appropriating faith. Think that you hear Jesus say, 'I have prayed for *thee* that thy faith fail not'. Think you see Him walking on the waters of thy trouble, for He is there, and He is saying, 'Fear not, it is I; be not afraid'. Oh, those sweet words of Christ! May the Holy Ghost make you feel them as spoken to *you*; forget others for a while - accept the voice of Jesus as addressed to you, and say, 'Jesus whispers consolation; I cannot refuse it; I will sit under His shadow with great delight'.

'*I will love them freely*'
Hosea 14:4

This sentence is a body of divinity in miniature. He who understands its meaning is a theologian, and he who can dive into its fulness is a true master in Israel. It is a condensation of the glorious message of salvation which was delivered to us in Christ Jesus our Redeemer. The sense hinges upon the word 'freely'. This is the glorious, the suitable, the divine way by which love streams from heaven to earth, a spontaneous love flowing forth to those who neither deserved it, purchased it, nor sought after it. It is, indeed, the only way in which God can love such as we are. The text is a death blow to all sorts of fitness: 'I will love them *freely*'. Now, if there were any fitness necessary in us, then He would not love us freely, at least, this would be a mitigation and a drawback to the freeness of it. But it stands, 'I will love you *freely*'. We complain, 'Lord, my heart is so hard'. 'I will love you freely.' 'But I do not feel my need of Christ as I could wish.' 'I will not love you because you feel your need; I will love you freely.' 'But I do not feel that softening of spirit which I could desire.' Remember, the softening of spirit is not a condition, for there are no conditions; the covenant of grace has no conditionality whatever; so that we without any fitness may venture upon the promise of God which was made to us in Christ Jesus, when He said, 'He that believeth on Him is not condemned'. It is blessed to know that the grace of God is free to us at all times, without preparation, without fitness, without money, and without price! 'I will love them freely.' These words *invite backsliders to return*: indeed, the text was specially written for such - 'I will heal their backsliding; I will love them freely'. Backslider! surely the generosity of the promise will at once break your heart, and you will return, and seek your injured Father's face.

'He shall take of Mine, and shall show it unto you'
John 16:15

There are times when all the promises and doctrines of
the Bible are of no avail, unless a gracious hand shall
apply them to us. We are thirsty, but too faint to crawl
to the waterbrook. When a soldier is wounded in battle
it is of little use for him to know that there are those at
the hospital who can bind up his wounds, and medi-
cines there to ease all the pains which he now suffers:
what he needs is to be carried thither, and to have the
remedies applied. It is thus with our souls, and to meet
this need there is one, even the Spirit of truth, who takes
of the things of Jesus, and applies them to us. Think not
that Christ hath placed His joys on heavenly shelves
that we may climb up to them for ourselves, but He
draws near, and sheds His peace abroad in our hearts.
O Christian, if thou art tonight labouring under deep
distresses, thy Father does not give thee promises and
then leave thee to draw them up from the word like
buckets from a well, but the promises He has written
in the word He will write anew on your heart. He will
manifest His love to you, and by His blessed Spirit,
dispel your cares and troubles. Be it known unto thee,
O mourner, that it is God's prerogative to wipe every
tear from the eye of His people. The good Samaritan
did not say, 'Here is the wine, and here is the oil for
you'; he actually poured in the oil and the wine. So
Jesus not only gives you the sweet wine of the promise,
but holds the golden chalice to your lips, and pours the
life-blood into your mouth. The poor, sick, way-worn
pilgrim is not merely strengthened to walk, but he is
borne on eagles' wings. Glorious gospel! which provides everything for the helpless, which draws nigh to
us when we cannot reach after it - brings us grace before
we seek for grace! Here is as much glory in the giving
as in the gift. Happy people who have the Holy Ghost
to bring Jesus to them.

'Will ye also go away?'
John 6:67

Many have forsaken Christ, and have walked no more with Him; but *what reason have YOU to make a change*? Has there been any reason for it in the *past*? Has not Jesus proved Himself all-sufficient? He appeals to you this morning - 'Have I been a wilderness unto you?' When your soul has simply trusted Jesus, have you ever been confounded? Have you not up till now found your Lord to be a compassionate and generous friend to you, and has not simple faith in Him given you all the peace your spirit could desire? Can you so much as dream of a better friend than He has been to you? Then change not the old and tried for new and false. As for *the present*, can that compel you to leave Christ? When we are hard beset with this world, or with the severer trials within the Church, we find it a most blessed thing to pillow our head upon the bosom of our Saviour. This is the joy we have today that we are saved in Him; and if this joy be satisfying, wherefore should we think of changing? Who barters gold for dross? We will not forswear the sun till we find a better light, nor leave our Lord until a brighter lover shall appear; and, since this can never be, we will hold Him with a grasp immortal, and bind His name as a seal upon our arm. As for *the future*, can you suggest anything which can arise that shall render it necessary for you to mutiny, or desert the old flag to serve under another captain? We think not. If life be long - He changes not. If we are poor, what better than to have Christ who can make us rich? When we are sick, what more do we want than Jesus to make our bed in our sickness? When we die, is it not written that 'neither death, nor life, nor things present, nor things to come, shall be able to separate us from the love of God, which is in Christ Jesus our Lord'! We say with Peter, 'Lord, to whom shall we go?'

> *'Why sleep ye? rise and pray,*
> *lest ye enter into temptation'*
> Luke 22:46

When is the Christian most liable to sleep? Is it not *when his temporal circumstances are prosperous*? Have you not found it so? When you had daily troubles to take to the throne of grace, were you not more wakeful than you are now? Easy roads make sleepy travellers. Another dangerous time is *when all goes pleasantly in spiritual matters*. Christian went not to sleep when lions were in the way, or when he was wading through the river, or when fighting with Apollyon, but when he had climbed half up the Hill Difficulty, and came to a delightful arbour, he sat down, and forthwith fell asleep, to his great sorrow and loss. The enchanted ground is a place of balmy breezes, laden with fragrant odours and soft influences, all tending to lull pilgrims to sleep. Remember Bunyan's description: 'Then they came to an arbour, warm, and promising much refreshing to the weary pilgrims; for it was finely wrought above head, beautified with greens, and furnished with benches and settles. It had also in it a soft couch, where the weary might lean.' 'The arbour was called the Slothful's Friend, and was made on purpose to allure, if it might be, some of the pilgrims to take up their rest there when weary.' Depend upon it, it is in easy places that men shut their eyes and wander into the dreamy land of forgetfulness. Old Erskine wisely remarked, 'I like a roaring devil better than a sleeping devil'. There is no temptation half so dangerous as not being tempted. The distressed soul does not sleep; it is after we enter into peaceful confidence and full assurance that we are in danger of slumbering. The disciples fell asleep after they had seen Jesus transfigured on the mountain top. Take heed, joyous Christian, good frames are near neighbours to temptations: be as happy as you will, only be watchful.

'The trees of the Lord are full of sap'
Psalm 104:16

Without sap the tree cannot flourish or even exist. *Vitality* is essential to a Christian. There must be *life* - a vital principle infused into us by God the Holy Ghost, or we cannot be trees of the Lord. The mere name of being a Christian is but a dead thing, we must be filled with the spirit of divine life. This life is *mysterious*. We do not understand the circulation of the sap, by what force it rises, and by what power it descends again. So the life within us is a sacred mystery. Regeneration is wrought by the Holy Ghost entering into man and becoming man's life; and this divine life in a believer afterwards feeds upon the flesh and blood of Christ and is thus sustained by divine food, but whence it cometh and whither it goeth who shall explain to us? What a *secret* thing the sap is! The roots go searching through the soil with their little spongioles, but we cannot see them suck out the various gases, or transmute the mineral into the vegetable; this work is done down in the dark. Our root is Christ Jesus, and our life is hid in him; this is the secret of the Lord. The radix of the Christian life is as secret as the life itself. How *permanently active* is the sap in the cedar! In the Christian the divine life is always full of energy - not always in fruit-bearing, but in inward operations. The believer's *graces*, are not every one of them in constant motion, but his life never ceases to palpitate within. He is not always working for God, but his heart is always living upon Him. As the sap *manifests itself in producing the foliage and fruit of the tree*, so with a truly healthy Christian, his grace is externally manifested in his walk and conversation. If you talk with him, he cannot help speaking about Jesus. If you notice his actions you will see that he has been with Jesus. He has so much sap within, that it must fill his conduct and conversation with life.

'He began to wash the disciples' feet'
John 13:5

The Lord Jesus loves His people so much, that every day He is still doing for them much that is analogous to washing their soiled feet. Their poorest actions He accepts; their deepest sorrow He feels; their slenderest wish he hears, and their every transgression He forgives. He is still their servant as well as their Friend and Master. He not only performs majestic deeds for them, as wearing the mitre on His brow, and the precious jewels glittering on His breastplate, and standing up to plead for them, but humbly, patiently, He yet goes about among His people with the basin and the towel. He does this when He puts away from us day by day our constant infirmities and sins. Last night, when you bowed the knee, you mournfully confessed that much of your conduct was not worthy of your profession; and even tonight, you must mourn afresh that you have fallen again into the selfsame folly and sin from which special grace delivered you long ago; and yet Jesus will have great patience with you; He will hear your confession of sin; he will say, 'I will, be thou clean'; He will again apply the blood of sprinkling, and speak peace to your conscience, and remove every spot. It is a great act of eternal love when Christ once for all absolves the sinner, and puts him into the family of God; but what condescending patience there is when the Saviour with much long-suffering bears the oft recurring follies of His wayward disciple; day by day, and hour by hour, washing away the multiplied transgressions of His erring but yet beloved child! To dry up a flood of rebellion is something marvellous, but to endure the constant dropping of repeated offences - to bear with a perpetual trying of patience, this is divine indeed! While we find comfort and peace in our Lord's daily cleansing, its legitimate influence upon us will be to increase our watchfulness, and quicken our desire for holiness. *Is it so?*

'For the truth's sake, which dwelleth in us,
and shall be with us for ever'
2 John 2

Once let the truth of God obtain an entrance into the human heart and subdue the whole man unto itself, no power human or infernal can dislodge it. We entertain it not as a guest but as the master of the house - this is a *Christian necessity*, he is no Christian who doth not thus believe. Those who feel the vital power of the gospel, and know the might of the Holy Ghost as He opens, applies, and seals the Lord's Word, would sooner be torn to pieces than be rent away from the gospel of their salvation. What a thousand mercies are wrapt up in the assurance that the truth will be with us for ever; will be our living support, our dying comfort, our rising song, our eternal glory; this is *Christian privilege*, without it our faith were little worth. Some truths we outgrow and leave behind, for they are but rudiments and lessons for beginners, but we cannot thus deal with Divine truth, for though it is sweet food for babes, it is in the highest sense strong meat for men. The truth that we are sinners is painfully with us to humble and make us watchful; the more blessed truth that whosoever believeth on the Lord Jesus shall be saved, abides with us as our hope and joy. Experience, so far from loosening our hold of the doctrines of grace, has knit us to them more and more firmly; our grounds and motives for believing are now more strong, more numerous than ever, and we have reason to expect that it will be so till in death we clasp the Saviour in our arms.

Wherever this abiding love of truth can be discovered, we are bound to exercise our love. No narrow circle can contain our gracious sympathies, wide as the election of grace must be our communion of heart. Much of error may be mingled with truth received, let us war with the error but still love the brother for the measure of truth which we see in Him; above all let us love and spread the truth ourselves.

'She gleaned in the field after the reapers: and her hap was to light on a part of the field belonging unto Boaz, who was of the kindred of Elimelech'
Ruth 2:3

Her *hap was*. Yes, it seemed nothing but an accident, but how divinely was it overruled! Ruth had gone forth with her mother's blessing under the care of her mother's God, to humble but honourable toil, and the providence of God was guiding her every step. Little did she know that amid the sheaves she would find a husband, that he should make her the joint owner of all those broad acres, and that she a poor foreigner, should become one of the progenitors of the great Messiah. God is very good to those who trust in Him, and often surprises them with unlooked for blessings. Little do we know what may happen to us tomorrow, but this sweet fact may cheer us, that no good thing shall be withheld. Chance is banished from the faith of Christians, for they see the hand of God in everything. The trivial events of today or tomorrow may involve consequences of the highest importance. O Lord, deal as graciously with Thy servants as Thou didst with Ruth.

How blessed would it be, if, in wandering in the field of meditation tonight, our hap should be to light upon the place where our next Kinsman will reveal Himself to us! O Spirit of God, guide us to Him. We would sooner glean in His field than bear away the whole harvest from any other. O for the footsteps of His flock, which may conduct us to the green pastures where He dwells! This is a weary world when Jesus is away - we could better do without sun and moon than without Him - but how divinely fair all things become in the glory of His presence! Our souls know the virtue which dwells in Jesus, and can never be content without Him. We will wait in prayer this night until our hap shall be to light on a part of the field belonging to Jesus wherein He will manifest Himself to us.

*'Ye looked for much, and, lo, it came to little; and
when ye brought it home, I did blow upon it. Why?
saith the Lord of hosts. Because of mine house that
is waste, and ye run every man unto his own house'*
Haggai 1:9

Churlish souls stint their contributions to the ministry
and missionary operations, and call such saving good
economy; little do they dream that they are thus
impoverishing themselves. Their excuse is that they
must care for their own families, and they forget that to
neglect the house of God is the sure way to bring ruin
upon their own houses. Our God has a method in
providence by which he can succeed our endeavours
beyond our expectation, or can defeat our plans to our
confusion and dismay; by a turn of His hand He can
steer our vessel in a profitable channel, or run it
aground in poverty and bankruptcy. It is the teaching of
Scripture that the Lord enriches the liberal and leaves
the miserly to find out that withholding tendeth to
poverty. In a very wide sphere of observation, I have
noticed that the most generous Christians of my
acquaintance have been always the most happy, and
almost invariably the most prosperous. I have seen the
liberal giver rise to wealth of which he never dreamed;
and I have as often seen the mean, ungenerous churl
descend to poverty by the very parsimony by which he
thought to rise. Men trust good stewards with larger
and larger sums, and so it frequently is with the Lord;
He gives by cartloads to those who give by bushels.
Where wealth is not bestowed the Lord makes the little
much by the contentment which the sanctified heart
feels in a portion of which the tithe has been dedicated
to the Lord. Selfishness looks first at home, but
godliness seeks first the kingdom of God and His
righteousness, yet in the long run selfishness is loss,
and godliness is great gain. It needs faith to act towards
our God with an open hand, but surely He deserves it
of us; and all that we can do is a very poor acknowledgment of our amazing indebtedness to His goodness.

'All the rivers run into the sea; yet the sea is not
full; unto the place from whence the rivers come,
thither they return again'
Ecclesiastes 1:7

Everything sublunary is on the move, time knows
nothing of rest. The solid earth is a rolling ball, and the
great sun himself a star obediently fulfilling its course
around some greater luminary. Tides move the rock,
winds stir the airy ocean, friction wears the rock:
change and death rule everywhere. The sea is not a
miser's storehouse for a wealth of waters, for as by one
force the waters flow into it, by another they are lifted
from it. Men are born but to die: everything is hurry,
worry, and vexation of spirit. Friend of the unchanging
Jesus, what a joy it is to reflect upon thy changeless
heritage; thy sea of bliss which will be for ever full,
since God Himself shall pour eternal rivers of pleasure
into it. We seek an abiding city beyond the skies, and
we shall not be disappointed.

The passage before us may well teach us gratitude.
Father Ocean is a great receiver, but he is a generous
distributor. What the rivers bring him he returns to the
earth in the form of clouds and rain. That man is out of
joint with the universe who takes all but makes no
return. To give to others is but sowing seed for
ourselves. He who is so good a steward as to be willing
to use his substance for his Lord, shall be entrusted
with more. Friend of Jesus, art thou rendering to Him
according to the benefit received? Much has been given
thee, what is thy fruit? Hast thou done all? Canst thou
not do more? To be selfish is to be wicked. Suppose the
ocean gave up none of its watery treasure, it would
bring ruin upon our race. God forbid that any of us
should follow the ungenerous and destructive policy of
living unto ourselves. Jesus pleased not Himself. All
fulness dwells in Him, but of His fulness have all we
received. O for Jesus' spirit, that henceforth we may
live not unto ourselves!

'It is a faithful saying'
2 Timothy 2:11

Paul has four of these *'faithful sayings'*. The first occurs in 1 Timothy 1:15, 'This is a faithful saying, and worthy of all acceptation, that Christ Jesus came into the world to save sinners'. The next is in 1 Timothy 4:8, 'Godliness is profitable unto all things, having the promise of the life that now is, and of that which is to come. This is a faithful saying, and worthy of all acceptation.' The third is in 2 Timothy 2:12, 'It is a faithful saying - If we suffer with Him we shall also reign with Him'; and the fourth is in Titus 3:8, 'This is a faithful saying, that they which have believed in God might be careful to maintain good works'. We may trace a connection between these faithful sayings. The first one lays the foundation of our eternal salvation in the free grace of God, as shown to us in the mission of the great Redeemer. The next affirms the double blessedness which we obtain through this salvation - the blessings of the upper and nether springs - of time and of eternity. The third shows one of the duties to which the chosen people are called; we are ordained to suffer for Christ with the promise that 'if we suffer, we shall also reign with Him'. The last sets forth the active form of Christian service, bidding us diligently to maintain good works. Thus we have the root of salvation in free grace; next, the privileges of that salvation in the life which now is, and in that which is to come; and we have also the two great branches of suffering with Christ and serving with Christ, loaded with the fruits of the Spirit. Treasure up these faithful sayings. Let them be the guides of our life, our comfort, and our instruction. The apostle of the Gentiles proved them to be faithful, they are faithful still, not one word shall fall to the ground; they are worthy of all acceptation, let us accept them now, and prove their faithfulness. Let these four faithful sayings be written on the four corners of my house.

'We are all as an unclean thing'
Isaiah 64:6

The believer is a new creature, he belongs to a holy generation and a peculiar people - the Spirit of God is in him, and in all respects he is far removed from the natural man; but for all that the Christian is a sinner still. He is so from the imperfection of his nature, and will continue so to the end of his earthly life. The black fingers of sin leave smuts upon our fairest robes. Sin mars our repentance, ere the great Potter has finished it, upon the wheel. Selfishness defiles our tears, and unbelief tampers with our faith. The best thing we ever did apart from the merit of Jesus only swelled the number of our sins; for when we have been most pure in our own sight, yet, like the heavens, we are not pure in God's sight; and as He charged His angels with folly, much more must He charge us with it, even in our most angelic frames of mind. The song which thrills to heaven, and seeks to emulate seraphic strains, hath human discords in it. The prayer which moves the arm of God is still a bruised and battered prayer, and only moves that arm because the sinless One, the great Mediator, has stepped in to take away the sin of our supplication. The most golden faith or the purest degree of sanctification to which a Christian ever attained on earth, has still so much alloy in it as to be only worthy of the flames, in itself considered. Every night we look in the glass we see a sinner, and had need confess, 'We are all as an unclean thing, and all our righteousnesses are as filthy rags'. Oh, how precious the blood of Christ to such hearts as ours! How priceless a gift is His perfect righteousness! And how bright the hope of perfect holiness hereafter! Even now, though sin dwells in us, *its power is broken*. It has no dominion; it is a broken-backed snake; we are in bitter conflict with it, but it is with a vanquished foe that we have to deal. Yet a little while and we shall enter victoriously into the city where nothing defileth.

'I have chosen you out of the world'
John 15:19

Here is distinguishing grace and discriminating regard; for some are made the special objects of divine affection. Do not be afraid to dwell upon this high doctrine of election. When your mind is most heavy and depressed, you will find it to be a bottle of richest cordial. Those who doubt the doctrines of grace, or who cast them into the shade, miss the richest clusters of Eshcol; they lose the wines on the lees well refined, the fat things full of marrow. There is no balm in Gilead comparable to it. If the honey in Jonathan's wood when but touched enlightened *the eyes*, this is honey which will enlighten *your heart* to love and learn the mysteries of the kingdom of God. Eat, and fear not a surfeit; live upon this choice dainty, and fear not that it will be too delicate a diet. Meat from the King's table will hurt none of his courtiers. Desire to have your mind enlarged, that you may comprehend more and more the eternal, everlasting, discriminating love of God. When you have mounted as high as election, tarry on its sister mount, the covenant of grace. Covenant engagements are the munitions of stupendous rock behind which we lie entrenched; covenant engagements with the surety, Christ Jesus, are the quiet resting-places of trembling spirits.

> His oath, His covenant, His blood,
> Support me in the raging flood;
> When every earthly prop gives way,
> This still is all my strength and stay.

If Jesus undertook to bring me to glory, and if the Father promised that He would give me to the Son to be a part of the infinite reward of the travail of His soul; then, my soul, till God himself shall be unfaithful, till Jesus shall cease to be the truth, thou art safe. When David danced before the ark, he told Michal that election made him do so. Come, my soul, exult before the God of grace and leap for joy of heart.

'His head is as the most fine gold,
His locks are bushy, and black as a raven'
Solomon's Song 5:11

Comparisons all fail to set forth the Lord Jesus, but the
spouse uses the best within her reach. By *the head* of
Jesus we may understand His deity, 'for the head of
Christ is God'; and then the ingot of purest gold is the
best conceivable metaphor, but all too poor to describe
one so precious, so pure, so dear, so glorious. Jesus is
not a grain of gold, but a vast globe of it, a priceless
mass of treasure such as earth and heaven cannot excel.
The creatures are mere iron and clay, they all shall
perish like wood, hay, and stubble, but the everliving
Head of the creation of God shall shine on for ever and
ever. In Him is no mixture, nor smallest taint of alloy.
He is for ever infinitely holy and altogether divine. *The
bushy locks* depict His manly vigour. There is nothing
effeminate in our Beloved. He is the manliest of men.
Bold as a lion, laborious as an ox, swift as an eagle.
Every conceivable and inconceivable beauty is to be
found in Him, though once He was despised and
rejected of men.

> His head the finest gold;
>> With secret sweet perfume,
> His curled locks hang all as black
>> As any raven's plume.

The glory of His head is not shorn away, He is eternally
crowned with peerless majesty. *The black hair* indicates youthful freshness, for Jesus has the dew of His
youth upon Him. Others grow languid with age, but He
is for ever a Priest as was Melchisedek; others come
and go, but He abides as God upon His throne, world
without end. We will behold Him tonight and adore
Him. Angels are gazing upon Him - His redeemed must
not turn away their eyes from Him. Where else is there
such a Beloved? O for an hour's fellowship with Him!
Away, ye intruding cares! Jesus draws me, and I run
after Him.

> *'After this manner therefore pray ye:*
> *Our Father which art in heaven, etc.'*
> Matthew 6:9

This prayer begins where all true prayer must commence, with the spirit of *adoption*, 'Our Father'. There is no acceptable prayer until we can say, 'I will arise and go unto my Father'. This childlike spirit soon perceives the grandeur of the Father 'in heaven', and ascends to *devout adoration*, 'Hallowed be Thy name'. The child lisping, 'Abba, Father', grows into the cherub crying, 'Holy, Holy, Holy'. There is but a step from rapturous worship to the *glowing missionary spirit*, which is a sure outgrowth of filial love and reverent adoration - 'Thy kingdom come, Thy will be done on earth as it is in heaven'. Next follows the heartfelt *expression of dependence* upon God - 'Give us this day our daily bread'. Being further illuminated by the Spirit, he discovers that he is not only dependent, but sinful, hence he *entreats for mercy*, 'Forgive us our debts as we forgive our debtors': and being pardoned, having the righteousness of Christ imputed, and knowing his acceptance with God, he humbly *supplicates for holy perseverance*, 'Lead us not into temptation'. The man who is really forgiven, is anxious not to offend again; the possession of justification leads to an anxious desire for sanctification. 'Forgive us our debts', that is justification; 'Lead us not into temptation, but deliver us from evil', that is sanctification in its negative and positive forms. As the result of all this, there follows a *triumphant ascription of praise*, 'Thine is the kingdom, the power, and the glory, for ever and ever, Amen'. We rejoice that *our* King reigns in providence and shall reign in grace, from the river even to the ends of the earth, and of His dominion there shall be no end. Thus from a sense of adoption, up to fellowship with our reigning Lord, this short model of prayer conducts the soul. Lord, teach us thus to pray.

> *'But their eyes were holden*
> *that they should not know Him'*
> Luke 24:16

The disciples ought to have known Jesus, they had heard His voice so often, and gazed upon that marred face so frequently, that it is wonderful they did not discover Him. Yet is it not so with you also? You have not seen Jesus lately. You have been to His table, and you have not met Him there. You are in a dark trouble this evening, and though He plainly says, 'It is I, be not afraid', yet you cannot discern Him. Alas! our eyes are holden. We know His voice; we have looked into His face; we have leaned our head upon His bosom, and yet, though Christ is very near us, we are saying, 'O that I knew where I might find Him'! We should know Jesus, for we have the Scriptures to reflect His image, and yet how possible it is for us to open that precious book and have no glimpse of the Wellbeloved! Dear child of God, are you in that state? Jesus feedeth among the lilies of the word, and you walk among those lilies and yet you behold Him not. He is accustomed to walk through the glades of Scripture, and to commune with His people, as the Father did with Adam in the cool of the day, and yet you are in the garden of Scripture, but cannot see Him, though He is always there. And why do we not see Him? It must be ascribed in our case, as in the disciples', to unbelief. They evidently did not expect to see Jesus, and therefore they did not know Him. To a great extent in spiritual things we get what we expect of the Lord. Faith alone can bring us to see Jesus. Make it your prayer, 'Lord, open Thou mine eyes, that I may see my Saviour present with me'. It is a blessed thing to *want* to see Him; but oh! it is better far to gaze upon Him. To those who seek Him He is kind; but to those who find Him, beyond expression is He dear!

'I will praise Thee, O Lord'
Psalm 9:1

Praise should always follow answered prayer; as the mist of earth's gratitude rises when the sun of heaven's love warms the ground. Hath the Lord been gracious to thee, and inclined his ear to the voice of thy supplication? Then praise Him as long as thou livest. Let the ripe fruit drop upon the fertile soil from which it drew its life. Deny not a song to Him who hath answered thy prayer and given thee the desire of thy heart. To be silent over God's mercies is to incur the guilt of ingratitude; it is to act as basely as the nine lepers, who after they had been cured of their leprosy, returned not to give thanks unto the healing Lord. To forget to praise God is to refuse to benefit ourselves; for praise, like prayer, is one great means of promoting the growth of the spiritual life. It helps to remove our burdens, to excite our hope, to increase our faith. It is a healthful and invigorating exercise which quickens the pulse of the believer, and nerves him for fresh enterprises in his Master's service. To bless God for mercies received is also the way to benefit our fellow-men, 'the humble shall hear thereof and be glad'. Others who have been in like circumstances shall take comfort if we can say, 'Oh! magnify the Lord with me, and let us exalt His name together; this poor man cried, and the Lord heard him'. Weak hearts will be strengthened, and drooping saints will be revived as they listen to our 'songs of deliverance'. Their doubts and fears will be rebuked, as we teach and admonish one another in psalms and hymns and spiritual songs. They too shall 'sing in the ways of the Lord', when they hear us magnify His holy name. Praise is the most heavenly of Christian duties. The angels pray not, but they cease not to praise both day and night; and the redeemed, clothed in white robes, with palm-branches in their hands, are never weary of singing the new song, 'Worthy is the Lamb'.

*'Thou that dwellest in the gardens, the companions
hearken to Thy voice: cause me to hear it'*
Solomon's Song 8:13

My sweet Lord Jesus remembers well the garden of
Gethsemane, and although He has left that garden, He
now dwells in the garden of His church: there He
unbosoms Himself to those who keep His blessed
company. That voice of love with which He speaks to
His beloved is more musical than the harps of heaven.
There is a depth of melodious love within it which
leaves all human music far behind. Tens of thousands
on earth, and millions above, are indulged with its
harmonious accents. Some whom I well know, and
whom I greatly envy, are at this moment hearkening to
the beloved voice. O that I were a partaker of their joys!
It is true some of these are poor, others bedridden, and
some near the gates of death, but O my Lord, I would
cheerfully starve with them, pine with them, or die with
them, if I might but hear Thy voice. Once I did hear it
often, but I have grieved Thy Spirit. Return unto me in
compassion, and once again say unto me, 'I am thy
salvation'. No other voice can content me; I know Thy
voice, and cannot be deceived by another, let me hear
it, I pray thee. I know not what Thou wilt say, neither
do I make any condition, O my Beloved, do but let me
hear Thee speak, and if it be a rebuke I will bless Thee
for it. Perhaps to cleanse my dull ear may need an
operation very grievous to the flesh, but let it cost what
it may I turn not from the one consuming desire, cause
me to hear Thy voice. Bore my ear afresh; pierce my
ear with Thy harshest notes, only do not permit me to
continue deaf to Thy calls. Tonight, Lord, grant Thine
unworthy one his desire, for I am Thine, and Thou hast
bought me with Thy blood. Thou hast opened mine eye
to see Thee, and the sight has saved me. Lord, open
Thou mine ear. I have read Thy heart, now let me hear
Thy lips.

'Renew a right spirit within me'
Psalm 51:10

A backslider, if there be a spark of life left in him will groan after restoration. In this renewal the same exercise of grace is required as at our conversion. We needed repentance then; we certainly need it now. We wanted faith that we might come to Christ at first; only the like grace can bring us to Jesus now. We wanted a word from the Most High, a word from the lip of the loving One, to end our fears then; we shall soon discover, when under a sense of present sin, that we need it now. No man can be renewed without as real and true a manifestation of the Holy Spirit's energy as he felt at first, because the work is as great, and flesh and blood are as much in the way now as ever they were. Let thy personal weakness, O Christian, be an argument to make thee pray earnestly to thy God for help. Remember, David when he felt himself to be powerless, did not fold his arms or close his lips, but he hastened to the mercy-seat with 'renew a right spirit within me'. Let not the doctrine that you, unaided, can do nothing, make you sleep; but let it be a goad in your side to drive you with an awful earnestness to Israel's strong Helper. O that you may have grace to plead with God, as though you pleaded for your very life - 'Lord, renew a right spirit within me'. He who *sincerely* prays to God to do this, will prove his honesty by using the means through which God works. Be much in prayer; live much upon the Word of God; kill the lusts which have driven your Lord from you; be careful to watch over the future uprisings of sin. The Lord has His own appointed ways; sit by the wayside and you will be ready when He passes by. Continue in all those blessed ordinances which will foster and nourish your dying graces; and, knowing that all the power must proceed from Him, cease not to cry, 'Renew a right spirit within me'.

> '*I did know thee in the wilderness,
> in the land of great drought*'
> Hosea 13:5

Yes, Lord, Thou didst indeed know me in my *fallen state*, and Thou didst even then choose me for Thyself. When I was loathsome and self-abhorred, Thou didst receive me as Thy child, and Thou didst satisfy my craving wants. Blessed for ever be Thy name for this free, rich, abounding mercy. Since then, *my inward experience* has often been a wilderness; but Thou hast owned me still as Thy beloved, and poured streams of love and grace into me to gladden me, and make me fruitful. Yea, when my *outward circumstances* have been at the worst, and I have wandered in a land of drought, Thy sweet presence has solaced me. Men have not known me when scorn has awaited me, but Thou hast know my soul in adversities, for no affliction dims the lustre of Thy love. Most gracious Lord, I magnify Thee for all Thy faithfulness to me in trying circumstances, and I deplore that I should at any time have forgotten Thee and been exalted in heart, when I have owed all to Thy gentleness and love. Have mercy upon Thy servant in this thing!

My soul, if Jesus thus acknowledged thee in thy low estate, be sure that thou own both Himself and His cause now that thou art in thy prosperity. Be not lifted up by thy worldly successes so as to be ashamed of the truth or of the poor church with which thou hast been associated. Follow Jesus into the wilderness: bear the cross with Him when the heat of persecution grows hot. He owned thee, O my soul, in thy poverty and shame - never be so treacherous as to be ashamed of Him. O for more shame at the thought of being ashamed of my best Beloved! Jesus, my soul cleaveth to Thee.

> I'll turn to Thee in days of light,
>   As well as nights of care,
> Thou brightest amid all that's bright!
>   Thou fairest of the fair!

November

'The Church in thy house'
Philemon 2

Is there a Church in this house? Are parents, children, friends, servants, all members of it? Or are some still unconverted? Let us pause here and let the question go round - *Am I a member of the Church in this house?* How would father's heart leap for joy, and mother's eyes fill up with holy tears if from the eldest to the youngest all were saved! Let us pray for this great mercy until the Lord shall grant it to us. Probably it has been the dearest object of Philemon's desires to have all his household saved; but it was not at first granted him in its fulness. He had a wicked servant, Onesimus, who, having wronged him, ran away from his service. His master's prayers followed him, and at last, as God would have it, Onesimus was led to hear Paul preach; his heart was touched, and he returned to Philemon, not only to be a faithful servant, but a brother beloved, adding another member to the Church in Philemon's house. Is there an unconverted servant or child absent this morning? Make special supplication that such may, on their return to their home, gladden all hearts with good news of what grace has done! Is there one present? Let him partake in the same earnest entreaty.

If there be such a Church in our house, let us order it well, and let all act as in the sight of God. Let us move in the common affairs of life with studied holiness, diligence, kindness, and integrity. More is expected of a Church than of an ordinary household; family worship must, in such a case, be more devout and hearty; internal love must be more warm and unbroken, and external conduct must be more sanctified and Christlike. We need not fear that the smallness of our number will put us out of the list of Churches, for the Holy Spirit has here enrolled a *family-church in the inspired* book of remembrance. As a Church let us now draw nigh to the great head of the one Church universal, and let us beseech Him to give us grace to shine before men to the glory of His name.

*'And knew not until the flood came, and took them
all away: so shall also the coming of the Son of man be'*
Matthew 24:39

Universal was the doom, neither rich nor poor escaped:
the learned and the illiterate, the admired and the
abhorred, the religious and the profane, the old and the
young, all sank one common ruin. Some had doubtless
ridiculed the patriarch - where now their merry jests?
Others had threatened him for his zeal which they
counted madness - where now their boastings and hard
speeches? The critic who judged the old man's work is
drowned in the same sea which covers his sneering
companions. Those who spoke patronisingly of the
good man's fidelity to his convictions, but shared not
in them, have sunk to rise no more, and the workers
who for pay helped to build the wondrous ark, are all
lost also. The flood swept them *all* away, and made no
single exception. Even so, out of Christ, final destruction is sure to every man of woman born; no rank,
possession, or character, shall suffice to save a single
soul who has not believed in the Lord Jesus. My soul,
behold this widespread judgment and tremble at it.

   How marvellous the general apathy! They were all
eating and drinking, marrying and giving in marriage,
till the awful morning dawned. There was not one wise
man upon earth out of the ark. Folly duped the whole
race, folly as to self-preservation - the most foolish of
all follies. Folly in doubting the most true God - the
most malignant of fooleries. Strange, my soul, is it
not? All men are negligent of their souls till grace gives
them reason, then they leave their madness and act like
rational beings, but not till then.

   All, blessed be God, were safe in the ark, no ruin
entered there. From the huge elephant down to the tiny
mouse all were safe. The timid hare was equally secure
with the courageous lion, the helpless cony as safe as
the laborious ox. All are safe in Jesus. My soul, art thou
in Him?

'I am the Lord, I change not'
Malachi 3:6

It is well for us that, amidst all the variableness of life, there is One whom change cannot affect; One whose heart can never alter, and on whose brow mutability can make no furrows. All things else have changed - all things are changing. The sun itself grows dim with age; the world is waxing old; the folding up of the worn-out vesture has commenced; the heavens and earth must soon pass away; they shall perish, they shall wax old as doth a garment; but there is One who only hath immortality, of whose years there is no end, and in whose person there is no change. The delight which the mariner feels, when, after having been tossed about for many a day, he steps again upon the solid shore, is the satisfaction of a Christian when, amidst all the changes of this troublous life, he rests the foot of his faith upon this truth - *'I am the Lord, I change not'*.

The stability which the anchor gives the ship when it has at last obtained a hold-fast, is like that which the Christian's hope affords him when it fixes itself upon this glorious truth. With God 'is no variableness, neither shadow of turning'. Whatever His attributes were of old, they are now; His power, His wisdom, His justice, His truth, are alike unchanged. He has ever been the refuge of his people, their stronghold in the day of trouble, and He is their sure helper still. He is unchanged in His *love*. He has loved his people with 'an everlasting love'; He loves them now as much as ever He did, and when all earthly things shall have melted in the last conflagration, His love will still wear the dew of its youth. Precious is the assurance that He changes not! The wheel of providence revolves, but its axle is eternal love.

> Death and change are busy ever,
>   Man decays, and ages move;
> But His mercy waneth never;
>   God is wisdom, God is love.

'Horror hath taken hold upon me because of the
wicked that forsake Thy law'
Psalm 119:53

My soul, feelest thou this holy shuddering at the sins of others? for otherwise thou lackest inward holiness. David's cheeks were wet with rivers of waters because of prevailing unholiness; Jeremiah desired eyes like fountains that he might lament the iniquities of Israel, and Lot was vexed with the conversation of the men of Sodom. Those upon whom the mark was set in Ezekiel's vision, were those who sighed and cried for the abominations of Jerusalem. It cannot but grieve gracious souls to see what pains men take to go to hell. They know the evil of sin experimentally, and they are alarmed to see others flying like moths into its blaze. Sin makes the righteous shudder, because it violates a holy law, which it is to every man's highest interest to keep; it pulls down the pillars of the commonwealth. Sin in others horrifies a believer, because it puts him in mind of the baseness of his own heart: when he sees a transgressor he cries with the saint mentioned by Bernard, 'He fell today and I may fall tomorrow'. Sin to a believer is horrible, because it crucified the Saviour; he sees in every iniquity the nails and spear. How can a saved soul behold that cursed kill-Christ sin without abhorrence? Say, my heart, dost thou sensibly join in all this? It is an awful thing to insult God to his face. The good God deserves better treatment, the great God claims it, the just God will have it, or repay His adversary to his face. An awakened heart trembles at the audacity of sin, and stands alarmed at the contemplation of its punishment. How monstrous a thing is rebellion! How direful a doom is prepared for the ungodly! My soul, never laugh at sin's fooleries, lest thou come to smile at sin itself. It is thine enemy, and thy Lord's enemy - view it with detestation, for so only canst thou evidence the possession of holiness, without which no man can see the Lord.

'Behold, he prayeth'
Acts 9:11

Prayers are instantly noticed in heaven. The moment Saul began to pray the Lord heard him. Here is comfort for the distressed but praying soul. Oftentimes a poor broken-hearted one bends his knee, but can only utter his wailing in the language of sighs and tears; yet that groan has made all the harps of heaven thrill with music; that tear has been caught by God and treasured in the lachrymatory of heaven. 'Thou puttest my tears into thy bottle', implies that they are caught as they flow. The suppliant, whose fears prevent his words, will be well understood by the Most High. He may only look up with misty eye; but 'prayer is the falling of a tear'. Tears are the diamonds of heaven; sighs are a part of the music of Jehovah's court, and are numbered with 'the sublimest strains that reach the majesty on high'. Think not that your prayer, however weak or trembling, will be unregarded. Jacob's ladder is lofty, but our prayers shall lean upon the Angel of the covenant and so climb its starry rounds. Our God not only *hears* prayer but also *loves* to hear it. 'He forgetteth not the cry of the humble.' True, He regards not high looks and lofty words; he cares not for the pomp and pageantry of kings; He listens not to the swell of martial music; He regards not the triumph and pride of man; but wherever there is a heart big with sorrow, or a lip quivering with agony, or a deep groan, or a penitential sigh, the heart of Jehovah is open; He marks it down in the registry of His memory; He puts our prayers, like rose leaves, between the pages of His book of remembrance, and when the volume is opened at last, there shall be a precious fragrance springing up therefrom.

> Faith asks no signal from the skies,
>   To show that prayers accepted rise,
> Our Priest is in His holy place,
>   And answers from the throne of grace.

*'Their prayer came up to His holy
dwelling place, even unto heaven'*
2 Chronicles 30:27

Prayer is the never-failing resort of the Christian in any case, in every plight. When you cannot use your sword you may take to the weapon of all-prayer. Your powder may be damp, your bow-string may be relaxed, but the weapon of all-prayer need never be out of order. Leviathan laughs at the javelin, but he trembles at prayer. Sword and spear need furbishing, but prayer never rusts, and when we think it most blunt it cuts the best. Prayer is an open door which none can shut. Devils may surround you on all sides, but the way upward is always open, and as long as that road is unobstructed, you will not fall into the enemy's hand. We can never be taken by blockade, escalade, mine, or storm, so long as heavenly succours can come down to us by Jacob's ladder to relieve us in the time of our necessities. Prayer is never out of season: in summer and in winter its merchandise is precious. Prayer gains audience with heaven in the dead of night, in the midst of business, in the heat of noonday, in the shades of evening. In every condition, whether of poverty, or sickness, or obscurity, or slander, or doubt, your covenant God will welcome your prayer and answer it from His holy place. Nor is prayer ever *futile*. True prayer is evermore true power. You may not always get what you ask, but you shall always have your real wants supplied. When God does not answer His children according to the letter, He does so according to the spirit. If thou askest for coarse meal, wilt thou be angered because He gives thee the finest flour? If thou seekest bodily health, shouldst thou complain if instead thereof He makes thy sickness turn to the healing of spiritual maladies? Is it not better to have the cross sanctified than removed? This evening, my soul, forget not to offer thy petition and request, for the Lord is ready to grant thee thy desires.

'For my strength is made perfect in weakness'
2 Corinthians 12:9

A primary qualification for serving God with any amount of success, and for doing God's work well and triumphantly, is a sense of our own weakness. When God's warrior marches forth to battle, strong in his own might, when he boasts, 'I know that I shall conquer, my own right arm and my conquering sword shall get unto me the victory', defeat is not far distant. God will not go forth with that man who marches in his own strength. He who reckoneth on victory thus has reckoned wrongly, for 'it is not by might, nor by power, but by my Spirit, saith the Lord of hosts'. They who go forth to fight, boasting of their prowess, shall return with their gay banners trailed in the dust, and their armour stained with disgrace. Those who serve God must serve Him in His own way, and in His strength, or He will never accept their service. That which man doth, unaided by divine strength, God can never own. The mere fruits of the earth He casteth away; He will only reap that corn, the seed of which was sown from heaven, watered by grace, and ripened by the sun of divine love. God will empty out all that thou hast before He will put His own into thee; He will first clean out thy granaries before He will fill them with the finest of the wheat. The river of God is full of water; but not one drop of it flows from earthly springs. God will have no strength used in His battles but the strength which He Himself imparts. Are you mourning over your own weakness? Take courage, for there must be a consciousness of weakness before the Lord will give thee victory. Your emptiness is but the preparation for your being filled, and your casting down is but the making ready for your lifting up.

When I am weak then am I strong,
Grace is my shield, and Christ my song.

'In Thy light shall we see light'
Psalm 36:9

No lips can tell the love of Christ to the heart till Jesus Himself shall speak within. Descriptions all fall flat and tame unless the Holy Ghost fills them with life and power; till our Immanuel reveals Himself within, the soul sees Him not. If you would see the sun, would you gather together the common means of illumination, and seek in that way to behold the orb of day? No, the wise man knoweth that the sun must reveal itself, and only by its own blaze can that mighty lamp be seen. It is so with Christ. 'Blessed art thou, Simon Bar-jona,' said He to Peter, 'for flesh and blood hath not revealed this unto thee.' Purify flesh and blood by any educational process you may select, elevate mental faculties to the highest degree of intellectual power, yet none of these can reveal Christ. The Spirit of God must come with power, and overshadow the man with His wings, and then in that mystic holy of holies the Lord Jesus must display Himself to the sanctified eye, as He doth not unto the purblind sons of men. Christ must be His own mirror. The great mass of this blear-eyed world can see nothing of the ineffable glories of Immanuel. He stands before them without form or comeliness, a root out of a dry ground, rejected by the vain and despised by the proud. Only where the Spirit has touched the eye with eye-salve, quickened the heart with divine life, and educated the soul to a heavenly taste, only there is He understood. 'To you that believe He is precious'; to you He is the chief cornerstone, the Rock of your salvation, your all in all; but to others He is 'a stone of stumbling and a rock of offence'. Happy are those to whom our Lord manifests Himself, for His promise to such is that He will *make His abode with them*. O Jesus, our Lord, our heart is open, come in, and go out no more for ever. Show Thyself to us now! Favour us with a glimpse of Thine all-conquering charms.

'No weapon that is formed against thee shall prosper'
Isaiah 54:17

This day is notable in English history for two great deliverances wrought by God for us. On this day the plot of the Papists to destroy our Houses of Parliament was discovered, 1605.

> While for princes they prepare
> In caverns deep a burning snare,
> He shot from heaven a piercing ray,
> And the dark treachery brought to day.

And secondly - today is the anniversary of the landing of King William III at Torbay, by which the hope of Popish ascendancy was quashed, and religious liberty was secured, 1688.

This day ought to be celebrated, not by the saturnalia of striplings, but by the songs of the saints. Our Puritan forefathers most devoutly made it a special time of thanksgiving. There is extant a record of the annual sermons preached by Matthew Henry on this day. Our Protestant feeling, and our love of liberty, should make us regard its anniversary with holy gratitude. Let our hearts and lips exclaim, 'We have heard with our ears, and our fathers have told us the wondrous things which Thou didst in their day, and in the old time before them'. Thou hast made this nation the home of the gospel; and when the foe has risen against her, Thou hast shielded her. Help us to offer repeated songs for repeated deliverances. Grant us more and more a hatred of Antichrist, and hasten on the day of her entire extinction. Till then and ever, we believe the promise, 'No weapon that is formed against thee shall prosper'. Should it not be laid upon the heart of every lover of the gospel of Jesus on this day to plead for the overturning of false doctrines and the extension of divine truth? Would it not be well to search our own hearts, and turn out any of the Popish lumber of self-righteousness which may lie concealed therein?

'Be thankful unto Him, and bless His name'
Psalm 100:4

Our Lord would have all His people rich in high and happy thoughts concerning His blessed person. Jesus is not content that His brethren should think meanly of Him; it is His pleasure that His espoused ones should be delighted with His beauty. We are not to regard Him as a bare necessary like to bread and water, but as a luxurious delicacy, as a rare and ravishing delight. To this end He has revealed Himself as the 'pearl of great price' in its peerless beauty, as the 'bundle of myrrh' in its refreshing fragrance, as the 'rose of Sharon' in its lasting perfume, as the 'lily' in its spotless purity.

As a help to high thoughts of Christ, remember the estimation that Christ is had in beyond the skies, where things are measured by the right standard. Think how God esteems the Only Begotten, His unspeakable gift to us. Consider what the angels think of Him, as they count it their highest honour to veil their faces at His feet. Consider what the blood-washed think of Him, as day without night they sing His well deserved praises. High thoughts of Christ will enable us to act consistently with our relations towards Him. The more loftily we see Christ enthroned, and the more lowly we are when bowing before the foot of the throne, the more truly shall we be prepared to act our part towards Him. Our Lord Jesus desires us to think well of Him, that we may submit cheerfully to His authority. High thoughts of Him increase our love. Love and esteem go together. Therefore, believer, think much of your Master's excellencies. Study Him in His primeval glory, before He took upon Himself your nature! Think of the mighty love which drew Him from His throne to die upon the cross! Admire Him as He conquers all the powers of hell! See Him risen, crowned, glorified! Bow before Him as the Wonderful, the Counsellor, the mighty God, for only thus will your love to Him be what it should.

'I will pour water upon him that is thirsty'
Isaiah 44:3

When a believer has fallen into a low, sad state of feeling, he often tries to lift himself out of it by chastening himself with dark and doleful fears. Such is not the way to rise from the dust, but to continue in it. As well chain the eagle's wing to make it mount, as doubt in order to increase our grace. It is not the law, but the gospel which saves the seeking soul at first; and it is not a legal bondage, but gospel liberty which can restore the fainting believer afterwards. Slavish fear brings not back the backslider to God, but the sweet wooings of love allure him to Jesus' bosom. Are you this morning thirsting for the living God, and unhappy because you cannot find him to the delight of your heart? Have you lost the joy of religion, and is this your prayer, 'Restore unto me the joy of Thy salvation'? Are you conscious also that you are barren, like the dry ground; that you are not bringing forth the fruit unto God which He has a right to expect of you; that you are not so useful in the Church, or in the world, as your heart desires to be? Then here is exactly the promise which you need, 'I will pour water upon him that is thirsty'. You shall receive the grace you so much require, and you shall have it to the utmost reach of your needs. Water refreshes the thirsty: you shall be refreshed; your desires shall be gratified. Water quickens sleeping vegetable life: you life shall be quickened by fresh grace. Water swells the buds and makes the fruits ripen; you shall have fructifying grace: you shall be made fruitful in the ways of God. Whatever good quality there is in divine grace, you shall enjoy it to the full. All the riches of divine grace you shall receive in plenty; you shall be as it were drenched with it: and as sometimes the meadows become flooded by the bursting rivers, and the fields are turned into pools, so shall you be - the thirsty land shall be springs of water.

*'Saying, This is the blood of the testament
which God hath enjoined unto you'*
Hebrews 9:20

There is a strange power about the very name of blood,
and the sight of it is always affecting. A kind heart
cannot bear to see a sparrow bleed, and unless famil-
iarised by use, turns away with horror at the slaughter
of a beast. As to the blood of men, it is a consecrated
thing: it is murder to shed it in wrath, it is a dreadful
crime to squander it in war. Is this solemnity occasioned by the fact that the blood is the life, and the
pouring of it forth the token of death? We think so.
When we rise to contemplate the blood of the Son of
God, our awe is yet more increased and we shudder as
we think of the guilt of sin, and the terrible penalty
which the Sin-bearer endured. Blood, always precious,
is priceless when it streams from Immanuel's side.
The blood of Jesus seals the *covenant* of grace, and
makes it for ever sure. Covenants of old were made by
sacrifice, and the everlasting covenant was ratified in
the same manner. Oh, the delight of being saved upon
the sure foundation of divine engagements which
cannot be dishonoured! Salvation by the works of the
law is a frail and broken vessel whose shipwreck is
sure; but the covenant vessel fears no storms, for the
blood ensures the whole. The blood of Jesus made His
testament valid. Wills are of no power unless the
testators die. In this light the soldier's spear is a
blessed aid to faith, since it proved our Lord to be really
dead. Doubts upon that matter there can be none, and
we may boldly appropriate the legacies which He has
left for His people. Happy they who see their title to
heavenly blessings assured to them by a dying Saviour.
But has this blood no voice to us? Does it not bid us
sanctify ourselves unto Him by whom we have been
redeemed? Does it not call us to newness of life, and
incite us to entire consecration to the Lord? O that the
power of the blood might be known, and felt in us this
night!

*'Behold, I have graven thee
upon the palms of my hands'*
Isaiah 49:16

No doubt a part of the wonder which is concentrated in the word *'Behold'*, is excited by the unbelieving lamentation of the preceding sentence. Zion said, 'The Lord hath forsaken me, and my God hath forgotten me'. How amazed the divine mind seems to be at this wicked unbelief! What can be more astounding than the unfounded doubts and fears of God's favoured people? The Lord's loving word of rebuke should make us blush; He cries, 'How can I have forgotten thee, when I have graven thee upon the palms of my hands? How darest thou doubt my constant remembrance, when the memorial is set upon my very flesh?' O unbelief, how strange a marvel thou art! We know not which most to wonder at, the faithfulness of God or the unbelief of His people. He keeps His promise a thousand times, and yet the next trial makes us doubt Him. He never faileth; He is never a dry well; He is never as a setting-sun, a passing meteor, or a melting vapour; and yet we are as continually vexed with anxieties, molested with suspicions, and disturbed with fears, as if our God were the mirage of the desert. *'Behold', is a word intended to excite admiration.* Here, indeed, we have a theme for marvelling. Heaven and earth may well be astonished that rebels should obtain so great a nearness to the heart of infinite love as to be written upon the palms of His hands. 'I have graven *thee.*' It does not say, 'Thy name'. The name is there, but that is not all: 'I have graven *thee*'. See the fulness of this! I have graven thy person, thine image, thy case, thy circumstances, thy sins, thy temptations, thy weaknesses, thy wants, thy works; I have graven *thee*, everything about thee, all that concerns thee; I have put thee altogether there. Wilt thou ever say again that thy God hath forsaken thee when He has graven *thee* upon His own palms?

'And ye shall be witnesses unto Me'
Acts 1:8

In order to learn how to discharge your duty as a witness for Christ, look at His example. He is always witnessing: by the well of Samaria, or in the Temple of Jerusalem: by the lake of Gennesaret, or on the mountain's brow. He is witnessing night and day; His mighty prayers are as vocal to God as His daily services. He witnesses under all circumstances; Scribes and Pharisees cannot shut His mouth; even before Pilate He witnesses a good confession. He witnesses so clearly and distinctly that there is no mistake in Him. Christian, make your life a clear testimony. Be you as the brook wherein you may see every stone at the bottom - not as the muddy creek, of which you only see the surface - but clear and transparent, so that your heart's love to God and man may be visible to all. You need not *say*, 'I am true': *be* true. Boast not of integrity, but *be* upright. So shall your testimony be such that men cannot help seeing it. Never, for fear of feeble man, restrain your witness. Your lips have been warmed with a coal from off the altar; let them speak as like heaven-touched lips should do. 'In the morning sow thy seed, and in the evening withhold not thine hand.' Watch not the clouds, consult not the wind - in season and out of season witness for the Saviour, and if it shall come to pass that for Christ's sake and the gospel's you shall endure suffering in any shape, shrink not, but rejoice in the honour thus conferred upon you, that you are counted worthy to suffer with your Lord; and joy also in this - that your sufferings, your losses, and persecutions shall make you a platform, from which the more vigorously and with greater power you shall witness for Christ Jesus. Study your great Exemplar, and be filled with His Spirit. Remember that you need much teaching, much upholding, much grace, and much humility, if your witnessing is to be to your Master's glory.

'*As ye have received Christ Jesus the Lord*'
Colossians 2:6

The life of faith is represented as *receiving - an act which implies the very opposite of anything like merit.* It is simply the acceptance of a gift. As the earth drinks in the rain, as the sea receives the stream, as night accepts light from the stars, so we, giving nothing, partake freely of the grace of God. The saints are not, by nature, wells, or streams, they are but cisterns into which the living water flows; they are empty vessels into which God pours His salvation. The idea of receiving implies *a sense of realisation*, making the matter *a reality*. One cannot very well receive a shadow; we receive that which is substantial: so is it in the life of faith, Christ becomes real to us. While we are without faith, Jesus is a mere name to us - a person who lived a long while ago, so long ago that His life is only a history to us now! By an act of faith Jesus becomes a real person in the consciousness of our heart. But receiving also means *grasping* or *getting possession of.* The thing which I receive becomes my own: I appropriate to myself that which is given. When I receive Jesus, He becomes *my* Saviour, so mine that neither life nor death shall be able to rob me of Him. All this is to receive Christ - to take Him as God's free gift; to realise Him in my heart, and to appropriate Him as mine.

Salvation may be described as the blind receiving sight, the deaf receiving hearing, the dead receiving life; but we have not only received these blessings, we have received CHRIST JESUS Himself. It is true that He gave us life from the dead. He gave us pardon of sin; He gave us imputed righteousness. These are all precious things, but we are not content with them; we have received *Christ Himself*. The Son of God has been poured into us, and we have received Him, and appropriated Him. What a heartful Jesus must be, for heaven itself cannot contain Him!

*'The Master saith, Where is the guestchamber,
where I shall eat the passover with My disciples?'*
Mark 14:14

Jerusalem at the time of the passover was one great inn;
each householder had invited his own friends, but no
one had invited the Saviour, and He had no dwelling of
His own. It was by His own supernatural power that He
found Himself an upper room in which to keep the
feast. It is so even to this day - Jesus is not received
among the sons of men save only where by His
supernatural power and grace He makes the heart anew.
All doors are open enough to the prince of darkness, but
Jesus must clear a way for Himself or lodge in the
streets. It was through the mysterious power exerted by
our Lord that the householder raised no question, but
at once cheerfully and joyfully opened his guestchamber.
Who he was, and what he was, we do not know, but he
readily accepted the honour which the Redeemer proposed to confer upon him. In like manner it is still
discovered who are the Lord's chosen, and who are not;
for when the gospel comes to some, they fight against
it, and will not have it, but where men receive it,
welcoming it, this is a sure indication that there is a
secret work going on in the soul, and that God has
chosen them unto eternal life. Are you willing, dear
reader, to receive Christ? Then there is no difficulty in
the way; Christ will be your guest; His own power is
working with you, making you willing. What an
honour to entertain the Son of God! The heaven of
heavens cannot contain Him, and yet He condescends
to find a house within our hearts! We are not worthy
that He should come under our roof, but what an
unutterable privilege when He condescends to enter!
For then He makes a feast, and causes us to feast with
Him upon royal dainties, we sit at a banquet where the
viands are immortal, and give immortality to those who
feed thereon. Blessed among the sons of Adam is he
who entertains the angels' Lord.

'So walk ye in Him'
Colossians 2:6

If we have received Christ Himself in our inmost hearts, our new life will manifest its intimate acquaintance with Him by a *walk of faith in Him*. Walking implies *action*. Our religion is not to be confined to our closet; we must carry out into practical effect that which we believe. If a man walks in Christ, then he so acts as Christ would act; for Christ being in him, his hope, his love, his joy, his life, he is the reflex of the image of Jesus; and men say of that man, 'He is like his Master; he lives like Jesus Christ'. Walking signifies *progress*. 'So walk ye in Him'; proceed from grace to grace, run forward until you reach the uttermost degree of knowledge that a man can attain concerning our Beloved. Walking implies *continuance*. There must be a perpetual abiding in Christ. How many Christians think that in the morning and evening they ought to come into the company of Jesus, and may then give their hearts to the world all the day: but this is poor living; we should always be with Him, treading in His steps and doing His will. Walking also implies *habit*. When we speak of a man's walk and conversation, we mean his habits, the constant tenor of his life. Now, if we sometimes enjoy Christ, and then forget Him; sometimes call Him ours, and anon lose our hold, that is not a habit; we do not *walk* in Him. We must keep to Him, cling to Him, never let Him go, but live and have our being in Him. 'As ye have received Christ Jesus the Lord, so walk ye in Him'; persevere in the same way in which ye have begun, and, as at the first Christ Jesus was the trust of your faith, the source of your life, the principle of your action, and the joy of your spirit, so let him be the same till life's end; the same when you walk through the valley of the shadow of death, and enter into the joy and the rest which remain for the people of God. O Holy Spirit, enable us to obey this heavenly precept.

*'His place of defence shall be the munitions of rocks:
bread shall be given him; his waters shall be sure'*
Isaiah 33:16

Do you doubt, O Christian, do you doubt as to whether
God will fulfil His promise? Shall the munitions of
rock be carried by storm? Shall the storehouses of
heaven fail? Do you think that your heavenly Father,
though He knoweth that you have need of food and
raiment, will yet forget you? When not a sparrow falls
to the ground without your Father, and the very hairs
of your head are all numbered, will you mistrust and
doubt Him? Perhaps your affliction will continue upon
you till you dare to trust your God, and then it shall end.
Full many there be who have been tried and sore vexed
till at last they have been driven in sheer desperation to
exercise faith in God, and the moment of their faith has
been the instant of their deliverance; they have seen
whether God would keep His promise or not. Oh, I pray
you, doubt Him no longer! Please not Satan, and vex
not yourself by indulging any more those hard thoughts
of God. Think it not a light matter to doubt Jehovah.
Remember, it is a *sin*; and not a little sin either, but in
the highest degree criminal. The angels never doubt
Him, nor the devils either: we alone, out of all the
beings that God has fashioned, dishonour Him by
unbelief, and tarnish His honour by mistrust. Shame
upon us for this! Our God does not deserve to be so
basely suspected; in our past life we have proved Him
to be true and faithful to His word, and with so many
instances of His love and of His kindness as we have
received, and are daily receiving, at His hands, it is base
and inexcusable that we suffer a doubt to sojourn
within our heart. May we henceforth wage constant war
against doubts of our God - enemies to our peace and
to His honour; and with an unstaggering faith believe
that what He has promised He will also perform. 'Lord,
I believe, help Thou mine unbelief.'

'The eternal God is thy refuge'
Deuteronomy 33:27

The word refuge may be translated 'mansion', or 'abiding-place', which gives the thought that *God is our abode, our home.* There is a fulness and sweetness in the metaphor, for dear to our hearts is our home, although it be the humblest cottage, or the scantiest garret; and dearer far is our blessed God, in whom we live, and move, and have our being. It is at home that we *feel safe*: we shut the world out and dwell in quiet security. So when we are with our God we 'fear no evil'. He is our shelter and retreat, our abiding refuge. At home, *we take our rest*; it is there we find repose after the fatigue and toil of the day. And so our hearts find rest in God, when, wearied with life's conflict, we turn to Him, and our soul dwells at ease. At home, also, we *let our hearts loose*; we are not afraid of being misunderstood, nor of our words being misconstrued. So when we are with God we can commune freely with Him, laying open all our hidden desires; for if the 'secret of the Lord is with them that fear Him', the secrets of them that fear Him ought to be, and must be, with their Lord. Home, too, is the place of our *truest and purest happiness*: and it is in God that our hearts find their deepest delight. We have joy in Him which far surpasses all other joy. *It is also for home that we work and labour.* The thought of it gives strength to bear the daily burden, and quickens the fingers to perform the task; and in this sense we may also say that God is our home. Love to Him strengthens us. We think of Him in the person of His dear Son; and a glimpse of the suffering face of the Redeemer constrains us to labour in His cause. We feel that we must work, for we have brethren yet to be saved, and we have our Father's heart to make glad by bringing home His wandering sons; we would fill with holy mirth the sacred family among whom we dwell. Happy are those who have thus the God of Jacob for their refuge!

'It is enough for the disciple that he be as His Master'
Matthew 10:25

No one will dispute this statement, for it would be unseemly for the servant to be exalted above his Master. When our Lord was on earth, what was the treatment he received? Were His claims acknowledged, His instructions followed, His perfections worshipped, by those whom He came to bless? No; 'He was despised and rejected of men'. Outside the camp was His place: cross-bearing was His occupation. Did the world yield Him solace and rest? 'Foxes have holes, and the birds of the air have nests; but the Son of man hath not where to lay His head.' This inhospitable country afforded Him no shelter: it cast Him out and crucified Him. Such - if you are a follower of Jesus, and maintain a consistent, Christ-like walk and conversation - you must expect to be the lot of that part of your spiritual life which, in its outward development, comes under the observation of men. They will treat it as they treated the Saviour - they will despise it. Dream not that worldlings will admire you, or that the more holy and the more Christ-like you are, the more peaceably people will act towards you. They prized not the polished gem, how should they value the jewel in the rough? 'If they have called the Master of the house Beelzebub, how much more shall they call them of His household?' If we were more like Christ, we should be more hated by His enemies. It were a sad dishonour to a child of God to be the world's favourite. It is a very ill omen to hear a wicked world clap its hands and shout, 'Well done' to the Christian man. He may begin to look to his character, and wonder whether he has not been doing wrong, when the unrighteous give him their approbation. Let us be true to our Master, and have no friendship with a blind and base world which scorns and rejects Him. Far be it from us to seek a crown of honour where our Lord found a coronet of thorns.

'Underneath are the everlasting arms'
Deuteronomy 33:27

God - the eternal God - is Himself *our support* at all times, and especially when we are sinking in deep trouble. There are seasons when the Christian *sinks very low in humiliation*. Under a deep sense of his great sinfulness, he is humbled before God till he scarcely knows how to pray, because he appears, in his own sight, so worthless. Well, child of God, remember that when thou art at thy worst and lowest, yet 'underneath' thee 'are the everlasting arms'. Sin may drag thee ever so low, but Christ's great atonement is still under all. You may have descended into the deeps, but you cannot have fallen so low as *the uttermost*; and to the uttermost He saves. Again, the Christian sometimes sinks very deeply in *sore trial from without*. Every earthly prop is cut away. What then? Still underneath him are 'the everlasting arms'. He cannot fall so deep in distress and affliction but what the covenant grace of an ever-faithful God will still encircle him. The Christian may be sinking under *trouble from within* through fierce conflict, but even then he cannot be brought so low as to be beyond the reach of the 'everlasting arms' - they are underneath him; and, while thus sustained, all Satan's efforts to harm him avail nothing.

This assurance of support is a comfort to any *weary but earnest worker* in the service of God. It implies a promise of strength for each day, grace for each need, and power for each duty. And, further, *when death comes*, the promise shall still hold good. When we stand in the midst of Jordan, we shall be able to say with David, 'I will fear no evil, for Thou art with me'. We shall descend into the grave, but we shall go no lower, for the eternal arms prevent our further fall. All through life, and at its close, we shall be upheld by the 'everlasting arms' - arms that neither flag nor lose their strength, for 'the everlasting God fainteth not, neither is weary'.

'He shall choose our inheritance for us'
Psalm 47:4

Believer, if your inheritance be a lowly one you should be satisfied with your earthly portion; for you may rest assured that it is the fittest *for you*. Unerring wisdom ordained your lot, and selected for you the safest and best condition. A ship of large tonnage is to be brought up the river; now, in one part of the stream there is a sandbank; should some one ask, 'Why does the captain steer through the deep part of the channel and deviate so much from a straight line?' His answer would be, 'Because I should not get my vessel into harbour at all if I did not keep the deep channel'. So it may be, you would run aground and suffer shipwreck, if your divine Captain did not steer you into the depths of affliction where waves of trouble follow each other in quick succession. Some plants die if they have too much sunshine. It may be that you are planted where you get but little, you are put there by the loving Husbandman, because only in that situation will you bring forth fruit unto perfection. Remember this, had any other condition been better for you than the one in which you are, divine love would have put you there. You are placed by God in the most suitable circumstances, and if you had the choosing of your lot, you would soon cry, 'Lord, choose my inheritance for me, for by my self-will I am pierced through with many sorrows'. Be content with such things as you have, since the Lord has ordered all things for your good. Take up your own daily cross; it is the burden best suited for your shoulder, and will prove most effective to make you perfect in every good word and work to the glory of God. Down busy self, and proud impatience, it is not for you to choose, but for the Lord of Love!

> Trials must and will befall -
> But with humble faith to see
> Love inscribed upon them all;
> This is happiness to me.

'The trial of your faith'
1 Peter 1:7

Faith untried may be true faith, but it is sure to be little faith, and it is likely to remain dwarfish so long as it is without trials. Faith never prospers so well as when all things are against her: tempests are her trainers, and lightnings are her illuminators. When a calm reigns on the sea, spread the sails as you will, the ship moves not to its harbour; for on a slumbering ocean the keel sleeps too. Let the winds rush howling forth, and let the waters lift up themselves, then, though the vessel may rock, and her deck may be washed with waves, and her mast may creak under the pressure of the full and swelling sail, it is then that she makes headway towards her desired haven. No flowers wear so lovely a blue as those which grow at the foot of the frozen glacier; no stars gleam so brightly as those which glisten in the polar sky; no water tastes so sweet as that which springs amid the desert sand; and no faith is so precious as that which lives and triumphs in adversity. Tried faith brings experience. You could not have believed your own weakness had you not been compelled to pass through the rivers; and you would never have known God's strength had you not been supported amid the water-floods. Faith increases in solidity, assurance, and intensity, the more it is exercised with tribulation. Faith is precious, and its trial is precious too.

Let not this, however, discourage those who are young in faith. You will have trials enough without seeking them: the full portion will be measured out to you in due season. Meanwhile, if you cannot yet claim the result of long experience, thank God for what grace you have; praise Him for that degree of holy confidence whereunto you have attained: walk according to that rule, and you shall yet have more and more of the blessing of God, till your faith shall remove mountains and conquer impossibilities.

> '*And it came to pass in those days,*
> *that He went out into a mountain to pray,*
> *and continued all night in prayer to God*'
> Luke 6:12

If ever one of woman born might have lived without prayer, it was our spotless, perfect Lord, and yet none was ever so much in supplication as He! Such was His love to His Father, that He loved much to be in communion with Him: such His love for His people, that He desired to be much in intercession for them. *The fact* of this eminent prayerfulness of Jesus is a lesson for us - He hath given us an example that we may follow in His steps. *The time* He chose was admirable, it was the hour of silence, when the crowd would not disturb Him; the time of inaction, when all but Himself had ceased to labour; and the season when slumber made men forget their woes, and cease their applications to Him for relief. While others found rest in sleep, He refreshed Himself with prayer. *The place* was also well selected. He was alone where none would intrude, where none could observe: thus was He free from Pharisaic ostentation and vulgar interruption. Those dark and silent hills were a fit oratory for the Son of God. Heaven and earth in midnight stillness heard the groans and sighs of the mysterious Being in whom both worlds were blended. *The continuance* of His pleadings is remarkable; the long watches were not too long; the cold wind did not chill His devotions; the grim darkness did not darken His faith, or loneliness check His importunity. We cannot watch with Him one hour, but He watched for us whole nights. *The occasion* for this prayer is notable; it was after His enemies had been enraged - prayer was His refuge and solace; it was before He sent forth the twelve apostles - prayer was the gate of His enterprise, the herald of His new work. Should we not learn from Jesus to resort to special prayer when we are under peculiar trial, or contemplate fresh endeavours for the Master's glory? Lord Jesus, teach us to pray.

'The branch cannot bear fruit of itself'
John 15:4

How did you begin to bear fruit? It was when you came to Jesus and cast yourselves on His great atonement, and rested on His finished righteousness. Ah! what fruit you had then! Do you remember those early days? Then indeed the vine flourished, the tender grape appeared, the pomegranates budded forth, and the beds of spices gave forth their smell. Have you declined since then? If you have, we charge you to remember that time of love, and repent, and do thy first works. *Be most in those engagements which you have experimentally proved to draw you nearest to Christ*, because it is from Him that all your fruits proceed. Any holy exercise which will bring you to Him will help you to bear fruit. The sun is, no doubt, a great worker in fruit-creating among the trees of the orchard: and Jesus is still more so among the trees of His garden of grace. When have you been the most fruitless? Has not it been when you have lived farthest from the Lord Jesus Christ, when you have slackened in prayer, when you have departed from the simplicity of your faith, when your graces have engrossed your attention instead of your Lord, when you have said, 'My mountain standeth firm, I shall never be moved'; and have forgotten where your strength dwells - has not it been *then* that your fruit has ceased? Some of us have been taught that we have nothing out of Christ, by terrible abasements of heart before the Lord; and when we have seen the utter barrenness and death of all creature power, we have cried in anguish, 'From Him all my fruit must be found, for no fruit can ever come from me'. We are taught, by past experience, that the more simply we depend upon the grace of God in Christ, and wait upon the Holy Spirit, the more we shall bring forth fruit unto God. Oh! to trust Jesus for fruit as well as for life.

'Men ought always to pray'
Luke 18:1

If *men* ought always to pray and not to faint, much more *Christian men*. Jesus has sent His church into the world on the same errand upon which He Himself came, and this mission includes intercession. What if I say that the church is the world's priest? Creation is dumb, but the church is to find a mouth for it. It is the church's high privilege to pray with acceptance. The door of grace is always open for her petitions, and they never return empty-handed. The veil was rent *for her*, the blood was sprinkled upon the altar *for her*, God constantly invites *her* to ask what she wills. Will she refuse the privilege which angels might envy her? Is she not the bride of Christ? May she not go in unto her King at every hour? Shall she allow the precious privilege to be unused? The church always has need for prayer. There are always some in her midst who are declining, or falling into open sin. There are lambs to be prayed for, that they may be carried in Christ's bosom. The strong, lest they grow presumptuous; and the weak, lest they become despairing. If we kept up prayer-meetings four-and-twenty hours in the day, all the days in the year, we might never be without a special subject for supplication. Are we ever without the sick and the poor, the afflicted and the wavering? Are we ever without those who seek the conversion of relatives, the reclaiming of backsliders, or the salvation of the depraved? Nay, with congregations constantly gathering, with ministers always preaching, with millions of sinners lying dead in trespasses and sins; in a country over which the darkness of Romanism is certainly descending; in a world full of idols, cruelties, devilries, if the church doth not pray, how shall she excuse her base neglect of the commission of her loving Lord? Let the church be constant in supplication, let every private believer cast his mite of prayer into the treasury.

*'I will cut off them that worship and that swear by
the Lord, and that swear by Malcham'*
Zephaniah 1:5

Such persons thought themselves safe because they
were with both parties: they went with the followers of
Jehovah, and bowed at the same time to Malcham. But
duplicity is abominable with God, and hypocrisy his
soul hateth. The idolater who distinctly gives himself
to his false god, has one sin less than he who brings his
polluted and detestable sacrifice unto the temple of the
Lord, while his heart is with the world and the sins
thereof. To hold with the hare and run with the hounds,
is a dastard's policy. In the common matters of daily
life, a double-minded man is despised, but in religion
he is loathsome to the last degree. The penalty pronounced in the verse before us is terrible, but it is well
deserved; for how should divine justice spare the
sinner, who knows the right, approves it, and professes
to follow it, and all the while loves the evil, and gives
it dominion in his heart?

My soul, search thyself this morning, and see
whether thou art guilty of double-dealing. Thou
professest to be a follower of Jesus - dost thou truly
love Him? Is thy heart right with God? Art thou of the
family of old Father Honest, or art thou a relative of Mr
By-ends? A name to live is of little value if I be indeed
dead in trespasses and sins. To have one foot on the
land of truth, and another on the sea of falsehood, will
involve a terrible fall and a total ruin. Christ will be all
or nothing. God fills the whole universe, and hence
there is no room for another god; if, then, He reigns in
my heart, there will be no space for another reigning
power. Do I rest alone on Jesus crucified, and live alone
for Him? Is it my desire to do so? Is my heart set upon
so doing? If so, blessed be the mighty grace which has
led me to salvation; and if not so, O Lord, pardon my
sad offence, and unite my heart to fear Thy name.

*'And Laban said, It must not be so done in our
country, to give the younger before the firstborn'*
Genesis 29:26

We do not excuse Laban for his dishonesty, but we
scruple not to learn from the custom which he quoted as
his excuse. There are some things which must be taken
in order, and if we would win the second we must secure
the first. The second may be the more lovely in our eyes,
but the rule of the heavenly country must stand, and the
elder must be married first. For instance, many men
desire the beautiful and well-favoured Rachel of joy and
peace in believing, but they must first be wedded to the
tender-eyed Leah of repentance. Every one falls in love
with happiness, and many would cheerfully serve twice
seven years to enjoy it, but according to the rule of the
Lord's kingdom, the Leah of real holiness must be
beloved of our soul before the Rachel of true happiness
can be attained. Heaven stands not first but second, and
only by persevering to the end can we win a portion in
it. The cross must be carried before the crown can be
worn. We must follow our Lord in His humiliation, or
we shall never rest with Him in glory.

My soul, what sayest thou, art thou so vain as to
hope to break through the heavenly rule? Dost thou
hope for reward without labour, or honour without toil?
Dismiss the idle expectation, and be content to take the
ill-favoured things for the sake of the sweet love of
Jesus, which will recompense thee for all. In such a
spirit, labouring and suffering, thou wilt find bitters
grow sweet, and hard things easy. Like Jacob, thy years
of service will seem unto thee but a few days for the
love thou hast to Jesus; and when the dear hour of the
wedding feast shall come, all thy toils shall be as
though they had never been - an hour with Jesus will
make up for ages of pain and labour.

Jesus, to win Thyself so fair,
   Thy cross I will with gladness bear:
Since so the rules of heaven ordain,
   The first I'll wed the next to gain.

'The Lord's portion is His people'
Deuteronomy 32:9

How are they His? By His own sovereign *choice*. He chose them, and set His love upon them. This He did altogether apart from any goodness in them at the time, or any goodness which He foresaw in them. He had mercy on whom He would have mercy, and ordained a chosen company unto eternal life; thus, therefore, are they His by His unconstrained election.

They are not only His by choice, but by *purchase*. He has bought and paid for them to the utmost farthing, hence about His title there can be no dispute. Not with corruptible things, as with silver and gold, but with the precious blood of the Lord Jesus Christ, the Lord's portion has been fully redeemed. There is no mortgage on His estate; no suits can be raised by opposing claimants, the price was paid in open court, and the Church is the Lord's freehold for ever. See the blood-mark upon all the chosen, invisible to human eye, but known to Christ, for 'the Lord knoweth them that are His'; He forgetteth none of those whom He has redeemed from among men; He counts the sheep for whom He laid down His life, and remembers well the Church for which He gave Himself

They are also his by *conquest*. What a battle He had in us before we would be won! How long He laid siege to our hearts! How often He sent us terms of capitulation! But we barred our gates, and fenced our walls against Him. Do we not remember that glorious hour when He carried our hearts by storm? When He placed His cross against the wall, and scaled our ramparts, planting on our strongholds the blood-red flag of His omnipotent mercy? Yes, we are, indeed, the conquered captives of His omnipotent love. Thus chosen, purchased, and subdued, the rights of our divine possessor are inalienable: we rejoice that we never can be our own; and we desire, day by day, to do *His* will, and to show forth *His* glory.

'Strengthen, O God,
that which thou hast wrought for us'
Psalm 68:28

It is our wisdom, as well as our necessity, to beseech God continually to strengthen that which He has wrought in us. It is because of their neglect in this, that many Christians may blame themselves for those trials and afflictions of spirit which arise from unbelief. It is true that Satan seeks to flood the fair garden of the heart and make it a scene of desolation, but it is also true that many Christians leave open the sluice-gates themselves, and let in the dreadful deluge through carelessness and want of prayer to their strong Helper. We often forget that the Author of our faith must be the Preserver of it also. The lamp which was burning in the temple was never allowed to go out, but it had to be daily replenished with fresh oil; in like manner, our faith can only live by being sustained with the oil of grace, and we can only obtain this from God Himself. Foolish virgins we shall prove, if we do not secure the needed sustenance for our lamps. He who built the world upholds it, or it would fall in one tremendous crash; He who made us Christians must maintain us by His Spirit, or our ruin will be speedy and final. Let us, then, evening by evening, go to our Lord for the grace and strength we need. We have a strong argument to plead, for it is *His own work of grace* which we ask Him to strengthen - '*that which Thou hast wrought for us*'. Think you He will fail to protect and sustain *that*? Only let your faith take hold of His strength, and all the powers of darkness, led on by the master fiend of hell, cannot cast a cloud or shadow over your joy and peace. Why faint when you may be strong? Why suffer defeat when you may conquer? Oh! take your wavering faith and drooping graces to Him who can revive and replenish them, and earnestly pray, 'Strengthen, O God, that which thou hast wrought for us'.

'The Lord is my portion, saith my soul'
Lamentations 3:24

It is not 'The Lord is *partly* my portion', nor 'The Lord is *in* my portion'; but He Himself makes up the sum total of my soul's inheritance. Within the circumference of that circle lies all that we possess or desire. The *Lord* is my portion. Not His grace merely, nor His love, nor His covenant, but Jehovah Himself. He has chosen us for His portion, and we have chosen Him for ours. It is true that the Lord must first choose our inheritance for us, or else we shall never choose it for ourselves; but if we are really called according to the purpose of electing love, we can sing:

> Lov'd of my God for Him again
>   With love intense I burn;
> Chosen of Him ere time began,
>   I choose Him in return.

The Lord is our *all-sufficient* portion. God fills Himself; and if God is all-sufficient in Himself, He must be all-sufficient for us. It is not easy to satisfy man's desires. When he dreams that he is satisfied, anon he wakes to the perception that there is somewhat yet beyond, and straightway the horse-leech in his heart cries, 'Give, give'. But all that we can wish for is to be found in our divine portion, so that we ask, 'Whom have I in heaven but Thee? and there is none upon earth that I desire beside Thee'. Well may we 'delight ourselves in the Lord' who makes us to drink of the river of His pleasures. Our faith stretches her wings and mounts like an eagle into the heaven of divine love as to her proper dwelling-place. 'The lines have fallen to us in pleasant places; yea, we have a goodly heritage.' Let us rejoice in the Lord always; let us show to the world that we are a happy and a blessed people, and thus induce them to exclaim, 'We will go with you, for we have heard that God is with you'.

'Thine eyes shall see the King in His beauty'
Isaiah 33:17

The more you know about Christ, the less will you be satisfied with superficial views of Him; and the more deeply you study His transactions in the eternal covenant, His engagements on your behalf as the eternal Surety, and the fulness of His grace which shines in all His offices, the more truly will you see the King in His beauty. Be much in such outlooks. Long more and more to see Jesus. *Meditation and contemplation* are often like windows of agate, and gates of carbuncle, through which we behold the Redeemer. Meditation puts the telescope to the eye, and enables us to see Jesus after a better sort than we could have seen Him if we had lived in the days of His flesh. Would that our conversation were more in heaven, and that we were more taken up with the person, the work, the beauty of our incarnate Lord. More meditation, and the beauty of the King would flash upon us with more resplendence. Beloved, it is very probable that we shall have such a sight of our glorious King as we never had before, *when we come to die.* Many saints in dying have looked up from amidst the stormy waters, and have seen Jesus walking on the waves of the sea, and heard Him say, 'It is I, be not afraid'. Ah, yes! when the tenement begins to shake, and the clay falls away, we see Christ through the rifts, and between the rafters the sunlight of heaven comes streaming in. But if we want to see face to face the 'King in His beauty', *we must go to heaven* for the sight, or the King must come here in person. O that he would come on the wings of the wind! He is our Husband, and we are widowed by His absence; He is our Brother dear and fair, and we are lonely without Him. Thick veils and clouds hang between our souls and their true life: when shall the day break and the shadows flee away? Oh, long-expected day, begin!

'To whom be glory for ever. Amen'
Romans 11:36

'To whom be glory for ever.' This should be *the single*
desire of the Christian. All other wishes must be
subservient and tributary to this one. The Christian
may wish for prosperity in his business, but only so far
as it may help him to promote this - 'To Him be glory
for ever'. He may desire to attain more gifts and more
graces, but it should only be that 'To Him may be glory
for ever'. You are not acting as you ought to do when
you are moved by any other motive than a single eye to
your Lord's glory. As a Christian, you are 'of God, and
through God', then live 'to God'. Let nothing ever set
your heart beating so mightily as love to Him. Let this
ambition fire your soul; be this the foundation of every
enterprise upon which you enter, and this your sustaining motive whenever your zeal would grow chill; make
God your *only* object. Depend upon it, where self
begins sorrow begins; but if God be my supreme
delight and only object,

'To me 'tis equal whether love ordain
My life or death - appoint me ease or pain.'

Let your desire for God's glory be a *growing*
desire. You blessed him in your youth, do not be
content with such praises as you gave Him then. Has
God prospered you in business? Give Him more as He
has given you more. Has God given you experience?
Praise Him by stronger faith than you exercised at first.
Does your knowledge grow? Then sing more sweetly.
Do you enjoy happier times than you once had? Have
you been restored from sickness, and has your sorrow
been turned into peace and joy? Then give Him more
music; put more coals and more sweet frankincense
into the censer of your praise. Practically in your life
give Him honour, putting the 'Amen' to this doxology
to your great and gracious Lord, by your own individual service and increasing holiness.

'*He that cleaveth wood shall be endangered thereby*'
Ecclesiastes 10:9

Oppressors may get their will of poor and needy men
as easily as they can split logs of wood, but they had
better mind, for it is a dangerous business, and a
splinter from a tree has often killed the woodman.
Jesus is persecuted in every injured saint, and He is
mighty to avenge His beloved ones. Success in treading
down the poor and needy is a thing to be trembled at:
if there be no danger to persecutors here there will be
great danger hereafter.

*To cleave wood is a common every-day business,
and yet it has its dangers*; so then, reader, there are
dangers connected with your calling and daily life
which it will be well for you to be aware of. We refer
not to hazards by flood and field, or by disease and
sudden death, but to perils of a spiritual sort. Your
occupation may be as humble as log splitting, and yet
the devil can tempt you in it. You may be a domestic
servant, a farm labourer, or a mechanic, and you may
be greatly screened from temptations to the grosser
vices, and yet some secret sin may do you damage.
Those who dwell at home, and mingle not with the
rough world, may yet be endangered by their very
seclusion. Nowhere is he safe who thinks himself so.
Pride may enter a poor man's heart; avarice may reign
in a cottager's bosom; uncleanness may venture into
the quietest home; and anger, and envy, and malice may
insinuate themselves into the most rural abode. Even in
speaking a few words to a servant we may sin; a little
purchase at a shop may be the first link in a chain of
temptations; the mere looking out of a window may be
the beginning of evil. O Lord, how exposed we are!
How shall we be secured! To keep ourselves is work
too hard for us: only Thou Thyself art able to preserve
us in such a world of evils. Spread Thy wings over us,
and we, like little chickens, will cower down beneath
Thee, and feel ourselves safe!

'A spring shut up, a fountain sealed'
Canticles 4:12

In this metaphor, which has reference to the inner life of a believer, we have very plainly the idea of *secrecy*. It is a spring *shut up*: just as there were springs in the East, over which an edifice was built, so that none could reach them save those who knew the secret entrance; so is the heart of a believer when it is renewed by grace: there is a mysterious life within which no human skill can touch. It is a secret which no other man knoweth; nay, which the very man who is the possessor of it cannot tell to his neighbour. The text includes not only secrecy, but *separation*. It is not the common spring, of which every passer-by may drink, it is one kept and preserved from all others; it is a fountain bearing a particular mark - a king's royal seal, so that all can perceive that it is not a common fountain, but a fountain owned by a proprietor, and placed specially by itself alone. So is it with the spiritual life. The chosen of God were separated by God in the day of redemption; and they are separated by the possession of a life which others have not; and it is impossible for them to feel at home with the world, or to delight in its pleasures. There is also the idea of *sacredness*. The spring shut up is preserved for the use of some special person: and such is the Christian's heart. It is a spring kept for Jesus. Every Christian should feel that he has God's seal upon him - and he should be able to say with Paul, 'From henceforth let no man trouble me, for I bear in my body the marks of the Lord Jesus'. Another idea is prominent - it is that of *security*. Oh! how sure and safe is the inner life of the believer! If all the powers of earth and hell could combine against it, that immortal principle must still exist, for He who gave it pledged His life for its preservation. And who 'is He that shall harm you', when God is your protector?

'Thou art from everlasting'
Psalm 93:2

Christ is EVERLASTING. Of Him we may sing with
David, 'Thy throne, O God, is for ever and ever'.
Rejoice, believer, in Jesus Christ, the same yesterday,
today, and for ever. Jesus always *was*. The Babe born
in Bethlehem was united to the Word, which was in the
beginning, by whom all things were made. The title by
which Christ revealed Himself to John in Patmos was,
'Him which is, and which was, and which is to come'.
If He were not God from everlasting, we could not so
devoutly love Him; we could not feel that He had any
share in the eternal love which is the fountain of all
covenant blessings; but since he was from all eternity
with the Father, we trace the stream of divine love to
Himself equally with His Father and the blessed Spirit.
As our Lord always *was*, so also he *is* for evermore.
Jesus is not dead; 'He ever liveth to make intercession
for us'. Resort to Him in all your times of need, for He
is waiting to bless you still. Moreover, Jesus our Lord
ever *shall be*. If God should spare your life to fulfil
your full day of threescore years and ten, you will find
that His cleansing fountain is still opened, and His
precious blood has not lost its power; you shall find
that the Priest who filled the healing fount with His own
blood, lives to purge you from all iniquity. When only
your last battle remains to be fought, you shall find that
the hand of your conquering Captain has not grown
feeble - the living Saviour shall cheer the dying saint.
When you enter heaven you shall find Him there
bearing the dew of His youth; and through eternity the
Lord Jesus shall still remain the perennial spring of
joy, and life, and glory to His people. Living waters
may you draw from this sacred well! Jesus always was,
He always is, He always shall be. He is eternal in all His
attributes, in all His offices, in all His might, and
willingness to bless, comfort, guard, and crown His
chosen people.

'Avoid foolish questions'
Titus 3:9

Our days are few, and are far better spent in doing good, than in disputing over matters which are, at best, of minor importance. The old schoolmen did a world of mischief by their incessant discussion of subjects of no practical importance; and our Churches suffer much from petty wars over abstruse points and unimportant questions. After everything has been said that can be said, neither party is any the wiser, and therefore the discussion no more promotes knowledge than love, and it is foolish to sow in so barren a field. Questions upon points wherein Scripture is silent; upon mysteries which belong to God alone; upon prophecies of doubtful interpretation; and upon mere modes of observing human ceremonials are all foolish, and wise men avoid them. Our business is neither to ask nor answer foolish questions, but to avoid them altogether; and if we observe the apostle's precept (Titus 3:8) to be careful to maintain good works, we shall find ourselves far too much occupied with profitable business to take much interest in unworthy, contentious, and needless strivings.

There are, however, some questions which are the reverse of foolish, which we must not avoid, but fairly and honestly meet, such as these: Do I believe in the Lord Jesus Christ? Am I renewed in the spirit of my mind? Am I walking not after the flesh, but after the Spirit? Am I growing in grace? Does my conversation adorn the doctrine of God my Saviour? Am I looking for the coming of the Lord, and watching as a servant should do who expects his master? What more can I do for Jesus? Such enquiries as these urgently demand our attention; and if we have been at all given to cavilling, let us now turn our critical abilities to a service so much more profitable. Let us be peacemakers, and endeavour to lead others both by our precept and example, to 'avoid foolish questions'.

'O that I knew where I might find Him!'
Job 23:3

In Job's uttermost extremity he cried after the Lord. The longing desire of an afflicted child of God is once more to see his Father's face. His first prayer is not 'O that I might be healed of the disease which now festers in every part of my body!' nor even 'O that I might see my children restored from the jaws of the grave, and my property once more brought from the hand of the spoiler!' but the first and uppermost cry is, 'O that I knew where I might find HIM, who is my God! that I might come even to His seat!' God's children run home when the storm comes on. It is the heaven-born instinct of a gracious soul to seek shelter from all ills beneath the wings of Jehovah. 'He that hath made his refuge God', might serve as the title of a true believer. A hypocrite, when afflicted by God, resents the infliction, and, like a slave, would run from the Master who has scourged him; but not so the true heir of heaven, he kisses the hand which smote him, and seeks shelter from the rod in the bosom of the God who frowned upon him. Job's desire to commune with God was intensified by the failure of all other sources of consolation. The patriarch turned away from his sorry friends, and looked up to the celestial throne, just as a traveller turns from his empty skin bottle, and betakes himself with all speed to the well. He bids farewell to earthborn hopes, and cries, 'O that I knew where I might find my God!' Nothing teaches us so much the preciousness of the Creator, as when we learn the emptiness of all besides. Turning away with bitter scorn from earth's hives, where we find no honey, but many sharp stings, we rejoice in Him whose faithful word is sweeter than honey or the honeycomb. In every trouble we should first seek to realise God's presence with us. Only let us enjoy His smile, and we can bear our daily cross with a willing heart for His dear sake.

'O Lord, Thou hast pleaded the causes of my soul'
Lamentations 3:58

Observe how *positively* the prophet speaks. He doth not say, 'I hope, I trust, I sometimes think, that God hath pleaded the causes of my soul'; but he speaks of it as a matter of fact not to be disputed. 'Thou *hast* pleaded the causes of my soul.' Let us, by the aid of the gracious Comforter, shake off those doubts and fears which so much mar our peace and comfort. Be this our prayer, that we may have done with the harsh croaking voice of surmise and suspicion, and may be able to speak with the clear, melodious voice of full assurance. Notice how *gratefully* the prophet speaks, ascribing all the glory to God alone! You perceive there is not a word concerning himself or his own pleadings. He doth not ascribe his deliverance in any measure to any man, much less to his own merit; but it is *'thou'* - 'O Lord, Thou hast pleaded the causes of my soul; *Thou* hast redeemed my life'. A grateful spirit should ever be cultivated by the Christian; and especially after deliverances we should prepare a song for our God. Earth should be a temple filled with the songs of grateful saints, and every day should be a censer smoking with the sweet incense of thanksgiving. How *joyful* Jeremiah seems to be while he records the Lord's mercy. How triumphantly he lifts up the strain! He has been in the low dungeon, and is even now no other than the weeping prophet; and yet in the very book which is called 'Lamentations', clear as the song of Miriam when she dashed her fingers against the tabor, shrill as the note of Deborah when she met Barak with shouts of victory, we hear the voice of Jeremy going up to heaven - 'Thou hast pleaded the causes of my soul; thou hast redeemed my life'. O children of God, seek after a vital experience of the Lord's loving-kindness, and when you have it, speak positively of it; sing gratefully; shout triumphantly.

*'The conies are but a feeble folk,
yet make they their houses in the rocks'*
Proverbs 30:26

Conscious of their own natural defencelessness, the conies resort to burrows in the rocks, and are secure from their enemies. My heart, be willing to gather a lesson from these feeble folk. Thou art as weak and as exposed to peril as the timid cony, be as wise to seek a shelter. My best security is within the munitions of an immutable Jehovah, where His unalterable promises stand like giant walls of rock. It will be well with thee, my heart, if thou canst always hide thyself in the bulwarks of His glorious attributes, all of which are guarantees of safety for those who put their trust in Him. Blessed be the name of the Lord, I have so done, and have found myself like David in Adullam, safe from the cruelty of my enemy; I have not now to find out the blessedness of the man who puts his trust in the Lord, for long ago, when Satan and my sins pursued me, I fled to the cleft of the rock Christ Jesus, and in His riven side I found a delightful resting-place. My heart, run to Him anew tonight, whatever thy present grief may be; Jesus feels for thee; Jesus consoles thee; Jesus will help thee. No monarch in his impregnable fortress is more secure than the cony in his rocky burrow. The master of ten thousand chariots is not one whit better protected than the little dweller in the mountain's cleft. In Jesus the weak are strong, and the defenceless safe; they could not be more strong if they were giants, or more safe if they were in heaven. Faith gives to men on earth the protection of the God of heaven. More they cannot need, and need not wish. The conies cannot build a castle, but they avail themselves of what is there already: I cannot make myself a refuge, but Jesus has provided it, His Father has given it, His Spirit has revealed it, and lo, again tonight I enter it, and am safe from every foe.

'Grieve not the Holy Spirit'
Ephesians 4:30

All that the believer has must come from Christ, but it comes solely through the channel of the Spirit of all grace. Moreover, as all blessings thus flow to you through the Holy Spirit, so also no good thing can come out of you in holy thought, devout worship, or gracious act, apart from the sanctifying operation of the same Spirit. Even if the good seed be sown in you, yet it lies dormant except He worketh in you to will and to do of His own good pleasure. Do you desire to speak for Jesus - how can you unless the Holy Ghost touch your tongue? Do you desire to pray? Alas! what dull work it is unless the Spirit maketh intercession for you! Do you desire to subdue sin? Would you be holy? Would you imitate your Master? Do you desire to rise to superlative heights of spirituality? Are you wanting to be made like the angels of God, full of zeal and ardour for the Master's cause? You cannot without the Spirit - 'Without me ye can do nothing'. O branch of the vine, thou canst have no fruit without the sap! O child of God, thou hast no life within thee apart from the life which God gives thee through His Spirit! Then let us not grieve Him or provoke Him to anger by our sin. Let us not quench Him in one of His faintest motions in our soul; let us foster every suggestion, and be ready to obey every prompting. If the Holy Spirit be indeed so mighty, let us attempt nothing without Him; let us begin no project, and carry on no enterprise, and conclude no transaction, without imploring His blessing. Let us do Him the due homage of feeling our entire weakness apart from Him, and then depending alone upon Him, having this for our prayer, 'Open Thou my heart and my whole being to Thine incoming, and uphold me with Thy free Spirit when I shall have received that Spirit in my inward parts'.

> '*Lazarus was one of them
> that sat at the table with Him*'
> John 12:2

He *is to be envied*. It was well to be Martha and serve, but better to be Lazarus and commune. There are times for each purpose, and each is comely in its season, but none of the trees of the garden yield such clusters as the vine of fellowship. To sit with Jesus, to hear His words, to mark His acts, and receive His smiles, was such a favour as must have made Lazarus as happy as the angels. When it has been our happy lot to feast with our Beloved in His banqueting-hall, we would not have given half a sigh for all the kingdoms of the world, if so much breath could have bought them.

He is to be imitated. It would have been a strange thing if Lazarus had not been at the table where Jesus was, for he had been dead, and Jesus had raised him. For the risen one to be absent when the Lord who gave him life was at his house, would have been ungrateful indeed. We too were once dead, yea, and like Lazarus stinking in the grave of sin; Jesus raised us, and by His life we live - can we be content to live at a distance from Him? Do we omit to remember Him at His table, where He deigns to feast with His brethren? Oh, this is cruel! It behoves us to repent, and do as *He* has bidden us, for His least wish should be law to us. To have lived without constant intercourse with one of whom the Jews said, 'Behold how He loved him', would have been disgraceful to Lazarus, is it excusable in us whom Jesus has loved with an everlasting love? To have been cold to Him who wept over his lifeless corpse, would have argued great brutishness in Lazarus. What does it argue in us over whom the Saviour has not only wept, but bled? Come, brethren, who read this portion, let us return unto our heavenly Bridegroom, and ask for His Spirit that we may be on terms of closer intimacy with Him, and henceforth sit at the table with Him.

*'Israel served for a wife,
and for a wife he kept sheep'*
Hosea 12:12

Jacob, while expostulating with Laban, thus describes his own toil, 'This twenty years have I been with thee. That which was torn of beasts I brought not unto thee: I bare the loss of it; of my hand didst thou require it, whether stolen by day, or stolen by night. Thus I was; in the day the drought consumed me, and the frost by night; and my sleep departed from mine eyes.' Even more toilsome than this was the life of our Saviour here below. He watched over all His sheep till he gave in as His last account, 'Of all those whom Thou hast given me I have lost none'. His hair was wet with dew, and His locks with the drops of the night. Sleep departed from His eyes, for all night He was in prayer wrestling for His people. One night Peter must be pleaded for; anon, another claims His tearful intercession. No shepherd sitting beneath the cold skies, looking up to the stars, could ever utter such complaints because of the hardness of his toil as Jesus Christ might have brought, if He had chosen to do so, because of the sternness of His service in order to procure His spouse:

Cold mountains and the midnight air,
    Witnessed the fervour of His prayer;
The desert His temptations knew,
    His conflict and His victory too.

It is sweet to dwell upon the spiritual parallel of Laban having required all the sheep at Jacob's hand. If they were torn of beasts, Jacob must make it good; if any of them died, he must stand as surety for the whole. Was not the toil of Jesus for His Church the toil of one who was under suretyship obligations to bring every believing one safe to the hand of Him who had committed them to His charge? Look upon toiling Jacob, and you see a representation of Him of whom we read, 'He shall feed His flock like a shepherd'.

'The power of His resurrection'
Philippians 3:10

The doctrine of a risen Saviour is exceedingly precious. The resurrection is the cornerstone of the entire
building of Christianity. It is the key-stone of the arch
of our salvation. It would take a volume to set forth all
the streams of living water which flow from this one
sacred source, the resurrection of our dear Lord and
Saviour Jesus Christ; but to *know* that he has risen, and
to have fellowship with Him as such - communing with
the risen Saviour by possessing a risen life - seeing
Him leave the tomb by leaving the tomb of worldliness
ourselves, this is even still more precious. The doctrine
is the basis of the experience, but as the flower is more
lovely than the root, so is the experience of fellowship
with the risen Saviour more lovely than the doctrine
itself. I would have you *believe* that Christ rose from
the dead so as to sing of it, and derive all the consolation
which it is possible for you to extract from this well-
ascertained and well-witnessed fact; but I beseech you,
rest not contented even there. Though you cannot, like
the disciples, see Him visibly, yet I bid you aspire to
see Christ Jesus by the eye of faith; and though, like
Mary Magdalene, you may not 'touch' Him, yet may
you be privileged to converse with Him, and to know
that He is risen, you yourselves being risen in Him to
newness of life. To know a crucified Saviour as having
crucified all my sins, is a high degree of knowledge; but
to know a risen Saviour as having justified me, and to
realise that He has bestowed upon me new life, having
given me to be a new creature through His own newness
of life, this is a noble style of experience: short of it,
none ought to rest satisfied. May you both 'know Him,
and the power of His resurrection'. Why should souls
who are quickened with Jesus, wear the grave-clothes
of worldliness and unbelief? Rise, for the Lord is risen.

'Fellowship with Him'
1 John 1:6

When we were united by faith to Christ, we were brought into such complete fellowship with Him, that we were made one with Him, and His interests and ours became mutual and identical. We have fellowship with Christ in His *love*. What He loves we love. He loves the saints - so do we. He loves sinners - so do we. He loves the poor perishing race of man, and pants to see earth's deserts transformed into the garden of the Lord - so do we. We have fellowship with Him in His *desires*. He desires the glory of God - we also labour for the same. He desires that the saints may be with Him where He is - we desire to be with Him there too. He desires to drive out sin - behold we fight under His banner. He desires that His Father's name may be loved and adored by all His creatures - we pray daily, 'Let Thy kingdom come and Thy will be done on earth, even as it is in heaven'. We have fellowship with Christ in His *sufferings*. We are not nailed to the cross, nor do we die a cruel death, but when He is reproached, we are reproached; and a very sweet thing it is to be blamed for His sake, to be despised for following the Master, to have the world against us. The disciple should not be above His Lord. In our measure we commune with Him in His *labours*, ministering to men by the word of truth and by deeds of love. Our meat and our drink, like His, is to do the will of Him who hath sent us and to finish His work. We have also fellowship with Christ in His *joys*. We are happy in His happiness, we rejoice in His exaltation. Have you ever tasted that joy, believer? There is no purer or more thrilling delight to be known this side heaven than that of having Christ's joy fulfilled in us, that our joy may be full. His *glory* awaits us to complete our fellowship, for His Church shall sit with Him upon His throne, as His well-beloved bride and queen.

'Get thee up into the high mountain'
Isaiah 40:9.

Each believer should be thirsting for God, for the living God, and longing to climb the hill of the Lord, and see Him face to face. We ought not to rest content in the mists of the valley when the summit of Tabor awaits us. My soul thirsteth to drink deep of the cup which is reserved for those who reach the mountain's brow, and bathe their brows in heaven. How pure are the dews of the hills, how fresh is the mountain air, how rich the fare of the dwellers aloft, whose windows look into the New Jerusalem! Many saints are content to live like men in coal mines, who see not the sun; they eat dust like the serpent when they might taste the ambrosial meat of angels; they are content to wear the miner's garb when they might put on king's robes; tears mar their faces when they might anoint them with celestial oil. Satisfied I am that many a believer pines in a dungeon when he might walk on the palace roof, and view the goodly land and Lebanon. Rouse thee, O believer, from thy low condition! Cast away thy sloth, thy lethargy, thy coldness, or whatever interferes with thy chaste and pure love to Christ, thy soul's Husband. Make Him the source, the centre, and the circumference of all thy soul's range of delight. What enchants thee into such folly as to remain in a pit when thou mayst sit on a throne? Live not in the lowlands of bondage now that mountain liberty is conferred upon thee. Rest no longer satisfied with thy dwarfish attainments, but press forward to things more sublime and heavenly. Aspire to a higher, a nobler, a fuller life. Upward to heaven! Nearer to God!

> When wilt Thou come unto me, Lord?
> Oh come, my Lord most dear!
> Come near, come nearer, nearer still,
> I'm blest when Thou art near.

> *'The glorious Lord will be unto us
> a place of broad rivers and streams'*
> Isaiah 33:21

Broad rivers and streams produce fertility, and abundance in the land. Places near broad rivers are remarkable for the variety of their plants and their plentiful harvests. God is all this to His Church. Having God she has *abundance*. What can she ask for that He will not give her? What want can she mention which He will not supply? 'In this mountain shall the Lord of Hosts make unto all people a feast of fat things.' Want ye the bread of life? It drops like manna from the sky. Want ye refreshing streams? The rock follows you, and that Rock is Christ. If you suffer any want it is your own fault; if you are straitened you are not straitened in Him, but in your own bowels. Broad rivers and streams also point to *commerce*. Our glorious Lord is to us a place of heavenly merchandise. Through our Redeemer we have commerce with the past; the wealth of Calvary, the treasures of the covenant, the riches of the ancient days of election, the stores of eternity, all come to us down the broad stream of our gracious Lord. We have commerce, too, with the future. What galleys, laden to the water's edge, come to us from the millennium! What visions we have of the days of heaven upon earth! Through our glorious Lord we have commerce with angels; communion with the bright spirits washed in blood, who sing before the throne; nay, better still, we have fellowship with the Infinite One. Broad rivers and streams are specially intended to set forth the idea of *security*. Rivers were of old a defence. Oh! beloved, what a defence is God to His Church! The devil cannot cross this broad current, but fear not, for God abideth immutably the same. Satan may worry, but he cannot destroy us; no galley with oars shall invade our river, neither shall gallant ship pass thereby.

*'Yet a little sleep, a little slumber, a little folding of
the hands to sleep: so shall thy poverty come as one
that travelleth; and thy want as an armed man'*
Proverbs 24:33, 34

The worst of sluggards only ask for a little slumber;
they would be indignant if they were accused of
thorough idleness. A little folding of the hands to sleep
is all they crave, and they have a crowd of reasons to
show that this indulgence is a very proper one. Yet by
these littles the day ebbs out, and the time for labour is
all gone, and the field is grown over with thorns. It is
by little procrastinations that men ruin their souls.
They have no intention to delay for years - a few
months will bring the more convenient season - tomorrow if you will, they will attend to serious things; but
the present hour is so occupied and altogether so
unsuitable, that they beg to be excused. Like sands
from an hour-glass, time passes, life is wasted by
driblets, and seasons of grace lost by little slumbers.
Oh, to be wise, to catch the flying hour, to use the
moments on the wing! May the Lord teach us this
sacred wisdom, for otherwise a poverty of the worst
sort awaits us, eternal poverty which shall want even a
drop of water, and beg for it in vain. Like a traveller
steadily pursuing his journey, poverty overtakes the
slothful, and ruin overthrows the undecided: each hour
brings the dreaded pursuer nearer; he pauses not by the
way, for he is on his master's business and must not
tarry. As an armed man enters with authority and
power, so shall want come to the idle, and death to the
impenitent, and there will be no escape. O that men
were wise betimes, and would seek diligently unto the
Lord Jesus, or ere the solemn day shall dawn when it
will be too late to plough and to sow, too late to repent
and believe. In harvest, it is vain to lament that the seed
time was neglected. As yet, faith and holy decision are
timely. May we obtain them this night.

'To preach deliverance to the captives'
Luke 4:18

None but Jesus can give deliverance to captives. Real liberty cometh from Him only. It is a liberty *righteously bestowed*; for the Son, who is Heir of all things, has a right to make men free. The saints honour the justice of God, which now secures their salvation. It is a liberty which has been *dearly purchased*. Christ speaks it by His power, but He bought it by His blood. He makes thee free, but it is by His own bonds. Thou goest clear, because He bare thy burden for thee: thou art set at liberty, because He has suffered in thy stead. But, though dearly purchased, *He freely gives it*. Jesus asks nothing of us as a preparation for this liberty. He finds us sitting in sackcloth and ashes, and bids us put on the beautiful array of freedom; He saves us just as we are, and all without our help or merit. When Jesus sets free, the liberty is *perpetually entailed*; no chains can bind again. Let the Master say to me, 'Captive, I have delivered thee', and it is done for ever. Satan may plot to enslave us, but if the Lord be on our side, whom shall we fear? The world, with its temptations, may seek to ensnare us, but mightier is He who is for us than all they who be against us. The machinations of our own deceitful hearts may harass and annoy us, but He who hath begun the good work in us will carry it on and perfect it to the end. The foes of God and the enemies of man may gather their hosts together and come with concentrated fury against us, but if God acquitteth, who is he that condemneth? Not more free is the eagle which mounts to his rocky eyrie, and afterwards outsoars the clouds, than the soul which Christ hath delivered. If we are no more under the law, but free from its curse, let our liberty be *practically exhibited* in our serving God with gratitude and delight. 'I am Thy servant, and the son of thine handmaid: Thou hast loosed my bonds.' 'Lord, what wilt Thou have me to do?'

*'For He saith to Moses, I will have mercy on whom
I will have mercy, and I will have compassion on
whom I will have compassion'*
Romans 9:15

In these words the Lord in the plainest manner claims
the right to give or to withhold His mercy according to
His own sovereign will. As the prerogative of life and
death is vested in the monarch, so the Judge of all the
earth has a right to spare or condemn the guilty, as may
seem best in His sight. Men by their sins have forfeited
all claim upon God; they deserve to perish for their sins
- and if they all do so, they have no ground for
complaint. If the Lord steps in to save any, He may do
so if the ends of justice are not thwarted; but if He
judges it best to leave the condemned to suffer the
righteous sentence, none may arraign Him at their bar.
Foolish and impudent are all those discourses about the
rights of men to be all placed on the same footing;
ignorant, if not worse, are those contentions against
discriminating grace, which are but the rebellions of
proud human nature against the crown and sceptre of
Jehovah. When we are brought to see our own utter ruin
and ill desert, and the justice of the divine verdict
against sin, we no longer cavil at the truth that the Lord
is not bound to save us; we do not murmur if He
chooses to save others, as though He were doing us an
injury, but feel that if He deigns to look upon us, it will
be His own free act of undeserved goodness, for which
we shall for ever bless his name.

How shall those who are the subjects of divine
election sufficiently adore the grace of God? They have
no room for boasting, for sovereignty most effectually
excludes it. The Lord's will alone is glorified, and the
very notion of human merit is cast out to everlasting
contempt. There is no more humbling doctrine in
Scripture than that of election, none more promotive of
gratitude, and, consequently, none more sanctifying.
Believers should not be afraid of it, but adoringly
rejoice in it.

'Whatsoever thy hand findeth to do,
do it with thy might'
Ecclesiastes 9:10

'Whatsoever thy hand findeth to do' refers to works
that are *possible*. There are many things which our
heart findeth to do which we never shall do. It is well
it is in our heart; but if we would be eminently useful,
we must not be content with forming schemes in our
heart, and talking of them; we must practically carry
out *'whatsoever our hand findeth to do'*. One good
deed is more worth than a thousand brilliant theories.
Let us not wait for large opportunities, or for a different
kind of work, but do just the things we 'find to do' day
by day. We have no other time in which to live. The past
is gone; the future has not arrived; we never shall have
any time but time *present*. Then do not wait until your
experience has ripened into maturity before you attempt to serve God. Endeavour now to bring forth fruit.
Serve God now, but be careful as to the way in which
you perform what you find to do - *'do it with thy might'*.
Do it *promptly*; do not fritter away your life in thinking
of what you intend to do tomorrow as if that could
recompense for the idleness of today. No man ever
served God by doing things tomorrow. If we honour
Christ and are blessed, it is by the things which we do
today. Whatever you do for Christ throw your whole
soul into it. Do not give Christ a little slurred labour,
done as a matter of course now and then; but when you
do serve Him, do it with heart, and soul, and strength.

But where is the might of a Christian? It is not in
himself, for he is perfect weakness. His might lieth in
the Lord of Hosts. Then let us seek His help; let us
proceed with prayer and faith, and when we have done
what our 'hand findeth to do', let us wait upon the Lord
for his blessing. What we do thus will be well done, and
will not fail in its effect.

'They shall rejoice, and shall see the plummet
in the hand of Zerubbabel'
Zechariah 4:10

Small things marked the beginning of the work in the hand of Zerubbabel, but none might despise it, for the Lord had raised up one who would persevere until the headstone should be brought forth with shoutings. *The plummet was in good hands.* Here is the comfort of every believer in the Lord Jesus; let the work of grace be ever so small in its beginnings, the plummet is in good hands, a master builder greater than Solomon has undertaken the raising of the heavenly temple, and He will not fail nor be discouraged till the topmost pinnacle shall be raised. If the plummet were in the hand of any merely human being, we might fear for the building, but the pleasure of the Lord shall prosper in Jesus' hand. The works did not proceed irregularly, and without care, for *the master's hand carried a good instrument.* Had the walls been hurriedly run up without due superintendence, they might have been out of the perpendicular; but the plummet was used by the chosen overseer. Jesus is evermore watching the erection of His spiritual temple, that it may be built securely and well. We are for haste, but Jesus is for judgment. He will use the plummet, and that which is out of line must come down, every stone of it. Hence the failure of many a flattering work, the overthrow of many a glittering profession. It is not for us to judge the Lord's church, since Jesus has a steady hand, and a true eye, and can use the plummet well. Do we not rejoice to see judgment left to Him?

The plummet was in active use - it was in the builder's hand; a sure indication that he meant to push on the work to completion. O Lord Jesus, how would we indeed be glad if we could see Thee at Thy great work. O Ziona, the beautiful, thy walls are still in ruins! Rise, Thou glorious Builder, and make her desolations to rejoice at Thy coming.

> *'Joshua the high priest standing*
> *before the angel of the Lord'*
> Zechariah 3:1

In Joshua *the high priest* we see a picture of each and every child of God, who has been made nigh by the blood of Christ, and has been taught to minister in holy things, and enter into that which is within the veil. Jesus has made us priests and kings unto God, and even here upon earth we exercise the priesthood of consecrated living and hallowed service. But this high priest is said to be *'standing* before the angel of the Lord', that is, standing to minister. This should be the perpetual position of every true believer. Every place is now God's temple, and His people can as truly serve Him in their daily employments as in His house. They are to be always 'ministering', offering the spiritual sacrifice of prayer and praise, and presenting themselves a 'living sacrifice'. But notice where it is that Joshua stands to minister, it is *before the angel* of Jehovah. It is only through a mediator that we poor defiled ones can ever become priests unto God. I present what I have before the messenger, the angel of the covenant, the Lord Jesus; and through Him my prayers find acceptance wrapped up in *His* prayers; my praises become sweet as they are bound up with bundles of myrrh, and aloes, and cassia from Christ's own garden. If I can bring Him nothing but my tears, He will put them with His own tears in His own bottle, for He once wept; if I can bring Him nothing but my groans and sighs, He will accept these as an acceptable sacrifice, for He once was broken in heart, and sighed heavily in spirit. I myself, standing in Him, am accepted in the Beloved; and all my polluted works, though in themselves only objects of divine abhorrence, are so received, that God smelleth a sweet savour. He is content and I am blessed. See, then, the position of the Christian - 'a priest - standing - before the angel of the Lord'.

'*The forgiveness of sins,
according to the riches of His grace*'
Ephesians 1:7

Could there be a sweeter word in any language than that word 'forgiveness', when it sounds in a guilty sinner's ear, like the silver notes of jubilee to the captive Israelite? Blessed, for ever blessed be that dear star of pardon which shines into the condemned cell, and gives the perishing a gleam of hope amid the midnight of despair! Can it be possible that sin, such sin as mine, can be forgiven, forgiven altogether, and for ever? Hell is my portion as a sinner - there is no possibility of my escaping from it while sin remains upon me - can the load of guilt be uplifted, the crimson stain removed? Can the adamantine stones of my prison-house ever be loosed from their mortices, or the doors be lifted from their hinges? Jesus tells me that I may yet be clear. For ever blessed be the revelation of atoning love which not only tells me that pardon is possible, but that it is secured to all who rest in Jesus. I have believed in the appointed propitiation, even Jesus crucified, and therefore my sins are at this moment, and for ever, forgiven by virtue of His substitutionary pains and death. What joy is this! What bliss to be a perfectly pardoned soul! My soul dedicates all her powers to Him who of His own unpurchased love became my surety, and wrought out for me redemption through His blood. What riches of grace does free forgiveness exhibit! To forgive at all, to forgive fully, to forgive freely, to forgive for ever! Here is a constellation of wonders; and when I think of how great my sins were, how dear were the precious drops which cleansed me from them, and how gracious was the method by which pardon was sealed home to me, I am in a maze of wondering worshipping affection. I bow before the throne which absolves me, I clasp the cross which delivers me, I serve henceforth all my days the Incarnate God, through whom I am this night a pardoned soul.

*'For I rejoiced greatly, when the brethren came and
testified of the truth that is in thee,
even as thou walkest in the truth'*
3 John 3

The truth was in Gaius, and Gaius walked in the truth. If the first had not been the case, the second could never have occurred; and if the second could not be said of him the first would have been a mere pretence. Truth must enter into the soul, penetrate and saturate it, or else it is of no value. Doctrines held as a matter of creed are like bread in the hand, which ministers no nourishment to the frame; but doctrine accepted by the heart, is as food digested, which, by assimilation, sustains and builds up the body. In us truth must be a living force, an active energy, an indwelling reality, a part of the woof and warp of our being. If it be *in us*, we cannot henceforth part with it. A man may lose his garments or his limbs, but his inward parts are vital, and cannot be torn away without absolute loss of life. A Christian can die, but he cannot deny the truth. Now it is a rule of nature that the inward affects the outward, as light shines from the centre of the lantern through the glass: when, therefore, the truth is kindled within, its brightness soon beams forth in the outward life and conversation. It is said that the food of certain worms colours the cocoons of silk which they spin: and just so the nutriment upon which a man's inward nature lives gives a tinge to every word and deed proceeding from him. To walk in the truth, imports a life of integrity, holiness, faithfulness, and simplicity - the natural product of those principles of truth which the gospel teaches, and which the Spirit of God enables us to receive. We may judge of the secrets of the soul by their manifestation in the man's conversations. Be it ours today, O gracious Spirit, to be ruled and governed by Thy divine authority, so that nothing false or sinful may reign in our hearts, lest it extend its malignant influence to our daily walk among men.

'*Seeking the wealth of his people*'
Esther 10:3

Mordecai was a true patriot, and therefore, being exalted to the highest position under Ahasuerus, he used his eminence to promote the prosperity of Israel. In this he was a type of Jesus, who, upon His throne of glory, seeks not His own, but spends His power for His people. It were well if every Christian would be a Mordecai to the church, striving according to his ability for its prosperity. Some are placed in stations of affluence and influence, let them honour their Lord in the high places of the earth, and testify for Jesus before great men. Others have what is far better, namely, close fellowship with the King of kings, let them be sure to plead daily for the weak of the Lord's people, the doubting, the tempted, and the comfortless. It will redound to their honour if they make much intercession for those who are in darkness and dare not draw nigh unto the mercy seat. Instructed believers may serve their Master greatly if they lay out their talents for the general good, and impart their wealth of heavenly learning to others, by teaching them the things of God. The very least in our Israel may at least *seek* the welfare of his people; and his desire, if he can give no more, shall be acceptable. It is at once the most Christlike and the most happy course for a believer to cease from living to himself. He who blesses others cannot fail to be blessed himself. On the other hand, to seek our own personal greatness is a wicked and unhappy plan of life, its way will be grievous and its end will be fatal.

Here is the place to ask thee, my friend, whether thou art to the best of thy power seeking the wealth of the church in thy neighbourhood? I trust thou art not doing it mischief by bitterness and scandal, nor weakening it by thy neglect. Friend, unite with the Lord's poor, bear their cross, do them all the good thou canst, and thou shalt not miss thy reward.

> *'Thou shalt not go up and down as a talebearer*
> *among thy people... Thou shalt in any wise rebuke*
> *thy neighbour and not suffer sin upon him'*
> Leviticus 19:16, 17

Tale-bearing emits a threefold poison; for it injures the teller, the hearer, and the person concerning whom the tale is told. Whether the report be true or false, we are by this precept of God's Word forbidden to spread it. The reputations of the Lord's people should be very precious in our sight, and we should count it shame to help the devil to dishonour the Church and the name of the Lord. Some tongues need a bridle rather than a spur. Many glory in pulling down their brethren, as if thereby they raised themselves. Noah's wise sons cast a mantle over their father, and he who exposed him earned a fearful curse. We may ourselves one of these dark days need forbearance and silence from our brethren, let us render it cheerfully to those who require it now. Be this our family rule, and our personal bond - SPEAK EVIL OF NO MAN.

The Holy Spirit, however, permits us to censure sin, and prescribes the way in which we are to do it. It must be done by rebuking our brother to his face, not by railing behind his back. This course is manly, brotherly, Christlike, and under God's blessing will be useful. Does the flesh shrink from it? Then we must lay the greater stress upon our conscience, and keep ourselves to the work, lest by suffering sin upon our friend we become ourselves partakers of it. Hundreds have been saved from gross sins by the timely, wise, affectionate warnings of faithful ministers and brethren. Our Lord Jesus has set us a gracious example of how to deal with erring friends in His warning given to Peter, the prayer with which He preceded it, and the gentle way in which He bore with Peter's boastful denial that he needed such a caution.

'Spices for anointing oil'
Exodus 35:8

Much use was made of this anointing oil under the law, and that which it represents is of primary importance under the gospel. The Holy Spirit, who anoints us for all holy service, is indispensable to us if we would serve the Lord acceptably. Without His aid our religious services are but a vain obligation, and our inward experience is a dead thing. Whenever our ministry is without unction, what miserable stuff it becomes! Nor are the prayers, praises, meditations, and efforts of private Christians one jot superior. A holy anointing is the soul and life of piety, its absence the most grievous of all calamities. To go before the Lord without anointing is as though some common Levite had thrust himself into the priest's office - his ministrations would rather have been sins than services. May we never venture upon hallowed exercises without sacred anointings. They drop upon us from our glorious Head; from His anointing we who are as the skirts of His garments partake of a plenteous unction.

Choice spices were compounded with rarest art of the apothecary to form the anointing oil, to show forth to us how rich are all the influences of the Holy Spirit. All good things are found in the divine Comforter. Matchless consolation, infallible instruction, immortal quickening, spiritual energy, and divine sanctification all lie compounded with other excellencies in that sacred eye-salve, the heavenly anointing oil of the Holy Spirit. It imparts a delightful fragrance to the character and person of the man upon whom it is poured. Nothing like it can be found in all the treasuries of the rich, or the secrets of the wise. It is not to be imitated. It comes alone from God, and it is freely given, through Jesus Christ, to every waiting soul. Let us seek it, for we may have it, may have it this very evening. O Lord, anoint Thy servants.

'*And Amaziah said to the man of God,*
But what shall we do for the hundred talents
which I have given to the army of Israel?
And the man of God answered,
The Lord is able to give thee much more than this'
2 Chronicles 25:9

A very important question this seemed to be to the king of Judah, and possibly it is of even more weight with the tried and tempted Christian. To lose money is at no times pleasant, and when principle involves it, the flesh is not always ready to make the sacrifice. 'Why lose that which may be so usefully employed? May not the truth itself be bought too dear? What shall we do without it? Remember the children, and our small income!' All these things and a thousand more would tempt the Christian to put forth his hand to unrighteous gain, or stay himself from carrying out his conscientious convictions, when they involve serious loss. All men cannot view these matters in the light of faith; and even with the followers of Jesus, the doctrine of 'we must live' has quite sufficient weight.

The Lord is able to give thee much more than this is a very satisfactory answer to the anxious question. Our Father holds the purse-strings, and what we lose for His sake He can repay a thousand-fold. It is ours to obey His will, and we may rest assured that He will provide for us. The Lord will be no man's debtor at the last. Saints know that a grain of heart's-ease is of more value than a ton of gold. He who wraps a threadbare coat about a good conscience has gained a spiritual wealth far more desirable than any he has lost. God's smile and a dungeon are enough for a true heart; His frown and a palace would be hell to a gracious spirit. Let the worst come to the worst, let all the talents go, we have not lost our treasure, for that is above, where Christ sitteth at the right hand of God. Meanwhile, even now the Lord maketh the meek to inherit the earth, and no good thing doth He withhold from them that walk uprightly.

*'Michael and his angels fought against the dragon;
and the dragon fought and his angels'*
Revelation 12:7

War always will rage between the two great sovereignties until one or other be crushed. Peace between good and evil is an impossibility; the very pretence of it would, in fact, be the triumph of the powers of darkness. *Michael will always fight*; his holy soul is vexed with sin, and will not endure it. Jesus will always be the dragon's foe, and that not in a quiet sense, but actively, vigorously, with full determination to exterminate evil. All His servants, whether angels in heaven or messengers on earth, will and must fight; they are born to be warriors - at the cross they enter into covenant never to make truce with evil; they are a warlike company, firm in defence and fierce in attack. The duty of every soldier in the army of the Lord is daily, with all his heart, and soul, and strength, to fight against the dragon.

The dragon and his angels will not decline the affray; they are incessant in their onslaughts, sparing no weapon, fair or foul. We are foolish to expect to serve God without opposition: the more zealous we are, the more sure are we to be assailed by the myrmidons of hell. The church may become slothful, but not so her great antagonist; his restless spirit never suffers the war to pause; he hates the woman's seed, and would fain devour the church if he could. The servants of Satan partake much of the old dragon's energy, and are usually an active race. War rages all around, and to dream of peace is dangerous and futile.

Glory be to God, we know the end of the war. The great dragon shall be cast out and for ever destroyed, while Jesus and they who are with Him shall receive the crown. Let us sharpen our swords tonight, and pray the Holy Spirit to nerve our arms for the conflict. Never battle so important, never crown so glorious. Every man to his post, ye warriors of the cross, and may the Lord tread Satan under your feet shortly!

December

'Thou hast made summer and winter'
Psalm 74:17

My soul begin this wintry month with thy God. The cold snows and the piercing winds all remind thee that He keeps His covenant with day and night, and tend to assure thee that He will also keep that glorious covenant which He has made with thee in the person of Christ Jesus. He who is true to His Word in the revolutions of the seasons of this poor sin-polluted world, will not prove unfaithful in His dealings with His own well-beloved Son.

Winter in the soul is by no means a comfortable season, and if it be upon thee just now it will be very painful to thee: but there is this comfort, namely, that *the Lord* makes it. He sends the sharp blasts of adversity to nip the buds of expectation: He scattereth the hoar-frost like ashes over the once verdant meadows of our joy: He casteth forth his ice like morsels freezing the streams of our delight. He does it all, He is the great Winter King, and rules in the realms of frost, and therefore thou canst not murmur. Losses, crosses, heaviness, sickness, poverty, and a thousand other ills, are of the Lord's sending, and come to us with wise design. Frosts kill noxious insects, and put a bound to raging diseases; they break up the clods, and sweeten the soil. O that such good results would always follow our winters of affliction!

How we prize the fire just now! How pleasant is its cheerful glow! Let us in the same manner prize our Lord, who is the constant source of warmth and comfort in every time of trouble. Let us draw nigh to Him, and in Him find joy and peace in believing. Let us wrap ourselves in the warm garments of His promises, and go forth to labours which befit the season, for it were ill to be as the sluggard who will not plough by reason of the cold; for he shall beg in summer and have nothing.

*'O that men would praise the Lord for His goodness,
and for His wonderful works to the children of men'*
Psalm 107:8

If we complained less, and praised more, we should be happier, and God would be more glorified. Let us daily praise God for *common mercies* - common as we frequently call them, and yet so priceless, that when deprived of them we are ready to perish. Let us bless God for the eyes with which we behold the sun, for the health and strength to walk abroad, for the bread we eat, for the raiment we wear. Let us praise Him that we are not cast out among the hopeless, or confined amongst the guilty; let us thank Him for liberty, for friends, for family associations and comforts; let us praise Him, in fact, for everything which we receive from His bounteous hand, for we deserve little, and yet are most plenteously endowed. But, beloved, the sweetest and the loudest note in our songs of praise should be of *redeeming love*. God's redeeming acts towards His chosen are for ever the favourite themes of their praise. If we know what redemption means, let us not withhold our sonnets of thanksgiving. We have been redeemed from the power of our corruptions, uplifted from the depth of sin in which we were naturally plunged. We have been led to the cross of Christ - our shackles of guilt have been broken off; we are no longer slaves, but children of the living God, and can antedate the period when we shall be presented before the throne without spot or wrinkle or any such thing. Even now by faith we wave the palm-branch and wrap ourselves about with the fair linen which is to be our everlasting array, and shall we not unceasingly give thanks to the Lord our Redeemer? Child of God, canst thou be silent? Awake, awake, ye heritors of glory, and lead your captivity captive, as ye cry with David, 'Bless the Lord, O my soul: and all that is within me, bless His holy name'. Let the new month begin with new songs.

'Thou art all fair, my love'
Solomon's Song 4:7

The Lord's admiration of His Church is very wonderful, and His description of her beauty is very glowing. She is not merely *fair*, but '*all* fair'. He views her in Himself, washed in His sin-atoning blood and clothed in His meritorious righteousness, and He considers her to be full of comeliness and beauty. No wonder that such is the case, since it is but his own perfect excellency that He admires; for the holiness, glory, and perfection of His Church are His own glorious garments on the back of His own well-beloved spouse. She is not simply pure, or well-proportioned; she is positively lovely and fair! She has actual merit! Her deformities of sin are removed; but more, she has through her Lord obtained a meritorious righteousness by which an actual beauty is conferred upon her. Believers have a positive righteousness given to them when they become 'accepted in the beloved' (Ephesians 1:6). Nor is the Church barely lovely, she is *superlatively so*. Her Lord styles her 'Thou fairest among women'. She has a real worth and excellence which cannot be rivalled by all the nobility and royalty of the world. If Jesus could exchange His elect bride for all the queens and empresses of earth, or even for the angels in heaven, He would not, for He puts her first and foremost - 'fairest among women'. Like the moon she far outshines the stars. Nor is this an opinion which he is ashamed of, for he invites all men to hear it. He sets a 'behold' before it, a special note of exclamation, inviting and arresting attention. '*Behold*, thou art fair, my love; *behold*, thou art fair' (Solomon's Song 4:1). His opinion He publishes abroad even now, and one day from the throne of His glory He will avow the truth of it before the assembled universe. 'Come, ye blessed of my Father' (Matthew 25:34), will be His solemn affirmation of the loveliness of His elect.

'Behold, all is vanity'
Ecclesiastes 1:14

Nothing can satisfy the entire man but the Lord's love and the Lord's own self. Saints have tried to anchor in other roadsteads, but they have been driven out of such fatal refuges. Solomon, the wisest of men, was permitted to make experiments for us all, and to do for us what we must not dare to do for ourselves. Here is his testimony in his own words: 'So I was great, and increased more than all that were before me in Jerusalem: also my wisdom remained with me. And whatsoever mine eyes desired I kept not from them, I withheld not my heart from any joy; for my heart rejoiced in all my labour: and this was my portion of all my labour. Then I looked on all the works that my hands had wrought, and on the labour that I had laboured to do: and, behold, all was vanity and vexation of spirit, and there was no profit under the sun.' 'Vanity of vanities, all is vanity.' What! the whole of it vanity? O favoured monarch, is there nothing in all thy wealth? Nothing in that wide dominion reaching from the river even to the sea? Nothing in Palmyra's glorious palaces? Nothing in the house of the forest of Lebanon? In all thy music and dancing, and wine and luxury, is there nothing? 'Nothing,' he says, 'but weariness of spirit.' This was his verdict when he had trodden the whole round of pleasure. To embrace our Lord Jesus, to dwell in His love, and be fully assured of union with Him - this is all in all. Dear reader, you need not try other forms of life in order to see whether they are better than the Christian's: if you roam the world around, you will see no sights like a sight of the Saviour's face; if you could have all the comforts of life, if you lost your Saviour, you would be wretched; but if you win Christ, then should you rot in a dungeon, you would find it a paradise; should you live in obscurity, or die with famine, you will yet be satisfied with favour and full of the goodness of the Lord.

'There is no spot in thee'
Solomon's Song 4:7

Having pronounced His Church positively full of
beauty, our Lord confirms His praise by a precious
negative, 'There is no spot in thee'. As if the thought
occurred to the Bridegroom that the carping world
would insinuate that He had only mentioned her comely
parts, and had purposely omitted those features which
were deformed or defiled, He sums up all by declaring
her universally and entirely fair, and utterly devoid of
stain. A spot may soon be removed, and is the very least
thing that can disfigure beauty, but even from this little
blemish the believer is delivered in his Lord's sight. If
He had said there is no hideous scar, no horrible
deformity, no deadly ulcer, we might even then have
marvelled; but when He testifies that she is free from
the slightest spot, all these other forms of defilement
are included, and the depth of wonder is increased. If
He had but promised to remove all spots by-and-by, we
should have had eternal reason for joy; but when he
speaks of it as already done, who can restrain the most
intense emotions of satisfaction and delight? O my
soul, here is marrow and fatness for thee; eat thy fill,
and be satisfied with royal dainties.

Christ Jesus has no quarrel with His spouse. She
often wanders from Him, and grieves His Holy Spirit,
but He does not allow her faults to affect His love. He
sometimes chides, but it is always in the tenderest
manner, with the kindest intentions: it is 'my love'
even then. There is no remembrance of our follies, He
does not cherish ill thoughts of us, but He pardons and
loves as well after the offence as before it. It is well for
us it is so, for if Jesus were as mindful of injuries as
we are, how could He commune with us? Many a time
a believer will put himself out of humour with the Lord
for some slight turn in providence, but our precious
Husband knows our silly hearts too well to take any
offence at our ill manners.

'The Lord mighty in battle'
Psalm 24:8

Well may our God be glorious in the eyes of His
people, seeing that He has wrought such wonders for
them, in them, and by them. *For them,* the Lord Jesus
upon Calvary routed every foe, breaking all the weapons of the enemy in pieces by His finished work of
satisfactory obedience; by His triumphant resurrection
and ascension He completely overturned the hopes of
hell, leading captivity captive, making a show of our
enemies openly, triumphing over them by His cross.
Every arrow of guilt which Satan might have shot at us
is broken, for who can lay anything to the charge of
God's elect? Vain are the sharp swords of infernal
malice, and the perpetual battles of the serpent's seed,
for in the midst of the church the lame take the prey, and
the feeblest warriors are crowned.

The saved may well adore their Lord for His
conquests *in them,* since the arrows of their natural
hatred are snapped, and the weapons of their rebellion
broken. What victories has grace won in our evil
hearts! How glorious is Jesus when the will is subdued,
and sin dethroned! As for our remaining corruptions,
they shall sustain an equally sure defeat, and every
temptation, and doubt, and fear, shall be utterly destroyed. In the Salem of our peaceful hearts, the name
of Jesus is great beyond compare: He has won our love,
and He shall wear it. Even thus securely may we look
for victories *by us.* We are more than conquerors
through Him that loved us. We shall cast down the
powers of darkness which are in the world, by our faith,
and zeal, and holiness; we shall win sinners to Jesus,
we shall overturn false systems, we shall convert
nations, for God is with us, and none shall stand before
us. This evening let the Christian warrior chant the war
song, and prepare for tomorrow's fight. Greater is He
that is in us than he that is in the world.

'*I have much people in this city*'
Acts 18:10

This should be a great encouragement to try to do good, since God has among the vilest of the vile, the most reprobate, the most debauched and drunken, an elect people who *must* be saved. When you take the Word to them, you do so because God has ordained you to be the messenger of life to their souls, and *they must* receive it, for so the decree of predestination runs. They are as much redeemed by blood as the saints before the eternal throne. They are Christ's property, and yet perhaps they are lovers of the ale-house, and haters of holiness; but if Jesus Christ purchased them He will have them. God is not unfaithful to forget the price which His Son has paid. He will not suffer His substitution to be in any case an ineffectual, dead thing. Tens of thousands of redeemed ones are not regenerated yet, but regenerated they must be; and this is our comfort when we go forth to them with the quickening Word of God.

Nay, more, these ungodly ones are prayed for by Christ before the throne. 'Neither pray I for these alone,' saith the great Intercessor, 'but for *them also which shall believe* on Me through their word.' Poor, ignorant souls, they know nothing about prayer for themselves, but Jesus prays for them. Their names are on his breastplate, and ere long they must bow their stubborn knee, breathing the penitential sigh before the throne of grace. 'The time of figs is not yet.' The predestinated moment has not struck; but, when it comes, *they shall obey*, for God will have His own; *they must*, for the Spirit is not to be withstood when He cometh forth with fulness of power - *they must* become the willing servants of the living God. 'My people shall be willing in the day of my power.' 'He shall justify many.' 'He shall see of the travail of His soul.' 'I will divide him a portion with the great, and He shall divide the spoil with the strong.'

'Even we ourselves groan within ourselves, waiting for the adoption, to wit, the redemption of our body'
Romans 8:23

This groaning is universal among the saints: to a greater or less extent we all feel it. It is not the groan of murmuring or complaint: it is rather the note of desire than of distress. Having received an earnest, we desire the whole of our portion; we are sighing that our entire manhood, in its trinity of spirit, soul and body, may be set free from the last vestige of the fall; we long to put off corruption, weakness, and dishonour, and to wrap ourselves in incorruption, in immortality, in glory, in the spiritual body which the Lord Jesus will bestow upon His people. We long for the manifestation of our adoption as the children of God. 'We groan,' but it is *'within ourselves'*. It is not the hypocrite's groan, by which he would make men believe that he is a saint because he is wretched. Our sighs are sacred things, too hallowed for us to tell abroad. We keep our longings to our Lord alone. Then the apostle says we are *'waiting'*, by which we learn that we are not to be petulant, like Jonah or Elijah, when they said, 'Let me die'; nor are we to whimper and sigh for the end of life because we are tired of work, nor wish to escape from our present sufferings till the will of the Lord is done. We are to groan for glorification, but we are to wait patiently for it, knowing that what the Lord appoints is best. Waiting implies being ready. We are to stand at the door expecting the Beloved to open it and take us away to Himself. This 'groaning' is a *test*. You may judge of a man by what he groans after. Some men groan after wealth - they worship Mammon; some groan continually under the troubles of life - they are merely impatient; but the man who sighs after God, who is uneasy till he is made like Christ, that is the blessed man. May God help us to groan for the coming of the Lord, and the resurrection which He will bring to us.

'Ask, and it shall be given you'
Matthew 7:7

We know of a place in England still existing, where a dole of bread is served to every passer-by who chooses to ask for it. Whoever the traveller may be, he has but to knock at the door of St Cross Hospital, and there is the dole of bread for him. Jesus Christ so loved sinners that He has built a St Cross Hospital, so that whenever a sinner is hungry, he has but to knock and have his wants supplied. Nay, He has done better; He has attached to this Hospital of the Cross a bath; and whenever a soul is black and filthy, it has but to go there and be washed. The fountain is always full, always efficacious. No sinner ever went into it and found that it could not wash away his stains. Sins which were scarlet and crimson have all disappeared and the sinner has been whiter than snow. As if this were not enough, there is attached to this Hospital of the Cross a wardrobe, and a sinner making application simply as a sinner, may be clothed from head to foot; and if he wishes to be a soldier, he may not merely have a garment for ordinary wear, but armour which shall cover him from the sole of his foot to the crown of his head. If he asks for a sword, he shall have that given to him, and a shield too. Nothing that is good for him shall be denied him. He shall have spending-money so long as he lives, and he shall have an eternal heritage of glorious treasure when he enters into the joy of his Lord.

If all these things are to be had by merely knocking at mercy's door, O my soul, knock hard this morning, and ask large things of thy generous Lord. Leave not the throne of grace till all thy wants have been spread before the Lord, and until by faith thou hast a comfortable prospect that they shall be all supplied. No bashfulness need retard when Jesus invites. No unbelief should hinder when Jesus promises. No coldheartedness should restrain when such blessings are to be obtained.

'And the Lord shewed me four carpenters'
Zechariah 1:20

In the vision described in this chapter, the prophet saw
four terrible horns. They were pushing this way and
that way, dashing down the strongest and the mightiest;
and the prophet asked, 'What are these?' The answer
was, 'These are the horns which have scattered Israel.'
He saw before him a representation of those powers
which had oppressed the church of God. There were
four horns; for the church is attacked from all quarters.
Well might the prophet have felt dismayed; but on a
sudden there appeared before him *four carpenters*. He
asked, 'What shall these do?' These are the men whom
God hath found to break those horns in pieces. *God will
always find men for His work*, and He will find them
at the right time. The prophet did not see the carpenters
first, when there was nothing to do, but first the
'horns', and then the 'carpenters'. Moreover, the Lord
finds *enough men*. He did not find *three* carpenters, but
four; there were four horns, and there must be four
workmen. God finds *the right men*; not four men with
pens to write; not four architects to draw plans; but four
carpenters to do rough work. Rest assured, you who
tremble for the ark of God, that when the 'horns' grow
troublesome, the 'carpenters' will be found. You need
not fret concerning the weakness of the church of God
at any moment; there may be growing up in obscurity
the valiant reformer who will shake the nations:
Chrysostoms may come forth from our Ragged Schools,
and Augustines from the thickest darkness of London's poverty. The Lord knows where to find His
servants. He hath in ambush a multitude of mighty
men, and at His word they shall start up to the battle;
'for the battle is the Lord's', and He shall get to
Himself the victory. Let us abide faithful to Christ, and
He, in the right time, will raise up for us a defence,
whether it be in the day of our personal need, or in the
season of peril to His Church.

*'As is the heavenly,
such are they also that are heavenly'*
1 Corinthians 15:48

The head and members are of one nature, and not like that monstrous image which Nebuchadnezzar saw in his dream. The head was of fine gold, but the belly and thighs were of brass, the legs of iron, and the feet, part of iron and part of clay. Christ's mystical body is no absurd combination of opposites; the members were mortal, and therefore Jesus died; the glorified head is immortal, and therefore the body is immortal too, for thus the record stands, 'Because I live, ye shall live also'. As is our loving head, such is the body, and every member in particular. A chosen Head and chosen members; an accepted Head, and accepted members; a living Head, and living members. If the head be pure gold, all the parts of the body are of pure gold also. Thus is there a double union of nature as a basis for the closest communion. Pause here, devout reader, and see if thou canst without ecstatic amazement, contemplate the infinite condescension of the Son of God in thus exalting thy wretchedness into blessed union with his glory. Thou art so mean that in remembrance of thy mortality, thou mayest say to corruption, 'Thou art my father', and to the worm, 'Thou art my sister'; and yet in Christ thou art so honoured that thou canst say to the Almighty, 'Abba, Father', and to the Incarnate God, 'Thou art my brother and my husband'. Surely if relationships to ancient and noble families make men think highly of themselves, *we* have whereof to glory over the heads of them all. Let the poorest and most despised believer lay hold upon this privilege; let not a senseless indolence make him negligent to trace his pedigree, and let him suffer no foolish attachment to present vanities to occupy his thoughts to the exclusion of this glorious, this heavenly honour of union with Christ.

'Girt about the paps with a golden girdle'
Revelation 1:13

'One like unto the Son of Man' appeared to John in
Patmos, and the beloved disciple marked that he wore
a girdle of gold. *A girdle*, for Jesus never was ungirt
while upon earth, but stood always ready for service,
and now before the eternal throne He stays not His holy
ministry, but as a priest is girt about with 'the curious
girdle of the ephod'. Well is it for us that He has not
ceased to fulfil His offices of love for us, since this is
one of our choicest safeguards that He ever liveth to
make intercession for us. Jesus is never an idler; His
garments are never loose as though His offices were
ended; He diligently carries on the cause of His people.
A golden girdle, to manifest the superiority of His
service, the royalty of His person, the dignity of His
state, the glory of His reward. No longer does He cry
out of the dust, but He pleads with authority, a King as
well as a Priest. Safe enough is our cause in the hands
of our enthroned Melchisedek.

Our Lord presents all His people with an example.
We must never unbind our girdles. This is not the time
for lying down at ease, it is the season of service and
warfare. We need to bind the girdle of truth more and
more tightly around our loins. It is a golden girdle, and
so will be our richest ornament, and we greatly need it,
for a heart that is not well braced up with the truth as
it is in Jesus, and with the fidelity which is wrought of
the Spirit, will be easily entangled with the things of
this life, and tripped up by the snares of temptation. It
is in vain that we possess the Scriptures unless we bind
them around us like a girdle, surrounding our entire
nature, keeping each part of our character in order, and
giving compactness to our whole man. If in heaven
Jesus unbinds not the girdle, much less may we upon
earth. Stand, therefore, having your loins girt about
with truth.

'Base things of the world hath God chosen'
1 Corinthians 1:28

Walk the streets by moonlight, if you dare, and you will see sinners then. Watch when the night is dark, and the wind is howling, and the picklock is grating in the door, and you will see sinners then. Go to yon jail, and walk through the wards, and mark the men with heavy over-hanging brows, men whom you would not like to meet at night, and there are sinners there. Go to the Reformatories, and note those who have betrayed a rampant juvenile depravity, and you will see sinners there. Go across the seas to the place where a man will gnaw a bone upon which is reeking human flesh, and there is a sinner there. Go where you will, you need not ransack earth to find sinners, for they are common enough; you may find them in every lane and street of every city, and town, and village, and hamlet. It is for such that Jesus died. If you will select me the grossest specimen of humanity, if he be but born of woman, I will have hope of him yet, because Jesus Christ is come to seek and to save *sinners*. Electing love has selected some of the worst to be made the best. Pebbles of the brook grace turn into jewels for the crown-royal. Worthless dross he transforms into pure gold. Redeeming love has set apart many of the worst of mankind to be the reward of the Saviour's passion. Effectual grace calls forth many of the vilest of the vile to sit at the table of mercy, and therefore let none despair.

Reader, by that love looking out of Jesus' tearful eyes, by that love streaming from those bleeding wounds, by that faithful love, that strong love, that pure, disinterested, and abiding love; by the heart and by the bowels of the Saviour's compassion, we conjure you turn not away as though it were nothing to you; but believe on Him and you shall be saved. Trust your soul with Him and He will bring you to His Father's right hand in glory everlasting.

> *'I am made all things to all men,*
> *that I might by all means save some'*
> 1 Corinthians 9:22

Paul's great object was not merely to instruct and to improve, but to save. Anything short of this would have disappointed him; he would have men renewed in heart, forgiven, sanctified, in fact, *saved*. Have our Christian labours been aimed at anything below this great point? Then let us amend our ways, for of what avail will it be at the last great day to have taught and moralised men if they appear before God unsaved? Blood-red will our skirts be if through life we have sought inferior objects, and forgotten that men needed to be saved. Paul knew the ruin of man's natural state, and did not try to educate him, but to save him; he saw men sinking to hell, and did not talk of refining them, but of saving from the wrath to come. To compass their salvation, he gave himself up with untiring zeal to telling abroad the gospel, to warning and beseeching men to be reconciled to God. His prayers were importunate and his labours incessant. To save souls was his consuming passion, his ambition, his calling. He became a servant to all men, toiling for his race, feeling a woe within him if he preached not the gospel. He laid aside his preferences to prevent prejudice; he submitted his will in things indifferent, and if men would but receive the gospel, he raised no questions about forms or ceremonies: the gospel was the one all-important business with him. If he might save some he would be content. This was the crown for which he strove, the sole and sufficient reward of all his labours and self-denials. Dear reader, have you and I lived to win souls at this noble rate? Are we possessed with the same all-absorbing desire? If not, why not? Jesus died for sinners, cannot we live for them? Where is our tenderness? Where our love to Christ, if we seek not His honour in the salvation of men? O that the Lord would saturate us through and through with an undying zeal for the souls of men.

> *'Thou hast a few names even in Sardis*
> *which have not defiled their garments;*
> *and they shall walk with me in white:*
> *for they are worthy'*
> Revelation 3:4

We may understand this to refer to *justification*. 'They shall walk in white'; that is, they shall enjoy a constant sense of their own justification by faith; they shall understand that the righteousness of Christ is imputed to them, that they have all been washed and made whiter than the newly-fallen snow.

Again, it refers to *joy and gladness*: for white robes were holiday dresses among the Jews. They who have not defiled their garments shall have their faces always bright; they shall understand what Solomon meant when he said, 'Go thy way, eat thy bread with joy, and drink thy wine with a merry heart. Let thy garments be always white, for God hath accepted thy works.' He who is accepted of God shall wear white garments of joy and gladness, while he walks in sweet communion with the Lord Jesus. Whence so many doubts, so much misery, and mourning? It is because so many believers defile their garments with sin and error, and hence they lose the joy of their salvation, and the comfortable fellowship of the Lord Jesus, they do not here below walk in white.

The promise also refers to *walking in white before the throne of God*. Those who have not defiled their garments here shall most certainly walk in white up yonder, where the white-robed hosts sing perpetual hallelujahs to the Most High. They shall possess joys inconceivable, happiness beyond a dream, bliss which imagination knoweth not, blessedness which even the stretch of desire hath not reached. The 'undefiled in the way' shall have all this - not of merit, nor of works, but of grace. They shall walk with Christ in white, for He has made them 'worthy'. In His sweet company they shall drink of the living fountains of waters.

> *'Thou, O God, hast prepared*
> *of Thy goodness for the poor'*
> Psalm 68:10

All God's gifts are prepared gifts laid up in store for wants foreseen. He anticipates our needs; and out of the fulness which He has treasured up in Christ Jesus, He provides of His goodness for the poor. You may trust Him for all the necessities that can occur, for He has infallibly foreknown every one of them. He can say of us in all conditions, 'I knew that thou wouldst be this and that'. A man goes a journey across the desert, and when he has made a day's advance, and pitched his tent, he discovers that he wants many comforts and necessaries which he has not brought in his baggage. 'Ah!' says he, 'I did not foresee this: if I had this journey to go again, I should bring these things with me, so necessary to my comfort.' But God has marked with prescient eye all the requirements of His poor wandering children, and when those needs occur, supplies are ready. It is goodness which He has prepared for the poor in heart, goodness and goodness only. 'My grace is sufficient for thee.' 'As thy days, so shall thy strength be.'

Reader, is your heart heavy this evening? God knew it would be; the comfort which your heart wants is treasured in the sweet assurance of the text. You are poor and needy, but He has thought upon you, and has the exact blessing which you require in store for you. Plead the promise, believe it and obtain its fulfilment. Do you feel that you never were so consciously vile as you are now? Behold, the crimson fountain is open still, with all its former efficacy, to wash your sin away. Never shall you come into such a position that Christ cannot aid you. No pinch shall ever arrive in your spiritual affairs in which Jesus Christ shall not be equal to the emergency, for your history has all been foreknown and provided for in Jesus.

*'Therefore will the Lord wait,
that He may be gracious unto you'*
Isaiah 30:18

God often DELAYS IN ANSWERING PRAYER.
We have several instances of this in sacred Scripture.
Jacob did not get the blessing from the angel until near
the dawn of day - he had to wrestle all night for it. The
poor woman of Syrophoenicia was answered not a
word for a long while. Paul besought the Lord *thrice*
that 'the thorn in the flesh' might be taken from him,
and he received no assurance that it should be taken
away, but instead thereof a promise that God's grace
should be sufficient for him. If thou hast been knocking
at the gate of mercy, and hast received no answer, shall
I tell thee why the mighty Maker hath not opened the
door and let thee in? Our Father has reasons peculiar to
Himself for thus keeping us waiting. Sometimes it is
to show His power and His sovereignty, that men may
know that Jehovah has a right to give or to withhold.
More frequently the delay is for our profit. Thou art
perhaps kept waiting in order that thy desires may be
more fervent. God knows that delay will quicken and
increase desire, and that if He keeps thee waiting thou
wilt see thy necessity more clearly, and wilt seek more
earnestly; and that thou wilt prize the mercy all the
more for its long tarrying. There may also be something wrong in thee which has need to be removed,
before the joy of the Lord is given. Perhaps thy views
of the Gospel plan are confused, or thou mayest be
placing some little reliance on thyself, instead of
trusting simply and entirely to the Lord Jesus. Or, God
makes thee tarry awhile that He may the more fully
display the riches of His grace to thee at last. Thy
prayers are all filed in heaven, and if not immediately
answered they are certainly not forgotten, but in a little
while shall be fulfilled to thy delight and satisfaction.
Let not despair make thee silent, but continue instant in
earnest supplication.

'My people shall dwell in quiet resting places'
Isaiah 32:18

Peace and rest belong not to the unregenerate, they are
the peculiar possession of the Lord's people, and of
them only. The God of Peace gives perfect peace to
those whose hearts are stayed upon Him. When man
was unfallen, his God gave him the flowery bowers of
Eden as his quiet resting places; alas! how soon sin
blighted the fair abode of innocence. In the day of
universal wrath when the flood swept away a guilty
race, the chosen family were quietly secured in the
resting-place of the ark, which floated them from the
old condemned world into the new earth of the rainbow
and the covenant, herein typifying Jesus, the ark of our
salvation. Israel rested safely beneath the blood-
besprinkled habitations of Egypt when the destroying
angel smote the first-born; and in the wilderness the
shadow of the pillar of cloud, and the flowing rock,
gave the weary pilgrims sweet repose. At this hour we
rest in the promises of our faithful God, knowing that
His words are full of truth and power; we rest in the
doctrines of His word, which are consolation itself; we
rest in the covenant of His grace, which is a haven of
delight. More highly favoured are we than David in
Adullam, or Jonah beneath his gourd, for none can
invade or destroy our shelter. The person of Jesus is the
quiet resting-place of His people, and when we draw
near to Him in the breaking of bread, in the hearing of
the word, the searching of the Scriptures, prayer, or
praise, we find any form of approach to Him to be the
return of peace to our spirits.

'I hear the words of love, I gaze upon the blood,
    I see the mighty sacrifice, and I have peace with God.
'Tis everlasting peace, sure as Jehovah's name,
    'Tis stable as His steadfast throne, for evermore the same;
The clouds may go and come, and storms may sweep my sky,
    This blood-sealed friendship changes not, the cross is ever
                                                                nigh.'

'*So shall we ever be with the Lord*'
1 Thessalonians 4:17

Even the sweetest visits from Christ, how short they are - and how transitory! One moment our eyes see Him, and we rejoice with joy unspeakable and full of glory, but again a little time and we do not see Him, for our beloved withdraws Himself from us; like a roe or a young hart he leaps over the mountains of division; He is gone to the land of spices, and feeds no more among the lilies.

> If today he deigns to bless us
>> With a sense of pardoned sin,
> He tomorrow may distress us,
>> Make us feel the plague within.

Oh, how sweet the prospect of the time when we shall not behold Him at a distance, but see Him face to face: when He shall not be as a wayfaring man tarrying but for a night, but shall eternally enfold us in the bosom of His glory. We shall not see Him for a little season but:

> Millions of years our wandering eyes,
>> Shall o'er our Saviour's beauties rove;
> And myriad ages we'll adore,
>> The wonders of his love.

In heaven there shall be no interruptions from care or sin; no weeping shall dim our eyes; no earthly business shall distract our happy thoughts; we shall have nothing to hinder us from gazing for ever on the Sun of Righteousness with unwearied eyes. Oh, if it be so sweet to see Him now and then, how sweet to gaze on that blessed face for aye, and never have a cloud rolling between, and never have to turn one's eyes away to look on a world of weariness and woe! Blest day, when wilt thou dawn? Rise, O unsetting sun! The joys of sense may leave us as soon as they will, for this shall make glorious amends. If to die is but to enter into uninterrupted communion with Jesus, then death is indeed gain, and the black drop is swallowed up in a sea of victory.

'Whose heart the Lord opened'
Acts 16:14

In Lydia's conversion there are many points of interest. It was brought about by *providential circumstances*. She was a seller of purple, of the city of Thyatira, but just at the right time for hearing Paul we find her at Philippi; providence, which is the handmaid of grace, led her to the right spot. Again, *grace was preparing her soul for the blessing* - grace preparing for grace. She did not know the Saviour, but as a Jewess, she knew many truths which were excellent stepping-stones to a knowledge of Jesus. Her conversion took place in the use of the means. On the Sabbath she went when prayer was wont to be made, and there prayer was heard. Never neglect the means of grace; God *may* bless us when we are not in His house, but we have the greater reason to hope that He *will* when we are in communion with His saints. Observe the words, 'Whose heart *the Lord* opened'. She did not open her own heart. Her prayers did not do it; Paul did not do it. The Lord Himself must open the heart, to receive the things which make for our peace. He alone can put the key into the hole of the door and open it, and get admittance for Himself. He is the heart's master as He is the heart's maker. The first outward evidence of the opened heart was *obedience*. As soon as Lydia had believed in Jesus, she was baptized. It is a sweet sign of a humble and broken heart, when the child of God is willing to obey a command which is not essential to his salvation, which is not forced upon him by a selfish fear of condemnation, but is a simple act of obedience and of communion with his Master. The next evidence was *love*, manifesting itself in acts of grateful kindness to the apostles. Love to the saints has ever been a mark of the true convert. Those who do nothing for Christ or His church, give but sorry evidence of an 'opened' heart. Lord, evermore give me an opened heart.

'Faithful is He that calleth you, who also will do it'
1 Thessalonians 5:24

Heaven is a place where we shall never sin; where we shall cease our constant watch against an indefatigable enemy, because there will be no tempter to ensnare our feet. There the wicked cease from troubling, and the weary are at rest. Heaven is the 'undefiled inheritance'; it is the land of perfect holiness, and therefore of complete security. But do not the saints even on earth sometimes taste the joys of blissful security? The doctrine of God's word is, that all who are in union with the Lamb are safe; that all the righteous shall hold on their way; that those who have committed their souls to the keeping of Christ shall find him a faithful and immutable preserver. Sustained by such a doctrine we can enjoy security even on earth; not that high and glorious security which renders us free from every slip, but that holy security which arises from the sure promise of Jesus that none who believe in Him shall ever perish, but shall be with Him where He is. Believer, let us often reflect with joy on the doctrine of the perseverance of the saints, and honour the faithfulness of our God by a holy confidence in Him.

May our God bring home to you a sense of your safety in Christ Jesus! May He assure you that your name is graven on His hand; and whisper in your ear the promise, 'Fear not, I am with thee'. Look upon Him, the great Surety of the covenant, as faithful and true, and, therefore, bound and engaged to present you, the weakest of the family, with all the chosen race, before the throne of God; and in such a sweet contemplation you will drink the juice of the spiced wine of the Lord's pomegranate, and taste the dainty fruits of Paradise. You will have an antepast of the enjoyments which ravish the souls of the perfect saints above, if you can believe with unstaggering faith that 'faithful is He that calleth you, who also will do it'.

'*Ye serve the Lord Christ*' - Colossians 3:24

To what choice order of officials was this word spoken? To kings who proudly boast a right divine? Ah, no! too often do they serve themselves or Satan, and forget the God whose sufferance permits them to wear their mimic majesty for their little hour. Speaks then the apostle to those so-called 'right reverend fathers in God', the bishops, or 'the venerable the archdeacons'? No, indeed, Paul knew nothing of these mere inventions of man. Not even to pastors and teachers, or to the wealthy and esteemed among believers, was this word spoken, but to servants, ay, and to slaves. Among the toiling multitudes, the journeymen, the day labourers, the domestic servants, the drudges of the kitchen, the apostle found, as we find still, some of the Lord's chosen, and to them he says, 'Whatsoever ye do, do it heartily, as to the Lord, and not unto men; knowing that of the Lord ye shall receive the reward of the inheritance: for ye serve the Lord Christ.' This saying ennobles the weary routine of earthly employments, and sheds a halo around the most humble occupations. To wash feet may be servile, but to wash *His* feet is royal work. To unloose the shoe-latchet is poor employ, but to unloose the great Master's shoe is a princely privilege. The shop, the barn, the scullery, and the smithy become temples when men and women do all to the glory of God! Then 'divine service' is not a thing of a few hours and a few places, but all life becomes holiness unto the Lord, and every place and thing, as consecrated as the tabernacle and its golden candlestick.

'Teach me, my God and King, in all things Thee to see;
And what I do in anything to do it as to Thee.
All may of Thee partake, nothing can be so mean,
Which with this tincture, *for Thy sake*, will not grow bright
                                                    and clean.
A servant with this clause makes drudgery divine;
Who sweeps a room, as for Thy laws, makes that and the action
                                                    fine.'

'His ways are everlasting'
Habakkuk 3:6

What He hath done at one time, He will do yet again. Man's ways are variable, but God's ways are everlasting. There are many reasons for this most comforting truth: among them are the following - the Lord's ways are *the result of wise deliberation*; He ordereth all things according to the counsel of His own will. Human action is frequently the hasty result of passion, or fear, and is followed by regret and alteration; but nothing can take the Almighty by surprise, or happen otherwise than He has foreseen. His ways are *the outgrowth of an immutable character*, and in them the fixed and settled attributes of God are clearly to be seen. Unless the Eternal One Himself can undergo change, His ways, which are Himself in action, must remain for ever the same. Is He eternally just, gracious, faithful, wise, tender? - then His ways must ever be distinguished for the same excellences. Beings act according to their nature: when those natures change, their conduct varies also; but since God cannot know the shadow of a turning, His ways will abide everlastingly the same. Moreover there is no reason from without which could reverse the divine ways, since they are *the embodiment of irresistible might*. The earth is said, by the prophet, to be cleft with rivers, mountains tremble, the deep lifts up its hands, and sun and moon stand still, when Jehovah marches forth for the salvation of His people. Who can stay His hand, or say unto Him, What doest Thou? But it is not might alone which gives stability; God's ways are *the manifestation of the eternal principles of right*, and therefore can never pass away. Wrong breeds decay and involves ruin, but the true and the good have about them a vitality which ages cannot diminish.

This morning let us go to our heavenly Father with confidence, remembering that Jesus Christ is the same yesterday, today, and for ever, and in Him the Lord is ever gracious to His people.

'They have dealt treacherously against the Lord'
Hosea 5:7

Believer, here is a sorrowful truth! Thou art the beloved of the Lord, redeemed by blood, called by grace, preserved in Christ Jesus, accepted in the Beloved, on thy way to heaven, and yet, 'thou hast dealt treacherously' with God thy best friend; treacherously with Jesus, whose thou art; treacherously with the Holy Spirit, by whom thou hast been quickened unto life eternal! How treacherous you have been in the matter of vows and promises. Do you remember the love of your espousals, that happy time - the springtide of your spiritual life? Oh, how closely did you cling to your Master then, saying, 'He shall never charge me with indifference; my feet shall never grow slow in the way of His service; I will not suffer my heart to wander after other loves; in Him is every store of sweetness ineffable. I give all up for my Lord Jesus' sake.' Has it been so? Alas! if conscience speak, it will say, 'He who promised so well has performed most ill. Prayer has oftentimes been slurred - it has been short, but not sweet; brief, but not fervent. Communion with Christ has been forgotten. Instead of a heavenly mind, there have been carnal cares, worldly vanities and thoughts of evil. Instead of service, there has been disobedience; instead of fervency, lukewarmness; instead of patience, petulance; instead of faith, confidence in an arm of flesh; and as a soldier of the cross there has been cowardice, disobedience, and desertion, to a very shameful degree.' 'Thou hast dealt treacherously.' Treachery to Jesus! what words shall be used in denouncing it? Words little avail: let our penitent thoughts execrate the sin which is so surely in us. Treacherous to Thy wounds, O Jesus! Forgive us, and let us not sin again! How shameful to be treacherous to Him who never forgets us, but who this day stands with our names engraven on His breastplate before the eternal throne.

'*Salt without prescribing how much*'
Ezra 7:22

Salt was used in every offering made by fire unto the
Lord, and from its preserving and purifying properties
it was the grateful emblem of divine grace in the soul.
It is worthy of our attentive regard that, when Artaxerxes
gave salt to Ezra the priest, he set no limit to the
quantity, and we may be quite certain that when the
King of kings distributes grace among His royal
priesthood, the supply is not cut short by *Him*. Often
are we straitened in ourselves, but never in the Lord. He
who chooses to gather much manna will find that he
may have as much as he desires. There is no such
famine in Jerusalem that the citizens should eat their
bread by weight and drink their water by measure.
Some things in the economy of grace are measured; for
instance our vinegar and gall are given us with such
exactness that we never have a single drop too much,
but of the salt of grace no stint is made, 'Ask what thou
wilt and it shall be given unto thee'. Parents need to
lock up the fruit cupboard, and the sweet jars, but there
is no need to keep the salt-box under lock and key, for
few children will eat too greedily from that. A man may
have too much money, or too much honour, but he
cannot have too much grace. When Jeshurun waxed fat
in the flesh, he kicked against God, but there is no fear
of a man's becoming too full of grace: a *plethora* of
grace is impossible. More wealth brings more care, but
more grace brings more joy. Increased wisdom is
increased sorrow, but abundance of the Spirit is fulness
of joy. Believer, go to the throne for a large supply of
heavenly salt. It will season thine afflictions, which are
unsavoury without salt; it will preserve thy heart which
corrupts if salt be absent, and it will kill thy sins even
as salt kills reptiles. Thou needest much; seek much,
and have much.

> *'I will make thy windows of agates'*
> Isaiah 54:12

The church is most instructively symbolised by a building erected by heavenly power, and designed by divine skill. Such a spiritual house must not be dark, for the Israelites had light in their dwellings; there must therefore be windows to let the light in and to allow the inhabitants to gaze abroad. These windows are *precious* as agates: the ways in which the church beholds her Lord and heaven, and spiritual truth in general, are to be had in the highest esteem. Agates are *not the most transparent* of gems, they are but semi-pellucid at the best:

> Our knowledge of that life is small,
> Our eye of faith is dim.

Faith is one of these precious agate windows, but alas, it is often so misty and beclouded, that we see but darkly, and mistake much that we do see. Yet if we cannot gaze through windows of diamonds and know even as we are known, it is a glorious thing to behold the altogether lovely One, even though the glass be hazy as the agate. *Experience* is another of these dim but precious windows, yielding to us a subdued religious light, in which we see the sufferings of the Man of Sorrows, through our own afflictions. Our weak eyes could not endure windows of transparent glass to let in the Master's glory, but when they are dimmed with weeping, the beams of the Sun of Righteousness are tempered, and shine through the windows of agate with a soft radiance inexpressibly soothing to tempted souls. *Sanctification*, as it conforms us to our Lord, is another agate window. Only as we become heavenly can we comprehend heavenly things. The pure in heart see a pure God. Those who are like Jesus see Him as He is. Because we are so little like Him, the window is but agate; because we are somewhat like Him, it is agate. We thank God for what we have, and long for more. When shall we see God and Jesus, and heaven and truth, face to face?

'They go from strength to strength'
Psalm 84:7

They go *from strength to strength*. There are various renderings of these words, but all of them contain the idea of progress.

Our own good translation of the authorised version is enough for us this morning. 'They go from strength to strength.' That is, they grow stronger and stronger. Usually, if we are walking, we go from strength to weakness; we start fresh and in good order for our journey, but by-and-by the road is rough, and the sun is hot, we sit down by the wayside, and then again painfully pursue our weary way. But the Christian pilgrim having obtained fresh supplies of grace, is as vigorous after years of toilsome travel and struggle as when he first set out. He may not be quite so elated and buoyant, nor perhaps quite so hot and hasty in his zeal as he once was, but he is much stronger in all that constitutes real power, and travels, if more slowly, far more surely. Some gray-haired veterans have been as firm in their grasp of truth, and as zealous in diffusing it, as they were in their younger days; but, alas, it must be confessed it is often otherwise, for the love of many waxes cold and iniquity abounds, but this is their own sin and not the fault of the promise which still holds good: 'The youths shall faint and be weary, and the young men shall utterly fall, but they that wait upon the Lord shall renew their strength; they shall mount up with wings as eagles, they shall run and not be weary, and they shall walk and not faint.' Fretful spirits sit down and trouble themselves about the future. 'Alas!' say they, 'we go from affliction to affliction.' Very true, O thou of little faith, but then thou goest from strength to strength also. Thou shalt never find a bundle of affliction which has not bound up in the midst of it sufficient grace. God will give the strength of ripe manhood with the burden allotted to full-grown shoulders.

'I am crucified with Christ'
Galatians 2:20

The Lord Jesus Christ acted in what He did as a great public representative person, and His dying upon the cross was the virtual dying of all His people. Then all His saints rendered unto justice what was due, and made an expiation to divine vengeance for all their sins. The apostle of the Gentiles delighted to think that as one of Christ's chosen people, he died upon the cross in Christ. He did more than believe this doctrinally, he accepted it confidently, resting his hope upon it. He believed that by virtue of Christ's death, he had satisfied divine justice, and found reconciliation with God. Beloved, what a blessed thing it is when the soul can, as it were, stretch itself upon the cross of Christ, and feel, 'I am dead; the law has slain me, and I am therefore free from its power, because in my Surety I have borne the curse, and in the person of my Substitute the whole that the law could do, by way of condemnation, has been executed upon me, for I am crucified with Christ.'

But Paul meant even more than this. He not only believed in Christ's death, and trusted in it, but he actually felt its power in himself in causing the crucifixion of his old corrupt nature. When he saw the pleasures of sin, he said, 'I cannot enjoy these: I am dead to them'. Such is the experience of every true Christian. Having received Christ, he is to this world as one who is utterly dead. Yet, while conscious of death to the world, he can, at the same time, exclaim with the apostle, 'Nevertheless, I live'. He is fully alive to God. The Christian's life is a matchless riddle. No worldling can comprehend it; even the believer himself cannot understand it. Dead, yet alive! crucified with Christ, and yet at the same time risen with Christ in newness of life! Union with the suffering, bleeding Saviour, and death to the world and sin, are soul-cheering things. O for more enjoyment of them!

'Orpah kissed her mother-in-law;
but Ruth clave unto her'
Ruth 1:14

Both of them had an affection for Naomi, and therefore set out with her upon her return to the land of Judah. But the hour of test came; Naomi most unselfishly set before each of them the trials which awaited them, and bade them if they cared for ease and comfort to return to their Moabitish friends. At first both of them declared that they would cast in their lot with the Lord's people; but upon still further consideration Orpah with much grief and a respectful kiss left her mother-in-law, and her people, and her God, and went back to her idolatrous friends, while Ruth with all her heart gave herself up to the God of her mother-in-law. It is one thing to love the ways of the Lord when all is fair, and quite another to cleave to them under all discouragements and difficulties. The kiss of outward profession is very cheap and easy, but the practical cleaving to the Lord, which must show itself in holy decision for truth and holiness, is not so small a matter. How stands the case with us, is our heart fixed upon Jesus, is the sacrifice bound with cords to the horns of the altar? Have we counted the cost, and are we solemnly ready to suffer all worldly loss for the Master's sake? The after gain will be an abundant recompense, for Egypt's treasures are not to be compared with the glory to be revealed. Orpah is heard of no more; in glorious ease and idolatrous pleasure her life melts into the gloom of death; but Ruth lives in history and in heaven, for grace has placed her in the noble line whence sprung the King of kings. Blessed among women shall those be who for Christ's sake can renounce all; but forgotten and worse than forgotten shall those be who in the hour of temptation do violence to conscience and turn back unto the world. O that this morning we may not be content with the form of devotion, which may be no better than Orpah's kiss, but may the Holy Spirit work in us a cleaving of our whole heart to our Lord Jesus.

'And lay thy foundations with sapphires'
Isaiah 54:11

Not only that which is seen of the church of God, but that which is unseen, is fair and precious. Foundations are out of sight, and so long as they are firm it is not expected that they should be valuable; but in Jehovah's work everything is of a piece, nothing slurred, nothing mean. The deep foundations of the work of grace are as sapphires for preciousness, no human mind is able to measure their glory. We build upon *the covenant of grace*, which is firmer than adamant, and as enduring as jewels upon which age spends itself in vain. Sapphire foundations are eternal, and the covenant abides throughout the lifetime of the Almighty. Another foundation is *the person of the Lord Jesus*, which is clear and spotless, everlasting and beautiful as the sapphire; blending in one the deep blue of earth's ever-rolling ocean and the azure of its all-embracing sky. Once might our Lord have been likened to the ruby as He stood covered with His own blood, but now we see Him radiant with the soft blue of love, love abounding, deep, eternal. Our eternal hopes are built upon *the justice and the faithfulness of God*, which are clear and cloudless as the sapphire. We are not saved by a compromise, by mercy defeating justice, or law suspending its operations; no, we defy the eagle's eye to detect a flaw in the groundwork of our confidence - our foundation is of sapphire, and will endure the fire.

The Lord Himself has laid the foundation of His people's hopes. It is matter for grave enquiry whether *our* hopes are built upon such a basis. Good works and ceremonies are not a foundation of sapphires, but of wood, hay, and stubble; neither are they laid by God, but by our own conceit. Foundations will all be tried ere long: woe unto him whose lofty tower shall come down with a crash, because based on a quicksand. He who is built on sapphires may await storm or fire with equanimity, for he shall abide the test.

'Come unto me'
Matthew 11:28

The cry of the Christian religion is the gentle word, 'Come'. The Jewish law harshly said, 'Go, take heed unto thy steps as to the path in which thou shalt walk. Break the commandments, and thou shalt perish; keep them, and thou shalt live.' The law was a dispensation of terror, which drove men before it as with a scourge; the gospel draws with bands of love. Jesus is the good Shepherd going before His sheep, bidding them follow Him, and ever leading them onwards with the sweet word, 'Come'. The law repels, the gospel attracts. The law shows the distance which there is between God and man; the gospel bridges that awful chasm, and brings the sinner across it.

From the first moment of your spiritual life until you are ushered into glory, the language of Christ to you will be, *'Come, come* unto me'. As a mother puts out her finger to her little child and woos it to walk by saying, 'Come', even so does Jesus. He will always be ahead of you, bidding you follow Him as the soldier follows his captain. He will always go before you to pave your way, and clear your path, and you shall hear His animating voice calling you after Him all through life; while in the solemn hour of death, His sweet words with which He shall usher you into the heavenly world shall be - 'Come, ye blessed of my Father'.

Nay, further, this is not only Christ's cry to you, but, if you be a believer, this is your cry to Christ - 'Come! come!'. You will be longing for his second advent; you will be saying, 'Come quickly, even so come Lord Jesus'. You will be panting for nearer and closer communion with Him. As His voice to you is 'Come', your response to Him will be, 'Come, Lord, and abide with me. Come, and occupy alone the throne of my heart; reign there without a rival, and consecrate me entirely to Thy service.'

*'Yea, thou heardest not; yea, thou knewest not; yea,
from that time that thine ear was not opened'*
Isaiah 48:8

It is painful to remember that, in a certain degree, this
accusation may be laid at the door of *believers*, who too
often are in a measure *spiritually insensible*. We may
well bewail ourselves that *we* do not hear the voice of
God as we ought, 'Yea, thou heardest not'. There are
gentle motions of the Holy Spirit in the soul which are
unheeded by us: there are whisperings of divine command and of heavenly love which are alike unobserved
by our leaden intellects. Alas! we have been *carelessly
ignorant* - 'Yea, thou knewest not'. There are matters
within which we ought to have seen, corruptions which
have made headway unnoticed; sweet affections which
have been blighted like flowers in the frost, untended
by us; glimpses of the divine face which might be
perceived if we did not wall up the windows of our soul.
But we 'have not known'. As we think of it we are
humbled in the deepest self-abasement. How must we
adore the grace of God as we learn from the context that
all this folly and ignorance on our part, was *foreknown
by God*, and, notwithstanding that foreknowledge, He
yet has been pleased to deal with us in a way of mercy!
Admire the marvellous sovereign grace which could
have chosen us in the sight of all this! Wonder at the
price that was paid for us when Christ knew what we
should be! He who hung upon the cross, foresaw us as
unbelieving, backsliding, cold of heart, indifferent,
careless, lax in prayer, and yet He said, 'I am the Lord
thy God, the Holy One of Israel, thy Saviour... Since
thou wast precious in My sight, thou hast been honourable, and I have loved thee: therefore will I give men for
thee, and people for thy life'! O redemption, how
wondrously resplendent dost thou shine when we think
how black we are! O Holy Spirit, give us henceforth the
hearing ear, the understanding heart!

'I remember thee'
Jeremiah 2:2

Let us note that Christ delights to think upon His Church, and to look upon her beauty. As the bird returneth often to its nest, and as the wayfarer hastens to his home, so doth the mind continually pursue the object of its choice. We cannot look too often upon that face which we love; we desire always to have our precious things in our sight. It is even so with our Lord Jesus. From all eternity 'His delights were with the sons of men'; His thoughts rolled onward to the time when His elect should be born into the world; He viewed them in the mirror of His foreknowledge. 'In Thy book,' He says, 'all my members were written, which in continuance were fashioned, when as yet there was none of them' (Psalm 139:16). When the world was set upon its pillars, He was there, and He set the bounds of the people according to the number of the children of Israel. Many a time before his incarnation, He descended to this lower earth in the similitude of a man; on the plains of Mamre (Genesis 18), by the brook of Jabbock (Genesis 32:24-30), beneath the walls of Jericho (Joshua 5:13), and in the fiery furnace of Babylon (Daniel 3:19, 25) the Son of Man visited His people. Because His soul delighted in them, He could not rest away from them, for His heart longed after them. Never were they absent from His heart, for He had written their names upon His hands, and graven them upon His side. As the breastplate containing the names of the tribes of Israel was the most brilliant ornament worn by the high priest, so the names of Christ's elect were His most precious jewels, and glittered on His heart. We may often forget to meditate *upon the perfections* of our Lord, but He never ceases to remember us. Let us chide ourselves for past forgetfulness, and pray for grace ever to bear Him in fondest remembrance. Lord, paint upon the eyeballs of my soul the image of thy Son.

'I am the door: by Me if any man enter in, he shall be saved, and shall go in and out, and find pasture'
John 10:9

Jesus, the great I AM, is the entrance into the true church, and the way of access to God Himself. He gives to the man who comes to God by Him four choice privileges.

1. *He shall be saved.* The fugitive manslayer passed the gate of the city of refuge and was safe. Noah entered the door of the ark, and was secure. None can be lost who take Jesus as the door of faith to their souls. Entrance through Jesus into peace is the guarantee of entrance by the same door into heaven. Jesus is the only door, an open door, a wide door, a safe door; and blessed is he who rests all his hope of admission to glory upon the crucified Redeemer.

2. *He shall go in.* He shall be privileged to go in among the divine family, sharing the children's bread, and participating in all their honours and enjoyments. He shall go in to the chambers of communion, to the banquets of love, to the treasures of the covenant, to the storehouses of the promises. He shall go in unto the King of kings in the power of the Holy Spirit, and the secret of the Lord shall be with him.

3. *He shall go out.* This blessing is much forgotten. We go out into the world to labour and suffer, but what a mercy to go in the name and power of Jesus! We are called to bear witness to the truth, to cheer the disconsolate, to warn the careless, to win souls, and to glorify God; and as the angel said to Gideon, 'Go in this thy might', even thus the Lord would have us proceed as His messengers in His name and strength.

4. *He shall find pasture.* He who knows Jesus shall never want. Going in and out shall be alike helpful to him: in fellowship with God he shall grow, and in watering others he shall be watered. Having made Jesus his all, he shall find all in Jesus. His soul shall be as a watered garden, and as a well of water whose waters fail not.

'Rend your heart, and not your garments'
Joel 2:13

Garment-rending and other outward signs of religious emotion, are *easily manifested* and are *frequently hypocritical*: but to feel true repentance is far more difficult, and consequently far less common. Men will attend to the most multiplied and minute ceremonial regulations - for such things are *pleasing to the flesh* - but true religion is too humbling, too heart-searching, too thorough for the tastes of carnal men; they prefer something more ostentatious, flimsy, and worldly. Outward observances are *temporarily comfortable*; eye and ear are pleased; self-conceit is fed, and self-righteousness is puffed up: but they are *ultimately delusive*, for in the article of death, and at the day of judgment, the soul needs something more substantial than ceremonies and rituals to lean upon. Apart from vital godliness all religion is *utterly vain*; offered without a sincere heart, every form of worship is a solemn sham and an impudent mockery of the majesty of heaven.

HEART-RENDING is *divinely wrought* and *solemnly felt*. It is a secret grief which is *personally experienced*, not in mere form, but as a deep, soul-moving work of the Holy Spirit upon the inmost heart of each believer. It is not a matter to be merely talked of and believed in, but keenly and sensitively felt in every living child of the living God. It is *powerfully humiliating*, and *completely sin-purging*; but then it is *sweetly preparative* for those gracious consolations which proud unhumbled spirits are unable to receive; and it is *distinctly discriminating*, for it belongs to the elect of God, and to them alone.

The text commands us to rend our hearts, but they are naturally hard as marble: how, then, can this be done? We must take them to Calvary: a dying Saviour's voice rent the rocks once, and it is as powerful now. O blessed Spirit, let us hear the death-cries of Jesus, and our hearts shall be rent even as men rend their vestures in the day of lamentation.

*'Be thou diligent to know the state of thy flocks,
and look well to thy herds'*
Proverbs 27:23

Every wise merchant will occasionally hold a stock-taking, when he will cast up his accounts, examine what he has on hand, and ascertain decisively whether his trade is prosperous or declining. Every man who is wise in the kingdom of heaven, will cry, 'Search me, O God, and try me'; and he will frequently set apart special seasons for self-examination, to discover whether things are right between God and his soul. The God whom we worship is a great heart-searcher; and of old His servants knew Him as 'the Lord which searcheth the heart and trieth the reins of the children of men'. Let me stir you up in His name to make diligent search and solemn trial of your state, lest you come short of the promised rest. That which every wise man does, that which God Himself does with us all, I exhort you to do with yourself this evening. Let the oldest saint look well to the fundamentals of his piety, for grey heads may cover black hearts: and let not the young professor despise the word of warning, for the greenness of youth may be joined to the rottenness of hypocrisy. Every now and then a cedar falls into our midst. The enemy still continues to sow tares among the wheat. It is not my aim to introduce doubts and fears into your mind; nay, verily, but I shall hope the rather that the rough wind of self-examination may help to drive them away. It is not security, but carnal security, which we would kill; not confidence, but fleshly confidence, which we would overthrow; not peace, but false peace, which we would destroy. By the precious blood of Christ, which was not shed to make you a hypocrite, but that sincere souls might show forth His praise, I beseech you, search and look, lest at the last it be said of you, 'Mene, Mene, Tekel: thou art weighed in the balances and art found wanting'.

'The lot is cast into the lap;
but the whole disposing thereof is of the Lord'
Proverbs 16:33

If the disposal of the lot is the Lord's, whose is the arrangement of our whole life? If the simple casting of a lot is guided by Him, how much more the events of our entire life - especially when we are told by our blessed Saviour: 'The very hairs of your head are all numbered: not a sparrow falleth to the ground without your Father.' It would bring a holy calm over your mind, dear friend, if you were always to remember this. It would so relieve your mind from anxiety, that you would be the better able to walk in patience, quiet, and cheerfulness as a Christian should. When a man is anxious he cannot pray with faith; when he is troubled about the world, he cannot serve his Master, his thoughts are serving himself. If you would 'seek first the kingdom of God and His righteousness', all things would then be added unto you. You are meddling with Christ's business, and neglecting your own when you fret about your lot and circumstances. You have been trying 'providing' work and forgetting that it is yours to obey. Be wise and attend to the obeying, and let Christ manage the providing. Come and survey your Father's storehouse, and ask whether He will let you starve while He has laid up so great an abundance in His garner? Look at His heart of mercy; see if that can ever prove unkind! Look at His inscrutable wisdom; see if that will ever be at fault. Above all, look up to Jesus Christ your Intercessor, and ask yourself, while He pleads, can your Father deal ungraciously with you? If He remembers even sparrows, will He forget one of the least of His poor children? 'Cast thy burden upon the Lord, and He will sustain thee. He will never suffer the righteous to be moved.'

My soul, rest happy in thy low estate,
   Nor hope nor wish to be esteem'd or great;
To take the impress of the Will Divine,
   Be that thy glory, and those riches thine.

'*And there was no more sea*'
Revelation 21:1

Scarcely could we rejoice at the thought of losing the glorious old ocean: the new heavens and the new earth are none the fairer to our imagination, if, indeed, literally there is to be no great and wide sea, with its gleaming waves and shelly shores. Is not the text to be read as a metaphor, tinged with the prejudice with which the Oriental mind universally regarded the sea in the olden times? A real physical world without a sea it is mournful to imagine, it would be an iron ring without the sapphire which made it precious. There must be a spiritual meaning here. In the new dispensation there will be no *division* - the sea separates nations and sunders peoples from each other. To John in Patmos the deep waters were like prison walls, shutting him out from his brethren and his work: there shall be no such barriers in the world to come. Leagues of rolling billows lie between us and many a kinsman whom tonight we prayerfully remember, but in the bright world to which we go there shall be unbroken fellowship for all the redeemed family. In this sense there shall be no more sea. The sea is the emblem of *change*; with its ebbs and flows, its glassy smoothness and its mountainous billows, its gentle murmurs and its tumultuous roarings, it is never long the same. Slave of the fickle winds and the changeful moon, its instability is proverbial. In this mortal state we have too much of this; earth is constant only in her inconstancy, but in the heavenly state all mournful change shall be unknown, and with it all fear of *storm* to wreck our hopes and drown our joys. The sea of glass glows with a glory unbroken by a wave. No tempest howls along the peaceful shores of paradise. Soon shall we reach that happy land where partings, and changes, and storms shall be ended! Jesus will waft us there. Are we in Him or not? This is the grand question.

'Yea, I have loved thee with an everlasting love'
Jeremiah 31:3

Sometimes the Lord Jesus tells His Church His love thoughts. 'He does not think it enough behind her back to tell it, but in her very presence He says, "Thou art all fair, my love". It is true, this is not His ordinary method; He is a wise lover, and knows when to keep back the intimation of love and when to let it out; but there are times when He will make no secret of it; times when He will put it beyond all dispute in the souls of His people' (R Erskine's *Sermons*). The Holy Spirit is often pleased, in a most gracious manner, to witness with our spirits of the love of Jesus. He takes of the things of Christ and reveals them unto us. No voice is heard from the clouds, and no vision is seen in the night, but we have a testimony more sure than either of these. If an angel should fly from heaven and inform the saint personally of the Saviour's love to him, the evidence would not be one whit more satisfactory than that which is borne in the heart by the Holy Ghost. Ask those of the Lord's people who have lived the nearest to the gates of heaven, and they will tell you that they have had seasons when the love of Christ towards them has been a fact so clear and sure, that they could no more doubt it than they could question their own existence. Yes, beloved believer, you and I have had times of refreshing from the presence of the Lord, and then our faith has mounted to the topmost heights of assurance. We have had confidence to lean our heads upon the bosom of our Lord, and we have no more questioned our Master's affection to us than John did when in that blessed posture; nay, nor so much: for the dark question, 'Lord, is it I that shall betray thee?' has been put far from us. He has kissed us with the kisses of His mouth, and killed our doubts by the closeness of His embrace. His love has been sweeter than wine to our souls.

'Call the labourers, and give them their hire'
Matthew 20:8

God is a good paymaster; He pays His servants while at work as well as when they have done it; and one of His payments is this, *an easy conscience.* If you have spoken faithfully of Jesus to one person, when you go to bed at night you feel happy in thinking, 'I have this day discharged my conscience of that man's blood'. There is a great *comfort in doing something for Jesus.* Oh, what a happiness to place jewels in His crown, and give Him to see of the travail of His soul! There is also very great reward in *watching the first buddings of conviction in a soul*! To say of that girl in the class, 'She is tender of heart, I do hope that there is the Lord's work within'. To go home and pray over that boy, who said something in the afternoon which made you think he must know more of divine truth than you had feared! Oh, the joy of hope! But as for the *joy of success*! It is unspeakable. This joy, overwhelming as it is, is a hungry thing - you pine for more of it. To be a soul-winner is the happiest thing in the world. With every soul you bring to Christ, you get a new heaven upon earth. But who can conceive the bliss which awaits us above! Oh, how sweet is that sentence, 'Enter thou into *the joy of thy Lord*!' Do you know what the joy of Christ is over a saved sinner? This is the very joy which we are to possess in heaven. Yes, when He mounts the throne, you shall mount with Him. When the heavens ring with 'Well done, well done!', you shall partake in the reward; you have toiled with Him, you have suffered with Him, you shall now reign with Him; you have sown with Him, you shall reap with Him; your face was covered with sweat like His, and your soul was grieved for the sins of men as His soul was, now shall your face be bright with heaven's splendour as is His countenance, and now shall your soul be filled with beatific joys even as His soul is.

'Yet He hath made with me an everlasting covenant'
2 Samuel 23:5

This covenant is *divine in its origin*. 'HE hath made with me an everlasting covenant.' Oh, that great word HE! Stop, my soul. God, the everlasting Father, has positively made a covenant with thee; yes, that God who spake the world into existence by a word; He, stooping from His majesty, takes hold of thy hand and makes a covenant with thee. Is it not a deed, the stupendous condescension of which might ravish our hearts for ever if we could really understand it? 'HE hath made with me a covenant.' A king has not made a covenant with me - that were somewhat; but the Prince of all the kings of the earth, Shaddai, the Lord All-sufficient, the Jehovah of ages, the everlasting Elohim, 'He hath made with me an everlasting covenant'. But notice, *it is particular in its application*. 'Yet hath he made with ME an everlasting covenant.' Here lies the sweetness of it to each believer. It is nought for me that He made peace for the world; I want to know whether He made peace for *me*! It is little that He hath made a covenant, I want to know whether He has made a covenant *with me*. Blessed is the assurance that He hath made a covenant with me! If God the Holy Ghost gives me assurance of this, then His salvation is mine, His heart is mine, He Himself is mine - *He is my God*.

 This covenant is *everlasting in its duration*. An everlasting covenant means a covenant which had no beginning, and which shall never, never end. How sweet amidst all the uncertainties of life, to know that 'the foundation of the Lord standeth sure', and to have God's own promise, 'My covenant will I not break, nor alter the thing that is gone out of my lips'. Like dying David, I will sing of this, even though my house be not so with God as my heart desireth.

*'I clothed thee also with broidered work, and shod
thee with badgers' skin, and I girded thee about
with fine linen, and I covered thee with silk'*
Ezekiel 16:10

See with what matchless generosity the Lord provides for His people's apparel. They are so arrayed that the divine skill is seen producing an unrivalled *broidered work*, in which every attribute takes its part and every divine beauty is revealed. No art like the art displayed in our salvation, no cunning workmanship like that beheld in the righteousness of the saints. Justification has engrossed learned pens in all ages of the church, and will be the theme of admiration in eternity. God has indeed 'curiously wrought it'. With all this elaboration there is mingled utility and durability, comparable to our being *shod with badgers' skins*. The animal here meant is unknown, but its skin covered the tabernacle, and formed one of the finest and strongest leathers known. The righteousness which is of God by faith endureth for ever, and he who is shod with this divine preparation will tread the desert safely, and may even set his foot upon the lion and the adder. Purity and dignity of our holy vesture are brought out in *the fine linen*. When the Lord sanctifies His people, they are clad as priests in pure white; not the snow itself excels them; they are in the eyes of men and angels fair to look upon, and even in the Lord's eyes they are without spot. Meanwhile the royal apparel is delicate and rich as *silk*. No expense is spared, no beauty withheld, no daintiness denied.

What, then? Is there no inference from this? Surely there is gratitude to be felt and joy to be expressed. Come, my heart, refuse not thy evening hallelujah! Tune thy pipes! Touch thy chords!

> Strangely, my soul, art thou arrayed
>   By the Great Sacred Three!
> In sweetest harmony of praise
>   Let all thy powers agree.

'I will strengthen thee'
Isaiah 41:10

God has a strong reserve with which to discharge this engagement; for he is able to do all things. Believer, till thou canst drain dry the ocean of omnipotence, till thou canst break into pieces the towering mountains of almighty strength, thou never needest to fear. Think not that the strength of man shall ever be able to overcome the power of God. Whilst the earth's huge pillars stand, thou hast enough reason to abide firm in thy faith. The same God who directs the earth in its orbit, who feeds the burning furnace of the sun, and trims the lamps of heaven, has promised to supply thee with daily strength. While He is able to uphold the universe, dream not that He will prove unable to fulfil His own promises. Remember what He did in the days of old, in the former generations. Remember how He spake and it was done; how He commanded, and it stood fast. Shall He that created the world grow weary? He hangeth the world upon nothing; shall he who doth this be unable to support His children? Shall He be unfaithful to His word for want of power? Who is it that restrains the tempest? Doth not He ride upon the wings of the wind, and make the clouds His chariots, and hold the ocean in the hollow of His hand? How can He fail thee? When He has put such a faithful promise as this on record, wilt thou for a moment indulge the thought that He has outpromised Himself, and gone beyond His power to fulfil? Ah, no! Thou canst doubt no longer.

O thou who art my God and my strength, I can believe that this promise shall be fulfilled, for the boundless reservoir of Thy grace can never be exhausted, and the overflowing storehouse of Thy strength can never be emptied by Thy friends or rifled by Thine enemies.

> Now let the feeble all be strong,
> And make Jehovah's arm their song.

'The spot of His children'
Deuteronomy 32:5

What is the secret spot which infallibility betokens the child of God? It were vain presumption to decide this upon our own judgment; but God's word reveals it to us, and we may tread surely where we have revelation to be our guide. Now, we are told concerning our Lord, 'to as many as *received Him*, to them gave He power to become the sons of God, even to as many as believed on His name'. Then, if I have received Christ Jesus into my heart, I am a child of God. That reception is described in the same verse as *believing on the name of Jesus Christ*. If, then, I believe on Jesus Christ's name - that is, simply from my heart trust myself with the crucified, but now exalted, Redeemer, I am a member of the family of the Most High. Whatever else I may not have, if I have this, I have the privilege to become a child of God. Our Lord Jesus puts it in another shape. 'My sheep hear My voice, and I know them, and they follow Me.' Here is the matter in a nutshell. Christ appears as a shepherd to His own sheep, not to others. As soon as He appears, His own sheep perceive Him - they trust Him, they are prepared to follow Him; He knows them, and they know Him - there is a mutual knowledge - there is a constant connection between them. Thus the one mark, the sure mark, the infallible mark of regeneration and adoption is a hearty faith in the appointed Redeemer. Reader, are you in doubt, are you uncertain whether you bear the secret mark of God's children? Then let not an hour pass over your head till you have said, 'Search me, O God, and know my heart'. Trifle not here, I adjure you! If you must trifle anywhere, let it be about some secondary matter: your health, if you will, or the title deeds of your estate; but about your soul, your never-dying soul and its eternal destinies, I beseech you to be in earnest. Make sure work for eternity.

'Friend, go up higher'
Luke 14:10

When first the life of grace begins in the soul, we do indeed draw near to God, but it is with great fear and trembling. The soul conscious of guilt and humbled thereby, is overawed with the solemnity of its position; it is cast to the earth by a sense of the grandeur of Jehovah, in whose presence it stands. With unfeigned bashfulness it takes the lowest room.

But, in after life, as the Christian grows in grace, although he will never forget the solemnity of his position, and will never lose that holy awe which must encompass a gracious man when he is in the presence of the God who can create or can destroy; yet his fear has all its terror taken out of it; it becomes a holy reverence, and no more an overshadowing dread. He is called up higher, to greater access to God in Christ Jesus. Then the man of God, walking amid the splendours of Deity, and veiling his face like the glorious cherubim, with those twin wings, the blood and righteousness of Jesus Christ, will, reverent and bowed in spirit, approach the throne; and seeing there a God of love, of goodness, and of mercy, he will realise rather the covenant character of God than his absolute Deity. He will see in God rather His goodness than His greatness, and more of His love than of His majesty. Then will the soul, bowing still as humbly as aforetime, enjoy a more sacred liberty of intercession; for while prostrate before the glory of the Infinite God, it will be sustained by the refreshing consciousness of being in the presence of boundless mercy and infinite love, and by the realisation of acceptance 'in the beloved'. Thus the believer is bidden to come up higher, and is enabled to exercise the privilege of rejoicing in God, and drawing near to Him in holy confidence, saying, 'Abba, Father'.

So may we go from strength to strength,
    And daily grow in grace,
Till in Thine image raised at length,
    We see Thee face to face.

'The night also is Thine'
Psalm 74:16

Yes, Lord, Thou dost not abdicate Thy throne when the sun goeth down, nor dost Thou leave the world all through these long wintry nights to be the prey of evil; Thine eyes watch us as the stars, and Thine arms surround us as the zodiac belts the sky. The dews of kindly sleep and all the influences of the moon are in Thy hand, and the alarms and solemnities of night are equally with Thee. This is very sweet to me when watching through the midnight hours, or tossing to and fro in anguish. There are precious fruits put forth by the moon as well as by the sun: may my Lord make me to be a favoured partaker in them.

The night of affliction is as much under the arrangement and control of the Lord of Love as the bright summer days when all is bliss. Jesus is in the tempest. His love wraps the night about itself as a mantle, but to the eye of faith the sable robe is scarce a disguise. From the first watch of the night even unto the break of day the eternal Watcher observes His saints, and overrules the shades and dews of midnight for His people's highest good. We believe in no rival deities of good and evil contending for the mastery, but we hear the voice of Jehovah saying, 'I create light, and I create darkness; I, the Lord, do all these things'.

Gloomy seasons of religious indifference and social sin are not exempted from the divine purpose. When the altars of truth are defiled, and the ways of God forsaken, the Lord's servants weep with bitter sorrow, but they may not despair, for the darkest eras are governed by the Lord, and shall come to their end at His bidding. What may seem defeat to us may be victory to Him.

> Though enwrapt in gloomy night,
>   We perceive no ray of light;
> Since the Lord Himself is here,
>   'Tis not meet that we should fear.

'For your sakes he became poor'
2 Corinthians 8:9

The Lord Jesus Christ was eternally *rich*, glorious, and exalted; but 'though *He was rich*, yet for your sakes He became poor'. As the rich saint cannot be true in his communion with his poor brethren unless of his substance he ministers to their necessities, so (the same rule holding with the head as between the members), it is impossible that our Divine Lord could have had fellowship with us unless He had imparted to us of His own abounding wealth, and had become poor to make us rich. Had He remained upon His throne of glory, and had we continued in the ruins of the fall without receiving His salvation, communion would have been impossible on both sides. Our position by the fall, apart from the covenant of grace, made it as impossible for fallen man to communicate with God as it is for Belial to be in concord with Christ. In order, therefore, that communion might be compassed, it was necessary that the rich kinsman should bestow his estate upon his poor relatives, that the righteous Saviour should give to His sinning brethren of His own perfection, and that we, the poor and guilty, should receive of his fulness grace for grace; that thus in giving and receiving, the one might descend from the heights, and the other ascend from the depths, and so be able to embrace each other in true and hearty fellowship. Poverty must be enriched by Him in whom are infinite treasures before it can venture to commune; and guilt must lose itself in imputed and imparted righteousness ere the soul can walk in fellowship with purity. Jesus must clothe His people in His own garments, or He cannot admit them into His palace of glory; and He must wash them in His own blood, or else they will be too defiled for the embrace of His fellowship.

O believer, herein is love! For *your sake* the Lord Jesus 'became poor' that He might lift you up into communion with Himself.

*'The glory of the Lord shall be revealed,
and all flesh shall see it together'*
Isaiah 40:5

We anticipate the happy day when the whole world shall be converted to Christ; when the gods of the heathen shall be cast to the moles and the bats; when Romanism shall be exploded, and the crescent of Mohammed shall wane, never again to cast its baleful rays upon the nations; when kings shall bow down before the Prince of Peace, and all nations shall call their Redeemer blessed. Some despair of this. They look upon the world as a vessel breaking up and going to pieces, never to float again. We know that the world and all that is therein is one day to be burnt up, and afterwards we look for new heavens and for a new earth; but we cannot read our Bibles without the conviction that:

> Jesus shall reign where'er the sun
> Does his successive journeys run.

We are not discouraged by the length of His delays; we are not disheartened by the long period which He allots to the church in which to struggle with little success and much defeat. We believe that God will never suffer this world, which has once seen Christ's blood shed upon it, to be always the devil's stronghold. Christ came hither to deliver this world from the detested sway of the powers of darkness. What a shout shall that be when men and angels shall unite to cry, 'Hallelujah, hallelujah, for the Lord God Omnipotent reigneth'! What a satisfaction will it be in that day to have had a share in the fight, to have helped to break the arrows of the bow, and to have aided in winning the victory for our Lord! Happy are they who trust themselves with this conquering Lord, and who fight side by side with Him, doing their little in His name and by His strength! How unhappy are those on the side of evil! It is a losing side, and it is a matter wherein to lose is to lose and to be lost for ever. On whose side are you?

'Behold, a virgin shall conceive, and bear a son,
and shall call his name Immanuel'
Isaiah 7:14

Let us today go down to Bethlehem, and in company with wondering shepherds and adoring Magi, let us see Him who was born King of the Jews, for we by faith can claim an interest in Him, and can sing, '*Unto us* a child is born, *unto us* a son is given'. Jesus is Jehovah incarnate, our Lord and our God, and yet our brother and friend; let us adore and admire. Let us notice at the very first glance *His miraculous conception*. It was a thing unheard of before, and unparalleled since, that a virgin should conceive and bear a Son. The first promise ran thus, *The seed of the woman*, not the offspring of the man. Since venturous woman led the way in the sins which brought forth Paradise lost, she, and she alone, ushers in the Regainer of Paradise. Our Saviour, although truly man, was as to His human nature the Holy One of God. Let us reverently bow before the holy Child whose innocence restores to manhood its ancient glory; and let us pray that He may be formed in us, the hope of glory. Fail not to note *His humble parentage*. His mother has been described simply as 'a virgin', not a princess, or prophetess, nor a matron of a large estate. True the blood of kings ran in her veins; nor was her mind a weak and untaught one, for she could sing most sweetly a song of praise; but yet how humble her position, how poor the man to whom she stood affianced, and how miserable the accommodation afforded to the new-born King!

Immanuel, God with us in our nature, in our sorrow, in our lifework, in our punishment, in our grave, and now with us, or rather we with Him, in resurrection, ascension, triumph, and Second Advent splendour.

'And it was so, when the days of their feasting were gone about, that Job sent and sanctified them, and rose up early in the morning, and offered burnt offerings according to the number of them all: for Job said, It may be that my sons have sinned, and cursed God in their hearts. Thus did Job continually'

Job 1:5

What the patriarch did early in the morning, after the family festivities, it will be well for the believer to do for himself ere he rests tonight. Amid the cheerfulness of household gatherings it is easy to slide into sinful levities, and to forget our avowed character as Christians. It ought not to be so, but so it is, that our days of feasting are very seldom days of sanctified enjoyment, but too frequently degenerate into unhallowed mirth. There is a way of joy as pure and sanctifying as though one bathed in the rivers of Eden: holy gratitude should be quite as purifying an element as grief. Alas! for our poor hearts, that facts prove that the house of mourning is better than the house of feasting. Come, believer, in what have you sinned today? Have you been forgetful of your high calling? Have you been even as others in idle words and loose speeches? Then confess the sin, and fly to the sacrifice. The sacrifice sanctifies. The precious blood of the Lamb slain removes the guilt, and purges away the defilement of our sins of ignorance and carelessness. This is the best ending of a Christmas day - to wash anew in the cleansing fountain. Believer, come to this sacrifice continually; if it be so good tonight, it is good every night. To live at the altar is the privilege of the royal priesthood; to them sin, great as it is, is nevertheless no cause for despair, since they draw near yet again to the sin-atoning victim, and their conscience is purged from dead works.

> Gladly I close this festive day,
>   Grasping the altar's hallow'd horn;
> My slips and faults are washed away,
>   The Lamb has all my trespass borne.

'The last Adam'

1 Corinthians 15:45

Jesus is the federal head of his elect. As in Adam, every heir of flesh and blood has a personal interest, because he is the covenant head and representative of the race as considered under the law of works; so under the law of grace, every redeemed soul is one with the Lord from heaven, since he is the Second Adam, the Sponsor and Substitute of the elect in the new covenant of love. The apostle Paul declares that Levi was in the loins of Abraham when Melchisedek met him: it is a certain truth that the believer was in the loins of Jesus Christ, the Mediator, when in old eternity the covenant settlements of grace were decreed, ratified, and made sure for ever. Thus, whatever Christ hath done, he hath wrought for the whole body of His Church. We were crucified in Him and buried with Him (read Colossians 2:10-13), and to make it still more wonderful, we are risen with Him and even ascended with Him to the seats on high (Ephesians 2:6). It is thus that the Church has fulfilled the law, and is 'accepted in *the beloved*'. It is thus that she is regarded with complacency by the just Jehovah, for he views her in Jesus, and does not look upon her as separate from her covenant head. As the Anointed Redeemer of Israel, Christ Jesus has nothing distinct from His Church, but all that He has He holds for her. Adam's righteousness was ours so long as he maintained it, and his sin was ours the moment that he committed it; and in the same manner, all that the Second Adam is or does, is ours as well as His, seeing that He is our representative. Here is the foundation of the covenant of grace. This gracious system of representation and substitution, which moved Justin Martyr to cry out, 'O blessed change, O sweet permutation!', this is the very groundwork of the gospel of our salvation, and is to be received with strong faith and rapturous joy.

'*Lo, I am with you alway*'
Matthew 28:20

The Lord Jesus is in the midst of His church; He walketh among the golden candlesticks; His promise is, 'Lo, I am with you alway'. He is as surely with us now as He was with the disciples at the lake, when they saw coals of fire, and fish laid thereon and bread. Not carnally, but still in real truth, Jesus is with us. And a blessed truth it is, for where Jesus is, *love becomes inflamed*. Of all the things in the world that can set the heart burning, there is nothing like the presence of Jesus! A glimpse of Him so overcomes us, that we are ready to say, 'Turn away Thine eyes from me, for they have overcome me'. Even the smell of the aloes, and the myrrh, and the cassia, which drop from His perfumed garments, causes the sick and the faint to grow strong. Let there be but a moment's leaning of the head upon that gracious bosom, and a reception of His divine love into our poor cold hearts, and we are cold no longer, but glow like seraphs, equal to every labour, and capable of every suffering. If we know that Jesus is with us, *every power will be developed*, and every grace will be strengthened, and we shall cast ourselves into the Lord's service with heart, and soul, and strength; therefore is the presence of Christ to be desired above all things. *His presence will be most realised by those who are most like Him.* If you desire to see Christ, you must grow in conformity to Him. Bring yourself, by the power of the Spirit, into union with Christ's desires, and motives, and plans of action, and you are likely to be favoured with His company. Remember *His presence may be had.* His promise is as true as ever. He delights to be with us. If He doth not come, it is because we hinder Him by our indifference. He will reveal Himself to our earnest prayers, and graciously suffer Himself to be detained by our entreaties, and by our tears, for these are the golden chains which bind Jesus to His people.

'Can the rush grow up without mire?'
Job 8:11

The rush is spongy and hollow, and even so it is a hypocrite; there is no substance or stability in him. It is shaken to and fro in every wind just as formalists yield to every influence; for this reason the rush is not broken by the tempest, neither are hypocrites troubled with persecution. I would not willingly be a deceiver or be deceived; perhaps the text for this day may help me to try myself whether I be a hypocrite or no. The rush by nature lives in water, and owes its very existence to the mire and moisture wherein it has taken root; let the mire become dry, and the rush withers very quickly. Its greenness is absolutely dependent upon circumstances, a present abundance of water makes it flourish, and a drought destroys it at once. Is this my case? Do I only serve God when I am in good company, or when religion is profitable and respectable? Do I love the Lord only when temporal comforts are received from His hands? If so I am a base hypocrite, and like the withering rush, I shall perish when death deprives me of outward joys. But can I honestly assert that when bodily comforts have been few, and my surroundings have been rather adverse to grace than at all helpful to it, I have still held fast my integrity? Then have I hope that there is genuine vital godliness in me. The rush cannot grow without mire, but plants of the Lord's right hand planting can and do flourish even in the year of drought. A godly man often grows best when his worldly circumstances decay. He who follows Christ for his bag is a Judas; they who follow for loaves and fishes are children of the devil; but they who attend him out of love to Himself are His own beloved ones. Lord, let me find my life in *Thee*, and not in the mire of this world's favour or gain.

'And the LORD shall guide thee continually'
Isaiah 58:11

'The *Lord* shall guide thee.' Not an angel, but JE-
HOVAH shall guide thee. He said He would not go
through the wilderness before His people, an angel
should go before them to lead them in the way; but
Moses said, 'If *Thy* presence go not with me, carry us
not up hence'. Christian, God has not left you in your
earthly pilgrimage to an angel's guidance: He Himself
leads the van. You may not see the cloudy, fiery pillar,
but Jehovah will never forsake you. Notice the word
shall - 'The Lord shall guide thee'. How certain this
makes it! How sure it is that God will not forsake us!
His precious 'shalls' and 'wills' are better than men's
oaths. 'I will never leave thee, nor forsake thee.' Then
observe the adverb *continually*. We are not merely to
be guided sometimes, but we are to have a perpetual
monitor; not occasionally to be left to our own understanding, and so to wander, but we are continually to
hear the guiding voice of the Great Shepherd; and if we
follow close at His heels, we shall not err, but be led by
a right way to a city to dwell in. If you have to change
your position in life; if you have to emigrate to distant
shores; if it should happen that you are cast into
poverty, or uplifted suddenly into a more responsible
position than the one you now occupy; if you are
thrown among strangers, or cast among foes, yet
tremble not, for 'the Lord shall guide thee continually'.
There are no dilemmas out of which you shall not be
delivered if you live near to God, and your heart be kept
warm with holy love. He goes not amiss who goes in
the company of God. Like Enoch, walk with God, and
you cannot mistake your road. You have infallible
wisdom to direct you, immutable love to comfort you,
and eternal power to defend you. 'Jehovah' - mark the
word - 'Jehovah shall guide thee continually'.

'The life which I now live in the flesh,
I live by the faith of the Son of God'
Galatians 2:20

When the Lord in mercy passed by and saw us in our blood, He first of all said, 'Live'; and this he did *first*, because life is one of the absolutely essential things in spiritual matters, and until it be bestowed we are incapable of partaking in the things of the kingdom. Now the life which grace confers upon the saints at the moment of their quickening is none other than the life of Christ, which, like the sap from the stem, runs into us, the branches, and establishes a living connection between our souls and Jesus. Faith is the grace which perceives this union, having proceeded from it as its first-fruit. It is the neck which joins the body of the Church to its all-glorious Head.

> *O Faith!* thou bond of union with the Lord,
>   Is not this office thine? and thy fit name,
> In the economy of gospel types,
>   And symbols apposite - the Church's *neck*;
>   Identifying her in will and work
> With Him ascended?

Faith lays hold upon the Lord Jesus with a firm and determined grasp. She knows his excellence and worth, and no temptation can induce her to repose her trust elsewhere; and Christ Jesus is so delighted with this heavenly grace, that He never ceases to strengthen and sustain her by the loving embrace and all-sufficient support of His eternal arms. Here, then, is established a living, sensible, and delightful union which casts forth streams of love, confidence, sympathy, complacency, and joy, whereof both the bride and bridegroom love to drink. When the soul can evidently perceive this oneness between itself and Christ, the pulse may be felt as beating for both, and the one blood as flowing through the veins of each. Then is the heart as near heaven as it can be on earth, and is prepared for the enjoyment of the most sublime and spiritual kind of fellowship.

'I came not to send peace on earth, but a sword'
Matthew 10:34

The Christian will be sure to make enemies. It will be one of his objects to make none; but if to do the right, and to believe the true, should cause him to lose every earthly friend, he will count it but a small loss, since his great Friend in heaven will be yet more friendly, and reveal Himself to him more graciously than ever. O ye who have taken up His cross, know ye not what your Master said? 'I am come to set a man at variance against his father, and the daughter against her mother; and a man's foes shall be they of his own household.' Christ is the great Peacemaker; but before peace, He brings war. Where the light cometh, the darkness must retire. Where truth is, the lie must flee; or, if it abideth, there must be a stern conflict, for the truth cannot and will not lower its standard, and the lie must be trodden under foot. If you follow Christ, you shall have all the dogs of the world yelping at your heels. If you would live so as to stand the test of the last tribunal, depend upon it the world will not speak well of you. He who has the friendship of the world is an enemy to God; but if you are true and faithful to the Most High, men will resent your unflinching fidelity, since it is a testimony against their iniquities. Fearless of all consequences, you must do the right. You will need the courage of a lion unhesitatingly to pursue a course which shall turn your best friend into your fiercest foe; but for the love of Jesus you must thus be courageous. For the truth's sake to hazard reputation and affection, is such a deed that to do it constantly you will need a degree of moral principle which only the Spirit of God can work in you; yet turn not your back like a coward, but play the man. Follow right manfully in your Master's steps, for He has traversed this rough way before you. Better a brief warfare and eternal rest, than false peace and everlasting torment.

'Hitherto hath the Lord helped us'
1 Samuel 7:12

The word 'hitherto' seems like a hand pointing in the direction of the *past*. Twenty years or seventy, and yet, 'hitherto the Lord hath helped'! Through poverty, through wealth, through sickness, through health, at home, abroad, on the land, on the sea, in honour, in dishonour, in perplexity, in joy, in trial, in triumph, in prayer, in temptation, 'hitherto hath the Lord helped us'!

We delight to look down a long avenue of trees. It is delightful to gaze from end to end of the long vista, a sort of verdant temple, with its branching pillars and its arches of leaves; even so look down the long aisles of your years, at the green boughs of mercy overhead, and the strong pillars of lovingkindness and faithfulness which bear up your joys. Are there no birds in yonder branches singing? Surely there must be many, and they all sing of mercy received 'hitherto'.

But the word also points *forward*. For when a man gets up to a certain mark and writes 'hitherto', he is not yet at the end, there is still a distance to be traversed. More trials, more joys; more temptations, more triumphs; more prayers, more answers; more toils, more strengths; more fights, more victories; and then come sickness, old age, disease, death. Is it over now? No! there is more yet - awakening in Jesu's likeness, thrones, harps, songs, psalms, white raiment, the face of Jesus, the society of saints, the glory of God, the fulness of eternity, the infinity of bliss. O be of good courage, believer, and with grateful confidence raise thy 'Ebenezer' for:

> He who hath helped thee hitherto
> Will help thee all thy journey through.

When read in heaven's light how glorious and marvellous a prospect will thy 'hitherto' unfold to thy grateful eye!

'What think ye of Christ?'
Matthew 22:42

The great test of your soul's health is, *'What think you of Christ?'* Is He to you 'fairer than the children of men' - 'the chief among ten thousand' - the 'altogether lovely'? Wherever Christ is thus esteemed, all the faculties of the spiritual man exercise themselves with energy. I will judge of your piety by this barometer: does Christ stand high or low with you? If you have thought little of Christ, if you have been content to live without His presence, if you have cared little for His honour, if you have been neglectful of His laws, then I know that your soul is sick - God grant that it may not be sick unto death! But if the first thought of your spirit has been, How can I honour Jesus? If the daily desire of your soul has been, 'O that I knew where I might find Him!', I tell you that you may have a thousand infirmities, and even scarcely know whether you are a child of God at all, and yet I am persuaded, beyond a doubt, that you are safe, since Jesus is great in your esteem. I care not for thy rags, what thinkest thou of *His* royal apparel? I care not for thy wounds, though they bleed in torrents, what thinkest thou of *His* wounds? Are they like glittering rubies in thine esteem? I think none the less of thee, though thou liest like Lazarus on the dunghill, and the dogs do lick thee - I judge thee not by thy poverty: what thinkest thou of the King in His beauty? Has He a glorious high throne in thy heart? Wouldst thou set Him higher if thou couldst? Wouldst thou be willing to die if thou couldst but add another trumpet to the strain which proclaims His praise? Ah! then it is well with thee. Whatever thou mayst think of thyself, if Christ be great to thee, thou shalt be with Him ere long.

> Though all the world my choice deride,
>   Yet Jesus shall my portion be;
> For I am pleased with none beside;
>   The fairest of the fair is He.

'Better is the end of a thing than the beginning thereof'
Ecclesiastes 7:8

Look at David's Lord and Master; see His beginning.
He was despised and rejected of men; a man of sorrows
and acquainted with grief. Would you see the end? He
sits at His Father's right hand, expecting until His
enemies be made His footstool. 'As He is, so are we
also in this world.' You must bear the cross, or you
shall never wear the crown; you must wade through the
mire, or you shall never walk the golden pavement.
Cheer up, then, poor Christian. 'Better is the end of a
thing than the beginning thereof.' See that creeping
worm, how contemptible its appearance! It is the
beginning of a thing. Mark that insect with gorgeous
wings, playing in the sunbeams, sipping at the flower
bells, full of happiness and life; that is the end thereof.
That caterpillar is yourself, until you are wrapped up in
the chrysalis of death; but when Christ shall appear you
shall be like Him, for you shall see Him as He is. Be
content to be like Him, a worm and no man, that like
Him you may be satisfied when you wake up in His
likeness. That rough-looking diamond is put upon the
wheel of the lapidary. He cuts it on all sides. It loses
much - much that seemed costly to itself. The king is
crowned; the diadem is put upon the monarch's head
with trumpet's joyful sound. A glittering ray flashes
from that coronet, and it beams from that very diamond
which was just now so sorely vexed by the lapidary.
You may venture to compare yourself to such a
diamond, for you are one of God's people; and this is
the time of the cutting process. Let faith and patience
have their perfect work, for in the day when the crown
shall be set upon the head of the King, Eternal,
Immortal, Invisible, one ray of glory shall stream from
you. 'They shall be Mine,' saith the Lord, 'in the day
when I make up My jewels.' 'Better is the end of a thing
than the beginning thereof.'

'Knowest thou not that it
will be bitterness in the latter end?'
2 Samuel 2:26

If, O my reader, thou art merely a professor, and not a possessor of the faith that is in Christ Jesus, the following lines are a true sketch of thine end.

You are a respectable attendant at a place of worship; you go because others go, not because your heart is right with God. This is your beginning. I will suppose that for the next twenty or thirty years you will be spared to go on as you do now, professing religion by an outward attendance upon the means of grace, but having no heart in the matter. Tread softly, for I must show you the deathbed of such a one as yourself. Let us gaze upon him gently. A clammy sweat is on his brow, and he wakes up crying, 'O God, it is hard to die. Did you send for my minister?' 'Yes, he is coming.' The minister comes. 'Sir, I fear that I am dying!' 'Have you any hope?' 'I cannot say that I have. I fear to stand before my God; oh! pray for me.' The prayer is offered for him with sincere earnestness, and the way of salvation is for the ten-thousandth time put before him; but before he has grasped the rope, I see him sink. I may put my finger upon those cold eyelids, for they will never see anything here again. But where is the man, and where are the man's true eyes? It is written, 'In hell he lifted up his eyes, being in torment'. Ah! why did he not lift up his eyes before? Because he was so accustomed to hear the gospel that his soul slept under it. Alas! if you should lift up your eyes, how bitter will be your wailings. Let the Saviour's own words reveal the woe: 'Father Abraham, send Lazarus, that he may dip the tip of his finger in water, and cool my tongue, for I am tormented in this flame.' There is a frightful meaning in those words. May you never have to spell it out by the red light of Jehovah's wrath!

> *'In the last day, that great day of the feast, Jesus
> stood and cried, saying, If any man thirst, let him
> come unto Me, and drink'*
> John 7:37

Patience had her perfect work in the Lord Jesus, and
until the last day of the feast He pleaded with the Jews,
even as on this last day of the year He pleads with us,
and waits to be gracious to us. Admirable indeed is the
longsuffering of the Saviour in bearing with some of us
year after year, notwithstanding our provocations,
rebellions, and resistance of His Holy Spirit. Wonder
of wonders that we are still in the land of mercy!

Pity expressed herself most plainly, for Jesus
cried, which implies not only the loudness of His
voice, but the tenderness of His tones. He entreats us
to be reconciled. 'We *pray* you,' says the Apostle, 'as
though God did *beseech* you by us.' What earnest,
pathetic terms are these! How deep must be the love
which makes the Lord weep over sinners, and like a
mother woo His children to His bosom! Surely at the
call of such a cry our willing hearts will come.

Provision is made most plenteously; all is provided that man can need to quench his soul's thirst. To
his conscience the atonement brings peace; to his
understanding the gospel brings the richest instruction;
to his heart the person of Jesus is the noblest object of
affection; to the whole man the truth as it is in Jesus
supplies the purest nutriment. Thirst is terrible, but
Jesus can remove it. Though the soul were utterly
famished, Jesus could restore it.

Proclamation is made most freely, that every
thirsty one is welcome. No other distinction is made
but that of thirst. Whether it be the thirst of avarice,
ambition, pleasure, knowledge, or rest, he who suffers
from it is invited. The thirst may be bad in itself, and
be no sign of grace, but rather a mark of inordinate sin
longing to be gratified with deeper draughts of lust; but
it is not goodness in the creature which brings him the

invitation, the Lord Jesus sends it freely, and without respect of persons.

Personality is declared most fully. The sinner must come to *Jesus*, not to works, ordinances, or doctrines, but to a personal Redeemer, who His own self bare our sins in His own body on the tree. The bleeding, dying, rising Saviour, is the only star of hope to a sinner. Oh for grace to come now and drink, ere the sun sets upon the year's last day!

No waiting or preparation is so much as hinted at. Drinking represents a reception for which no fitness is required. A fool, a thief, a harlot can drink; and so sinfulness of character is no bar to the invitation to believe in Jesus. We want no golden cup, no bejewelled chalice, in which to convey the water to the thirsty; the mouth of poverty is welcome to stoop down and quaff the flowing flood. Blistered, leprous, filthy lips may touch the stream of divine love; they cannot pollute it, but shall themselves be purified. Jesus is the fount of hope. Dear reader, hear the dear Redeemer's loving voice as He cries to each of us,

'IF ANY MAN THIRST,
LET HIM
COME UNTO ME
AND DRINK.'

'The harvest is past, the summer is ended,
and we are not saved'
Jeremiah 8:20

Not *saved*! Dear reader, is this your mournful plight?
Warned of the judgment to come, bidden to escape for
your life, and yet at this moment *not saved*! You know
the way of salvation, you read it in the Bible, you hear
it from the pulpit, it is explained to you by friends, and
yet you neglect it, and therefore are *not saved*. You will
be without excuse when the Lord shall judge the quick
and the dead. The Holy Spirit has given more or less of
blessing upon the word which has been preached in
your hearing, and times of refreshing have come from
the divine presence, and yet you are without Christ.

All these hopeful seasons have come and gone -
your summer and your harvest have passed - and yet
you are *not saved*. Years have followed one another
into eternity, and your last year will soon be here: youth
has gone, manhood is going, and yet you are *not saved*.
Let me ask you - *will you ever be saved*? Is there any
likelihood of it? Already the most propitious seasons
have left you unsaved; will other occasions alter your
condition? Means have failed with you - the best of
means, used perseveringly and with the utmost affection - what more can be done for you?

Affliction and prosperity have alike failed to impress you; tears and prayers and sermons have been
wasted on your barren heart. Are not the probabilities
dead against your ever being saved? Is it not more than
likely that you will abide as you are till death for ever
bars the door of hope? Do you recoil from the supposition? Yet it is a most reasonable one: he who is not
washed in so many waters will in all probability go
filthy to his end. The convenient time never has come,
why should it ever come?

It is logical to fear that it never will arrive, and that
Felix-like, you will find no convenient season till you
are in hell. O bethink you of what that hell is, and of the

dread possibility that you will soon be cast into it!

Reader, suppose you should die unsaved, your doom no words can picture. Write out your dread estate in tears and blood, talk of it with groans and gnashing of teeth: you will be punished with everlasting destruction from the glory of the Lord, and from the glory of His power. A brother's voice would fain startle you into earnestness. O be wise, be wise in time, and ere another year begins, believe in Jesus, who is able to save to the uttermost. Consecrate these last hours to lonely thought, and if deep repentance be bred in you, it will be well; and if it lead to a humble faith in Jesus, it will be best of all. O see to it that this year pass not away, and you an unforgiven spirit. Let not the new year's midnight peals sound upon a joyless spirit! *Now*, Now, NOW believe, and live.

'Escape for thy life;
   Look not behind thee,
      Neither stay thou in all the plain;
     Escape to the mountain,
       Lest thou be consumed.'

"Escape for thy life;
Look not behind thee,
Neither stay thou in all the plain.
Escape to the mountain,
Lest thou be consumed."